MARKETING RESEARCH

AN APPLIED APPROACH

McGraw-Hill Series in Marketing

MARKETING RESEARCH

AN APPLIED APPROACH

THIRD EDITION

Thomas C. Kinnear

Professor of Marketing
Graduate School of Business Administration
University of Michigan

James R. Taylor

Sebastian S. Kresge Professor of Marketing
Graduate School of Business Administration
University of Michigan

McGR

New York   St. Louis   San Francisc
Johannesburg   London   Madrid   Mexi
Panama   Paris   São Paulo   Sing

This book was set in Optima by Syntax International.
The editor was Sam Costanzo;
the cover was designed by John Hite;
the production supervisor was Phil Galea.
Project supervision was done by The Total Book.
R. R. Donnelley & Sons Company was printer and binder.

MARKETING RESEARCH

An Applied Approach

1 2 3 4 5 6 7 8 9 0 DOCDOC 8 9 4 3 2 1 0 9 8 7

ISBN 0-07-034748-4

Library of Congress Cataloging-in-Publication Data

Kinnear, Thomas C.
   Marketing research.

   Includes bibliographies and indexes.
   1. Marketing research.   2. Marketing—Management.
I. Taylor, James R. (James Ronald), 1938–
II. Title.
     .2.K53   1987   658.8′3   86–20844
   –07–034748–4

To Connie, Maggie, and Jamie

Linda, Pam, and Sandy

CONTENTS

PREFACE

The quality of marketing decisions is to a great extent dependent on the information available to the marketing decision maker. It is the function of marketing research to provide information for this decision making. A marketing manager who does not know how to use or evaluate marketing research is much like a general manager who does not understand the income statement for the company. Both individuals are severely limited in their ability to effectively perform their jobs.

OBJECTIVES

The main purpose of this book is to provide the prospective marketing manager with an understanding of marketing research. It may also serve as a first book for people with career objectives in the field of marketing research. The book is designed for use either in a junior or a senior undergraduate course in marketing research or in a first graduate course in marketing research.

UNIQUE FEATURES

There are certain attributes of this book that define its competitive positioning. These are:

1 It is designed to be easily read and understood. Great care has been taken to explain the basic technical issues in a step-by-step fashion.

2 It presents marketing research as a managerially and decision-making-oriented subject.

3 It presents marketing research in a pragmatic, "here's how to do it" fashion.

4 Advanced quantitative procedures are not dealt with in detail. It is not a text on quantitative techniques in marketing research.

5 It contains 30 real cases that are designed to allow students to apply material presented in the chapters.

6 Its accompanying volume, *Exercises in Marketing Research*, is designed to allow for the actual undertaking of certain parts of the research process described in the text. Thus, learning by doing is encouraged.

7 It contains one whole chapter that presents an actual research project from beginning stages to completion. Managerial interactions are described along with study objectives and some results.

8 It contains "application" chapters in the major areas of demand measurement and forecasting, product research and test marketing, and advertising research.

9 It has been designed for flexibility of use; the more complex chapters and appendixes may be skipped without disrupting the flow of the book.

10 It contains a glossary of important marketing research terms.

11 Each chapter is concluded with a point-by-point summary.

12 Each chapter has questions and/or problems for student discussion.

13 The book contains many extended real-world illustrations labeled Marketing Research in Action. These inserts add life to the chapter materials and present the real-world of marketing research to the reader.

The use of the term "applied" in the subtitle of this text signals three important aspects of the book:

1 It is highly concerned with the managerial use of marketing research and with the role of managers and researchers in this process.

2 It deals with the technical aspects of marketing research in a manner that allows the reader to apply these procedures to real applications.

3 It presents materials on major application areas within marketing research such as demand measurement and forecasting, product research and test marketing, and advertising research, plus extensive applications in the Marketing Research in Action inserts.

ORGANIZATION OF THE BOOK

The book is organized around the steps one would actually take in conducting a marketing research project. Part One presents an overview of marketing research. Chapter 1 defines marketing research and positions it within marketing management. Chapter 2 describes a number of the aspects of the business of marketing research, including types of institutions, jobs, use of outside suppliers, and ethics. Chapter 3 presents a detailed example of a real marketing research project.

Part Two consists of three chapters that examine issues that are usually dealt with early in the process of marketing research. Chapter 4 discusses when marketing research should be undertaken and includes a discussion of problem definition and a nonquantitative discussion regarding the cost and value of information. (A quantitative discussion of the latter topic appears in the appendix to Chapter 4.) Alternative research designs and data sources, including syndicated sources, are the subject of Chapter 5. Chapter 6 presents a detailed review of available secondary data, including census and library data.

Part Three considers various aspects of sampling. Chapter 7 presents an overview of sampling and a discussion of nonprobability sampling procedures. Chapter 8 discusses the most straightforward type of probability sampling: simple random sampling. Statistical concepts are reviewed as they apply to marketing research, with the emphasis on usefulness, not theory. Also, various aspects of determining sample size are presented. In Chapter 9 more complex but more useful sampling procedures are discussed, including stratified sampling and cluster sampling.

In Part Four the questions of measurement and causality are dealt with. Chapter 10 discusses how numbers can properly be assigned to the types of variables one attempts to measure in marketing research. This is a necessary step in quantitative analysis of marketing data. Chapter 11 covers in detail one area of measurement that is extremely important in marketing research: attitude measurement. Different scaling techniques are examined. Chapter 12 discusses the use of experimental procedures in marketing research by outlining the preconditions necessary for one to be able to infer causality in marketing situations; Chapter 12 also discusses certain research designs that aid this process.

In Part Five the steps necessary for actually collecting information from respondents are discussed. Chapter 13 reviews the different types of procedures available, including mail, phone, and in-person interviews, and examines focus-group interviews and other qualitative procedures. Chapter 14 presents a discussion of how to design effective data collection forms, including questionnaires. In Chapter 15 the interviewing process and the control of the actual interviews in the field are examined.

Once the research has been designed, the sample drawn, and the field work completed, the data must be analyzed and reported. The six chapters that make up Part Six deal with this area. Chapter 16 describes how data on data collection instruments can be converted into computer readable form. Chapter 17 presents data analysis techniques of the simplest type—those for analyzing only one variable at a time. Data analysis involving two variables at a time is discussed in Chapter 18. The emphasis is on the pragmatics of data analysis. More advanced topics in the analysis of data are presented in Chapters 19 and 20. They are not examined in the detail in which other material in the book is presented, however. Our objective is to acquaint readers with this material so that they are familiar with the terms and concepts and have some understanding of how these procedures might be used. Chapters 19 and 20 offer an overview of data analysis procedures that analyze more than two variables at a time. Specifically, Chapter 19 discusses factor analysis, cluster analysis, and multidimensional scaling, while Chapter 20 examines such procedures as multiple regression, discriminant analysis, analysis of variance, conjoint measurement, and AID. Chapter 21 discusses reporting research findings both orally and in written form.

Part Seven presents selected important application areas within marketing research. Chapter 22 discusses demand measurement and forecasting terminology and procedures. The emphasis is on the conceptual foundation of various procedures and not on their mathematical complexities. Chapter 23 examines various marketing research procedures used in product development and presents a detailed look at the field-testing tool of test marketing and its laboratory based alternative, simulated test marketing. Chapter 24 discusses the marketing research procedures and issues that arise in the measurement of media audiences and the copy testing of advertising messages.

CASES AND EXERCISES

Throughout the book, the thrust is pragmatic in terms of showing what it is like to actually do a marketing research project in the context of providing the decision maker with relevant information. This approach is aided by 30 real cases and by the companion volume, *Exercises in Marketing Research*. These cases and exercises allow the student to actually do the things presented in the chapters.

ALTERNATIVE USAGE PATTERNS

The book is designed for flexibility of use. We have opted for a large number of relatively short chapters and appendixes to accomplish this. More complex material can easily be skipped without disrupting the flow of the book. We have employed this approach in order to use this text at both the undergraduate and graduate levels. Some possible usage patterns might be:

1 A course designed to provide a managerial overview with little quantitative material (Chapters 1–7, 13–18, and 21–24).

2 A course designed to provide both a managerial overview and a good understanding of the basic quantitative concepts (Chapters 1–18, and 21–24).

3 A course designed to provide a managerial overview and a more detailed understanding of quantitative material (Chapters 1–24).

ACKNOWLEDGMENTS

We owe thanks to many people in preparing this manuscript. Our McGraw-Hill editor, Sam Costanzo, provided most insightful guidance. Helpful reviewer comments were provided by Andrew A. Brogowicz, Western Michigan University; James H. Leigh, Texas A&M University; Danny L. Moore, University of Florida; and Gary J. Russell, University of California at Berkeley.

We are grateful to the Literary Executor of the late Sir Ronald A. Fisher, F.R.S.; to Dr. Frank Yates, F.R.S.; and to Longman Group Ltd., London, for permission to reprint Table III from their book *Statistical Tables for Biological, Agricultural and Medical Research* (6th ed., 1974).

Finally, we owe special thanks to Sheryl Petras, who helped develop many of the Marketing Research in Action inserts and who coauthored many of the new cases.

Thomas C. Kinnear

James R. Taylor

INTRODUCTION

CHAPTER 1

THE MARKETING RESEARCH SYSTEM

MARKETING RESEARCH IN ACTION

Mercedes-Benz Develops the "Baby Benz"

Marketing research played a key role in Mercedes-Benz's 1983 introduction of the 190 class—the "Baby Benz." The 190 is smaller and less expensive (about $23,000) than Mercedes' other models, yet comparable in quality and performance. According to David M. McCall, chairman of the board at McCaffrey and McCall, Inc., Mercedes' New York–based ad agency, "What was learned from [research] helped guide us through the most successful and exciting new-model launch Mercedes has ever staged in the U.S." The research for the Baby Benz included focus groups, automobile clinics, ad impact and awareness studies, measurements of consumer reaction after test drives, a survey of early buyers, and a follow-up survey.

Mercedes-Benz did not use marketing research until 1965, just after the creation of Mercedes-Benz of North America. "Under the previous U.S. distributor, advertising and marketing had been a hip-shot affair. Nothing was known about the market or the buyer," said McCall. U.S. sales at that point were barely 12,000 units (compared to over 80,000 units in 1984). Thus, initial research was undertaken both to gain insight into the affluent U.S. auto-buying market and to discover buyers' perceptions of the Mercedes. This research yielded some very interesting results. For example, sales per capita were the highest in Anchorage, Alaska. Also, consumers were trading in Chevrolets, rather than higher-priced Cadillacs or Jaguars as one might expect.

This early research also suggested that, as luxury car buyers, Mercedes owners were unique. They wanted a well-designed, well-engineered, high-performance automobile values. "Frills" were both unnecessary and unwanted. Consequently, ads for Mercedes-Benz discussed its engineering and design, and were without flashy copy or gimmicks. These ads were extremely successful. According to McCall, they have "been proven through every known research measurement ever applied to be among the best-read print copy year after year."

Source: Adapted from *Marketing News,* vol. 19, no. 1, pp. 20–21, Jan. 4, 1985.

The importance of marketing research to Mercedes-Benz is clearly illustrated in the above example. While the importance of marketing research has grown rapidly during the last three decades, organizations vary substantially as to its role and responsibility. Some, for example, view research as mainly an ad hoc data gathering and analysis function, while others broadly define the role and responsibility of research and view the marketing research department as an information center for decision making. This latter view of research is what we refer to as a *marketing research system.*

The concept of a marketing research system implies a deeply involved role for research in the marketing management process. This includes the active participation of research in the decision-making process, with particular emphasis on the provision of meaningful information for the planning and control functions. The purpose of this information input is to narrow decision-making error and broaden the decision-making perspective. Better decisions should result from better information inputs.

Organizations which embrace the marketing concept tend to view marketing research as a research system. The marketing concept suggests that the resources and activities of the organization be focused in an integrated way on the *needs and wants of the consumer* as opposed to the needs and wants of the organization. As an organization adopts this concept, marketing research is seen as a way to integrate the organization's activities and focus them on the needs of the marketplace. The growing acceptance of the marketing concept implies a more important role for marketing research in the marketing management process.

The central problem confronting many organizations is how to monitor the needs of the marketplace and anticipate the future. In response to this situation, the concept of a formalized system for acquiring information to assist in understanding the marketplace and to facilitate the decision-making process has emerged.

The marketing concept has expanded to many types of organizations. Producers and distributors of consumer and industrial goods were the first to formalize and implement the marketing concept, but this consumer-oriented philosophy has now been extended to service and nonprofit organizations such as financial institutions, the entertainment industry, hospitals, universities, churches, fund-raising groups, museums, and government agencies. Nations are beginning to adopt the marketing concept in their efforts to sell goods and services in the world's markets. As we see the marketing concept adopted by more and more organizations, the need for understanding the nature and role of marketing research has expanded. This textbook is designed to serve the needs of students training for, and practitioners serving in, these organizations.

Let's begin by noting some examples of the use of marketing research in consumer product organizations, industrial product organizations, and nonprofit organizations.

EXAMPLES OF MARKETING RESEARCH

The importance of marketing research to the success of marketing actions can be seen in the following examples.

United Airlines[1]

After the 1978 deregulation act, United Airlines was forced for the first time to take a serious look at the competition. There were 33 percent more carriers, but the passenger volume and the number of miles flown had declined 4 percent. Also, fewer cities were being served, making competition in the remaining cities even stiffer. Marketing research became a necessity, according to Charles M. Lamar, director of marketing research at United Airlines, Chicago.

Research revealed that prices could be varied according to arrival and departure times, and that they could be based on destination city rather than departure city. Analysis of existing data on first-class passenger volume indicated that United could further increase profits by varying fares on certain routes. Forecasts were developed to determine how many seats on each flight should be set aside for full fares and how many for discount fares.

The Mileage Plus program, instituted to increase loyalty among frequent flyers, was maintained as a direct result of marketing research. Mileage Plus is a program in which passengers could receive free first-class upgrades and flights by accumulating a certain mileage with United. Before any research findings were known, top management was skeptical of the idea. According to Lamar, "They didn't see any point in giving away flights . . . [but research showed that] the program not only maintained brand loyalty, it made people fly more often!" Research revealed that members booked an average one or two extra flights for every free flight received.

United Airlines surveyed 1000 passengers to determine what factors they deemed most important in choosing an airline. Through conjoint analysis, they found that (in order of importance) fare price, prompt departures and arrivals, scheduling, the length of check-in lines, and the quality of baggage handling service were considered the most significant attributes. Interestingly, United's "friendly skies" were perceived as less friendly than either Delta's or American's, but friendly personnel were relatively unimportant factors in a customer's selection of a carrier.

According to Lamar, marketing research has become an integral part of United Airlines. "Since 1981, our research department has doubled in size. Our influence extends to virtually every area of the business and we help to determine corporate strategies and tactics. United Airlines has made a strong commitment to marketing research."

---

[1] *Source: Marketing News,* vol. 19, no. 1, p. 17, Jan. 4, 1985.

Corning Glass Works[2]

Corning, long successful in ovenware, had not been represented in cookware for the top of the range, a segment that accounted for 60 percent of all cookware sales. While developing and successfully marketing a new line of top-of-the-range products, Corning did extensive marketing research. One of Corning's vice presidents noted, "Corning also made considerable investment in marketing research. In fact, the marketing studies were the most expensive ever undertaken by us in terms of time, cost, number of people involved, locations used and even in the type of research used."

Tonka and Hasbro Toys[3]

Every year 3000 to 4000 new toy products are introduced into the marketplace. More than 99 percent of them fail. To help meet the challenge of creating "winners" in a fickle children's toy market, increasing numbers of toymakers have begun to adopt a marketing orientation. "Companies are getting more disciplined in their approach," said Raymond E. McDonald, director of marketing for Tonka Toys in Spring Park, Minnesota.

Spurred ahead by marketing research, both Tonka and Hasbro Bradley, Inc., introduced a line of robot toys into the 1984 market. Hasbro Bradley's Transformers sold $90 million in the first year to lead the industry; Tonka's GoBots weren't far behind with sales of $82 million. Hasbro Bradley and Tonka were the first to create personalities for what the industry calls "boy dolls." Each of the robot toys was given a different personality: half of them good and half of them evil.

"Girl dolls have always had personalities associated with them," explained McDonald. "With boy dolls, we're [also] dealing with fantasy, and you need to give the doll a specific characteristic. It's important to the child to know that one is good and one is bad.

"It's not just enough to do a character line; you have to verify that the character line will hold the interest of the target audience. If they don't care about your character, everything else is for naught." That verification requires marketing research. Although conducting research with children aged 5 to 9 is often a nightmare, McDonald emphasized its importance. "You'd be surprised how much information you can get from young kids," he said. "They're articulate—and if you listen closely, you can get some valuable information."

According to Stephen A. Schwartz, Hasbro Bradley's senior vice president, marketing, "You really can't do a major product launch without developing a personality—kids won't accept it." And a personality can't be developed without conducting marketing research. In a recent report entitled "The Market for Children's Toys & Games," Find/SVP, a New York–based marketing research firm, points to the extensive use of focus groups, diary panels, concept and theme testing, name and package testing, and simulated test models as research tools. They estimate that industry leaders, such as Mattel, Hasbro Bradley, and Fisher-Price, spend 3 to 5 percent of sales on R&D. By conducting

---

[2] Adapted from "Corning's New Product Kick," *Marketing and Media Decisions,* p. 66, January 1981.
[3] Based on Kevin T. Higgins, "Research, Marketing Not Playthings for Toymakers," *Marketing News,* vol. 19, no. 14, p. 1, July 5, 1985.

thorough marketing research before the introduction of a new toy, manufacturers increase their product's chance of being among that 1 percent that makes it in the marketplace.

Union Carbide

Union Carbide, a diversified industrial products company, makes extensive use of marketing research to guide research and development activity and to provide information for other marketing management decisions. Two of their executives observe: "Marketing research can make a significant contribution toward improved effectiveness [of R&D]. Marketing-oriented R&D relies heavily on marketing research to identify needs and monitor changes in the external environment." A person in charge of a new product proposal screens it and transmits it to marketing research if the proposal has merit. Then "marketing research gathers pertinent information including marketing potential, competing technology, and cost/performance requirements. This analysis, together with appropriate recommendations, is presented to the product manager who may then either abandon the idea or develop an integrated business plan."[4] Union Carbide has developed zeolite (an industrial product used in absorption, catalysis, and ion exchange) and many other products using this type of marketing research.

Federal Trade Commission

In an important piece of regulatory action, the Federal Trade Commission (FTC) reached an agreement with the STP Corporation that directed STP to run "corrective advertising" (advertisements that attempt to correct consumer misperception of the truth about a product) for its oil additive product. The claim to be corrected was that the use of STP reduced oil consumption. The FTC then undertook market research to determine whether the corrective advertising had had the desired impact. This research involved interviews with about 2400 people in an experimental research design. Results showed some corrective impact on consumer perceptions.

We see in these examples and in the Baby Benz example the power of marketing research to aid marketing decision makers. The details of the specific techniques mentioned will become clear as we progress through the book. We now turn our attention to how marketing research fits into marketing management.

THE MARKETING SYSTEM

It is tempting to turn immediately to a discussion of contemporary research techniques and methodology. But this would be hasty; several introductory concepts and issues

---

[4] K. D. Marchanda and D. G. Driscoll, "The Role of Marketing Research in R&D—A Case Study," in Merit G. Marbach (ed.), *Marketing Research and R&D—The Vital Partnership,* Proceedings of the Chemical Marketing Research Association, Sea Island, Ga., Sept. 23–26, 1979 pp. 72–82.

FIGURE 1-1   Model of the marketing system.

must be discussed first. In particular, we must address the following questions:

1 What is the character of marketing activity?
2 What is the task of marketing management?
3 What type of information is needed by marketing management?
4 What are the sources of information for marketing decision making?
5 What is the role of marketing research in the marketing system?

To facilitate our understanding of the nature and role of marketing research, we must first characterize the marketing system of which it is a part. Figure 1-1 presents a diagrammatic model of this system. This conceptual scheme depicts the marketing system from the perspective of the selling organization. The model specifies one or more performance measures for the organization, identifies relevant variables in the process, and classifies the variables as independent or dependent.

Marketing Mix

By *variable* we mean a property that takes on different values at different times. For example, an organization may vary its advertising budget or change its selling price. An *independent variable* is the presumed cause of the dependent variable, which is the presumed effect.[5] The independent variables are classified as to whether they can be

---

[5] Fred N. Kerlinger, *Foundations of Behavioral Research,* 2d ed. (New York: Holt, Rinehart, 1973), p. 35.

manipulated or controlled by the selling organization. Those variables that can be controlled are identified as the marketing mix components of *product, price, place,* and *promotion.*[6] Different levels of these variables can be combined to form alternative marketing programs or courses of action.

Situational Factors

The situational variables represent independent variables that are not under the control of the marketing organization. These variables make up the state of nature which the selling organization must adapt to in formulating and implementing a marketing program. The state of nature consists of factors such as the energy crisis, competitive actions, economic climate, market trends, and government regulation.

Behavioral Response

Both sets of independent variables, marketing mix and situational factors, combine to influence a behavioral response such as purchase, buying intentions, preference, attitudes, and so on. This behavioral response is the dependent variable, or the presumed effect. A complicating factor is that the behavioral response is influenced by the consequences of past behavior in addition to the immediate influence of the independent variables.[7] Consequently, developing an effective marketing program is a challenging and complicated process involving a dynamic set of variables and a behavioral response which changes as a result of learning. This situation requires skilled managers who can give proper perspective to past experience and effectively use marketing research information in their decision making.

Formally identifying the functional relationships among the independent and dependent variables is obviously a difficult assignment. Regardless of how difficult, it is important to recognize that the nature of these relationships is *implicit* to the manager's choice of alternative courses of action. In attempting to use marketing research to formalize these relationships, the manager must consider the cost of gathering the information relative to the level of confidence gained in selecting the optimum course of action.[8] In practice, management experience and judgment, combined with information from the marketing research system, form the basis for management decision making.

It should be clearly understood that managers can and do make decisions without using marketing research. These decisions may be very sound if the manager's experience is relevant and his or her judgment is good. The idea is to make an effective decision, not to spend money on marketing research that will not be used to aid a decision. It is when the decision maker needs additional information to decrease the uncertainty associated with a decision that marketing research is used.

---

[6] E. Jerome McCarthy, *Basic Marketing: A Managerial Approach,* 4th ed. (Homewood, Ill.: Richard D. Irwin, 1971), p. 44.

[7] See B. F. Skinner, *Science and Human Behavior* (New York: The Free Press, 1953).

[8] The cost and value of information will be discussed more fully in Chapter 4.

For example, the development of Softsoap by Minnetonka was done without the use of much marketing research. It promptly took over 7 percent of the $1 billion personal-care soap market. In the words of Wallace A. Marx, vice president of Minnetonka, "Softsoap emerged without a great deal of formal research but with a great deal of personal evaluation, personal judgment, and experience as to what would work and what wouldn't work."[9]

Performance Measures

The behavior responses form the basis for the organization's monetary and nonmonetary performance measures. Monetary measures are sales, market share, profit, internal rate of return, and so on. Nonmonetary measures are the organization's image, consumer attitudes toward the organization, and so on. Developing valid performance measures is central to the effective management of the marketing system. Marketing research plays an important role in supplying the tools and data sources for performance measurement.

THE MARKETING MANAGEMENT PROCESS

What do marketing managers do? One of their key roles is to make decisions about marketing mix elements. This involves them in the decision-making process. Fundamental to the decision-making process is information. Marketing managers rely on two information inputs, namely their own experience and judgment and the more formalized information available from the marketing research system. Let's discuss the components of the marketing management process in more detail.

The Decision-Making Process

A characteristic of fundamental importance to the marketing management process is decision making. The decision-making process permeates the management process, and the two terms are often considered synonymous.[10]

The organization's well-being is dependent on the wisdom of the decisions made by its managers. The vast majority of decisions made by managers are *programmed*[11] and involve recurring situations which have been dealt with previously. We will refer to these as *routine decision situations* since they contain practically no uncertainty and have a low potential for surprise. Managers rely heavily, if not exclusively, on their experience and judgment in making such decisions.

A second type of decision involves situations where past experience and judgment are less relevant. These are called *nonroutine decision situations*. Here, the problem is new or the situation is unique in some way so that the manager's normal decision-making approach does not fit neatly into the new setting. Confronted with this non-

---

[9] "Minnetonka Credits 'Thinking,' Not Research, for Success of Softsoap," *Marketing News*, p. 1, Dec. 26, 1980.

[10] Herbert A. Simon, *The New Science of Management Decision* (New York: Harper & Row, 1960), p. 1.

[11] Ibid.

routine decision situation, the manager would follow a more formal approach which we will call the decision-making process.

The decision-making process may be thought of as involving a series of steps (see Figure 1-2). *The first step is the recognition that a unique marketing problem exists or that an opportunity is present.* Marketing problems and opportunities result from the dynamic nature of the situational factors and/or the implementation of the marketing program. Performance measures often signal the presence of problems, while the monitoring of the situational factors can signal the presence of both problems and opportunities. For example, the manager may be informed that a product's market share has declined, or that a competitor will be introducing a new product, or that primary demand for a product has risen faster than anticipated, or that government action has negatively influenced the sale of a competitor's product, and so on. Consequently, managers will make decisions to solve problems or to capitalize on opportunities.

The second step in the decision-making process is the definition of the decision problem. The manager needs to define and clarify the main issues and causal factors operating in the decision situation. It is not always easy to identify what fundamental variables are causing trouble and what needs correcting. Marketing research personnel and techniques play an important role here. By involving the research function in this early phase of the decision-making process, the marketing manager can benefit from more effective formulation of problems and opportunities, while at the same time assuring more effective use of marketing research in later stages of the decision process.

The third step in the decision process is the identification of alternative courses of action. In marketing, a course of action involves the specification of some combination of the marketing mix variables. "Do nothing new" or "maintain the status quo" is just as much a course of action as one denoting a change in marketing activities.

FIGURE 1-2   Steps in the decision-making process.

The effectiveness of management decision making is constrained by the quality of the alternatives considered. Consequently, it is critical that the "best" alternative be identified. The process of identifying courses of action is a *creative process* similar to the first stage of the decision-making process. The manager and marketing researcher have to search for new ideas, which come from creative thinking and imagination. Various marketing research approaches are available that can stimulate the manager's creative process and broaden the domain of alternatives identified.

The fourth and fifth steps in the decision process include the evaluation of alternatives and the selection of a course of action. In order that a decision can be made, there must be at least two courses of action identified and uncertainty as to which course of action will maximize the attainment of management objectives. If the decision maker is faced with a situation where there is only one realistic course of action, and that is to "do nothing," then there is no decision involved, even though the problem or opportunity confronting management has significant consequences for the organization.

Marketing research is a valuable tool in the evaluation of alternative courses of action. Often, nonroutine decision situations involve substantial uncertainty and risk. The manager is interested in marketing research information as a way to reduce the uncertainty inherent in the selection of a course of action.

The final step in the decision-making process is the implementation of the selected course of action. Again, marketing research supplies the means for monitoring the effectiveness of the action selected and the situational variables that influence the program's performance.

Decision making involving nonroutine decision situations can never be as well done as managers would like. This is caused partly by the uncertainty regarding the future state of the situational factors, partly by the limitations of gathering clear and precise information regarding the outcomes of the alternatives considered, and partly by the fact that decision making is a human process. The long time span between making decisions and receiving definite feedback plus the uncertainty regarding the nature of the cause-and-effect relations in the marketing system contribute substantially to this situation.

Figure 1-3 links the informational inputs of management experience and marketing research, the decision-making process, and the marketing system. Managers make decisions about the marketing system based upon their information about this system. Basically, they plan their future actions and control the performance of these implemented plans by comparing actual performance against objectives.

It is useful to make a distinction between the terms "information" and "data." *Data* are observations and evidence regarding some aspect of the marketing system. *Information* refers to data which reduce the uncertainty in a decision situation. This definition makes the uses of the term "information" dependent upon the manager and the decision-making situation. An example will clarify this distinction. A ship's captain is confronted with the problem of piloting his ship into a treacherous harbor at night. To aid the decision-making process, the captain is radioed the following data: (1) channel depth, (2) wind speed and direction, (3) score of the local baseball game, (4) tide speed and direction. Given the captain's problem, which data could be labeled information? Most readers, it is hoped, will find this distinction fairly easy, but given a

FIGURE 1-3   The marketing management process.

typical marketing decision making situation, distinguishing between data and information becomes substantially more challenging.

Information Needs

There are certain essential groups of information required by the marketing manager for planning and control purposes.[12] Exhibit 1-1 illustrates this type of information. While this listing is not intended to be complete, it does indicate that information is needed regarding the controllable and uncontrollable variables in the marketing system plus the measurement of their influence on the behavioral response.

Marketing research plays a central role in supplying information for the planning and control functions. It is in response to the need for formal planning and control that research is able to develop a systematic approach to the information needs of management. The activities of research can be built to a large extent around the needs of the planning process. The responsibility of research is not only to have such information on hand but also to organize and present it in a manner that contributes to the organization's planning and control activities. With a continually updated library of information available to facilitate decision making, the manager should be able to do an effective job of (1) developing the objectives, (2) allocating marketing resources, and (3)

---

[12] The discussion that follows is based on Murray A. Cayley, "Marketing Research Planning and Evaluation," *The Business Quarterly,* Spring 1975.

EXHIBIT 1-1

TYPES OF INFORMATION NEEDED FOR PLANNING AND CONTROL

I Situational analysis
  A Demand analysis
    1 Buyer behavior and characteristics:
      a What do they buy?
      b Who buys?
      c Where do they buy?
      d Why do they buy?
      e How do they buy?
      f When do they buy?
      g How much do they buy?
      h How will buyer behavior and characteristics change in the future?
    2 Market characteristics:
      a Market size potential
      b Segments
      c Selective demand
      d Future market trends
  B Competition
    1 Who are competitors?
    2 Competitor characteristics:
      a Marketing programs
      b Competitive behavior
      c Resources
    3 Major strengths and weaknesses
    4 Future competitive environment
  C General environment
    1 Economic conditions and trends
    2 Government regulation and trends
    3 Pollution, safety, consumerism concerns
    4 Technological trends
    5 Political climate
  D Internal environment
    1 Marketing resources/skills
    2 Production resources/skills
    3 Financial resources/skills
    4 Technological resources/skills
    5 Future trends in internal environment
II Marketing mix
  A Product
    1 What product attributes/benefits are important?
    2 How should the product be differentiated?
    3 What segments will be attracted?
    4 How important is service, warranty, and so on?
    5 Is there a need for product variation/product line?
    6 How important is packaging?
    7 How is the product perceived relative to competitive offerings?

B Place
    1 What types of distributors should handle the product?
    2 What are the channel attitudes and motivations for handling the product?
    3 What intensity of wholesale/retail coverage is needed?
    4 What margins are appropriate?
    5 What forms of physical distribution are needed?
C Price
    1 What is the elasticity of demand?
    2 What pricing policies are appropriate?
    3 How should the product line be priced?
    4 How do we establish price variations for a product?
    5 How should we react to a competitive price threat?
    6 How important is price to the buyer?
D Promotion
    1 What is the optimal promotional budget?
    2 How important is sales promotion, advertising, personal selling in stimulating demand?
    3 What is the proper promotion mix?
    4 How do you measure the effectiveness of the promotion tools?
    5 What copy is most effective?
    6 What media are most effective?
III Performance measures
    1 What are current sales by product line?
    2 What are current market shares by product line?
    3 What are current sales/market share by customer types, sales region, so on?
    4 What is our product/company image among customers, distributors, public?
    5 What is the awareness level to our promotion?
    6 What is the recall level of our brand name?
    7 What percentage distributorship do we have in large retailers, medium, small? By geography, customer type?
    8 What percentage of the channel is selling below suggested retail price? What is the average retail price of our product?

auditing performance. The balance of the research activities will arise ad hoc as problems and opportunities develop in the course of implementing the marketing plan.

WHAT ORGANIZATIONS DO

What types of information do organizations collect for decision making? Who collects the information? Table 1-1 presents the findings of a survey conducted by the American Marketing Association to answer these questions.[13]

[13] Dik Warren Twedt, *Survey of Marketing Research, 1978* (Chicago: American Marketing Association, 1978). This survey, the sixth in a series begun in 1947, was sent to 2780 companies, and the tabulation in Table 1-1 is based on the returns from the 798 usable questionnaires.

TABLE 1-1 TYPES OF RESEARCH ACTIVITY CONDUCTED BY COMPANIES

	Companies conducting research, %	Change, %	Done by marketing research dept., %*	Change, %	Done by another dept., %	Change, %	Done by outside firm, %*	Change, %
I Situational research								
A Demand research								
1 Determination of market characteristics	97	+4†	88	+6	3	−50	6	+33
2 Measurement of market potential	97	+4	88	+7	4	−43	5	+25
3 Short-range forecasting (up to 1 year)	89	+5	51	−2	36	+16	2	0
4 Long-range forecasting (over 1 year)	87	+6	49	−2	34	+13	4	+100
5 Export and international studies	49	−4	22	−8	25	0	2	0
6 Motivation	47	−2	30	+7	2	−33	15	−12
B Competition research								
1 Competitive product studies	87	−2	71	0	10	+11	6	+20
C General environment research								
1 Studies of business trends	91	+6	68	+11	20	−5	3	−25
2 Studies of legal constraints on advertising and promotion	46	−10	10	−17	31	−9	5	0
3 Ecological impact studies	23	−30	2	−60	17	−32	4	+33
4 Social values and policies studies	39	−3	19	+6	13	−24	7	+40
5 Consumers' "right to know" studies	18	−31	7	−36	9	−25	2	−33
D Internal environment research								
1 Internal company employee studies (attitudes, communication, etc.)	76	+17	25	+39	45	+7	6	0

II Marketing mix research

	Done by marketing research department		Done by other departments		Done by both inside depts. and outside firms		Done by outside firm	
	%	Change†	%	Change	%	Change	%	Change
A Product research								
1 New product acceptance and potential	76	−10	59	−17	11	+57	6	0
2 Testing of existing products	80	+7	55	+12	19	−5	6	0
3 Acquisition studies	73	+6	33	+14	38	0	2	0
4 Packaging research	65	+8	44	+22	12	−25	9	+13
B Place research								
1 Distribution channel studies	71	+3	32	+3	38	+3	1	0
2 Plant and warehouse location	68	−4	29	−3	35	−8	4	+33
C Price research	83	+2	34	−6	47	−7	2	+100
D Promotion research								
1 Studies of ad effectiveness	76	+13	42	+11	5	0	29	+21
2 Sales compensation studies	60	0	13	−7	43	0	4	+33
3 Media research	68	+11	22	−8	14	+27	32	+23
4 Promotional studies of premiums, coupons, sampling, deals, etc.	58	+12	38	+12	14	−7	6	+100
5 Copy research	61	+32	30	+36	6	0	25	+19
III Performance research								
1 Market share analysis	97	+5	85	+6	6	−33	6	+100
2 Sales analysis	92	+3	67	+3	23	−4	2	+100
3 Establishment of sales quotas, territories	78	+4	23	−15	54	+13	1	0
4 Test markets, store audits	59	+9	43	+13	7	−22	9	+29
5 Consumer panel operations	63	+26	46	+44	2	−60	15	+15
IV Decision aids								
1 MIS (management information system)	80	+11	25	−4	53	+20	2	0
2 Operations research	65	+8	14	−18	50	+19	1	0

* The total of the percentages "done by marketing research department," "done by other departments," "done by outside firm" is greater than "percentage of companies doing" because some firms have studies done by both inside departments and outside firms.

† The change is calculated with 1978 survey as the base year.

Source: D. W. Twedt, *Survey of Marketing Research, 1983* (Chicago: American Marketing Association, 1983), p. 41.

Companies collect information on all aspects of the marketing system, i.e., situational variables, marketing mix variables, and performance measures. Over 90 percent of the companies surveyed conducted some research on the situational variables. This included research on demand (market characteristics, market potential, short- and long-range forecasting), competitive research studies, and research on business trends. Over 80 percent did some studies on the marketing mix variables of product (new products, existing products, acquisition studies, and product mix studies) and price. Over 90 percent of the companies collected some type of performance information (market share and sales analysis). Also note the growth in the use of marketing research in many areas over the 1978 survey. This is a continuation of a long-term trend.

The vast majority of these studies were conducted by the companies' own marketing research departments. Of the studies not done by the marketing research department, the bulk were conducted by another department within the organization. Only a few studies (media research, copy research, ad effectiveness research, and motivation research) tend to be conducted by an outside firm.

MARKETING RESEARCH DEFINED

What is marketing research? There are many excellent definitions.[14] For our purposes, there are four terms that need to be included in such a definition. These are (1) systematic, (2) objective, (3) information, and (4) decision making. Thus,

> Marketing research is the systematic and objective approach to the development and provision of information for the marketing management decision-making process.

A few comments are in order regarding this definition. "Systematic" refers to the requirement that the research project should be well organized and planned: the strategic and tactical aspects of the research design must be detailed in advance, and the nature of the data to be gathered and the mode of analysis to be employed must be anticipated. "Objectivity" implies that marketing research strives to be unbiased and unemotional in performing its responsibilities. One often hears that marketing research is "the application of the scientific method to marketing." The hallmark of the scientific method is the objective gathering, analysis, and interpretation of data. While one may learn of a scientist who violates the rule of objectivity, this is rare and often results in sanctions by the scientific community. Marketing research may operate in different settings from those of the physical, social, and medical sciences, but it shares their common standard of objectivity.

The remaining two elements of this definition, information and the decision-making process, have been discussed previously. It is important to recognize that these are the two elements that differentiate marketing research from research in other fields. The primary purpose of marketing research is to provide information, not data, for the management decision-making process.

---

[14] A very popular definition is "the systematic gathering, recording, and analyzing of data about problems relating to the marketing of goods and services" (report of the Definitions Committee of the American Marketing Association, Chicago, 1961).

Does the definition of marketing research apply to management experience and judgment? The answer is—not completely. The definition's two elements of information and the management decision-making process are characteristics of experience and judgment. As discussed previously, the latter qualities even have an advantage over marketing research in that they are almost always in the form of information rather than data.

It is in regard to the remaining elements, being objective and systematic, that experience and judgment fail to fit this definition. "Systematic" refers to being well organized in the collecting and processing of data. Since experience and judgment involve the acquisition of knowledge about the marketing system through personal observations and experiences, they are subject to bias and frailty resulting from this rather casual approach to data collection. The element of objectivity involves the unemotional and unbiased description of reality. Knowledge gained through personal experience and observation can be biased by our selective perception of reality, distorting facts to benefit personal objectives and to conform with existing attitudes regarding the marketing system.

Biases of this nature are likely to be minimized in routine decision situations because of the feedback about the accuracy of decision making in other similar decisions. Here, effective decision making can result from information inputs based on experience and judgment. However, with nonroutine decision situations, these biases can be serious and may result in a conflict with information emanating from the marketing research system. A skilled manager recognizes and attempts to control such biases in executing the decision-making process.

BASIC AND APPLIED RESEARCH

Marketing research studies can be classified as being basic or applied in nature. *Basic* (pure or fundamental) *research* seeks to extend the boundaries of knowledge regarding some aspect of the marketing system. There is little concern with how this knowledge can be used in the marketing management process. In contrast, *applied research* studies or investigations are concerned with assisting managers in making better decisions. These studies are directed toward the orgnization's specific situation and guided by the requirements of the decision-making process. Basic research studies tend to be less organization-specific, broader in purpose, and guided by marketing hypotheses and theory.

Applied and basic research can be differentiated with regard to the thoroughness of the research. A desirable characteristic for basic research is that it be thorough and complete. For applied research, the thoroughness of the research is dictated by the information needs of the decision maker. Consequently, the time and money required to do a thorough study may be inappropriate given the information required for an effective and efficient decision.

It should be noted, however, that marketing research that will be used in a broader political context must meet basic research standards. Studies done by the Federal Trade Commission or by organizations trying to influence government agencies or make product claims are in this category.

This textbook is primarily concerned with applied research. This is reflected in the definition of marketing research discussed earlier. While many of the concepts, approaches, and techniques discussed in this book are applicable to those interested in basic research, our primary focus is on applied marketing research.

THE RESEARCH PROCESS

The formal marketing research project can be viewed as a series of steps called the *research process*. Figure 1-4 illustrates the nine steps in this process. To effectively conduct a research project it is essential to anticipate all the steps and recognize their interdependence. These nine steps represent the framework for the chapters in the book. We will touch briefly on each of these steps now in order to emphasize their sequencing and interdependence.

1 Need for Information

Establishing the need for marketing research information is, of course, the first step in the research process. Rarely does the manager's initial request for help adequately es-

FIGURE 1–4   Steps in the research process.

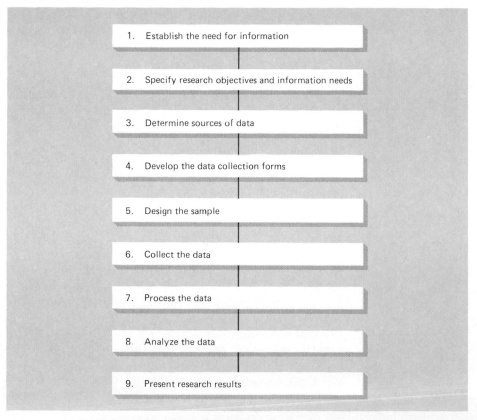

1. Establish the need for information

2. Specify research objectives and information needs

3. Determine sources of data

4. Develop the data collection forms

5. Design the sample

6. Collect the data

7. Process the data

8. Analyze the data

9. Present research results

tablish the need for research information. The researcher must thoroughly understand why the information is needed. The manager is responsible for explaining the situation surrounding the request for help and establishing that research information will facilitate the decision-making process. If the research project is to provide pertinent information for the decision making, the need for research information must be precisely defined. Chapter 4 will discuss this area in more detail along with issues related to the management-research interface.

Managers often react to hunches and symptoms rather than clearly identified decision situations. Consequently, establishing the need for research information is a critical and difficult phase of the research process. Too often the importance of this initial step is overlooked in the excitement of undertaking a research project. This results in research findings that are not decision oriented.

2 Research Objectives and Information Needs

Once the need for research information has been clearly established, the researcher must specify the objectives of the proposed research and develop a specific list of information needs. Research objectives answer the question "Why is this project being conducted?" Typically, research objectives are put in writing before the project is undertaken. Information needs answer the question "What specific information is needed to attain the objectives?" In practice, information needs may be thought of as a detailed listing of research objectives.

3 Data Sources

Once the study objectives have been determined and the information needs listed, the next step is to determine whether the data are currently available from sources internal or external to the organization. Internal sources include previous research studies and company records. External sources include commercial research reports, trade magazine or industry reports, government reports, and so on. If data are found which fit the information needs, the researcher must examine the research design to determine their accuracy. The reputation of the organization which collected and analyzed the data is often a guide to reliability.

If the data are not available from internal or external sources, the next step is to collect new data by means of mail, telephone, and personal interviews, observation, experimentation, or simulation. The remaining steps in the research process relate to data collected through these sources.

4 Data Collection Forms

In preparing the data collection forms, the researcher must establish an effective link between the information needs and the questions to be asked or the observations to be recorded. The success of the study is dependent upon the researcher's skill and creativity in establishing this link. The responsibility for this task rests mainly with the researcher.

5 Sample Design

The first issue in designing the sample concerns who or what is to be included in the sample. This means that a clear definition is needed of the population from which the sample is to be drawn. The next issue concerns the method used to select the sample. These methods can be classified as to whether they involve a probability or nonprobability procedure. The third issue involves the size of the sample.

6 Data Collection

The process of collecting data is critical since it typically involves a large proportion of the research budget and a large proportion of the total error in the research results. Consequently, the selection, training, and control of interviewers is essential to effective marketing research studies.

7 Data Processing

Once they have been recorded, the processing of the data begins. This includes the functions of editing and coding. Editing involves reviewing the data forms as to legibility, consistency, and completeness. Coding involves establishing categories for responses or groups of responses so that numerals can be used to represent the categories. The data are then ready for hand tabulation or computer data analysis.

8 Data Analysis

It is important that the data analysis be consistent with the requirements of the information needs identified in step 2. It is usually done using appropriate data analysis software packages.

9 Presentation of Results

The research results are typically communicated to the manager through a written report and oral presentation. It is imperative that the research finding be presented in a simple format and addressed to the information needs of the decision situation. "No matter what the proficiency with which all previous steps have been dispatched, the project will be no more successful that the research report."[15]

ERRORS IN MARKETING RESEARCH

At every step in the marketing research process, errors can occur that result in misinformation being communicated to managers. The control of these errors is of critical concern in marketing research. Much of the rest of this book is concerned with under-

---

[15] Harper Boyd and Ralph Westfall, *Marketing Research: Text and Cases* (Homewood, Ill.: Richard D. Irwin, 1956), p. 195.

MARKETING RESEARCH IN ACTION

HERTZ VERSUS AVIS AND AVIS'S MARKETING RESEARCH SUPPLIER

Avis, famous for its "We're number two so we try harder" campaign, may not have tried hard enough in obtaining and verifying its marketing research results, alleges Thomas Werbe, Hertz Corporation's vice president of marketing research and planning. Werbe's claims were initiated by an Avis press conference, during which Avis announced a gain in market share relative to Hertz. Avis said this gain was reflected in a recently conducted poll. But, according to Werbe, Avis's survey was timed to yield optimum results. People were interviewed after receiving a free promotional gift from Avis, which materially altered the results of the survey. The poll was conducted for Avis by Garth-Mariorana-Connelly, a subsidiary of the political campaign management company, Garth Organization, Ltd.

Werbe's assertions implied that the Garth organization's research was tailored and in its own self-interest. He called Garth's sampling procedures "so lax, so sloppy, that they have [even] been interviewing Hertz managers." Werbe went on to say that the Hertz manager at Chicago's O'Hare airport was approached and interviewed in one of the surveys.

David Garth, the head of Garth-Mariorana-Connelly, vehemently denied the Werbe-Hertz allegations. He said, "We don't tailor our polls. If anything, we go the other way; we are twice as tough on our clients . . . as their opponents are."

Mr. Garth compared his polling strategy to the political strategy his corporation used in political surveys. "It's the exact same thing you do in a political campaign," he said. "You want to look at the candidate (Avis), you want to look at the person you are running against (Hertz) and the people who are his or her supporters." Mr. Mariorana, a partner in Garth-Mariorana-Connelly, called Werbe's claims "hysterical, assumptive, and inaccurate."

This type of allegation of incompetence in field work has the potential to damage both the research firm's and the client's reputations. Furthermore, poor research techniques open the door to a host of potentially injurious lawsuits from the competition, making the costs of the research far outweigh any potential benefits.

Source: Based on *Advertising Age,* Feb. 28, 1983.

standing and controlling these errors. In this section we note that basically there are two types: (1) sampling errors and (2) nonsampling errors. The Marketing Research in Action feature on the Hertz versus Avis illustrates the critical nature of error control in marketing research.

Sampling Errors

Most marketing research studies utilize samples of people or products or stores. Based upon these sample results, the researcher and the manager make conclusions about the whole population from which the sample was selected. For example, the attitudes of all Chevrolet owners could be inferred from a sample of a thousand owners. Because the sample is used to estimate the population, differences exist between the sample value and the true underlying population value. This difference is called sam error and is discussed in Chapters 8 and 9.

Nonsampling Errors

Nonsampling errors are all the errors that may occur in the marketing research process except the sampling error. This concept simply includes all the aspects of the research process where mistakes and deliberate deceptions can occur. Unfortunately, these mistakes and deceptions occur with great frequency in the marketing research process. We must therefore be aware of (1) what nonsampling errors may occur, (2) what effect these errors may have on our results, and (3) what steps we can take to reduce these errors. This chapter deals with the first two issues, identification of nonsampling errors and possible effects of these errors. The details of how to reduce nonsampling errors will be left to the remaining chapters of the book, since most of them focus on that topic. The chapters that deal with the reduction of nonsampling errors will be identified with the specific error in the list of errors described below.

The Effect of Nonsampling Errors

Sampling error has two properties that make it useful to the researcher: (1) it is measurable and (2) it decreases as the sample size increases. Unfortunately, nonsampling errors are not easily measurable, and they do not decrease with sample size. In fact, in all likelihood, nonsampling errors increase as sample size increases. What nonsampling errors do is put a bias in our results of unknown direction and magnitude. One practicing researcher put forth the following view of the effect of nonsampling errors:

> Over the years I have used a simple rule of thumb that the true mean square error of field studies is at least twice the size of reported theoretical sampling error, though there is evidence to suggest that it is larger in many commercial surveys.[16]

Indeed, nonsampling error can render the results of a study useless. Examples of different types of these errors follow.

Types of Nonsampling Errors

Faulty Problem Definition   A product manager requests a study to test a media mix. If the true problem is pricing strategy, then any research that is conducted, no matter how technically correct, will not be helpful to the manager. This issue is discussed in detail in Chapter 4.

Defective Population Definition   The study population must be defined to fit the study objectives. Consider the case of the manager of one of the restaurants in a major metropolitan airport. She would like to know what sort of image the restaurant has among those who have some likelihood of eating in the airport. The population is defined as people over 18 years old, getting off planes in the week of September 12 to 19. If the sample is selected from this population, one might get misleading results. It does not include significant numbers of potential customers, i.e., people who are

---

[16] Benjamin Lipstein, "In Defense of Small Samples," *Journal of Advertising Research*, vol. 15, p. 39, February 1975.

visting the airport but who are not landing on planes, and people who are just taking off. Also, the sample includes people who have no chance of eating at the restaurant, i.e., people who change planes without going into the main terminal where the restaurants are located. Conclusions from the study are questionable.

Frame Is Nonrepresentative of the Population   The sampling frame must match the defined population. Consider the case of an investment company that uses the telephone book (the frame) to select a sample of "potential stock buyers." This frame would not cover the defined population well, as a significant number of high-income people have unlisted phone numbers. These high-income people are the prime potential stock buyers. Again, conclusions are suspect.

Nonresponse Errors   Errors occur because people in the selected sample either refuse to be a part of the sample or are not at home during the sampling period. A sample is a representative sample as selected. If some of the selected elements do not form part of the realized sample, it is not a truly representative sample. The resulting error is called nonresponse error.

As an example of this problem, consider the case of a resort developer who attempts to interview people during the day. The study yields some refusals and a lot of "not at homes." We must wonder if the refusals as a group hold different attitudes about the development from those who responded. Also, by interviewing only in the day, the developer missed all families where both the spouses work. This group may be a prime prospect.

Frame problems and nonresponse errors are discussed in Chapter 15. The remaining nonsampling errors, which follow, are related to areas of the research process other than sampling.

Measurement Error   Measurement is the process of assigning numbers to observed phenomena. A researcher may try to develop a scale of interest in a new product, but the scaling may be done improperly. This is a complex area which will be discussed in detail in Chapters 10 and 11.

Improper Causal Inferences   A producer of heavy equipment changes the compensation scheme of its sales force, and the following year sales double. Management infers that the new compensation plan caused the sales increase. It is also possible that other factors could have caused it—for example, the economy could have improved, the product was improved, or the salespersons have become more experienced. Management has observed an association between sales and compensation and has inferred the cause. The search for causes is discussed in Chapter 12.

Poor Questionnaire Design   In a survey of his constituents, a congressman asked: "Should the Congress challenge the do-nothing administration and take action on unemployment?" This is hardly the way to find their true feeling on a complex issue. What good is measuring sampling error here? Most questionnaire design problems are more complex than this, relating to question sequence, length, word usage, etc., and the topic is discussed fully in Chapter 14.

Auspices Bias   Error can occur because of the respondents' perception of who is conducting the study. Consider the following question: "We represent the Procter and Gamble Company, and we would like to know your opinion of our product, Pampers." People's true feelings may not come out when they know the source of the study.

Interviewer-Related Errors   Interviewers can lead respondents to answer in a particular way either by accident or on purpose. They also have been known to record responses improperly and even to fill out questionnaires without interviewing anyone. In other words, they cheat. This issue is discussed in Chapter 15.

Data Processing Errors   Questionnaires must be prepared for analysis. This involves coding the responses, recording the codes, punching the codes onto computer cards, and so on. Mistakes can occur in all these activities, or a bias could be exhibited in coding responses. These issues are discussed in Chapter 16.

Data Analysis Errors   Simple mistakes can occur in data analysis, such as adding numbers incorrectly. Most errors here are more complex than this. They usually involve the misapplication of data analysis procedures. This topic is discussed in Chapters 17, 18, 19, and 20.

Interpretation Errors   We have all observed that people can interpret a set of data to suit their own purposes. This bias may be explicitly deliberate or subconscious. It can also be related to misunderstandings of study results. This issue is discussed in Chapter 4 and will be treated further in Chapter 21.

Total Error

What should be clear now is that a small sampling error does not necessarily indicate an accurate result. What the user of research must be concerned about is *total error,* where

$$\text{Total error} = \text{sampling error} + \text{nonsampling error}$$

SUMMARY

1 The need for marketing research parallels acceptance of the marketing concept. Organizations of all types are integrating and directing their activities to meet the needs of the marketplace. The growing acceptance of the marketing concept has increased the need for a formal process of acquiring information, namely, marketing research.

2 Marketing research can supply information regarding many aspects of the marketing system. This domain ranges from monitoring and describing situational factors to evaluating marketing programs and measuring the performance of these programs.

3 The primary purpose of marketing research is to provide information for decision making. Marketing research information can be useful in all stages of the decision-making process. This ranges from information to aid in recognizing that a decision situation is present to information that will guide the selection of a course of action.

4 Marketing management's increased emphasis on the planning and control functions has influenced the nature of marketing research activity. A more systematic and continuous flow of information is required. The activities of marketing research must be designed in accord with the requirements of the planning and control process. Marketing research is required to have available a continually updated library of information to facilitate the decision-making process.

5 Most marketing decisions involve limited marketing research input. These decisions are repetitive in nature, and the manager's experience and judgment provide adequate information for sound decisions. Marketing information is typically the main input to nonrepetitive decision situations.

6 The concept of a marketing research system implies a broadly defined role for marketing research in the marketing management process. Here, marketing research is viewed by management as an information center for decision making as opposed to an activity that merely gathers and analyzes data.

7 Marketing research is defined as the systematic and objective approach to the development and provision of information for the marketing management decision-making process. This definition emphasizes the applied-research focus of this book. Information based on management experience and judgment differs from marketing research information in terms of objectivity and of how systematically the data was collected and processed.

8 The research process is composed of nine steps, starting with the establishment of the need for information and ending with the presentation of the research results. To effectively conduct a research project it is essential to anticipate the nine steps and recognize their interdependence. What is done in one step can greatly influence the other steps.

9 The researcher should be concerned with total error, which is the sum of sampling and nonsampling errors.

DISCUSSION QUESTIONS

1 What effect has the increasing adoption of the marketing concept by organizations had on marketing research?

2 Present the four essential components of the marketing system and examples of each.

3 In what aspects of the marketing system is marketing research of limited applicability?

4 Outline the steps involved in the decision-making process.

5 What factors determine the relative importance of managerial experience versus marketing research in a given situation?

6 What is the difference between "data" and "information"?

7 What is a marketing research system?

8 Define marketing research. Elaborate on the components of your definition.

9 Contrast basic and applied marketing research.

10 Specify the sequence of steps in the research process.

11 Why is it essential that a researcher anticipate all of the steps of the research process?

12 What is a nonsampling error?

13 What are the properties of nonsampling errors?

14 Define and then give an example of each type of nonsampling error listed in this chapter.

15 A major marketing research firm once declared one of its survey-based services to be "free from all error, except sampling error." Do you think this could be a true statement?

CHAPTER 2

THE MARKETING RESEARCH BUSINESS

In Chapter 1, we discussed the nature and role of marketing research as it relates to marketing decision making. Now our objective is to add life to the marketing research process by presenting a description of a very exciting business, the marketing research business; unfortunately, no words on paper can do justice to its dynamic nature.

This chapter will first present a brief history of marketing research and then describe the amount of money that is spent on marketing research and the types of institutions that use and perform such research. In this context, we shall discuss how companies organize the marketing research function, the types of job opportunities that are available, and the procedures by which the users of marketing research select those who will actually perform it. With a good understanding of the practice of marketing research in hand, we will then address the ethical constraints that affect this field and finally its legal dimensions.

HISTORY OF MARKETING RESEARCH

To put the nature of marketing research in perspective, let's review the history of the field. The development of marketing research during the early part of the twentieth century parallels the rise of the marketing concept. Over this period, the management philosophy guiding organizations gradually changed to the consumer orientation of today. During the period 1900–1930, management concern was focused primarily on the problems and opportunities associated with production; between 1930 and the late 1940s, this orientation shifted to the problems and opportunities associated with distribution; since the late 1940s, increased attention has been focused on consumer needs and desires.[1] The nature and role of marketing activity in these organizations reflects this shift in management philosophy.

Pioneers and Institutions

While numerous people and institutions were involved in the occasional use of marketing research prior to 1910, the period 1910–1920 is recognized as the formal beginning of marketing research.[2] In 1911, J. George Frederick established a research firm called The Business Bourse. Charles Coolidge Parlin was appointed manager of the Commercial Research Division of the Curtis Publishing Company that same year. The use of the name "commercial research" had special significance, since most business people considered the term research too eloquent for a business service. Parlin managed one of the leading research organizations of this period.

The success of Parlin's work inspired several industrial firms and advertising media to establish research divisions. In 1915, the United States Rubber Company hired Dr. Paul H. Nystrom to manage a newly established Department of Commercial Research. In 1917, Swift and Company hired Dr. Louis D. H. Weld from Yale University to become manager of their Commercial Research Department.

In 1919, Professor C. S. Duncan of the University of Chicago published *Commercial Research: An Outline of Working Principles*. This was considered to be the first major book on commercial research. In 1921, Percival White's *Market Analysis* was published. This was the first research book to gain a large readership, and it went through several editions. *Market Research and Analysis* by Lyndon O. Brown was published in 1937.[3] This became one of the most popular college textbooks of the period, reflecting the growing interest in marketing research on the college campus. After 1940, numerous research textbooks were published, and the number of business schools offering research courses rapidly expanded.

Following World War II, the growth of marketing research activity dramatically increased, paralleling the growing acceptance of the marketing concept. By 1948, over 200 marketing research organizations had been formed in the United States.[4] Expenditures on marketing research activities were estimated to be $50 million a year in 1947.[5] Over the next three decades this expenditure level increased more than tenfold.[6]

The growing acceptance of the marketing concept brought a change in emphasis from "market research" to "marketing research." Market research implied that the focus of research was on the analysis of markets. The shift to marketing research broad-

---

[1] Robert L. King, "The Marketing Concept," in G. Schwartz (ed.), *Science in Marketing* (New York: Wiley, 1965).

[2] Material in this section draws heavily from the work of Lawrence C. Lockley, "History and Development of Marketing Research," in Robert Ferber (ed.), *Handbook of Marketing Research* (New York: McGraw-Hill, 1974), pp. 1-3 to 1-15.

[3] Lyndon O. Brown, *Market Research and Analysis* (New York: Ronald Press, 1937).

[4] "Market Detectives," *Wall Street Journal*, September 1947, p.1.

[5] Donald M. Hobart (ed.), *Marketing Research Practice* (New York: Ronald Press, 1950), p. 9.

[6] "Marketing Research Investment to Hit $600,000,000: Dutka," *Advertising Age*, vol. 39, p. 88, Dec. 9, 1968.

ened the nature and role of research, with the emphasis on contact between research-ers and the marketing management process. The publication of *Marketing Research* by Harper Boyd and Ralph Westfall in 1956 reflected this change in orientation.[7]

Methodological Development

Advances in marketing research methodology parallel the development of research methodology in the social sciences, of which marketing is a part. The methodological advances made by psychologists, economists, sociologists, political scientists, statisti-cians, and so on had a pronounced influence on marketing research methodology, and consequently its history is interwoven with the historical development of the social sciences.

Marketing research made major methodological advances from 1910 to 1920. Ques-tionnaire studies or surveys became popular modes of data collection. With the growth of survey research came improvements in questionnaire design and question construc-tion, along with the awareness of biases resulting from the questioning and the inter-viewing process. Several social scientists who entered the field were interested in working on these applied methodological problems. This established a methodological communi-cation link between marketing and the other social sciences that exists to this day.

During the 1930s, sampling became a serious methodological issue. As statistical training developed beyond descriptive statistics (calculation of means, variances, simple correlation, and construction of index numbers) to an emphasis on inferential statistics, nonprobability sampling procedures came under heavy attack. Modern probability sampling approaches slowly gained acceptance during this period.

Methodological innovation occurred at a fairly steady pace from 1950 through the early 1960s. At this time a major development occurred, the commercialization of the large-scale digital computer. The computer rapidly increased the pace of methodological innovation, especially in the area of quantitative marketing research.

In response to this methodological explosion, two new journals appeared in the 1960s: the *Journal of Marketing Research* and the *Journal of Advertising Research*. In 1966, professors Paul Green and Donald Tull authored an innovative textbook which emphasized the methodological advances made in marketing research.[8] In 1974, the *Journal of Consumer Research* appeared, sponsored by an impressive list of organiza-tions representing the social sciences. This latter publication reflects the growing emphasis on consumer behavior research in business, government, and academia. This focus on consumer behavior reflects the shift of management philosophy to the mar-keting concept.

The 1980s find technological advances in computer and related areas having major impact on many aspects of the marketing research profession. These include checkout scanners in supermarkets which provide panel data, computer-assisted telephone inter-viewing, data analysis by microcomputer and remote terminals, and the potential for

---

[7] Harper Boyd and Ralph Westfall, *Marketing Research: Text and Cases* (Homewood, Ill.: Richard D. Irwin, 1956).

[8] Paul E. Green and Donald S. Tull, *Research for Marketing Decisions* (Englewood Cliffs, N.J.: Prentice-Hall, 1966).

interviewing through two-way cable television systems. All of these are amplified later in this book.

THE PRACTICE OF MARKETING RESEARCH

Dollar Expenditures

It is difficult to obtain exact dollar figures for the amount of money expended for marketing research activity. However, some good estimates are available to help us understand the magnitude of this business.

A 1983 American Marketing Association study[9] reported that 559 companies surveyed in the United States and Canada spent $429 million for marketing research in 1983. If one allows for reasonable growth since 1983, this figure is likely to be well over $500 million in 1986. These figures understate the expenditures for marketing research, as can be seen by examining Table 2-1. This table presents the worldwide and United States revenues for the top 44 marketing research suppliers. These are companies that do research for other organizations on both an ad hoc and a syndicated basis. Most are large suppliers of syndicated data. Note that the top 100 companies had worldwide revenues of $1785 million in 1985 and United States revenues of well over $1400 million. If one considers all the money that was spent on research where outside research suppliers were not used, and the research done by the thousands of other marketing research supply firms not in the top 100, then annual expenditures on marketing research in the United States should easily be in excess of $1400 million. In the AMA survey a 62 percent increase in dollar expenditures on the average over 1978 was reported in marketing research budgets.[10]

Table 2-2a presents estimates that were made by marketing researchers of the consumer ad hoc marketing research expenditures outside the United States in 1975. If syndicated services were added to the $212 million in Table 2-2a, the total was estimated by the researchers to be over $400 million. It is likely to be over $500 million now. Table 2-2b itemizes the 10 largest research groups.

Marketing research is a big and rapidly growing business offering interesting employment opportunities. We now turn our attention to where the employment opportunities are by examining the institutional structure of the industry.

Institutional Structure

The institutional structure of the marketing research business is complex, with many thousands of different types of organizations being part of the industry. To simplify our discussion we will position each of these organizations in one of three categories. These categories are (1) users, (2) users/doers, and (3) doers. Figure 2-1 presents a graphic representation of this structure. Different types of organizations are listed under each of the three categories. The arrows indicate the direction of the flow of marketing re-

---

[9] Dik Warren Twedt, *1983 Survey of Marketing Research* (Chicago: American Marketing Association, 1983), p. 28.
[10] Twedt, op. cit., p. 8.

TABLE 2-1   HOW THEY RANK: 1985 REVENUE RECORD OF THE 44 LEADING U.S. RESEARCH COMPANIES

1985 rank	1984 rank	Organization	Research revenues, millions	% change vs. 1984[†]	Research revenues from outside U.S., millions
1	1	A.C. Nielsen Co.	$517.0	+ 7.7%	$268.8 est.
2	2	IMS International	171.1	+11.4	86.9
3	3	SAMI	138.5	+17.0	—
4	4	Arbitron Ratings Co.	122.0	+15.3	—
5	8	Information Resources	75.1	+22.9	3.0 est.
6	5	Burke Marketing Services	73.1	+10.8	3.7
7	6	M/A/R/C	46.3	+23.0	—
8	7	Market Facts	37.8	+ 5.1	—
9	9	NFO Research	34.3	+16.3	—
10	10	NPD Group	33.1	+13.4	—
11	11	Maritz Market Research	30.0	+21.4	—
12	12	Westat	25.2	+ 3.3	—
13	13	Elrick and Lavidge	24.6	+ 5.6	—
14	14	Walker Research	20.7	+ 7.1	—
15	15	YSW/Clancy Shulman	19.5	+14.7	1.0
16	16	Chilton Research	19.1	+15.8	—
17	22	Simmons Market Research Bureau	16.5	+32.0	—
18	18	Louis Harris and Associates	15.8	+ 3.3	5.5
19	17	ASI Market Research	15.7	− 4.3	—
20	19	Opinion Research Corp.	14.5	0.0	—
21	21	Winona Research	14.4	+11.6	—
22	24	Decisions Center	13.8	+35.3	—
23	20	Ehrhart-Babic Group	13.8	+ 4.2	—
24	25	Harte-Hanks Marketing Services Group	11.7	+20.3	—
25	23	Data Development Corp.	10.9	+ 3.8	—
26	28	Custom Research	9.7	+12.8	—
27	29	National Analysts	9.6	+21.5	—
28	34	Mediamark Research	9.5	+23.1	—
29	27	Admar Research	8.9	− 4.3	—
30	33	Starch INRA Hooper	8.9	+18.5	—
31	26	McCollum/Speilman Research	8.8	− 6.4	—
32	32	Gallup Organization	8.6	+11.7	—
33	—	National Research Group	8.0	+73.1	.9
34	38	Response Analysis	7.6	+35.0	—
35	39	Decision Research Corp.	6.8	+23.6	—
36	30	Decision/Making/Information	6.7	−14.1	—
37	35	Market Opinion Research	6.5	− 5.0	—
38	—	Guideline Research	6.5	+18.0	—
39	37	Ad Factors Marketing Research	5.9	− 1.0	—
40	—	J.D. Power & Associates	5.8	+ 6.0	—
41	—	Lieberman Research West	5.3	− 2.6	—
42	—	Marketing Research Services	5.1	+59.0	—
43	40	Oxtoboy-Smith	5.0	+ 2.7	—
44	36	Kapuler Marketing Research	4.8	−19.5	—
Subtotal, top 44			$1,652.5	+11.5%	$369.8
All other (56 CASRO companies not listed in top 44)			132.8[‡]	+10.9%	
Total (100 organizations)			$1,785.3	+11.5%	$369.8

* Total revenues that include nonresearch activities, for some companies, are significantly higher. This information is given in the individual company profiles in the main article.

† Rate of growth from year to year has been adjusted so as to not include revenue gains from acquisition. See main article for explanation.

‡ Total revenues of 56 survey research companies—over and beyond those listed in top 44 list—that provide financial information on a confidential basis to CASRO.

Source: Advertising Age study, p. S-5, May 19, 1986.

TABLE 2-2a   WORLDWIDE PERSPECTIVE ON MARKETING
RESEARCH: EXPENDITURES

	Prevailing year exchange rates, billions		
	1983	**1979**	**1977**
North America*	$1.4	$1.1	$0.6
Europe	1.1	0.8	0.5
Asia/Oceania	0.3	0.2	0.15
Central/South America	0.08	0.05	0.04
Africa	0.04	0.03	0.02
Middle East	0.02	0.02	0.01
Total world market	$2.94	$2.20	$1.32

*Source: Eileen Cole. The United States represents approximately $1.3 billion of these totals in 1983.

search services. As one would expect, services flow from doers to users. In actuality the industry is more complex than this representation. To show it in all its complexity would reduce any graphic display to chaos.

Users   In Figure 2-1 certain organizations are placed in two categories, namely, users and users/doers. These organizations are manufacturers, wholesalers, retailers,

TABLE 2-2b   WORLDWIDE PERSPECTIVE ON ADVERTISING/MARKETING RESEARCH:
TEN LARGEST RESEARCH GROUPS

Organization	Home country	Approx. research revenues, 1982*, millions	Number of countries[†]
1 A.C. Nielsen Co.	U.S.	$433.1	25
2 IMS International	U.S.	124.8	34
3 SAMI	U.S.	85.0	1
4 Arbitron Ratings Co.	U.S.	80.3	1
5 AGB Research PLC	U.K.	73.6	20
6 Burke Marketing Serv.	U.S.	52.1	2
7 Research International	U.K.	48.2	29
8 Infratest Forschung GmbH & Co.	W. Germany	32.2	5
9 Market Facts Inc.	U.S.	25.4[††]	1
10 GFK Nurnberg Gesellschaft F Konsum	W. Germany	23.9	6
Total		$978.6	

 * In many cases, total company revenues are significantly larger; see individual company profiles.
 [†] Through subsidiary company or branch office.
 [††] Does not include Market Facts of Canada, with volume of about $2.3 million, in which the parent owns about 50 percent.
 Source: Advertising Age, pp. 35–36, Nov. 1, 1984.

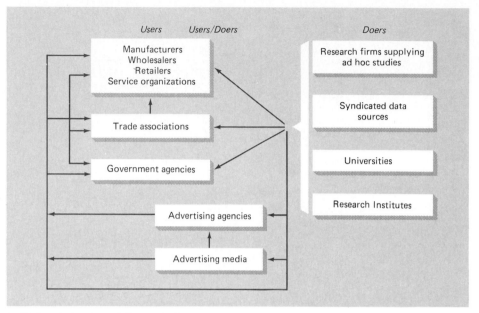

FIGURE 2-1 Institutional structure of the marketing research business.

service organizations, trade associations, and government agencies. All of these organizations use marketing research data for the purpose of making marketing decisions of various kinds: product planning and evaluation, distribution planning and evaluation, promotional activity development and assessment, and pricing. However, some do not do any of their own research. These are the organizations designated as users only. Others do some of their own research, while making use of outsiders for the rest. Thus, the graphic representation has these organizations in both categories.

Users/Doers Certain other institutions are almost always users/doers. Foremost among these are advertising agencies, which undertake research studies for their own planning purposes but also do a great deal of research on behalf of clients. This latter research is usually specially funded by client organizations if large, and often absorbed by the agency for their standard 15 percent of media billings if small. Most agencies have their own research departments, but they also make use of outside suppliers for some studies.

Advertising media are also users/doers. It is important to them to be able to provide accurate information about the size and composition of their audiences, since their advertising revenues per insertion depend on this. This information is communicated to advertising agencies and the clients of agencies. Most media have good reputations for doing competent research in this regard and for providing accurate information. However, the media often make use of outside research suppliers in order to add even more credibility to their audience estimates.

Doers   Doer institutions undertake marketing research solely to provide information for the use of other institutions. Marketing research firms supplying ad hoc studies are one type of doer. We need to distinguish between full-service and limited-service research suppliers. Full-service suppliers will undertake complete research studies for client organizations. That is, they will do problem definition work, questionnaire design, sampling, interviewing, coding, editing, and data analysis and interpretation, and they are prepared to do this for the full range of marketing decision problems. Limited-service suppliers do only some of these activities. There are firms that do only field interviewing or data analysis, for example, or firms that specialize in, say, advertising research or product testing. These limited-service firms often concentrate on one geographic region of the country. This is especially true in interviewing work. These local interviewing firms make themselves available to users/doers and doers. The cost and trouble of maintaining a national interviewing force is too much for most users/doers and doers, and so local firms have set up arrangements with other firms to be able to put together a national interviewing system as needed. (It would not be uncommon for two studies performed through two different doers to end up using the same field interviewers.)

Marketing research supply firms can range from large multinational organizations all the way down to one-person businesses operating out of a basement office. The common denominator is that they all have a client or clients that will pay for the services they provide.

It is important to note the difference between ad hoc studies and syndicated studies. All ad hoc studies are designed to solve *client-specific problems; syndicated data sources* provide information that is *not client-specific*. Syndicated data sources collect certain types of data and then sell these data on a subscription basis to any organization that will buy them. Common types of syndicated data measure retail sales, wholesale product shipments, consumer panels, advertising media audiences, advertising effectiveness, and consumer attitudes. Significant companies in this field include A. C. Nielsen, Selling Areas–Marketing Inc., Audits and Surveys, and Daniel Starch and Staff. A detailed description of the types of syndicated data available and some of the better-known organizations providing it is presented in Chapter 5. We should recognize that many of the firms doing syndicated studies are also in the ad hoc study business. The big users of syndicated data are consumer products companies, advertising agencies, and the advertising media.

Universities, through their division of business research, are also doers. Research may be undertaken for specific client organizations, but usually it is made public because of university regulations. Government agencies are the biggest users of this group of doers. Commercial firms rarely use universities. Individual professors doing marketing research work on a consulting basis would be included as suppliers of ad hoc studies.

Research institutes can be located within a university structure or independent of the arrangement. They can be providers of both ad hoc and syndicated information. Their ad hoc clients are usually government agencies. An example of such a syndicated service would be the "Index of Consumer Sentiment" published by the Survey Research Center of the University of Michigan.

Career Aspects

A discussion of institutions can hide the fact that it is people pursuing individual careers who actually do the work of marketing research. This section presents an overview of some of the careers available in marketing research. In corporations and suppliers, there are basically four types of jobs: (1) research directors, (2) analysts, (3) technical specialists, and (4) clerical workers.

Research Directors   These individuals are responsible for all activities of the other people in a department. A study by Krun[11] gives us a good portrait of research directors in large companies. The majority (55 percent) hold a master's degree, with a significant number (33 percent) holding a bachelor's degree, and a few (8 percent) a doctoral degree. Most became the research director after holding positions in marketing research or some other marketing staff job. Their role was seen to be largely advisory to top management, but with some policy-making aspects. The average marketing research director in a large company earns between $80,000 and $120,000. Many firms now have a vice president of marketing research earning from $125,000 to over $150,000 (see Figure 2-2).

Analysts   These individuals do the bulk of the designing and supervision of actual marketing research studies. They are sometimes referred to as *research generalists* because they act as intermediaries between marketing managers and technical people. Table 2-3 lists the responsibilities of the research generalist.

There are different grades of analysts. Senior analysts in large organizations usually supervise other analysts who do the majority of project work. In turn, these more junior analysts may have apprentice analysts assisting them. The position of analyst can be an entry-level job for someone pursuing either a B.B.A. or M.B.A. Most large organizations pay competitive salaries to attract new graduates. In the long run, a successful career in marketing research usually pays less than a successful line career in marketing. However, many find the nature of marketing research work worth the sacrifice.

A study by Blankenship[12] gives insight into the background and characteristics desired for marketing research generalists. Most managers wanted their new analysts to have a master's degree (51 percent) or a bachelor's degree (40 percent). Most wanted an interdisciplinary degree, with the major to be marketing (68 percent), statistics (60 percent), economics (44 percent), general business (42 percent), or psychology (35 percent). Most managers (89 percent) indicated that they would hire analysts right out of school. The characteristics they most desired were brightness/intelligence (89 percent), analytic ability (87 percent), imagination/creativity (78 percent), interpersonal skills (66 percent), curiosity (65 percent), writing proficiency (63 percent), and drive/ambition (60 percent). A competent analyst is a person of many analytical and interpersonal skills

---

[11] James R. Krun, "Marketing Research Chiefs Tend to Progress in Company or Out of It—1975 Study Reveals." *Marketing News*, p. 18, Jan. 28, 1977.

[12] Al Blankenship, "What Marketing Research Managers Want in Trainees," *Journal of Advertising Research*, vol. 15, pp. 7–14, February 1975.

VICE PRESIDENT
MARKETING RESEARCH
$125,000

Our client, a prestigious package goods company, has created a new position that will have appeal to the research professional who has grown beyond the traditional research function.

The successful candidate must be conspicuously intelligent and articulate with a boardroom appearance, presence and demeanor. You will have achieved your current prominent status in either a corporate, agency, supplier or consulting environment, where consumer behaviorism is emphasized.

As an integral member of the executive committee, you will have responsibility for determining the strategic marketing direction of this billion dollar organization.

Please send resume, in strictest confidence, to:

Robert Maiorino, President

MAIORINO & WESTON

701 Westchester Avenue, Suite 308 West
White Plains, N.Y. 10604
(914) 328-7500

FIGURE 2-2   An example of an upper-end marketing research job.

TABLE 2-3   RESPONSIBILITIES OF THE RESEARCH GENERALIST

1 Develop knowledge and judgment about various businesses
2 Understand the research process and language
3 Define problems and identify opportunities
4 Identify management alternatives
5 Marshall evidence to evaluate alternatives
6 Propose profit-oriented research to close information gaps
7 Balance decision risks and research costs to achieve high payoff research projects
8 Provide an element of entrepreneurial spirit in the planning of research
9 Bring an element of creativity and insight to research findings and their implications for decision making
10 Provide perspective on the long-range research needs for a business
11 Be an educator, liaison person, communicator, and counselor

with a solid understanding of both marketing and marketing research. (A more detailed look at three different analysts is presented below.)

Technical Specialists   These individuals are available to solve very narrow aspects of marketing research problems. They include, for example, experts in questionnaire design, sampling, data analysis, and computers. Analysts make use of their knowledge when needed.

Clerical Workers   These individuals perform functions as directed by analysts. For example, they type reports, pull sample elements as directed, prepare computer runs, etc.

A Week in the Life of . . .

After the brief overview of the available jobs, let us now focus on the analyst's job by outlining the activities undertaken by analysts in three different types of organizations. Excerpts from their daybooks are given below.

Sandra Jenkins, Consumer Products Analyst   The following is a typical week for Ms. Jenkins, who works for a large consumer products company.

Monday A.M.   Made oral presentation to VP of marketing on just-completed product test for new brand.

P.M.   Completed work on a questionnaire for advertising evaluation study; in evening attended group interview done by supplier.

Tuesday   Flew to Denver to supervise the setup of a test market.

Wednesday A.M.   Met with brand manager to discuss problem definition for new study on his brand.

P.M.   Discussed this brand problem with research director and brand manager.

Thursday A.M.   Met with contact analyst from research supplier who is handling field work on pricing study; discussed design issues and timing.

P.M.   Wrote part of report on product test study.

Friday A.M.   Received solicitation from new research supplier seeking our business.

P.M.   Briefed computer people on data analysis runs to be made on image and distribution penetration study involving 2000 respondents. Did some sample run and demonstration graphs on my personal computer.

William Brunner, Industrial Products Analyst   The following is a typical week for Mr. Brunner, who works for a large industrial products company.

Monday A.M.   Returned from Boston after completing a set of interviews with engineers about the potential for a new electrical component we have developed; interviewed a total of 20 engineers in six industries.

	P.M.	Began writing report on the project.
Tuesday	A.M.	Met with director of sales to design study on sales force turnover.
	P.M.	Gave oral report to top management on corporate image advertising results.
Wednesday	A.M.	Met with Department of Commerce people to find if they had industry data on the potential for one of our products.
	P.M.	Worked with data provided to try to make an estimate.
Thursday		Flew to Chicago to talk to trade association people about their database and our problems.
Friday	A.M.	Began designing a new questionnaire for second round of corporate image advertising.
	P.M.	Explained the type of work I do to a new analyst.

Dan Razinski, Supplier Analyst   The following is a typical week for Mr. Razinski, who works for a full-service marketing research supplier.

Monday		Met with client to give findings on branding study; handed in written report, gave oral presentation.
Tuesday	A.M.	Prepared bid for field work portion of national study by large petroleum company.
	P.M.	Made call on new director of research at large company; explained why we should be one of their suppliers.
Wednesday		Worked on study design for product taste test as directed by client.
Thursday	A.M.	Briefed interviewers on media habits questionnaire, made sure their task was clear.
	P.M.	Flew to Los Angeles for Friday presentation.
Friday		Made oral presentation to client on study; discussed possible followup work.

These three analysts have much in common. They all give oral and written reports, define problems in concert with management, design studies, and execute parts of studies and delegate parts to other people. All would get much enjoyment out of the researcher's prayer in Exhibit 2-1, since it deals with parts of the research process.

Note that the industrial products analyst and the consumer products analyst perform similar functions, except that the sample sizes used for industrial products are smaller and more time is spent searching out secondary data and doing interviewing.

Consumer and Industrial Marketing Research

We need to stress further some of the differences between marketing research in consumer organizations and marketing research in industrial product organizations. Table 2-4 presents a summary of the major differences that relate to the areas of size of populations dealt with, respondent accessibility, respondent cooperation, sample sizes used, respondent definition, interviewers, and study costs. As Table 2-4 indicates,

EXHIBIT 2-1

A RESEARCHER'S PRAYER*

Though this prayer seems lengthy,
It merely is designed
To ask the simple blessing to
Be furnished peace of mind.

Make interviewers speedy,
Make terminations small,
Let users not be hard to find
And book high-traffic malls.

Give interviewers training
And have them follow rules,
Make supervisors supervise
And respondents not be fools.

Have skip instruction followed,
Open ends probed well,
Key questions not omitted,
Give respondents much to tell.

May markets not be altered
Once arrangements have been made,
Nor questionnaires revised
When the printer's just been paid.

Let studies not be challenged
For how they were designed,
Make code books never criticized
For codes that were combined.

Make focus groups be noisy,
Let the leader stay in charge.
Cause recruiting to be bountiful,
Grant viewing rooms be large.

Have all products shipped on schedule,
Let bottles never leak.
Make labels always sticky
And boxes never weak.

Furnish matched test panels,
Bring not flood nor strike nor snow.
Let no one steal test product,
Have shelf stock not run low.

Let major chains reject
No store co-op request
And may undue competition
Upset no market test.

Let regressions show relationships,
Residuals show none.
Let computers never break down
Before the final run.

Suffer changes to be measurable,
Error ranges small.
Let norms be ever handy
And results show winners all.

Make top line always come on time,
Reports rush through the mail
And have syndicated service
Monthly schedules never fail.

Make conclusions logical,
Analysis concise
And let research implications
Be adopted once or twice.

Make brand requests be simple,
Phone calls all be quick,
Questions always answerable,
Rejoinders never slick.

May jobs be always authorized
Ere field work has begun
And if one slips through just make sure
No cancellations come.

Please grant the brand group reason,
Let account execs be sane,
Make suppliers competent,
Have r&d abstain.

Make the sales force happy
With research in their stores
And let management perceive
Some value in our chores.

But if all else is impossible,
Would it be out of line
To ask to be allowed to face
One crisis at a time?

*Source: Douglas Hanauer, senior marketing analyst, Texize Chemicals Co., Greenville, S.C.: reprinted from *Newsletter,* Association for Consumer Research, vol. 11, no. 4, p. 14, December 1981. Used with permission.

TABLE 2-4   CONSUMER VERSUS INDUSTRIAL MARKETING REASEARCH; WHAT ARE THE DIFFERENCES?

	Consumer	Industrial
Universe/ population	Large. Dependent on category under investigation but usually unlimited. 72.5 million U.S. households and 215 million persons.	Small. Fairly limited in total population and even more so if within a defined industry or SIC category.
Respondent accessibility	Fairly easy. Can interview at home, on the telephone, or using mail techniques.	Difficult. Usually only during working hours at plant, office, or on the road. Respondent is usually preoccupied with other priorities.
Respondent cooperation	Over the years has become more and more difficult, yet millions of consumers have never been interviewed.	A major concern. Due to the small population, the industrial respondent is being over-researched. The purchaser and decision makers in an industrial firm are the buyers of a variety of products and services from office supplies to heavy equipment.
Sample size	Can usually be drawn as large as required for statistical confidence since the population is in the hundreds of millions.	Usually much smaller than consumer sample, yet the statistical confidence is equal due to the relationship of the sample to the total population.
Respondent definitions	Usually fairly simple. Those aware of a category or brand, users of a category or brand, demographic criteria, etc., etc. The ultimate purchaser is also a user for most consumer products and services.	Somewhat more difficult. The user and the purchasing decision maker in most cases are not the same. Factory workers who use heavy equipment, secretaries who use typewriters, etc., are the users and, no doubt, best able to evaluate these products and services. However, they tend not to be the ultimato purchasers and in many cases do not have any influence on the decision-making process.
Interviewers	Can usually be easily trained. They are also consumers and tend to be somewhat familiar with the area under investigation for most categories.	Difficult to find good executive interviewers. At least a working knowledge of the product class or subject being surveyed is essential. Preferably more than just a working knowledge.
Study costs	Key dictators of cost are sample size and incidence. Lower incidence usage categories (for example, users of soft-moist dog food, powdered breakfast beverages, etc.) or demographic or behavioral screening criteria (attend a movie at least once a month, over 65 years of age, and do not have direct deposit of social security payments, etc.) can up costs considerably.	Relative to consumer research, the critical element resulting in significantly higher per-interview costs are: the lower incidence levels, the difficulties in locating the "right" respondent (that is, the purchase decision maker), and securing cooperation (time and concentration of effort) for the interview itself.

Source: Marvin Katz, "Use Same Theory, Skills for Consumer, Industrial Research," *Marketing News,* p. 16, Jan. 12, 1979.

there are many differences arising from the nature of the products and markets for the two types of organizations.

Despite these differences, the underlying methods and skills are the same for both consumer and industrial marketing research. Both are concerned with problem definition, research design, use of secondary data, sampling, measurement, field work, data processing and analysis, and presentation of results. One practicing researcher with experience in both areas of marketing research has noted:

> Many marketers and marketing researchers perceive consumer and industrial marketing research as two entirely different fields of endeavor. Having worked in both environments, I see more, and more important, similarities than differences.
>
> Of course, the markets and respondents are different, but the skillful marketing researcher can apply his or her art to an infinite variety of markets, products, and services in both the consumer and industrial environments. The theory and basic skills required are the same.
>
> Whether it's a consumer or industrial marketing research study:
>
> • The overall administration, design, execution, and analysis of research tend to follow the same basic rules and procedures;
>
> • The research study design should address the problem and the information needed in a valid and reliable manner;
>
> • The data processing procedures—coding, editing, keypunching, and weighting—are consistent;
>
> • The analysis of data requires the same type of skill and knowledge;
>
> • The marketing researcher in a business environment is a problem solver and marketing consultant; and
>
> • The researcher's "tools of the trade" are the application of valid and reliable research techniques to uncover information that aids in problem solution and helps make a better business or marketing decision.[13]

The service section is also now learning to effectively utilize marketing research, as noted in the Marketing Research In Action in this section.

As can be seen, analysts work in an organization context. The next section discusses the organization of the marketing research function in corporations.

Organization[14]

This section considers the question: "Where should the marketing research function be positioned within an organizational structure?" Unfortunately, there is no easy or technically right way to answer this question, for two reasons. First, every organization will differ in the relative importance attached to marketing research and the scale and complexity of research methods employed. Therefore, the marketing research department should be custom tailored to fit the firm's informational requirements. Second, within each firm the organization of the research department is inevitably going to demonstrate dynamism. Despite these limitations, it is possible to give a company and its officers some guidelines as to where the research deparment should be located within its organization. This discussion applies most directly to large organizations. More will be said about smaller research operations later.

Centralized Organization   The first structural option to be considered is that of completely centralizing the research function of a company by locating it at corporate

[13] Marvin Katz, "Use Same Theory, Skills for Consumer, Industrial Research," *Market News*, p. 16, Jan. 12, 1979. Used with permission.

[14] This section is based upon an unpublished paper by J. Craig DeNooyer of the University of Michigan.

MARKETING RESEARCH IN ACTION

SERVICE SECTOR GETS MARKETING RESEARCH ATTENTION

The service sector comprises 64 percent of the U.S. GNP, but it has been relatively ignored by the marketing research sector, which has typically centered around the packaged goods industry.

Despite basic differences between the product and service sectors, their marketing information needs are very similar. They both need sales data, information regarding consumers' wants and needs, and measurements of consumers' attitudes toward the company.

The differences arise in the performance monitoring aspect of marketing research. Because service organizations deal with people rather than machines, it is more difficult to institute quality control measures. Ingrained employee behavior patterns are difficult to change. But a firm in the service sector still must deliver on its advertising promises, otherwise consumers' expectations will not be met, resulting in their rejection of future claims.

Marketing research can actually assist in controlling the human element within companies. Through customer surveys, trouble areas can be easily identified. Besides pinpointing problem areas, the survey technique can be used to measure employee competence and friendliness, as well as consumer wants, needs, and overall satisfaction with a company's service department.

Marketing research should prove to be an increasingly useful tool for the service sector in the future.

Based on *Marketing News*, vol. 17, no. 10, sec. 1, p. 13, May 13, 1983.

headquarters. In such a case, all research would be under the control of the vice president in charge of marketing. Table 2-5 shows the advantages and disadvantages of this structure.

Decentralized Organization The second option open to a divisionalized firm wishing to position its marketing research function is to completely decentralize the department along divisional lines. In this system the market researcher would be responsible to the division manager and not to a top corporate executive. Divisions of companies may be organized by products, by customers, or by geographic regions. The divisional assignment of research personnel would exactly parallel the type of divisional basis used by the company. Thus, research people would be expected to become expert in the research problems of particular products, customer markets, or geographic regions. In many cases decentralization's advantages and disadvantages are inverse arguments of our previous discussion on centralization. Still, there are a few pros and cons that should be highlighted. Table 2-6 lists these advantages and disadvantages.

Integrated Organization A viable alternative form to the extremes of centralization and decentralization has proved to be the "integrated" organization structure. This increasingly popular research structure makes use of a central staff (which includes a

TABLE 2-5 CENTRALIZED ORGANIZATION

Advantages

1 Effective coordination and control of the research activity is possible
2 Encouragement of economical and flexible use of facilities and personnel occurs
3 Increased usefulness and objectivity of research results to corporate executives develops
4 Greater prestige to marketing research occurs
5 Better likelihood of attracting top-notch researchers is possible
6 Cross-fertilization of ideas occurs
7 Greater likelihood of obtaining an adequate budget is possible

Disadvantages

1 Isolates researchers from day-to-day activities and problems
2 Corporate problems receive all of the time and attention, at the expense of the divisions
3 Separates researchers from the action programs based on the research; takes no responsibility for their implemented recommendations

highly qualified marketing research function) available as needed to counsel with and reinforce individual research departments within each division. This central staff is responsible to a top-level corporate executive, usually the vice president in charge of marketing. Divisional work is conducted by division research staffs directly responsible to division managers. Their research projects deal with divisional marketing problems. The thought behind this matrix organization is that it combines the best features of centralization and decentralization into one effective system. Unfortunately, there are also pluses and minuses to this type of research structure.

All the advantages of the hybrid relationship can be summed up as "more coordinated and effective research." Both levels of the research function contribute to this process. The central research staff arranges for the exchange of pertinent marketing data to the various divisions, acts as a central purchasing agent for all services common

TABLE 2-6 DECENTRALIZED ORGANIZATION

Advantages

1 Researchers are close to the action of marketing problems and implementation of their recommendations
2 More specialization is available on product, customers, or markets
3 More attention will be paid by divisional managers to marketing research
4 Breakdown of the corporate/divisional barriers can occur

Disadvantages

1 Tendency to bias results in favor of the marketing group the researcher works for
2 Inadequate research controls, standards, and procedures
3 Difficulty in finding qualified people
4 High cost
5 Duplication of effort
6 Central management's needs not attended to

to the needs of the research teams, and carries out research projects with company-wide implications. In addition, the central corporate staff sets and explains company research standards, undertakes projects for departments too small to have their own research staffs, and assists divisional research staffs when they become overloaded with research requests. By having additional research teams located at the divisional level, a company achieves its goal of making the research function part of the firm's marketing team. This allows researchers to become experts in their fields and places their infomation-gathering techniques closer to the consumer of research.

The main disadvantage to the integrated system is the potential occurrence of control conflicts over the research staffs and their projects. Control conflicts can result when the lines of authority in a company are not clearly delineated. Theoretically the central research staff is organized solely as a helping, advisory branch. But all too often divisional researchers look to corporate staffers as their ultimate bosses instead of their divisional heads. Any other disadvantages inherent in the integrated system resemble the disadvantages attributed to decentralized research departments—such as high cost, duplication of efforts, and lack of an adequate number of competent specialists. Nonetheless, the control conflict problem is by far the most serious obstacle to implementing the integrated marketing research system.

Choosing a Structure   Now that the main alternatives to organizing the marketing research function have been outlined, the question becomes: "How is one to choose the structure that is 'best' for one's particular firm?" There are no simple answers, no handy "cookbook" ways to determine the optimum choice. There are, however, a number of criteria which can be followed to help narrow the selection alternatives. In the final analysis, there is no completely right or wrong organizational structure for marketing research in a firm.

The first criterion, and perhaps the most important, is this: The marketing research function should be placed where the marketing decisions are made. The researcher's task is to provide information to marketers to help them in their decision-making process. At whatever level decision making is performed, the research function should be there to help. For example, if a firm makes one or two industrial goods for a few customers, a research staff located at the corporate level might suffice. However, if the firm is like General Foods, which produces a myriad of products for a host of different customers, it would be better to decentralize or integrate the research function. This would allow all market information to be closer to the person who uses it. In essence, the research function should reside where the marketing decision-making power resides. Figure 2-3 shows General Foods' integrative structure.

The second criterion to consider when organizing the research department is: Researchers should be free from undue influence or manipulation by those areas or people for whom they conduct research projects. A third criterion is: The marketing research function should be organized so that the firm can satisfy the demand for research projects quickly and efficiently. If the firm's divisions exhibit a steady volume of requests for research projects, it would be advisable to decentralize the research function. On the other hand, if the demand for research within a firm is sparse or fluctuates widely, it may be more expedient to centralize all research activities in a

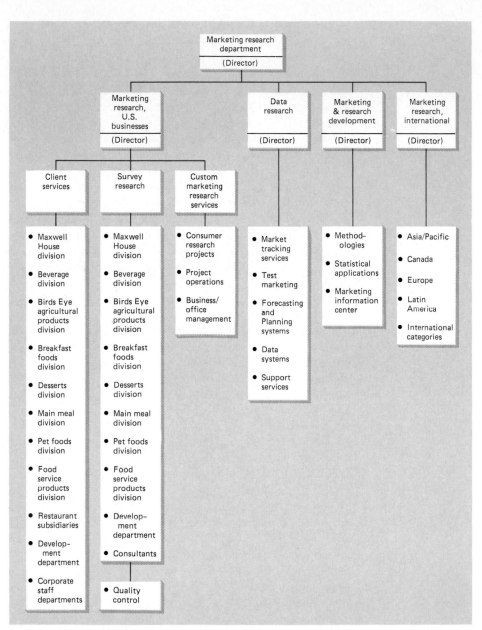

FIGURE 2-3 General Foods' marketing research organization. *(Source: "Marketing Research: Career Opportunities at General Foods," General Foods Corporation, White Plains, N.Y.)*

TABLE 2-7   ORGANIZATIONS WITH MARKETING RESEARCH DEPARTMENTS

	Formal department, %	One person, %	No one assigned, %
Consumer products	83	14	3
Industrial products	69	22	9
Advertising agencies	85	12	3
Financial services	71	26	3
Publishing and broadcasting	93	7	0
All others	65	32	3

Source: Dik Warren Twedt, *Survey of Marketing Research, 1983* (Chicago: American Marketing Association, 1983), p. 11.

corporate office. The final criterion is a matter of practicality that many times is over-looked: The research department should report to an executive who has a genuine interest in marketing research, understands how it operates, knows its potentials, and possesses sufficient authority to ensure that the actions called for by the research are undertaken.

Characteristics of Marketing Research Departments[15]

No matter what type of business organizations engage in, most have formal marketing research departments. Table 2-7 shows that over 70 percent of organizations have formal marketing research departments. There has been a rapid growth in the number of formal marketing research departments over the 1968–1986 period. This reflects the continued growth in acceptance of the use of marketing research in marketing decision making and especially in nontraditional areas like financial services.

Marketing research departments are usually quite small. Table 2-7 indicates a significant number of organizations with only one person assigned to marketing research. Additionally, Table 2-8 shows the median number of full-time employees in marketing

[15] This section is based upon Twedt, op cit., pp. 11, 18–19, and 38.

TABLE 2-8   MEDIAN NUMBER OF FULL-TIME MARKETING RESEARCH EMPLOYEES

	Annual sales, millions			
	$50–$100	$100–$200	$200–$500	Over $500
Consumer products	2	4	5	10
Industrial products	2	2	2	6
Advertising agencies	6	8	18	18
Financial services	2	2	3	4
Not listed—publishing and broadcasting	4	3	10	20

Source: Dik Warren Twedt, *Survey of Marketing Research, 1983* (Chicago: American Marketing Association, 1983), p. 18–19.

TABLE 2-9 PERCENT OF TOTAL BUDGET SPENT ON
OUTSIDE RESEARCH

	1978	1983	Change, %
Consumer products	58	53	−9
Industrial products	31	18	−42
Advertising agencies	41	36	−12
Financial services	31	22	−29

Source: Dik Warren Twedt, *Survey of Marketing Research,
1983* (Chicago: American Marketing Association, 1983), p. 38.

research in organizations and relates this to the size of the organizations. Small marketing research departments are usually centralized in structure. This puts a great onus on the individual researcher not to remove himself or herself too far from the operating managers.

Utilizing Research Suppliers

One issue that confronts all marketing research directors and a great many analysts is the utilization of research suppliers. These suppliers may be involved with a few aspects of a research study or may be given total responsbility for all aspects of a study. Table 2-9 shows that the percentage of total marketing research conducted by research suppliers is sizable but on the decline. Table 2-10 indicates that outside suppliers have their primary utilization in brand attitude and usage tracking, consumer product

TABLE 2-10 AREAS OF OUTSIDE RESEARCH

	Major research applications, % (1)	Minor reasearch applications, % (2)	Total past year usage, % (3) = (1 + 2)
Brand attitude and usage tracking	43	50	93
Consumer product testing	34	38	72
New product screening and evaluation	32	55	87
Basic market strategy studies, such as image studies, trade-off or segmentation studies	32	53	85
Advertising pretesting and copy testing	29	56	85
Continuing advertising campaign evaluation and measurement	17	48	65
Test marketing	16	43	59

Source: Market Facts Inc., Chicago, 1979.

testing, new product screening and evaluation, strategy studies, various advertising testing, and test marketing.

The primary advantages of using research suppliers include: (1) the cost may be less than hiring additional personnel and paying the other costs of an internal project; (2) the supplier costs to the user are a variable cost, whereas internal personnel constitute a fixed expense—that is, if the work load varies in the department, outside suppliers can be used at peak times only; (3) suppliers offer special skills not available internally; (4) the users of outside services retain great flexibility, as they pick the best firm available for a specific type of problem; (5) outside suppliers have greater objectivity and are usually not involved in the politics of specific problems; (6) the sponsoring company can remain anonymous.

We must also recognize some disadvantages in the use of research suppliers. These are: (1) the firm may not be completely familiar with the objectives and problems of the company and/or industry; (2) there is a risk, especially in the first purchase from a firm, that the research will not be done well or not done on time; (3) there is a greater risk that results of studies or company activities will become known to competitors; (4) the costs can be higher, as suppliers must earn a profit that allows for slack periods and for studies that lose money.

Selecting a Supplier   Just how does one go about selecting a specific supplier for a project? First of all, a list of possible firms must be drawn up. Learning about and evaluating suppliers are subjects where word-of-mouth influences are high. Buyers seek recommendations from associates within their company, from other researchers outside their company, from advertising agencies, trade associations, and even university professors.[16] Impersonal sources such as trade publications, professional directories,[17] journals, and promotional material of suppliers may also provide prospective supply firms.

The evaluation of prospective suppliers usually involves direct contacts with the firms, discussions with other people for whom they have done work, and the examination of some piece of research they have done. These information sources are used to collect information about the criteria that will be used to make the actual choice. These criteria may include (1) the capabilities of individuals who will be assigned to the project, (2) the degree of specialization needed and provided, (3) technical competence, (4) orientation toward marketing management, (5) education of staff, (6) personal characteristics of key personnel, (7) facilities (field work, data processing, analysis), (8) creativity, (9) ethics, (10) communication skills, (11) ability to perform on time, (12) location close to buyer to allow for better communication, (13) stability, and (14) cost of the project.

---

[16] "Using Marketing Consultants and Research Agencies," National Industrial Conference Board *Studies in Business Policy*, no. 120 (New York: NICB, 1966), p. 1.

[17] For example, see *International Directory of Marketing Research Houses and Services* (New York: Marketing Review, New York Chapter of the American Marketing Association); Ernest S. Bradford, *Bradford's Directory of Marketing Research Agencies and Management Consultants* (Middleburg, VA), and *A Geographic Listing of Marketing Consultants and Research Agencies* (Chicago: American Marketing Association).

The list of firms may be reduced using these criteria, and then the remaining firms may be asked to submit proposals. Proposals are usually provided to prospective clients without charge. The average cost to the supplier of preparing a proposal is $2000 to $3000, with the high end being about $15,000 for a large project. The quality of the proposal constitutes another criterion on which firms would be evaluated.

Sometimes competitive bids for a project are asked for, but this approach is not now a significant way of selecting a supplier. A study[18] of 159 research suppliers found that only 14 percent of their business was via competitive bidding. The rest came through negotiations. Furthermore, 72 percent of all suppliers of ad hoc studies refuse to bid competitively, and firms that do bid usually face only one or two other firms in the competition. The 159 suppliers perceived price to be ranked eleventh on a list of important factors for firms choosing a supplier. Quality of work, understanding of the problem, reputation, integrity, experience, referrals, personality of key people, skill of individuals assigned to projects, specialization, and personal contact all ranked higher in perceived importance.

As in all buying decisions, customers will find some brands they prefer over others. Thus, most experienced buyers of research develop a short list of suppliers with whom they deal on a regular basis. It is often difficult for a new firm to get on the approved list.

Ground Rules for Buyer-Supplier Relationships   In the interaction between the buyers of research and the suppliers, certain ground rules should apply. The supplier should be able to expect certain things from the buyer. These include:

1 A statement of the general background of the management problem at hand
2 A statement of the management problem
3 A statement of the research problem and objectives, and the use to which the research result will be put
4 A chance to discuss these problem statements and background
5 A range of budget available for the project
6 The desired timing
7 An assurance that they will be approached only when there is a reasonable expectation that they will be selected

The supplier also must be able to satisfy certain requirements of the buyer. In general, the supplier must provide information on the list of criteria the buyer is using in making the selection.

Most clients desiring marketing research require that all interested research firms submit a proposal for research. Because this proposal is vital in securing a marketing research contract, we will spend some time discussing how a good proposal is put together.

The topics listed below create guidelines around which to write a research proposal. The number of topics covered in the proposal will depend upon the size of the project. Obviously, the proposal for a million-dollar research project will cover more topics and

[18] Joel B. Haynes and James T. Rothe, "Competitive Bidding for Marketing Research Services: Fact or Fiction," *Journal of Marketing,* vol. 38, pp. 69–71, July 1974.

go into much greater depth than the proposal for a $5000 project. You must use common sense to determine which topics to include in any specific proposal.

Topics to Consider[19]

1 *Problem.* The problem (or opportunity) must be clearly defined. Does it affect only one area of the firm or agency, or is it company—wide? What are the underlying causes of the decision situation?

2 *Objectives.* What are the decision objectives? What does management expect to gain from research? Objectives should be stated clearly and concisely.

3 *Alternatives.* What are the alternative courses of action?

4 *Information needs.* What information is needed? How will it be gathered? State your initial plan and organization, search of literature, interviews, questionnaires, experiments, etc.

5 *Personnel qualifications.* Cite your experience and success with problems of a similar nature. Include dates and references (with permission, of course) so your statements can be verified. Also, give job descriptions, names, and one-page résumés of key personnel who will be working on the project.

6 *Evaluation.* State how the data will be handled and stored. Tell whether or not the project can be duplicated in other branches of the company or other areas of the country. Show how you will evaluate the project while it is under way, and how you will determine whether to continue, change, or terminate it. What criteria will be used to recommend the best alternative? What is the likelihood of success? Be realistic—don't promise more than you can deliver.

7 *Budget.* Do not overbudget: a padded budget is quickly rejected. Show clients where their money will go—list the salaries, equipment and supplies, travel requirements, miscellaneous expenses and indirect costs, and allowances for the unexpected. Provide justification for each budget item.

8 *An accurate timetable.* After the appropriate topics have been covered in rough-draft form, assemble these answers into a logical, coherent format, such as the one presented below:

1 Prefatory parts
    Title page
    Letter of transmittal (short note accompanying the proposal which explains or
        justifies documents being transmitted)
    Table of contents
    List of tables (if any)
    List of figures (if any)
2 Body of proposal
    Introduction
      Problem
      Need
      Background
    Objectives/Purpose

---

[19] From H. A. Murphy and H. W. Hildebrandt, *Effective Business Communications*, 4th ed., (New York: McGraw-Hill, 1984) pp. 543–548.

TABLE 2-11 HOW TO IMPROVE OUTSIDE RESEARCH QUALITY

1 Increase your involvement—at the decision-making level—especially at the beginning stages of the research
2 Use suppliers with qualified personnel
3 Review the supplier's data validation procedures
4 Maintain continual evaluation and individual assessment of your suppliers
5 Use more than one supplier
6 Get several proposals for each project
7 Ask the supplier's views on the research findings' implications
8 Get involved in the specifications of the tabulation (data analysis)
9 Consult with outside agencies about the reputation of the outside agencies under consideration

Source: Adapted from "Six Consultants Counsel Clients on How to Improve the Marketing Research They Buy," *Marketing News*, pp. 1, 11–14, Jan. 28, 1977.

Procedures
    Methods and sources
    Plan of attack
    Sequence of activities
    Equipment and facilities available
    Personnel qualifications
Evaluation
Budget
3 Supplementary parts
    Agency forms
        Budget justification (if any)
        References
    Tables or figures (if any)

Getting the highest quality from outside marketing research suppliers is of great concern to marketing research directors and analysts. It is necessary to maintain control of all aspects of the suppliers' work. Some practitioners suggest the approach presented in Table 2-11.

We can see that marketing research involves complex relationships among buyers and suppliers. Furthermore, in the process of collecting marketing research information, the doers of research are dealing with providers of the required information, who may be respondents to a survey, subjects in an experiment, etc. In all these relationships among buyers, suppliers, and providers, the chance for unethical behavior exists. Thus, a very relevant part of the domain of any practitioner of marketing research is to be aware of the ethics of the field. This is the topic to which we now direct our attention.

ETHICS

Ethics as related to marketing research deal with the judgment that (1) certain types of activities are inappropriate, and (2) certain types of activities must be undertaken. An example of the former would be the prohibition against using marketing research as a trick to sell products. An example of the latter would be to present the details of how a sample was selected to a client. Ethical issues arise in both the relationship between users and doers of research and the relationship between doers and providers (respondents) of research data.

Codes of Ethics

Because of actual and potential abuses in these areas, a number of codes of ethics have been developed to guide researchers. Exhibit 2-2 presents the American Marketing Association's Marketing Research Code of Ethics as adopted in 1962, with 1972 revisions included. This code deals with user-doer and doer-provider relationships. Some feel that the code does not go far enough, as it deals mostly with prohibition. The Market Research Council developed a code of ethics that deals with things that ought to be done in marketing research. Shown in Exhibit 2-3, the code gives details on what should be included in a marketing research report. Both of these codes focus on ethical issues between users and doers and deal with some issues between respondents and doers/ users as well.

Tybout and Zaltman argued that respondents in marketing research studies are not subject to high enough ethical behavior on the part of doers. Drawing on codes of ethics from nonmarketing consumer researchers (American Psychological Association, American Sociological Association, etc.), they suggest that respondents should have the following basic rights:[20]

1 The right to choose whether or not to participate in a study; included in this are the right to be made aware of this right, to be given sufficient information about the study to decide, and to be explicitly given a chance to choose

2 The right to safety; this includes protection of the respondent's anonymity, freedom from a stressful experience, and freedom from deception as to the nature and objectives of the study.

3 The right to be informed; this includes a debriefing of the respondent as to what went on and why, and dissemination of data to respondents if desired.

The focus here is on relationships between respondents and doer/users. These views are not generally accepted yet.[21]

The ethical dimensions of marketing research will confront anyone who works in marketing research or even in marketing management. What would you do if (1) a study design error came to your attention after a report was written, (2) a study design required that respondents be misled as to the actual purpose of a study, or (3) a manager deliberately withheld details of a study in order to make his or her pet project look better? These and other similar situations are tough to deal with, since questions of ethical standards, not law, are involved.

---

[20] Alice M. Tybout and Gerald Zaltman, "Ethics in Marketing Research: Their Practical Relevance," *Journal of Marketing Research,* vol. 11, pp. 357–368, November 1974.

[21] For a commentary, see Robert L. Day, "A Comment on Ethics in Marketing Research," *Journal of Marketing Research,* vol. 12, pp. 232–233, May 1975, and Alice M. Tybout and Gerald Zaltman, "A Reply to Comments on 'Ethics in Marketing Research,'" *Journal of Marketing Research,* vol. 12, pp. 234–237, May 1975.

EXHIBIT 2-2

AMERICAN MARKETING ASSOCIATION'S MARKETING
RESEARCH CODE OF ETHICS

The American Marketing Association, in furtherance of its central objective of the advancement of science in marketing and in recognition of its obligation to the public, has established these principles of ethical practice of marketing research for the guidance of its members. In an increasingly complex society, marketing management is more and more dependent upon marketing information intelligently and systematically obtained. The consumer is the source of much of this information. Seeking the cooperation of the consumer in the development of information, marketing management must acknowledge its obligation to protect the public from misrepresentation and exploitation under the guise of research.

Similarly the research practitioner has an obligation to the discipline he practices and to those who provide support for his practice—an obligation to adhere to basic and commonly accepted standards of scientific investigation as they apply to the domain of marketing research.

It is the intent of this code to define ethical standards required of marketing research in satisfying these obligations.

Adherence to this code will assure the users of marketing research that the research was done in accordance with acceptable ethical practices. Those engaged in research will find in this code an affirmation of sound and honest basic principles which have developed over the years as the profession has grown. The field interviewers who are the point of contact between the profession and the consumer will also find guidance in fulfilling their vitally important role.

For Research Users, Practitioners, and Interviewers

1 No individual or organization will undertake any activity which is directly or indirectly represented to be marketing research, but which has as its real purpose the attempted sale of merchandise or services to some or all of the respondents interviewed in the course of the research.

2 If a respondent has been led to believe, directly or indirectly, that he is participating in a marketing research survey and that his anonymity will be protected, his name shall not be made known to anyone outside the research organization or research department, or used for other than research purposes.

For Research Practitioners

1 There will be no intentional or deliberate misrepresentation of research methods or results. An adequate description of methods employed will be made available upon request to the sponsor of the research. Evidence that field work has been completed according to specifications will, upon request, be made available to buyers of research.

2 The identity of the survey sponsor and/or the ultimate client for whom a survey is being done will be held in confidence at at times, unless this identity is to be revealed as part of the research design. Research information shall be held in confidence by the research organization or department and not used for personal gain or made available to any outside party unless the client specifically authorizes such release.

3 A research organization shall not undertake marketing studies for competitive clients when such studies would jeopardize the confidential nature of client-agency relationships.

For Users of Marketing Research

1 A user of research shall not knowingly disseminate conclusions from a given research project or service that are inconsistent with or not warranted by the data.

2 To the extent that there is involved in a research project a unique design involving techniques, approaches, or concepts not commonly available to research practitioners, the prospective user of research shall not solicit such a design from one practitioner and deliver it to another for execution without the approval of the design originator.

For Field Interviewers

1 Research assignments and materials received, as well as information obtained from respondents, shall be held in confidence by the interviewer and revealed to no one except the research organization conducting the marketing study.

2 No information gained through a marketing research activity shall be used, directly or indirectly, for the personal gain or advantage of the interviewer.

3 Interviews shall be conducted in strict accordance with specifications and instructions received.

4 An interviewer shall not carry out two or more interviewing assignments simultaneously unless authorized by all contractors or employees concerned.

Members of the American Marketing Association will be expected to conduct themselves in accordance with the provisions of this Code in all of their marketing research activities.

EXHIBIT 2-3

MARKET RESEARCH COUNCIL'S CODE OF ETHICS

The following "position papers" were developed by the Ethics Committee of the Market Research Council during 1967–1968 and were adopted by an overwhelming vote of the membership as official positions of the Market Research Council in July 1968.

These papers are intended as a first step, not a final step—the thought being that additional papers on other subjects may be added in the future or that these papers may be amended as future developments might warrant.

The Respondent's Right to Privacy

The goodwill and cooperation of the public are necessary to successful public opinion and market research. Actions by researchers which tend to dilute or dissipate these resources do a disservice both to the research profession and to the public.

By its very nature, research must in some measure invade the privacy of respondents. The ringing of a respondent's doorbell or his telephone is an intrusion. If he agrees to participate in a study, his private world of attitudes, knowledge, and behavior is further invaded.

Researchers should recognize that the public has no obligation to cooperate in a study. Overly long interviews and subject matter which causes discomfort or apprehension serve to reduce respondent cooperation. When such interviews cannot be avoided, efforts should be made to explain the reasons to the respondent and to mitigate his anxieties to the extent possible.

One of the greatest invasions of the privacy of respondents is through the use of research techniques such as hidden microphones and cameras. When such a research technique has been used, a respondent should be told and, if the respondent requests it, any portion of the interview that serves to identify the respondent should be deleted.

Even after the respondent has been interviewed, his privacy is endangered while his interview is being coded, processed, and analyzed. Research agencies have the same responsibility as other professional groups to take all reasonable steps to insure that employees with access to these data observe the canons of good taste and discretion in handling this information.

Since public opinion and market researchers must infringe on the privacy of the public at several stages of the research process, it is unlikely that any set of rules or code of ethics can prevent abuses by unscrupulous or careless researchers, even though such abuses are inexcusable. The best hope of maintaining an attitude of goodwill and cooperation among the public will depend on researchers':

1 Being constantly mindful of the problem
2 Keeping in mind the recommendations above
3 Doing everything in their power to inform the public of the benefits of market and opinion research

Maintaining Respondent Anonymity

Good and accurate research requires obtaining honest and frank expressions of opinions and beliefs. Respondents are more likely (*a*) to participate in a survey and (*b*) to speak honestly and frankly if they believe that they will remain anonymous and will not be called to account for their expressed opinions or stated behavior. For this reason, every researcher should do everything in his power to protect the anonymity of the people he interviews unless he obtains their permission to reveal their names.

This does not preclude follow-up contacts for further research or for verification purposes. However, if there seems to be a reasonable possibility that there will be contacts for any other purposes, it is incumbent on the researcher to warn the respondent of this possibility.

The researcher should be willing to make reasonable efforts to provide evidence on the authenticity of the interviews he has made, providing this does not subject the respondent to harassment.

Disclosure or Release of Survey Results

Implicit in the nature of surveys is the fact that they purport to reflect the opinions or behavior of the population under study. It is the obligation of the researcher to present survey results in such a manner that they do not give a distorted or biased picture of his findings. The client also has this same obligation in reporting survey findings. When others report his findings, the researcher has an additional responsibility to make all reasonable effort to see that they, likewise, present the results impartially.

It is not incumbent on the researcher to insist on an "all-or-nothing" policy in the release of his findings. Only part of the results may be released provided this part does not give a distorted picture of the subject matter it covers.

If the client misuses, misstates, or distorts a survey finding, the researcher should release such other findings and information about how the data were obtained as will put it in proper perspective. Client-researcher agreement prior to release would minimize misunderstandings in this respect.

Any release of findings should include appropriate information about objectives, sample, research techniques, the name of the research organization, etc., that will be helpful in evaluating the results.

Buyer-Seller Relationships

A successful marketing research study is a joint operation involving a research company and its client. It requires mutual respect and confidence between the two parties and imposes certain obligations on each of them.

The buyer of research services has the right to make sure that the work he has contracted for meets all the specifications. He has the right to examine all operations of the research company to see that they are being carried out in the manner agreed upon. However, in doing so he should respect the research company's obligations to the public in matters of anonymity and invasion of respondents' privacy.

The buyer should recognize that the research company is a professional organization engaged in collecting marketing and/or opinion data. The buyer should not, therefore, ask or expect the research company to violate any of the suggested rules of procedure covered elsewhere in this statement. The buyer should not publicly identify the research agency in any release of findings, implying the endorsement of the research agency without prior agreement from the agency.

It is understood that in seeking a research agency the buyer may request proposals from more than one research company. However, generating ideas and planning research designs to solve specific problems are an important part of the services a research agency offers. The buyer, therefore, should not (1) lift ideas from one proposal and give them to another research agency or (2) ask for a proposal from a company which he knows has little or no chance of obtaining his business, unless he so informs them in advance. Soliciting bids for the purpose of obtaining free ideas which will be turned over to another bidder, or for purely technical compliance with a company's policy of obtaining competitive bids, does a disservice to the research firms involved, reflects on the integrity of the client company, and generally lessens the professional level of the research profession.

Kickbacks, rebates, and other "inducements" similarly destroy the professional character of research and should not be solicited, offered, or agreed to.

The research agency has the obligation to express, as they become apparent, any reservations about the usefulness of the proposed research in solving the client's problem. The agency also has the obligation, of course, to do the study contracted for in the manner agreed on. No additional questions designed for another purpose should be included in interviews done for a client without the client's knowledge and consent.

Unless otherwise agreed on by the seller and the buyer, the study report and the compiled tabulated data on which it is based are the property of the buyer. No by-product information should be sold to another buyer unless express permission is obtained from the original buyer.

In the course of conducting research, the researcher may become privy to confidential information relating to the client company. The researcher should not reveal any of this material to any outsider at any time.

Information to Be Included in the Research Firm's Report

Every research project differs from all others. So will every research report. All reports should nonetheless contain specific references to the following items:

1 The objectives of the study (including statement of hypotheses)
2 The name of the organization for which the study is made and the name of the organization that conducted it
3 Dates the survey was in the field and date of submission of final report
4 A copy of the full interview questionnaire, including all cards and visual aids used in the interview; alternatively, exact question wording, sequence of questions, etc.
5 Description of the universe(s) studied
6 Description of the number and types of people studied:
  a Number of people (or other units)
  b Means of their selection
  c If sample, method of sample selection
  d Adequacy of sample representatives and size
  e Percentage of original sample contacted (number and type of call-backs)

f Range of tolerance
g Number of cases for category breakouts
h Weighting and estimating procedures used

Where trend data are being reported and the methodology or question wording has been changed, these changes should be so noted.

On request—clients and other parties with legitimate interests may request and should expect to receive from the research firm the following:

a Statistical and/or field methods of interview verification (and percentage of interviews verified)
b Available data re validation of interview techniques
c Interviewing instructions
d Explanation of scoring or index number devices

Source: Paper developed by The Market Research Council's Ethics Committee. Reprinted with permission from Leo Bogart.

LEGAL ASPECTS

Recently certain activities related to marketing research have come under legal examination. Specific examples include:[22]

1 The Federal Trade Commission (FTC) successfully moved against encyclopedia firms who were using marketing research as a trick to solicit sales.

2 The FTC successfully moved against firms using research to identify prospects for a direct-mail scheme.

3 The FTC successfully moved against supply firms who purported that their data were free from all nonsampling error.

4 The Internal Revenue Service classified freelance field interviewers as part-time employees of supply firms, thus requiring these firms to pay social security, unemployment insurance, etc.

5 The Privacy Act of 1974 gives to respondents in federal government-related projects the rights suggested previously by Tybout and Zaltman. It is as yet unclear if and when these rights will be legislated for all marketing research studies.

6 The Privacy Protection Study Commission of the U.S. Government made 162 recommendations to protect the privacy of individuals. If put into law by Congress and held to apply to government and other research, they could seriously affect the ability of research to obtain respondent information.

[22] For a more detailed discussion of this issue see: Cynthia J. Frey and Thomas C. Kinnear, "Legal Constraints and Marketing Research: Review and Call to Action," *Journal of Marketing Research*, vol. XVI, pp. 295–302, August 1979.

MARKETING RESEARCH IN ACTION

UNFAIR SURVEYS TARGETED BY CALIFORNIA BILL

A bill that would enable public personalities to sue for damages if a survey used to evaluate their public appeal did not properly represent Hispanics, blacks and other minority groups, moved closer to law in the California state legislature last week. Presumably, this stricture also would apply to radio and TV ratings developed by A. C. Nielsen Co. or Arbitron.

The law would be administered by the California Department of Fair Employment and Housing. For example, if a locally produced TV show with an Hispanic emcee was discontinued, presumably because of low audience ratings, the performer could, under the Torres bill, request a review of the rating service's sample, and if the Department of Fair Employment and Housing found the sample did not accurately reflect the Hispanic population, the stage would be set for a civil suit for damages. It's not clear who gets sued—the station or the rating service, or both.

This is not an academic question. According to a story last month both Grey and Young & Rubicam recently switched from Nielsen to make Arbitron their main vehicle for ratings in spotty media buys. One reason for such switches, according to Steven Ball, vice president and general manager of KTLN, was that the Nielsen sample in Los Angeles was not fully reflective of minority audiences.

The Torres bill, apparently, stems from an interview Steven Levitt, president of a Port Washington, N.Y.–based survey company, Marketing Evaluations, did last December on the TV show "Entertainment Tonight."

The peg for Mr. Levitt's interview were two Marketing Evaluation services, TVQ Program Ratings and TVQ Performer Ratings, regularly scheduled nationwide surveys that measure public familiarity and likability of performers and celebrities. Advertising agencies, casting directors and producers use TVQ in casting work.

News stories quoted Mr. Levitt as saying Hispanics had been underrepresented in TVQ surveys because many could not read or write and had no telephone. Mr. Levitt claims his remarks were taken out of context, but still it was enough to set off a press brouhaha.

A minority entertainer refused a part in a TV pilot film or commercial, who could prove that his or her rejection was due to a low recognition score in a survey such as TVQ, or if his or her identiy was not explicit in such surveys, or if the sample was not representative, would then have legal recourse under the Torres bill.

Opposition to the Torres bill, mainly, has been organized by CASRO (a survey research trade association), its legal counsel and membership—which has been asked to pay legal costs.

Source: Jack Honomichl, "Unfair Surveys Targeted by California Bill," *Advertising Age,* June 18, 1984.

In a recent legal proceeding the FTC barred certain ads for Litton microwave ovens and in doing this established guidelines for the use of marketing research in support of advertising claims.[23] The relevant parts of the FTC order required Litton to cease

[23] "Certain Litton Ads for Microwave Ovens Barred as FTC Offers Guides on Surveys," *The Wall Street Journal,* p. 1, Jan. 14, 1981.

and desist from:[24]

> **1** Misrepresenting in any manner, directly or by implication, the purpose, sample, content, reliability, results, or conclusions of any survey or test.
> **2** Advertising the results of a survey unless the respondents in such survey are a census or a representative sample of the population referred to in the advertisement, directly or by implication. A representative sample need not be a probability sample so long as when the ad is first disseminated respondents have a reasonable basis to expect the sampling method used would not produce biased results.
> **3** Representing, directly or by implication, that experts were surveyed, unless reasonable care was taken to insure that the survey respondents possessed sufficient expertise to qualify as respondents for the survey and to answer the survey questions. For purposes of this order, an "expert" is an individual, group or institution held out as possessing, as a result of experience, study, or training, knowledge of a particular subject, which knowledge is superior to that generally acquired by ordinary individuals.

This order sets a high standard for research that will be used in a public forum. In this context, research quality and results must stand on their own; in contrast, studies that are used internally, where management judgment plays a role, need not be quite as comprehensive or systematic.

An example of ethics and legal aspects of marketing research merging is illustrated in the Marketing Research In Action concerning "unfair surveys."

SUMMARY

1 The history of marketing research parallels the rise of the marketing concept. Early practitioners were concerned with gathering information on markets and developing the applied aspects of survey research. The gradual shift to a focus on marketing research broadened the nature and role of research activities. The emphasis was on gathering information for marketing management decision making. Methodological development in marketing research parallels the development of research methodology in the social sciences. Early methodological development focused on data collection and sampling issues. More contemporary methodological advances relate to computer-based technologies for data analysis and interviewing.

2 Marketing research is a big and dynamic business.

3 Institutions in the marketing research business can be classified as users, users/doers, or doers.

4 Doers supply both ad hoc studies and syndicated data, on a full- or limited-service basis.

5 Careers are available as research directors, analysts, technical specialists, or clerical workers.

6 A firm may organize the marketing research function so that it is centralized, decentralized, or integrated.

---

[24] Federal Trade Commission Final Order in the Matter of Litton Industries, Inc. and Litton Systems, Inc., Docket no. 9123, p. 3, Jan. 5, 1981.

7 There are many differences between consumer and industrial marketing research in the areas of population, respondent accessibility, respondent cooperation, sample size, respondent definitions, interviews, and study costs.

8 The fundamental marketing research process and required skills are the same for both consumer and industrial marketing research.

9 Over 70 percent of organizations have formal marketing research departments. There has been rapid growth in the formation of marketing research departments in the last ten years.

10 Most marketing research departments are small in terms of number of employees.

11 A large percentage of total marketing research budgets is spent for outside research.

12 The effective use of outside marketing research suppliers is important.

13 Ethical issues arise in user-doer and doer-provider relationships. Various codes of ethics have been developed to direct researchers.

14 Legal constraints are becoming more important in marketing research.

DISCUSSION QUESTIONS

1 What is the institutional structure of the marketing research business?

2 What type of person would make a good research analyst?

3 How can the marketing research function be organized?

4 What are the advantages and disadvantages of each organizational alternative?

5 On what basis should an organizational structure be selected?

6 How should a research supplier be selected?

7 What should buyers and suppliers of research expect from each other?

8 Should legal action be taken to regulate marketing research activity? If so, state specifics.

CHAPTER 3

AN EXAMPLE OF
MARKETING RESEARCH

This chapter is designed to put into operation many of the concepts presented in Chapter 1 and serve the frequently expressed desire of students to see what a research project looks like.[1] The project presented here is not intended to be illustrative of good or effective marketing research. The focus is on the stages of the research process and the types of research that can be utilized.

In addition to being an initial overview of a research project, this chapter is intended to serve as a unifying reference when reading subsequent chapters dealing with specialized aspects of the research process. At several points in the chapter, you may encounter terms and techniques which are new. In such cases, we have tried to identify the chapters where these are explained in detail. The intent is not to have you turn to these chapters for explanation but rather to develop an understanding of the sequencing and role of future topics as they relate to the marketing research process. When studying subsequent chapters dealing with specialized aspects of the research process, you may find that reference to this chapter will help to bring perspective to the area being studied.

THE PROBLEM SETTING

The research project described here was conducted for the Rigid Container Division of the Society of the Plastic Industry (SPI) by a leading marketing research firm. The Rigid Container Division of SPI represents the majority of U.S. manufacturers of rigid

[1] We wish to acknowledge the assistance of Lawrence A. Crosby, associate professor of marketing, Arizona State University, in preparing this chapter.

plastic containers. Many of these companies are small manufacturing units with limited marketing and marketing research capabilities. A six-member executive board administers the activities of the Rigid Container Division.

Problem Recognition and Definition

In the last ten years, the plastic packaging industry has experienced dynamic growth, making significant penetration into the markets of more conventional packaging materials such as paper, paperboard, glass, and metal. Sales of plastic packaging totaled around $6 billion in 1982, up from approximately $2 billion in 1970. Plastic containers represent about 10 percent of the industry volume.

Several SPI research studies indicated that rigid plastic containers offer important advantages over other container materials. The consumer advantages include their light weight, resistance to breakage, toughness, resealability, and potential for reuse. Plastic containers are attractive to producers in that they are often less expensive than other containers. They store easily because they can be "nested," a feature which reduces shipping costs and warehouse space. In addition, they can be printed with an unlimited variety of colors and designs.

Much of the growth in plastic container sales had stemmed from the initiative of food manufacturers in seeking new packaging concepts for new products being developed. An example of this situation was the development of soft margarine. The manufacturer had requested the development of a reusable container specifically designed for this new product. Similar situations could be cited for other plastic containers for dairy products. An example of a plastic container replacing the traditional package is found with cottage cheese. Here, the advantages of the plastic container were reflected in the consumer's preference for brands of cottage cheese packaged in plastic rather than paper containers. Today, plastic is the dominant packaging form for soft margarine and cottage cheese.

The future outlook for further penetration of the packaging business was optimistic, but expectations were for a much slower growth rate than had been experienced in the previous decade. There were several constraints on future growth:

1 Growing uncertainty regarding the cost of raw materials and the competitive influence this would have on container selection.

2 Future competitive moves from glass, metal, and paper manufacturers. Many of these firms were large and had extensive research and development (R&D) and marketing capabilities.

3 Debate over environmental and safety issues regarding packaging containers. The nonbiodegradable property of plastic was a matter of concern, and the SPI commissioned a leading marketing research firm to analyze the issues in this area. A report was prepared titled "Resource and Environmental Profile Analysis of Plastic and Nonplastic Containers."

4 Growing concern among SPI members that possibly the high potential markets for plastic containers had been saturated (for example, soft margarine and cottage cheese).

The rapid growth of plastic container sales over the last·decade resulted in the modernization and expansion of production facilities to meet this demand. As a result, manufacturing capacity was currently in excess of demand for the majority of SPI members. It was the concern of these members that new markets for plastic products should be identified and programs developed to capture the market potential. Such action would help solve the excess-capacity problem and would continue the trend of plastic penetration of the container industry. Consequently, the executive board of the Rigid Container Division of SPI concluded that a marketing research study was needed to identify and evaluate the market opportunities for rigid plastic containers.

A leading marketing research firm in Chicago was recommended by the SPI New York office as highly qualified to conduct the study. A preliminary meeting was then arranged. The SPI representatives included a staff member from the New York office and three members representing the Rigid Container Division executive board. The three board members were managers of plastic container manufacturing operations. The purpose of the meeting was to explain why marketing research information was needed. This was to be accomplished by a series of presentations which characterized the plastic container industry and the past, current, and future situation that faced the industry. The previous discussion on problem recognition and definition summarizes the focus of this initial meeting with the marketing research firm. At the end of this meeting, the research firm requested one week to review the problem situation and formulate specific questions.

At the second meeting, the research firm requested a formal statement of objectives and potential courses of action available for reaching the objectives. A lengthy discussion was required before the SPI members committed themselves to specific statements in this regard. They indicated that these two matters had been discussed previously but only in general terms. The SPI members finally agreed to the following statement:

I SPI objective:
To increase the market penetration of plastic containers to 20 percent by 1990.
II Courses of action:
  A Develop and implement a marketing program to maintain or improve the acceptance of plastic containers in markets where plastic now dominates.
  B Develop and implement a marketing program to expand the acceptance of plastic containers in markets where plastic has a low or moderate penetration.
  C Develop and implement a marketing program to enter new markets currently dominated by paper, paperboard, glass, or metal.
  D Develop and implement a marketing program to work actively with manufacturers of new products.

The discussion turned to the type of information needed to select and implement one or more of the alternatives identified. Again, a lengthy discussion followed, reflecting the complexity of the problem (see Chapter 4).

The Problem Setting in Perspective

The marketing alternatives of concern to the Rigid Container Division involved broad and extensive information requirements. A program of research for developing a marketing plan was required. This implied the use of multiple data sources and specialized research projects.

One research approach involved studying the reactions of individuals and organizations who influenced the market acceptance of plastic containers. The ultimate consumers can be an influential group in this acceptance process. Consumers may have preferences for packaging characteristics that favor plastic over other packaging materials. The retailer and wholesaler may find packaging characteristics important in the selection of products to handle. Characteristics such as stacking ability, display appeal, and potential for breakage may influence their selection. Manufacturers who must decide on a packaging container for their product may consider many areas in making a decision. The preferences and reactions of consumers, retailers, and wholesalers may be important considerations. Container costs and related investment would be important. Manufacturing considerations, degree of product protection, promotional features, and ecological issues could all enter into the decision. Several research projects would be required to study this complex chain of influence for each market under consideration.

Another area of investigation concerned an analysis of current markets. The task here would be to quantify markets on characteristics such as size, trends in size, current mix of packaging forms, and fit of packaging requirements with existing plastic container manufacturing processes. This research approach involves the use of published data sources such as research reports, trade association data, and trade periodicals.

Additional studies could be required depending on the breadth of the sponsor's information needs. These might include profitability analysis of current lines of plastic containers, customer analysis, competitive analysis, and environmental analysis.

The information needs of this project were extensive and required a variety of research approaches and studies. These could range from small exploratory studies with consumers, retailers, wholesalers, and manufacturers to more formal studies using observation, interrogation, and experimentation. In addition, studies using published data sources internal and external to the sponsoring organizations could be required.

THE STUDY PROPOSAL

After several weeks of preparation, a research proposal was developed and sent to each of the executive board members for review. At a subsequent meeting with the research firm and after several changes, the proposal was approved. The following is a summary of the finalized proposal which contains two sections: (1) packaging markets and (2) consumer acceptance.

Study of Packaging Markets

Rationale for the Study The purpose of this study is to identify and characterize packaging markets and screen these markets as to their potential for penetration by plastic containers. The high-potential markets identified through this study will be further screened in the study of consumer acceptance.

Research Objectives

1 To compare current and potential packaging markets with regard to dimensions indicative of market potential.

2 To categorize packaging markets as to the degree of plastic container penetration.

3 To evaluate the high-potential markets in terms of the compatibility of packaging requirements with existing production and material capabilities.

Information Needs

1 Rank container markets by number of containers used per year. Illustrate trends over the past five years.

2 Classify markets as to the most likely plastic manufacturing process (thermoforming, injection molding, spin welding, or blow molding).

3 Classify markets by proportion of containers that are paper, paperboard, glass, metal, and plastic. Illustrate trends over the past five years.

4 Rank container markets by retail price of the product. Illustrate trends over the past five years.

5 Rank container markets by proportion of retail price represented by packaging costs. Illustrate trends over the past five years.

6 Rank container markets by magnitude of packaging cost increase or decrease resulting from a change to a plastic container.

7 Classify markets as to the degree of fit with existing production and material capabilities—high, medium, and low fit.

8 Calculate the plastic container manufacturer's break-even volume for each market. Determine the proportion of market penetration required to break even for each market. Rank the markets or proportion of market penetration required to break even.

Data Sources   The data used to meet the information needs will include internal and external reports, publications, and records. (See Chapter 5.) Data that are not available in published form will be gathered by interviews with knowledgeable people in the industry.

The following published sources have been identified:

1 "The Plastic Industry in the Year 2000," by SPI

2 "The Packaging Revolution" from *A Note on the Metal Container Industry*, by Harvard Business School

3 "New Container Push Accents Packaging," *Industrial Marketing,* December 1977

4 "Packaging Seen as Effective Marketing Tool," *Advertising Age,* September 1980

5 *Standard and Poor's Industry Surveys—Containers*

6 *1972 Census of Manufacturers*
   a Food Sales—Standard Industrial Classification #20
   b Plastic Sales—Standard Industrial Classification #30794

    7 *Standard and Poor's Industry Surveys—Retailing Food*
    8 *Modern Plastics*
    9 *Modern Plastics Encyclopedia*
   10 *Plastics Journal*
   11 *Society of Petroleum Engineering Journal*
   12 *Modern Packaging*
   13 *Modern Packaging Encyclopedia*
   14 *Resource and Environmental Profile Analysis of Plastic and Non-Plastic Containers,*
Midwest Research Institute

Study of Consumer Acceptance

    Rationale for the Study   It was the opinion of the research firm that demonstrating consumer acceptance or preference would be the critical factor in influencing a manufacturer to use a plastic container, in the absence of an unfavorable cost differential or excessive distribution problems. Consumer preference for a plastic container over existing packaging would provide strong evidence for a potential sales increase resulting from a change to a plastic container. In addition, understanding the underlying characteristics of the plastic container which cause this preference would be useful in developing a promotional program directed to manufacturers. The same information would be useful to manufacturers in developing a promotional program for trade and consumer acceptance.

    Research Objectives

    1 To determine which container markets have the greatest consumer acceptance of plastic containers.
    2 To determine the characteristics of plastic containers which represent advantages compared with paper, paperboard, glass, and metal containers.

    Information Needs

    1 Identify the characteristics or attributes which differentiate alternative packaging materials.
    2 Determine the importance of packaging attributes in container markets.
    3 Determine consumer preference for alternative packaging materials in container markets.
    4 Identify the characteristics of packaging containers which influence consumer preference.
    5 Determine which attributes of plastic containers represent important selling points.
    6 Determine the characteristics of the ideal packaging container.
    7 Determine the likes and dislikes of consumers regarding current packaging containers.
    8 Determine what suggestions consumers have for packaging improvement in container markets.

9 Determine which markets have the most inadequate packaging and whether plastic containers represent an improvement.

10 Determine consumer attitudes toward ecological aspects of packaging materials, specifically plastic.

11 Determine consumers' perceptions regarding the cost of alternative packaging materials. Do some containers have a "high price/high quality" image?

12 Determine the nature of the trade-offs consumers will make in selecting a brand/package. How large a price increase will be accepted for a superior packaging form? How much will a lower price offset packaging deficiencies?

13 Determine the characteristics (demographic, life cycle, usage rates) of consumers who are most receptive to plastic containers.

Data Sources   Acquiring data to meet the information needs will involve the interrogation of consumers. The first phase will include a series of focus group interviews (see Chapter 13). The purpose is to explore consumer attitudes, feelings, and motives concerning the information need areas such as attributes of packaging, pros and cons of packaging, and ecological issues. Based on these findings, specific questions can be developed for more systematic data collection. The second phase will involve a survey of consumers using a questionnaire administered by personal interview (see Chapters 13 and 14). The main conclusions of the study will be based on the results of this survey.

THE RESEARCH PROJECT

Results of the Study of Packaging Markets

The starting point for this phase of the research project was an extensive list of packaging markets which, at least superficially, seemed to hold good potential for rigid plastic containers. The list was furnished by the SPI, where it had been developed through continuous monitoring and contact with the packaging industry. This list was further screened by SPI to include only those markets where rigid plastic containers were judged to be feasible from the standpoint of both technology and cost.

The next step was to trim from the list those markets with obviously undesirable demand characteristics based on research using secondary data sources (see Chapter 6). While length prohibits presenting these detailed findings, the markets which survived this process appear in Exhibit 3-1, where they are classified according to the current penetration of plastic containers. A "major plastics market," for example, is one in which there is already high penetration.

By now, it may have occurred to the discerning reader that there are at least two types of markets with high potential for rigid plastic containers. One would be rapidly growing markets where plastic already has significant penetration, while the other would be large or growing markets where the pentration of plastic could be significantly improved. On the other hand, high-penetration markets with stable or declining primary demand afford little opportunity and therefore do not appear on the list.

The study of packaging markets can be viewed as exploratory research (see Chapter 4) for the purpose of identifying specific alternative courses of action to reach the

EXHIBIT 3-1

POTENTIAL MARKETS FOR RIGID PLASTIC CONTAINERS

Major plastics markets

Cultured dairy (cottage cheese, yogurt, etc.)
Butter and margarine
Portion packs (e.g., meat cold cuts)
Pantyhose

Minor plastics markets

Shortening	Cosmetic creams and gels
Ice cream	Auto oil and grease
Spreads and dips	Food sauces
Frozen juice	Meat trays

Non-plastics market

Jelly and preserves	Pet foods
Salad dressing	Auto parts and kits
Baby food	Cheese
Coffee	Household cleaners,
Drink powders	wax, car care
(e.g., Kool-Aid)	

SPI objectives previously discussed. In this case, "alternative courses of action" can be construed as different container markets at which the members' efforts might be directed. The study of consumer acceptance, to which we now turn, concerns not only the identification and evaluation of these specific container market alternatives but the selection of a course of action as well. This study involves both exploratory and conclusive research.

Results of the Study of Consumer Acceptance

Group Studies   This state of the project involved a series of group discussion sessions to explore consumer attitudes on the advantages and disadvantages of different types of containers. The sort of information derived from these sessions was qualitative in nature and served to guide the quantitative research conducted later. Group sessions are a fairly well-established technique in the marketing research business for probing a topic that is not yet well defined. Chapter 13 will discuss the area of qualitative research in detail.

Design and Procedure   Anywhere from eight to twelve paid participants attended each of the sessions, which were held at a special facility for group sessions run by the research firm. The sessions took place in a family-living-room environment made as comfortable as possible to help put the participants at ease. The sessions were video tape-recorded for later analysis, but an effort was made to keep the equipment as unobtrusive as possible, again to minimize anxiety.

In order to ensure that the sessions were of reasonable length (1½ hours is usually optimal), it was necessary to restrict the number of uses of plastic containers discussed in depth in any one session. A master plan was devised whereby each use was discussed in more than one session but usually in the context of a different set of other possible uses. Of course, when uses such as baby food and pet food containers were discussed, it was necessary to have panel members who were all purchasers of these products. To assure this, a screening process was employed which we will now examine.

Sample Selection Each session was conducted with a panel of consumers who were largely homogeneous in terms of their position in the family life cycle. While pros and cons exist for this sort of design, recruiting along life-cycle lines helped in the identification of the most probable users of certain sets of products. To facilitate the selection process, a screening questionnaire was constructed to determine marital status, number and ages of any children living at home, occupational status of the adult family members, and usage rates of those products previously defined as markets for plastic containers. Using this questionnaire, interviewers then selected a convenient sample at a nearby shopping center (see Chapter 7). Those who agreed to participate were given a time and place at which to appear.

Moderator and Guide Questions The group discussions were led by trained moderators whose function was to channel the conversation along particular lines. They in turn were directed by a "moderator's guide," which specified the minimum set of topics which the group was to cover and how the topics were to be broached. A few sample questions from the guide appear in Exhibit 3-2.

EXHIBIT 3-2

EXAMPLES FROM THE MODERATOR'S GUIDE

When was the last time you found yourself extremely dissatisfied with the container used for a product you had purchased?

Certain types of containers are best suited for certain types of products. Describe for me the kind of product you would expect to find in a glass jar. How about a metal can? Paper or cardboard? Plastic?

In general, what do you consider to be the advantages and disadvantages of glass, metal, paper, and plastic containers?

Let's discuss the kinds of experiences you have had with the container's used for ice cream, jelly, coffee, meat.

Do you think it usually costs more to package a product in plastic rather than glass? Metal? Paper?

Assume that the brand of ice cream you buy was available in the standard paper carton, a plastic container, or a sturdy cardboard container (the cylindrical kind with the separate top). If the price were the same for the three versions, which would you buy? What sort of person can you visualize buying the other two versions?

The job of moderating a group session tends to be a very sensitive task. To be most useful, the conversation needs to be lively and uninhibited but should not be dominated by a few panel members and should not stray too far from the assigned topics. The moderators applied various techniques to help achieve this result. One such technique was to identify panel members holding widely divergent points of view and then guide them into a debate. Another was to call on shy or retiring members directly for their opinions.

Analysis   After all the sessions were completed, the tapes were replayed and transcribed, and summary reports were written based on what they contained. Given that the data were qualitative, no statistics were formally presented, such as what percentage said this or that. Instead, the format was to categorize and list comments in such a way as to define the domain of the problem without trying to determine the relative importance of its various aspects. As an aid to the analysis, the individual tapes were edited into a summary tape that included only the most meaningful dialog from each session. In the research business, such tapes are often used for management presentations.

Results   At the general level, what emerged from these sessions was as follows:

1 A better understanding of how consumers think about containers, the terms they use, and the attributes and characteristics they consider relevant
2 A more thorough list of the advantages and disadvantages associated with different container types, depending on how they are used
3 Some new ideas on the kinds of products that might be contained in rigid plastic

To help make this discussion more concrete, however, we might consider the results obtained for one packaging market in particular, namely, ice cream. Although per capita consumption of ice cream declined 5 percent from 1970 to 1980, it represents a market with minor plastic penetration and would therefore seem to offer good potential for the future. Most ice cream is now contained in paper cartons, which, according to the panel members, have these deficiencies:

1 When the ice cream melts, they leak.
2 They are flimsy and tear easily.
3 Children don't know which end is the top, and they open both.
4 They are susceptible to freezer burn.
5 They tend to absorb moisture.

In comparison, the participants tended to view plastic containers mainly in positive terms, such as the following:

1 They are reusable.
2 They are resealable.
3 They are strong.
4 They are less messy, because they don't leak.
5 They prevent freezer burn.

6 Sherbet comes like this, and experiences with it have been good.

7 Plastic has a higher quality/price image.

8 They are easy to use and have a wide mouth.

9 There is an incentive value in seeing the ice cream.

In spite of these positive findings from the qualitative research there was not sufficient evidence to say that ice cream in rigid plastic containers would definitely have consumer acceptance. For one thing, the sample was small and not representative. There were no statistics projectable to the general population as to the level of acceptance. Also, it was possible that all nine positive aspects on the list could be easily outweighed by a single important disadvantage not uncovered for some reason. Finally, some other use might exist where the acceptance of plastic would be much more certain. For these reasons and others, the conclusive research discussed in the next section was undertaken.

Survey of Consumers   In contrast to the focus group sessions discussed above, the methodology of the survey of consumers was more heavily influenced by an existing body of scientific knowledge. That body of knowledge specifies the manner in which surveys should be conducted and analyzed so as to minimize the amount of error in the results. This survey employed some error-reducing techniques that are not always used in marketing research because the benefits of the reduction in uncertainty do not, in every case, justify the increased cost.

As is the case with most well-developed areas of science, survey research has its own terminology, some of which may be confusing to the uninitiated. Various technical terms are introduced in the rest of this chapter without elaboration or apology, because considerable effort will be expended in defining them in detail in the remainder of the book.

The survey of consumers followed what is a fairly standard series of steps for doing this type of research. The processes which will be discussed are, in the order of their occurrence: questionnaire design and pretesting; sample selection and field work; editing, coding, and data processing; and analysis and reporting.

Questionnaire Design and Pretesting   Some say that questionnaire design is as much an art as it is a science. While this may be true, there is much more to designing a questionnaire than its literary aspects (see Chapter 14). Perhaps one scientific principle in the design of a questionnaire is that the questions should proceed from the general to the specific. For example, in this study respondents were asked to recall some products they had seen contained in plastic. It made sense that this question should occur before one that specifically mentioned product names. A few other refinements incorporated in the questionnaire were alternate question wordings to avoid an acquiescence bias, the rotation of item lists to avoid an order bias (e.g., the list of attributes and the list of container uses), and precoding of the response categories for machine processing. Some of the questions used in this study have been paraphrased in Exhibit 3-3.

The questionnaire was pretested on a convenience sample of about 75 consumers to make sure that the proper flow existed and that the questions were understandable

EXHIBIT 3-3

EXAMPLE OF QUESTIONS ON THE QUESTIONNAIRE

1 Of the packages you currently purchase, which do you feel could be improved? Why?

2 What products do you currently purchase which come packaged in a plastic container?

3 What are the advantages of a plastic container?

4 What are the disadvantages of a plastic container?

5 Would you please evaluate (packaging container) in regard to the degree it possesses the characteristic of (attribute)? (rating scale)

6 How important is the packaging characteristic of (attribute) for a (packaging container)? (rating scale)

7 (Interviewer checks "male" or "female.")

8 What is your marital status?

9 How many people are there in your household?

10 How many children do you have at home?

11 What are their ages?

12 What is the highest grade of school or college that you have completed?

to ordinary individuals. The pretesting also provided the opportunity to analyze the items for redundancy. This was accomplished by taking the data for the total sample and subjecting them to a technique known as factor analysis (see Chapter 19). The procedure revealed that several of the attributes actually measured the same underlying characteristic, so it was possible to eliminate a few of the items.

Sample Selection and Field Work It was determined that the interviews could be successfully conducted over the telephone. Telephone numbers were selected using the method of random-digit dialing (see Chapter 13). Under this procedure, three-digit exchange codes supplied by the telephone company are combined with four-digit random numbers to give every operating telephone in the country an equal probability of selection. An advantage of random-digit dialing is that there is no bias against newly listed or unlisted numbers, as occurs when samples are selected from telephone directories. However, households without telephones are excluded from the target population, and there is some inefficiency in connections made to business numbers. In addition, households with two or more phone listings have a higher probability of being included in the sample. The interviews were conducted at various times of the day over WATS lines. A number of call-backs were made when there was no answer or the line was busy. In all, about 500 interviews were completed over the course of several weeks.

Editing, Coding, and Data Processing At this stage, completed interviews were edited to make sure that they were legible, complete, consistent, and accurate and that all the instructions had been properly followed (see Chapter 16). In some cases where data were missing, estimates were made of what the responses would have been based on other information in the questionnaire. This was only necessary in a few critical places in the questionnaire. Open-ended questions were then coded to make the data machine-readable. As the coding process was getting under way, a "round robin" was used whereby several individuals coded the same questionnaire. This revealed a few ambiguities in the code book.

As soon as the completed interviews were edited and coded, they were keypunched onto computer cards and verified 100 percent. The research firm had available standard computer programs to process the survey data.

Analysis and Reporting The objectives of this chapter, together with space limitations, restrict the presentation of the results of the study and the course of action selected and implemented by SPI. Consequently, the following discussion is designed to illustrate the data analysis state and to discuss a few of the research findings.

The first step in the analysis process was to obtain a description of the sample in terms of demographic characteristics. The sample demographics were then compared with U.S. census data to determine whether the sample was representative of the population. Except for minor sampling variations, the sample and population distributions were very similar.

In like fashion, descriptive statistics were obtained on the response to every item in the questionnaire (see Chapter 17). These statistics included measures of central tendency and dispersion. Among the benefits of doing this was the identification of a number of "wild codes" that needed to be corrected. Some of these univariate statistics were used to make interval estimates of the proportion of consumers in the general population who felt a particular way on a certain issue. For example, it was of interest to the SPI to know that, at the 95 percent confidence level, somewhere between 43 and 51 percent of the population would prefer that their ice cream came in a rigid plastic container. These statistics were especially valuable when compared with similar figures for other products.

There were other cases, however, where a simple univariate analysis was not revealing enough and a cross tabulation or bivariate analysis seemed necessary (see Chapter 18). For instance, 25 percent of the respondents said they would switch brands of ice cream to obtain a plastic container. However, a cross tabulation revealed that the result varied depending on the level of educational attainment, as evidenced in Table 3-1. Only 17 percent of those who graduated from high school said they would switch brands to get plastic, compared with 37 percent of those who had not graduated. Was it safe to conclude, then, that educational attainment was a causal factor affecting the intention to switch brands? The fallacy of this conclusion is evident in

TABLE 3-1   INTENTION TO SWITCH BRANDS BY LEVEL OF EDUCATIONAL ATTAINMENT

	Total, %	Did not graduate, %	Graduated from high school, %
Would switch	25	37	17
Would not	75	63	83
Total	100	100	100

TABLE 3-2   INTENTION TO SWITCH BRANDS BY LEVEL OF EDUCATIONAL ATTAINMENT AND
BIO-AWARENESS

	Did not graduate from high school			Graduated from high school		
	Total, %	Aware, %	Not aware, %	Total, %	Aware, %	Not aware, %
Would switch	37	20	43	17	20	43
Would not	63	80	57	83	80	57
Total	100	100	100	100	100	100

Table 3-2. Note that regardless of the level of educational attainment, only 20 percent of those who were aware that plastic is nonbiodegradable said they would switch brands, compared with 43 percent of those who were not aware. The influence of education was that more people with a high school education were aware that plastic was nonbiodegradable (50 percent compared with 25 percent).

Many other two-way relationships were studied, and in addition some more complex multivariate analysis was performed (see Chapter 19 and 20). These results are not reported here, but they were useful to management in decision making.

SUMMARY

1 The purpose of this chapter was to illustrate the character and flow of a research project.

2 The first phase of the project involved the recognition by the Rigid Container Division's executive board that a problem existed. The problem was defined as the need to identify and evaluate the market opportunities for rigid plastic containers.

3 The next phase involved specifying the objective of the executive board and identifying potential courses of action to accomplish the objective.

4 The project next turned to identifying the type of information needed to select and implement one or more of the alternatives identified.

5 The information requirements suggested that a series of projects were required. Research objectives and specific information needs were specified for a study of packaging markets and a study of consumer acceptance. The study of packaging markets was an exploratory research study using secondary data sources to identify specific alternative courses of action. The study of consumer acceptance was mainly concerned with conclusive research directed at the selection of a course of action. This study involved a national probability sample of households, with interviews conducted over the telephone.

6 The results of the telephone survey were analyzed by means of univariate and bivariate analysis. Illustrative results were presented for the ice cream container market.

7 The presentation of the research project was not intended to illustrate how a research report should be organized and written. Chapter 21 discusses this in detail.

DISCUSSION QUESTIONS

1 How did the marketing research firm ascertain the information needs of SPI?
2 What type of research did the study of packaging markets involve? Why?
3 What type of research did the study of consumer acceptance involve? Why?
4 Evaluate the manner in which the group phase of the study of consumer acceptance was carried out.

CASES FOR PART ONE

CASE 1-1: National Markets—Nutritional Labeling*

Jose Martinez was the president of Midwest Marketing Research Associates (MMRA). He was in the process of preparing a marketing research proposal for National Markets, the largest supermarket chain in the midwestern United States. National's market share had been declining steadily for the past year and a half, and the marketing department was determined to turn things around. The senior members in the department had formulated a plan, but they needed marketing research data in order to verify the plan's validity to other National departments. MMRA was one of three major marketing research firms vying for this research project. The completed research proposal was due in 2 weeks.

Martinez had had a meeting with National's marketing department earlier in the month to roughly define the purpose of the project. Michelle Stead, vice president in charge of marketing at National, hadn't outlined the specific information needs; rather, she had gone over the problems that were facing National. She had indicated to Martinez that it would be up to him to formulate research objectives based on his perception of the information needs.

Stead told him that National's sales had been increasing at a slower pace than its competitors' and that National wanted to reverse this trend through "goodwill gestures" aimed at consumers. The tentative plan was to provide shoppers with detailed nutritional information about the packaged foods sold in National stores. But National executives weren't sure exactly how the information should be presented to consumers,

* Coauthored by Sheryl Petras.

how the consumers would react to it, or even if they would use the information. Because of these concerns, initiation of the program had been delayed until consumers' attitudes could be researched.

Bart Russell, National's district manager for Illinois and Indiana, foresaw several potential problems with the proposed "solution." First of all, he related to Martinez, stores would be reluctant to post information that might cut their profits. Since many of the high-margin items were also the least nutritious, consumers might avoid the nonnutritious—but highly profitable—foods if nutrition information were available. Second, the cost to provide this information would be high unless the stores were subsidized by the National main office. The majority of National's stores could not afford to offer additional services to shoppers without boosting prices. But, said Russell, store managers would furnish nutrition information readily if they were shown that the cost of providing this information would be offset by the benefits gained if more people began shopping at National. The marketing department hoped that presenting favorable marketing research results to the store managers would make them more willing to accept the idea of forgoing some short-term profits for long-range benefits.

The nutrition information had already been gathered by National, so the only cost to the individual stores would come from disseminating this data to consumers. The information had, for the most part, been obtained from outside sources. For 85 percent of all products, the required nutrition information had been collected from the manufacturers—either directly from the food labels, or in response to a written request. For another 9 percent of the products, National managers had weighed the contents of the packages and combined that data with information from the manufacturers, or from the U.S. Department of Agriculture, to determine the nutrient content of the foods. For the remaining 6 percent, National could not acquire nutrition information. Most of these foods were "mixed" foods with low sales volume, like frozen mixed vegetables, or multipacks of single-serving breakfast cereals.

National executives from other (nonmarketing) departments had indicated a willingness to help stores implement the program, but only if marketing research showed that:

1 Shoppers would actually benefit from the information.
2 They would make use of the information.

Even if sales did not increase right away, National top management felt that providing this extra service to consumers would benefit National in the long run by increasing customer loyalty.

Because this project was such a major undertaking, Martinez spent a great of time conversing with Stead, as she would be very influential in choosing which company got the research grant. Martinez wanted to be absolutely certain that he had enough information to identify the problem areas National was most concerned with so that he could define the research objectives correctly. Stead had not set an upper limit on the project's budget, but Martinez wanted to keep it at a reasonable level so as to remain competitive. In the end, though, he knew that the quality of his research proposal would determine whether or not MMRA would be awarded the project.

CASE QUESTIONS

1 Develop a statement of research objectives. Think about: Why the request for information was made. Who the decision makers are. The goals or objectives of the decision makers. The decision-making environment.

2 What are the key information needs? List the five you feel are most important, and be prepared to defend your reasons for listing each.

3 One possible research design would be to interview (either in person, by telephone, or through the mail) grocery store shoppers. What are other possible designs?

4 Make a detailed outline of the research proposal you would submit if you were Jose Martinez. (Think about the information that National will be looking for in a research proposal.)

5 Prepare a research proposal. Use the outline you developed in Question 4.

CASE 1-2: Weston Food Company

The following five episodes deal with the relationship between research and management. In each episode, ask yourself: What is going on? Is the research/management connection effective? Why or why not? How could the situations be improved? What generalizations can be made about how to establish an effective research/management relationship in an organization?

Episode A

Tom Murphy, director of research for the Weston Food Company, has been striving to establish a cordial relationship with the advertising department for several months. He feels that the research department can supply very useful information regarding the advertising programs of the Weston Food Company.

In response to these efforts, Sam Jones, the advertising manager, calls Murphy, asking for help in developing a new advertising program. "We need to know customers' perceptions, attitudes, and preferences toward our new line of diet products."

Murphy personally directs an extensive research study on the diet product line. Seven weeks later, a thorough report and presentation on current users' attitudes, perceptions, and preference patterns is presented to Jones and his staff. After the presentation, Jones' reaction is: "Certainly a lot of interesting data that we weren't aware of; but how does this help us design a new advertising campaign to switch buyers from competitive diet lines to ours and entice potential dieters to try our line?"

Episode B

John Phelps, product manager for Weston's "Magic" scouring pads, calls upon Tom Murphy, director of research, to discuss a problem he has. "Good to see you again, Tom. As you know, sales volume on 'Magic' has not reached the targeted market share. We are seven points off target. I feel it is time to do some research on this problem. It's obvious to me that the culprit is our package design. We just don't catch the eye of the consumer like SOS does. Also, the package does a poor job in conveying the product concept and our point of difference from SOS."

Murphy concurs with John Phelps that the packaging is poorly done and that the research department could provide useful information concerning the selection of a new package design.

He goes on to say, "This type of problem lends itself to controlled experimentation very well. As you know, Barbra Kindle is an expert on experimental design and would be delighted to develop a research proposal that would get right at this problem."

Phelps reacts: Sounds excellent to me. Can you have a proposal put together by Thursday?

Murphy replies: I'll have to check with Barbra first, but let's plan on a Thursday afternoon meeting in Conference Room C.

Phelps: That's great. I know I can always count on the cooperation of the research department.

Episode C

Tom Murphy, director of research, cautious about vaguely stated research study objectives, has been impressing on a senior staff member, Sid Alsen, the need for clearly written research proposals including management objectives, information requirements, and anticipated uses of expected results. During their conversation, Murphy receives a call from the marketing department asking for a research staff member to participate in a planning meeting where research needs will be discussed. Tom tells Sid about the call and suggests that he attend the meeting. Before leaving, Alsen is advised: "Be sure to develop a careful specification of how the information required will be used."

Later in the afternoon, Sid returns from the meeting thoroughly defeated. "They told me it wasn't any of my damn business what they were going to do with the information. We are just supposed to get it and they will decide what to do with it."

Episode D

Ellen Tod, senior research analyst, reviews the marketing plan for the instant potato line and reports to her manager, Tom Murphy: "If they had paid any attention to my research report they wouldn't be doing these things. They must be stupid up there; why, I could run that program better!"

Murphy later receives a call from the planning manager, telling him: "If that analyst (Ellen Tod) can't just report the facts and stop trying to make us look stupid, we would rather do without!"

Episode E

The following dialogue takes place between a product manager, Jim Phiel, and Ellen Tod, senior research analyst.

Tod: I understand you are interested in a consumer test on product C-11.
Phiel: Yes, we definitely need to get some good market feedback.
Tod: What will you do if the results are favorable?
Phiel: National introduction, of course. This product has a great future.

Tod: What if the results are negative?

Phiel: Don't worry about that. I know C-11 will be accepted with enthusiasm.

Tod: But what happens if your expectations are wrong?

Phiel: Look, if you design a good test, we won't have any problems. There are a lot of hopes riding on the success of this product, and we need some good information behind it.

CASE 1-3: Detroit Public Library (A)*

In order to improve the effectiveness of library services in its 31-branch system and their relevance to community needs, the Detroit Public Library initiated a market-oriented community study. The mission of the study was:

> To identify and analyze informational and cultural needs, patterns of present library use and nonuse, sociological obstacles to effective library use, and other factors basic to the development of a comprehensive plan of library services to a modern urban community.

In a departure from the traditional community survey, which focuses on the composition of the population and projected population trends, the study designed for the Detroit Public Library was to emphasize the identification of library users and nonusers as market segments and to analyze those differences between segments which might be useful in expanding the service base of the branch library system. Further evaluations of the attitudes of both current users and branch library personnel were to provide a review of the effectiveness of existing programming. A proposal submitted by a marketing research supplier follows.

PROPOSAL FOR RESEARCH

Phase 1—Exploratory Research

Two focus group interview sessions will be conducted to identify important attributes that should be examined and included in the conclusive phases outlined in the following two sections. Two separate groups of 7 to 10 library users and two similar-sized groups of nonusers will be selected to participate. Individuals for the user sessions will be solicited at several branch locations. The nonuser groups will be screened prior to the focus group sessions. Each participant will be remunerated for cooperating and completing sessions lasting 1 to 2 hours.

Phase 2—Study of Branch Personnel

This portion of the research project will examine factors common to one or both of two important library groups: the general public and the branch personnel who interact directly with the using public. Since the primary emphasis will be directed toward examining individual factors relating to use and nonuse of the library and its branches,

* This case was coauthored by Cynthia Frey, Patricia Braden, and Denise Hoyer.

it makes sense to consider first the opinions and observations of personnel concerning these factors prior to asking respondents from the general Detroit population to report their "true" attitudes and behavior regarding library-related factors. Selected branch personnel will be asked questions concerning what they feel are the attitudinal and behavioral characteristics of users, nonusers, and fellow personnel. Furthermore, these employees will be asked to speculate about the attitudes of library users concerning such factors as the library personnel, the branch environment, and the services provided. Crucial to understanding if individual employee characteristics may be affecting responses or possibly even library usage, questions will be addressed which concern employee perceptions of their roles and the overall image of the library and of the branch, as well as characteristics and level of satisfaction with the work environment in general and the job in particular.

The survey instrument will be distributed by designated library or research administrators to all branch personnel meeting the criterion of direct daily interaction with the public. Only anonymous responses will be solicited and this will be achieved by having respondents mail the completed questionnaire to the research firm. No attempt will be made to draw a sample from this population since the incremental costs of taking a census are minimal and the impact on the employees of participating in a study of this nature should be positive. Finally, samples can be drawn from the final set of returned questionnaires in order to compute estimates of sampling error and therefore allow comparisons between employees and the general public and its subgroups to be made.

Phase 3—Study of the General Public

Following the pattern of the branch personnel study, the survey instrument administered to respondents from the general population will contain similar attribute dimensions for examination, except that questions will be framed from the perspectives of users and nonusers. For example, these respondents will be asked to state their attitudes toward factors that relate to the library environment such as the personnel, other users, and the level of service. In addition, questions will be asked to determine what library users and nonusers think that other groups (such as library personnel, users, and nonusers) perceive as being characteristic of each of the remaining groups. As one example, we would like to understand the dynamics of why users visit a particular branch. Is it done because the branch personnel are perceived as being similar to the user in certain respects, because some branches have more friendly or less intimidating atmospheres than others, strictly because of location factors, or some combination of the aforementioned? Furthermore, we will also examine factors which may be contributing to nonuse of library facilities and services such as perceptual distortions, unfamiliarity, and fear. Finally, the nature and extent of library participation and usage will be examined, with provisions made for delineating unbiased self-reports of behavior from their biased counterparts.

Several different sample designs must be used in order to achieve an adequate representation of the entire Detroit library market (including Highland Park and Hamtramck).

A multistage area sampling procedure will be employed for selecting probabilistically a sample of respondents from two of the following three segments of the general population. One segment will consist of those residences that have a listed phone number; another segment comprises those residences that have a phone, but the number is unlisted. Within each of these segments, the list of applicable phone numbers will be divided into areas and potential respondents will be selected from these area lists using a systematic random sampling procedure. Respondents selected at the second stage will become part of the final sample if the quota based on reported usage has not been satisfied at the time of selection. These phone interviews should require no more than 30 minutes of each respondent's time and, like the study of branch personnel (and the portion of this study requiring personal interviews), data submitted for analysis will not reveal identifying characteristics of the individual respondent.

Personal interviews will be used to obtain information from the segment of residences lacking telephone service. Rather than attempting to select no-phone residences on a strict probability basis, we will concentrate instead on those areas in which the telephone coverage is much lower than the average for the city. Within these areas, however, blocks and ultimately residences will be selected probabilistically.

In all segments, a fixed ratio of reported users to nonusers will be used as quotas and will be coupled with a fixed sample size of 1000 for the phone segments and 50 for the nonphone segment.

The proposal also contained a detailed timetable, a reporting plan, and a budget estimate of $50,000 broken down as follows: personnel costs, $24,000; field cost of interviewing, $19,000; data processing and analysis, $3000; and travel and overhead, $4000.

CASE QUESTIONS

1 Evaluate the statement of research mission. How well does it guide the research process?
2 Evaluate each phase of the research proposal in terms of content and presentation.
3 How could the research design be improved?
4 What is the value of this research to the Detroit Public Library? Is it worth $50,000?
5 What potential sources of errors should be of concern to the researchers in this study? How does the proposal attempt to control these errors?

CASE 1-4: Ethical Dimensions in Marketing Research*

The following situations and questions have occurred many times in the real world of marketing research. Each raises ethical concerns about the practice of marketing research. For each situation and question, identify what you believe to be the ethical issue and indicate what you would do.

* This case was developed using a number of sources, including: *Marketing Educator*, vol. 3, no. 1, Winter 1984; Richard Crosby, "Uniform Ethical Cost Is Impractical due to Shifting Marketing Research Circumstances," *Marketing News*, p. 16, Sept 19, 1981; C. Merle Crawford, "Attitudes of Marketing Executives toward Ethics in Marketing Research," *Journal of Marketing*, pp. 46–52, April 1970; plus suggestions by Philip Hendrix.

1 A research buyer asks for competitive proposals from a number of research suppliers. The buyer takes ideas from a number of these proposals without offering payment for the ideas and then awards the contract to one of the research suppliers to conduct the study using all the ideas.

2 A research organization uses questions developed for one client in designing a questionnaire for another client.

3 Without obtaining the approval of the client, a simple set of questions for that client is added to another client's questionnaire.

4 A major error is discovered by a research supplier in a study that has been completed and submitted to the client.

5 A research firm is asked to conduct a study by a firm that is in direct competition with one of the research firm's clients.

6 A research firm accepts an assignment with the knowledge that it cannot complete the project in the designated time.

7 A research firm wonders what the ethical issues are, if any, in using entertainment and gifts to help in soliciting business.

8 The director of marketing research presented to senior management the results of a study conducted by a member of the marketing research staff. No mention of this staff member was made during the presentation. In a footnote in the written report, the staff member was given credit for this contribution.

9 A consultant was asked by a highly conservative publication to conduct a readership survey. Although the consultant was well qualified to do the research, the magazine's philosophy was quite inconsistent with her own. She was having difficulty resolving this professional/moral dilemma.

10 A project director has proposed to use ultraviolet ink on a questionnaire in a mail survey. The letter with the survey promises that the respondent will not be identified. The director thinks that the ink identification is needed to save money in the mailing of a follow-up questionnaire to those who do not respond to the first mailing. Without the ink marking, the questionnaire will have to be mailed to all subjects in the sample, including those who responded to the first mailing.

11 An interviewer tells a respondent that an interview will only last 15 minutes, fully knowing that it takes a half hour. Experience has shown that many respondents granting a 15-minute interview would refuse a 30-minute interview. However, once subjects agree to participate, they usually complete the interview process—even if it runs longer than the originally cited time. Thus, nonresponse error can be reduced, and data accuracy increased.

12 As part of a study on family buying processes, a family is videotaped as it examines automobiles in a dealer showroom. Also, conversations within the family are recorded by a "shopper"/researcher. The family is not aware that it is being monitored.

13 A family places its trash in a public alley for pickup. Without asking permission, a researcher sorts through the garbage as part of a brand-preference survey.

EARLY STAGES OF THE RESEARCH PROCESS

CHAPTER 4

THE DECISION TO UNDERTAKE RESEARCH

It has been stated that there are three basic components in any marketing research undertaking: (1) making certain that the right questions are being asked, (2) using appropriate research techniques and controls, and (3) presenting research findings in a clear, comprehensible format that leads to management action.[1]

The purpose of this chapter is to highlight the first component, namely, making certain that the right questions are being asked. Subsequent chapters will deal with the remaining two.

There is probably no activity more critical to the success of the research project than the analysis leading to the decision to undertake research. Frequently, this analysis is poorly executed or superficially passed over in the excitement of doing a research study. The consequences are inadequate information for decision making, wasted research funds, and management dissatisfaction with the marketing research system.

The decision-making process and the management process are often considered synonymous. An organization's well-being is dependent on the wisdom of the decisions made by its managers. When confronted with decision situations where the setting is unique, the manager turns to a more formal approach to decision making called the decision-making process. A central issue in this process involves the use of marketing research. The nature and role of marketing research vary with the needs of management at various stages of this process.

---

[1] William B. Loeander and A. Benton Cocanougher (eds.), *Problem Definition in Marketing*, American Marketing Association, Marketing Research Techniques, ser. 2, Chicago, p. i, 1975.

TYPES OF RESEARCH

Marketing research can be classified as (1) exploratory research, (2) conclusive research, and (3) performance-monitoring (routine feedback) research. The stage in the decision-making process for which the research information is needed determines the type of research required. Figure 4-1 illustrates this interdependence, while Exhibit 4-1 presents a real-world example of using different types of research in the decision-making process involving a cereal product.

Exploratory Research

Exploratory research is appropriate for the early stages of the decision-making process. This research is usually designed to obtain a preliminary investigation of the situation with a minimum expenditure of cost and time. The research design is characterized by flexibility in order to be sensitive to the unexpected and to discover insights not previously recognized. Wide-ranging and versatile approaches are employed. These include secondary data sources, observation, interviews with experts, group interviews with knowledgeable persons, and case histories.

Exploratory research is appropriate in situations where management is searching for potential problems or opportunities; seeks new insights, ideas, or hypotheses regarding

FIGURE 4-1   Types of research.

EXHIBIT 4-1

**USING DIFFERENT TYPES OF RESEARCH—
REPOSITIONING TOTAL CEREAL**

Problem Recognition

Research Type: Performance-monitoring research
Method: *SAMI Reports* (from a marketing research supply company) audit the warehouse movement of food products
Finding: Gradual decline in Total's share of market during the mid-1970s

Definition of Decision Problem

Research Type: Exploratory research
Method: Focus group interviews with current and former Total users
Finding: The cause of declining share of market was hypothesized as consumer misperception of granola or natural cereal as having high nutrition value in comparison to Total and was therefore being viewed as a substitute for Total.

Identifying Courses of Action

Research Type: Exploratory research
Method: Focus group interviews with adult cereal buyers
Finding: Presenting consumers with the nutrition labeling information (percentage of U.S. Recommended Daily Allowance) existing on the Total and granola containers lowered their perception of granola's nutritional value and increased their preference for Total

Evaluating Courses of Action

Research Type: Conclusive research
Method: Advertising copy testing using experimental design
Finding: Several copy approaches were tested. One approach compared the amount of granola cereal one must eat (25 oz.) to get the same nutrient value as a bowl of Total. An alternate approach compared Total's percent of recommended daily allowance of vitamins and iron to that of granola cereal (100% vs. 6%). The first approach tested the highest and was selected for the national advertising campaign. The second approach was used later in the campaign.

Implementation and Control

Research Type: Performance-monitoring research
Method: *SAMI Reports*
Finding: There was a substantial increase in Total's share of the market over the next several years and a serious decline in granola's market penetration.

Based upon a presentation by General Mills, Inc., at the Graduate School of Business Administration, the University of Michigan.

the situation; or desires a more precise formulation of the problem and the identification of the relevant variables in the decision situation. Once these issues have been adequately investigated and the decision situation is thoroughly defined, exploratory research can be useful in identifying alternative courses of action. Here the manager seeks clues to innovative marketing approaches. The objective is to broaden the domain of alternatives identified, with the hope of including the "best" alternative in the set of alternatives to be evaluated.

Conclusive Research

Conclusive research provides information which helps the manager evaluate and select a course of action. The research design is characterized by formal research procedures. This involves clearly defined research objectives and information needs. Often a detailed questionnaire is drawn up, along with a formal sampling plan. It should be clear how the information to be collected relates to the alternatives under evaluation. Possible research approaches include surveys, experiments, observations, and simulation.

Performance-Monitoring Research

Once a course of action is selected and the marketing program is implemented, performance-monitoring research is needed to answer the question "What is happening?" Performance monitoring is the essential element needed to control marketing programs in accordance with plans. Deviation from the plan can result from improper execution of the marketing program and/or unanticipated changes in the situational factors. Consequently, effective performance monitoring involves monitoring both the marketing mix variables and the situational variables in addition to traditional performance measures such as sales, share of market, profit, and return on investment.

PRELIMINARY STEPS IN THE DECISION-MAKING PROCESS

According to some sources, the analysis that was done leading to the decision to build the aircraft carrier *Enterprise* resulted in reports that weighed more than the ship itself. While this is obviously an exaggeration, it does emphasize the importance of adequate planning and analysis preceding the decision to undertake an important project such as research. The quality of this preparatory activity largely determines the success of the research project.

In marketing research, this preparatory activity should establish an effective link between the early stages of the decision process and the research process. Figure 4-2 illustrates the nature of this link. The relevance of the research findings to the information requirements of management is established at this crucial stage.

This section will cover the issues involved in the first three stages of the decision-making process: (1) recognition of a decision situation, (2) definition of the decision problem, and (3) identification of alternative courses of action. The next section will focus on the remaining steps: (4) evaluating courses of action, (5) selecting a course of

FIGURE 4-2   Link between the decision process and the research process.

action, and (6) implementing and modifying the action. The discussion will emphasize the requirements for each of the stages and the role of research in each stage.

Recognition of a Decision Situation

Figure 4-3 presents the preliminary steps in the decision-making process and illustrates how the marketing system triggers the recognition of a situation calling for a decision. Here, the behavioral response and performance measures signal symptoms, while the marketing mix and situational factors produce the underlying problems and opportunities. The decision maker's task is to respond to symptoms and analyze the underlying problems and opportunities to determine whether a situation is present that calls for a decision. If the answer is affirmative, the decision maker proceeds to the second and third stages of the decision process—developing a clear statement of the decision problem and identifying alternative courses of action.

Problems   The word "problem" carries a connotation of trouble; something is wrong and needs attention. The existence of a problem is detected when objectives are established and a measurement of performance indicates that the objectives are not being

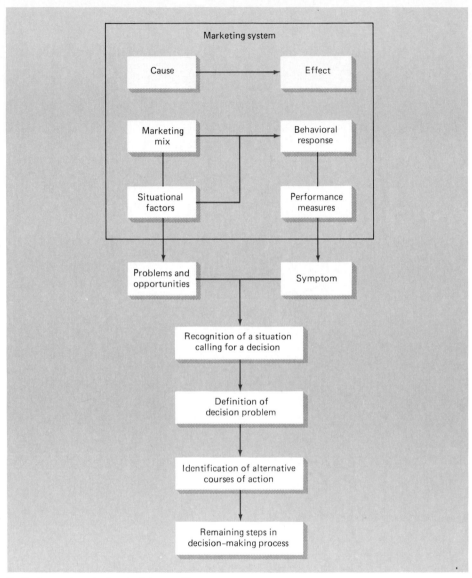

FIGURE 4-3   Preliminary steps in the decision-making process.

met. For example, a product's share of market could be below forecasted share. The effectiveness of a new advertising campaign could be below desired awareness levels. The expenses associated with the introduction of a new product could be over budget. Consequently, a problem results when actual performance does not match expected performance.

By "problem" we refer to those independent variables that cause the organization's performance measures to not meet objectives. Problems can result from an ineffective marketing program (product, price, distribution, and promotion), from changes in the situational factors, or from a combination of both.

Opportunities   Managers make decisions regarding opportunities as well as problems. By "opportunity" we refer to the presence of a situation where performance can be improved by undertaking new activities. An opportunity may result in the establishment of even higher objectives. Opportunities differ from problems in that the manager may not be required to do anything about them. In fact, they may not even be recognized. Most opportunities do not force themselves on managers in the same way that problems do, since most firms have formal methods for detecting the presence of problems via their performance measures but less formal methods for monitoring the opportunities.

The distinction between problems and opportunities is not clear-cut. Problems are usually associated with adversity, but even adversity may be an opportunity in disguise. It has been said that "we are all continually faced with a series of great opportunities brilliantly disguised as insoluble problems."[2]

Symptoms   A symptom is a condition that signals the presence of a problem or opportunity.[3] Performance measures act as this signal for marketing management. It is important to recognize that symptoms are not the same as problems and opportunities. For example, a decline in sales volume from forecasted levels is not a problem; it is the symptom of a problem yet to be identified. A symptom can be viewed as the result of a problem or opportunity.

Symptoms occupy a critical position in the process of recognizing that a situation exists calling for a management decision. Once the existence of a problem or opportunity has been recognized, the main issues and causal factors need to be identified. Effective decision making is dependent upon a clear statement regarding the basic problem or opportunity. This statement is often developed only after a thorough investigation of the marketing program and/or the situational factors. Rarely can the problem or opportunity be adequately identified solely on the knowledge that a symptom is present. Decisions are made to solve problems and/or to take advantage of opportunities, not to treat symptoms.

Symptoms often trigger the analysis process designed to identify and define the problems or opportunities. During this process, one may find that the initial variables identified as causing the symptom are the result of even more fundamental variables. An intensive investigation may uncover a complicated sequence of influences which interact to produce the symptom. Once this analysis is completed, the manager can formulate the decision problem and determine the course of action which, it is hoped, will attack the problem and/or exploit the opportunity.

[2] Quotation by John W. Gardner in Philip Kotler, *Marketing Management,* 3d ed. (Englewood Cliffs, N.J.: Prentice-Hall, 1976), p. 45.

[3] David J. Luck, Hugh G. Wales, and Donald A. Taylor, *Marketing Research,* 4th ed. (Englewood Cliffs, N.J.: Prentice-Hall, 1974), p. 16.

Definition of the Decision Problem

Once the manager recognizes that a situation exists which calls for a decision, the next step is to clearly define the decision problem. A clearly defined decision problem has two components: (1) a thorough understanding of the objectives surrounding the decision situation and (2) a statement of the problems and opportunities present in the decision situation.

The decision maker has two approaches to defining the decision problem. They can be used in combination, or a single approach can be employed. The first approach is to formulate the decision problem based on the analysis of existing information. This approach relies upon the manager's experience and judgment plus skills in analyzing existing data regarding the decision situation. The second approach is to use exploratory research to aid in defining the decision problem. If the latter route is selected, there will be a process of interaction between hypotheses previously formulated based on existing information and hypotheses developed from the exploratory research findings. At some point in this interactive process, the decision maker must clearly define the decision problem and proceed to the remaining steps of the decision-making process.

The remainder of this section will discuss the issues involved in the process of defining the decision problem. First, it is important to understand clearly what is meant by a decision problem. Second, the role and responsibility of the decision maker in guiding the definition of the decision problem are emphasized. Next, the two components of the decision problem are reviewed: (1) objectives and (2) statement of problems and opportunities.

What Is a Decision Problem?   A decision problem exists whenever management has an objective to accomplish and is confronted with a situation involving two or more courses of action to reach the objective. In addition, uncertainty must exist regarding the best course of action. If the manager is certain as to the best course of action, there is no decision problem. If there is only one course of action available, and that is to "do nothing," there is no decision problem.

Decision problems can exist for situations involving both problems and opportunities. Uncertainty can exist regarding the best course of action to solve a problem as well as how to take advantage of an opportunity. Consequently, a decision problem is present in situations regarding problems and opportunities whenever the manager faces a choice among alternative courses of action in which uncertainty exists about the outcome of the decision.

Role of the Decision Maker   The decision maker plays a central role in the definition of the decision problem. After recognizing that a potential decision problem exists, it is his or her responsibility to ensure that the decision objectives are specified and the problems and opportunities are clearly identified.

Decision Objective   The decision-making process typically has two sources for objectives. The primary source for objectives is the organization. For example, an organization may have an objective to increase earnings per share by 10 percent next year. The second source involves the personal objectives of the decision maker(s) and those who influence that individual. For example, a marketing manager may have the personal objective of becoming the vice president of marketing or of acquiring more prestige among his or her peers.

In order to understand the motivation for a decision, we must be sensitive to the role played by both organization and personal objectives. When both sets of objectives coincide, the decision-making process flows more smoothly than when there is conflict between them. The question of how to resolve this conflict in favor of organizational objectives is obviously a complex one, but one approach is to have organizational objectives stated explicitly to others in the organization. In addition, the development of explicit decision criteria for the selection among alternative courses of action often ensures that organizational objectives will predominate in the decision. More will be said on this issue shortly.

In many decision situations the "decision maker" may not be a single individual. Decision making in organizations can involve two or more people who must make decisions as a group. Other situations involve one predominant decision maker who is strongly influenced by other individuals who are part of the decision-making process. In such situations, not only is there potential conflict between organizational and personal objectives, but there is also conflict among the personal objectives of the individuals involved in the decision process.

It is a serious mistake to assume that the decision maker clearly knows what the organizational objectives are and that formulating an explicit statement of these objectives will be viewed with favor. An explicit statement of organizational objectives can force the decision maker to suppress personal objectives. In addition, some individuals may feel that making certain aspects of the decision process explicit can threaten one's status and position as a decision maker.[4]

Statement of Problems and Opportunities   The process of identifying problems and opportunities is called _situational analysis_.[5] Its purpose is to analyze the past and future situations facing an organization to uncover those variables that cause poor performance or represent opportunities for future growth. Specifically, this means that a diagnosis and prognosis must be made of the marketing program and situational variables in the marketing system.

The situational analysis is a creative process in which an attempt is made to isolate and understand the causal variables influencing the marketing system. During this investigation, one must be sensitive to the fact that symptoms are not the same thing as problems and opportunities.

In conducting a situational analysis, diversity of information sources may be needed to develop insight and hypotheses regarding the causal factors. Flexibility in thinking and the use of multiple information sources are often critical to a successful situational analysis.

---

[4] Joseph W. Newman, "Put Research into Marketing Decisions," _Harvard Business Review,_ vol. 40, no. 2, pp. 105–112, March–April 1962.

[5] William B. Loeander and A. Benton Cocanougher (eds.), _Problem Definition in Marketing,_ American Marketing Association, Marketing Research Techniques, ser. 2, Chicago, 1975.

MARKETING RESEARCH IN ACTION. .

RENAULT'S ALLIANCE

The AMC sales picture was bleak in the spring of 1978. In order to survive in the U.S. market, AMC had to do something drastic—hence the birth of the AMC-Renault agreement. AMC was to be the exclusive U.S./Canadian distributor of all Renault-made automobiles. And in 1979, AMC was told that Renault would be producing a new car, code-named X-42, in the United States. It would be 75 percent American made. AMC's job was to decide both the model name and the company name under which the car would be marketed.

To resolve these issues, David G. Garfield, manager of marketing services at AMC, and Joseph G. Smith, president of the New York–based survey research firm Oxtoby-Smith, Inc., designed a marketing research plan. "We were trying to figure out how to sell the car (X-42), and we didn't know what we didn't know," said Garfield. What did "European" mean to U.S. consumers? What connotations did "Renault" and "imported" carry? Exploratory research in the form of six focus group interviews was undertaken, followed by an automobile clinic held in Anaheim, California.

At the clinic, people from the target market were recruited to look at a prototype of the car (exterior only), which was displayed next to competitive automobiles whose nameplates had been removed. Their responses were recorded and used both to suggest minor modifications and to gain insight in how to best market the X-42.

Another clinic, which displayed both the interior and the exterior of the X-42, resulted in two key findings: first, the car itself got very positive scores; and second, when the car was coupled with the either the Renault or AMC name, the results were less positive than when it had no identification.

AMC was also faced with the unenviable task of choosing a model name. Over 1000 possible names had judgmentally been narrowed down to 10, and it was these 10 names AMC commissioned Burke Marketing Research to test. The result: "Alliance."

A third series of clinics was held in July 1981 to measure the attractiveness of the Alliance vs. competitive cars. In the fall of that year, focus group sessions were held to develop ideas on how to best position the Alliance in the American marketplace.

These ideas were tested in face-to-face interviews with 605 respondents in eight cities. The Alliance was presented as a solely AMC, a solely Renault, and a joint AMC/Renault product.

The results of the study were threefold: (1) interest in the Alliance overcame consumers' negative attitudes toward Renault and AMC; (2) the Renault name alone generated a strong purchase interest; and (3) the target consumers emphasized durability and technology as the most important attributes when considering a new car purchase.

The final decision, suggested and supported by marketing research, was to market the X-42 under the name Renault Alliance, and to position it as a technically sound automobile. These decisions led to one of the most effective new-car introductions that the auto industry has ever seen.

Source: Jack J. Honomichl, *Marketing/Research People: Their Behind-the-Scenes Stories* (Chicago: Crain Books, 1984), pp. 39–56.

Alternative Courses of Action

Given a clear statement of the decision problem, the next stage of the decision process is to identify alternative courses of action. (Remember that a decision problem exists only when there are two or more actions to be taken and uncertainty as to which is the best one to take.)

A *course of action* specifies how the organization's resources are to be deployed in a given time period. Maintaining the status quo or "doing nothing new" is a course of action just as much as one that designates a change in the status quo.

The development of alternative courses of action is a crucial stage in the formulation of the decision problem. The management decision can be no better than the best alternative under evaluation. Identifying mediocre courses of action is often an easy task. Implementation of a mediocre action may partially solve a problem or take advantage of an opportunity to some degree. The real management challenge is to identify the best course of action which will result in high performance and give the organization a competitive edge.

Creativity is needed to identify innovative and highly effective courses of action. Various approaches are available that can stimulate the manager's creative process and broaden the domain of alternatives identified.[6] Exploratory research can be especially helpful in identifying innovative courses of action.

Remaining Steps in the Decision Process

Once the alternative courses of action are identified, the next step is one of evaluation. At this point, the manager is faced with the question "What information is needed to properly choose among the courses of action?" This may be answered with the help of information inputs from the manager's experience and judgment plus information currently available through the marketing research system. Alternatively, the manager may decide that new information is needed and request that a formal marketing research study be conducted. The decision to use research implies that the desired information can be obtained and that the cost and time delay associated with collecting it are more than offset by its potential value. The value or benefit of research is typically commensurate with the ability of research information to reduce the management uncertainty regarding the selection of a course of action. Once this information is obtained and presented in a meaningful format, the manager can proceed to the final stage of the decision-making process, namely, the selection of a course of action and the development of a plan for implementation.

A research study designed to evaluate alternative courses of action is called conclusive research. Let us turn now to a discussion of how to get this formal research project under way.

---

[6] See Sidney J. Parnes and Harold F. Harding (eds.), *Source Book for Creative Thinking* (New York: Scribner, 1962), and Alex F. Osborn, *Applied Imagination,* 3d ed. (New York: Scribner, 1963).

PRELIMINARY CONSIDERATIONS FOR CONDUCTING CONCLUSIVE RESEARCH

Conclusive research provides information which helps the decision maker evaluate and select a course of action. This formal research project contains a series of steps called the research process. The nine steps in this process were outlined in Chapter 1 and in Figure 1-4. Our discussion here will focus on the initial three stages of the research process: (1) establishing the need for information, (2) determining research objectives, and (3) specifying information needs. During our discussion of these initial research stages, the role of the researcher in establishing an effective link with the early stages of the decision-making process will be emphasized.

Establish the Need for Information

Establishing the need for marketing research information is a critical step in the research process. The wisdom of this initial step largely determines the success or failure of the research project.

Role of the Researcher   Rarely does the manager's initial request for help adequately establish the need for research information. Consequently, the researcher has an important role to play in making sure that information is in fact needed and that the research study will provide useful information for decision making. The following questions should be thoroughly addressed by the researcher at this initial stage:

1 Who is the decision maker?
2 What are his or her objectives?
3 Has a clear and concise statement of problems and/or opportunities been developed?
4 What courses of action are to be evaluated?

Decision Maker   The researcher must distinguish between the decision maker and those who represent the decision maker. Often the person who first requests assistance from the marketing research system is not the decision maker. This individual may or may not know how the decision maker views the specifics of the decision situation. Valuable time and effort can be saved if the researcher insists on meeting directly with the individual who has major responsibility for making the decision.

A meeting with the decision maker may be difficult in practice. Many organizations have complicated formal and informal command structures; also, the organizational status of the researcher or the research department may make it difficult to reach the ultimate decision maker in the early stages of the research process. Finally, in many decision situations a number of individuals may influence the decision or act together as the decision maker. Meeting with them as a group or individually may be difficult, and the coordination of a clear statement regarding the decision situation may be even more so. Despite these potential problems, it is essential that the researcher understand the problem situation from the perspective of the decision maker.

Objectives of the Decision Maker   Decisions are made to accomplish objectives. The success of a research study is dependent on a clear understanding of the decision objectives. A major task of the marketing researcher is to skillfully identify the organizational objectives and be sensitive to the personal objectives lurking in the background of the decision process. A successful researcher may be one who can design research to serve the needs of the organization effectively while at the same time enhancing the personal objectives of the decision maker.

The identification of objectives can be a difficult assignment in practice.

> Despite a popular misconception to the contrary, objectives are seldom given to the researcher. The decision maker seldom formulates his objectives accurately. He is likely to state his objectives in the form of platitudes which have no operational significance. Consequently, objectives usually have to be extracted by the researcher. In so doing, the researcher may well be performing his most useful service to the decision maker.
>
> Direct questioning of the decision maker seldom reveals all the relevant objectives. One effective technique for uncovering these objectives consists of confronting the decision maker with each of the possible solutions to a problem and asking him whether he would follow that course of action. Where he says "no," further probing will usually reveal objectives which are not served by the course of action.[7]

Effective Statement of Problems and Opportunities   There is probably no activity more critical to the success of the formal research process than a clear and concise statement of problems and/or opportunities. Far too often this task is the most neglected phase in initiating the research project. Improper definition of the problem or opportunity can easily lead astray all subsequent efforts to provide useful information for decision making.

The researcher must be sensitive to managers who are reacting to symptoms or vague feelings regarding a possible problem and/or opportunity. The researcher's task is to ask probing questions of the manager to determine the existing degree of knowledge regarding the underlying causes of the decision situation. As discussed previously, exploratory research may be needed to facilitate the development of the statement of problems and opportunities.

Courses of Action   The researcher must be satisfied that the relevant courses of action have been identified and approved by management. Nothing can destroy an otherwise successful research study more than to find that a key alternative was not evaluated.

Given a clear understanding of the courses of action relevant to the decision situation, the researcher can turn to the task of establishing the research objectives and identifying the scientific information needs for evaluating the courses of action.

Research Objectives

Research objectives answer the question "What is the purpose of the research project?" For example, the research study discussed in Chapter 3 had the following objectives:

1 To determine which container markets have the greatest consumer acceptance of plastic containers

2 To determine the characteristics of plastic containers which represent advantages compared with paper, paperboard, glass, and metal containers

[7] Russell L. Ackoff, *Scientific Method* (New York: Wiley, 1962), p. 71.

The research objectives should be put in writing and communicated to the decision maker; they explain why the project is being conducted, and it is important that the researcher and decision maker be in agreement.

Research objectives can be stated so broadly that they fail to communicate the specifics of why the study is being conducted. For example, the following lacks the precise detail of the research objective given previously: *To study consumer reactions to containers.*

A broad statement like this does not indicate what type of container is to be studied, what is to be measured, and how the information might be used. While the degree of detail in the research objectives is dependent upon the nature of the decision situation, generally the more specific the statement of objectives, the lower the risk that management will misperceive the purpose of the study.

In some respects, the more detailed the statement of research objectives, the more it coincides with the listing of information needs. Figure 4-4 highlights the pyramiding aspect of research objectives, information needs, and questions on the data collection forms.

Specify Information Needs

After the research objectives have been specified, the next question concerns "What specific information is needed by the decision maker?" A listing of specific information needs is designed to answer this question.

Research objectives which are specified in great detail often coincide with a more general listing of information needs. In the same manner, a more detailed listing of information needs coincides with the specific questions developed for the questionnaire. Consequently, research objectives serve to guide the research project by giving direction to the specific information to be gathered and the specific questions to be developed for the questionnaire.

From the other perspective, we can say that each question on the questionnaire should have a direct correspondence to an information need, and each information need should have a direct correspondence to a research objective. If such a correspondence is not established, unneeded data will be collected.

The decision maker should be actively involved in formulating the research objectives and in specifying the information needs, because only the decision maker has a clear

FIGURE 4-4 Pyramid of research objectives and information needs.

perspective as to the character and specificity of the information needed to reduce the uncertainty surrounding the decision situation. Failure to involve the decision maker in this regard can severely hamper the success of the research project.

(An example of specifying research objectives and listing information needs was presented in Chapter 3; a review of this chapter should provide a concrete illustration of the points discussed here.)

In developing the list of information needs, both the manager and researcher should ask, for each item, "Can this information be obtained?" The skills and judgment of the researcher come to the fore at this point.

The data collection process imposes many limitations on the type of information that can be collected. In surveys, buyers or distributors may refuse to disclose certain types of information, or they may not have the knowledge to answer the questions accurately. Consequently, many excellent information needs may be developed, but if it is not possible to collect the information, time and effort will be wasted in the research process. The manager and researcher need to work closely in this regard to assure a correspondence between the information required and the ability of the marketing research system to gather it.

Visualize the Research Findings

Assuming that the information can be gathered, it is important that the potential research findings be visualized and the question asked, "Of what use are these data to the decision situation?" Many managers and researchers find that mocking up the potential research findings is a valuable way to ensure that the data to be collected fit the information needs specified by the decision maker. Often, the decision maker can identify gaps in the original list of needs which can be easily corrected at this preliminary stage of the research project.

The concept of mocking up the potential research findings means that each stage of the research process must be anticipated. For example, in survey research specific questions must first be developed for the questionnaire. Next, the data processing and analysis must be established; then the resulting data can be visualized. At this point, the decision maker would be presented with a mock-up of the data in the form of various tables or graphs containing potential research findings. In essence, the research presentation or report is simulated prior to conducting the project.

The actual data presented may represent a range of optimistic, most likely, and pessimistic results. From this mock-up of findings, the manager and researcher may be able to determine whether the data intended to be collected will serve to reduce the uncertainty surrounding the decision situation. If not, the wisdom of collecting the data should be challenged.

Often, the manager can more clearly specify how the data should be analyzed and presented after seeing a mock-up of the potential findings. Additional cross tabulations may be requested, and several multivariate analysis approaches may be required. Often, certain data analysis approaches require that the questionnaire be developed in a certain format, that specific questions be asked, or that the data be tabulated in a certain manner. If these issues are not addressed prior to executing the project, it may be that added costs and delays are incurred at later stages or that the data cannot be obtained. Consequently, the directions received from the manager before beginning the project can be invaluable to its success.

Develop Decision Criteria

Once the research findings have been visualized and the decision maker and researcher are confident that the information needs are complete and the data analysis appropriate, the issue of *decision criteria* should be addressed. Decision criteria are concerned with the rules for selecting among courses of action given various data outcomes.

Developing decision criteria often means setting up a series of "if then" statements. For example:

1 If the research finds a 5 percent potential market share or larger for our new product, then we will proceed to test-market.

2 If the research finds a 3 to 5 percent potential market share, then we will reformulate the new product.

3 If the research finds less than a 3 percent potential market share, then we will abandon the project.[8]

It is important that decision criteria be developed before the decision maker and researcher experience the actual results. Having clear decision rules prior to the research results ensures that organizational objectives take priority over personal objectives and that they assist the data analysis and reporting stages. In addition, decision rules maintain a balance between the weight assigned to information existing prior to the research and the research findings. The absence of decision criteria can result in an inappropriate weight assigned to the research findings depending upon the research outcome and the reaction of management to experiencing the outcome for the first time.

Cost and Value of Research

The evaluation of most activities in an organization is approached on a cost-benefit basis. While it is fairly easy to quantify the costs directly associated with a research project, it is very difficult to quantify the benefits. Benefits are often subjective in nature. Consequently, the evaluation of research is inherently subjective.

Given the cost of research, it is possible to determine the number of units of a product that need to be sold to break even on the cost of the research project. Table 4-1 illustrates this type of thinking for two market sizes and two contribution levels. For example, if the research project costs $10,000 and the contribution margin is $0.10 per unit (selling price = $1; variable cost = $0.90), the break-even point is 100,000 units. However, if the contribution margin is $0.90 per unit (selling price = $1; variable cost $0.10), the break-even point is reduced to 11,111 units. Given a large market size (e.g.,

---

[8] Eric Marder, "Use One Measure, Do Analysis Before Looking at Data," *Marketing News,* vol. 7, no. 12, p. 1, December 1973.

TABLE 4-1 RESEARCH VALUE AS FUNCTION OF CONTRIBUTION MARGIN AND MARKET SIZE

Market size	Contribution margin	
	Small	**Large**
Small	Unlikely research can be supported e.g., hobby glue (Elmers), nail clippers (Trim), screwdriver (Stanley)	Can support some small research e.g., specialty tape (3M), specialty drugs (Upjohn), executive aircraft (Lear)
Large	Can support large amount of research e.g., razor blades (Gillette), soap powder (Tide), soft drinks (Coca-Cola)	Easy to support large amount of research e.g., automobiles (Ford), appliances (Hotpoint), long-distance calls (Bell System)

1 million units), the break-even points represent a small share of market (i.e., 1 percent and .1 percent). Assuming a smaller market size (e.g., 10,000 units), the break-even points are substantially higher (i.e., 100 percent and 10 percent).

Extending this thinking to real products, the contribution margin of $100 per automobile in a market of 500,000 units is a total contribution of $50 million. This level of contribution can easily support a research project of $10,000. However, the contribution margin of $0.20 per screwdriver in a market of 100,000 units is $20,000. Spending half of this contribution on a $10,000 research project is obviously difficult to justify.

In general, these calculations suggest that it is easier to justify the cost of research as the market size increases and as the ratio of variable cost to selling price decreases. Therefore, the benefits resulting from a $10,000 research project designed to evaluate alternative advertising campaigns to stimulate demand for long-distance phone calls may be easier to justify than a similar study dealing with a new hobby kit glue. While this type of calculation does not determine the actual benefit derived from such a study, it does indicate the level of benefit needed to cover the cost of research.

There is an additional concept that relates directly to the manager's evaluation of the benefits of marketing research. This concept is the degree of certainty that the manager holds about particular outcomes of the organization's courses of action. For example, a manager might say, "I am 95 percent sure that this advertising theme will be a success." This manager should be much less likely to undertake research on the new advertising theme than a manager who says, "I am about 50 percent sure that this advertising theme will be a success." The purpose of marketing research is to reduce the uncertainty about the outcomes of alternative courses of action. Thus, the value of research to a manager increases as the degree of certainty decreases. Again, it is a subjective evaluation by the manager.

In summary, the value of research to a manager increases as (1) the market size increases, (2) the ratio of variable cost to selling price decreases, and (3) the degree of certainty held about outcomes of actions decreases. All three of these factors will be discussed in detail in the appendix at the end of this chapter, and a dollar value for specific marketing research proposals will be calculated.

Controlling the Use of Research

The success of the research project depends heavily upon the ability of the managers and researchers to work effectively together. For most managers, decision making is a highly personalized process which is influenced by the individual's management style and the specifics of the decision situation. The researcher must be sensitive to this situation in developing an effective working relationship with the decision maker. The success of the research project rests upon the quality of this marriage. There are several ways to ensure that research is being used effectively in the decision-making process.

Organizational Design The various organizational designs discussed in Chapter 2 can serve to control the effectiveness of contacts between decision makers and researchers. One design is to assign management responsibility for the initial and final stages of the research process; here the responsibility for the effectiveness of the research rests predominantly in the management camp. The researcher's responsibility is that of adviser regarding the initial and final stages, with primary responsibility for the middle stages of data collection and processing. Typically, the researcher has the right to refuse to conduct a study which he or she views as inappropriate.

An alternative organizational design involves keeping the responsibility for the research process within the research camp while giving the researcher a more powerful organizational role in dealing with management. For example, the researcher may be required to participate in the majority of management meetings regardless of whether the use of research is an issue. Here, the researcher is viewed as part of the management team and is assigned responsibility for identifying decision situations where research is appropriate.

A compromise between these two organizational designs involves the creation of the position of research generalist, someone who serves as an intermediary between the research and management camps. The generalist's main responsibility is to promote effective contacts between decision makers and researchers. The research generalist concept was discussed in Chapter 2.

Research Request Forms Most organizations require that the decision to undertake research be in writing and approved by upper management and the director of marketing research. This formal request typically involves a standard form which is completed by the decision maker and/or the marketing researcher. Exhibit 4-2 illustrates the type of information requested on such a form.

The purpose of the research request form is to ensure that all of the areas identified on the form have been covered by the decision makers and researchers. There is a degree of commitment associated with things in writing that rarely exists with informal agreements.

Additional forms may be used in some companies for the remaining steps in the research process—for example, project budget estimate forms, project control forms, and project evaluation forms.[9]

[9] For an expanded discussion of this area, see Lawrence D. Gibson, "Use of Marketing Research Contractors," in Robert Ferber (ed.), *Handbook of Marketing Research* (New York: McGraw-Hill, 1975), pp. 1-128 to 1-141.

EXHIBIT 4-2

RESEARCH REQUEST FORM

Title: _____ Date prepared: _____
Requested by: _____ Start of project: _____
Approved by: _____ Report due: _____
Date approved: _____ Budget: _____
Project number: _____ Supplier: _____

1 *Background:* What led to the recognition that research was needed?
2 *Objectives:* What are the decision objectives?
3 *Problem/opportunity:* What are the underlying causes of the decision situation?
4 *Decision alternatives:* What are the alternative courses of action?
5 *Research objectives:* What is the purpose of the research?
6 *Information needs:* What type of information is needed?
7 *Example of questions:* What kind of questions should be asked?
8 *Decision criteria:* What criteria should be used to select the best alternative?
9 *Value of research:* Why is the research useful?

Proposal for Research

For projects conducted predominantly within the organization, the research request form usually serves as the research proposal. In practice, most research projects have some phase of the study conducted by outside contractors. Typically, this involves the field interviewing phase. A growing number of organizations are expanding their reliance on outside contractors and using them to conduct more phases of the research process. In some situations, an organization may rely entirely on an outside contractor to conduct the research study. Here, several outside contractors could be asked to submit a proposal for research.

THE MANAGEMENT-RESEARCH RELATIONSHIP

The effectiveness of the research system is dependent upon its relationship with marketing management. Many factors influence the success of this interpersonal contact, such as differences between some managers and researchers in job responsibilities, career objectives, and educational backgrounds.

The research system requires the skills and knowledge of specialized people. A research department may have individuals specializing in various steps of the research process—for example, questionnaire design, field supervision, data processing, data analysis, and report preparation. Specialization involving the marketing mix decision areas is common; individuals or groups may specialize in advertising research, distribution research, product development research, and so on. People trained in statistics, mathematics, psychology, computer science, and economics often qualify for many of these specialized positions. Frequently, these individuals have limited training and perspective regarding the role of applied research in the management decision-making process.

The research specialist who is not management oriented will often accept the request for research help without clearly establishing the need for research. This person may fail to ask perceptive questions regarding the decision situation and be uncritical of whether research will facilitate the decision-making process. In addition, many specialists are more concerned with the technical sophistication of the research design and methodology than the information needs of management. This focus leads many researchers to look for decision situations where they can apply the latest research techniques. Many managers view researchers as more concerned with finding an application for their techniques than with supplying information for decision making. This emphasis on technique results in technical jargon and standardized ways of presenting research findings, which tends to inhibit the management research communication process, especially in the reporting of research results.

In reporting research findings, some researchers fail to recognize that their role is advisory; they are not being asked to make the decision for management. The researcher can play a very active and supportive role in the decision-making process, but the responsibility for making the decision rests with management. The researcher may become frustrated by the constraints of this advisory role and develop the feeling that "I can make better decisions than management."[10]

Why shouldn't the researcher participate in making the decision? First, the objectivity of the research process could be influenced. The researcher's personal biases and vested interests associated with various decision outcomes could decrease the objectivity of the research design and the analysis of the findings. Second, the researcher would weigh the research findings heavily in selecting a course of action. In contrast, the manager can evaluate and weigh the significance of the research findings in the context of experience and knowledge plus the broader policy considerations associated with the decision.

While many researchers are not sufficiently management oriented, many managers are not sufficiently research oriented. Far too many managers have no training in marketing research and a limited perspective as to the nature and role of research in the decision-making process. This inhibits their active involvement in the stages of the research project. This lack of participation can diminish the usefulness of the research findings. If the manager does not view research as a natural aspect of the decision-making process, the researcher is forced to solicit research studies from the manager. This results in myopic and fragmented studies which rarely make a significant contribution to the decision-making process. The effectiveness of marketing research is dependent on the skills and perspective of the manager in using the research function in decision making.

Some managers operate as if the researcher is clairvoyant regarding the nature of the decision situation, the courses of action that appear reasonable, the objective to be accomplished, and the information needed to reduce the decision uncertainty. Few managers explain these areas lucidly to the researcher. In some cases the manager may be unwilling or unable to communicate this type of information. Consequently, many

---

[10] Murray Cayley, "The Role of Research in Marketing," *The Business Quarterly,* p. 33, Autumn 1968.

research projects are not decision oriented because of the manager's poor communication skills.

The manager may view research as a way to satisfy needs other than those related to decision making. This has been called "pseudo-research."[11]

1 The manager can use marketing research as a way to gain visibility and power in the organization.

2 Marketing research can be used to justify decisions already made. If the research results contradict the decision, the manager can declare the research invalid or simply ignore it altogether.

3 Marketing research can be conducted to establish a scapegoat for marketing decisions that do not accomplish objectives. If the decision is successful, the manager can take full credit; if it is not successful, marketing research is to blame.

4 Marketing research can be used as a promotion tool for service organizations like advertising agencies and media to attract new business and impress current clients.

5 Marketing research can serve to soothe an anxious manager with the knowledge that "something is being done."

6 Managers may support marketing research studies and new research methodology because they believe it is the "faddish thing to do" or the current trend in management practice.

Several barriers to the effective management utilization of marketing research have been identified.[12]

1 Some managers view research as a threat to their personal status as decision makers. They fear that marketing research information may conflict with or invalidate the "knowledge" gained from experience and judgment. These managers may believe that this "knowledge" is what justifies their status and position.

2 The absence of systematic planning procedures in many organizations contributes to the lack of common organizational objectives for managers. In the absence of clear organizational objectives, the managers will substitute their own objectives, which can result in conflict among managers. Research may be seen as a way to support one's view in this internal struggle for power. Managers who believe that marketing research will enhance their position will favor it, while others will oppose it.

3 Some managers are unable to effectively work with, understand, and use the knowledge and skills of research specialists. The interdisciplinary training of specialists makes communication difficult.

4 The isolation of marketing research personnel from the managers can be a problem. The effective use of marketing research assumes that research personnel will have a close and continuous relationship with the managers. Often marketing research departments are handicapped in this regard by low organizational status. The weakness of this organizational arrangement is that it depends on the initiative of the manager

---

[11] Stewart A. Smith, "Research and Pseudo-Research in Marketing," *Harvard Business Review,* pp. 73–76, March–April 1974.
[12] Joseph W. Newman, "Put Research into Marketing Decisions," *Harvard Business Review,* vol. 40, no. 2, pp. 105–112, March–April 1962.

for effective use of marketing research. Too often managers are unfamiliar with the nature and role of research and are unable to identify problems well enough to ask for the help they need. Those research departments that operate on management request tend to be occupied with routine, short-range operating problems.

Recent studies by the Marketing Science Institute have made several observations regarding the effectiveness of the manager-researcher interaction.[13]

1 Researchers love a surprise. Managers do not like surprises; when they are surprised, they tend to reject the research.

2 Researchers like to explore. Managers prefer to confirm. Researchers should be sensitive to managerial "comfort zones."

3 Technical quality does not speak for itself. Working together influences perceptions of technical quality and creates trust in the research results.

4 Political acceptability of research results is perceived by researchers as a major consideration for use. An effective working relationship between researcher and manager can enhance political acceptability.

5 Manager-researcher interaction, of all variables studied, has the highest total influence on research use. Open and frequent communications with managers are vital to marketing research effectiveness.

6 Good horizontal relationships (teaming of researchers with product managers) are more important than vertical relationships (e.g., reporting to the senior marketing executive).

7 Involvement in the strategic planning process separates more effective from less effective marketing research departments. But most research is tactical, and researchers feel excluded from strategy formulation.

8 Managers expect research to come up with innovative solutions or courses of action. Research is not perceived as doing so. More involvement in strategy formulations might help.

9 Smooth planning and delivery of marketing research services have a strong influence on management satisfaction. On the other hand, researchers perceive managers as making sudden changes in data needs, priorities, or deadlines.

The previous discussion has emphasized many of the factors that can influence the effectiveness of the management-research relationship. The most basic causes of conflict have been identified as research responsibility, research personnel, budget, assignments, problem definition, research reporting, and the use of research. Table 4-2 presents the typical positions of top management and marketing research staff on these areas of conflict.[14]

What can be done to minimize this organizational conflict? The research system re-

[13] Speech by Alden G. Clayton, managing director, Marketing Science Institute, before the American Marketing Association Conference, New Orleans, 1980. Based upon Marketing Science Institute Working Papers by Gerald Zaltman and Rohit Deshpande, "The Use of Marketing Research: An Exploratory Study of Managers and Researchers Perspectives," Report No. 80–115, December 1980, and by David J. Luck and James R. Krum, "Conditions Conducive to the Effective Use of Marketing Research in the Corporation," Report No. 81–100, May 1981.

[14] John G. Keane, "Some Observations on Marketing Research in Top Managemeent Decision Making," *Journal of Marketing*, vol. 33, pp. 10–15, October 1969.

TABLE 4-2   PROBABLE AREAS OF TOP MANAGEMENT-MARKETING RESEARCH CONFLICT

Top management position	Area	Marketing research position
MR lacks sense of accountability. ¯ Sole MR function is as an information provider.	Research responsibility	Responsibility should be explicitly defined and consistently followed. Desire decision-making involvement with TM.
Generally poor communicators. Lack enthusiasm, salesmanship, and imagination.	Research personnel	TM is anti-intellectual. Researchers should be hired, judged, and compensated on research capabilities.
Research costs too much. Since MR contribution difficult to measure, budget cuts are relatively defensible.	Budget	"You get what you pay for" defense. Needs to be continuing, long-range TM commitment.
Tend to be over-engineered. Not executed with proper sense of urgency. Exhibit ritualized, staid approach.	Assignments	Too many nonresearchable requests. Too many "fire-fighting" requests. Insufficient time and money allocated.
MR best equipped to do this. General direction sufficient. . . . MR must appreciate and respond. Can't help changing circumstances.	Problem definition	TM generally unsympathetic to this widespread problem. Not given all the relevant facts. Changed after research is under way.
Characterized as dull, with too much "researchese" and too many qualifiers. Not decision-oriented. Too often reported after the fact.	Research reporting	TM treats superficially. Good research demands thorough reporting and documentation. Insufficient lead time given.
Free to use as it pleases. . . . MR shouldn't question. Changes in need and timing of research are sometimes unavoidable. MR deceived by not knowing all the facts.	Use of research	TM uses to support a predetermined position represents misuse. Isn't used after requested and conducted . . . wasteful. Uses to confirm or excuse past actions.

quires the skills and knowledge of specialists. It also must be sensitive to the needs of management and communicate in management language. Those specialists who find it difficult to communicate with management must be restricted to an analytic role within the research system. The specialist's work can be guided by the use of people who have been referred to as "research generalists."[15] (See Chapter 2.)

SUMMARY

1 The analysis underlying the decision to undertake research largely determines the success of the research project. Failure to establish an effective link between the decision process and the research process can result in inadequate research findings and management dissatisfaction with the marketing research system.

2 Marketing research can be classified according to the way it interacts with the decision-making process. Exploratory research is designed to facilitate recognition of a decision situation and aid in identifying alternative courses of action. Conclusive

[15] Newman, "Put Research into Marketing Decisions," p. 111.

research is concerned with providing information to evaluate and select a course of action. Performance-monitoring research serves to control the marketing program in accordance with objectives by providing feedback regarding performance. Effective management is dependent upon an effective control system which can signal the existence of problems and/or opportunities.

3 The decision process begins with the recognition that a unique marketing problem exists or that an opportunity is present. Problems are detected when objectives are established and a measure of performance indicates that the objectives are not being met. Opportunities are present in situations where performance can be improved by undertaking new activities. A symptom is a condition that signals the presence of a problem or opportunity. It often triggers the analysis process designed to identify and define problems and opportunities.

4 A decision problem is present in situations where the manager faces a choice among alternative courses of action in which uncertainty exists regarding the outcome of the decision. Implicit in any decision problem is a clear statement of objectives plus the identification of problems and/or opportunities.

5 A situational analysis is the process which leads to the identification of problems and opportunities. This involves a diagnosis and prognosis of the marketing program and situational variables in the marketing system.

6 Once the decision problem has been formulated, the next step is to identify alternative courses of action. A course of action is the specification of how the organization's resources are to be developed in a given period. Creativity is needed to identify innovative and highly effective courses of action. Exploratory research can be very useful in this regard.

7 Once the alternatives have been established, the manager may turn to the use of conclusive research. Conclusive research provides information for the evaluation of courses of action.

8 The first step in the conclusive research process is to establish the need for information. The researcher plays a vital role in this process. The decision maker must be clearly identified and the objectives of the decision situation established. A clear statement of problems and/or opportunities must be developed and the alternative courses of action identified. Based on this information, the researcher can formulate the research objectives.

9 Research objectives establish the purpose of the study. They should be in writing and clearly communicated to the decision maker.

10 The specific types of information needed by the decision maker should be identified in writing. The researcher must determine whether it is indeed possible to obtain the type of information requested.

11 The potential research findings should be visualized prior to conducting the study. Preparing a mock-up of the results is a valuable way to ensure that the data to be collected meet the information needs of the decision situation.

12 Decision criteria for selecting among courses of action given various data outcomes should be established prior to conducting the study.

13 The cost of obtaining the information should be weighed against the benefits which result from a reduction in the decision uncertainty. This type of evaluation is inherently subjective.

14 Various organizational designs can facilitate the establishment of an effective link between the decision process and the research process. Requiring research request forms to be completed prior to undertaking research also strengthens the effectiveness of this link.

15 For research projects conducted within an organization, the research request form serves as the proposal for research. When outside contractors bid on the research project, more elaborate research proposals are required. It is important that clear decision criteria be established for the evaluation of the proposals submitted.

16 Many factors influence the effectiveness of the management-research relationship. An effective research system is one which is respected by management and focuses on the needs of management. Many sources of conflict can be reduced by proper training of both research and management regarding the role of research in the decision-making process. The creation of the position "research generalist" has substantially increased the effectiveness of the management-research relationship.

DISCUSSION QUESTIONS

1 Why is the analysis preceding the decision to undertake research so crucial to the success of the project?

2 Discuss the types of marketing research appropriate for various stages of the decision-making process.

3 Distinguish among problems, opportunities, and symptoms.

4 What are the essential elements of a decision problem?

5 What are the implications for the marketing researcher of a decision situation characterized by primary (organizational) and secondary (personal) objectives?

6 What is the purpose and nature of a situational analysis?

7 What is the basic criterion in deciding whether or not to conduct a research project?

8 What are the responsibilities of the researcher in establishing the need for marketing research information?

9 What characteristics should research objectives possess?

10 Should the decision maker be involved in formulating research objectives and listing information needs? Why or why not?

11 Of what use is a mock-up of potential research findings?

12 What are decision criteria? When should they be developed?

13 Why is the evaluation (a priori) of marketing research inherently subjective?

14 How might an organization ensure that marketing research is being used effectively in the decision-making process?

15 What are some of the factors which impinge upon the management-research relationship?

APPENDIX: A Decision Theory Approach to Marketing Research

In Chapter 4 it was noted that the value of research information is related to the degree of uncertainty held by the manager and the likely benefits of marketing activity (contribution per unit, market size, and market share). The more uncertainty, or the larger the market size or contribution margin, the more value would accrue to research information. In Chapter 4 we made no attempt to measure uncertainty or benefit. An approach to marketing research which allows the researcher to do this is called the *decision theory* or *bayesian approach*, and it constitutes the topic of this appendix.[1]

THE DECISION THEORY APPROACH

To use the decision theory or bayesian approach, the decision maker must undertake the following steps:

1 Identify the objectives toward which the decision making should be directed.

2 Identify the alternative courses of action that should be considered.

3 Identify the possible events (environmental conditions) that would influence the payoff of each course of action.

4 Assign a numerical value to the payoff of each course of action, given each possible event.

5 Assign a subjective probability to the occurrence of each possible event.

6 Using the probabilities, compute the weighted average (expected value) of the payoffs assigned to each course of action.

7 Assess the exposure to both gain and loss associated with each course of action.

8 Choose among the alternative courses of action on the basis of the combination of (a) expected monetary value and (b) exposure to gain and loss that is most consistent with the decision maker's objectives and attitude toward risk;[2] i.e., convert the payouts to utility values.

The decision theory approach is then based on the belief that a decision maker can assign meaningful subjective probabilities to events or outcomes. Instead of saying, for example, "There is a good chance of S_1 occurring," the decision maker must be prepared to say, "There is a .70 probability of S_1 occurring." This probability is not based on relative frequencies, as in classical statistics, but on the belief of the manager.

The two decision criteria generally used in a decision theory analysis are (1) the expected monetary value criterion and (2) the expected utility criterion.

Expected Monetary Value Criterion (EMV)

According to the EMV criterion, one simply selects the alternative with the highest EMV. Table A4-1 presents the payoffs associated with the various combinations of two courses of action, A_1 and A_2, with three outcomes, S_1, S_2, and S_3. Note that the decision maker has assigned different probabilities, $P(S_i)$ to various outcomes depending on the alternative and that the sum of the probabilities for outcomes of any action equals 1.0. This latter point is true because the identified outcomes must be mutually exclusive and collectively exhaustive of all possible outcomes.

The EMV of an alternative is calculated by multiplying the probability of an outcome by the value of that outcome and adding this to the probability-multiplied values associated with other outcomes. In symbols,

$$\text{EMV}(A_j) = \sum_{i=1}^{k} S_i P(S_i)$$

---

[1] This appendix follows an excellent discussion of this material in Joseph W. Newman, *Management Applications of Decision Theory* (New York: Harper & Row, 1971), pp. 3–27.

[2] Adapted from Newman, op. cit., pp. 6–7.

TABLE A4-1   PAYOUT MATRIX AND SUBJECTIVE PROBABILITIES

Courses of action	Outcomes and probabilities					
	S_1	$P(S_1)$	S_2	$P(S_2)$	S_3	$P(S_3)$
A_1	115	.2	64	.5	15	.3
A_2	101	.4	80	.4	3	.2

$$\text{EMV}(A_1) = 115(.2) + 64(.5) + 15(.3) = 59.5$$
$$\text{EMV}(A_2) = 101(.4) + 80(.4) + 3(.2) = 73.0$$

where A_j is the jth alternative and k is the number of possible outcomes of an alternative. Here

$$\text{EMV}(A_1) = \sum_{i=1}^{3} S_i P(S_i)$$
$$= 115(.2) + 64(.5) + 15(.3) = 59.5$$

For A_2 the EMV is 73.0. Since the EMV (A_2) is greater than the EMV (A_1), the decision maker would select A_2.

Expected Utility Value Criterion (EUV)

The EMV criterion assumes that the decision maker's utility function with respect to money is linear, but this may not be the case. For example, the utility to a small company of a $100,000 loss may be much greater than the same loss to a giant corporation. Here the differences in exposure to gain or loss are large enough to be relevant to the decision and should be incorporated into the analysis. This can be done by converting the monetary payouts to utility values,[3] a procedure which allows one explicitly to incorporate one's attitude toward risk into the analysis. One then selects the alternative with the highest EUV.

We will not make use of the EUV criterion in this appendix. All decision theory illustrations in this appendix will use the EMV criterion. We have now laid the necessary foundation to present the first type of decision theory analysis, namely, *prior analysis,* which is performed before additional information is collected.

PRIOR ANALYSIS

Prior analysis involves the application of the decision theory approach where the probabilities of outcomes are assessed on the basis of the manager's present judgments, without the benefit of additional information. Consider the situation faced by a marketing manager for a soft drink company who is considering whether to undertake a special promotion.[4] Table A4-2 represents the manager's structuring of the problem. On this table we note that (1) alternative A_1 is "run a special promotion" and alternative A_2 is "have no special promotion"; (2) the possible consumer reactions are considered to be "very favorable," "favorable," and "unfavorable"; (3) the

---

[3] For a discussion of how to do this, see Robert Schlaifer, *Analysis of Decisions under Uncertainty* (New York: McGraw-Hill, 1969), pp. 140–170.

[4] Adapted from Newman, op. cit., pp. 10–13.

TABLE A4-2   EXPECTED PAYOFFS: SOFT-DRINK SPECIAL PROMOTION

Possible consumer reactions	Alternative courses of action		Probabilities of consumer reactions
	A_1	A_2	
Very favorable	$300,000	$0	.4
Favorable	100,000	0	.3
Unfavorable	−200,000	0	.3
Expected payoffs	$ 90,000	$0	1.0

Source: Joseph W. Newman, *Management Applications of Decision Theory* (New York: Harper & Row, 1971), p.10.

associated probabilities of reactions are .4, .3, and .3, respectively; and (4) the associated payoffs are listed in the body of the table. The EMV (A_1) is $300,000(.4) + $100,000(.3) − $200,000(.3) = $90,000. The EMV (A_2) is $0. The manager would decide to run the special promotion.

Decision Trees

A decision situation can be much more complex than this example. It might have many more alternatives and possible outcomes. As an aid in understanding decision problems, we may use a decision tree. Figure A4-1 presents a decision tree for the soft-drink promotion problem. Basically a graphic representation of the problem, it is composed of a series of nodes and branches. Decision nodes are represented by square boxes, and outcome or event nodes by circles. The decision to be made is always to the leftmost node point. Event branches then appear as they are related to the alternatives in chronological order. Note that for alternative A_1, run the special promotion, the manager has identified the same three outcomes as in Table A4-2 and has assigned the same subjective probabilities. For alternative A_2, do not run the special promotion, the manager's judgment is that it is certain no change will occur. The associated monetary value of each end point has been assigned.

FIGURE A4-1   Decision tree: soft drink promotion problem. [*Source: Joseph W. Newman, Management Applications of Decision Theory (New York: Harper & Row, 1971), p. 13.*]

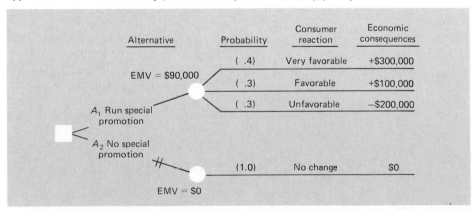

The tree is solved as follows: (1) Calculate the EMV of each node, beginning with the right-most node; (2) adopt the alternative for the branch with the highest EMV. On Figure A4-1 the EMV of each alternative is presented at the outcome nodes following each alternative. Alternatives A_1 and A_2 have EMVs of $90,000 and $0, respectively, as before. The fact that we reject alternative A_2 is indicated by the fact that we have drawn double slash marks through the A_2 branch.

A decision tree may be much more complicated than the one presented in Figure A4-1. It may have many event nodes and branches or forks in sequence and may even have a decision node in the middle of some parts of the tree. These complications really present no problem, for the same rules for solving the tree apply. We just begin at the right side and work to the left. For event branches we calculate the EMVs and record them at the node, and for decision points we simply select the decision with the highest EMV.

Expected Monetary Value of Perfect Information

The structure of a prior analysis allows one to calculate the absolute theoretical limit to marketing research expenditures, known as the *expected monetary value of perfect information* (EMVPI). To calculate this value we must subtract the EMV of the decision under uncertainty from the EMV of the decision in the situation where certainty about outcomes exists. In symbols,

$$EMVPI = EMV(C) - EMV(UC)$$

where EMV(C) is the EMV with certainty and EMV(UC) is the EMV with uncertainty. The rationale for this approach is that if we were certain about outcomes, we would make the correct decision in each outcome situation. The EMV of these correct decisions represents some gain over the EMV where outcomes are uncertain. The amount of the gain is the difference between EMV(C) and EMV(UC).

For the soft drink promotion problem, we already calculated the EMV(UC) as $90,000. Table A4-3 presents the calculation of the EMV(C) for this problem, which is performed as follows: If one had perfect information that a particular outcome would occur, one would select the associated alternative with the highest payout. Thus one would select A_1 if consumer responses were known to be "very favorable" or "favorable" and A_2 if they were known to be "unfavorable." The resultant EMV(C) is then

$$EMV(C) = \$300,000(.4) + \$100,000(.3) + \$0(.3)$$
$$= \$150,000$$

TABLE A4-3   EXPECTED PAYOFFS UNDER CERTAINTY—SOFT-DRINK SPECIAL-PROMOTION PROBLEM

Possible consumer reactions	Alternative courses of action		Probabilities of consumer reactions
	A_1	A_2	
Very favorable	$300,000	$0	.4
Favorable	100,000	0	.3
Unfavorable	0	0	.3
Expected payoff	$150,000	$0	1.0

Source: Joseph W. Newman, *Management Applications of Decision Theory* (New York: Harper & Row, 1971), p. 18.

Therefore

$$EMVPI = \$150,000 - \$90,000 = \$60,000$$

Under no circumstances should the manager making these judgments be willing to spend more than $60,000 on marketing research. Marketing research information is never perfect. Many errors are likely to be in the findings, so the amount this manager should in fact be willing to spend will be substantially less than $60,000; the exact amount depends on the value of imperfect information. We will develop procedures for valuing imperfect information later in this appendix. To understand this material properly, we must first grasp certain rules of probability theory.

THE NECESSARY PROBABILITY THEORY

We begin this section on probability theory by considering a number of definitions.

Some Definitions

Conditional Probability   Conditional probability is the probability assigned to an event when another event is known or assumed to have occurred. In symbols we can write $P(A|B)$, which reads "the probability of A given B." For example, one might assign a probability of .9 that a certain football team will win the big game, given that the star quarterback is not injured.

Joint Probability   Joint probability is the probability that two or more events will occur. In symbols we can write $P(A$ and $B)$, which reads "the probability of A and B." For example, one might assign a probability of .2 that both the football and basketball teams will win their weekend games.

Unconditional Probability   Unconditional probability is the probability assigned to an event that is independent of other events. It is also called *marginal probability*. It can be calculated by adding the probabilities of all the joint events of which it is a part. For example, if $P(A$ and $B) = .2$ and $P(A$ and $C) = .3$, then $P(A) = .5$.

The decision theory approach makes use of relationships among all these probability concepts. To apply these concepts properly we must be familiar with certain rules of probability theory.

Rules

Addition Rule   The addition law states that given the two events A and B,

$$P(A \text{ or } B) = P(A) + P(B) - P(A \text{ and } B)$$

If the two events are mutually exclusive, then

$$P(A \text{ or } B) = P(A) + P(B)$$

Multiplication Rule   The multiplication law states that given the two events A and B,

$$P(A \text{ and } B) = P(A|B) \cdot P(B) \tag{A4-1}$$

If the two events are independent, then

$$P(A \text{ and } B) = P(A) \cdot P(B)$$

Bayes' Rule   We could rearrange Equation A4-1 to yield what is called Bayes' rule, which is that

$$P(A|B) = \frac{P(A \text{ and } B)}{P(B)}$$

In words, the conditional probability of A given B is equal to the joint probability of A and B divided by the unconditional probability of B. This formula could be rewritten in the following way:

$$P(A|B) = \frac{P(A) \cdot P(B|A)}{P(A) \cdot P(B|A) + P(A') \cdot P(B|A')}$$

The numerator is simply the application of the multiplication rule for nonindependent events, and the denominator is simply the application of the fact that an unconditional or marginal probability is the sum of the joint probabilities where it occurs. In this latter formula A' represents events other than A.

We now have the necessary probability theory stated. We are ready to undertake the remaining two types of decision theory analysis.

POSTERIOR ANALYSIS

Posterior analysis requires the straightforward application of Bayes' rule; prior information is combined with additional information to provide revised probability estimates. Posterior analysis values both present and additional information. These posterior (revised) probabilities are then used to calculate a posterior $EMV/(A_i)$.

An example will make this clear. Suppose that, on the basis of pretest results, we wish to revise our prior probabilities of A_1 in our soft-drink promotion problem. Table A4-4 presents

TABLE A4-4   AN EXAMPLE OF POSTERIOR ANALYSIS

Outcome S_i (1)	Probabilities			
	Prior $P(S_i)$ (2)	Conditional* $P(R/S_i)$ (3)	Joint $P(R \text{ and } S_i)$ (4)	Posterior $P(S_i/R)$ (5)
S_1	.400	.700	.280	.757†
S_2	.300	.200	.060	.162
S_3	.300	.100	.030	.081
Totals	1.00		$P(R) = .370$	1.00

$$\text{Posterior EMV}(A_1) = \$300,000(.757) + \$100,000(.162) - \$200,000(.081)$$
$$= \$227,100$$

*R = very favorable pretest result.
†$P(S_1/R) = 280/.370 = .757$.

the necessary information. In the first two columns of this table we have identified the three possible outcomes and their respective prior probabilities. Now suppose a pretest result on this promotion was "very favorable." To update the prior probabilities, the manager must assess the conditional probability of getting a very favorable pretest given the various possible outcomes. In symbols, the manager must assess $P(R|S_i)$, where R is the very favorable pretest. Column 3 of Table A4-4 presents one such assessment. For example, this manager has assigned a probability of .7 of getting the very favorable pretest, given that the true outcome is indeed very favorable. The joint probability of R and S_i, $P(R$ and $S_i)$, is obtained by multiplying columns 2 and 3. This is just an application of the multiplication rule. The unconditional probability of getting a very favorable pretest, $P(R)$, is equal to the sum of all the joint probabilities where R occurs, $P(R) = .370$ in this example. The posterior probabilities are obtained by applying Bayes' rule. Here we want the $P(S_i|R)$. That is, we want the probability of various outcomes given the test results. For example, to calculate $P(S_1|R)$ we use the formula

$$P(S_1|R) = \frac{P(R \text{ and } S_1)}{P(R)}$$

$$= 280/.370 = .757$$

Thus the posterior probability of S_1 given this pretest result is .757. The probabilities of the other outcomes are calculated in a similar manner.

The posterior $EMV(A_1) = \$300,000(.757) + \$100,000(.162) - \$200,000(.081) = \$227,100$. Thus on the basis of the pretest the manager is able to recalculate the EMV of each alternative. At this point the EMV(C) will have changed to $\$300,000(.757) + \$100,000(.162) + \$0(.081) = \$243,300$. Therefore the new EMVPI $= \$243,300 - \$227,100 = \$16,200$. Prior to doing the pretest the EMVPI was $\$60,000$. This should make sense. New information has reduced the uncertainty and thus the value of additional information.

The decision theory approach may also be used to evaluate the worth of research before this research is undertaken. This type of decision theory analysis is called preposterior analysis, the topic to which we now turn our attention.

PREPOSTERIOR ANALYSIS

If one is willing to make certain probability assessments, *preposterior analysis* will allow the value of alternative research studies to be measured prior to the research being undertaken. This value is referred to as the *expected monetary value of imperfect information* (EMVII). In our soft-drink example we know the EMVII must be less than $\$60,000$, since this was the amount of the EMVPI. What follows is a simple example of how to calculate the EMVII for one specific study design. In performing this type of analysis we must recognize that a research study will cost money; thus, we also need to calculate this expected monetary value net of the cost of the research. We define this value as the expected monetary gain of imperfect information (EMGII). In symbols,

$$\text{EMGII} = \text{EMVII} - \text{cost of information}$$

In our example, we shall also calculate the EMGII. Actually, many alternative research designs could be considered in this fashion. We would select that design with the most positive EMGII. Clearly if the EMGII were negative, we would not undertake the research.

Preposterior analysis involves the following steps:

1. List the possible research outcomes and calculate their unconditional or marginal probabilities.

2. Assume, in turn, that each of the research outcomes has been obtained. For each research outcome: (a) calculate posterior probabilities; (b) calculate the expected payoff of each course of action under consideration and select the act with the highest expected payoff; (c) multiply the expected payoff of the best course of action by the marginal probability of the research outcome.

3. Sum the products of step 2c (taken for each research outcome) to get the expected payoff of the strategy that includes ordering research before taking final action.[5]
4. Calculate the EMVII.
5. Calculate the EMGII.
6. Choose the strategy with the highest EMGII if at least one strategy has a positive EMGII; otherwise choose the strategy without research that has the highest EMV.

An example should make these steps clear. Suppose that the manager was considering undertaking a market test of the special soft-drink promotion. The cost of this test would be $3500. Figure A4-2 presents the structure of the problem in decision tree form. Note that the decision to be

[5] Items 1–3, ibid., p. 24.

FIGURE A4-2 Decision tree for soft drink special promotion problem: no market test versus market test.
[*Source: Joseph W. Newman, Management Applications of Decision Theory (New York: Harper & Row, 1971), p. 25.*]

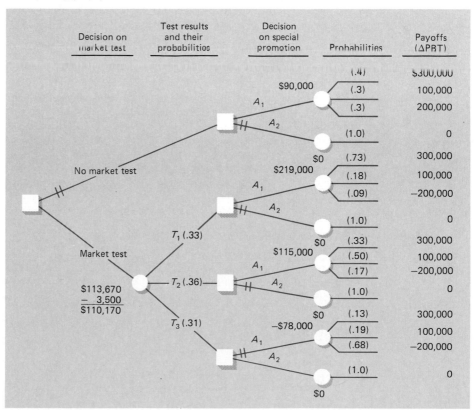

TABLE A4-5   CONDITIONAL PROBABILITIES OF MARKET TEST RESULTS

States of consumer reactions to special promotion if run as proposed	Test results		
	T_1 (+ 15%)	T_2 (+ 5%)	T_3 ($\pm$ 0)
S_1 (very favorable)	.6	.3	.1
S_2 (favorable)	.2	.6	.2
S_3 (unfavorable)	.1	.2	.7

Source: Joseph W. Newman, *Management Applications of Decision Theory* (New York: Harper & Row, 1971), p. 25.

made is whether to market-test and that the internal branches of the tree contain the original decision problem about whether to run the special promotion. The sequence is in chronological order. The test market decision comes first, then the test market (if it is undertaken), then the choice of decision alternatives about the promotion, then the possible outcomes of this latter decision. Also note that the prior probabilities of various outcomes are assigned to the top fork of the tree and that the EMV of the best decision without research is $90,000, as calculated in our prior analysis. Now we shall proceed to go through the steps of a preposterior analysis.

Step 1   Three market-test outcomes are thought possible: a 15 percent increase in sales (T_1), a 5 percent increase in sales (T_2), and no sales increase (T_3). To obtain the marginal probabilities of T_1, T_2, and T_3, one could reason as follows: If the promotion were run as planned and received a very favorable consumer reaction, what is the probability of T_1, T_2, and T_3 occurring? This is the $P(T_i|S_1)$. One such set of assessments is given in the first line of Table A4-5. For example, we note that the conditional probability of finding T_1 given that S_1 would be found is .6. The other two lines of this table present the conditional probabilities of various test results given other possible consumer reactions, S_2 and S_3. These assessments are in essence a judgment about the ability of particular research designs to find the true situation. These $P(T_i|S_i)$'s are multiplied by the prior probabilities, $P(S_i)$, to yield joint probabilities, as found in Table A4-6. For example, $P(S_1 \text{ and } T_1) = P(S_1) \cdot P(T_1|S_1) = (.4)(.6) = .24$. The marginal probability of each T_i can be obtained by adding the joint probabilities where T_i occurs. Thus we find: $P(T_1) = .33$, $P(T_2) = .36$, and $P(T_3) = .31$. These probabilities are recorded on the decision tree in Figure A4-2.

TABLE A4-6   JOINT PROBABILITIES OF STATES AND MARKET TEST RESULTS

States of consumer reactions to special promotion if run as proposed	Test results			Marginal probabilities
	T_1 (+ 15%)	T_2 (+ 5%)	T_3 ($\pm$ 0%)	
S_1 (very favorable)	.24	.12	.04	.4
S_2 (favorable)	.06	.18	.06	.3
S_3 (unfavorable)	.03	.06	.21	.3
Marginal probabilities	.33	.36	.31	1.00

Source: Joseph W. Newman, *Management Applications of Decision Theory* (New York: Harper & Row, 1971), p. 26.

Step 2 Next we can revise the prior probabilities of the possible outcomes given that various test results have occurred. To do this we use Bayes' rule. For example,

$$P(S_1|T_1) = \frac{P(S_1 \text{ and } T_1)}{P(T_1)} = \frac{.24}{.33} = .73$$

$$P(S_2|T_1) = .06/.33 = .18$$

$$P(S_3|T_1) = .03/.33 = .09$$

These calculations are recorded for the possible outcomes along the T_1 branch of the tree. Similar calculations are easily made for the S_i's given T_2 and T_3. These results are recorded on the decision tree. The expected payout of each alternative is recalculated using the revised probabilities. Thus, if a 15 percent sales increase is observed in the market test (T_1), the expected payoff is $219,000; similarly for T_2, $115,000; and T_3, $-$78,000. If T_1 or T_2 were observed, we would choose A_1, but if T_3 were observed we would choose A_2. Thus the best courses of action and payoffs are $T_1 = $219,000, $T_2 = $115,000, and $T_3 = $0. These three best payoffs are then multiplied by their associated $P(T_i)$.

Step 3 The sum of the best outcomes, each multiplied by its respective $P(T_i)$, equals $113,670 [$219,000(.33) + $115,000(.36) + $0(.31)].

Step 4 Now we are in a position to calculate EMVII:

$$
\begin{aligned}
\text{FMVII} &= \text{EMV(with test)} - \text{EMV(without test)} \\
&= \$113,670 \quad\quad - \$90,000 \\
&= \$23,670
\end{aligned}
$$

This is the absolute maximum we would be willing to pay for this research.

Step 5 The net gain of the study can also be calculated:

$$
\begin{aligned}
\text{EMVII} &= \text{EMV(with test)} - \text{EMV(without test)} \\
&= \$113,670 \quad\quad - \$90,000 \\
&= \$23,670
\end{aligned}
$$

Step 6 Since the EMGII is positive, we would choose to do the market test. It is possible that alternative designs for this test may be possible, each having different costs and conditional probabilities, $P(T_i|S_i)$. We could calculate the EMGII for each of these, just as we have done here, and select that study with the highest EMGII. Clearly if EMGII is negative, we are better off making the decision without research.

ADVANTAGES AND LIMITATIONS

The decision theory approach has a number of advantages, including (1) the rigor of requiring the manager to structure the problem completely; (2) the rigor of having to specify the value of each outcome; (3) the ability to determine the expected value of alternatives before and after research; and (4) the ability to determine the expected value of alternative research projects before undertaking the research. These are indeed major benefits of this approach. However, we must temper these positive aspects with some strong limitations—for example, (1) the lack of knowledge among managers and researchers of the procedures of this approach; (2) the inability or unwillingness of managers to structure problems completely and identify outcomes; (3) the inability or unwillingness of managers to make the necessary conditional probability judgments; and (4) the general unwillingness of managers to expose their thinking in such an explicit manner. For the present, therefore, the decision theory approach remains a powerful theoretical tool that has obtained some usage in sophisticated organizations.[6] It is for the future to judge its long-term practical value.

[6] For some applications, see Rex V. Brown, "Do Managers Find Decision Theory Useful?" *Harvard Business Review,* pp. 78–89, May–June 1970.

CHAPTER 5

RESEARCH AND DATA SOURCES

The previous chapter discussed the importance of the planning and analysis leading to the decision to undertake a formal research project. It was stressed that the decision problem must be clearly stated and the alternative courses of action specified. The role research can play in both formulating the problem and stimulating the creative process involved in identifying alternative courses of action was emphasized, along with the importance of clearly stated research objectives and detailed information needs. The success of the formal research project is highly dependent upon how skillfully these preliminary issues are addressed.

Once the initial phase of the research process has been adequately performed, the researcher can turn to designing the formal research project and identifying the appropriate sources of data for the study. The primary task of the formal research project is to supply the decision maker with conclusive research information which will increase the level of confidence regarding the best course of action to accomplish objectives.

In this chapter, we first discuss the research designs and the data sources appropriate for exploratory, conclusive, and performance-monitoring research. Next we turn to a more detailed discussion of the basic sources of marketing data. These data sources include (1) interrogation of respondents, (2) observation, (3) study of analogous situations, (4) experimentation, and (5) secondary data. We conclude the chapter with a discussion of marketing decision support systems.

RESEARCH DESIGN

A research design is the basic plan which guides the data collection and analysis phases of the research project. It is the framework which specifies the type of information to be collected, the sources of data, and the data collection procedure. A good design will make sure that the information gathered is consistent with the study objectives and that the data are collected by accurate and economical procedures. There is no standard or idealized research design to guide the researcher, since many different designs may accomplish the same objective.[1]

The objective of the research project logically determines the characteristics desired in the research design. Research objectives are dependent upon the stages of the decision-making process for which information is needed. Three types of research have been identified in this regard: exploratory, conclusive, and performance-monitoring research.

Research designs are typically classified according to the nature of the research objectives or types of research. While this classification is far from perfect, it will organize our discussion of research design. It is important to remember that research designs can serve many research objectives and types of research. The following classification reflects a judgment about the research objectives more predominantly associated with a design; it does not imply exclusive association. (See Figure 5-1.)

Exploratory Research

Exploratory research is appropriate when the research objectives include (1) identifying problems or opportunities, (2) developing a more precise formulation of a vaguely identified problem or opportunity, (3) gaining perspective regarding the breadth of variables operating in a situation, (4) establishing priorities regarding the potential significance

---

[1] Julian L. Simon, *Basic Research Methods in Social Sciences: The Art of Empirical Investigation* (New York: Random House, 1969), p. 4.

FIGURE 5-1   Research design.

of various problems or opportunities, (5) gaining management and researcher perspective concerning the character of the problem situation, (6) identifying and formulating alternative courses of action, and (7) gathering information on the problems associated with doing conclusive research.

Exploratory research is often the initial step in a series of studies designed to supply information for decision making. The purpose of this research is to formulate hypotheses regarding potential problems and/or opportunities present in the decision situation. By "hypothesis" we refer to a conjectural statement about the relationship between two or more variables. This statement should carry clear implications for measuring the variables and testing the stated relationship.[2] For example, exploratory research would be appropriate in a situation where management responds to the symptom of declining share of market by asking. "What is the problem?" The task of exploratory research would be to identify tentative hypotheses concerning the cause of this decline. Potential hypotheses may be narrowed by further research to the point where a statement of problems and opportunities can be developed. This statement represents the formal hypotheses regarding the causes of the decision situation. These hypotheses can be tested at a later stage of the decision process with conclusive research methods.

Examples of hypotheses developed from exploratory research are as follows:

1 An advertising theme emphasizing the "nutrition value" of food product X will increase brand awareness more than a theme emphasizing "good flavor."

2 A change in the ingredients of product X from artificial chocolate to real chocolate will increase the preference for product X compared with its competition.

3 A 10 percent cut in the retail price of product X will result in a 1 percent market share gain within 6 months.

Because exploratory research deals with a decision situation where limited knowledge exists, the research design is characterized by flexibility in order to be sensitive to the unexpected and to discover ideas and insights not previously recognized. The formulation of hypotheses rarely comes to the mind of the manager or researcher through the application of fixed and rigid procedures. Of all the stages of the decision-making process, identification of problems and opportunities eludes formal description. While the ability to formulate the decision problem must be relegated in part to the realm of inspiration, it is also true that various procedures can assist this creative process. These procedures are (1) searching secondary sources, (2) interviewing knowledgeable persons, and (3) compiling case histories.

Conclusive Research

Conclusive research is designed to provide information for the evaluation of alternative courses of action. It can be subclassified into descriptive research and causal research.[3]

---

[2] See Fred N. Kerlinger, *Foundations of Behavioral Research,* 2d ed. (New York: Holt, Rinehart, 1973), pp. 18–26, for a detailed discussion of the characteristics and role of hypotheses in research.

[3] This classification follows that of Daniel Katz, "Field Studies," in Leon Festinger and Daniel Katz (eds.), *Research Methods in the Behaviorial Sciences* (New York: Holt, Rinehart, 1953), p. 74, and Claire Selltiz et al., *Research Methods in Social Relations,* rev. ed. (New York: Holt, Rinehart, 1959), p. 50.

Descriptive Research The vast majority of marketing research studies involve descriptive research. Most studies of this nature rely heavily on interrogation of respondents and data available from secondary data sources. Descriptive research is appropriate when the research objectives include (1) portraying the characteristics of marketing phenomena and determining the frequency of occurrence, (2) determining the degree to which marketing variables are associated, and (3) making predictions regarding the occurrence of marketing phenomena.

A significant share of research falls under the first of these objectives, portraying the characteristics of marketing phenomena and determining the frequency of occurrence. Consumer profile studies are conducted by firms like General Motors and Procter & Gamble to describe the characteristics of the users of a product or service. Such profiles can use demographic, socioeconomic, geographic, and psychographic characteristics, as well as consumption rates. Descriptive studies determine buyer perceptions of product characteristics and audience profiles for media such as television and magazines. Market potential studies describe the size of the market, buying power of consumers, availability of distributors, and buyer profiles for a product; product usage studies describe consumption patterns; market share studies determine the proportion of total sales received by both a company and its competitors; sales analysis studies describe sales patterns by geographic region, type, size of account, and product line characteristics; distribution research determines the number and location of distributors; pricing research describes the range and frequency of prices charged for both a company's products and those of its competitors. These examples of descriptive research represent only a sampling of the numerous studies conducted in this area.

Descriptive research often involves determining the degree to which marketing variables are associated. For example, a company may study the degree of association between sales of a product and such buyer characteristics as income and age.

Descriptive information can be used to make predictions about the occurrence of marketing phenomena. While data regarding the presence of an association among variables can be used for predictive purposes, these data are not adequate to establish a causal relationship. However, it is not always necessary to understand causal relations in order to make accurate predictive statements. A company may establish an association between the sales of a product and the months of the year, and a sales forecast based on this association may have a high probability of success regarding future sales volume even though the causal relationship has not been established. The concept is to identify variables which are associated with the variable to be predicted and are measurable at the time the prediction is required.

While descriptive research may characterize marketing phenomena and demonstrate an association among variables, statements regarding cause-and-effect relationships are not possible with descriptive research. The decision maker may make predictions that certain actions will result in certain performance outcomes based on the evidence provided from a descriptive study, but this evidence in itself does not demonstrate a cause-and-effect relationship. (Where such evidence is needed, causal research designs are required, which will be discussed shortly.)

The character and purpose of descriptive research are substantially different from that of exploratory research. Effective descriptive research is marked by a clear statement of the decision problem, specific research objectives, and detailed information needs. It is characterized by a carefully planned and structured research design. Since the purpose is to provide information regarding specific questions or hypotheses, the research must be designed to ensure accuracy of the findings. By accuracy we mean a design that minimizes systematic error and maximizes the reliability of the evidence collected. Systematic error refers to a constant bias in the measurement process, while reliability refers to the extent to which the measurement process is free from random errors. For a detailed discussion of systematic error and reliability in connection with the measurement process, see Chapter 10.

Cross-Sectional Design   Descriptive research typically makes use of a cross-sectional research design, i.e., taking a sample of population elements at one point in time. Frequently this is called the *survey research design*. This is the most popular type of research design and the one with which people are most familiar. The survey design is useful in describing the characteristics of consumers and determining the frequency of marketing phenomena, although it is often expensive and requires skillful and competent research personnel to conduct it effectively.

Decision Maker's Implicit Causal Model   The evidence provided by descriptive research can be very useful when combined with the decision maker's implicit model of how the marketing system functions in regard to the specific area under investigation. This causal model is typically based on the experience and judgment of the decision maker and represents key assumptions regarding the cause-and-effect relationships present in the marketing system. A descriptive study can provide evidence regarding specific questions or hypotheses relating to the current state of the variables present in this causal model. Given this descriptive evidence, the decision maker can draw conclusions about the effects of various courses of action and reach a decision as to which course of action will best accomplish objectives. Consequently, descriptive research in itself may not provide evidence directly related to the selection of a course of action. It is when descriptive evidence is incorporated in the decision maker's personal model of the marketing system that it contributes directly to the decision-making process.

To illustrate, a marketing manager wishes to test the hypothesis that the reason for the decline in share of market for the firm's aspirin-free analgesic product is due to the consumer's misperception that the product contains aspirin. This hypothesis was developed from several exploratory group interviews with former users of the firm's product. Descriptive research was conducted to test this hypothesis, and an extensive survey of several hundred former and potential consumers supported it. The marketing manager combined this descriptive evidence with a personal causal model of how the analgesic market functions to reach a decision on a course of action. The decision was to develop an advertising campaign stressing the product's absence of aspirin and the benefits associated with a nonaspirin product. The strategy was to correct the market misperception about the presence of aspirin in the product and to reposition the product in the growing aspirin-free segment of the analgesic market. The result was a substantial increase in the product's share of market.

As this example points out, descriptive research presupposes that a sound causal model of the marketing system exists in the mind of the decision maker. The lower the decision maker's confidence in the wisdom of the causal model, the lower the value of descriptive research in the decision-making process. For example, descriptive research for the positioning of a brand is of little value if the decision maker does not know how brand positioning relates to the success of the brand.

Descriptive studies cover an array of research interests, but they require skillful planning if they are to be used effectively in decision making. Far too often, descriptive research is viewed as a fact-gathering expedition.

> Facts do not lead anywhere. Indeed, facts as facts are the commonest, cheapest, and most useless of all commodities. Anyone with a questionnaire can gather thousands of facts a day—and probably not find much real use for them. What makes facts practical and valuable is the glue of explanation and understanding, the framework of theory, the tie-rod of conjecture. Only when facts can be fleshed to a skeletal theory do they become meaningful in the solution of problems.[4]

Descriptive research is easy to conduct when the decision maker gives free rein to collect what are believed to be interesting facts. Too often, research objectives are vague, specific research questions or hypotheses have not been formulated, and limited thought has been given to how the evidence can be used in the decision-making process. The results are that the majority of the data turn out to be useless and management has wasted both funds and time. In this situation, possibly an exploratory research study would provide better information, faster and at a lower cost, than a fact-finding descriptive study. Since descriptive studies often cost several thousand dollars, the collection of interesting but useless facts can be very costly.

Descriptive research designs can utilize one or more of the following sources of data: (1) interrogation of respondents, (2) secondary data, and (3) simulation.

Causal Research   The decision-making process calls for assumptions regarding the cause-and-effect relationships present in the marketing system, and causal research is designed to gather evidence regarding these relationships. It requires a planned and structured design that will not only minimize systematic error and maximize reliability, but will also permit reasonably unambiguous conclusions regarding causality.

Causal research is appropriate given the following research objectives: (1) to understand which variables are the cause of what is being predicted (the effect)— here the focus is on understanding the reasons why things happen; (2) to understand the nature of the functional relationship between the causal factors and the effect to be predicted.

Marketing executives continually think and make decisions based on an implicit causal model of the marketing system. If prices are reduced on a product or the promotion budget is increased, and subsequent unit sales of the product show an upward surge, this effect could be assumed to be caused by the changes in price level and/or the promotion budget. However, can we confidently say that the change in unit sales was caused by the change in price and promotion levels? Certainly not with a high degree of confidence. Many other variables could be the cause. Consequently, causal research must be designed such that the evidence regarding

[4] Robert Ferber, Donald F. Blankertz, and Sidney Hollander, Jr., *Marketing Research* (New York: Ronald, 1964), p. 153.

causality is clear. Research designs vary substantially in the degree of ambiguity present in the evidence regarding causality.

The main sources of data for causal research are (1) interrogating respondents through surveys and (2) conducting experiments.

While surveys can determine the degree of association among variables and test hypotheses, they cannot distinguish causality as well as experiments. A skillfully designed experiment can ensure that the evidence regarding causality is reasonably unambiguous in interpretation.

Because of the complexity of the research designs appropriate for experimental research, a separate section of this book has been devoted to their explanation. Chapter 12 discusses the principles of experimentation and alternative research designs.

Our discussion of conclusive research has emphasized the distinction between descriptive and causal research. In practice, these two approaches may be combined to meet the varied research objectives of a particular study. Even so, it is important to recognize the distinction between them, since they do serve different types of research objectives and differ in the character of the evidence provided for decision making. For example, with causal research, especially in the case of an experiment, the research design may directly evaluate the alternative courses of action under consideration. Here, the independent variables (courses of action) can be manipulated to determine the effect on purchase behavior, attitudes, and so forth. In the case of descriptive research, the evidence is more indirect, and the decision maker's experience and judgment regarding the nature of the causal relationships are required for the effective use of this evidence in the decision-making process.

Performance-Monitoring Research

Performance-monitoring research provides information regarding the monitoring of the marketing system. It is an essential element in the control of marketing programs in accordance with plans. The purpose of this research is to signal the presence of potential problems or opportunities.

The objectives of performance-monitoring research are to monitor and report changes (1) in performance measures, such as sales and market share, to determine whether plans are accomplishing desired objectives; (2) in subobjectives, such as awareness and knowledge levels, distribution penetration, and price levels, to determine whether the marketing program is being implemented according to plans; and (3) in the situational variables, such as competitive activity, economic conditions, and demand trends, to determine whether the situational climate is an anticipated when plans were formulated.

The data sources appropriate for performance-monitoring research include (1) interrogation of respondents, (2) secondary data, and (3) observation.

Performance-monitoring research can involve a special (ad hoc) study or a continuous research program.

Ad hoc performance monitoring consists of research programs designed to monitor new or special marketing programs of the organization or competitor. Typical here is the monitoring of a test market for a new product. Recent years have shown growing interest in monitoring such situational variables as government regulation, availability of resources, changing life-styles of buyers, concerns of consumer groups, and so forth. The previously discussed cross-sectional research design is appropriate in this situation. This typically involves survey research.

Continuous performance measures are, in general, formal systems designed to monitor the dependent variables in the marketing system. In recent years, increased effort has been directed to monitoring the independent variables as well. The most common performance measures involve product movement data such as units sold, sales volume, and market share. Many organizations, such as General Foods and Westinghouse, have formal systems to monitor the performance of the distribution system, sales force, and promotional programs. Most firms have the sales force submit to management, on a routine basis, formal reports concerning market and competitive conditions.

Longitudinal Design   Continuous performance monitoring typically requires a *longitudinal research design,* that is, one in which a fixed sample of population elements is measured repeatedly. The term "panel" is often used synonymously with longitudinal design. Two types of panels exist: the traditional panel and the omnibus panel. The *traditional panel* is a fixed sample where the same variables are repeatedly measured; for example, the Nielsen Retail Store Audit involves a fixed sample of 2500 stores which are measured monthly to estimate the sales of various food and drug items.[5] The *omnibus panel* is a fixed sample of respondents which is measured repeatedly, but the variables measured are different each time. For example, a food company maintains a panel of households who are asked to evaluate different food products at different times.

The motivation for longitudinal data derives from the decision makers' need to measure the effect of marketing variables over time for the same buying units. The following examples illustrate situations where panel data are useful.[6]

1 *Measuring the effect of a soft-drink promotional offer.* A sample of families are interviewed repeatedly over several weeks about their purchases of soft drinks in order to establish their "steady state" purchasing patterns. A special soft-drink promotional deal is introduced to the families, and their purchases are monitored every week for 4 weeks. This allows researchers to measure the short-term and long-term effects of the promotional deal.

2 *Tracking brand purchases of frozen food.* Detailed data are collected every week for several years regarding family purchases of frozen food. Estimates are derived regarding the extent to which purchasers remain loyal to different brands and how market shares shift over time among different groups of consumers.

3 *Monitoring the acceptance of a new toy line.* Information is obtained every month on the toy purchases of families with children. Such information allows marketers to determine the types of families that are buying new toys and how soon after market introduction they make their purchases.

[5] Nielsen Retail Index Service (Northbrook, Ill.: A. C. Nielsen Company, 1975).

[6] Adapted from Seymour Sudman and Robert Ferber, *Consumer Panels,* American Marketing Association, Chicago, Ill., 1979, p. 5.

A study by Hardin and Johnson of consumer panel users found that most used the data for monitoring trends, making demographic profiles, conducting brand-switching analyses, examining new tryer–repeat buyer patterns, checking combination purchases, predicting product success in test markets, and evaluating special promotions.[7] This diverse list of uses illustrates that panel studies come in many different forms and varying time intervals and involve different data collection methods. Panels need not be limited to individuals or to individual households but can consist of stores, business firms, or some other type of entity.

A major advantage of longitudinal data over cross-sectional data is their ability to reflect the true extent of change taking place in a population. This is possible due to the repeated measurement of a topic with the same sample of respondents. Cross-sectional data can be very misleading, since surveys at two points in time with different respondents in the sample can show no change when in fact very dramatic changes are taking place in the population.

Table 5-1 shows how cross-sectional reported purchases of brands A and B remain the same in time periods 1 and 2 but show dramatic differences when longitudinal purchases are reported. In the cross-sectional surveys the purchase of brands A and B both represent 20 percent of purchases in each time period. In the longitudinal data we see that the total purchases within a time period reflects the cross-sectional data in that 20 percent of purchases are brands A and B. However, substantial variation exists when we observe the repeat purchase patterns. In particular, none of the individuals who purchase brand B in time period 1 repeat their purchase in time period 2. Conversely, all individuals who purchased brand A in time period 1 repurchase brand A in time period 2. These dramatic differences in the repurchase patterns for brands A and B are not reflected in the cross-sectional data and have significant implications for the marketing strategies of the two brands.

Various data analysis approaches have been developed to analyze this type of data set.[8] These approaches allow the study of changes in attitudes, knowledge, and behavior for the same respondents or households at different points in time. Such changes (or lack of change) can be related to changes in marketing program variables (price, promotion, distribution, and product) as well as to changes in situational variables (e.g., competition, economic conditions, and so forth).

Another advantage of the panel design relates to the amount of information which can be collected. Since panel members are often compensated for their participation, they are more cooperative regarding longer and more demanding interviews. Consequently, panels are able to gather extensive background data on the respondents in addition to more detailed data regarding the primary variables of interest.

It is argued that panel data can be more accurate than cross-sectional data. Research evidence suggests that professionally administered panels using the diary reporting procedure (self-administered questionnaire) yield reasonably accurate estimates

---

[7] David K. Hardin, and Richard M. Johnson, "Patterns of Use of Consumer Purchase Panels," *Journal of Marketing Research,* vol. 8, pp. 364–367, August 1971.

[8] Francesco M. Nicosia, "Panel Designs and Analysis in Marketing," in Peter D. Bennett (ed.), *Marketing and Economic Development* (Chicago: American Marketing Association, 1965), pp. 222–243.

TABLE 5-1   CROSS-SECTIONAL DATA MAY NOT REFLECT LONGITUDINAL DATA

Cross-sectional data

	Period 1 survey	Period 2 survey
Brand A		
Purchase	100	100
No purchase	400	400
Total	500	500
Brand B		
Purchase	100	100
No purchase	400	400
Total	500	500

Longitudinal data

Period 2 panel reporting	Period 1 panel reporting		
	Brand A		
	Purchase	No purchase	Total
Brand A			
Purchase	100	0	100
No purchase	0	400	400
Total	100	400	500
	Brand B		
	Purchase	No purchase	Total
Brand B			
Purchase	0	100	100
No purchase	100	300	400
Total	100	400	500

Source: Adapted from Seymour Sudman and Robert Ferber, *Consumer Panels,* American Marketing Association, Chicago, Ill., p. 5, 1979.

of retail sales for an array of food and drug items.[9] A comparison of panel and survey estimates of retail sales indicates that more accurate estimates of retail sales exist with panel data.[10] The survey design requires the respondent to recall past purchases, which can be biased because of forgetting and misassociation; bias is reduced in the panel design since there is continuous recording of purchases in the diary as they occur. Additional research suggests that panel members must be paid in order to

[9] Seymour Sudman, "On the Accuracy of Recording of Consumer Panels: II," *Journal of Marketing Research,* vol. 1, pp. 69–83, August 1964.
[10] J. H. Parfitt, "A Comparison of Purchase Recall with Diary Panel Records," *Journal of Advertising Research,* vol. 7, pp. 16–31, September 1967.

maintain reporting accuracy. Small payments can produce very accurate reporting. Variations in work loads imposed on the panel members do not significantly influence the reporting accuracy.[11]

The cost of panel data can be lower than the cost of comparable data collected through a survey. The fixed costs associated with developing and maintaining a panel can be spread over the many clients who use it, while a comparable survey requires that the incurred fixed cost be charged directly to a single client.

The main disadvantages of panels stem from the fact that they are not representative. The two major problems are (1) unrepresentative sampling and (2) response bias.

The unrepresentative sampling problem arises from the need to have panel members serve for a long period. As an inducement to serve, they are offered gifts and money. It is argued that individuals who are mobile, employed, and uninterested in panel activities, gifts, or money, and individuals who are unable to perform the tasks required will not serve on the panel. Despite attempts to match the sample on selected population characteristics such as age, education, occupation, and so on, it is feared that the sample may be unrepresentative of the particular variable being measured.

Another issue relates to the mortality rates of existing panel members and the representativeness of the new members chosen to replace them. Mortality rates (resulting from members moving, losing interest, and dying) can range as high as 20 percent per year for panels operating over a long period of time.

Despite these potential biases in representativeness of the sample, the available research evidence suggests that this problem is not a serious issue for professionally administered panels.[12]

The response bias issue is not serious for well-managed panels. The response biases that need to be controlled result from the panel members believing they are "experts," wanting to look good or give the "right" answer, becoming biased from boredom and fatigue, and not routinely completing diary entries.

Research evidence does suggest that new panel members are often biased in their initial responses.[13] New members tend to increase the behavior being measured, e.g., television viewing and food purchasing.[14] Professionally managed panels minimize this type of bias by initially excluding the data of new members from panel results. After the novelty of being on the panel declines, the accuracy of the data increases.

DATA SOURCES

There are four basic sources of marketing data. These are (1) respondents, (2) analogous situations, (3) experimentation, and (4) secondary data.

---

[11] Sudman, "On the Accuracy of Recording of Consumer Panels: II."

[12] W. N. Cordell and H. A. Rahmel, "Are Nielsen Ratings Affected by Non-Cooperation, Conditioning, or Response Error?" *Journal of Advertising Research,* vol. 2, pp. 45–49, September 1962.

[13] D. G. Morrison, R. E. Frank, and W. F. Massy, "A Note on Panel Bias," *Journal of Marketing,* vol. 3, pp. 85–88, February 1966.

[14] A. S. C. Ehrenberg, "A Study of Some Potential Biases in the Operation of a Consumer Panel," *Applied Statistics: A Journal of the Royal Statistical Society,* vol. 9, pp. 20–27, March 1960.

MARKETING RESEARCH IN ACTION . . .

THE KODAK DISC CAMERA

"The photographic industry was an excellent example of widespread consumer satisfaction with existing products," according to John J. Powers, vice president and director of marketing communications at Eastman Kodak Co., Rochester, N.Y. Yet, Kodak was able to successfully market the highly innovative disc camera. What was Kodak's key to success in this highly "consumer-satisfied" industry?

Eastman Kodak recognized an opportunity in the photographic market and seized upon it. They proceeded to develop, test, and market a product which met photography needs never before addressed at the amateur level.

Kodak began its exploratory research process by setting a goal: to determine under what conditions amateur photographers were and were not taking pictures. Next, Kodak created a photographic system that would take the quality pictures amateur photographers were not currently able to take. This system was the disc camera and its accompanying film.

To narrow the alternatives regarding product usage and features, Kodak did further marketing research, this time in the form of a feasibility study. They went first to their own employees. According to Powers, "More than 500 people, from throughout Kodak, put 64 different camera configurations through a battery of 14 tests. . . . . From this, the basic design parameters began to emerge."

Employee testing alone, though, could not supply sufficient data to begin marketing the camera. Before undertaking more research, Eastman Kodak had to determine exactly who the target market was. Then they had to see how this target group perceived the product and if this perception was the same among demographically different consumer groups. Consumer research was also necessary to determine if (1) consumers would notice the benefits of the disc camera, and (2) whether or not these benefits would motivate consumers enough to buy a new camera. Furthermore, said Powers, "Kodak needed to know more specifically what features people liked most, and whether they would perceive these features as allowing them to take pictures where they previously didn't. [Kodak] needed to translate those advantages into benefits the consumer would quickly recognize."

To this end, Kodak took a prototype disc camera into 1000 U.S. homes. Kodak was not identified as the sponsor of study. First, consumers were shown the camera and asked to write down the features they recognized. After that, the camera's features were explained in detail. Respondents were then asked to rank 18 specific features in order of preference.

From these data, Kodak was able to determine that preferences for features were constant across all demographic groups. They also learned which of the 18 features consumers considered most appealing. Most important, though, Kodak discovered that intent to purchase nearly doubled after respondents were shown all the features of the disc.

This information, gathered through marketing research, gave Kodak insight which enabled them to market one of the biggest selling new items of 1980!

Source: Marketing News, vol. 17, no. 2, sec. 1, pp. 8–9, Jan. 21, 1983.

Respondents

Respondents are a major source of marketing data. There are two principal methods of obtaining data from respondents—communication and observation. Communication requires the respondent to actively provide data through verbal response, while observation requires the recording of the respondent's passive behavior.

Communication with Respondents   The most common source of marketing data is communication with respondents. It is logical to acquire data from people by asking questions. In our daily activities we gather information by asking questions of persons whom we consider knowledgeable. Marketing research is just a more formal and scientific way of gathering such information.

When the information needs of a study require data about respondents' attitudes, perceptions, motivations, knowledge, and intended behavior, asking people questions is essential. The respondents can be consumers, industrial buyers, wholesalers, retailers, or any knowledgeable persons who can provide data useful to a decision situation. Effective communication with respondents requires special training and skill if the data are to be useful. Misleading data can result when the questions are biased or require respondents to provide data which they do not possess or choose not to disclose.

The research design can range from questioning a few knowledgeable individuals (qualitative research) to surveys involving hundreds of respondents (quantitative research). *Qualitative or exploratory research* usually consists of questioning knowledgeable respondents individually or in small groups (i.e., five to six people). *Group interviews* provide free-flowing unstructured situations designed to stimulate ideas and insights into a problem situation through group interaction. This typically means asking deeply probing questions over a long time span (i.e., one or two hours). *Depth interviews* use extensive questioning of respondents individually to explore the reasons underlying attitudes and behavior. The focus is on developing hypotheses and insight regarding the "why" of past and future behavior. In contrast, *quantitative research* is designed to explain what is happening and the frequency of occurrence; it is normally conducted by asking a large sample of respondents a few simple questions in a brief time span (i.e., 10−20 minutes). Formal and structured research procedures designed to control bias in the data are employed.

The data collection methods used in communicating with respondents include personal interviews, telephone interviews, and mail questionnaires. The questions are asked of the respondent and answered verbally with the personal and telephone interview, in writing with the mail questionnaire. The popularity of the telephone interview has increased significantly in recent years.

Observation of Respondents   Observation is the process of recognizing and recording relevant objects and events. It is an important and commonplace activity in our daily routines. Similarly, in marketing, valuable information pertaining to a decision situation can be obtained by observing either present behavior or the results of past behavior.

Observational methods allow the recording of behavior when it occurs, thus eliminating those errors associated with the recall of behavior. This is often less costly and/or more accurate than asking the respondent to recall the same behavior at another point in time. While observation can accurately record what people do and how it is done, it cannot be used to determine the motivations, attitudes, and knowledge that underlie the behavior.

The many issues involved in obtaining data from respondents through communication and observation are discussed in Chapters 13 to 15.

Analogous Situations

A logical way to study a decision situation is to examine analogous or similar situations. Analogous situations include the study of case histories and simulations.

Case Histories   The case history approach is an old and established method in the behavioral sciences and has been used successfully in marketing research for decades.[15] The design involves the intensive investigation of situations which are relevant to the problem situation. The concept is to select several target cases where an intensive analysis will (1) identify relevant variables, (2) indicate the nature of the relationship among variables, and (3) identify the nature of the problem and/or opportunity present in the original decision situation. For example, the research might investigate selected retail stores, sales territories, markets, salespeople, or industrial buyers. The purpose is to obtain a comprehensive description of the cases and to formulate a better understanding of the variables operating.

The case history method is especially useful in situations where a complicated series of variables interact to produce the problem or opportunity. Cases which can be studied are those reflecting (1) contrasting performance levels, e.g., good and poor markets; (2) rapid changes in performance, e.g., entry of a competitor into a market; and (3) the order in which events occurred, e.g., sales regions which are in various stages of transition from indirect to direct selling efforts.[16]

Data can be obtained through the search of records and reports, observation of key variables, and interrogation of knowledgeable persons. The research style is one of flexibility in the analysis to take advantage of the unexpected and develop insights into the problem situation.

Simulation   This means the creation of an analogy or likeness of a real-world phenomenon. It is an incomplete representation of reality which tries to duplicate the essence of the phenomenon without actually attaining reality itself. Common examples of simulation are model airplanes, road maps, and planetariums.

---

[15] This method of investigation has been widely used in the behavioral sciences and marketing research under the label of "case study." The term "case history" is used here to differentiate the research-oriented case study from the classroom case study most familiar to students. The classroom case study is a pedagogical device designed to put the student in a situation similar to that encountered by a management group. The student's task is to analyze the situation and logically proceed through the decision-making process, ending with a recommendation for action. Research case histories or case studies are typically more myopic than classroom case studies and are intended to aid the decision-making process by providing ideas and insight into a decision situation. The classroom case study may include one or more case histories as part of the background information in the case.

[16] Gilbert A. Churchill, Jr., *Marketing Research* (Hinsdale, Ill.: Dryden Press, 1976), p. 67.

What is a *marketing simulation*? It can be defined as an incomplete representation of the marketing system or some aspect of this system. It is a relatively new source of data which is largely computer based. Simulation can be used to gain insight into the dynamics of the marketing system by manipulating the independent variables (marketing mix and situational factors) and observing their influence on the dependent variable(s). A marketing simulation requires data inputs regarding the characteristics of the phenomenon to be represented and the relationships present.

The development of a marketing simulation requires that the builder conceptualize and document the structural components of the system and establish probabilities to represent the behavior of the components.[17] The components or units of the marketing simulation represent objects in the marketing system. Depending on the marketing phenomenon under study, the units can be buyers, households, retailers, etc. The variables in the system establish how the units behave. Variables can be price levels, advertising expenditures, product quality, deals, competitive strategy, and so forth. Probabilities are assigned to the units corresponding to their response to the variables. The objective is to make the simulation units imitate the behavior of the marketing system units which they represent. The behavior of these units results in the numerical output, or data, from the simulation. For example, the numerical output could be share of market, sales, or profitability. The parameters of the simulation represent the constraints that can be changed only at the direction of the user. These might be level of advertising, price elasticity, proportion of children in the market, competitive advertising levels, and so forth. Parameters allow the user to experiment with the simulation, explore alternative marketing strategies, and determine the influence of changes in situational factors.

The development of a marketing simulation requires the skills of a specialist and the cooperation of management. The simulation builder's task is to reduce the complex phenomenon under study to manageable proportions while at the same time replicating the interactions found in the marketing system. The inputs to the simulation represent existing data regarding the system and the organization's experience and judgment as to how the system operates. Once the simulation has been constructed, it can be tested to determine whether the output is consistent with the known performance of the actual system being simulated. "A valid simulation model should behave in a manner similar to the underlying phenomena. This is a necessary validation criterion, but alone may not be sufficient to permit us to rely on its predictive abilities."[18]

Developing a simulation can be a complicated process. A central issue concerns the extent to which the simulation should be abstracted from reality. Simulations should neither oversimplify nor overcomplicate. A simulation which is too simple may not be trusted by a decision maker because of its lack of detail or likeness to the real marketing system. However, if it is too complex, the decision maker again may not have confidence in the simulation since it is difficult to understand how it operates. A good

---

[17] This discussion follows that of William D. Wells, "Computer Simulation of Consumer Behavior," in Edward C. Bursk and John F. Chapman (eds.), *Modern Marketing Strategy* (Cambridge, Mass.: Harvard Univ. Press, 1964), pp. 104–115.

[18] Robert C. Meier, Willian T. Newell, and Harold L. Pazer, *Simulation in Business and Economics* (Englewood Cliffs, N.J.: Prentice-Hall, 1969), p. 23.

simulation model should possess the characteristics of being (1) simple enough for easy comprehension and manipulation by the user, (2) reasonably representative of the domain of implications existing in the marketing system, and (3) complex enough to represent accurately the system being studied.[19]

Simulation models can be classified many different ways. One of the more common classifications is based on the management purpose served by the simulation and includes three types: descriptive, predictive, and prescriptive.

A *descriptive simulation model* is one which illustrates or describes the marketing system under investigation.

> Descriptive models are relatively easy to construct but difficult to manipulate. For this reason, the descriptive model is limited in application to the particular situation which it portrays and does not have general applicability to other situations. For the same reason, descriptive models usually do not lend themselves to portraying dynamic situations or causal relationships between variables, although they may sometimes do so. Descriptive models, however, are valuable for obtaining a "feel" for a situation and for providing a stepping stone for the development of other models with more abstract representation.[20]

A *predictive model* is designed to assist in the prediction of the performance of the marketing system when variables in the system change. For example, a simulation of the distribution system for a product might predict the loss of sales and shelf space resulting from an interruption in the supply of the product to wholesalers and retailers. A predictive model is useful in studying the effect of different levels of variables in the system but is limited in that it does not allow for the manipulation of the system for purposes of evaluating new courses of action.

A *prescriptive model* is one that allows the user to experiment with changes in the system. This model permits the evaluation of changes in situational factors (e.g., competitive changes) and of the effects of alternative marketing strategies.

How does simulation differ from other data-gathering methods? Simulation requires that a model of the system be conceptualized, developed, and manipulated. The data obtained from simulation consist of numerical outputs resulting from this model. In contrast, the data obtained from respondents, experiments, and secondary sources result directly from the situation being studied.

What are the advantages of simulation compared with other data sources? It can be less expensive than conducting a survey of respondents or test marketing, and the time required to collect and analyze the data may be less. Simulation can be conducted with complete secrecy within an organization; other data sources may not assure this degree of security. Simulation allows the evaluation of alternative marketing strategies and provides "proof" regarding the superiority of one strategy over another. In addition, the consequences of changes in the marketing system can be evaluated without the risk of making changes in the real system. This allows the evaluation of multiple strategies and encourages creativity in that radical strategy changes can be evaluated.

---

[19] Dimitris N. Chorafas, *Systems and Simulation* (New York: Academic Press, 1965), p. 31.
[20] M. D. Richards and Paul S. Greenlaw, *Management Decision Making* (Homewood, Ill.: Richard D. Irwin, 1966), p. 65.

Simulation can be useful in determining the sensitivity of a strategy option to departures in the initial assumptions. This is called *sensitivity analysis*. Finally, simulation can be used as a training device for members of the organization. Individuals not directly involved in marketing activities may develop an appreciation of how the marketing system operates and how it affects decisions in their areas, e.g., research and development (R&D) or manufacturing.

The limitations of simulation are the difficulty of developing a valid simulation model and the time and cost of updating the model as conditions change. In situations where the organization has limited background and experience regarding the marketing phenomenon under investigation (e.g., new markets), simulation may not be a feasible data source.

Experimentation

Experimentation is a relatively new source of marketing data. The data from an experiment are organized in such a way that relatively unambiguous statements can be made regarding cause-and-effect relationships.

An experiment is conducted when one or more independent variables are consciously manipulated or controlled and their effect on the dependent variable(s) is measured. The objective of an experiment is to measure the effect of the independent variables on a dependent variable, while controlling for other variables that might confuse one's ability to make valid causal inferences. Various experimental designs have been developed to reduce or eliminate the possible influence of extraneous variables on the dependent variable. Chapter 12 deals exclusively with the concept of experimentation and the research designs used in this area.

Secondary Data

There are two general types of marketing data—primary and secondary. *Primary data* are collected specifically for the research needs at hand. *Secondary data* are already published data collected for purposes other than the specific research needs at hand. Consequently, this distinction is defined by the purpose for which the data were collected.

Secondary data can be classified as coming from *internal sources* or *external sources*, the former being available within the organization and the latter originating outside it. External data come from an array of sources such as government publications, trade association data, books, bulletins, reports, and periodicals. Data from these sources are available at minimal cost or free in libraries. The next chapter deals specifically with the data sources available in a library. External data sources not available in a library are usually standardized data which are expensive to acquire. We refer to these data sources as *syndicated sources*. Such sources are predominantly profit-making organizations who provide standardized data to an array of clients. The remainder of this section will discuss internal data sources and syndicated external data sources.

Internal Data   As stated already, these data originate within the organization for which the research is conducted. Internal data collected for purposes other than the research being conducted are *internal secondary data*.

All organizations collect internal data as part of their normal operations. Sales and cost data are recorded, sales reports submitted, advertising and promotion activities recorded, research and development and manufacturing reports made; these are but a few of the data sources available for research purposes within a modern organization. A researcher must be thoroughly familiar with all of these.

Sales and cost data collected for accounting purposes represent particularly promising sources for many research projects. For example, if the research objectives of a project are to evaluate previous marketing activity or to determine the organization's competitive position, sales and cost data can be very helpful.

Many organizations do not collect and maintain sales and cost data in sufficient detail to be used for many research purposes. Sales records should allow for classification by type of customer, payment procedure (cash or credit), product line, sales territory, time period, and so forth. By simple analysis of this type of data the researcher can determine the level and trend in sales, costs, and profitability by customer, territory, and product. More sophisticated analysis could attempt to measure the effect of changes in the marketing program and/or situational variables on sales, costs, and profitability.

The advantages of internal secondary data are their low cost and availability. Unfortunately, many organizations fail to recognize that they have or could have useful internal data available at low cost. These organizations could benefit from specially designed programs to organize and maintain secondary internal data for marketing research purposes.

External Data—Syndicated The growing demand for marketing data has produced a number of companies which collect and sell standardized data designed to serve information needs shared by a number of organizations; the most common are information needs associated with performance-monitoring research.

Syndicated data sources can be classified as (1) consumer data, (2) retail data, (3) wholesale data, (4) industrial data, (5) advertising evaluation data, and (6) media and audience data. The following section presents an overview of the main types of data available in each of these classifications. A more comprehensive listing and discussion of syndicated data sources is provided in the appendix.

Consumer Data Several services collect data from consumers regarding purchases and the circumstances surrounding the purchase. The National Purchase Diary Panel, Inc. (NPD) maintains a panel of 13,000 households who keep diaries in which they record all purchases in 50 food and personal care product categories. The Marketing Research Corporation of America (MRCA) maintains a diary panel of 7500 households who record the significant details regarding the purchase of grocery and personal care products. Panel services of this type provide data on sales by brand, type, flavor, or variety purchased; the quantities bought; the price paid; the store patronized; brand switching; demographic and socioeconomic characteristics of the purchase; and so forth.

Various services survey large groups of consumers regarding purchases and the buying situation. Audits and Surveys, Inc., conducts an annual survey of 5000 consumers who participate in leisure sports and recreational activity. The Gallup Organization, Inc., has an annual survey of 15,000 households about the purchase of consumer goods and services. Trendex, Inc., conducts a quarterly survey of 15,000 households regarding the ownership and acquisition of consumer durables.

The National Menu Census conducted by Marketing Research Corporation of America provides data regarding the consumption of food products in the home. Data are provided on the menu at each meal, snack items, carry-out foods, and so forth.

Numerous services survey consumers' attitudes and opinions regarding consumption behavior and a variety of contemporary topics relevant to marketing. The Gallup Organization, Inc., Louis Harris and Associates, Inc., The Roper Organization, Inc., and Yankelovich, Skelly and White, Inc., conduct large surveys which monitor consumers' attitudes and opinions on a broad range of social, political, and economic issues as well as trends in life-style and consumption patterns. The Survey Research Center, University of Michigan, monitors consumer consumption patterns, attitudes, and intentions as related to financial issues and the purchase of durable goods. Other services monitor consumers' attitudes and opinions regarding the food-shopping process and their awareness levels for brands and advertisements.

Retail Data Numerous services rely on retailing establishments for their data. The data collected focus on the products or services sold through the outlets and/or the characteristics of the outlets themselves. Two of the better-known services are A. C. Nielsen's Retail Index and Audits and Surveys' National Total-Market Audit. The Nielsen Retail Index involves a store audit of supermarkets, drugstores, and mass merchandisers taken every two weeks. The data reported to a client include total sales by product class, sales by brand, and sales of competing brands. Audits and Surveys' National Total-Market Audit provides bimonthly reports which contain data similar to the Nielsen Retail Index. Many of the product categories included in the audit are different from the Nielsen service.

Wholesale Data A growing number of services rely on warehouse shipment data to estimate sales at retail. SAMI (Selling Areas—Marketing, Inc.) is a well-known service to manufacturers who sell through retail food stores. Clients who buy SAMI reports can receive monthly data on the movement of each brand in each of 425 product categories. SAMI data estimate sales of a brand and competitive brands in each of 36 markets. Such data allow the client to analyze trends in sales or package size and the impact of promotions and competitive actions. The Nielsen Retail Index and SAMI are competitive services in that they provide similar data for similar product categories. SAMI reports become available more quickly than Nielsen data, but the latter represent actual retail purchases, whereas SAMI data represent retail orders from the warehouse.

Industrial Data There are substantially more syndicated data services available to consumer goods manufacturers than to industrial goods suppliers. The services available for industrial goods are fairly recent and still evolving; an example is Dun & Bradstreet's "Market Identifiers," which provides data on 390,000 Dun & Bradstreet–rated companies. The data can be used to construct sales prospect lists, identify sales territories, establish sales potentials, and so forth. Other industrial services include *Fortune* magazine's *Input/Output* matrix reports and McGraw-Hill's *Dodge Reports.*

Advertising Evaluation Data Billions of advertising dollars are spent each year on media such as magazines and television with the expectation that these expenditures will result in sales. Consequently, advertisers are interested in data which measure the effectiveness of these expenditures. Our discussion will focus on those services which evaluate advertisements in broadcast and print media.

Several services evaluate advertising in print media. Two of the well-known syndicated readership services are the Starch *Readership Reports* and Gallup and Robinson *Magazine Impact Studies.*

Starch reports measure an advertisement's effectiveness by classifying magazine readership into three groups: (1) those who remember seeing a particular advertisement ("Noted"), (2) those who associated the sponsor's name with the advertisement ("Seen-Associated"), and (3) those who read half or more of its copy ("Read Most"). This evaluation is provided for most consumer magazines and selected business and industrial publications. Starch is the most widely used syndicated readership service.

Gallup and Robinson (G&R) is Starch's major competitor. It uses a more rigorous method in gathering data from magazine readers. G&R first asks the reader to recall and describe advertisements from the closed issue of the magazine, whereas Starch shows the reader the advertisements by turning through the magazine. G&R measures three levels of advertising effectiveness: (1) "Proved Name Registration" (PNR) score, which gives the percentage of readers who remembered the ad and proved its recall by describing the ad; (2) "Idea Playback Profile," a measure of sales message recall; and (3) "Favorable Buying Attitude" score, which measures message persuasiveness. Both Starch and G&B allow the assessment of individual advertisement effectiveness and the tracking of successive campaigns over time.

The services which evaluate television commercials use two basic approaches—the recruited audience method and the normal viewing environment method.

With the recruited audience method, respondents are recruited and brought to a viewing center (theater or mobile viewing laboratory) for purposes of pretesting television commercials. Data are gathered regarding the viewers' attitudes, knowledge, preference, and selection of products. Services which use this approach are McCollum/Spielman Company Audience Studies (ASI), Burgoyne, Inc., PACE (Persuasion and Communication Effectiveness), and Tele-Research, Inc.

With the second approach, the normal viewing environment method, commercials are evaluated in the home. New commercials are pretested by substituting the test commercial for a regular commercial on established programming. This can be done at the network level or in local markets. A sample of viewers is then interviewed to determine the new advertisement's effectiveness. The services which use this approach are AdTel, Ltd.; ARS Division, Research Systems, Inc.; Audience Studies/Com. Lab., Inc.; and Television Testing Company.

Gallup and Robinson, with its Total Prime Time (TPT) Studies, is very prominent in the posttesting of TV commercials. A sample of television viewers are asked to recall their viewing behavior of the previous evening. The recall of sales points and the persuasiveness of the commercial are probed. Two scores—"Commercial Recognition" (CR) and "Proved Commercial Registration" (PCR)—are reported for commercials shown during prime viewing time.

Media and Audience Data   The task of media planner is to identify media that have audience characteristics similar to those of the target market to be reached. The types of data used in matching markets and media typically include demographics, psychographics, and product usage rates. A number of syndicated audience measurement services provide this type of data. The A. C. Nielsen Company and the American Research Bureau provide audience data for television programs. Other services specialize in providing audience measurement data for a particular medium.

The Simmons Market Research Bureau, on the other hand, offers a multimedia service which allows the media planner to compare audience characteristics over an array of media. Simmons describes the audiences of magazines and newspapers and their supplements as well as all network television programs. Audience data are provided on demographic characteristics and usage of products and services.

Media planners need data regarding the advertising effects of competitors. It is important to know how much competitors are spending, where they are spending their advertising dollars, and in what media mix. Several syndicated services provide this type of data.

Perhaps the best-known competitive data service is Leading National Advertisers (LNA). This service monitors over 150,000 ads each year in 86 consumer magazines and 3 national newspaper supplements. Data regarding other media are supplied by services such as BAR (Broadcast Advertisers Report), Media Records, Inc., ACB (Advertising Checking Bureau), and others.

Scanner Data   The age of retail scanner data has arrived. Scanner data represent an improved data source for both retailers and manufacturers. As the number of supermarkets and other retail stores equipped with computerized checkout scanners increases, the resulting proliferation of data will revolutionize packaged goods marketing, retailing, and marketing research.

Scanner data are recorded by passing merchandise over a laser scanner which optically reads the bar-coded description printed on the merchandise. This code is then linked to the current price held in the computer memory, and the amount due is calculated and printed out on an itemized sales slip giving descriptions as well as prices of all items purchased.

In 1980, approximately 2500 U.S. supermarkets had checkout scanners, and that number could rapidly grow to 20,000, representing 66 percent of all U.S. grocery sales.[21] Growth has been driven primarily by potential labor productivity and inventory control improvements. These so-called "hard" benefits will grow even more important as labor and inventory costs continue to increase for retailers.

The "soft" benefits will also contribute to the acceptance of scanners by retailers. These include the use of scanner information to make better decisions in a variety of merchandising areas, such as product assortment, promotion, and pricing. These additional benefits, combined with the expectation that scanner equipment will fall in price relative to labor and inventory cost, suggest that scanners will penetrate a high proportion of retail outlets, including relatively smaller stores.

Advantages of Scanner Data   Scanner data have a number of advantages over the traditional store audit data, such as the Nielsen Retail Index, and warehouse withdrawal data, such as SAMI.[22] First, scanning more accurately measures consumer sales, in that

---

[21] Derek Bloom, "Point of Sale Scanners and Their Implications for Market Research," *Journal of Market Research Society,* vol. 22, no. 4, p. 223, 1981.

[22] "Utilizing UPC Scanning Data for New Product Decisions," *The Nielsen Researcher,* A. C. Nielsen Company, no. 1, 1981, pp. 2-3.

sales are free of breakage and pilferage. In addition, comprehensive historical data are available. Second, scanner data measure consumer sales by specific item. The economics of auditing and reporting often dictate that some items are not audited or that broad categories of items are reported. Contrasted with SAMI data, scanner data measure store-door-delivered merchandise, such as soft drinks, ice cream, and dairy products. Third, scanner data offer fast response reporting systems based on consolidated weekly data. In contrast, A. C. Nielsen generally operates on a bimonthly or monthly basis and SAMI data are reported monthly. Finally, scanner data generate better consumer price information than has previously been available. The remaining major source of discrepancy from actual price would be due to coupons redeemed during the transaction.

Disadvantages of Scanner Data The major limitation of scanner data relates to the restricted coverage across retail store types and geographic areas. Scanner stores are not representative of all stores. With an installation cost of up to $150,000, the typical scanner store is part of a large chain and is located in an upscale neighborhood in a large metropolitan area. In fact, 35 percent of all scanner installations are accounted for by 10 large grocery chains. It has been estimated that "once the percentage of grocery transactions that are scanned passes 30 percent, they will become the basis for the measurement of market sizes and brand shares—since by then it will be practical to draw a sample of scanner stores geographically representative of the top 70 to 80 percent of the grocery trade, on which the fortunes of most packaged goods manufacturers depend."[23] Consequently, scanner data will remain more of a special-use data source and will not immediately be viewed as a substitute for Nielsen or SAMI data.

A second problem has to do with data comparability. Scanner software is often chain-specific, and data are gathered and reported differently for each chain. The "data week," that is, the time period over which the data are recorded, often differs from store to store. Furthermore, sales periods, display periods, and test variables within a given store may not coincide. Test variables must be carefully scheduled to ensure concurrence with the store's data schedule.

Finally, researchers must realize that scanner data may be inaccurate. Not all product categories are always scanned. For example, many flavors of the same item are often purchased at once. If three different flavors of yogurt are being purchased, the checkout clerk may scan the first item three times, or scan it once and then hit the multiply button on the cash register. Occasionally an item won't scan on the first try, and cashiers often key in the price and ignore the bar code. Sometimes individual retailers cut prices to clear the shelves, but the host computer has on file only what was supposed to have been charged. Thus, the marketing researcher has no way of knowing from the scanner data what the customer actually paid.

Scanner data are very useful marketing research tools, but researchers must be aware the costs—in terms of bias, comparability, and accuracy—that accompany the benefits.

Scanning Diary Panels Scanning diary panels involve recruiting shoppers in the market area to participate in the panel. Panel members are compensated for their participation. Each household member is given an ID card which looks like a credit card.

---

[23] Derek Bloom, "Point of Sale Scanners and Their Implications for Marketing Research," p. 225.

The panel member goes to the store and shops normally but presents the ID card at the beginning of the checkout process. The checker keys in the ID number, and each item of that customer's order is isolated and inputted into the computer. The information is stored by day of week and time of day.

There are several advantages in the use of this technique over traditional diary panels.[24] First, there is less selection bias in scanner panels owing to the minimal effort required by the panelists. They simply present their ID card at the checkout counter instead of filling out the lengthy forms of the traditional diary panel. Second, there is less price sensitivity bias in that the panelist is not required to be overly conscious of price levels and changes imposed by the traditional diary recording process. Third, the data are more accurate in that the panelist's memory is not relied upon for the recording of purchases. Fourth, there is a complete record of purchases. Fifth, in-store variables such as pricing, promotions, and displays are part of the data set. Finally, since the diary and sales data come from the same source, there is no need to adjust the diary sales data.

Cable TV   An even more advanced use of scanning combines diary panels with new technologies growing out of the cable TV industry. Diary panel households receive all their at-home television programming via cable relay from the local metropolitan area. Commercials are controlled by means of a cable TV "split." For example, half the households may see commercial A during the 6 P.M. newscast while the other half watches commercial B. A fully automated experimental facility can control and manipulate almost all the components of the marketing plan.[25] For example, it is possible to control the length and character of the product line, pricing, and other in-store conditions. Promotional materials including door-to-door delivery, mail, newspaper features, and TV advertising also can be managed. Copy and ad weight, as well as multiple levels and combinations of those variables, can be tested.

Scanner Data Services   The A. C. Nielsen Company offers its National Scan Track service as a sample projection for all scanner stores doing $4 million or more in retail sales. This service is designed to supplement and eventually replace part of the Nielsen Retail Index. The Newspaper Advertising Bureau offers a service called NABSCAN. This nonprofit service processes scanner data free for retailers and supplies them with confidential monthly reports on brand movement and promotion in their stores contrasted with other stores in the database. The data are also sold to national marketers, and the revenue is divided with retailers on a 50-50 basis. A similar service is provided by Tele-Research, Inc. (TRIM). The TRIM service draws scanner data from larger supermarkets (over $4 million) across the country. TRIM tabulates data at no charge for cooperating stores and shares its revenues from reports sold to national marketers.

The two leading services which combine scanner data, panels, and cable TV systems are Behavior Scan (Information Resources, Inc.) and Adtel Scanner Markets (Burke Marketing Services, Inc.). Behavior Scan has two test-market cities equipped with scanners

---

[24] "Utilizing UPC Scanning Data for New Product Decisions," *The Nielsen Researcher*, A. C. Nielsen Company, no. 1, 1981, pp. 6–7.

[25] General J. Eskin, "Advances in Scanner-Based Research Systems Yield Fast, Accurate New Product Test Results," *Marketing News*, American Marketing Association, Section 2, p. 20, Sept. 18, 1981.

and dual-cable television. Adtel Scanner Markets combines the SAMSCAN scanner store system of Selling Areas–Marketing, Inc., with their dual-cable CATV system. Both of these services provide marketing researchers with a unique controlled laboratory for the manipulating of marketing variables.

MARKETING DECISION SUPPORT SYSTEM (MDSS)

In today's dynamic and competitive business environment, marketing managers find themselves making more frequent and far-reaching decisions. This situation has resulted in growing concern regarding the availability, accuracy, and scope of marketing information for decision making.

Every organization has procedures for acquiring the basic data needed to perform daily activities and assist in the decision-making function. In recent years, many of these procedures have evolved into formal systems for collecting, storing, analyzing, and reporting such data. The introduction of the computer has supported and expanded this trend. From a marketing perspective, we shall refer to this system as a marketing decision support system (MDSS).

MDSS Concept

A *marketing decision support system* is defined as an integrated system of data, statistical analysis, modeling, and display formats using computer hardware and software technology to provide information for the marketing decision-making process. Figure 5-2 presents the MDSS concept. We now turn to a discussion of the components of the marketing decision support systems.

MDSS Components

Marketing decision support systems can be classified into five components: (1) data sources; (2) database management; (3) display; (4) statistical analysis; and (5) modeling.

Data sources represent the backbone of a marketing decision support system. Before developing an MDSS, an organization must review and overhaul its relevant data sources, identifying and organizing them into systematic structures.

As discussed in a previous section, data sources can be classified as internal and external to the organization. An organization's accounting system and sales organization are important internal data sources for a marketing information system. Syndicated services and library sources represent key external data sources.

The organization's accounting system is a critical data source for marketing decision makers.[26] This system contains data regarding sales, inventory levels, cost allocations, accounts receivable, and so on. Such information is important in monitoring the performance of marketing programs and signaling problems and opportunities.

The organization's sales organization is an excellent source of data.[27] Sales personnel can provide data regarding many aspects of the marketing system. They literally are

---

[26] See *Information for Marketing Management*, National Association of Accountants, New York, 1971.

[27] See *Salesmen's Call Reports*, Conference Board Report No. 570, The Conference Board, New York, 1972.

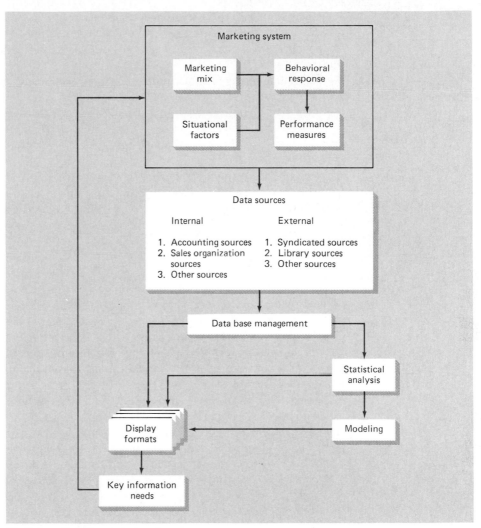

FIGURE 5-2   Marketing decision support system.

the organization's eyes and ears in the marketplace. Data can be provided on (1) number of calls made in a time period; (2) circumstances surrounding the sales call; (3) products used by customers; (4) customer expansion plans; (5) competitive activity; and (6) economic and social trends in an area. Many of these data can be standardized and collected through salespeople's periodically completed call reports.

Data purchased from syndicated services can be a valuable input to the MDSS. As presented in the appendix to this chapter, these services provide an array of data such as (1) consumer sales, (2) warehouse withdrawals, (3) sales by retail outlet, (4) buyer profiles, (5) pricing and point-of-sale promotional data, (6) media characteristics and evaluation, (7) advertising campaign evaluations, (8) economic, social, and demographic trends, (9) prospect lists, and (10) advertisting expenditures in various media. To a substantial degree these data are standardized and can be used for performance-monitoring purposes.

There are a variety of library sources, such as government publications, trade association data, reports, periodicals, and the like. Again, data from these sources are for the most part standardized and can be used for a wide range of information needs.

For a particular organization or industry, other data sources may be as important as those discussed above. For example, valuable data can be provided by an organization's production department and distribution system. Research studies can be conducted periodically to collect standardized data for input to the MDSS.

Database management involves capturing relevant marketing data from an array of data sources, establishing common time frames, determining the appropriate level of detail, and putting the data in an accessible form. This component of MDSS is very critical and difficult to accomplish.

Display formats allow marketing people to access the database. More specifically, they must be able to retrieve and manipulate the data easily and quickly. Required capabilities range from simple ad hoc retrieval to more formal displays that monitor product performance or flag problem areas using exception reports. Such reports could involve the use of a graphics display. A graphics display package should include a wide range of options, from time-series plots to bar and pie charts to scatterplots for comparing two measures, such as advertising expenditures and brand awareness. With the latest display software, marketers can move from one data display to another in a user-friendly environment.

Statistical analysis involves manipulating data such as arithmetic calculations and performing statistical operations such as standard deviation and regression. Statistical analysis can bring insight regarding relationships among marketing data and better understanding of marketing issues. Such manipulations are required for the modeling of advertising, new product introductions, and pricing and distribution systems.

Modeling involves developing a representation of how marketing phenomena behave. Such models may be implicit in the manager's mind and used as theories about the marketing system to determine what data to look at and what manipulations of them are meaningful to the decision at hand. Models can be made explicit in the form of mathematical and computational representation. In applying marketing data to the model, they can be transformed into approximate representations of the marketing phenomena under investigation. With such a model, marketing decisions can be tested against the model to determine what outcomes are likely.

MDSS Stages

MDSS typically evolve from a performance-monitoring, or tracking, system to a more sophisticated system where the association among variables is studied (linkage system), and finally to a more complex system with modeling capability. We will briefly review this evolution.

The first stage of MDSS evolution involves establishing an effective database and display capability. This *monitoring* stage addresses the question: What is happening to my business? It reports on areas such as sales levels, share of market, and daily production and inventory levels. The output of this system generally requires the data to be manipulated in order to meet the management information needs. This data manipulation may involve the calculation of means, proportions, or indexes. Typically the system allows the data to be presented in various display formats.

The second stage is a *linkage system* where the association among variables can be studied. This stage addresses the more complex question: What causes my business to behave as it does? Sophisticated statistical procedures are required to answer this question.

The third stage involves *modeling*. This is the most sophisticated phase of MDSS evolution. It addresses the question: What would happen if . . . ? Models have been developed to represent new product acceptance, advertising effectiveness, sales force performance, and pricing-revenue relationships.

MDSS Attributes

The output of an MDSS must have certain attributes if it is to be useful for decision-making purposes.[28] These include (1) timeliness—the information must be available when needed; (2) flexibility—the information must be available in varied formats and in detail so that the specific information needs of alternative decision situations can be served; (3) inclusiveness—the information must cover the entire range of information needs; (4) accuracy—the accuracy of the information must fit the needs of the decision situation; and (5) convenience—the information must be easily accessible to the decision maker and presented in a clear and usable manner.

MDSS Current Status

The growing acceptance of the computer in the business community and its significant achievements in data processing and analysis created a movement which advocated an idealized MDSS concept—a total system which encompasses a significant proportion of the information requirements of the decision maker. This excitement was soon dampened by the practical difficulties of implementing such a concept.[29]

Part of the problem with the idealized MDSS concept relates to the failure of its proponents to recognize that the information needs of decision makers are varied, often complicated, and specific to the skills, knowledge, experience, and personality of the decision maker.[30] No simple combination of data inputs and information out-

---

[28] Ibid., pp. 11–13.

[29] Russell L. Ackoff, "Management Misinformation Systems," *Management Science*, vol. 14, no. 4, December 1967; John Dearden, "MIS Is a Mirage," *Harvard Business Review*, vol. 50, no. 1, pp. 90–99, January–February 1972.

[30] Henry Mintzberg, "The Manager's Job: Folklore and Fact," *Harvard Business Review*, vol. 53, no. 4, pp. 49–61, July–August 1975.

puts is going to meet a significant proportion of the decision maker's requirements for information. This becomes more of a problem the higher the decision maker is in the organization.

Several companies are making progress with systems designed to serve the information needs of middle and lower management. The key lessons learned by those developing these systems are as follows:[31]

• Thoroughly understand what information is needed by management and build systems consistent with these needs.

• While retrieval systems are important, systems with analysis capabilities are more important to managers.

• If the database does not contain the key data needed by management, the whole system is doomed to failure.

• Managers do express a need for models. Some can be prepackaged while others are ad hoc.

• A computer science intermediary is needed to interface between the manager and the system. Rarely will the manager use the system directly.

• The systems must respond to management's request for information very, very quickly. Slow systems result in nonusage by management.

John D. C. Little, a leading researcher in the MDSS area, foresees the following trends:[32]

• An order-of-magnitude increase in the amount of marketing data used
• A similar tenfold increase in computer power available for marketing analysis
• Widespread adoption of analytic computer languages
• A shift from market status reporting to market response reporting
• New methodology for supporting strategy development
• A shortage of marketing scientists

While significant progress is being made in the development of marketing decision support systems, many hurdles must be overcome before reaching the final goal.[33] Presently, we appear to be at a more intermediate stage previously defined as the marketing research system (see Chapter 1). The marketing research system includes many of the diverse data sources found in an MDSS but does not have the degree of structure and interactive people-machine concepts found in the complete MDSS concept. The objective of a marketing research system is to become an information center for marketing decision making by using a combination of research approaches and philosophies which fit the special needs of the organization and individual decision makers.

---

[31] John D. C. Little, "Decision Support Systems for Marketing Managers," *Journal of Marketing,* vol. 43, pp. 9–26, Summer 1979.

[32] Ibid., p. 25.

[33] Charles D. Schewe, "Management Information Systems in Marketing—A Promise Not Yet Realized," *Management Informatics,* vol. 3, no. 5, 1974.

SUMMARY

1 A research design is the basic plan which guides the data collection and analysis phases of the research project. An effective design assures that the information gathered is consistent with the research objectives and that the data collection and analysis phases involve accurate and economical procedures.

2 The research design for exploratory research is best characterized by its lack of structure and its flexibility. The data collection and analysis strategy is one of diversity and searching in new directions until new ideas or better ideas can no longer be discovered. It facilitates the development of hypotheses regarding potential problems and/or opportunities.

3 Conclusive research provides information for the evaluation of alternative courses of action. It can be subclassified into descriptive and causal research.

4 Descriptive research characterizes marketing phenomena, determines the association among variables, and predicts future marketing phenomena. It is characterized by a carefully planned and structured research design. A cross-sectional design or survey research design is typically used in descriptive research projects. This design involves taking a sample of population elements at one point in time. The evidence provided by descriptive research can be very useful in evaluating courses of action when combined with the decision maker's implicit model of how the marketing system functions.

5 Causal research is designed to gather evidence regarding cause-and-effect relationships. The appropriate research designs vary substantially in complexity and in the degree of ambiguity present in the evidence regarding causality. With causal research, the research design may directly evaluate the alternative courses of action under consideration.

6 Performance-monitoring research provides evidence regarding the monitoring of the marketing system. It can involve either an ad hoc study or a continuous program of research. Continuous performance monitoring typically requires a longitudinal research design which is often called a panel design. In this design, a fixed sample of population elements is measured repeatedly. In a traditional panel, the same variables are measured every time, as opposed to an omnibus panel where different variables are measured each time. In both types of panels, the sample of respondents remains fixed.

7 The basic sources of marketing data are (1) respondents, (2) analogous situations, (3) experiments, and (4) secondary data.

8 There are two main types of data from respondents—those obtained by communication and those obtained by observation. Communication requires the respondent to actively provide data through verbal responses, while observation involves the recording of the respondent's behavior.

9 The study of analogous situations includes the study of case histories and simulations. With the case history approach, there is an intensive investigation of situations which are relevant to a particular problem setting. With simulation, an analog or likeness of a real world phenomenon is created. Simulation models can be classified as descriptive, predictive, and prescriptive.

10 Experimentation calls for the organization of data in such a way as to permit relatively unambiguous statements regarding cause-and-effect relationships.

11 Secondary data are data collected for purposes other than the specific research needs at hand. Internal secondary data are those available within the organization, whereas external secondary data are provided by sources outside the organization. The latter can be classified into library sources and syndicated sources.

12 External syndicated data sources are predominantly profit-making organizations that provide standardized data. Such data can be classified into (1) consumer data, (2) retail data, (3) wholesale data, (4) industry data, (5) advertising evaluation data, (6) media and audience data, and (7) scanner data.

13 A marketing decision support system is defined as an integrated system of data, statistical, modeling, and display formats using computer hardware and software technology to provide information for the marketing decision-making process. An organization's accounting system and sales organization are important internal data sources, while syndicated services and library sources are key external data sources for an MDSS. The five components of an MDSS are: (1) data sources; (2) database management; (3) display; (4) statistical analysis; and (5) modeling. The output of an MDSS should have the attributes of timeliness, flexibility, inclusiveness, accuracy, and convenience. The current status of the MDSS is marked by growing acceptance of the staged evolution of more customized decision support systems but limited acceptance of the idealized MDSS concept.

DISCUSSION QUESTIONS

1 Discuss the nature and role of research design in marketing research.
2 What type of research design is associated with exploratory research?
3 Why is exploratory research often utilized in the initial steps of the decision process?
4 What is descriptive research?
5 How does the research design in descriptive research differ from that in exploratory research?
6 How does the cross-sectional design differ from the longitudinal design?
7 What role does an implicit causal model play in descriptive research?
8 What are the objectives of performance-monitoring research?
9 What advantages does the longitudinal design offer relative to the cross-sectional design?
10 What problems are associated with longitudinal designs?
11 Discuss the four basic sources of marketing data.
12 What is the primary distinction between qualitative and quantitative research?
13 What are the benefits and limitations of simulation?
14 What is meant by a "syndicated source"?
15 What types of data are available from syndicated data sources?
16 What is the role of a marketing information system within an organization?
17 What attributes should MDSS output possess?
18 What is the current state of the MDSS concept?

APPENDIX: Syndicated Sources of Marketing Data

The purpose of this appendix is to catalog the leading syndicated sources of marketing data. For each service, the name of the sponsoring organization, the name of the service, and a brief abstract are presented. Because of the evolving nature of syndicated services and the rapid entry and withdrawal of services, omissions and inaccuracies are unavoidable. More detailed and contemporary information regarding a particular service can be obtained by contacting the organization directly. For information on how to contact these data services, consult such publications as the American Marketing Association's *International Directory of Marketing Research Houses and Services* (Greenbook), AMA—New York Chapter, 420 Lexington Ave., New York, NY 10017, or *Bradford's Directory of Marketing Research Agencies and Management Consultants in the U.S. and the World*, P.O. Box 276, Dept. A, Fairfax, VA 22030.

The data services have been classified as follows:

A Consumer Data: Purchase and Consumption Patterns
B Consumer Data: Attitudes, Opinions, and Behavior Patterns
C Retail Data
D Wholesale Data
E Industrial Data
F Advertising Evaluation Data: Broadcast Media
G Advertising Evaluation Data: Print Media
H Media and Audience Data: Media-Market Fit
I Media and Audience Data: Competitive Efforts

A. CONSUMER DATA: PURCHASE AND CONSUMPTION PATTERNS

A.1 *Organization:* Audits and Surveys Company, Inc.
  Service: National Sportsman's Consumer Audit

This is an annual survey which provides data regarding consumer participation in leisure sports and recreation activity, plus buying patterns and brand preferences. The data are cross-classified by demographic and media characteristics. The sample size is 5000 and the sampling unit consists of males age 15 years and over. The data are gathered by telephone interviews.

A.2 *Organization:* MRCA (Market Research Corporation of America) Information Services, Inc.
  Service: Menu Census

The Menu Census is an ongoing consumer food usage information service with over 20 years of comparative data on preparation and consumption habits of the people who use products at home and away from home. Over 20,000 specific food items are tracked by Menu Census in 2000 households (totaling more than 5500 individual consumers) on a continuous basis.

A.3 *Organization:* MRCA Information Services, Inc.
  Service: National Consumer Panel

The NCP database contains very specific cross-referenced data on actual consumer purchases in over 50 categories of prepared foods, household products, and health and beauty aids. This diary-based data bank contains a wealth of reliable information—everything needed to track and analyze the behavior of a single household or an entire market, over time, and on time—within 10 days of when it happens.

A.4 *Organization:* NPD Research, Inc.
  Service: National Purchase Diary Panels (NPD)

This panel is composed of 50,000 households who report monthly; 15,000 are nationally representative, and the other 35,000 are concentrated in 25 selected local markets. Preprinted diaries are used to record household purchasing activities. The data pertain to products purchased frequently in 50 food and personal care product categories: brand name purchased, data, price, store name, special price offer, and so forth. Extensive socioeconomic and demographic characteristics exist for each household. Other industries reported on are: restaurant, toy, textile, gasoline, and record and tape.

A.5   *Organization:* Trendex, Inc.
   Service: Trendex Buyership Service

This survey is conducted quarterly. The data concern the purchase or acquisition of consumer durables and allow the tracking of durable purchasing patterns. The sample size is 70,000 households, which allows reliable estimates of low-purchase-frequency durable goods. Telephone interviews are employed.

B. CONSUMER DATA: ATTITUDES, OPINIONS, AND BEHAVIOR PATTERNS

B.1   *Organization:* Burgoyne, Inc.
   Service: Burgoyne Consumer Surveys

In testing merchandising alternatives, this in-store consumer survey zeros in on the people who are actually buying your test products in order to measure on-the-spot reactions to merchandising and product innovations. These are far more revealing than random interviews by phone or door-to-door calls.

B.2   *Organization:* The Gallup Organization, Inc.
   Service: The Gallup Omnibus

This is a survey conducted at 3-week intervals. The data involve attitudes and opinions on a variety of contemporary topics. Trends are analyzed from questions which are repeatedly asked on each survey. The data can be cross-classified with demographic and socioeconomic characteristics. The sample size is 1500 households, and the sampling unit is an adult. In addition, other omnibus services are available including the Hispanic Consumer Omnibus and the College Student Omnibus.

B.3   *Organization:* Louis Harris and Associates, Inc.
   Service: Harris Survey

This is a reprint of the column written three times a week by Louis Harris and syndicated through the Chicago *Tribune*–New York *Daily News* Syndicate. Surveys are conducted nationwide, approximately monthly, on a wide variety of public affairs issues. Occasionally, the survey deals with consumer issues and consumer purchase intentions. Sample size is usually 1500 adults.

B.4   *Organization:* The Roper Organization, Inc.
   Service: Roper Reports

This survey is conducted 10 times a year, monitoring public opinion and consumer behavior on a broad range of existing and emerging social, political, and economic subjects and issues, as well as the public's interests in and attitudes toward various services, products, and lifestyles. The sample size is 2000 men and women, age 18 and up. Personal interviews are conducted.

B.5   *Organization:* Survey Research Center, University of Michigan
   Service: Survey of Consumer Finances

From 1946 to 1970, the Survey Research Center, with the support of the Federal Reserve Board, conducted an annual Survey of Consumer Finances. These surveys are now updated and enlarged periodically and provide cross-sectional and trend data on the distribution of assets, debts, durable goods, and financial transactions among American families. The surveys include 2500 personal interviews. The reporting frequency is irregular.

B.6 *Organization:* Survey Research Center, University of Michigan
      Service: Survey of Consumer Attitudes

This survey provides data regarding consumer consumption patterns, attitudes, and intentions as related to personal finances, business conditions, and market conditions for housing, automobiles, and durables as well as topics of particular timeliness and interest. The Index of Consumer Sentiment, an overall measure of consumer attitudes toward the economy, is developed from these data. Seven hundred households are interviewed by telephone each month. Reports and data books are available monthly.

B.7 *Organization:* Yankelovich, Skelly and White, Inc.
      Service: Yankelovich, Skelly and White Monitor (VALS)

This survey is conducted annually. The data include statistics on over 40 social trends which measure the country's mood and outlook on life. Annual changes in these trends are analyzed by demographic and socioeconomic segments. The sample consists of 2500 households. The data are collected by personal interview. Implications relative to the marketing of consumer products and services are discussed.

B.8 *Organization:* Opinion Research Corporation
      Service: Public Opinion Index

The index is a continuing program of attitude research to help companies deal with the problems and opportunities of fast-moving social, economic, and political trends affecting business now and in the future. The index regularly tracks, analyzes, and interrelates changes in opinion among members of the general public and many target groups, including members of Congress, federal regulatory officials, union leaders, corporate social activists, and the Washington press corps. Reports, issued monthly, present data graphically and contain "Implications for Management."

B.9 *Organization:* Opinion Research Corporation
      Service: Corporate Reputations Survey

This survey covers 2000 adults' familiarity/favorability/image of 20 major industries, 60 major companies; a custom questions option is available. Included are long-term trend data on attitudes toward business and related subjects.

B.10 *Organization:* Opinion Research Corporation
      Service: Caravan Surveys

Three services are offered: (1) a semimonthly survey by way of telephone interviews with a probability sample of 1000 adults nationwide; (2) a quarterly survey by way of personal interviews with 500 top and middle-management executives in the 1000 largest industrial companies; (3) a semiannual survey by way of telephone interviews with 500 executives in midsize companies.

C. RETAIL DATA

C.1 *Organization:* Audits and Surveys, Inc.
      Service: Retail Census of Product Distribution

This study of products and brands is based on personal interviews and inspections conducted in some 40,000 retail outlets. The data focus on the number of kinds of outlets in the United States carrying various product categories and the specific brands in stock. The data are analyzed by city size, geographic region, type of outlet, annual store volume, and chain versus independent. The product categories could include automotive supplies, electrical appliances, household products, food, health and beauty aids, photographic supplies, tobacco, and writing instruments. The reporting frequency is annual, and the study results are projectable to all U.S. retail outlets.

C.2   *Organization:* Audits and Surveys, Inc.
    Service: National Total-Market Audit

This service provides bimonthly retail (consumer) sales, retail distribution, and retailer inventory for product categories such as automotive, electrical, food, tobacco, photographic, health and beauty aids, household products, and writing instruments. The service provides data on market size and market shares; sales by outlet type, region, and size of city; inventory levels, and percentage of distribution and out-of-stock situations. Retail stores are the sampling units, and the sample size is 5000. The study results are projectable to all U.S. retail outlets.

C.3   *Organization:* Audits and Surveys, Inc.
    Service: National Restaurant Market Index

This service provides data on the commercial restaurant market. Trained enumerators personally call on a national probability sample of 6000 restaurants, projectable to all commercial restaurants in the United States. The clients of this service are institutional food product distributors. The service provides data by product category on brand usage, package sizes, and product types. The data are reported separately for five restaurant types, nine geographic regions, and six city sizes or client sales regions. The reporting frequency is annual.

C.4   *Organization:* Audits and Surveys, Inc.
    Service: Selling-Areas Distribution Index

This service is designed to provide companies using SAMI (warehouse withdrawals to food stores—see next section) with measurement of in-store conditions important in evaluating warehouse movement data. For example, the service reports on number of facings, shelf price, promotional activity, and so forth. The sampling units are 2375 supermarkets in all 38 SAMI areas. The reporting frequency is bimonthly.

C.5   *Organization:* Burgoyne, Inc.
    Service: In-store Observation Systems

This service combines an in-store observation and reporting system with panels composed of store managers (over $20,000 weekly volume). The panel data are available by area and store type to tie in with the audit data. Reporting frequency is monthly. The observed measurements include shelf position, out-of-stock, average price, shelf facings, package type, P.O.P. displays, age of stock, and condition of product.

C.6   *Organization:* Ehrhart-Babic Group
    Service: National Retail Tracking Index, Inc.

This service provides syndicated in-store distribution data in six types of retail outlets in all SAMI areas, over 8000 stores in total.

C.7   *Organization:* Ehrhart-Babic Group
    Service: Ehrhart-Babic Associates, Inc.

This service provides custom in-store research in all types of retail outlets. Services include trended and projectable sales audits, controlled store tests, mini-markets, custom distribution studies, product purchases, and new product introduction performance data.

C.8   *Organization:* Information Resources, Inc.
    Service: Behavior Scan

This service provides multiple test marketing capability with a highly controlled testing environment by installing its own checkout scanners, recruiting panel members, and measuring different advertising strategies and weight by cable TV split viewing. The system can identify a family's purchases by price, brand, and size and then relate this information to various promotional tools.

C.9   *Organization:* NABSCAN USA, Inc.
    Service: National Scanning Services, Inc. (NSS)

This service processes scanner data collected from participating supermarkets every week. Participating chains/stores are contrasted with activity in all stores participating. The data are sold to national and regional marketers. Subscribers receive weekly product movement and retail price data. The data are utilized to track advertising and promotion programs on a market basis along with the basic brand performance measurements.

C.10   *Organization:* A. C. Nielsen Company
    Service: ERIM

This service competes directly with Information Resources' Behavior Scan. Consumer buying habits and effectiveness of commercials are measured by comparing store purchases with advertising beamed to cable and noncable TV participants' homes. The information is collected by entering a participant's card in a store cash register each time a purchase is made. This service is in operation at present in two markets.

C.11   *Organization:* A. C. Nielsen Company
    Service: National Scan Track

This service provides clients with a sample projection to the national scanner universe of supermarkets doing $4 million or more retail sales. Scanner data are combined with regular staff visits to supermarkets to monitor displays and other in-store promotions. Weekly reports are available.

C.12   *Organization:* A. C. Nielsen Company
    Service: Nielsen Retail Index

This service involves a store audit of 1300 supermarkets, 700 drugstores, and 150 mass merchandisers taken every 2 months. The types of data provided include share of market, prices, displays, inventory, and promotional efforts. Nielsen retail indexes are available for grocery, drug, pharmaceutical, confectionery, liquor, appliance, perfume, and photographic products.

C.13   *Organization:* TRIM, Inc. (Division of Harte-Hanks Communications, Inc.)
    Service: TRIM In-Store Testing; SALESCAN; TELE-SCAN

Services designed to analyze sales movement information from grocery and drug chains for manufacturers, advertising agencies, and retailers. SALESCAN is a proprietary set of PC software designed to integrate scanner data with in-store causal information, such as feature ads, reduced prices, displays, and margins.

D. WHOLESALE DATA

D.1   *Organization:* A. C. Nielsen Company
    Service: Nielsen Early Intelligence Service

This service collects data from warehouses concerning movement of new products through 150 food chains and independent warehouses. The reporting frequency is bimonthly.

D.2   *Organization:* Pipeline Research, Inc.
    Service: National Drug Warehouse Audit

This service audits the warehouse movement and inventories of drug products through major drug chains and independent drug wholesalers. The reporting frequency is monthly.

D.3   *Organization:* P-O-S Research, Inc.
    Service: Warehouse Withdrawal Brand Movement Data

P-O-S audits the warehouse movement of products sold through food store distribution, including grocery, frozen, dairy, household, non-foods/health and beauty aids. Two services are offered:

(1) National RE-CON Service furnishing national data from a select "blue-ribbon panel" of high-volume distributors. RE-CON provides national sales data detailed by brand, size, item, and trend line. Reports are provided semiannually and show cumulative movement including national case sales, national retail dollar sales or tonnage, and national shares of market. (2) Individual market service furnishes exclusive warehouse withdrawal coverage in 24 small and medium-sized markets. It can be used for measuring new product tests, media-level spending tests, etc. Reports are delivered every 4 weeks.

D.4   *Organization:* Selling Areas—Marketing, Inc. (Subsidiary of Time Inc.)
    Service: SAMI Reports

This service audits the warehouse movement of products through food chains, co-ops and wholesalers servicing independent food stores. The sample size varies by market ranging from 4 to 25 food operators with an average market coverage factor in excess of 70 percent of all commodity volume. There are 54 major market areas reported on, representing more than 85 percent of total U.S. food store volume. Four hundred and fifty different product categories are monitored, and data are available on volume (dollars, units, poundage, cases, and other appropriate tonnage equivalents). Data can be provided on an individual market basis, markets by group or by region, or on a projected total U.S. basis. Reports are issued 13 times a year, each covering 28-day periods.

    SAMI also provides online access to data in all categories reported (SOLO-SAMI Online Operations), distribution data based upon shipments to specified food outlets (SARDI-SAMI Retail Distribution Index), and store-by-store point-of-sale data in key markets where electronic scanning has achieved a high level of penetration.

E. INDUSTRIAL DATA

E.1   *Organization:* Dun & Bradstreet, Inc.
    Service: Dun's Marketing Services

Dun's Marketing Services provides comprehensive market planning and information services to business-to-business marketers and publishes reference directories for business planners and information specialists. DMS's Industrial Marketing Services are designed to help managers develop targeted marketing programs—which analyze potential markets (domestic and international), identify likely prospects, and deliver an effective sales message to the right audience. DMS's Business Reference Publications provide extensive information on U.S. and foreign businesses and business executives to serve a wide variety of planning and reference needs. DMS delivers its services in hard copy (books, sales prospecting cards, mailing labels, personalized computer letters, and analytical reports), on computer-readable media (magnetic tape and personal computer diskettes), or via online transmission.

E.2   *Organization:* McGraw-Hill Information Systems Company
    Service: Dodge Reports: Dodge Construction Potential

This service collects data from 165,000 building material manufacturers and distributors, and from governmental and educational institutions. The data, useful in the marketing of building products, cover public and private contract totals by type and number of projects, square feet, and dollar value. Possible geographic classifications include counties, metropolitan areas, states, and individual sales territories. The reporting frequency is monthly.

E.3   *Organization:* McGraw-Hill Publications Company, Department of Economics
    Service: Annual Survey of U.S. Business' Plans for New Plants and Equipment

This service surveys about 900 industrial or commercial companies regarding planned capital investments. Thirty major industries are reported for the coming 4-year period. The data are collected by mail questionnaire, and the reporting frequency is annual.

E.4 *Organization:* R. L. Polk & Company
  Service: Motor Statistics

The Motor Statistical Division, using state motor vehicle registration records, compiles statistical information on both new vehicle registration and the total number of vehicles registered each year in the United States and Canada. Reports on new vehicles registered by make and model are compiled monthly, with counts available for the entire United States as well as by state, county, city and town, census tract, and other designated market areas. An annual census of all registered vehicles is compiled as of July 1 each year. More detailed reports are also compiled showing engine size, body style, and other information.

F. ADVERTISING EVALUATION DATA: BROADCAST MEDIA

F.1 *Organization:* AdTel, Ltd (Division of Burke International Research Corp.)
  Service: AdTel

This service measures the sales response over a period of time that results from alternative television commercials and consumer promotions. A dual-cable CATV system and two balanced consumer purchase diary panels of 1000 households each are used as controls for variables other than those being tested. The panel members keep a diary of the products purchased every week. The impact that a particular television commercial has on sales can be determined by comparing panel sales results. In addition, AdTel can track buying habits of both test and control groups with supermarket scanner systems.

F.2 *Organization:* Research Systems Corporation
  Service: ARS—Advertising Research Service

This copy-testing service assesses the impact of television advertising on consumer behavior by simulating the advertising process. From 400 to 600 randomly selected respondents preview pilot programs and commercials via closed-circuit television monitors. Pre- and posttest measures of brand preferences are taken at the beginning and end of each preview. Three days later, respondents are telephoned to determine delayed recall. The reliability of persuasion and recall measures is established by automatically retesting every nth commercial within 1 to 3 weeks of actual testing. The validity of these measures is established by comparisons with actual consumer behavior studies in controlled markets.

F.3 *Organization:* Research Systems Corporation
  Service: ACE_{sm} (Advertising Competitive Effectiveness)

A unique syndicated tracking service providing competitive advertising effectiveness/elasticity data three times a year. ACE_{sm} measures the selling power of the TV advertising aired by competitive brands.

F.4 *Organization:* Audience Studies/Com. Lab, Inc.
  Service: ASI Tests

This service is very similar in data collection and reporting procedures to ARS Division, Research Systems, Inc. discussed above. The sample is composed of 100 subscribers to one of two cable TV systems. The data are based on recalling seeing the commercial and unaided recalling of copy details.

F.5 *Organization:* Gallup and Robinson, Inc.
  Service: In-View

This service pretests rough or finished commercials on a weekly basis. The sample is drawn from three ADI (Pittsburgh, Louisville, San Diego) and is composed of 150 men and/or 150 women, aged 18–49. The audience is recruited in advance to watch the normal program braodcast and then interviewed 24 hours after exposure to measure recall and persuasiveness.

F.6   *Organization:* Television Testing Company
    Service: Commercial Pretesting
This service uses about 400 cable TV households to determine a commercial's impact on brand awareness and intention to purchase. The data are collected by telephone interviews.

G. ADVERTISING EVALUATION DATA: PRINT MEDIA

G.1   *Organization:* Chilton Company
    Service: Chilton Ad-Chart Services
This service evaluates the effectiveness of advertisements in magazines. The sample includes about 100 subscribers to the publication. A personal or telephone interview is used to determine the degree to which the subscribers noticed and/or were informed by the advertising or editorial content of the publication. The data are grouped by product category and purchase influence groups. Over 70 issues are studied annually. This service conducts Ad-Analysis studies for tutorial-"how-to" type publications with readership scores for Noticed, Started to Read, Read Half or More, and Informative level. Ad-Action studies conducted for tabloid publications also determine what actions readers may have taken as a result of reading the ad. Ad-Access is a quick, convenient, up-to-date online five-year database of Ad-Analysis and Ad-Action results.

G.2   *Organization:* Gallup and Robinson, Inc.
    Service: Magazine Impact Research Services (MIRS)
This service evaluates the effectiveness of advertisements in magazines. The sample includes 150 readers of the magazine type (news, women's wear, etc). The study method used is personal placement of the publication (in 10–20 SMSA) and a telephone interview the following day. Three levels of effectiveness are measured: (1) percentage of readers who remembered the ad, (2) sales message recall, and (3) message persuasiveness.

G.3   *Organization:* Harvey Research Organization, Inc.
    Service: The Harvey Communication Measurement Service
This service evaluates the effectiveness of advertisement in magazines. A sample of 100 readers is interviewed to determine the effectiveness of the advertising and editorial content of the publication. Open-ended questions are used to probe for ideas and impressions about the advertising. Another service, AD-Q Studies, uses a mailed questionnaire to perform the same function.

G.4   *Organization:* Majers Corporation
    Service: Grocery Ad Book
This service provides a visual overview of the advertising of major grocery chains across the nation in the top 50 markets. Copies of the actual advertising are included along with each advertiser's share of retail food volume in their metropolitan area. The country is divided into four regions. The service is available weekly, biweekly, or monthly.

G.5   *Organization:* Readex Research
    Service: Readership Studies
Readex measures readership of advertising and editorial material in magazines. An *n*th name selection of readers indicates which items in the test issue have been "found to be of interest." Publishers and advertisers then receive final reports indicating the percent of total responents marketing items of interest. Reports are based on the first 100 usable returns in addition to studies measuring reader interest in Ad Component Rating. This determines reader reaction to specific aspects of an ad's headline, illustration, and text. Other services include custom-designed research projects.

G.6 *Organization:* Daniel Starch and Staff, Inc.

Service: Starch Message Report

This service evaluates the effectiveness of advertisements in general magazines, business publications, and newspapers. Sample sizes per issue range from 100 to 150 adult males (aged 18 and over) plus the same number of adult females. A personal interview is used to determine those who remember seeing a particular ad, those who associated the sponsor's name with the ad, and those who read half or more of the copy. The data are reported on a weekly or monthly frequency, depending on the publication.

G.7 *Organization:* Gallup and Robinson, Inc.

Service: RAM (Rapid Ad Measurement)

This service is used to pretest magazine ads. It is done on a weekly basis with *People* magazine as the vehicle. The sample is composed of 150 men and/or 150 women from 10 major markets. Evaluative measures same as MIRS (see above).

H. MEDIA AND AUDIENCE DATA: MEDIA-MARKET FIT

H.1 *Organization:* The Arbitron Ratings Company

Services: Arbitron Radio Local Market Reports

Arbitron Television Local Market Reports

Arbitron Television Meter Reports

Condensed Radio Market Reports

Nationwide Radio Report

Syndicated Program Analysis

ADI Viewing Allocation Report

Network Program Analysis

County Coverage (Radio and Television)

Arbitrends Microcomputer Delivered Audience Estimates

Arbitron Television Information on Demand

Arbitron Radio Information on Demand

Consumer Lifestyle Audience Estimates

Arbitron measures viewing and listening audiences in 210 television and 269 radio markets nationwide. The information collected in diaries or by meters is reported in terms of sex and age demographic characteristics. Sample sizes range from 450 to 8000. All radio markets are measured from 12 weeks up to 48 weeks each year. The New York, Chicago, Los Angeles, Boston, Washington D.C., Miami, Detroit, Dallas, Houston, San Francisco, and Philadelphia television markets are measured continuously while all other markets are measured at least 4 months out of every year.

H.2 *Organization:* Audit Bureau of Circulations

Service: ABC Audit Reports

Semiannual publisher's statements from member newspapers, business publications, consumer magazines, and farm publications are verified or corrected through annual field audits and the resulting ABC Audit Reports. Services also include: Circulation Data Bank, Supplementary Data Reports, quarterly FAS-FAX reports, annual Magazine Trend Reports, semiannual Blue Books, and Advertising Coupon Distribution Verification Services.

H.3 *Organization:* A. C. Nielsen Company

Service: Nielsen Television Index

This service provides estimates of the size and nature of the audience for individual television programs. The data are collected by an audimeter device attached to the television receiver.

Data are available on the program's audience size and characteristics, viewing habits, switching, and so on. The sample size is over 1000 TV households. The frequency of reporting is both weekly and semiannual. Another service available is the Nielsen Station Index which measures television station audiences in over 200 local markets and provides season-to-season reports on viewing by time periods and programs.

H.4   *Organization:* Marketing Evaluations, Inc.
   Service: Performer Q

An annual survey of over 1100 personalities measuring the familiarity and popularity of each among large national samples. Used for selecting spokespeople for commercials and casting of series, specials, hosts, and guest stars.

H.5   *Organization:* Simmons Market Research Bureau, Inc.
   Service: Study of Media and Markets

This service reports on media exposure and product-usage behavior. The data include readership and exposure to magazines, newspapers, television, radio, and outdoor billboards. These data are cross-referenced with product-usage, demographic, and socioeconomic characteristics. The national probability sample includes 15,000 adult males and females. The data are collected through a series of interactions with the respondents, using personal interviews, a self-administered questionnaire, and a personal viewing diary. The reporting frequency is annual.

H.6   *Organization:* Lee Slurzberg Research, Inc.
   Service: LSR National Black Omnibus

This service reports on magazine readership of the U.S. black adult population. The service covers 16 major magazines and selected general magazines and includes data on demographic and socio-economic characteristics. The sample size is 1000 black adults in urban areas who are interviewed personally. The reporting frequency is quarterly.

H.7   *Organization:* Mediamark Research, Inc.
   Service: Mediamark Report

This service reports on magazine audiences. MRI executes an ongoing survey of the U.S. population and their media and consumer usage characteristics. The annual sample of 20,000 adults is conducted in two waves, and reports are published every six months (April and October) using a 12-month moving average. All basic media usage information (except TV programs) is single-source, collected in the personal interview. Product usage and TV program viewing are collected in a personally placed and picked up self-administered questionnaire.

I. MEDIA AND AUDIENCE DATA: COMPETITIVE EFFORTS

I.1   *Organization:* The Advertising Checking Bureau, Inc.
   Service: Magazine Checking; Newspaper Advertising Research

Newspaper Research and Magazine Checking provides advertising research information specifi-cally designed to meet client's research requirements. Information is provided on linage and cost of advertising for client brand and competitive brands, national and retail advertising reports, pricing reports, etc. Data are provided via tearsheets, manual and computer reports, data tapes, scrapbooks, etc. Reporting frequency determined by client.

I.2   *Organization:* Broadcast Advertisers Reports, Inc.
   Service: BAR Network Television and Radio Service
         BAR National Spot Television Service

These services monitor television, cable TV and radio networks, as well as spot television on over 300 stations in 75 major markets. Data are presented by brand, by parent company, and by product category. They are used by advertisers and agencies for proof-of-performance and are also the industry sources for competitive expenditures for the four media monitored.

I.3 *Organization:* Leading National Advertisers
  Service: Multi-Media Service
This service provides summaries of brand and company expenditures in six major media: magazines, newspaper supplements, network TV, spot TV, network radio, and outdoor. Data are presented in three easy-to-read reports: AD $ Summary, brands listed alphabetically showing total advertising expenditures and media used; Company/Brand, brands listed within parent company; and Class/Brand, brands listed within each of the 243 product classes, showing advertising dollars in each of the six media by brand, company, or class.

I.4 *Organization:* Media Records, Inc.
  Service: Blue Book, Green Book, Other Special Reports
This service measures newspaper advertising in linage (inches in 1985) and expenditures by advertiser. It is published monthly, quarterly, and at other frequencies for over 200 daily and Sunday papers. It reports on both national and retail advertising as well as giving an annual summary of newspaper advertising expenditures by classification and advertisers. Media Records' subsidiary, COMTRAC, provides competitive TV broadcast reports, recording from sign-on to sign-off all actual broadcast activity in a given market.

I.5 *Organization:* Publisher's Information Bureau, Inc.
  Service: PIB Magazine Advertising Analysis
This service determines the advertising space size and copy characteristics of 1937 consumer magazines and three Sunday supplements. The data are classified by industry, company, and product. The basic reports are published monthly. Specialized reports are also available.

I.6 *Organization:* Rome Reports, Inc.
  Service: The Rome Report of Business Publication Advertising
This service audits 575 industrial and professional magazines to determine the advertising space and investment of over 50,000 advertisers. The reporting frequency is semiannual.

1.7 *Organization:* Leading National Advertisers
  Service: PIB Magazine Analysis Service
A monthly detailed analysis of brand expenditures in about 140 consumer magazines and 3 national newspaper supplements, this service shows magazines used, size of ad, and cost of ad. This service denotes special sizes and types of advertisements, such as digest-sized units, partial-run, and geographic split-run. The firm's Regional Advertising Service provides the same type of data for 98 percent of the regional advertising. Quarterly and year-end summaries are included.

I.8 *Organization:* Leading National Advertisers
  Service: Outdoor Advertising Expenditures
A quarterly report of brand expenditures in outdoor (billboard) advertising showing poster or paint and markets used by each brand, it covers markets of over 100,000 population.

CHAPTER 6

SECONDARY DATA

Once the research objectives and information needs have been specified, the researcher turns to the task of formulating the research design and determining the appropriate sources of marketing data. The previous chapter discussed the research design options available to the researcher and presented an overview of the basic sources of marketing data. This chapter continues the discussion by focusing on secondary data and their role in the research process.[1]

ROLE OF SECONDARY DATA

Figure 6-1 presents the initial steps in the research process with an emphasis on the types of data sources available at the data collection stage. All too frequently the beginning researcher assumes that a survey of respondents is the only way to collect the data for a research project. Actually, survey research should be used only if the data cannot be collected using more efficient data sources. The authors of one book emphasize this point by stating that "a good operating rule is to consider a survey akin to surgery—to be used only after other possibilities have been exhausted."[2] Consequently, the first issue in the data collection stage is to determine whether the data have already been collected.

The data sources available to the marketing researcher can be classified as primary or secondary. *Secondary data* are already published data collected for purposes other

---

[1] The authors wish to acknowledge the valuable assistance of Nancy S. Karp, Librarian, Graduate School of Business Administration, The University of Michigan, in preparing this chapter.

[2] Robert Ferber and P. J. Verdoorn, *Research Methods in Economics and Business* (New York: Macmillan, 1962), p. 208.

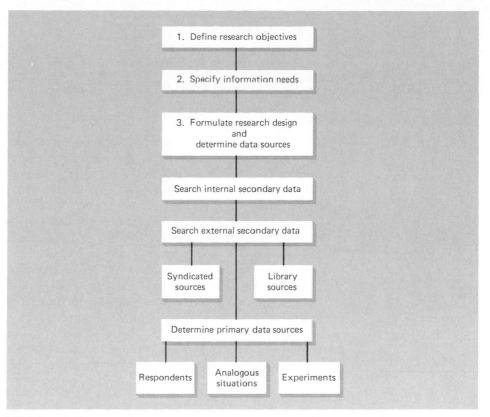

FIGURE 6-1 Initial steps in the research process.

than the specific research needs at hand. Such data can be classified as internal or external. *Internal secondary data* are available within the organization (e.g., accounting records and sales reports), whereas *external secondary data* are provided by sources outside the organization (e.g., reports, periodicals, books). *Primary data* are collected specifically for purposes of the research needs at hand. For example, if a retailer collects data from shoppers regarding store image, the resulting data would be primary.

As Figure 6-1 shows, internal secondary data sources should be searched thoroughly before turning to external sources. External secondary data are available from two main sources: (1) syndicated sources and (2) library sources. Syndicated sources, discussed in Chapter 5, are services which collect standardized data to serve the needs of an array of clients. These data are often expensive, and their availability may be restricted to certain clients. Library sources, the focus of this chapter, include an array of publicly circulated publications.

Once the search of secondary data is completed, the researcher typically will find that primary data must be collected to supplement the secondary data. Rarely will secondary data fulfill the data requirements of a research project. The remaining chapters in this book concentrate on the data collection, analysis, and reporting phases of the research process involving primary data.

It is important that the marketing researcher be familiar with the advantages and disadvantages of secondary data as well as the sources of such data, and these topics will occupy the remainder of this chapter.

Advantages of Secondary Data

The central advantage of secondary data is the saving in cost and time in comparison with primary data sources. Consider the research objective of estimating the market potential for a product. If secondary data are available, the researcher may be able to visit a library, identify the appropriate source, and collect the desired data relating to market potential. This may take a day of the researcher's time and involve minimal cost. Contrast this situation with collecting similar data via a survey. Several weeks or months may be required to design and pretest a questionnaire, train the interviewers, devise a sampling plan, and collect and process the data. In addition, the cost of such a project could involve thousands of dollars. Consequently, it is important to search secondary data sources first before proceeding to primary sources. While it is rare that secondary data completely fulfill the data requirements of a research project, typically they can (1) aid in the formulation of the decision problem, (2) suggest methods and types of data for meeting the information needs, and (3) serve as a source of comparative data by which primary data can be interpreted and evaluated.[3]

Another advantage of secondary data is that it may be beyond the means of the typical organization to collect such data on its own. For example, this would be true of the data available from the Bureau of the Census.

Disadvantages of Secondary Data

The major disadvantages of secondary data relate to (1) the extent that the data fit the information needs of the project and (2) the accuracy of the data.

Data Fit Problem   As discussed previously, since secondary data are collected for purposes other than those of the research project at hand, they will rarely completely serve the information needs of the project. The degree of fit can range from completely inadequate to very close. This degree of fit is influenced by three factors: (1) units of measurement, (2) definition of classes, and (3) publication currency.[4]

It is common for the researcher to discover that the secondary data are expressed in units different from those required by the project. For example, a project may require data regarding household income. The researcher may find that income is measured by individual, family, spending unit, or tax return rather than by household. Extreme caution should be exercised in estimating the desired data from measurements in other units.

---

[3] Jerry E. Drake and Frank J. Millar, *Marketing Research: Intelligence and Management* (Scranton, Pa.: International Textbook Company, 1969), p. 277.

[4] Harper W. Boyd, Ralph Westfall, and Stanley F. Stasch, *Marketing Research: Text and Cases*, 4th ed. (Homewood, Ill.: Irwin, 1977), p. 147.

Another problem relates to the class boundaries used to summarize the data. Assuming the unit of measurement is correct, a researcher could find that household income is composed of $7000 boundaries (0–6999, 7000–13,999, and so on) when the information needs require $5000 boundaries.

The final problem relates to the recency of the data. Marketing decision making typically requires up-to-date information. Many sources of secondary data have long time periods between the collection and publication of the data. For example, government sources, such as census data, can be as much as three years old before they are published. The value of these data for marketing purposes can diminish rapidly with time.

Accuracy Problem   The researcher must determine whether the secondary data are accurate enough for the purposes of the research project at hand. A serious limitation of secondary data is the difficulty of evaluating their accuracy. There are a number of sources of error in the sampling, data collection, analysis, and reporting stages of the research process that influence the accuracy of the data. These sources of error can be more easily evaluated when the researcher directly participates in the research process, as is the situation with primary research. The lack of participation in the research process in no way reduces the responsibility of the researcher to evaluate the accuracy of the data used. The following criteria can be used in the difficult task of assessing the accuracy of secondary data: (1) source, (2) purpose of the publication, and (3) evidence concerning quality.[5]

The source of the data is very important in evaluating its accuracy. Secondary data may be secured from an original source or an acquired source. An *original source* is the source that originated the data, while an *acquired source* is a source which procured the data from an original source. The *Statistical Abstract of the United States* is an example of an acquired source. All the data in the *Statistical Abstract* are taken from other government and trade sources. A fundamental rule in using secondary data is to secure data directly from the original source rather than using acquired sources. The reasons for this rule are two. First, the original source is in most cases the only place where the details of the data collection and analysis process are described. Knowledge of the research process is essential in evaluating the accuracy of the data. Second, the original source is generally more detailed and accurate than the acquired source. Errors in transcription and failure to reproduce footnotes and other textual comments can seriously influence the accuracy of the data.

Evaluation of the purpose of a publication is the second criterion for determining the accuracy of secondary data.

> Sources published to promote sales, to advance the interests of an industrial or commercial or other group, to present the cause of a political party, or to carry on any sort of propaganda, are suspect. Data published anonymously, or by an organization which is on the defensive, or under conditions which suggest a controversy, or in a form which reveals a strained attempt at "frankness," or to controvert inferences from other data, are generally suspect.[6]

---

[5] This discussion follows that of Gilbert A. Churchill, Jr., *Marketing Research: Methodological Foundations* (New York: Dryden Press, 1976), pp. 129–131.

[6] Erwin Esser Nemmers and John H. Myers, *Business Research: Text and Cases* (New York: McGraw-Hill, 1966), p. 43.

The above statement should not be interpreted to mean that data from such sources are useless. On the contrary, valuable information can be identified. However, the researcher needs to be sensitive to the purpose of the publication and more cautious in evaluating the data to detect those who would misrepresent and distort statistics to support a position or belief.

The third criterion for evaluating the accuracy of secondary data is to assess the general evidence regarding the quality of the data. If the primary source does not disclose details of the research design, be very cautious. This frequently suggests that the supplying organization has something to conceal. When the details of the research design are disclosed, the researcher should evaluate areas such as (1) sampling plan, (2) data collection procedure, (3) quality of field training, (4) questionnaire technique, and (5) data analysis procedures. A section discussing the limitations of the research design and data should be included. When limited information is available regarding the research design, the researcher can still evaluate the quality of the reporting of the data. Important here are items such as the labeling of tables and figures, the internal consistency of the data, and whether the data support the conclusions drawn in the report.

LIBRARY SOURCES OF SECONDARY DATA

Library sources of marketing data include an array of publicly circulated material, e.g., government documents, periodicals, books, research reports, and trade association publications. What types of research objectives and information needs might call for secondary data? Some examples would be: (1) to estimate the total market potential for corrugated and solid fiber boxes in a given area; (2) to develop a method for establishing sales quotas for television sets by states; (3) to establish national, state, and county sales quotas and a method for estimating the potential market for battery replacements for automobiles; (4) to determine the market potential for industrial lubricants in Cook County, Illinois; (5) to predict the potential market for paper and allied products to merchant wholesalers and the retail trades to 1988; (6) to estimate the market for clothes-washing machines and dryers, dishwashers, and television sets in the Fort Wayne, Indiana, Metropolitan Statistical Area, which consists of Allen County; (7) to select a county in the Syracuse, New York, Metropolitan Statistical Area to locate new supermarkets (the area is composed of Madison, Onondaga, and Oswego counties); or (8) to disperse an advertising budget in proportion to the potential markets, by states, in the South Atlantic region.

Secondary data can be used to meet the information needs represented by the above research objectives. The following types of secondary data would be appropriate: (1) employment data, (2) population data, (3) radio and television sales, (4) number of households with television, (5) family median income, (6) aggregate income of the population, (7) occupied housing units, (8) automobile registration, (9) housing units without automobiles, (10) grocery store sales, (11) value of box shipments by end use, and (12) employment by industry group. These data are available from library sources.

MARKETING RESEARCH IN ACTION:

GOODLIFE MAGAZINE

Sophisticated computer modeling played a key role in the successful introduction of *Goodlife*, a monthly magazine direct-mailed to 1 million affluent U.S. households. The model, called the "Goodlife Index" (GLI), was developed by Demographic Research Co., Inc., Santa Monica, Calif. According to E. Wayne Hansen, senior technical representative at Demographic Research, "Because the credibility of a controlled-circulation magazine rests entirely on its ability to efficiently reach its audience, the methodology and development of the mailing lists were carefully designed and evaluated." The magazine's publisher, Printcast Publishing Network, Toronto, used the GLI to choose which households—50,000 from each of 20 major metropolitan statistical areas (MSAs)—would qualify as *Goodlife* recipients.

The consumers targeted to receive *Goodlife* were aged 40–50 with incomes of $60,000 +. They were in professional or top management positions and held at least an undergraduate degree. "They must not only have money, they must also have style and taste," said Hansen. Thus, the GLI was a weighted, multivariate index combining measures of income, occupation, life-cycle stage, home value, and education.

Within each MSA it was assumed that smaller areas were more homogeneous than larger areas, so analysis was based upon the smallest unit for which census data was available—the block. For each MSA, data from the Current Population Survey, the Annual Housing Survey, and the Survey of Consumer Expenditures was entered into the GLI model. A GLI score was generated, and those neighborhoods with the highest scores were checked further for potential *Goodlife* recipients. Then, within the selected blocks, individual addresses were selected. Because census data is not available at the household level, *Goodlife* households were chosen on the basis of other "desirable characteristics . . . to maximize the likelihood that every selected address met the criteria needed for receiving *Goodlife*," said Hansen.

Finally, computer maps which highlighted the *Goodlife* neighborhoods were produced, enabling Printcast to attract lucrative advertising. These maps accurately demonstrated to the advertisers that *Goodlife* provided an effective advertising vehicle because it was, in fact, reaching only the specific market advertisers wanted to reach.

Source: Marketing News, vol. 16, no. 11, p. 22, Nov. 26, 1982.

Government Data Sources

The largest single source of statistical data is the United States government. For years, marketing researchers have relied on this source of data for developing market potential and sales forecasts, determining sales territories and sales quotas, and locating retail, wholesale, and manufacturing establishments. As the breadth and depth of government data have increased over the years, the relevance of this source of data to marketing information needs has increased dramatically. Consequently, effective marketing research requires a thorough knowledge of government data.

Census Data

Within the federal government, the Bureau of the Census is the leading source of data relevant to marketing. Its vast resources and years of experience combine to give census data a high reputation for quality. The data are generally detailed enough for most marketing information needs. They are reasonably priced and accessible in printed form or on computer tape. Unpublished data contained on the census computer tapes can be purchased on microfiche for $3 plus $0.25 per fiche or a complete tape reel can be purchased for $110. The Census Bureau will do individualized computer runs for those willing to pay a small fee.

The Bureau of the Census collects and publishes many types of data, including Census of Population, Census of Housing, Census of Manufacturing, Census of Retail Trade, Census of Wholesale Trade, Census of Transportation, Census of Agriculture, and Census of Business. Other publications which make use of Bureau information or which originate from the Bureau are described in the appendix to this chapter.

The available census data on population and housing are summarized in Table 6-1. Note that some census items are collected through the use of samples. Many census data can be very useful to marketers; examples are demographic profiles, housing patterns, and appliance ownership.

The census data are available at many different levels, ranging all the way from the nation as a whole down to city blocks. Figure 6-2 shows the hierarchical relationships among the geographic units used by the Census Bureau. Most census data are published only down to the "tract" level. Some of the levels are governmental units—states, counties, etc.—while others are just statistical units used by the Census Bureau—divisions, metropolitan statistical areas (MSAs), etc. Table 6-2 presents definitions of the geographic units shown in Figure 6-2.

Figure 6-3 further illustrates the type of geographic units used. It presents the geographic subdivision of an MSA all the way down to a city block. Clearly, many detailed data of relevance to marketers are available in the census reports.

Census data are not without defects. As with all secondary data, they have the limitation of not being collected for the specific information needs of a marketing research project. At times, definitions have been changed from census to census. Note in Table 6-1 the items that have been changed in definition in 1980 relative to the 1970 census and the new items that have been added. Even within a census, definitions can have different meanings. For the researcher who is not familiar with the details of census data, it can be very useful to seek the advice of a professional in this area regarding the specifics of how the data are to be used. Numerous publications, workshops, and conferences sponsored by the U.S. Department of Commerce and the Bureau of the Census are designed to aid the user of census data.

Additionally, the accuracy of the 1980 census has been questioned because of potential undercounts of minority groups, especially in urban areas. This situation underscores the necessity of approaching all data sources cautiously.

Standard Industrial Classification   Many sources of marketing data are classified according to the Standard Industrial Classification Code, or *SIC Code*. This system of

TABLE 6-1 SUBJECTS IN THE 1980 CENSUS CLASSIFIED AS COMPLETE-COUNT OR SAMPLE ITEMS

Population	Housing
Items collected at every household ("complete-count items")	
Household relationship[1]	Number of units at address
Sex	Complete plumbing facilities[1]
Race	Number of rooms
Age	Tenure (whether the unit is owned or rented)
Marital status	Condominium identification[1]
Spanish/Hispanic origin or descent[1]	Value of home (for owner-occupied units and condominiums)
	Rent (for renter-occupied units)
	Vacant for rent, for sale, and so forth; and period of vacancy
Additional items collected at sample households *	
School enrollment	Type of unit
Educational attainment	Stories in building and presence of elevator
State or foreign country of birth	Year built
Citizenship and year of immigration	Year moved into this house[1]
Current language and English proficiency[2]	Acreage and crop sales
Ancestry[2]	Source of water
Place of residence 5 years ago	Sewage disposal
Activity 5 years ago	Heating equipment
Veteran status and period of service	Fuels used for house heating, water heating, and cooking
Presence of disability or handicap	
Children ever born	Costs of utilities and fuels[1]
Marital history	Complete kitchen facilities
Employment status last week	Number of bedrooms
Hours worked last week	Number of bathrooms
Place of work	Telephone
Travel time to work[2]	Air-conditioning
Means of transportation to work[1]	Number of automobiles
Persons in carpool[2]	Number of light trucks and vans[2]
Year last worked	Homeowner shelter costs for mortgage, real-estate taxes, and hazard insurance[2]
Industry	
Occupation	
Class of worker	
Work in 1979 and weeks looking for work in 1979[2]	
Amount of income by source[1] and total income in 1979	
Derived variables (illustrative examples)	
Families	Persons per room ("crowding")
Family type and size	Household size
Poverty status	Plumbing facilities
Population density	Institutions and other group quarters
Size of place	Gross rent
	Farm residence

[1]Changed relative to 1970.
[2]New items.
*For most areas of the country in 1980, one out of every six housing units or households received the sample form. Areas estimated to contain 2500 or fewer persons in 1980 had a 3-out-of-every-6 sampling rate, which is required in order to obtain reliable statistics needed for participation in certain federal programs.
Source: Charles P. Kaplan and Thomas L. Van Valey, *Census '80: Continuing the Factfinder Tradition,* U.S. Bureau of the Census, p. 173, 1980.

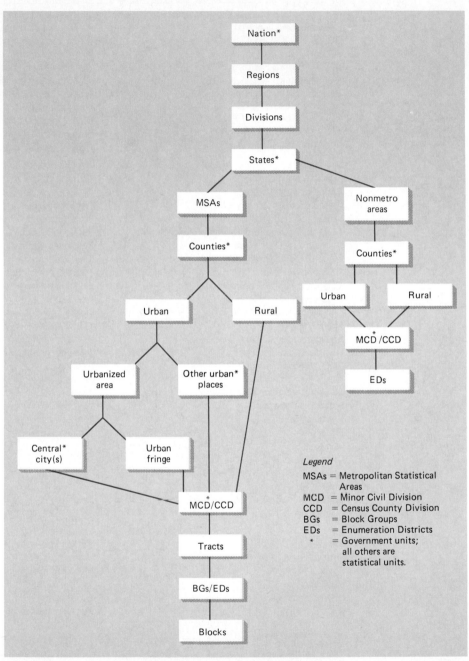

FIGURE 6-2 Census Bureau geographic units and their hierarchical relationships. *(Source: Teacher's Guide: Approaches to Census Data, U.S. Bureau of the Census, p. 16, 1977.)*

TABLE 6-2   DEFINITIONS OF GEOGRAPHIC UNITS USED BY THE CENSUS BUREAU

Nation	The U.S. as a whole.
Region	The U.S. is divided into four regions as follows: West: Wash., Oreg., Calif., Mont., Idaho, Nev., Utah, Ariz., N.Mex., Colo., Wyo., Alaska, Hawaii South: Tex., Okla., Ark., La., Miss., Ala., Ga., Fla., S.C., N.C., Tenn., Ky., W. Va., Va., Md., Del., D.C. Northeast: Pa., N.J., N.Y., Conn., R.I., Mass., Vt., N.H., Maine North Central: Ill., Ind., Ohio, Mich., Wisc., Minn., Iowa, Mo., Kan., Nebr., S.D., N.D.,
Divisions	The regions are divided into a total of nine geographic divisions, each of which is composed of a specific group of contiguous states as follows: Pacific: Wash., Oreg., Calif., Alaska, Hawaii Mountain: Mont., Idaho, Utah, Nev., Ariz., N.Mex., Colo., Wyo. West South Central: Tex., Okla., Ark., La East South Central: Miss., Ala., Tenn., Ky. South Atlantic: Fla., Ga., S.C., N.C., W. Va., Va., Md., Del., D.C. Middle Atlantic: Pa., N.J., N.Y. New England: Conn., R.I., Mass., Vt., N.H., Maine East North Central: Ill., Ind., Ohio, Mich., Wisc. West North Central: Minn., Iowa, Mo., Kan., Nebr., S.D., N.D.
States	The states of the union.
MSAs	Metropolitan statistical areas: (a) One city with 50,000 or more inhabitants, or (b) A Census Bureau-defined urbanized area of at least 50,000 inhabitants *and* a total MSA population of at least 100,000 (75,000 In New England). The standards provide that the MSA include as "central county(ies)" the county in which the central city is located, and adjacent counties, if any, with at least 50 percent of their population in the urbanized area. Additional "outlying counties" are included if they meet specified requirements of commuting to the central counties and of metropolitan character (such as population density and percent urban). In New England the MSAs are defined in terms of cities and towns rather than counties. There are 261 MSAs in the United States.
Counties	The primary divisions of a state as defined by state law (called parishes in Louisiana; there are none in Alaska).
Urban	The part of a county containing cities and towns of 2500 population or more.
Rural	The complement of the urban population, containing farm and nonfarm components.
Urbanized areas	A central city of 50,000 or more, or twin cities of 50,000 or more, with the smallest having 15,000 people or more, plus the surrounding urban buildup or fringe (suburbs).
Other urban places	Urban areas not qualifying as urbanized areas; i.e., places of over 2500 but less 50,000.
Central city	The area designated by the title of the urbanized area; e.g., Boston does not include Cambridge, etc.
Urban fringes:	Suburbs of central cities.
MCDs	Minor civil divisions are component parts of counties representing political or administrative subdivisions called townships, districts, precincts, etc.

TABLE 6-2 *(Continued)*

CCDs	Census county divisions were formed by the Census Bureau in 21 states for the purpose of dividing counties into statistical areas; they are used instead of townships, etc.
Tracts	Small areas into which large cities and their adjacent areas have been divided for statistical purposes.
BG	A block group is a subdivision of a tract made up of a number of city blocks.
ED	An enumeration district is a subdivision of a tract or county MCD/CCD for the purpose of assignment to enumerators for collecting questionnaires; no standard printed reports are available at this level.
Block	The smallest area for which data are available; it is usually a well-defined rectangular piece of land bounded by streets or roads.
Nonmetro areas	The parts of a state not included in an MSA.
Unincorporated places	A concentration of population of at least 1000 which is not legally a city.

classification was developed by the federal government in connection with taking its Census of Manufacturers. The classification system is based on the products produced or operations performed. The SIC Code classifies all manufacturing into 20 major industry groups, each having a two-digit code (e.g., 25 is Furniture and Fixtures). Each major industry group is further classified into approximately 150 industry groups which are identified with a three-digit code (e.g., 252 is Office Furniture). Each industry group is further classified into approximately 450 product categories designated by a four-digit code (e.g., 2522 is Metal Office Furniture). This kind of hierarchical system is also used to classify other areas of the economy. For detailed information on how to use the SIC Code, see the *Standard Industrial Classification Manual* and Chapter 22 of this book.

Additional Data Sources

In addition to government sources, a large number of other publications contain data applicable to a wide number of research objectives. The task of identifying relevant sources of data can be a difficult one for researchers who are not familiar with the area under investigation. Fortunately, there are many published guides and indexes (see the appendix) to assist them in this pursuit. In addition, researchers will find that a competent reference librarian can identify relevant sources of data.

In evaluating the quality of the data identified, the researcher must be sensitive to the origin of the data and the research design. At times, this may be difficult to determine. Library data originate from an array of sources such as federal, state, and local governments, colleges and universities, trade associations, chambers of commerce, commercial organizations, foundations, and publishing companies. Some publications mainly present the results of original research, some summarize the research findings of others, and some mainly present interpretations and conclusions regarding the research findings of others.

Area

Metropolitan Statistical Area
and component areas
(central city of 50,000+ population
and the surrounding metropolitan
county [s])

Central city

Urbanized area
(shaded area)

Place

Minor civil division

County

Population size

At least 50,000
(in an MSA)

Census tract (small, homogeneous,
relatively permanent area; all MSAs
recognized at the time of the 1980
census are entirely tracted)

Average 4000

Block (identified in all urbanized areas
and some selected areas)

Average 100

FIGURE 6-3 Geographic subdivisions of an MSA. *(Adapted from Charles P. Kaplan and Thomas L. Van Valey, Census '80: Continuing the Factfinder Tradition, U.S. Bureau of the Census, p. 141, 1980.)*

The appendix to this chapter gives a listing of the main guides and indexes to marketing data, as well as the more predominant sources of marketing data.

One development in the provision of demographic data to marketers is the growth of private companies that market census-related products. They provide the fastest way to get census data tailored to one's needs.[7] Additionally, they offer updates on census data at the tract level and above between census years, and provide clients with a range of services designed to assist in using demographics in planning, marketing, and forecasting.[8] Two products receiving heavy marketing from these companies are computer graphics and geocoding.[9] The former provides complex data display capabilities in color. The latter assigns demographic data to a geographic location. The user can then define pieces of geography and examine the demographic characteristics in these areas. This would be especially valuable in retail location studies, for example. One writer described these companies as providing "demographic supermarkets"[10] for marketers.

SUMMARY

1 Sources of marketing data can be classified as primary or secondary. Secondary data are defined as data collected for purposes other than the specific research needs at hand. Primary data are defined as data collected specifically for purposes of the research needs at hand.

2 Secondary data can be subclassified as internal or external. Internal secondary data are those available within the organization, while external secondary data are those provided by sources outside the organization.

3 External secondary data are available from syndicated and library sources. Syndicated sources refer to data services that collect standardized data to serve the needs of many clients. Library sources include an array of publicly circulated publications.

4 The first phase of the data collection stage of the research process involves a search of internal and external secondary data sources. Primary data sources should be employed after it is determined that the data are not available from secondary data sources. Rarely will secondary data completely meet the data requirements of a research project.

5 The advantage of secondary data are their lower cost and fast retrieval compared with primary data. Additionally, to collect the data using primary data research methods may be beyond the means of the organization.

6 The disadvantages of secondary data are related to the accuracy of the data and the degree of fit between the data and the information needs of the project. The accuracy of secondary data can be evaluated in terms of (1) the source, (2) the purpose of the publication, and (3) evidence regarding quality.

[7] Martha Farnsworth Riche, "Choosing 1980 Census Products," *American Demographics,* p. 13, December 1981.
[8] Ibid.
[9] Martha Farnsworth, Riche, "Demographic Supermarkets of the Eighties," *American Demographics,* p. 15, February 1981.
[10] Ibid.

DISCUSSION QUESTIONS

1 What is the role of secondary data in the research process?
2 What are the advantages of secondary data relative to primary data?
3 Discuss the shortcomings of secondary data.
4 Suggest some examples of census data useful to marketers.
5 Indicate the main components of the hierarchy of geographic units in descending order of level of aggregation.

APPENDIX: Library Sources of Marketing Data

The purpose of this appendix is to catalog the predominant library sources of marketing data and to identify the main guides and indexes to marketing data. For each listing, the name of the publication, the publisher, and a brief abstract are presented. Because of the ever-changing nature of library data sources, omissions and inaccuracies are unavoidable. More contemporary information regarding a particular data source can be obtained from a reference librarian. Where noted, the government printing office, not the producing agency, is the sales agency for government publications.

The information contained in some of the following sources can be accessed through computerized information retrieval systems. Bibliographic Retrieval Systems, Inc. (Scotia, N.Y.), System Development Corp. (Santa Monica, Calif.), and DIALOG Information Services, Inc. (Palo Alto, Calif.), are the major vendors offering access to a range of business-related databases. Additional relevant databases are available independently. Many libraries of all types now offer this service. Systems are also available for direct access by individuals.

GUIDES TO BUSINESS LITERATURE SOURCES

Business Information Sources, rev. ed. (Berkeley: University of California Press, 1985), Lorna M. Daniels, compiler. Excellent bibliography of reference tools in business and economics. Provides a general introduction to business reference sources. Valuable to the marketer for its coverage of statistics sources and its section on market research sources. Many sources listed are published on a recurrent basis.

Business Organizations and Agencies Directory, 2d ed. (Detroit: Gale Research Company, 1984), Anthony T. Kruzas et al., compilers. Focus is on business-related organizations and agencies in the U.S. Includes professional societies, trade associations, government agencies, research centers, educational institutions, and others. Includes a brief description of each organization's activities.

Dissertation Abstracts International (Ann Arbor, Mich.: Xerox University Microfilms, since 1952). Monthly. Includes title key-word and author indexes. The Humanities and Social Science section includes sections on marketing, business administration, banking, and other topics. This source abstracts doctoral dissertations of over 350 institutions.

Encyclopedia of Business Information Sources, 5th ed. (Detroit: Gale Research Company, 1983). Arranged by subject, this work lists periodicals, statistics sources, directories, bibliographies, general works, and other sources. Includes a supplement published in 1985.

Frank, Nathalie D., and John V. Ganly, *Data Sources for Business and Market Analysis,* 3d ed. (Metuchen, N.J.: Scarecrow Press, 1983). Annotated bibliography emphasizes original sources of qualitative data and business facts, and useful secondary sources. Covers such areas as government publications, professional and trade associations, advertising media, and company information. Also refers to relevant computerized databases.

University Research in Business and Economics (Morgantown, W. Va.: Bureau of Business Research, College of Business and Economics, West Virginia University, for the Association for University Business and Economics Research). Annual. Books, working papers, periodical articles, monographs, and other publications are indexed by author, subject, and institution.

GUIDES TO MARKETING SOURCES

American Marketing Association Bibliography Series (Chicago). Issued periodically. Contains a series of annotated bibliographies with emphasis on books and periodicals. Each covers a particular topic in some depth.

Communications Abstracts (Beverly Hills, Calif.: Sage Publications, Inc.). Issued quarterly. Indexes and abstracts major communication-related articles, reports, and books. In addition to advertising and marketing, covers such topics as mass communication, small-group communication, the media, and public opinion.

Journal of Marketing (Chicago). "Marketing Abstracts" section, each issue. Published quarterly by the American Marketing Association. Contains an annotated bibliography of articles published within the last year in major business, economic, and social science periodicals.

INDEXES: GENERAL BUT USEFUL

New York Times Index. Since 1913. Semimonthly, with quarterly and annual cumulations. Detailed subject index includes very brief summaries of articles.

Public Affairs Information Service Bulletin (New York). Since 1915. Biweekly, plus periodic cumulations. A subject index to books, pamphlets, government documents, periodical articles, and other publications dealing with economic and social conditions and public affairs. Includes English-language publications issued worldwide.

Reader's Guide to Periodical Literature (New York: H. W. Wilson). Since 1900. Semimonthly plus quarterly and annual cumulations. Contains a subject and author index of over 175 U.S. general periodicals.

Social Sciences Citation Index (Philadephia: Institute for Scientific Information). Since 1969. Three times yearly, with annual cumulations. Indexes all articles in about 1400 social science periodicals and selected articles in about 3000 periodicals of other disciplines. Subjects covered include marketing, economics, management, and other areas. Provides a citation index, author (source) index, and a subject index.

INDEXES: BUSINESS

Business Periodicals Index (New York: H. W. Wilson). Published since 1959. Important subject index to selected periodicals in all major fields of business. Covers over 300 English-language periodicals, primarily U.S. Monthly (except for August), with cumulations quarterly and annually.

Predicasts F&S Index, United States (Cleveland, Ohio: Predicasts, Inc.). Weekly, plus quarterly and annual cumulations. Indexes U.S. industry, product, and company information from over 750 business and financial publications. There are two sections: industry/product and company. Similar publications, *Predicasts F&S International* and *Predicasts F&S Europe* deal with international business articles.

Wall Street Journal Index (Princeton, N.J.: Dow Jones Books). Since 1957. Monthly, with annual cumulations. Subject index to the Eastern edition. There are two sections: general news and corporate news.

Business Index (Menlo Park, Calif.: Information Access Corporation). Since 1979. Cumulated and updated monthly. Comprehensive subject coverage of over 800 primarily U.S. periodicals and major newspapers. Also indexes *Area Business Databank* (Belmont, Calif.: Information Access Company) from 1984. This source includes the full text of articles about business trends and companies of all sizes, on a local, regional, and national level.

GUIDES TO STATISTICAL SOURCES

American Statistics Index: A Comprehensive Guide and Index to the Statistical Publications of the U. S. Government (Washington, D.C.: Congressional Information Service). Since 1973. Monthly, plus annual cumulations. Excellent guide to the statistical publications of federal government agencies, Congress, and other programs. A typical abstract includes a complete description of the data given. Material is indexed according to subject, author, title, report number, and demographic or other category.

Bureau of the Census Catalog (Government Printing Office). Annual. A comprehensive annotated guide to Census Bureau publications, including data files and special tabulations. Publications cover agriculture, foreign trade, governments, population, and the economic censuses; retail trade, wholesale trade, service industries, construction industries, manufacturers, mineral industries, and transportation. The catalog also lists available data files and special tabulations which contain data not found in printed reports. The catalog is updated by a monthly Census Bureau publication, *Data User News* (Government Printing Office).

Guide to Foreign Trade Statistics, Bureau of the Census (Government Printing Office). Issued periodically. A guide to foreign trade statistics. Description of Census Bureau publications dealing with foreign trade. Includes sample tables.

A Handbook for Business on the Use of Government Statistics, Eleanor G. May (Charlottesville, Va.: Tayloe Murphy Institute, 1979). Handbook of brief case descriptions of marketing-related problem solving through the use of available government statistics.

Statistical Reference Index: A Selective Guide to American Statistical Publications from Private Organizations and State Government Sources (Washington, D.C.: Congressional Information Service). Since 1980. Monthly, plus annual cumulations. Guide to statistical publications of associations, business organizations, commercial publishers, independent research organizations, state governments, and universities. Follows same format as *American Statistics Index.* Material is indexed by subject, author, title, geographic, economic, and demographic breakdowns, and issuing source.

Statistics Sources, Paul Wasserman et al., 9th ed. (Detroit: Gale Research Company, 1984). A subject guide to business, industrial, financial, social, and other topics. Detailed subheadings are used under each subject.

GENERAL SOURCES OF STATISTICS

Business Conditions Digest, Bureau of Economic Analysis, Department of Commerce (Government Printing Office). Monthly. This publication contains numerous indicators of current business activity in chart and table form. Researchers find this data useful for developing and updating industry and company forecasts.

Economic Indicators, Council of Economic Advisers (Government Printing Office). Monthly. Presents current statistical series considered to be key indicators of general business conditions. These include gross national product, personal consumption expenditures, and so forth. Researchers find this document useful in developing and updating industry and company forecasts.

Economic Report of the President (Government Printing Office). Annual. This publication documents the President's annual address to Congress regarding the economic condition of the United States. The annual report of the Council of Economic Advisers is included; it reviews economic policy and outlook. Included are statistical series from other documents published by the government dealing with numerous economic indicators.

Federal Reserve Bulletin (Washington, D.C.: Federal Reserve System Board of Governors). This monthly publication contains current financial data on banking activity, savings, interest rates, credit, and domestic nonfinancial statistics; an index of industrial production and some statistics on international trade and finance.

Handbook of Basic Economic Statistics (Economic Statistics Bureau of Washington, D.C.) Annual, plus monthly supplements. This publication is a compilation of statistics collected by federal government agencies dealing with all areas of the national economy. Historical data given for each statistical series.

Historical Statistics of the United States, Colonial Times to 1970, Bureau of the Census (Government Printing Office). This publication is a historical supplement to the *Statistical Abstract.* The comparison of historical data from the *Statistical Abstract* is difficult because of the changes in data classifications and definitions at various points in time. *Historical Statistics* presents these data comparisons using consistent classifications and definitions for all data in the statistical series. Over 12,500 different time series are presented in this document.

Monthly Labor Review, Bureau of Labor Statistics (Government Printing Office). Monthly. This publication presents current data and related articles on employment, earnings, wholesale and retail prices, and so forth. For more detailed data, see *Employment and Earnings, CPI Detailed Report,* and *Producer Prices and Price Indexes,* all produced by the U.S. Bureau of Labor Statistics (Government Printing Office).

Predicasts Forecasts (Cleveland, Ohio: Predicasts, Inc.). Quarterly with annual cumulations. Gives short and long range projection data for U.S. economic indicators, products, and industries. Also a guide to statistics; for further reference, the source of the data (trade journal, newspaper, government report, or other publication) is given with each entry. Other Predicast publications include separate digest, index, statistical, and research services.

Statistical Abstract of the United States, Bureau of the Census (Government Printing Office). Annual. The purpose of this valuable publication is to serve as a basic reference for those individuals searching for secondary data. Over 1400 tables presenting social, economic, political, and demographic data appear in this document. These tables serve as an abstract and reference for data available in other published sources. For many researchers, this publication is the initial reference in their search for external secondary data. Includes a "Guide to State Statistical Abstracts": sources listed contain statistical tables on a variety of subjects for states, counties, cities, and other areas.

Statistical Service (New York: Standard & Poor's Corporation). Basic material plus monthly supplements. The publication presents current and historical statistical data covering banking and finance, production and labor, price indexes, income and trade, transportation and communication, and some major industries.

Survey of Current Business, Bureau of Economic Analysis, Department of Commerce (Government Printing Office). Monthly. This important publication provides some 2600 current statistical series covering areas such as indicators of general business, domestic trade, industry statistics, personal consumption expeditures, earnings and employment by industry, and so forth. A historical record of the *Survey of Current Business* is provided in a biennial supplement by *Business Statistics,* Bureau of Economic Analysis, Department of Commerce.

World Almanac and Book of Facts (New York: Newspaper Enterprise Association). Annual. This publication is a handbook of statistics and factual information on a wide variety of subjects, e.g., industry, finance, religion.

Worldcasts (Cleveland, Ohio: Predicasts, Inc.). Quarterly. Two series: World Regional Casts and World Product Casts. Publishes forecast data from 800 foreign and domestic journals, bank letters, special studies, and other publications. The available information includes product, country, economic indicator, base period data, short- and long-range forecasts, and a key to indicate source of article. Country summary coverage includes 50 countries, ranging from detailed products to industries and general economics. Product summary volumes contain data for all major countries.

MARKET GUIDES AND DATA

County and City Data Book, Bureau of the Census (Government Printing Office, 1977). This publication contains census data pertaining to states, counties, and cities. Statistics are provided on population, income, education, employment, housing, retail and wholesale sales, and so forth. The data are compiled from numerous government and private agency publications with heavy emphasis in Census Bureau titles. A related publication, *State and Metropolitan Area Databook,* Bureau of the Census (Government Printing Office, 1982) focuses on MSAs and other metropolitan areas.

Market Guide (New York: *Editor and Publisher* magazine). Annual. This publication contains data for 1500 U.S. and Canadian newspaper markets. Data include principal industries, population, transportation facilities, households, banks, retail outlets. Includes estimates based on government data.

Rand McNally Commercial Atlas and Marketing Guide (Chicago: Rand McNally Company). Annual. This publication contains detailed statistics for counties, cities, metropolitan statistical areas (MSAs), and principal business centers, covering trade, manufacturing, transportation, population, and related data. Each state section includes maps and some business data for counties and cities. Includes estimates based on government data.

Registration Data. A wide variety of registration data are collected by government. Typically this information is difficult to locate and acquire in a convenient form. Examples of registration data are automobile and boat registrations; licenses for business activities, births, deaths, and marriages; income tax returns; and school enrollments.

Sales and Marketing Management, "Survey of Buying Power" issues (New York: *Sales and Marketing Management magazine). Annual: Part I, July and Part II, October. This publication con*tains data on population, effective buying income, and retail sales data for U.S. markets, also comparable data for Canada. Includes estimates based on government data. Provides tables ranking metropolitan areas and other markets according to population, income, and sales. Gives population, income, and retail sales data for TV markets. Projects data for U.S. and Canadian markets. A separate *Data Service* volume provides additional data. *Sales and Marketing Management* also publishes a "Survey of Industrial and Commercial Buying Power" issue (annual, April) and a "Survey of Selling Costs" issue (annual, February).

CONSUMER DATA

Census of Housing, Bureau of the Census (Government Printing Office). This census, taken in conjunction with the *Census of Population,* enumerates types of structures, size, year built, occupancy, equipment (such as clothes washers, stoves, and air conditioners), average value, monthly rent, number of persons per room, ethnic category of occupants, and so forth. The 1980 *Census of Housing* included a "general housing characteristics" series for places with a population of 1000 or more, a "detailed housing characteristics" series for places of 2500 or more, and a "metropolitan housing characteristics" series providing considerable detail and cross-classification of housing subjects. These data have been found to be very useful for marketing research purposes. Interim information regarding the percentage distribution of rental and home owner vacancies, general housing characteristics, urban and rural housing data, and other characteristics is furnished by the bureau's *Current Housing Report* series and *Annual Housing Survey.*

Census of Population, Bureau of the Census (Government Printing Office). This census presents population counts by states, counties, metropolitan statistical areas (MSAs), urbanized areas, county subdivisions, and other areas. The 1980 *Census of Population* identified the population by age, sex, race, national origin, marital status, citizenship, family composition, employment status, income, and other demographic characteristics. The census is taken every 10 years, in the years ending with a zero. Various interim reports are prepared by the Census Bureau. The *Current Population Report* series is a continual updating of population figures. U.S. aggregate data are presented on family characteristics, mobility, income, education, population estimates and projections, and other subjects.

Census of Population and Housing, Bureau of the Census (Government Printing Office). Taken in conjunction with the *Census of Population* and issued in three series: "Block Statistics," including data for individual city blocks on selected housing and population subjects for MSAs and other geographic areas; "Census Tracts," including data on most subjects for tracts (similar to neighborhoods) in each MSA and the tracted balance of each state; and "Summary Characteristics for Governmental Units," including additional data for each MSA and other areas.

BUSINESS AND INDUSTRY DATA

Agricultural Statistics, Department of Agriculture (Government Printing Office). Annual. This publication presents statistics on prices, production, costs, consumption, and so forth for various agricultural products.

Census of Construction Industries, Bureau of the Census (Government Printing Office). This census is taken every five years, in the years ending with 2 and 7; covers 27 industries. Data include number of establishments, receipts, employment, payments for materials, and other figures. Area statistics reports cover states. Data are arranged according to SIC code numbers. Interim data on housing starts, housing completions, new housing authorized, and other topics are published in the *Current Construction Reports* series and in *Construction Review,* U.S. Bureau of Industrial Economics (Government Printing Office), monthly.

Census of Manufacturers, Bureau of the Census (Government Printing Office). This census is an enumeration of establishments engaged in manufacturing activites. It is taken every five years in the years ending with 2 and 7. Manufacturing establishments are categorized under 450 industries. Statistics are provided on number and size of establishments, capital expenditures, quantity of output, inventories, employment, payroll, and consumption of fuel, materials, and energy. Additional reports cover special subjects, such as concentration ratios and plant and equipment expenditures. Separate state reports provide a geographical approach to the data. Interim reports include the *Annual Survey of Manufacturers,* which updates in part the *Census of Manufacturers,* and the *Current Industrial Reports,* which contain monthly, quarterly, and annual reports on production, inventories, and orders for commodities. In all three publications, data are arranged by SIC Code number.

Census of Mineral Industries, Bureau of the Census (Government Printing Office). This census is an enumeration of establishments primarily engaged in the extraction of minerals. It is taken every five years, in the years ending with 2 and 7. Statistics are available on some 42 mineral industries regarding such things as number of companies, production, number of employees, capital expenditures, water use, power equipment, and value of shipments. There are also area statistics, covering states, counties, and other areas. Data are arranged by SIC Code number. *Minerals Yearbook* provides annual data which supplement the *Census of Mineral Industries.*

Census of Retail Trade, Bureau of Census (Government Printing Office). This publication contains information on 100 kind-of-business classifications. Statistics are available on number of establishments, total sales, sales by merchandise lines, size of firm, employment and payroll for states, MSAs, counties, and cities of 2500 or more. The census is taken every five years in the years ending with 2 and 7, and the data are arranged by SIC code number. Interim publications include *Monthly Retail Trade.*

Census of Service Industries, Bureau of the Census (Government Printing Office). This publication provides data on more than 200 kind-of-business classifications. Statistics are available on number of establishments, receipts, and payrolls for states, MSAs, counties, and cities for service organizations such as hotels, barber shops, laundries, and so forth. The census does not include the finance, insurance, and real state industries. Some data relating to health, educational, legal, and other services are included. Data are not available on the professions (with the exception of legal services). The census is taken every five years in the years ending with 2 and 7, and the data are arranged by SIC Code number. An interim annual publication is *Service Annual Survey Report.*

Census of Transportation, Bureau of the Census (Government Printing Office). This census involves four separate studies—Truck Inventory and Use Survey, National Travel Survey, Commodity Transportation Survey, and Selected Statistics for Transportation Industries. The census is authorized every five years, in years ending with 2 and 7.

Census of Wholesale Trade, Bureau of the Census (Government Printing Office). This publication presents data on 118 kind-of-business classifications. Statistics are available on number of establishments, sales, personnel, and payroll for states, MSAs, counties, and cities. This census is taken every five years in the years ending with 2 and 7, and the data are arranged by SIC Code number. Interim publications include the *Monthly Wholesale Trade: Sales and Inventories* and *Wholesale Trade* (annual).

Commodity Yearbook (New York: Commodity Research Bureau). Annual. This publication contains data on production, prices, consumption, and import and export flow for approximately 100 individual commodities. A supplement, *Statistical Abstract Service,* is issued three times yearly.

County Business Patterns, Bureau of the Census (Government Printing Office). Annual. This publication presents a county breakdown of business by type, employment, and payroll. The data can be used to develop industrial market potential studies. There is a separate report for each state. Data are arranged by SIC Code number.

Enterprise Statistics, Bureau of the Census (Government Printing Office). Presents statistics based on data collected in the Census Bureau economic census program. Regroups census data records of establishments under common ownership or control to show various economic characteristics of owning or controlling companies. Issued every five years in years ending with 2 and 7.

Merchandising, "Statistical and Marketing Report" (New York: Billboard Publications). Annual, March issue. Presents tables (some with 5-year figures) and charts covering shipments, sales, product saturation, replacement and trade-in, and import/export figures for home electronics, major appliances, and housewares. "Consumers Survey" annual. Presents results from personal interviews regarding such areas as information seeking, discretionary spending, warranties, and so forth. Additional annual statistical and marketing reports include "Electronics," "House-wares," and "Appliances." Presents manufacturer-supplied projections for the coming year regarding unit sales an annual forecast article.

Standard and Poor's Industry Surveys (New York: Standard and Poor's Corporation). Updated regularly. Covers 69 major domestic industries, arranged into 36 major industry groups. Text and summary statistics in a basic (annual) and current (three times yearly) analysis for each group. Discussion of current situation, recent trends, outlook. The basic analysis includes financial data allowing comparison of major companies within an industry.

Standard Industrial Classification Manual (1972 and 1977 supplement), Office of Management and Budget (Government Printing Office). This document presents a numerical classification of business establishments according to the product or service involved. Covers all areas of the economy. Widely used by both governmental and private organizations to collect and tabulate data. Commonly known as the *SIC Code*. The Office of Federal Statistical Policy and Standards, U.S. Dept. of Commerce, is planning a major 1987 revision of the code.

Statistics of Income, Internal Revenue Service (Government Printing Office). Annual. This series presents data collected from corporate, proprietorship, and partnership income tax returns and those of individuals. The corporate report presents balance sheet and income statement data broken by industry type, asset size, and so forth. These publications are preceded by a series of preliminary summary reports.

U.S. Industrial Outlook, International Trade Administration, U.S. Dept of Commerce. (Government Printing Office). Annual. This publication presents a detailed analysis of about 350 manufacturing and nonmanufacturing industries. For each, information is given on recent developments and outlook. Researchers find this publication useful for forecasting and market planning.

COMPANY DATA AND FACTS: CONSULTANTS AND ASSOCIATIONS

Bradford's Directory of Marketing Research Agencies and Management Consultants in the U.S. and the World (Fairfax, Va.). Biennial. Listings arranged geographically—by state and city, and by foreign country. There is heavy emphasis on U.S. listings. Each entry describes type of research done. A separate list classifies agencies according to the specific service offered.

Consultants and Consulting Organizations Directory. Paul Wasserman (Detroit: Gale Research Company). 5th ed. 1984. Lists about 8000 firms and individuals, mostly U.S., some Canadian. Each entry briefly describes services and field interest. Includes an index of firms arranged by subject area and state. Updated by supplements called *New Consultants.* Also useful is the *Directory of Management Consultants* (Fitzwilliam, N.H.: Consultants News), 4th ed., 1985. Lists management consultants only. Each entry lists services and industries covered.

Encyclopedia of Associations (Detroit: Gale Research Company). Issued periodically; annually since 1975. Volume 1, *National Organizations of the United States,* lists active trade, business, professional, and other organizations; each entry briefly describes the organization's activities and lists available publications. Inactive, defunct, and "missing" organizations are identified as such in the index. Includes Volume 2, *Geographic and Executive Indexes, Volume 3, New Associations and Projects* (issued periodically); Volume 4, *International Organizations;* and Volume 5, *Research Activities and Funding Programs.* A related publication is the *National Trade and Professional Associations of the United States and Canada and Labor Unions* (Washington, D.C.: Columbia Books, Inc.), annual. Lists associations and publications of associations and has a key-word index.

FINDEX, the Directory of Market Research Reports, Studies and Surveys (New York: FIND/SVP). Annual plus midyear supplement. Guide to published, commercially available market and business research reports. Latest edition includes over 9000 reports from about 300 domestic and foreign research publishers. Many reports listed are moderately priced.

International Directory of Marketing Research Houses and Services (American Marketing Association, New York Chapter). Annual. Alphabetical listing of marketing research houses in the United States and some foreign countries. Each entry describes available services. Firms are also listed by geographic location.

Membership Directory and International Buyers' Guide to Marketing Services (Chicago: American Marketing Association, 1984). An alphabetic listing of organizations includes a description of each firm's services. Includes a geographic index and a listing of firms by specialty. Many areas of marketing research and consulting are covered.

Who's Who in Consulting (Detroit: Gale Research Company, 1973). Biographical information on consultants in a variety of fields. Also an index of consultants arranged by subject area and geographic location. Updated by supplements.

COMPANY DATA AND FACTS: DIRECTORIES

Directory of Corporate Affiliations (Skokie, Ill.: National Register Publishing Co., Inc.). Annual. Section 2 lists parent companies; each entry includes divisions, subsidiaries, and affiliates. Section 1 is a straight alphabetical listing of all entries in Section 2 to aid in identifying parent companies of subsidiaries. A geographical index lists all parents and subsidiaries by state and city. A related publication from the same publisher, *International Directory of Corporate Affiliations* (annual), lists foreign parent companies with their U.S. subsidiaries and U.S. parent companies and their foreign holdings.

Million Dollar Directory (New York: Dun & Bradstreet). Five volumes. Annual. Volumes 1–3 collectively list over 160,000 U.S. businesses with an indicated net worth of over $500,000. Each entry identifies officers, products, applicable SIC numbers, sales, and number of employees. Volume 4, a cross-reference volume, lists businesses geographically and by industry classification. An additional volume lists the "Top 50,000 companies."

Moody's Manuals (New York: Moody's Investors Service). Annual, plus weekly or twice weekly news issues. The seven manuals published by Moody's include *Industrial, OTC Industrial, Municipal and Government, Public Utility, Transportation, International,* and *Bank and Finance.* A typical listing includes location of agency or company, brief history, description of operation, officers, subsidiaries, detailed current and historical financial data, securities information. The *Banks and Finance* volume also covers insurance companies and real estate and investment companies.

Sheldon's Retail Directory of the United States and Canada and Phelon's Resident Buyers and Merchandise Brokers (New York: Phelon, Sheldon & Marsar, Inc.) Annual. Directory of the largest chain and independent department and specialty stores, arranged by state and city, also by Canadian province and city. Lists merchandise managers and buyers.

Standard and Poor's Register of Corporations, Directors and Executives. Three volumes, annual. Covers about 45,000 U.S., Canadian, and major international corporations, with same information as in the Dun's directories. There is very heavy emphasis on U.S. firms. A biographical volume provides brief information on 75,000 executives and directors. Companies also arranged in an index volume by state and major city, and by SIC Code number.

State manufacturing and service directories. Directories are published for every state. A typical listing is arranged by geographic location and includes company addresses, officers, products, and related data. A good source of available directories is *The Directory of Directories* (Detroit: Gale Research Co.). Biennial plus supplements.

Thomas Register of American Manufacturers and Thomas Register Catalog File (New York: Thomas Publishing Company). Annual. Multivolume source lists companies by specific product or service. A separate alphabetical listing of manufacturers aids in locating small companies. There is also a brand name/trademark index. If the city is known, *telephone directories* provide addresses for companies not listed elsewhere.

COMPANY DATA AND FACTS: FINANCIAL

BAR/LNA Multi-Media Service (New York: Leading National Advertisers, Inc.) A series of quarterly reports that provide advertising expenditure statistics in six major media. The "AD $ Summary Report" has statistics arranged by specific brand. Data in other reports are arranged by company and product class.

Company Reports. Company annual reports are useful sources of information. Business libraries and large public libraries with sizable business collections generally collect some of these reports, or they can be requested directly from the company. Among reports filed with the Securities and Exchange Commission, the annual 10-K report is the most detailed.

Corporation Records. Updated quarterly. Published by Standard and Poor's Corporation, this is a source of the latest financial statistics on companies. Contains brief background information and news items relating to a company's operation. Updates material in *Moody's Industrials* and corporation annual reports. Good source for quarterly financial data.

Fortune Double 500 Directory (New York: Time Inc.). Annual. Published in May–August issues of *Fortune* magazine. Provides information on sales, assets, profits, and so forth. Ranks by either sales or assets the 500 largest U.S. industrial corporations. In a separate Service 500 section, ranks the 100 largest diversified-financial, diversified-service, and commercial banking companies, and the 50 largest life insurance, retailing, utility, and transportation companies. Also ranks non-U.S. firms, non-U.S. banks, worldwide firms, and U.S. exporters.

ADVERTISING AND PROMOTION DATA

Advertising Age (Chicago: Crain Communications, Inc.). Selected special issues: "U.S. Advertising Agency Profiles," annual, March. Covers larger agencies. Each agency profile lists billings figure, accounts won and lost, billings breakdown by media, gross income. "Foreign Agency Income Reports," annual, April. Same data as above are given, when available. Agencies arranged by country. "100 Leading National Advertisers," annual, September. For each, data on advertising expenditures, sales and profits, rank of leading product lines and brands, market share, sales, advertising personnel. Other issues published include "Top 100 Leading Markets" (published every three years) and "100 Leading Media Companies" (annual, June).

Broadcasting (Washington, D.C.: Broadcasting Publications, Inc.). "Broadcasting Cablecasting Yearbook" issue, published each spring. Directory of U.S. and Canadian television and radio stations. Also includes television market data and additional industry-related information. A cable section includes information on cable systems in the U.S. and Canada. A related publication is *Television and Cable Factbook* (Washington, D.C.: Television Digest, Inc.). Annual. The *Stations* volume gives expanded information on television stations, including market data. The *Cable and Services* volume covers such areas as cable systems and TV household data.

Journal of Advertising Research (New York: Advertising Research Foundation). Bimonthly. This publication presents research studies, literature reviews, and listings.

Standard Directory of Advertisers (Skokie, Ill.: National Register Publishing Co., Inc.). Annual, plus supplements. Lists U.S. companies doing national or regional advertising. Data include company personnel, name of advertising agency, advertising budget figures, types of media used. Also a separate geographic index.

Standard Directory of Advertising Agencies (Skokie, Ill.: National Register Publication Co., Inc.). Issued three times yearly, plus supplements. Lists agency officers, accounts, and approximate annual billings of about 4400 U.S. and foreign agencies.

Standard Rate and Data Service, Inc. (Skokie, Ill.). Various titles, many issued monthly. Provides current advertising rates and related data for U.S. radio and TV stations, consumer magazines, business publications, newspapers, other media. Some market data included in the radio, TV, and newspaper volumes. The SRDS is considered the standard source of cost estimation for media planning.

Survey of World Advertising Expenditures (New York: Starch INRA Hooper). Annual. Provides estimates of expenditures in various media categories, arranged by country.

CASES FOR PART TWO

CASE 2-1: Computer Town, Inc.*

Computer Town, Inc. was formed by five recent graduates of Duke University's M.B.A. program. All of the group members were computer engineers or programmers as undergraduates, so each of them was experienced with computers. Their objective was to open a profitable retail store in Winston-Salem, North Carolina, a town of approximately 132,000 people. Since three of the founders came from the Winston-Salem area, the group felt it would be beneficial to locate the store there. Computer Town would stock both hardware and software. According to Renee Scott, one of the store's founders, "We'll sell anything related to a computer—monitors, printers, software, floppy disks. You name it, we'll sell it."

The group decided to locate Computer Town in a shopping center. Four malls were being considered, two located in the suburbs and two in downtown Winston-Salem. "Our goal is to be open within six months," said Scott, "but now, our foremost concern is to research all aspects of our entry into the retail computer market."

CASE QUESTIONS

1 What decisions must be made in order to open this retail·outlet?
2 What information is needed to make each of these decisions?
3 What marketing research can be used to provide the required information?

* Coauthored by Sheryl Petras.

CASE 2-2: Twin Pines Golf and Country Club (A)

In mid-May, the Capital Planning Committee of the Twin Pines Golf and Country Club met to discuss a research report that they had just received. This report gave the results of a survey of the club members on the issue of which projects the club should begin this fiscal year. Members of the committee intended to use the report as a basis for selecting among alternative capital projects. A biographical description of the committee members is given in Appendix 1.

Background to the Study

Twin Pines Golf and Country Club was a private club situated in the southwestern corner of Hinsdale, Illinois, a suburb of Chicago. The club was founded in 1936 as an 18-hole golf course and dining room. In 1956, an additional nine holes were built, and in 1969 three outdoor tennis courts were added to the club.

The Capital Planning Committee was a permanent committee of the Twin Pines Club. Its task in recent years involved the overseeing of the maintenance of current facilities. However, in this particular year the Board of Directors of the Club had given an additional task to the committee. They had been asked to make recommendations on new capital facilities. In this letter to the committee, the president of the club stated: "We must be prepared to add new facilities to serve the current and future interests of our members and to attract new members. It is your task to make recommendations in this matter."

In response to this request, the Capital Planning Committee held a series of meetings where they discussed possible projects requiring capital expenditures during the next few years. From these meetings they identified five potential projects and the associated capital costs and operating costs per year. These projects were:

	Capital cost	Operating cost per year
An additional nine golf holes complete with automatic watering system on existing lands	$400,000	$45,000
Swimming pool and clubhouse with lockers	80,000	30,000
Tennis clubhouse, court lighting, and bubble cover for winter	120,000	20,000
Three new tennis courts	30,000	10,000
Purchase of 150 acres of land adjacent to club as a buffer against city expansion or for club expansion	300,000	27,000

The committee decided to obtain the opinion of the membership on the five projects before reaching a decision. In December, a research subcommittee was formed which would obtain the views of the membership. It was the expressed intention of the whole committee to recommend the capital project or projects that the membership desired.

The Study

The research subcommittee developed a questionnaire (see Appendix 2) designed to measure the preference of the membership for the five projects. In March, this questionnaire was mailed to all senior and intermediate members of the club. Table 1 shows the number of questionnaires mailed to each class of membership and the associated return rate. The report prepared by the research subcommittee consisted of a set of tables giving what the committee members thought were the main findings of the survey. These are presented as Tables 2–4.

TABLE 1   QUESTIONNAIRE RETURNS BY CLASS OF MEMBERSHIP

	Number mailed	Number returned	Percent returned
Senior male (club shareholders)	710	540	76
Senior female	650	402	62
Intermediate male (age 21–26)	250	110	44
Intermediate female (age 21–26)	75	32	43
Total	1685	1084	66

TABLE 2   PROJECT PREFERENCE GIVEN KNOWLEDGE OF THE EFFECT ON ANNUAL FEES (Question 4 in the Questionnaire)

Response	Projects					Total responses
	Golf	Swimming pool	Tennis clubhouse	Tennis courts	Land	
Yes	32.5% (352)	37.1% (402)	32.9% (357)	27.4% (297)	23.7% (257)	1665
No	50.6% (549)	59.6% (646)	51.1% (554)	53.6% (581)	60.4% (655)	2995
No opinion	16.9% (183)	3.3% (36)	16.0% (173)	19.0% (206)	15.9% (172)	770
Total respondents	1084	1084	1084	1084	1084	5420

TABLE 3 PROJECT PREFERENCE BY TYPE OF MEMBERSHIP
(Yes to Question 4 and Categories of Question 1)

Membership type*	Projects					
	Golf	Swimming pool	Tennis clubhouse	Tennis courts	Land	Total responses
Senior male	30.2%† (163)	25.9% (140)	27.6% (149)	23.5% (127)	27.2% (147)	726
Senior female	36.4% (146)	38.8% (156)	28.1% (113)	28.7% (115)	19.7% (79)	609
Intermediate male	31.2% (34)	73.6% (81)	67.3% (74)	38.2% (42)	21.4% (24)	255
Intermediate female	29.7% (9)	78.1% (25)	65.6% (21)	40.1% (13)	20.7% (7)	75
Total responses	352	402	357	297	257	1665

*Total response per membership type adds up to more than 100% of the respondents because of multiple responses. Total number of respondents = 1084.
†That is, 30.2% of senior male members are in favor of the golf project.

TABLE 4 PRIORITY CLUB SHOULD ATTACH TO PROJECTS
(Responses to Question 3b)

	High	Medium	Low	No opinion
Additional nine holes	24.7	21.0	45.1	9.2
Swimming pool	28.5	18.7	45.9	6.9
Tennis clubhouse and lights	16.4	16.9	51.2	15.5
Three tennis courts	17.6	15.9	52.0	14.5
Land	19.7	21.4	46.0	12.9

Note: All numbers are percentages by rows. Total number of respondents = 1084.

May 15 Meeting

All members of the Capital Planning Committee were present for the meeting held in the Twin Pines boardroom on May 15. John Watts, the committee chairman, opened the meeting by thanking the research subcommittee for their efforts. He also noted that the Board of Directors of the club had asked him to be prepared to make a recommendation concerning capital expenditures at the next board meeting. This meeting was to be held on May 21. Because of this time pressure, it would be necessary for the Capital Planning Committee to reach a decision at the May 15 meeting.

CASE QUESTIONS

1 What action should the committee take?
2 Why?

BIOGRAPHICAL DESCRIPTION OF CAPITAL PLANNING COMMITTEE MEMBERS

	Age	Family	Occupation	Club activities
John B. Watts (Chairman)	62	Married, 2 sons, ages 29 and 27	President, Exeter Tool Company	Golf
Dr. L. Gary Johnston	45	Married, 1 daughter, age 20; 2 sons, ages 17 and 12	Dentist	Golf, tennis
Joseph R. Taylor	35	Married, 1 son, age 7	Lawyer	Golf
Robert H. Robertson*	59	Married, 3 daughters, ages 32, 30, and 27	President, Robertson Advertising	Golf
Dr. Malcolm R. Richardson	42	Unmarried	Internal medicine specialist	Golf, tennis
Kenneth L. Wecker*	69	Widower, 2 daughters, ages 42 and 38	Retired, president of Alpha Associates, Management Consultants	Golf
Dr. W. Lloyd Hains	53	Married, no children	General practitioner	Golf
Bruce A. Frederick*	46	Married, 1 son, age 16	Sales manager, Beta Electronics	Golf

*Member research subcommittee.

QUESTIONNAIRE

1 *Class of Membership*

Please indicate your membership class:

Senior male	( )
Senior female	( )
Intermediate male	( )
Intermediate female	( )

2 *Junior members living at home*

Ages of sons	( )	( )	( )	( )	( )
Ages of daughters	( )	( )	( )	( )	( )

3 *Proposed Capital Projects*

Your Capital Planning Committee is presently evaluating a number of possible projects. As part of this evaluation we would like your opinion on the projects listed below:

	Capital cost	Operating cost per year
Nine-hole golf course with automatic watering system	$400,000	$45,000
Swimming pool and clubhouse with lockers	80,000	30,000
Tennis clubhouse, court lighting, and bubble cover for winter	120,000	20,000
Three new tennis courts	30,000	10,000
Purchase of land adjacent (150 acres) to the 16th and 17th holes	300,000	27,000

a What is *your* interest in these projects?

	High	Medium	Low
Additional 9 holes	( )	( )	( )
Swimming pool	( )	( )	( )
Tennis clubhouse and lights	( )	( )	( )
Three tennis courts	( )	( )	( )
Land	( )	( )	( )

b What priority should the club attach to each of these projects?

	High	Medium	Low
Additional 9 holes	( )	( )	( )
Swimming pool	( )	( )	( )
Tennis clubhouse and lights	( )	( )	( )
Three tennis courts	( )	( )	( )
Land	( )	( )	( )

4 *Financing*

Your committee has expressed above the capital and operating costs for each project. Below we have stated these costs in terms of the effect these projects will have on the fees of senior members. Would you be in favor of proceeding with the following projects:

	To finance construction over 10 years	Operating costs	Total	In favor	
				Yes	No
Additional 9 holes	$29	$33	$62	( )	( )
Swimming pool	6	22	28	( )	( )
Tennis clubhouse and lights	9	15	24	( )	( )
Three tennis courts	2	7	9	( )	( )
Land	22	20	42	( )	( )

CASE 2-3: Automotive Supply, Inc. *

Automotive Supply, Inc. is a large wholesaler located in Tulsa, Oklahoma. It supplies auto parts to service stations, department stores, discount houses, and retail parts outlets in and around the Tulsa area. Bill Douglass, president of Automotive, was concerned about his company's declining sales. Between 1982 and 1986 revenues dropped from $8 million to $5 million, and he feared the business would go under unless something was done to improve its sales picture. "It's those foreign imports," lamented Douglass, "they're ruining my parts business." ASI only sold parts for domestic cars, and Douglass did not want to enter the foreign parts market.

In an effort to improve profits, Douglass contacted the Rightway Research firm to submit a proposal for marketing research which would help in formulating a long-range growth strategy for Automotive. Limited funds forced Douglass to set a low budget for the research project. Douglass received Rightway's proposal and was in the process of evaluating it. The submitted proposal is as follows:

RIGHTWAY RESEARCH

The influx of foreign cars into the American auto market has had an adverse effect on all suppliers of domestic parts. Success in this market is dependent on two things: accurate automobile demand forecasts and a sufficient inventory to meet retailers' needs. Lack of either can result in disaster. Automotive's research objective is thus:

> To obtain the data which would enable Automotive to (1) accurately forecast demand for autos, and (2) make proper inventory decisions.

A list of the information needs and sources of information to meet those needs follows.

Information needs	Source(s)
Auto industry	
Total demand	Wards Automotive
Demand by make and model	Reports
Proportion of new vs. used sales	Motor Statistics
Diesel car sales	(R.L. Polk & Co.)
Projected gasoline prices	City, county, and
Availability of parts from	state planning
manufacturers	commission
Government regulations	reports
	Manufacturers
Population	
Growth	Statistical Abstracts
Age and sex composition	of the U.S.

* Coauthored by Sheryl Petras.

Economic	
Number of dual-career households	Local employment bureau
Employment, payroll, and sales of the major industries in the market area	Statistical Abstracts
Labor market	
GNP for market area	
Availability of money for loans, status of interest rates	
Current government position on imports—quotas vs. free trade	

As you can see, most of the information needed is readily available in federal, state, and county publications, trade journals, manufacturer publications, and syndicated sources. This data can be obtained at a low or moderate cost. The above list is by no means complete; rather it represents the minimum sources that Automotive should be aware of and carefully monitor.

CASE QUESTIONS

1 Evaluate the stated research objective and the information needs presented in the proposal.
2 Are the data sources appropriate to the information needs and research objectives? Why or why not?
3 Evaluate the data collection framework.
4 What other possible research design and data sources could be used?

SAMPLING

CHAPTER 7

THE BASICS OF SAMPLING

Without sampling, marketing research as we know it today would not exist. Virtually every marketing research study requires the selection of some kind of sample. When a new product is placed in households for trial, we must select the households to use; when we want to monitor the sales we are experiencing in a geographical area, we must select the stores in the area in which we will record the sales; when we want to conduct a group interview about meat prices, we must select eight to ten people to take part in the group.

The alternative to sampling is to take a census. In a census, we execute our study using *all available elements of a defined population.* Thus, in the examples above, we would use all households for the product placement test, all stores in the area for the sales monitoring, etc.

In this chapter, we shall outline the basic terminology and concepts of sampling and then discuss three types of nonprobability sampling procedures. This chapter lays the basic groundwork necessary for an understanding of the probability sampling procedures that will be discussed in Chapters 8 and 9.

SAMPLING: AN INTRODUCTION

The Benefits of Sampling

Sampling is used very frequently in marketing research because it offers some major benefits over taking a census.

1 *A sample saves money:* The cost of an hour-long in-person interview may be about $30 to $55 per interview. Clearly, we would save money by interviewing 1000 people rather than the 1 million who make up the relevant population.

2 *A sample saves time:* In the above example, we would have 1000 hours of interviewing with a sample versus 1 million hours with a census. To this we must add the time for, say, printing questionnaires, training field interviewers, and preparing the completed questionnaires for data analysis. The problem that led to this study being undertaken is likely to be long forgotten before the census is complete.

3 *A sample may be more accurate:* Surprising as it may seem, this is indeed true. This results from several sources of inaccuracy, called *nonsampling errors,* that occur in the marketing research process. In a census study, we will need more interviewers, more supervisors of interviewers, more people to convert the raw questionnaires to computer input, etc. The smaller the study, the more likely we are to obtain more highly skilled people for each stage of the research process. As the staff gets bigger, the quality of people will fall, and the control and supervision of their activities will become more difficult. Also, a census may take so long that the marketing phenomenon of interest may have changed. For example, questions about the awareness of a new product have meaning only at one point in time. A census awareness level would be biased upward by the passage of time. All of this leads to more errors and less accurate results.

Like a census, a sample includes nonsampling errors too, but to a lesser degree. Unlike a census, a sample also gives us sampling error. This is a statistical concept that will be discussed in detail in Chapter 8. For now, we should just remember that a sample statistic provides an estimate of a population value. To the extent that the two values differ, sampling error has occurred.

Thus, a sample will be more accurate than a census if the total of sampling and nonsampling errors for the sample is less than nonsampling types of errors for the census.

4 *A sample is better in the event that the study results in the destruction or contamination of the element sampled:* Product usage tests result in the consumption of the product. Clearly, in a taste test, taking a census of Budweiser beer is not the way to run a profitable business. Similarly, interviewing people may sensitize them to the topic of the interview. We can say that they have been "contaminated" with respect to this topic. We may want to interview people again about the same topic to see whether, for example, our advertising campaign has had an impact. We would like to interview those who have not been contaminated by a previous interview. If a census were taken previously, all subjects of interest would have been contaminated.

Some Necessary Sampling Concepts

With the reasons for sampling established, we now turn to the question of how a sample is selected. First we must learn the definition of some basic sampling concepts, that is, the language of sampling. The taxonomy of sampling terms which follows is based on that used by Leslie Kish,[1] as adapted by Earl Babbie.[2]

---

[1] Leslie Kish, *Survey Sampling* (New York: Wiley, 1965), pp. 6–7.
[2] Earl Babbie, *Survey Research Methods* (Belmont, Calif.: Wadsworth, 1973), pp. 79–82.

Element   *An element is the unit about which information is sought.* It provides the basis of the analysis that we will undertake. The most common elements in marketing research sampling are individuals. In other instances, the elements could be products, stores, companies, families, etc. The elements in any specific sample would depend on the objectives of the study.

Population   A population, or universe, as it is also called, is the aggregate of all the elements defined prior to selection of the sample. A properly designated population must be defined in terms of (1) *elements,* (2) *sampling units,* (3) *extent,* and (4) *time.* For example, a survey of consumers might specify the relevant population as:

1 Element: females 18—50
2 Sampling units: females 18—50
3 Extent: Texas
4 Time: May 1—June 15, 1987

Alternatively, the population for a study designed to measure buyer reaction to a new industrial chemical might be:

1 Element: chemical engineers
2 Sampling units: companies purchasing over $300,000 of chemicals per year;
                     then chemical engineers
3 Extent: the continental United States
4 Time: 1987

Or, if we wished to monitor the sales of a new consumer product, the population might be:

1 Element: our product
2 Sampling units: supermarkets, drugstores, discount stores; then our product
3 Extent: Boston
4 Time: May 5—12, 1987

We cannot overstress how critical it is to define the population to this level of detail; nothing else constitutes proper sampling.

Sampling Unit   Previously, we used the term "sampling unit" in defining a relevant population. It is now time to define it more explicitly. A sampling unit is the element or elements available for selection at some stage of the sampling process. In the simplest type of sampling, single-stage sampling, the sampling units and the elements are the same. For example, in our first population illustration above, both the elements and the sampling units were "females 18—50." This indicates a direct, one-stage sampling process. We would select our sample of females 18—50 directly.

With more complex sampling procedures, different levels of sampling units may be utilized, and then the sampling units and elements differ in all but the last stage. Consider our second illustration above. Our elements of interest are chemical engineers. However, we are reaching these engineers indirectly, through a two-stage process. First, we will select a sample of "companies purchasing over $300,000 of chemicals per year." Then, within these selected companies we will select a sample of chemical engineers. This is a two-stage sampling process. Note that only at the final stage are elements and sampling units identical. Similarly, the third illustration above is also a two-stage process, with the stores constituting the first stage and "our product" the second.

A sampling process may have as many stages as the reseacher desires. All he or she must do is specify the sampling unit at each stage. For example, a four-stage sample might be:

Stage 1: Cities over 500,000 population
Stage 2: City blocks
Stage 3: Households
Stage 4: Males 50 and over

The elements of interest in this study would, of course, be "males 50 and over." The terms "primary sampling units," "secondary sampling units," "tertiary sampling units," and "final sampling units" are often used to designate the successive stages of the process.

Sampling Frame   A sampling frame is a list of all the sampling units available for selection at a stage of the sampling process. At the final stage, the actual sample is drawn from such a list. Some of the most creative thinking in a marketing research project may be related to the specification of a sampling frame. A frame may be a class list, a list of registered voters, a telephone book, an employee list, or even a map. In the case of a map we would be sampling pieces of geography. A city block would be an example. The frame list may be printed or stored in a computer file, on tape or disk. Once a population is specified, you then search for a good sampling frame. Often the availability of a sampling frame defines the population, as no per- fect fit is available between population and frame. Each stage of a sampling process requires its own sampling frame. Thus, the four-stage sampling process listed above would require four sampling frames as follows: (1) a list of cities of over 500,000 population, (2) a list of city blocks within the selected cities, (3) a list of households within the selected city blocks, and (4) a list of males 50 and over within the selected households. A direct, one-stage sampling selection procedure would require only one sampling frame, which would contain all the elements in the population.

Study Population   A study population is the aggregate of elements from which the sample is drawn. Previously, we defined a population as the "aggregate of the ele- ments defined prior to the selection of the sample." Unfortunately, practical difficulties arise that cause the actual sample to be drawn from a somewhat different population from the one we defined a priori. What happens is that elements of the population are omitted from the sampling frame. For example, a club membership list may be incomplete, some people have unlisted phone numbers, a map may not include a new street.

The study population, then, is the aggregation of elements from which the sample is actually selected. It is with regard to this study population that we can make proper inferences, even though our real interest is the original population.

The Sampling Process: An Overview

Armed with the sampling concepts we just defined, we can describe in overview the steps in selecting a sample. Figure 7-1 presents this overview.

Step 1   Define the population. This would, of course, include (1) the elements, (2) the sampling units, (3) the extent, and (4) the time.

Step 2   Identify the sampling frame from which the sample will be selected.

Step 3   Decide on a sample size. Here we determine how many elements to include in the sample. Deciding when a sample is too big or too small is a difficult problem. We will discuss this in Chapter 8.

FIGURE 7-1   Steps in selecting a sample.

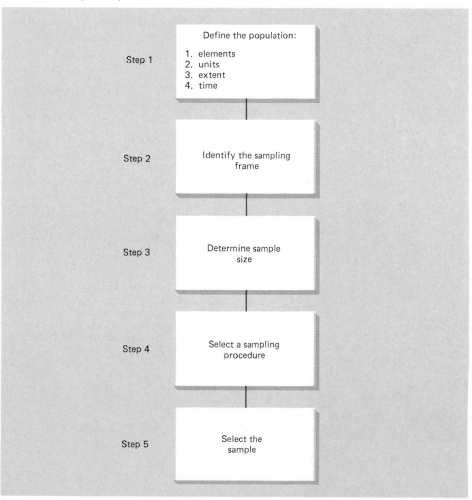

Step 4   Select a specific procedure by which the sample will be determined. Exactly how will the decision be made on which population elements to include in the sample? This issue is examined in this and the next two chapters. (In actuality, Steps 3 and 4 are often done at the same time.)

Step 5   Physically select the sample based upon the procedure previously described in Step 4.

SAMPLING PROCEDURES

There are many different procedures by which researchers may select their samples, but one fundamental concept must be established at the outset—the distinction between (1) a probability sample and (2) a nonprobability sample.

In *probability sampling,* each element of the population has a known chance of being selected for the sample. The sampling is done by mathematical decision rules that leave no discretion to the researcher or field interviewer. Note that we said a "known chance" and not an "equal chance" of being selected. Equal-chance probability sampling is only a very special case of probability sampling, called *simple random sampling.* What probability sampling allows us to do is calculate the likely extent to which the sample value differs from the population value of interest. This difference is called *sampling error.* We will discuss sampling error in more detail in Chapter 8.

In *nonprobability sampling,* the selection of a population element to be part of the sample is based in some part on the judgment of the researcher or field interviewer. There is no known chance of any particular element in the population being selected. We are therefore unable to calculate the sampling error that has occurred. We have absolutely no idea whether or not the sample estimates calculated from a nonprobability sample are accurate or not. We are in the realm of a wish and a prayer.

There are a number of different sampling procedures that fall into the category of nonprobability methods and a number that are probability methods. Figure 7-2 lists them. In the rest of this chapter we will discuss the three kinds of nonprobability

FIGURE 7-2   Sampling procedures.

samples: convenience, judgment, and quota. Chapter 8 presents a discussion of both the most elementary type of probability sampling, simple random sampling, and the determination of sample size. Chapter 9 discusses the more complex probability sampling procedures, stratified and cluster sampling.

Nonprobability Sampling Procedures

Convenience Sampling   Convenience samples are selected, as the name implies, on the basis of the convenience of the researcher. Examples here include (1) asking for people to volunteer to test products and then using these people, (2) stopping people in a shopping mall to get their opinion, (3) using students or church groups for conducting an experiment, (4) having "people in the street interviews" by a television station, and so on. In each instance, the sampling unit or element either is self-selected or has been selected because it was easily available. In all cases it is unclear as to what population the actual sample is drawn from. The television interviewer may state that her sample represents the community. Clearly, she is wrong. Most members of the community had no chance of being selected. It is only those who happened to be where the interviewer was at the time of the show who had a chance of being selected. Even the exact chance of these people being selected is unknown.

In such cases, the difference between the population value of interest and the sample value is unknown, in terms of both size and direction. We cannot measure sampling error, and clearly we cannot make any definitive or conclusive statements about the results from such a sample. However, convenience samples can be most easily justified at the exploratory stage of research, as a basis for generating hypotheses, and for conclusive studies where the manager is willing to accept the risk that the study results might have great inaccuracies. Convenience sampling is extensively used in practice.

Judgment Sampling   Judgment samples (or purposive samples, as they are also called) are selected on the basis of what *some expert thinks* those particular sampling units or elements will contribute to answering the particular research question at hand. For example, in test marketing, a judgment is made as to which cities would constitute the best ones for testing the marketability of a new product. In industrial marketing research, the decision to interview a purchasing agent about a given product constitutes a judgment sample. He or she must be regarded as a representative of the company by the person who draws the sample. Other examples could include an instructor's choice of someone to start a class discussion; expert witnesses presenting their views in court; and the selection of stores in an area to try out a new display.

Again, the degree and direction of error are unknown, and definite statements are not meaningful. However, if the expert's judgment is valid, the sample will be a better one than if a convenience sample were used. Judgment sampling is moderately used in practice.

Quota Sampling   Quota samples are a special type of purposive sample. Here the researcher takes explicit steps to obtain a sample that is similar to the population on some prespecified "control" characteristics. For example, an interviewer may be instructed to conduct half of the interviews with people 30 years old and over, and half with people under 30. Here, the control characteristic is the age of respondents. Specifying this particular control statement implies, of course, that the researcher knows the population of interest is equally divided among persons 30 years old and over and persons under 30. Obviously this is a simple example, as only one control characteristic was used.

More realistically, in order to be more representative of a population, we would have to "control" on a number of characteristics. Therefore, to properly select a quota sample we must (1) specify a list of relevant control characteristics and (2) know the distribution of these characteristics across our population. Let's look at an example. Suppose we have two control characteristics of interest, age and race, as follows:

1 Age: 2 categories—under 30 and 30 and over
2 Race: 2 categories—white and nonwhite

There are then four sampling cells of interest. They are (1) under 30 and white, (2) 30 and over and white, (3) under 30 nonwhite, and (4) 30 and over and nonwhite. What we must know is the proportion of the population in each of these cells. This is a much more complex question than just knowing the proportion of the population in a single control characteristic. Note what happens to the number of sampling cells as the number of control characteristics and associated categories increase. Suppose we had four characteristics for control, as follows:

1 Age: 4 categories—(1) under 18, (2) 18–30, (3) 31–50, (4) over 50
2 Race: 3 categories—(1) white, (2) black, (3) other
3 Education: 4 categories—(1) elementary school, (2) high school, (3) college, (4) graduate school
4 Incomes: 5 categories (1) under $5000 (2) $5000–$7499, (3) $7500–$9999, (4) $10,000–$14,999, (5) $15,000 and over

This would result in $4 \times 3 \times 4 \times 5 = 240$ sampling cells. We would have to have information on the proportion of the population in each of these 240 cells. Such a description of the particular population that interests us may be extremely difficult or impossible to find. As a matter of fact, often our intent is in measuring the population on these types of characteristics.

However, if up-to-date knowledge of the distribution of the control characteristics is available, we may determine the size of sample to select in each cell. Cell sample size is simply:

$$\text{Total sample size} \times \text{proportion desired in the cell}$$

For example, if our total sample is 1200 and the proportion in Cell 1 is .05 (5 percent), the number of people with those characteristics in our sample for Cell 1 would be:

$$1200 \times .05 = 60$$

We would then direct our interviewer to interview 60 people with these characteristics. The same procedure is repeated for all cells. The actual selection of specific sample elements is left to the judgment of the interviewer.

There are some problems with quota samples.

1 The proportion of respondents assigned to each cell must be accurate and up to date. This is often difficult or impossible.

2 The "proper" control characteristics must be selected; that is, all characteristics that are related to the measures of interest must be included. For example, if we want to learn people's attitudes toward males having long hair, it would be a mistake not to use age as a control factor, since age is probably related to the attitude toward long hair for males. In any particular study, we may omit a relevant control characteristic and not be aware of it. Consequently, our results can be misleading.

3 The third problem concerns the practical difficulties associated with including more and more control characteristics. As noted before, we end up with too many cells for the interviewers to work with; finding the desired respondents will not be easy.

4 A fourth difficulty concerns the interviewer's selection of the actual respondents to interview. In finding people who fit the desired description, he or she may avoid people who look unfriendly, live in poorly painted houses, live in apartment buildings, etc. An unknown bias is thus introduced into the study. Therefore, a quota sample and population may be exactly the same on measures for which we know the characteristics of both, but differ substantially on measures for which we have only the sample value. Indeed, it is these "sample only" measures that are the ones that really interest us to begin with. They are the reason for taking the sample. The sample provides estimates of the unknown population value. If we knew the population value, there would be no reason for sampling. The validity of a quota sample is often presented in terms of the match between known population and sample characteristics. Beware of this. The error in other sample measures is again of unknown size and direction.

Quota samples are useful in preliminary stages of research, and if done with great care they can provide more definitive answers. However, they are likely to be less valid than a probability sample. Quota sampling is very extensively used in practice.

Probability Sampling Procedures

Probability sampling is relatively new in terms of its actual application in marketing research. Before 1950, the nonprobability sample was almost the only kind used in real field studies. Advances in sampling theory and field sampling techniques since then have allowed probability sampling to become a real alternative for marketing researchers.

In probability sampling, the chance that a population element will be included in the sample is known, and the sample elements are selected by means of mechanical decision rules. No discretion is left to the researcher or field interviewer in selecting sample elements. There is no guarantee that the results obtained with a probability sample will be more accurate than those obtained with a nonprobability sample; what the former allows the researcher to do is to measure the amount of sampling error likely to occur in his or her sample. This provides a measure of the accuracy of the sample result. With nonprobability sampling no such error measure exists.

We will develop probability sampling concepts in more detail in the next two chapters.

SUMMARY

1 Sampling is an activity carried on in almost all marketing research.

2 The advantages of sampling over a census include saving money, saving time, obtaining more accurate information, and avoiding the destruction or contamination of all the elements in the population.

3 An element is the unit about which information is sought. A population is the aggregate of the elements defined prior to selection of the sample. It is defined in terms of (1) elements, (2) sampling units, (3) extent, and (4) time. A sampling unit is the element or elements available for selection at some stage of the sampling process. A sampling frame is a list of all the sampling units available for selection at a stage of the sampling process.

4 The steps in the sampling process are: (1) define the population, (2) identify the sampling frame, (3) decide on the sample size, (4) select a specific procedure by which the sample will be determined, and (5) physically draw the sample.

5 In probability sampling each element of the population has a known chance of being selected. In simple random sampling each element has an equal chance of being selected. In nonprobability sampling, the selection of elements is based in some part on the judgment of the researcher.

6 Nonprobability sampling procedures include the use of convenience, judgment, and quota samples. Convenience samples are selected at the convenience of the researcher, judgement samples on the basis of the expert opinion of the researcher, and quota samples on the basis of the distribution of the defined population across control characteristics.

DISCUSSION QUESTIONS

1 Why is sampling so often used in marketing research?
2 Distinguish among the following sample concepts: element, population, sampling unit, sampling frame, and study population.
3 Distinguish between probability and nonprobability sampling.
4 What is the nature of the error generated by a nonprobability sampling procedure?
5 Distinguish among three types of nonprobability sampling procedures.
6 Why are nonprobability sampling procedures so often used in practice?

CHAPTER 8

SIMPLE RANDOM SAMPLING AND SAMPLE SIZE

The previous chapter presented concepts essential for understanding sampling in marketing research and also drew the fundamental distinction between probability and nonprobability sampling procedures. This chapter presents a detailed description of the most elementary type of probability sampling, simple random sampling. Care is taken to present a step-by-step approach, because the principles developed here have direct application to the more frequently used and more complex sampling procedures discussed in Chapter 9. We will also look at the issue of the accuracy of sample results. For example, in 1936 a sample of over 2 million persons taken by the *Literary Digest* predicted a victory for Landon over Roosevelt by about 15 percent. "President" Landon must have wondered how the sample could have been so wrong. In contrast, in 1984 all major polls picked Reagan to win, and most estimated his vote percentage to be around 57 to 60 percent. He actually received 59 percent. How can a sample of 2000 persons be more accurate than a sample of 2 million? By the end of this chapter you will understand how.

Integral to the question of sample result accuracy is the issue of how to determine the sample size to use. This is discussed later in this chapter.

SIMPLE RANDOM SAMPLING

It is our assumption in writing this chapter that you have had one course in statistics. However, experience tells us that most students have found statistics difficult and welcome a review of basic concepts. Its usefulness to real problems may also have been obscure until now. Our discussion will therefore start with basics, stay at an elementary level, and sacrifice technical elegance for communication purposes. We hope to demonstrate that basic sampling concepts are fundamental to the practice of marketing research.

The discussion that follows is based on classical statistics. There is an alternative type of statistics, called bayesian statistics or decision theory statistics, that can be used in sampling. This approach is more complex and remains for the most part an academic exercise, as most organizations do not use it in practice. You are referred to the appendix to Chapter 4 for the presentation of this material.

Some Terms and Symbols Defined

To begin our discussion of simple random sampling, we must again define a few terms.

Parameter   A parameter is a summary description of a measure in the defined population. This is the true value we would obtain if we undertook a census that did not contain any nonsampling errors. The average age of a class in marketing research and the average income of new business school graduates are parameters.

Statistic   A statistic is a summary description of a measure in the selected sample. The sample statistic is used to estimate the population parameter. Thus, the average age of a class in marketing research and the average income of new business school graduates would also be statistics if measured by means of a sample.

Some Symbols to Get Straight   There are certain conventions that are used in sampling and statistics. The following symbols and associated meanings will be used in this book. Basically, Greek letters are used for population parameters and English letters for sample statistics. (See Appendix Table A-7 for a complete listing of the Greek alphabet.) We also distinguish between the symbols for population size, N, and sample size, n.

	Concept	Population symbol	Sample symbol
A. Continuous measures	Mean or average of continuous variable	μ	$\bar{X}$
	Variance of continuous variable	σ^2	s^2
B. Dichotomous or two-answer measures or binomial measures (e.g., Are you female— yes or no)	Proportion answering "yes"	π	p
	Proportion answering "no"	$(1 - \pi)$	$(1 - p)$ or q
	Variance of proportion	σ^2	s^2

A Population to Examine

Table 8-1 presents a population that we will use to illustrate sampling concepts. This population consists of students who are taking an Introduction to Marketing course

TABLE 8-1   CENSUS OF AGE AND ELECTION OF MARKETING RESEARCH COURSE
AS OPTION OF STUDENTS

(1) Student number	(2) Age (X_1)	(3) Election of marketing research course 1 = yes, 0 = no (X_2)	(4) $x = X_1 - \mu$	(5) $x^2 = (X_1 - \mu)^2$
1	25	1	1.3	1.69
2	27	0	3.3	10.89
3	29	1	5.3	28.09
4	31	1	7.3	53.29
5	25	0	1.3	1.69
6	29	0	5.3	28.09
7	27	0	3.3	10.89
8	24	0	.3	.09
9	27	1	3.3	10.89
10	28	1	4.3	18.49
11	33	0	9.3	86.49
12	29	1	5.3	28.09
13	26	0	2.3	5.29
14	28	0	4.3	18.49
15	28	1	4.3	18.49
16	26	0	2.3	5.29
17	26	1	2.3	5.29
18	36	1	12.3	151.29
19	29	0	4.3	18.49
20	26	0	2.3	5.29
21	21	0	−2.7	7.29
22	19	0	−4.7	22.09
23	24	0	.3	.09
24	22	0	−1.7	2.89
25	20	1	−3.7	13.69
26	22	0	−1.7	2.89
27	19	1	−4.7	22.09
28	20	0	−3.7	13.69
29	19	0	−4.7	22.09
30	24	0	.3	.09
31	25	0	1.3	1.69
32	22	1	−1.7	2.89
33	20	0	−3.7	13.69
34	21	1	−2.7	7.29
35	21	0	−2.7	7.29
36	23	1	−.7	.49
37	21	0	−2.7	7.29
38	23	0	−.7	.49
39	18	0	−5.7	32.49
40	21	1	−2.7	7.29
41	19	0	−4.7	22.09
42	23	0	−.7	.49
43	22	1	−1.7	2.89
44	19	0	−4.7	22.09
45	20	0	−3.7	13.69
46	20	0	−3.7	13.69

(Continued)

TABLE 8-1 (*Continued*)

(1) Student number	(2) Age (X_1)	(3) Election of marketing research course $1 = yes,$ $0 = no$ (X_2)	(4) $x = X_1 - \mu$	(5) $x^2 = (X_1 - \mu)^2$
47	21	0	-2.7	7.29
48	20	1	-3.7	13.69
49	19	0	-4.7	22.09
50	18	0	-5.7	32.49
	$\Sigma X_1 = 1184$	$\Sigma X_2 = 17$	$\Sigma(X_1 - \mu) = 0$	$\Sigma(X_1 - \mu)^2 = 844.90$

from a particular professor. The professor has collected three pieces of information from them:

1 The student number of each student (column 1)
2 The age of each student (column 2)
3 A statement as to whether the student intends to take the course in marketing research before graduation, with answers coded as follows: 1 = yes, the student intends to take marketing research; and 0 = no, the student does not intend to take marketing research (column 3)

The other columns in Table 8-1 will be used in later calculations. The student number will be used only to identify each population element. It is the other two items that interest us from a measurement point of view. We note that age is a continuous variable, and election of marketing research is a dichotomous variable. Let's identify them as follows:

$$Age = X_1$$
$$Election\ of\ marketing\ research = X_2$$

Calculation of Population Parameters for Continuous Variables

As a way of clarifying the nature of sample statistics, we will first look at the calculation of parameters taken from a census. Table 8-1 presents a census of the age and the election of a marketing research course as an option of students in an Introduction to Marketing course.

The measure in column 2, age, is a continuous variable. Let's calculate a measure of central tendency and a measure of dispersion for age as follows:

Central tendency: the mean or average $= \mu$
Dispersion: the variance and standard deviation $= \sigma^2$ and σ, respectively

For a population the mean is simply *the sum of the values divided by the number in the population*. Thus,

$$\mu = \frac{\sum\limits_{i=1}^{N} X_i}{N}$$

$$= \frac{25 + 27 + \cdots + 18}{50} = \frac{1184}{50}$$

$$= 23.7$$

So the average age in the class is 23.7.

The variance of a population measure is the *sum of the squared deviations about the mean divided by the number in the population.* Thus,

$$\sigma^2 = \frac{\sum\limits_{i=1}^{N} (X_i - \mu)^2}{N}$$

Column 4 of Table 8-1 lists the deviations from the mean, and column 5 lists the squares of these deviations. Here,

$$\sigma^2 = \frac{(25 - 23.7)^2 + (27 - 23.7)^2 + \cdots + (18 - 23.7)^2}{50}$$

$$= \frac{(1.3)^2 + (3.3)^2 + \cdots + (-5.7)^2}{50}$$

$$= \frac{1.69 + 10.89 + \cdots + 32.49}{50}$$

$$= \frac{844.90}{50}$$

$$= 16.9$$

The standard deviation is *the square root of the variance:*

$$\sigma = \sqrt{16.9}$$

$$= 4.1$$

Calculation of Population Parameters for Dichotomous Variables

Column 3 of Table 8-1 presents the values associated with the dichotomous variable, the election of marketing research as an option. It is dichotomous because only the answers yes or no are allowed. "Yes" is coded 1, and "no" is coded 0 (zero).

In the same way that we calculated the mean, variance, and standard deviation of age, let us now turn to the election of marketing research.

$$\pi = \frac{\sum\limits_{i=1}^{N} X_i}{N}$$

$$= \frac{(1 + 0 + \cdots + 0)}{50}$$

$$= \frac{17}{50}$$

$$= .34, \text{ and } (1 - \pi) = .66$$

The proportion of the population electing marketing research is .34. The variance, as before, is

$$\sigma^2 = \frac{\sum\limits_{i=1}^{N} (X_i - \pi)^2}{N}$$

$$= \frac{(1 - .34)^2 + (0 - .34)^2 + \cdots + (0 - .34)^2}{50}$$

We note that $(1 - .34)^2$ occurs every time $X_2 = 1$. Thus it occurs .34 of the time. Also we note that $(0 - .34)^2$ occurs every time $X_2 = 0$, or .66 of the time. Thus

$$\sigma^2 = (1 - .34)^2(.34) + (0 - .34)^2(.66)$$

$$= (.66)^2(.34) + (-.34)^2(.66)$$

$$= .2244$$

Then

$$\sigma = \sqrt{.2244}$$

$$= .473$$

The general formula for σ^2 is

$$\sigma^2 = \pi(1 - \pi)$$

$$= (.34)(.66)$$

$$= .2244$$

and

$$\sigma = \sqrt{\pi(1 - \pi)} = \sqrt{.2244} = .473$$

What we have done is calculate parameters that describe a known population. Let us now proceed to sample from this population. Our interest in the samples we draw will be to calculate statistics that describe the sample, and to make inferences about how well these statistics estimate the parameters of the population. In the terms of a statistics course, we are interested in descriptive and inferential statistics, respectively.

Calculation of Sample Statistics for Continuous Variables

Earlier we calculated population parameters for the age of students in Table 8-1. Let us now draw a sample from that population and calculate the mean, variance, and standard deviation of the sample. Our method of sampling will be simple random sampling.

There are two conditions that define the existence of simple random sampling. They are: (1) each element has an equal chance of being selected and (2) each combination of the n sample elements has an equal chance of being selected. Previously we noted only the first condition as defining simple random sampling; this was done to keep the discussion simple. Now we must note that there are other probability sampling procedures in which the elements have an equal chance of selection. However, in all other sampling procedures, constraints are put on the possible combinations of sampling elements such that all combinations of elements are not equally likely. Mechanically, we use a set of random numbers to make the selection. The list of random numbers in Appendix Table A-1 (at the end of the text), as the name implies, is composed of numbers that have no pattern of occurrence. Any number is as likely to appear in any spot on the table as any other. Each student is identified by a two-digit student number ranging from 01 to 50. Thus, we could use the table to give us a two-digit number between 01 and 50 to select an element for the sample. We would use as many of these two-digit numbers as we wanted elements in the sample.

An example will help make this clear. Suppose we wish to select a sample with $n = 5$. If we start on Appendix Table A-1 at an arbitrary point in the 36th row, first column, and move horizontally, we would select a sample consisting of elements numbered 32, 17, 05, 37, and 41. These are the first five two-digit numbers between 01 and 50 that we meet. Our sample values for age and election of marketing research would be:

Student number	Age	Election of marketing research
32	22	1
17	26	1
05	25	0
37	21	0
41	19	0

We have selected a sample of size 5 from a population of size 50. Thus we have selected n/N or 5/50 or 1/10 or .1 of the population elements. We say that the *sampling fraction* is .1.

The sampling fraction can be used to estimate total population usage of a product or service from the total sample usage. Suppose that our sample of five students uses a total of 35 gallons of gasoline a week. Then the estimated total population usage of gasoline would be

$$\frac{\text{Total sample usage}}{\text{Sampling fraction}} = \frac{35}{.1}$$

$$= 350 \text{ gallons}$$

The mean or average of the sample is simply *the sum of the values divided by the sample size.* Thus,

$$\bar{X} = \frac{\sum\limits_{i=1}^{n} X_i}{n}$$

$$= \frac{22 + 26 + 25 + 21 + 19}{5}$$

$$= \frac{113}{5}$$

$$= 22.6$$

Our mean sample statistics value for age is 22.6. We note that this is slightly lower than our true population mean age of 23.7. In most real problems we would not know the true mean age and so would use the sample mean as our best estimate of the true value.

The sample variance is *the sum of squared deviations about the mean divided by the degrees of freedom we have available.*

$$s^2 = \frac{\sum\limits_{i=1}^{n} (X_i - \bar{X})^2}{\text{degrees of freedom (df)}}$$

A sample is capable of allowing us to calculate a number of statistics. The first statistic limits the values that other statistics may take.[1] We say that one degree of freedom was used in calculating the first statistic. More generally, degrees of freedom equal *the number of independent observations on the variables of interest minus the number of statistics calculated.* Or

$$df = \text{sample size} - \text{number of statistics calculated}$$

In calculating the mean for our sample we used up one degree of freedom, and we must take this into consideration in calculating the variance. Thus, the degrees of

---

[1] An example might help. If we have two numbers, 2 and 3, we calculate the mean as 2.5. If someone is told that we have two numbers, that one number is 2, and that the mean of the numbers is 2.5, he or she knows the other number must be 3; it has no freedom to take any value except 3. Thus this sample of $n = 2$ has one degree of freedom $(n - 1)$.

freedom for our sample variance are $n - 1$. So

$$
\begin{aligned}
s^2 &= \frac{\sum_{i=1}^{n} (X_i - \bar{X})^2}{n - 1} \\
&= \frac{(22 - 22.6)^2 + (26 - 22.6)^2 + (25 - 22.6)^2 + (21 - 22.6)^2 + (19 - 22.6)^2}{5 - 1} \\
&= \frac{(-.6)^2 + (3.4)^2 + (2.4)^2 + (-1.6)^2 + (-3.6)^2}{4} \\
&= \frac{.36 + 11.56 + 5.76 + 2.56 + 12.96}{4} \\
&= \frac{33.20}{4} \\
&= 8.3
\end{aligned}
$$

Our population variance was 16.9, so our sample has understated it somewhat. Note that if we had divided by n instead of $n - 1$, the variance would have been even smaller. This is generally what happens. Division by n leads to an understatement of the variance.

The standard deviation would be

$$
\begin{aligned}
s &= \sqrt{8.3} \\
&= 2.88
\end{aligned}
$$

We have now calculated descriptive statistics for our continuous variable. Let's look at the numerator of our variance equation. It is

$$
\sum_{i=1}^{n} (X_i - \bar{X})^2
$$

In words, it is the sum of squared deviations about the mean. Or, more simply, we will refer to it as *the sum of squares*, or "SS." We will use this terminology throughout the book. We note, then, that the variance is simply

$$
\frac{SS}{df}
$$

Remember this!

We now introduce a simplification of our formula for calculating variance and standard deviation for a continuous variable. This new formula is called the *computational formula* for calculating variance. It is

$$
s^2 = \frac{\Sigma X^2 - [(\Sigma X)^2 / n]}{n - 1}
$$

and

$$s = \sqrt{\frac{\Sigma X^2 - [(\Sigma X)^2/n]}{n - 1}}$$

In our sample of 5,

$$\Sigma X^2 = (22)^2 + (26)^2 + (25)^2 + (21)^2 + (19)^2 = 2587$$

$$(\Sigma X)^2 = (22 + 26 + 25 + 21 + 19)^2 = (113)^2 = 12,769$$

Thus,

$$s^2 = \frac{2587 - (12,769/5)}{4}$$

$$= \frac{2587 - 2553.8}{4}$$

$$= \frac{33.2}{4}$$

$$= 8.3$$

and

$$s = \sqrt{8.3} = 2.88$$

We note that these values for s^2 and s are exactly the same as previously calculated. In all future calculations of s^2 and s we will use the computational formula, as it saves a great deal of work.

Calculation of Sample Statistics for Dichotomous Variables

Now let's calculate the mean, variance, and standard deviation of our dichotomous variable, election of marketing research.

$$p = \frac{\sum_{i=1}^{n} X_i}{n}$$

$$= \frac{1 + 1 + 0 + 0 + 0}{5}$$

$$= \frac{2}{5}$$

$$= .4$$

We note that $q = (1 - p) = (1 - .4) = .6$.

The variance:

$$s^2 = \frac{\sum_{i=1}^{n} (X_i - p)^2}{df}$$

$$= \frac{(1 - .4)^2 + (1 - .4)^2 + (0 - .4)^2 + (0 - .4)^2 + (0 - .4)^2}{5 - 1}$$

$$= \frac{(.6)^2 + (.6)^2 + (-.4)^2 + (-.4)^2 + (-.4)^2}{4}$$

$$= \frac{1.2}{4}$$

$$= .3$$

The standard deviation:

$$s = \sqrt{.3}$$
$$= .548$$

We note that the general formula for the variance is

$$s^2 - pq \left(\frac{n}{n - 1} \right) \quad \text{or} \quad \frac{npq}{n - 1}$$

$$= (.4)(.6)\left(\frac{5}{4} \right) = .3 \quad \text{or} \quad \frac{(5)(.4)(.6)}{4} = .3$$

The standard deviation formula is

$$s = \sqrt{\frac{npq}{n - 1}}$$

We have now calculated statistics for our dichotomous variable. These are estimates of the population parameters.

Drawing Inferences about Population Parameters from Sample Statistics for Continuous Variables

The Basic Theory   Earlier we calculated the mean age of a sample we randomly selected from our student population. In order to tell how good an estimate of the population parameter this sample statistic really is, we must understand the theory of statistical inference.

First we assume a second student population that consists of five elements. In this case, the students are identified by the letters A, B, C, D, and E. Suppose we wish to select a single random sample of size $n = 2$ from this population. There are a number of combinations of elements that could form the sample—that is, there are a number of possible samples. They are:

Sample number	Elements in sample
1	AB
2	AC
3	AD
4	AE
5	BC
6	BD
7	BE
8	CD
9	CE
10	DE

There are 10 possible combinations of two elements from a population of five. Mathematically, this is simply the calculation of the number of all possible combinations without replacement. The general formula for this is

$$C_n^N = \binom{N}{n} = C(N,n)$$

$$= \frac{N!}{n!(N-n)!}$$

In our example, $N = 5$ and $n = 2$, therefore

$$C(5,2) = \frac{5!}{2!\,3!} = \frac{5 \cdot 4 \cdot 3 \cdot 2 \cdot 1}{2 \cdot 1 \cdot 3 \cdot 2 \cdot 1}$$

$$= \frac{20}{2}$$

$$= 10$$

Each of the 10 possible samples would yield an estimate of the mean of the population.

We now turn our attention back to the population of 50 students in Table 8-1. Previously we selected one sample of five from this population. The number of possible samples of size 5 from this population is

$$C(50,5) = \frac{50!}{5!\,45!} = \frac{50 \cdot 49 \cdot 48 \cdot 47 \cdot 46}{5 \cdot 4 \cdot 3 \cdot 2 \cdot 1}$$

$$= \frac{254,251,200}{120}$$

$$= 2,118,760 \text{ possible samples}$$

So we selected one of the 2,118,760 possible samples of size $n = 5$. Just consider the number of possible samples from a realistic population of interest. For example, if there are 70 million voters in a presidential election and we select a sample of 1000, this sample is only one of C(70 million, 1000) possible samples.

$$C(70 \text{ million}, 1000) = \frac{70 \text{ million}!}{1000!(70 \text{ million} - 1000)!}$$

The important point is that in any population there are many possible samples. We must also understand that classical statistical inference is based on what happens when we repeatedly select different samples from a population.

Previously we did select one sample of $n = 5$ from our population, and this sample yielded a mean age of 22.6. Now suppose we select another sample of $n = 5$ and calculate the mean. In this sample the mean might be 23.4 years. If we again repeat the process, we might get a third sample mean of 24.2 years. Seemingly, we have confused ourselves in that we now have three estimates of the population parameter. However, in statistical theory we would not stop at three samples; we would sample again and again, and in repeating this process we would note that certain mean values repeat themselves. Specifically, we would note that sample means closer in value to the population mean tend to repeat themselves more often than those farther removed from the population mean. This should make intuitive sense. We could plot these mean values, and they would seem to be forming the familiar bell-shaped (or normal) curve. This distribution of sample means is called the *sampling distribution of the mean*, or simply the *sampling distribution*. The sampling distribution is important for two reasons: (1) the sample means in this distribution are distributed around the population mean in a known way; (2) using this distribution, we can determine how closely the sample statistics are distributed around the population parameter.

In order to derive these benefits from the sampling distribution, we must formalize the nature of the sampling distribution of the mean. To do this we turn to the *central-limit theorem* of statistics, which states that:

1 If a population distribution for a measure is normal, the sampling distribution of the mean will be normal for all sample sizes.

2 If a population is non-normal for a measure, the sampling distribution of the mean approaches normal as the sample size increases.

3 The mean of the sampling distribution of the mean is the population mean. In the type of situation where the expected value of an estimator (the mean of the sampling distribution for the statistic) is the parameter or population value, the statistic is said to be *unbiased*.

4 The standard deviation of the sampling distribution of the mean is the population standard deviation divided by the square root of the sample size. Thus,

$$\sigma_{\bar{X}} = \frac{\sigma}{\sqrt{n}}$$

This value is often called the *standard error of the mean*.

In practice we do not know μ or σ, so we estimate them with $\bar{X}$ and s, respectively, calculated from the one sample we do select; so,

$$s_{\bar{X}} = \frac{s}{\sqrt{n}}$$

Figure 8-1 demonstrates the central-limit theorem. Four different population distributions for a variable are presented. Only in the situation depicted at the right is this distribution normal. However, we note that for each population the sampling distribution of the mean is virtually normal when $n = 5$ (it is truly normal for the normal population) and truly normal when $n = 30$ or greater. So when we calculate the mean from any one sample of $n = 30$, we can be sure that this mean comes from a distribution that is normal with a mean of μ and standard error of $\sigma/\sqrt{n}$.

There is one other aspect about a normal curve that must be understood before we can put all this theory to work. This aspect relates to the area contained under a normal curve. Figure 8-2 shows a normal curve with an amount of area contained within different standard deviations from the mean. Specifically, we note that approximately

1 68 percent of cases will be within ± 1 standard deviation from the mean.
2 95 percent of cases will be within ± 2 standard deviations from the mean.
3 99.7 percent (almost all) cases will be within ± 3 standard deviations from the mean.

We now have all the pieces of theory in place that are needed to determine how good an estimate our sample mean is.

Using the Theory   Our sample of the ages of five students was selected from a population distribution that was close to normal, so we know that the mean we calculated is from a normal distribution of means. We estimate

1 The mean of the sampling distribution as $\bar{X}$
2 The standard deviation of the sampling distribution[2] (standard error) as

$$s_{\bar{X}} = \frac{s}{\sqrt{n}} = \frac{\sqrt{\sum_{i=1}^{n} (X_i - \bar{X})^2/(n-1)}}{\sqrt{n}}$$

In our example, $\bar{X} = 22.6$ and $s = 2.88$, thus

$$s_{\bar{X}} = \frac{2.88}{\sqrt{5}} = \frac{2.88}{2.24} = 1.3$$

[2] Technical purists will note that with a population as small as this one, we should apply a correction factor to the formula. However, in practice most populations are quite large, and the correction factor is not needed. So, to aid in student understanding, we are ignoring the point for now. We will address it later in the chapter.

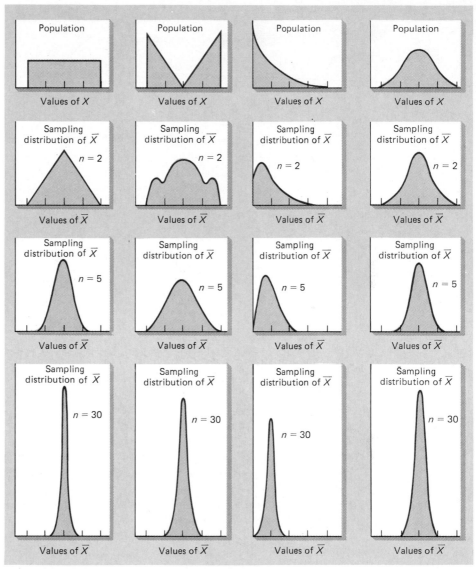

FIGURE 8-1 Distribution of sample means for samples of various sizes and different population distributions. [*Reproduced with permission from Ernest Kurnow, Gerald J. Glasser, and Frederick R. Ottman, Statistics for Business Decisions (Homewood, Ill.: Irwin, 1959), pp. 182–183.*]

Now let's calculate the size of the intervals at ± 1 standard deviation from the mean, then ± 2, then ± 3 standard deviations from the mean. At ± 1 standard deviation, the interval is

$$22.6 \pm 1.3 = 21.3–23.9$$

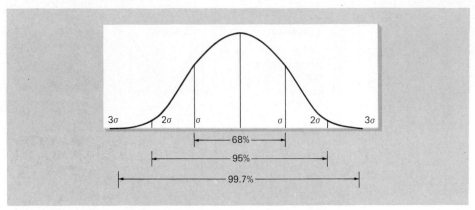

FIGURE 8-2   Area under the normal curve.

We know that 68 percent of the means from our sampling distribution are contained in this interval if our calculated sample mean $\bar{X}$ is truly the mean of the sampling distribution. (Remember $\mu = 23.7$.) At ± 2 standard deviations, the interval is

$$22.6 \pm 2(1.3) = 22.6 \pm 2.6 = 20.0–25.2$$

We know that 95 percent of the means from our sampling distribution are contained in this interval if our calculated sample mean $\bar{X}$ is truly the mean of the sampling distribution. At ± 3 standard deviations, the interval is

$$22.6 \pm 3(1.3) = 22.6 \pm 3.9 = 18.7–26.5$$

We know that 99.7 percent (virtually all) of the means from our sampling distribution are contained in this interval if our calculated mean $\bar{X}$ is truly the mean of the sampling distribution.

We refer to these intervals that we have calculated as *confidence intervals*. The first interval was a 68 percent confidence interval, the second a 95 percent, and the last one a 99.7 percent confidence interval. Note that we must designate the level of confidence before we can calculate an interval; it is our knowledge that the mean comes from a normal distribution of means that allows us to calculate an interval.

Exactly what does a confidence interval mean? Let's use the 95 percent confidence level as an illustration. We noted previously that the mean of the sampling distribution is the population mean, and that we use one sample mean, $\bar{X}$, as an estimator of the mean of the sampling distribution. But we have selected only one sample, and thus we do not know what the true mean of the sampling distribution is. It is therefore possible to select a sample such that the true population mean is not contained within the 95 percent (or other level) confidence interval calculated from the sample. The population mean either is or is not contained within the 95 percent confidence interval calculated from a sample. A 95 percent confidence interval does not mean that there are

95 chances in 100 that the population mean is contained within the interval; it means that if we selected 100 different random samples and calculated 100 different 95 percent confidence intervals, we could expect the true mean to be contained within the 95 percent confidence interval in 95 out of the 100 samples. So again we note that concepts of classical statistics have meaning in terms of repeated sampling.

The 95 percent confidence interval we calculated was 22.6 ± 2.6, or 20.0 to 25.2. Under repeated sampling, we would expect the true population mean to fall within such intervals in 95 samples out of 100. In our example we note that the population mean of 23.7 does fall within the 95 percent confidence interval we calculated from our sample of 5. Also, we can say that our estimate has a *precision* of ± 2.6 years at a 95 percent level of confidence. Note that the size of the precision has meaning only at a designated level of confidence. At 99.7 percent the precision of our estimate is ± 3.9 years. Precision then is the width of the confidence interval.

The calculation of a confidence interval provides us with the measure of *sampling error* and sample accuracy we were in search of earlier. Again it is only the use of probability-based selection procedures that allows us to properly calculate the confidence interval. We know nothing about the sampling distribution of means for non-probability sampling and thus cannot calculate a meaningful confidence interval. We should note that it is common practice for confidence intervals to be calculated from nonprobability samples; the manager who uses these intervals, however, is implicitly assuming that the non-probability sampling procedure has yielded a simple random sample.

The Effect of Sample Size on Precision   As stated previously, the formula for the standard deviation of the sampling distribution of the mean is

$$s_{\bar{X}} = \frac{\sqrt{\sum_{i=1}^{n} (X_i - \bar{X})^2 \Big/ (n - 1)}}{\sqrt{n}}$$

or more simply it is

$$s_{\bar{X}} = \frac{s}{\sqrt{n}}$$

where s is the standard deviation of the distribution of the variable of interest. We note that $s_{\bar{X}}$ will vary inversely with the square root of the sample size we select. That is, $s_{\bar{X}}$ will get smaller by the square root of the sample size as the sample size increases. Notice that the confidence interval around $\bar{X}$ will get smaller as $s_{\bar{X}}$ gets smaller, and we will be more certain of the accuracy of our estimate.

We can illustrate this by again using our student population, but this time assume that the population really has 500,000 elements and not 50 and that the population mean and variance are as before. Now let's assume we selected a number of simple random samples from this population, and in each case the mean and variance we calculated from these samples were identical, as follows:

$$\bar{X} = 22.6; \quad s^2 = 8.3; \quad s = 2.88$$

You will recognize these as the statistics calculated from our sample of 5 taken previously. The different sample sizes are

(1) $n = 5$ (4) $n = 1000$
(2) $n = 30$ (5) $n = 2000$
(3) $n = 100$

For each sample size we calculate $s_{\bar{X}}$.

(1) $s_{\bar{X}} = \dfrac{2.88}{\sqrt{5}} = 1.3$

(2) $s_{\bar{X}} = \dfrac{2.88}{\sqrt{30}} = \dfrac{2.88}{5.48} = .53$

(3) $s_{\bar{X}} = \dfrac{2.88}{\sqrt{100}} = \dfrac{2.88}{10} = .29$

(4) $s_{\bar{X}} = \dfrac{2.88}{\sqrt{1000}} = \dfrac{2.88}{31.7} = .09$

(5) $s_{\bar{X}} = \dfrac{2.88}{\sqrt{2000}} = \dfrac{2.88}{44.8} = .06$

The associated 95 percent confidence intervals are

(1) $22.6 \pm 2(1.3) = 22.6 \pm 2.6 = 20.0\text{–}25.2$
(2) $22.6 \pm 2(.53) = 22.6 \pm 1.06 = 21.5\text{–}23.7$
(3) $22.6 \pm 2(.29) = 22.6 \pm .58 = 22.0\text{–}23.2$
(4) $22.6 \pm 2(.09) = 22.6 \pm .18 = 22.4\text{–}22.8$
(5) $22.6 \pm 2(.06) = 22.6 \pm .12 = 22.5\text{–}22.7$

As n has increased from 5 to 2000, the width of confidence interval has decreased from 5.2 to .2, which shows how much more confident in our estimate we can be as the sample size increases. That is, for $n = 2000$, we would expect that the true mean would fall in an interval only .2 wide in 95 samples out of 100.

In this example, the true mean, 23.7, does not fall in the interval from 22.5 to 22.7. This has happened because we forced all the sample means to be the same, no matter what the sample size. We did this just to illustrate the effect of sample size on the size of a calculated confidence interval. In truth, as we increase the sample size, the sample mean would approach the population mean in value. A statistic that approaches the population parameter in value as the sample size increases is called a *consistent estimator*. Obviously we want consistent estimators, so our sample mean for $n = 2000$ would be much closer to 23.7 than the $n = 5$ mean we used above. This should make intuitive sense. The more elements we include, the more representative our sample should be.

The other component of the calculation that affects the size of $s_{\bar{x}}$, and thus our confidence interval, is the standard deviation of the distribution of the variable, s. It is the numerator of $s_{\bar{x}}$. Thus, we would like our estimate of $\bar{X}$ to have as small a variance and therefore as small a standard deviation as possible. An estimator that provides this minimum variance and thus the minimum standard error for any given sample size is called the *most efficient estimator*. We want efficient estimators.

Drawing Inferences about Population Parameters from Sample Statistics for Dichotomous Variables

All the theory and procedures we applied to continuous variables also apply to dichotomous variables. The sample mean of the proportion of students electing marketing research in our sample of 5 was .4. This is but one sample mean from a distribution of means of the proportion that would result from repeated samplings of size 5. Again, the central-limit theorem applies. In this case the mean of the sampling distribution of means is π, and the standard deviation of the sampling distribution is $\sqrt{\pi(1 - \pi)/n}$. We do not know these population values, so we estimate them as follows:

$$\text{Mean} = p \ .$$

$$\text{Standard error} = s_p = \sqrt{\frac{p(1 - p)}{n}} \qquad \text{or} \qquad \sqrt{\frac{pq}{n}}$$

We now calculate the 95 percent confidence interval for our sample of 5. The formula would be

$$p \pm 2 \sqrt{\frac{pq}{n}}$$

In our example, $p = .4$ and $n = 5$. The 95 percent interval is

$$.4 \pm 2 \sqrt{\frac{(.4)(.6)}{5}} = .4 \pm 2\sqrt{.048}$$

$$= .4 \pm 2(.22) = .4 \pm .44$$

$$= 0 - .84$$

This is a very wide interval because the sample size is small and the value pq of the variable is large. What we can say is that in 95 samples out of 100, we would expect the true proportion mean to be contained in this type of interval. The true mean, .27, is contained in this interval.

Again let us note the effect on the confidence interval of an increase in the sample size to 2000. If $p = .4$ again, the 95 percent confidence interval would be

$$.4 \pm 2 \sqrt{\frac{(.4)(.6)}{2000}} = .4 \pm 2\sqrt{.00012}$$

$$= .4 \pm 2(.011) = .4 \pm .022$$

$$= .38 - .42$$

Again because we constrained p to equal .4, a result obtained from a sample of 5, the true mean falls outside this tight interval. If the sample size were 2000, the sample mean would move closer to the population value. That is, p is a consistent estimator of π. We would then expect the true mean to fall in this type of small interval in 95 samples out of 100.

Note that for any given sample size the value of s_p is maximum when $p = .5$. This is because $pq = .25$. For no other value of p is pq this large. If $p = .6$, $pq = .24$; if $p = .7$, $pq = .21$; if $p = \sqrt{8}$, $pq = .16$; if $p = 9$, $pq = .09$; if $p = .99$, $pq = .0099$. What this indicates is that the more undefinitive the results (the closer p is to .5), the larger is the amount of error.

We have now calculated a measure of sampling error for both a continuous and a dichotomous variable.

The Question of Population Size

The discussion to date has made no mention of the size of the population as being important in our calculations. Technically this is not correct, but most marketing-related populations are large enough so that the concern about population size is not important, and this extra level of complexity would have made the previous discussion harder to follow.

The problem of population size is simply that for finite populations we must change the formula we use in calculating the standard error of the sampling distribution of the mean. What we do is apply the *finite population correction* or "finite correction factor" to our previous formula, so that

(1) $\quad \sigma_{\bar{x}} = \dfrac{\sigma_x}{\sqrt{n}} \sqrt{\dfrac{N - n}{N - 1}}$ and $s_{\bar{x}} = \dfrac{s}{\sqrt{n}} \sqrt{\dfrac{N - n}{N - 1}}$

(2) $\quad \sigma_p = \sqrt{\dfrac{\pi(1 - \pi)}{n}} \sqrt{\dfrac{N - n}{N - 1}}$ and $s_p = \sqrt{\dfrac{pq}{n}} \sqrt{\dfrac{N - n}{N - 1}}$

The value $\sqrt{(N - n)/(N - 1)}$ is the finite correction factor. For large values of N relative to n, the value of $\sqrt{(N - n)/(N - 1)}$ is approximately equal to 1. Thus we can just use the basic formula for $\sigma_{\bar{x}}$ and $s_{\bar{x}}$ and for σ_p and s_p.

The value of the correction factor is always between 0 and 1. It is zero when $N = n$. That is, when we take a complete census we cannot calculate a standard error. This is as we should expect. Standard error has meaning only for samples, not for a census. The value of the correction factor approaches 1 as N gets bigger relative to n. So we see that multiplying by the correction factor will always lower the size of the standard error (except when it equals 1). Thus, if we choose to ignore the correction factor, we overstate the standard error and increase the size of our confidence interval. We err on the side of conservatism.

In most marketing applications it is safe to ignore the correction factor. As a rule of thumb, some suggest applying the correction factor when the sample includes more than 5 percent of the population (when the sampling fraction exceeds .05). Like all rules of thumb, 5 percent is not a definite guide; others have suggested 10 percent as the magic number. Simply be sensitive to this issue when dealing with small populations.

In our example we selected 10 percent ($\frac{5}{50}$) of the population. We should have applied the correction factor.

A Warning about Nonsampling Errors

The calculation of confidence intervals about an estimator gives us the feeling that we know just how much error we are dealing with. For most marketing research studies this can be very misleading. Our measurement of error was that of sampling error only. A confidence interval does not take nonsampling errors into account at all. If nonsampling errors occur, a bias is introduced into our estimate of unknown degree and magnitude. Control of nonsampling errors is therefore critical. (Nonsampling errors were discussed in detail in Chapter 1.)

The Accuracy of Probability Samples

Probability samples can be extremely accurate. In fact, the Gallup and Harris polls have successfully predicted the outcome of every presidential election in which they have applied probability sampling procedures. What about 1948, you say. Didn't the polls predict that Dewey would defeat Truman? Indeed they did, but the samples were quota samples, as probability sampling was new at that time.

Let's return to our discussion of two presidential elections. In 1936 the *Literary Digest* conducted a poll by mail. Their sample size was over 2 million. They predicted a victory for Landon over Roosevelt by about 15 percent; in fact, Roosevelt won easily. In 1968, using a probability sample of less than 2000 out of over 70 million voters, Gallup predicted that Richard Nixon would get 43 percent of the vote. He got 42.9 percent. The sampling frame used by the *Literary Digest* was more well-to-do than the true population of voters. The poor people who supported Roosevelt did not get a chance to respond to the poll.

The sampling procedures outlined in this chapter provide the tools for the researcher to give accurate estimates of the parameters of interest. The major problem area lies in the nonsampling errors that arise.

In Chapter 9, we shall continue our discussion of probability sampling. Specifically, we shall discuss two types of sampling procedures—stratified sampling and cluster sampling. These procedures are more complex than simple random sampling but are used more often in practice. But before turning to these procedures, we must first address the issue of sample size.

THE DETERMINATION OF SAMPLE SIZE

Armed with an understanding of both sampling error and nonsampling error, we now turn our attention to the question of sample size determination. Both types of error bear on this question. First, let's examine sample size in statistical theory.

The Question of Sample Size in Statistical Theory

In simple random sampling for a known sample size, we calculated the confidence interval of our estimate at a given level of confidence. To do this for a continuous measure we had the following information, which sums up what we have covered in this chapter:

1 An estimate of the mean, $\bar{X}$.
2 An estimate of the standard deviation, s.
3 A sample size.
4 A level of confidence.
5 Using (2) and (3), we calculated the standard error, $s_{\bar{x}}$. We then calculated the relevant confidence interval. The equation to do this at the 95 percent confidence level was

$$\text{Confidence interval} = \bar{X} \pm 2\,\frac{s}{\sqrt{n}}$$

We have calculated $\bar{X}$ and s, and know n, so we can solve this equation for the confidence interval. Or, we could calculate the precision we obtained using part of the above equation as follows:

$$\text{Precision} = \pm 2\,\frac{s}{\sqrt{n}}$$

Now suppose we want to reach a given level of precision. If we have a value for s, we can solve this equation for the required sample size.[3]

Let's illustrate this conclusion. Suppose that at the 95 percent level of confidence we wish to obtain an estimate of the mean age of students that is within ± 3 years

---

[3] If we know the true standard deviation, σ, we can also calculate the required sample size. Here,

$$\text{Precision} = +2\,\frac{\sigma}{\sqrt{n}}$$

Our presumption is that it is unrealistic to think that we would know σ. In all likelihood this is one parameter we are trying to estimate. We will use statistical values in this section ($\bar{X}$, s, p), although parameters (μ, σ, π) are technically more correct.

of the true mean age. Additionally, we will assume that we have an estimate of $s = 3.0$. The required sample size is obtained by solving the following equation for n:

$$\text{Precision} = \pm 2 \frac{s}{\sqrt{n}}$$

$$\pm 3 \text{ years} = \pm 2 \frac{3.0}{\sqrt{n}}$$

$$3 = \frac{6}{\sqrt{n}}$$

$$3\sqrt{n} = 6$$

$$\sqrt{n} = \frac{6}{3}$$

$$\sqrt{n} = 2$$

$$n = 4$$

A sample size of 4 will assure us a precision of ± 3 years, if $s = 3.0$.

In this example we expressed the precision in units (years). When we use units to do this, it is called *absolute precision*. We might also have expressed precision as a percentage of the mean value we calculate. Here the precision in units varies depending on the size of the mean.

Precision expressed in percentages is called *relative precision*. Let's do an example to calculate sample size to assure a specified relative precision. Assume that $\bar{X} = 25$, $s = 3.0$, the required precision is ± 10 percent (.1), and a 99.7 percent level of confidence is desired. The required equation is

$$\pm .b\bar{X} = \pm 3 \frac{s}{\sqrt{n}}$$

where $.b$ is the precision percentage expressed as a decimal. In our example the equation becomes

$$\pm .1(25) = \pm 3 \frac{3.0}{\sqrt{n}}$$

$$2.5 = \frac{9}{\sqrt{n}}$$

$$2.5\sqrt{n} = 9$$

$$\sqrt{n} = \frac{9}{2.5}$$

$$\sqrt{n} = 3.6$$

$$n = 13$$

The required sample size is 13 if $\bar{X} = 25$ and $s = 3.0$.

We could rearrange our relative precision equation as follows (we can ignore the ± signs, as they drop out in the calculation):

$$.b\bar{X} = 3\,\frac{s}{\sqrt{n}}$$

$$.b\bar{X}\sqrt{n} = 3s$$

$$.b\sqrt{n} = 3\,\frac{s}{\bar{X}}$$

Rearranging the equation in this fashion demonstrates that we really do not need to know both $\bar{X}$ and s but only the ratio of the standard deviation to the mean, $s/\bar{X}$. This ratio is called the *coefficient of variation*.

The troublesome thing about our calculations of required sample size is that we need a value of s for absolute precision and a value for $s/\bar{X}$ for relative precision. If we do have these values, in all likelihood we already know what we want to know about a particular variable. Also, for absolute precision the required sample size varies (1) inversely with the size of the precision desired, (2) directly with s, and (3) directly with the size of the confidence level desired. In most studies we want to measure many variables. To the extent that they differ in terms of precision desired, s, or confidence level, the required sample sizes will differ. There is no one sample size that is statistically optimal for any study. The only way to assure the required precision would be to select the largest sample. In this way the variable requiring the largest sample size would reach its specified precision, and all the others would have tighter precision than specified.

All is not lost, however, in the search for optimal sample size. If a researcher has experience with the problem at hand, then very accurate estimates of s are likely to be available at the time the sample size is being planned. For example, suppliers of store audit data have a great deal of knowledge in this area because of their experience. Additionally, the scale on which the variable of interest is measured sets limits on the size of s. For example, a 7-point attitude rating scale is likely to have an s in the 2–3 range, and it is impossible for it to be as large as 7. In contrast, a 100-point rating scale could easily have an s of 20–30. Thus, if the experienced researcher understands the effects that the measurement scale being used will have on s, then a very good estimate can be made of optimal sample size.

To be sure that you understand how to calculate the required sample size and the limitations of such a calculation, let's now calculate n for a dichotomous variable. The confidence interval for a dichotomous variable at the 95 percent level of confidence is

$$p \pm 2\sqrt{\frac{pq}{n}}$$

Thus,

$$\text{Absolute precision} = \pm 2 \sqrt{\frac{pq}{n}}$$

Assume we have an estimate of $p = .3$ and that we want $\pm.04$ as the absolute precision at the 95 percent level of confidence. Then

$$.04 = 2 \sqrt{\frac{(.3)(.7)}{n}}$$

is the required equation. Solving for n, we get

$$.04 = 2 \sqrt{\frac{.21}{n}}$$

Dividing through by 2, we get

$$.02 = \sqrt{\frac{.21}{n}}$$
$$.02\sqrt{n} = \sqrt{.21}$$
$$\sqrt{n} = \frac{\sqrt{.21}}{.02}$$
$$\sqrt{n} = \frac{.46}{.02}$$
$$\sqrt{n} = 23$$
$$n = 529$$

The required sample size is 529.

To calculate relative precision at the 99.7 percent level of confidence, the equation is

$$.bp = 3 \sqrt{\frac{pq}{n}}$$

where $.b$ is the precision percentage expressed as a decimal. If the required precision is ± 5 percent (.05), the equation becomes

$$.05(.3) = 3 \sqrt{\frac{(.3)(.7)}{n}}$$

$$.015 = 3 \sqrt{\frac{.21}{n}}$$

Dividing through by 3, we get

$$.005 = \sqrt{\frac{.21}{n}}$$

$$.005\sqrt{n} = \sqrt{.21}$$

$$\sqrt{n} = \frac{.46}{.005}$$

$$\sqrt{n} = 92$$

$$n = 8464$$

The required sample size is 8464, reflecting our use of the 99.7 percent level of confidence and a very tight precision specification.

We note that in order to determine required sample size for a dichotomous variable we need to know the mean value p. Regrettably, p is probably the value we are trying to determine in the first place. So be wary of people who claim that they have determined the statistically optimal sample size for a study, for such a statement is nonsense—unless they are experienced in the problem being researched and know the effect of the measurement scales they are using. This does not mean that the calculation of required sample size is of no value. It can provide a general guide to the researcher as to the required sample size under differing types of findings. That is, assume different values for $\bar{X}$, s, p, etc., and see what sample sizes are required.

This would be one factor affecting the determination of sample size for the study. Other factors in the decision would be the study objectives, the cost involved, the time requirements, the type of data analysis planned, and the existence of nonsampling errors.

The sample size calculations we made here were for simple random samples only. In the more complex sampling procedures discussed in Chapter 9 the formulas become more complicated. However, the principle is exactly the same; that is, we must specify the level of confidence and precision, and then we use the relevant formula for standard error to find the sample size.

Sample Size and Nonsampling Error

No one should blindly accept the sample size generated by a statistical formula. One reason for not doing so is the existence of nonsampling errors. Some nonsampling errors will get larger as the sample size increases—for example, nonresponse errors, interviewer errors, data processing errors, and data analysis errors. Thus, a decrease in sampling error occurs at the expense of an increase in nonsampling error. A carefully done study with $n = 200$ may have a smaller total error than a study of $n = 2000$. The problem is that many researchers, managers, and media people like to refer to the statistical precision of estimates. Rarely do they mention other possible errors. Look beyond the statistical formulas to the details of how the study was done. The general public also seems to believe that larger samples are necessarily better than smaller ones, which is incorrect, but the company doing research that will be exposed in the public domain must be aware of this perception. It just seems more credible to say: "Based on a study of 3000 people" than to say: "Based on a study of 250." Researchers must respond to this perception for outside use, but they should never be fooled with the same reasoning for internal use reports. Larger is not necessarily better. Also, a very small sample may yield a statistical precision at a level suitable to the needs of marketing decision makers.

Sample Size and Other Factors

A marketing research study is always a compromise between technical elegance and practical constraints faced by researchers and managers. These constraints affect sample size decisions, and several are discussed below.

Study Objectives   The use that management intends to make of the information provided by a study affects the sample size. A decision that does not need precise informational inputs can make do with a very small sample size. A company may be happy to measure interest in its new product within 15 to 20 percent. In contrast, a political pollster can be off by less than 1 percent and fail in the study objective, to predict the election outcome. The latter obviously needs a larger sample than the former.

Time Constraints   Often research results are needed "yesterday." Of course, some time for presenting results is agreed upon. This time period may be too short to use anything except a small sample. The larger the study, the more time is needed.

Cost Constraints   A limit on the amount of money available for a study obviously could limit the sample size. Alternatively, the existence of a lot of money for a study should not be the sole motivation for a large sample size. Available dollars can be a downward constraint on sample size. It should never be the reason for increasing the sample size beyond that needed to meet the study objectives.

Data Analysis Procedures   Data analysis procedures have an effect on the sample size for a study. The most basic type of analysis that can be performed deals with only one variable at a time. This is called univariate analysis (see Chapter 17). The relationship between sample size and precision of estimates on one variable is exactly what we have been discussing in this chapter.

When we examine the relationship of two variables at a time, the sample size issue becomes more complex. This is called bivariate analysis (see Chapter 18). Suppose we wanted to examine the relationship between usage of a product and income. Suppose also that each variable is composed of five categories. Therefore, the cross tabulation of usage by income results in a table of 25 cells. Suppose we had a sample of 250 people. If these people were spread evenly across the crosstab table, there would be only 10 respondents per cell. An even distribution across cells is not likely. However, the point is that some cell sizes will be quite small, and the precision of estimates within cells will obviously be less than those obtained in a univariate analysis. Thus, the types of bivariate analysis planned and the precision required within cells will affect the choice of sample size. A study doing only univariate analysis may only require 200 respondents, whereas a similar study doing bivariate analysis may require over 1000 respondents.

We might want to examine the relationships among more than two variables at a time. This is called multivariate analysis (see Chapters 19 and 20). Different multivariate techniques require different sample sizes to allow the researcher to make valid estimates of population parameters. In general, the more parameters we are estimating, the larger the sample size must be. Beyond this statement it is difficult to make simple generalizations. Some multivariate techniques can be used legitimately with small sample sizes. These include factor analysis, cluster analysis, multidimensional scaling, and small regression and analysis of variance models. At the other extreme, some techniques were designed for very large samples. The AID (Automatic Interaction Detector) model is one example of this situation. The details of these analysis models and their sample size requirements are left to Chapters 19 and 20. In summary, the researcher must think ahead to the plan of data analysis in determining sample size.

It should now be clear that the choice of a sample size is situation-specific. It depends on statistical precision requirements, concern for nonsampling error, study objectives, time available, cost, and the data analysis plan. There is no one correct answer for the choice of sample size for a study.

SUMMARY

1 A parameter is a summary description of a measure in the defined population. A statistic is a summary description of a measure in the selected sample.

2 The ratio of sample size n to population size N is called the sampling fraction.

3 We are able to calculate the mean and standard deviation for a population and for a simple random sample. We can do this for both continuous and dichotomous variables. Variance is simply SS/df.

4 Any simple random sample that we draw is just one of the $C(N,n)$ samples that could have been drawn.

5 In simple random sampling, each element has an equal chance of being selected, and each combination of n sample elements has an equal chance of being selected.

6 The central-limit theorem tells us that the mean of the sample that we did select comes from a distribution of sample means that form a normal curve if $n \geq 30$, no matter what the shape of the underlying variable distribution. Also, if the variable distribution is normal, then the sampling distribution of the mean is always normal, no matter what the sample size is.

7 Using our knowledge of the area under a normal curve, we can calculate confidence intervals about our sample mean. Specifically, the 95 percent interval will be $\bar{X} \pm 2s_{\bar{x}}$, and the 99.7 percent interval will be $\bar{X} \pm 3s_{\bar{x}}$, where $s_{\bar{x}} = s/\sqrt{n}$.

8 Precision is the absolute size of the confidence interval about the mean. For example, at the 95 percent level of confidence, absolute precision $= \pm 2s/\sqrt{n}$.

9 A sample statistic whose expected value equals the population parameter is called an unbiased statistic. A sample statistic that has the minimum variance is the most efficient estimator.

10 The confidence interval provides a measure of accuracy of an estimator.

11 Beware of nonsampling errors.

12 Probability samples can provide very accurate estimates if properly executed.

13 Sample size should not be determined by the use of statistical formulas alone.

14 The choice of sample size is made involving trade-off among sampling error, nonsampling error, study objectives, time constraints, cost constraints, and data analysis plans,

DISCUSSION QUESTIONS

1 What is the difference (if any) between a parameter and a statistic?

2 Identify the symbols which denote common parameters and statistics of both continuous and dichotomous variables.

3 Define the mean and variance in words and in mathematical notation for both a population and a sample, first treating the variable as continuous and then as dichotomous.

4 Why is the central-limit theorem critical to measuring sampling error?

5 What is a confidence interval?

6 What affects the size of a confidence interval?

7 What are the desirable properties of estimators?

8 To what extent do confidence intervals increase our certainty with regard to making inferences?

9 Most political pollsters judged the 1980 presidential election to be too close to call. Explain how this could happen.

10 What problems are likely to occur in implementing a field study using simple random sampling?

11 Why do some researchers calculate confidence intervals from data generated from non-probability samples?

12 Since nonprobability samples do not yield a measure of sampling error, why are these procedures so extensively used in commercial and academic practice?

13 What is absolute precision? What is relative precision?

14 What information is necessary in order to calculate a statistically optimal sample size for (1) a continuous variable, (2) a dichotomous variable?

15 What factors should you consider in determining the sample size for a study?

CHAPTER 9

MORE COMPLEX SAMPLING PROCEDURES

We now continue our discussion of probability sampling procedures. The first part of this chapter deals with stratified sampling, and the remainder describes two types of cluster sampling: systematic sampling and area sampling. These three sampling procedures are more complex than simple random sampling, but they are also much more frequently used in practice.

STRATIFIED SAMPLING

Purpose

One property that we wanted in our estimators was efficiency—that is, we wanted them to have as small a standard error as possible. Stratified sampling may result in a *decrease in the standard error of the estimator*. Thus the confidence interval we calculate would be smaller.

Method of Selection

A stratified sample is selected as follows:

1 Divide the defined population into mutually exclusive and collectively exhaustive subgroups or strata. Strata are mutually exclusive if membership in one stratum precludes membership in any other stratum. For example, a population may be divided into two strata on the basis of sex; that is, there would be a male stratum and a female stratum. An individual person cannot belong to both strata, and thus they are mutually exclusive. Strata are collectively exhaustive if all possible categories of a variable are used to define the strata. That is, the categories "male and female" define the complete domain of the variable "sex." No other category is possible, and thus the defined strata are collectively exhaustive of the variable sex.

2 Select an independent simple random sample in each stratum.

An Illustration

How does such a two-stage procedure decrease the standard error of an estimator? It only does so if the designated strata are *more homogeneous* on the variable on which we are calculating our statistics. If the strata are as heterogeneous on this variable as the unstratified whole population, no decrease in the standard error will occur.

Let's illustrate the standard error–reducing property of stratified sampling. Again we use part of the data presented in Table 8-1. The student number and age of students are presented in Table 9-1. We will use the age data to illustrate the standard error–reducing property.

TABLE 9-1   CENSUS OF AGE OF STUDENTS

	(1) Student number	(2) Age (X_1)		(1) Student number	(2) Age (X_1)
Graduate students:	1	25	Undergraduate students:	21	21
	2	27		22	19
	3	29		23	24
	4	31		24	22
	5	25		25	20
	6	29		26	22
	7	27		27	19
	8	24		28	20
	9	27		29	19
	10	28		30	24
	11	33		31	25
	12	29		32	22
	13	26		33	20
	14	28		34	21
	15	28		35	21
	16	26		36	23
	17	26		37	21
	18	36		38	23
	19	28		39	18
	20	26		40	21
				41	19
				42	23
				43	22
				44	19
				45	20
				46	20
				47	21
				48	20
				49	19
				50	18

Perhaps you noted in reading Table 8-1 that the ages of students numbered 1–20 seemed higher than the ages of students numbered 21–50. This is indeed true. A piece of information that was missing in Table 8-1 was that students 1–20 are graduate students and students 21–50 are undergraduate students. We would expect graduate students to be older than undergraduates, and they are. Note that the group of students numbered 1–20 has a more homogeneous age profile than the population as a whole, and so does the group of students numbered 21–50. By using a *stratification variable,* "graduate versus undergraduate," we have identified two strata that are more homogeneous than the population on the variable of interest, age. We have present the necessary condition to take advantage of stratification.

The Sample

Now let us draw a simple random sample of $n = 2$ from the graduate stratum and a simple random sample of $n = 3$ from the undergraduate stratum. Note that the ratio of our sample sizes by strata is in proportion to the ratio of the number of population elements by strata. Here the sample ratio 2/3 is proportionate to the population ratio 20/30. This is called *proportionate stratified sampling,* and it occurs when the total sample elements are allocated to strata *in proportion to the number of population elements in the strata.* The researcher also has the option of allocating the total sample to strata on a basis disproportionate with the population distribution among strata. We shall discuss disproportionate stratified sampling later in this chapter.

As a basis for facilitating the discussion that follows, we identify the following notation:

$N_{st.1}$ = population size in stratum 1 $\bar{X}_{st.1}$ = sample mean of stratum 1

$N_{st.2}$ = population size in stratum 2 $\bar{X}_{st.2}$ = sample mean of stratum 2

$n_{st.1}$ = sample size in stratum 1 $s^2_{st.1}$ = sample variance of stratum 1

$n_{st.2}$ = sample size in stratum 2 $s^2_{st.2}$ = sample variance of stratum 2

Now let's draw a simple random sample of $n = 2$ from stratum 1 and $n = 3$ from stratum 2. Conveniently, the sample of $n = 5$ we drew in Chapter 8 was just this kind of sample, so we do not have to select a new sample. Specifically, the sample by strata is:

Student number	Age
Stratum 1	
05	25
17	26
Stratum 2	
32	22
37	21
41	19

Calculation of Statistics within Strata

In Chapter 8 we calculated the mean, variance, and standard deviation of the total sample without stratification. There,

$$\bar{X} = 22.6, \quad s^2 = 8.3, \quad \text{and} \quad s = 2.88$$

Now we calculate the mean, variance, and standard deviation within each stratum. For stratum 1,

$$
\begin{aligned}
\bar{X}_{st.1} &= \frac{\sum\limits_{i=1}^{n_{st.1}} X_i}{n_{st.1}} \\
&= \frac{25 + 26}{2} \\
&= \frac{51}{2} \\
&= 25.5
\end{aligned}
$$

To find $s^2_{st.1}$ using our computational formula, we calculate

$$\Sigma X^2_{st.1} = (25)^2 + (26)^2 = 625 + 676 = 1301$$

and

$$
\begin{aligned}
\frac{(\Sigma X_{st.1})^2}{n} &= \frac{(51)^2}{2} = \frac{2601}{2} = 1300.5 \\
s^2_{st.1} &= \frac{1301 - 1300.5}{1} \\
&= .5 \\
s_{st.1} &= .71
\end{aligned}
$$

For stratum 2,

$$
\begin{aligned}
\bar{X}_{st.2} &= \frac{22 + 21 + 19}{3} \\
&= \frac{62}{3} \\
&= 20.7
\end{aligned}
$$

$$
\begin{aligned}
\Sigma X^2_{st.2} &= (22)^2 + (21)^2 + (19)^2 \\
&= 484 + 441 + 361 \\
&= 1286
\end{aligned}
$$

$$\frac{(\Sigma X_{st.2})^2}{n} = \frac{(62)^2}{3}$$

$$= \frac{3844}{3}$$

$$= 1281.3$$

$$s^2_{st.2} = \frac{1286 - 1281.3}{2}$$

$$= \frac{4.7}{2}$$

$$= 2.35$$

$$s_{st.2} = 1.53$$

Table 9-2 summarizes these results. We note that the variance and standard deviation within each stratum are much lower than the variance and standard deviation of the total sample. This points out one advantage of stratified sampling—that is, we can do analysis within strata with a smaller standard error than that available for the whole sample. Our within-strata confidence interval would thus be smaller than that generated by the use of the standard error of the whole sample.

TABLE 9-2 TOTAL SAMPLE AND WITHIN-STRATA MEAN, AND VARIANCE OF SAMPLE

	Mean	Variance	Standard deviation
Without stratification	22.6	8.3	2.88
Within stratum 1	25.5	.5	.71
Within stratum 2	20.7	2.35	1.53

Calculation of the Mean and Standard Error for the Whole Sample

We next consider how to calculate the mean and the standard error for the whole sample on the basis of within-strata results. The overall sample mean, $\bar{X}_{st.}$, is simply a *weighted average of the within-strata means*. The weight for a stratum is the ratio of the population size of that stratum to the total population size,

$$\frac{N_{st.j}}{N}$$

where $N_{st.j}$ is the population size within stratum j. Therefore,

$$\bar{X}_{st.} = \sum_{j=1}^{A} \left(\frac{N_{st.j}}{N}\right) X_{st.j}$$

where A = the number of strata.

In our example we have two strata; thus $A = 2$, and so,

$$\bar{X}_{\text{st.}} = \sum_{j=1}^{2} \left(\frac{N_{\text{st.}j}}{N} \right) \bar{X}_{\text{st.}j} = \left(\frac{N_{\text{st.}1}}{N} \right) \bar{X}_{\text{st.}1} + \left(\frac{N_{\text{st.}2}}{N} \right) \bar{X}_{\text{st.}2}$$

$$= (^{20}\!/_{50})25.5 + (^{30}\!/_{50})20.7$$

$$= .4(25.5) + .6(20.7)$$

$$= 10.2 + 12.4$$

$$= 22.6$$

This is exactly the same mean we calculated without stratification.

The ratio $N_{\text{st.}j}/N$ is the relative weight attached to each stratum. For future reference, let's call this ratio W_j.

In our example,

$$W_1 = .4 \qquad \text{and} \qquad W_2 = .6$$

The calculation of the *standard error* of the mean from within-strata information is more complex. It is *the square root of the weighted combination of the square of the standard error within each stratum.* The weighting factor in this case is the square of the relative weight of each stratum.

The formula[1] is

$$s_{\bar{X}} = \sqrt{s_{\bar{X}}^2}$$

where

$$s_{\bar{X}}^2 = \sum_{j=1}^{A} \left(\frac{N_{\text{st.}j}}{N} \right)^2 s_{\bar{X}_{\text{st.}j}}^2$$

$$= \sum_{j=1}^{A} W_j^2 s_{\bar{X}_{\text{st.}j}}^2$$

In our example (using the values in Table 9-2), we have for stratum 1:

$$s_{\bar{X}_{\text{st.}1}} = \frac{.71}{\sqrt{2}} = \frac{.71}{1.41}$$

$$= .50$$

$$s_{\bar{X}_{\text{st.}1}}^2 = .25$$

and for stratum 2:

$$s_{\bar{X}_{\text{st.}2}} = \frac{1.53}{\sqrt{3}} = \frac{1.53}{1.73}$$

$$= .88$$

$$s_{\bar{X}_{\text{st.}2}}^2 = .78$$

---

[1] Again we will ignore the finite-population correction factor.

Therefore,

$$s_{\bar{X}}^2 = (.4)^2(.25) + (.6)^2(.78)$$
$$= (.16)(.25) + (.36)(.78)$$
$$= .04 + .28$$
$$= .32$$
$$s_{\bar{X}} = \sqrt{.32}$$
$$= .57$$

Note that we took the square of the weighting factor for each stratum and the square of the standard error. We cannot take a simple weighting of the strata weight and the associated standard errors.

Alternatively, we may calculate $s_{\bar{X}}^2$ directly without first calculating the standard errors within each stratum. The formula to do this is:

$$s_{\bar{X}}^2 = \sum_{j=1}^{A} \frac{\left(\dfrac{N_{st.j}}{N}\right)^2 s_{st.j}^2}{n_{st.j}}$$

$$= \sum_{j=1}^{A} \frac{(W_j)^2 s_{st.j}^2}{n_{st.j}}$$

In our example, with $A = 2$,

$$s_{\bar{X}}^2 = \frac{(W_1)^2 s_{st.1}^2}{n_{st.1}} + \frac{(W_2)^2 s_{st.2}^2}{n_{st.2}}$$
$$= \frac{(.4)^2(.5)}{2} + \frac{(.6)^2(2.35)}{3}$$
$$= (.16)(.25) + (.36)(.78)$$
$$= .04 + .28$$
$$= .32$$
$$s_{\bar{X}} = \sqrt{.32} = .57$$

The value of $s_{\bar{X}}$ is identical to that previously calculated.

In Chapter 8 we calculated the standard error of the mean, using the unstratified sample, to be 1.3. By stratifying the sample the standard error has been reduced to .57.

Calculation of Associated Confidence Interval

The 95 percent confidence interval for the stratified sample is $22.6 \pm 2(.57) = 22.6 \pm 1.1 = 21.5-23.7$. The unstratified 95 percent interval was $20.0-25.2$. Thus the size of the interval has been reduced from 5.2 to 2.2 and the absolute precision from ± 2.6 to ± 1.1. Note that the population mean, 23.7, does fall in this new interval. Note also that the stratified 99.7 percent confidence interval would be smaller than the unstratified 95 percent interval. The 99.7 percent interval is $22.6 \pm 3(.57) = 22.6 \pm 1.7 = 20.9 - 24.3$. Clearly a stratified sampling procedure is more efficient than an unstratified one. This fact helps account for the moderately high use of stratified sampling in practice.

Why do we get such a reduction in standard error and associated precision using a stratified sampling procedure? It is because we use only within-stratum variability in calculating the overall standard error. Across-strata variability becomes irrelevant.

The effect with stratified sampling is that we can increase the precision of our estimates with the same sample size we used in an unstratified fashion. Alternatively, we could obtain the same precision as with an unstratified sample with a smaller sample and thus a lower cost.

The Number of Possible Samples

The sampling fraction in stratum 1 was $2/20 = .1$, and in stratum 2 it was $3/30 = .1$. Both of these sampling fractions are identical with the sample we selected in Chapter 8, $5/50 = .1$. Under both stratified and unstratified procedures each population element had an equal chance, .1, of being selected. However, with stratified sampling *all possible combinations of elements are not equally likely*. To illustrate, we shall use a population of elements identified as A, B, C, D, and E. This of course is the population that yielded 10 possible simple random samples of size 2. Now assume that elements A and B are from one stratum, while C, D, and E are from another. Again we wish to draw a sample of $n = 2$, but this time we restrict the sample to one element from each stratum. The possible sample element from stratum 1 is either A or B, and within stratum 2 it is either C, D, or E. Combining possible elements from each stratum, we get the possible samples:

Sample number	Elements in sample
1	AC
2	AD
3	AE
4	BC
5	BD
6	BE

There are 6 possible samples with stratification, and 10 without. The possible samples that have been eliminated are those that could occur within one stratum before; for example, AB and CD are no longer possible as samples. Note that it is these within-strata means that are the outliers of our distribution of means in simple random sampling. To illustrate this result, we may assign scores to these population elements as follows:

Element	Score
Stratum 1	
A	1
B	2
Stratum 2	
C	3
D	4
E	5

The mean of this distribution of scores is $15/5 = 3.0$. The possible stratified samples of $n = 2$ are

Sample elements	Sample mean
AC	$(1 + 3)/2 = 2.0$
AD	$(1 + 4)/2 = 2.5$
AE	$(1 + 5)/2 = 3.0$
BC	$(2 + 3)/2 = 2.5$
BD	$(2 + 4)/2 = 3.0$
BE	$(2 + 5)/2 = 3.5$

These sample means cluster reasonably tightly about the true mean of 3.0.

Now we examine the mean values generated by samples that are not allowed to occur in this example of stratified sampling, that is, the within-stratum sample means. These means are

Sample elements	Sample mean
Stratum 1	
AB	$(1 + 2)/2 = 1.5$
Stratum 2	
CD	$(3 + 4)/2 = 3.5$
CE	$(3 + 5)/2 = 4.0$
DE	$(4 + 5)/2 = 4.5$

These means are less well clustered about the mean of 3.0, i.e., they are the outliers on the distribution of means. In our age example, we get means like 26, 27, etc., in stratum 1, or like 20 or 21 in stratum 2. These types of means are not as likely when we combine elements from different strata, as we do when we estimate the mean with a stratified procedure. Removal of some outliers in stratified sampling would thus decrease the variability of the distribution of sample means. That is, the standard error becomes smaller. All combinations of elements are not equally likely. This is one aspect that distinguishes stratified sampling from simple random sampling. Note that the number of possible samples with stratification is the product of the number of all possible samples within each stratum. In our example the formula with two strata is

$$
\begin{aligned}
\text{Number of possible samples} &= C(N,n)_{st.1} \cdot C(N,n)_{st.2} \\
&= C(2,1) \cdot C(3,1) \\
&= \frac{2!}{1!\,1!} \cdot \frac{3!}{1!\,2!} \\
&= 2 \cdot 3 = 6
\end{aligned}
$$

In our student age example, the number of possible samples with stratification is

$$
\begin{aligned}
C(20,2) \cdot C(30,3) &= \frac{20!}{2!\,18!} \cdot \frac{30!}{3!\,27!} \\
&= \frac{20 \cdot 19}{2 \cdot 1} \quad \frac{30 \cdot 29 \cdot 28}{3 \cdot 2 \cdot 1} \\
&= 190 \cdot 4{,}060 \\
&= 771{,}400 \text{ possible samples}
\end{aligned}
$$

In Chapter 8 we noted that there were over 2 million possible simple random samples of size 5 in a population of 50. The number of possible samples has decreased substantially, although it is still very large. Further, once again the sampling distribution of the means of these samples will form a normal curve. The standard error will be smaller than with simple random sampling, as we previously noted in our calculations. Thus, we can again calculate a legitimate confidence interval.

Usefulness in Marketing Research

Stratified sampling is used moderately in marketing research. The types of variables often measured in marketing research show high variability that can be reduced by stratification. As an example, suppose that we are asked to monitor the retail sales of Folger's coffee. To do this we want to measure the unit sales level of Folger's in a sample of stores. What stratification variables should we use? First we must answer another question: "What factors contribute to the variability in the variable we intend to measure?" In the Folger's example, variability contributing factors would include:

1 Size of store; big stores would have higher sales than small stores.
2 Day of the week; stores sell more coffee on weekends than early in the week.
3 Region of the country; Folger's is a more established brand in the Western states, so we would find higher sales there than in other regions.

Other factors may also contribute to the variability in sales. If we thought they were important contributors, we would also include them as stratification variables. If we distinguished three sizes of stores, two types of days of the week, and four regions of the country, we would have $3 \times 2 \times 4 = 24$ different cells or strata. The similarity to quota sampling in the way the number of cells expands is obvious. However, in quota sampling we have no error measure.

In the stratum composed of "large stores—weekends—Western regions," we might find case sale numbers like 150, 170, or 205. In the stratum labeled "small stores—weekdays—Eastern region," however, we might find case sale numbers like 10, 6, 7. The across-strata variability is much greater than that within each stratum. We would thus obtain more efficient estimates using stratification.

The stratification variables worked because they are all *correlated* with the sales of Folger's. In general, we add stratification variables as long as they contribute meaningfully to the variability of the variable we are measuring. Of course, we also consider the *cost* of stratification in deciding on the number of stratification variables.

Most studies are designed to measure many variables. What is a good stratification variable for some of these may not be as good for others. In selecting stratification variables, we want those that will contribute most meaningfully across all variables of interest.

Disproportionate Stratified Sampling

The overall sample size *n* can also be allocated to strata on a basis *disproportionate* with the population sizes of the strata. Proportionate allocation is straightforward, so why should we complicate things by allocating on some other basis? The answer lies in the differences in variability within strata. Generally, for a fixed sample size we can reduce the overall standard error of the estimate by sampling more heavily in strata with higher variability. Suppose that we had added another stratification variable to our age example and that by doing so we obtained a population stratum with the elements 21, 21, 21 in it. There is no variability in this stratum, and a sample of one is all that is needed to measure perfectly the mean of this stratum. Alternatively, a stratum with much variability will require a large sample size to produce an efficient estimate of the mean. This is true because in order to calculate the standard error within a stratum we divide the standard deviation within the stratum by the square root of the stratum sample size, $n_{\text{st}.j}$.

An optimal allocation of a fixed sample size among strata is one that generates the minimum standard error of the overall estimate. To find this optimal allocation we must know something about the variability within strata before sampling. Experience and past studies may provide such knowledge. Companies doing retail store audits often sample the larger stores at a disproportionately high level because these larger stores exhibit more variability in sales than small stores. The result is a smaller standard error and a more reliable estimate. There are mathematical formulas to determine the optimal allocation of a sample to strata, but they are complex and beyond the scope of this book. In general, these formulas indicate that (1) the larger the stratum, the larger the sample, and (2) the greater variability within a stratum, the larger the sample.

How are the overall mean and standard error calculated with a disproportionate stratified sample? Exactly the same formulas are used as before, in proportionate stratified sampling. This is the case because

$$W_j = \frac{N_{\text{st.}j}}{N}$$

That is, it is the size of the population within strata and the total population that determine the weighting factors. The sample sizes within strata are used only to calculate within-strata means and standard errors.

CLUSTER SAMPLING

Overview

In all the probability sampling methods we have discussed so far, the elements that form the sample are selected individually. In cluster sampling, *a cluster or group of elements are randomly selected at one time*. Thus, before we can select a cluster sample, the population must be divided into mutually exclusive and collectively exhaustive groups. We then select a random sample of these groups.

Suppose we had a population of 20 elements divided into 4 equal-sized groups as follows:

Group	Population element number
Group 1	1, 2, 3, 4, 5
Group 2	6, 7, 8, 9, 10
Group 3	11, 12, 13, 14, 15
Group 4	16, 17, 18, 19, 20

If we wanted to select a probability sample of 10 elements, we could select elements individually using simple random sampling, or we could randomly select two of the four groups and use all the elements in those two groups. The situation where we directly select groups and then use *all* the elements in these groups is called *one-stage cluster sampling*. If we had selected a random sample of elements from within the selected groups, we would call this a *two-stage cluster sample*. In both cluster and simple random sampling the sampling fraction would be the same, .5. However, all possible combinations of elements are not equally likely in cluster sampling. Most combinations are impossible.

What if the clusters we select have elements that are not representative of the population? Wouldn't our estimates be biased? The answer is yes. This points out the criterion we should use in forming groups. We want them to be as close in heterogeneity on the variables of interest as the population as a whole. If the groups are exactly as heterogeneous as the population, any one group we select will accurately represent the population; in practice, however, this ideal is never reached. Note that in cluster sampling the criterion used in forming groups is exactly the opposite of that used in stratified sampling. In stratified sampling we want homogeneous groups, whereas in cluster sampling we want heterogeneous groups.

How does the size of the standard error generated from a cluster sample compare with the size of the standard error generated from a simple random sample? The answer depends on the similarity of the heterogeneity in the formed groups compared with the population, as follows:

1 If the groups are exactly as heterogeneous as the population, both methods will yield the same standard error.

2 If the groups are less heterogeneous than the population, the standard error will be greater with cluster sampling than with simple random sampling.

We refer to this comparison of the standard errors generated by various sampling procedures as an assessment of the *statistical efficiency* of the procedures.

In practice, sample clusters are often much less heterogeneous than the population, which means that in most cases they are less statistically efficient than simple random samples. For reasons of cost, however, cluster samples are very extensively used in practice. They are often much cheaper than other procedures for a given sample size. Alternatively, for a given dollar budget we can generate a larger sample using cluster sampling. When we combine the statistical efficiency of a procedure with its cost, we refer to this as the *overall efficiency* or *total efficiency* of the procedure. Cluster sampling is often the most overall efficient procedure. That is, we get a smaller standard error per dollar spent. The next section discusses the most straightforward type of cluster sampling, systematic sampling.

SYSTEMATIC SAMPLING

The Method

In systematic sampling, the researcher selects *every kth element in the frame, after a random start somewhere within the first k elements.* Suppose we wanted to select a systematic sample of $n = 5$ from our student population in Tables 8-1 and 9-1. Here

$$k = \frac{50}{5} = 10$$

In general,

$$k = \frac{N}{n}$$

which is the reciprocal of the sampling fraction we desire and is called the *sampling interval*. Thus, to select our systematic sample of $n = 5$, we do the following:

1 Obtain a random number between 1 and 10. This element will be our starting point and the first element of the sample.

2 Add 10 to this random number. This element will be the second element of the sample. Add another 10 to get the third element, and so on.

If the random number were 2, our sample would include the elements

$$2, 12, 22, 32, 42$$

Once the sampling interval and random starting point have been specified, the elements that are included in the sample become automatic. They form a cluster of elements. In our population of 50, there are only 10 possible systematic samples of size $n = 5$ that can be drawn, because each cluster includes $\frac{1}{10}$ of the population. In general, the number of possible samples is equal to k, the sampling interval. With populations that are large relative to the sample size, the value of k, and therefore the number of possible samples, increases substantially.

Because we use all the elements in the cluster generated by systematic sampling, it is called a *one-stage cluster sampling procedure*. Also, it is clear that all possible combinations of elements are not equally likely. We have reduced the number of possible samples from over 2 million with simple random sampling to 10 with systematic sampling.

Fortunately, it can be shown that the mean of the sampling distribution of means generated by repeated systematic sampling is equal to the population mean. That is, the mean from any one systematic sample is an unbiased estimator of the population mean. We may then calculate meaningful confidence intervals as we did with simple random sampling.[2] In fact, if the frame from which we are sampling is truly random, a systematic sample may be thought of as being identical to simple random sampling. In most applications the results are almost identical.

The mean age for the systematic sample we drew is (reading the ages associated with the selected elements from Table 9-1)

$$\bar{X} = \frac{27 + 29 + 19 + 22 + 23}{5}$$

$$= \frac{120}{5}$$

$$= 24.0$$

---

[2] There are some very technical aspects related to the calculation of standard error that apply here. They are well beyond the scope of this book and have been ignored. In most situations these refinements add little to real managerial understanding of sampling results. We proceed here as if the formulas related to simple random sampling apply. For technical detail see Leslie Kish, *Survey Sampling* (New York: Wiley, 1965), pp. 117–118.

and

$$\Sigma X^2 = (27)^2 + (29)^2 + (19)^2 + (22)^2 + (23)^2$$
$$= 729 + 841 + 361 + 484 + 529$$
$$= 2944$$

$$\frac{(\Sigma X)^2}{n} = \frac{(120)^2}{5}$$
$$= \frac{14400}{5}$$
$$= 2880$$

Therefore,

$$s^2 = \frac{2944 - 2880}{4}$$
$$= \frac{64}{4}$$
$$= 16$$

Then

$$s = 4$$

The standard error is

$$\frac{4}{\sqrt{5}} = \frac{4}{2.24}$$
$$= 1.79$$

The 95 percent confidence interval is then

$$24.0 \pm 2(1.79) = 24.0 \pm 3.58$$
$$= 20.4 - 27.6$$

The true mean is again contained within the 95 percent interval. Because of the particular elements that formed the cluster we selected, the standard error is larger than in the simple random sample we selected earlier; thus, so is the confidence interval.

Systematic sampling is more often used in practice than simple random sampling, because it is much easier and cheaper to select a systematic sample. With systematic sampling we do not jump back and forth all over our sampling frame wherever our random number leads us, nor do we have to worry about checking for duplication of elements. In simple random sampling both of these problems occur. Because systematic sampling is a close substitute for simple random sampling, we may use it to select elements within strata in stratified sampling.

There is one other benefit of systematic sampling over simple random sampling: we do not need a complete sampling frame to draw a systematic sample. An interviewer instructed to interview every 20th customer can do so without a full list of all customers. Similarly, he or she could select a sample of every third house without a full list of the houses available.

The Problem of Periodicity

There is one major problem with systematic sampling, namely that we will obtain biased estimates if the list of elements forming the frame forms a cyclical pattern that coincides with a multiple of the size of the sampling interval. This type of frame is said to have *periodicity*. We may illustrate this problem with two examples. Suppose we wanted to interview residents of a student housing complex[3] and selected housing units from a list of all units arranged in numerical order: 1, 2, . . . , 599, 600. Suppose our sampling interval was 10 and our random starting number 5. Our sample would contain the 60 housing units numbered 5, 15, 25, . . . , 585, 595. Now suppose that the complex was built such that the units ending in 5, 25, 45, 65, and 85 were corner units. These corner units had one more bedroom than the other units and had higher rent. They also were allocated to students on the basis of seniority (number of years in the complex) and on the basis of having at least three children. So half of our sample would consist of people with at least three children who had been in the complex a number of years and were willing to pay the higher rent. Our sample would not be representative of the complex. Note here that the cyclical pattern is twice the size of the sampling interval. The pattern could be any multiple of the sampling interval and cause bias in our estimates.

As a second example,[4] consider the problem of a movie theater manager who wants to estimate total popcorn sales by using a sample of certain days' sales. Suppose it is decided to select one day from each week of the year—that is, $n = 52$. The sampling interval is then $365/52 = 7$. The sample would then allow the recording of popcorn sales only on the same day of the week for all 52 weeks. A sample of Saturdays would obviously overstate sales, whereas a sample of Tuesdays would understate sales.

The researcher must be sensitive to periodicity in a sampling frame if the intention is to use systematic sampling. If periodicity exists, is must be removed from the frame by rearranging the elements, or some other sampling procedure must be adopted.

Implicit Stratification with Systematic Sampling

Ordered frames are not always bad for systematic sampling. If the frame is ordered on what might be used as a stratification variable, selection of a systematic sample will

---

[3] This example is adapted from Earl Babbie, *Survey Research Methods* (Belmont, Calif.: Wadsworth, 1973), p. 93.

[4] This example is adapted from Gilbert A. Churchill, Jr., *Marketing Research: Methodological Foundations* (Hinsdale, Ill.: Dryden Press, 1976), p. 293.

automatically provide a stratified sample. In this situation, a systematic sample will produce a more statistically efficient result than simple random sampling.

Consider the systematic sample of students we selected. We know that the list of students is ordered by whether they are graduate or undergraduate students, in the ratio 20/30. With a sampling interval of 10, we know that the first two sample elements must come from the graduate stratum and the last three from the undergraduate stratum. Thus we automatically selected a proportionate stratified sample of students with our systematic sample.

If the researcher is aware of the implicit stratification that has occurred, it is possible to use stratified formulas to calculate the sample mean and standard error. The result is a smaller confidence interval. In our student age sample, the ages of the students within strata would be

Stratum 1: 27, 29

Stratum 2: 19, 22, 23

You are encouraged to do the necessary calculations to show the reduction in standard error. It should now be intuitively obvious by just looking at the numbers arranged in strata.

In summary, systematic sampling offers potential advantages in (1) ease of sample selection, (2) cost, (3) removal of the need for a complete frame, and (4) implicit stratification of properly ordered frames. Difficulties are related to (1) the problem of possible periodicity and (2) possible technical problems in calculating standard error. Systematic sampling is moderately used in practice.

AREA SAMPLING

The Basics

With simple random sampling, stratified sampling, and most applications of systematic sampling discussed so far, a complete and accurate listing of the elements of the population is required. Unfortunately, for a great many marketing research applications such lists are impossible to generate at a reasonable cost. Lists are not available for such populations as all the adults in the United States, all the inhabitants of a state or city, all users of a particular product, or all university students or church members. It may be possible to obtain such lists, but the cost would be extremely high, and they would probably contain many inaccuracies. Sampling practitioners have developed an ingenious solution to this problem. They reasoned that people reside on a specific piece of land, so why not sample pieces of land and interview the persons who reside there? So the word "area" in area sample originally referred to a piece of land. *An area sample is actually a sampling of areas.* It is extensively used in practice.

We shall illustrate this concept by outlining what a one-stage area sample might look like. Suppose we want to run an in-home usage test of a new formulation of a shampoo. We have decided to run this test in Atlanta. An accurate listing of all households in Atlanta is unavailable, since the city directory and telephone book are both very out of date even as they are published. So we select an area sample using the following method:

1 List all city blocks in Atlanta, N_B.
2 Choose a simple random or systematic sample of n_B city blocks from the population of N_B city blocks.
3 Attempt to place the product in all households in the chosen blocks, n_B.

This is a probability sampling procedure because the probability of any household being selected is equal to the sampling fraction, n_B/N_B. If Atlanta had 10,000 blocks and we selected a sample of 20 blocks, the probability of any household being selected would be $20/10,000 = .002$. The reason why this probability equals the sampling fraction for the blocks is that we are using all households in the selected blocks as part of the sample.

Multistage Area Samples

An area sample can have as many stages as the researcher desires. Most area samples have more than one stage. What would a two-stage area sample designed for our product usage look like? The steps would be:

1 List all city blocks in Atlanta, N_B.
2 Choose a simple random sample or systematic sample of n_B city blocks.
3 List the households located in the selected city blocks, N_H.
4 Select a simple random or systematic sample of n_H households from the selected n_B city blocks.

Note that the first two steps of two-stage area sampling are the same as in one-stage area sampling. With the latter, however, we were required to make one list (of blocks), and we used probability sampling procedures only once (to select the blocks). In two-stage area sampling we were required to make two lists (blocks and then households), and we used probability sampling procedures twice (to select blocks and then households). In a two-stage area sample we twice repeated the sequence "list population sampling units, and then sample." Thus, in a k-stage area sample we would go through this sequence k times.

A multistage area sample may be illustrated by describing the five-stage area sampling process used by the Survey Research Center of the Institute for Social Research of the University of Michigan for its many national studies.[5] Figure 9-1 gives a graphic view of the five stages of this process. The five stages are:

Stage 1 The continental United States is divided into 74 "primary areas." These areas are usually counties, groups of counties, or metropolitan areas. A probability sample of primary areas is then made. That is, the researchers list the areas and then sample from this list. The top row of Figure 9-1 depicts the primary areas on the map

---

[5] This section is based on the *Interviewer's Manual*, rev. ed., Survey Research Center, Institute for Social Research, the University of Michigan, Ann Arbor, 1976, pp. 35–37.

of the continental United States and shows the selection of one primary area. It is common for the researchers to stratify the primary-area population to assure themselves that their sample will include the proper proportion of primary areas of different types. For example, a geographic stratification would ensure that each region of the country is represented. Multiple stratification variables are often used.

Stage 2   A listing is made of the large cities, medium-sized towns, and remaining areas in the selected primary areas. In the example of Figure 9-1, the selected area consists of one large city, four medium-sized towns, and open space. This area would probably be stratified into three groups: (1) large cities, (2) smaller cities and towns, and (3) open space. Then one or more of what are called "sample locations" would be selected by probability methods from each stratum. Again the researchers list the population sampling units and select a probability sample.

We should also note that they have again been stratified to ensure a representative sample. The connected circles running from "primary area" to "sample location" in Figure 9-1 illustrate stage 2 for the selection of one sample location from one primary area previously selected.

Stage 3   A listing is made of the geographic areas within the sample location. These geographic areas must have identifiable boundaries—for example, city blocks, rural roads, rivers, or county lines. These geographic areas are referred to as "chunks." On the average, chunks are designed to contain from 16 to 40 dwellings, but they may contain more in large cities. A probability sample of chunks is then selected from each selected sample location obtained in stage 2. The theme of "list sampling units and select a probability sample" should be very obvious. The connected circles running from "sample location" to "chunk" on Figure 9-1 illustrate stage 3 for the selection of one chunk from one sample location previously selected.

Stage 4   A listing is made of all the housing units in the selected chunk, which is then divided into smaller units called "segments," containing from 4 to 16 housing units. A probability sample of segments is then selected. The connected circles running from "chunk" to "segment" on Figure 9-1 illustrate the selection of one segment from a chunk that was previously selected.

Stage 5   From the listing of housing units in segments, a probability sample of housing units is selected. The connected circles running from "segment" to "housing unit" on Figure 9-1 illustrate the selection of one housing unit from one segment that was previously selected. If this process continued to include the listing of persons within housing units and then selected a probability sample of persons, it would be a six-stage area sample. Note that a housing unit does not have to be a single-family dwelling. A full 70-unit apartment building would count as 70 housing units.

The Properties of Multistage Area Samples

Multistage area sampling is much less statistically efficient than simple random sampling. In a simple random sample a single sampling error is calculated. A two-stage area sample is subject to two sampling errors. The selection of the clusters at the

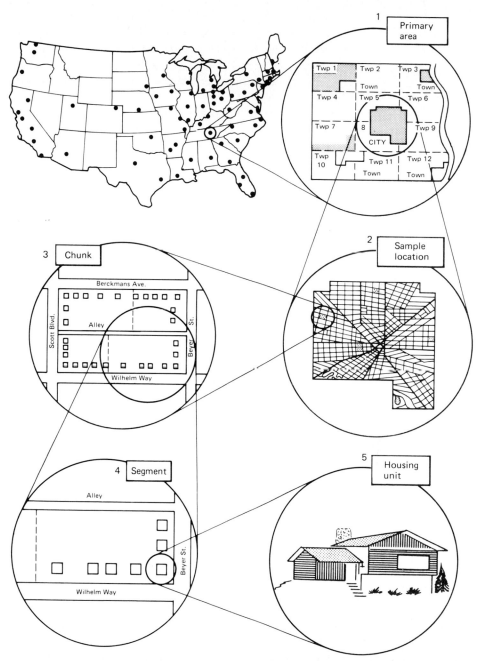

FIGURE 9-1   An illustration of area sampling. [*Adapted from Interviewer's Manual, rev. ed. (Ann Arbor: Survey Research Center, Institute for Social Research, the University of Michigan, 1976), p. 36.*]

first stage is only an estimate of the population of clusters; that is, sampling error occurs. In this way, the selection of elements from within a cluster is only an estimate of the population of elements within that cluster. Thus, a five-stage area sample would contain five sampling errors. The formulas to calculate the standard error from a multistage area sample are too complex to be discussed here. Researchers should be sensitive to this issue and prepared to consult a technical expert for the proper calculation. In practice, the results obtained from the final stage are often treated as if they came from a direct probability sampling of a list of final elements. That is, the formulas used are those for simple random sampling and stratified sampling. The net effect of doing this is to understate the sampling error that has occurred. However, for decisions where the risk of such an understatement is explicitly tolerated, we cannot be too critical of such a shortcut procedure.

The technical aspects may seem complex enough at this point, but there are still some basics concerning the sampling error generated in multistage area sampling that should be understood.[6] Sampling error is decreased by an increase in (1) sample size and (2) the homogeneity of the elements being sampled. Sample size and homogeneity affect sampling error at each stage of a multistage sample design. Thus, to have a small sampling error at the time of selecting clusters, we would like to select a large number from a group of very similar clusters. Similarly, to have a small sampling error at the time of selecting elements from a given cluster, we would like to select a large number from a group of very similar elements. For any given sample size, we cannot increase the number of clusters without decreasing the number of elements within each cluster. Therefore, cluster-level error would seem to be decreased at the expense of element-level error. This is true, but the effect is limited by the fact that elements within area sample clusters tend to be more homogeneous than the population as a whole. For example, the residents of a city block are more similar than those in the country or even city as a whole. Therefore, the sample size within clusters of this type can be quite small and still yield a reasonable sampling error. Clusters, on the other hand, tend to be more heterogeneous. Thus, a large number of clusters may be necessary to reduce the sampling error to a reasonable size at the cluster selection level. This discussion leads to the conclusion that we should select a large number of clusters and a small number of elements within each cluster in order to have the best statistical efficiency.

But what about total efficiency? It does have a role to play. The more clusters we select, the more lists of elements we have to prepare, the more geographical areas we have to send interviewers to, and the more administrative complications we will have to deal with. All these factors increase the cost of the study, so the final sample design involves a tradeoff between statistical efficiency and cost, There is no optimal choice available. The researcher must make this tradeoff based on the objectives of the study, the amount of money available, and the amount of error that is acceptable. The accuracy of these types of samples is clearly illustrated in the Marketing Research In Action in this section. Every election was called correctly with an average deviation of only 1.6 percent.

---

[6] This discussion follows an excellent one in Babbie, op. cit., pp. 98–99.

MARKETING RESEARCH IN ACTION

FOUR DECADES OF POLLING EXPERIENCE:

Accuracy Record of the Michigan Poll by Market Opinion Research
Statewide Poll of Election Trends (1944–1982)

Year	MOR final survey, %	Majority vote election result, %	Error on winning candidate, percentage points
*1944	60.7 Roosevelt	61.5 Roosevelt	−0.8 Roosevelt
*1948	52.1 Truman	58.3 Truman	−6.2 Truman
1952	52.6 Eisenhower	55.8 Eisenhower	−3.2 Eisenhower
1956	57.8 Eisenhower	55.8 Eisenhower	+2.0 Eisenhower
1960	52.9 Kennedy	51.0 Kennedy	+1.9 Kennedy
1962	50.9 Romney	51.5 Romney	−0.6 Romney
1964	68.0 Johnson	66.8 Johnson	+1.2 Johnson
1966	61.0 Romney	60.7 Romney	+0.3 Romney
1968	47.0 Humphrey	48.6 Humphrey	−1.6 Humphrey
1970	50.5 Milliken	50.9 Milliken	−0.4 Milliken
1972	53.8 Nixon	57.3 Nixon	−3.5 Nixon
1974	50.9 Milliken	51.6 Milliken	−0.7 Milliken
1976	50.0 Ford	51.8 Ford	−1.8 Ford
1978	52.6 Milliken	56.7 Milliken	−4.1 Milliken
1980	49.0 Reagan	49.1 Reagan	−0.1 Reagan
1982	50.0 Blanchard	51.4 Blanchard	−1.4 Blanchard

Average deviation for 14 statewide elections since 1952 = 1.6%.
The final survey figures and the majority vote figures are based on percentaging the vote for the two major candidates, plus in 1968, 1980 and 1982 the minority candidate votes, to equal 100%.

* Detroit metropolitan area poll.

Equal-Probability Area Sampling

Earlier we defined probability sampling as a technique where each element has a known chance of being selected. In all the types of sampling discussed so far, except disproportionate statistical sampling, each element has had an equal chance of being selected. This is the easiest way to ensure that the sample selected represents the population. In this section we shall discuss how we obtain equal probabilities for each element. Later in the chapter we shall discuss sampling with unequal probabilities for the elements.

There are two ways to assure equal-chance selection of elements in an area sample.

1 Equal-Chance Selection of Clusters—Equal-Proportion Selection of Elements within Clusters   In this method each cluster is given an equal chance of selection regardless of size; then the same proportion of the elements is selected from within each cluster. Thus, each element has an equal chance of being selected. To illustrate, suppose we have 1000 elements divided into 50 clusters of different sizes. If we select a sample of 5 clusters, each cluster has a $\frac{5}{50}$ chance of being selected. If we then select one-fifth of the elements within each cluster, the total probability of an element being selected is

$$\tfrac{5}{50} \times \tfrac{1}{5} = .1 \times .2 = .02$$

In this way bigger clusters have more elements selected. This balances the fact that these clusters had only as high a chance of being selected as smaller clusters. This process would require a sample size of $.02 \times 1000 = 20$ elements. Note that for equal-probability sampling, the probability of an element being selected is equal to the sampling fraction. In this case $\frac{20}{1000} = .02$.

More typically we would have a specified sample size and would be asked to select the number of clusters and proportion of elements within each cluster. A number of combinations of numbers of clusters and within-cluster proportions could accomplish this task. For example, the following combinations yield a probability of selection of .02;

(1)   10 clusters and $\frac{1}{10}$ of the elements $= \frac{10}{50} \times \frac{1}{10}$
$$= .2 \times .1 = .02$$
(2)   20 clusters and $\frac{5}{100}$ of the elements $= \frac{20}{50} \times \frac{5}{100}$
$$= .4 \times .05 = .02$$

We can apply this procedure to multistage designs, as long as we continue to select the elements at each stage with equal proportion. Let's use the Institute for Social Research design to illustrate this. Suppose that at stage 1 we selected 10 of the 74 "primary areas." These primary areas vary in size, so at stage 2 we select $\frac{2}{5}$ of the "sample location sections" in each primary area; each sample location section therefore has an equal probability of being selected equal to

$$\tfrac{10}{74} \times \tfrac{2}{5} = .14 \times .4 = .056$$

Now for stage 3, if we select a sample of "chunks" from each sample location section at the rate of $\frac{7}{400}$, each chunk will have an equal chance of being selected even if the sample location sections are of different sizes. If the stage 4 proportion to select "segments" is $\frac{1}{4}$ and the stage 5 proportion to select "housing units" is $\frac{1}{5}$, the probability of selecting any housing unit is

$$\begin{array}{l} \text{House-} \\ \text{hold unit} \\ \text{probability} \end{array} = \dfrac{\text{stage 1}}{\text{proportion}} \times \dfrac{\text{stage 2}}{\text{proportion}} \times \dfrac{\text{stage 3}}{\text{proportion}} \times \dfrac{\text{stage 4}}{\text{proportion}} \times \dfrac{\text{stage 5}}{\text{proportion}}$$

$$= \tfrac{10}{74} \times \tfrac{2}{5} \times \tfrac{7}{400} \times \tfrac{1}{4} \times \tfrac{1}{5}$$
$$= .14 \times .4 \times .018 \times .25 \times .2$$
$$= .00005$$

In a household population of 70 million this design would require a sample size of $.00005 \times 70$ million $= 3500$. Of course, given a sample size of 3500 and a sampling fraction objective of .00005, we can adjust the proportions of sampling units selected at various stages as long as their product continues to equal .00005.

What makes this yield equal probability for each household is that we select an equal proportion within each cluster at each stage. Thus different-size clusters are automatically taken care of. Clearly, if we had selected the same number of sampling units at each stage, the household unit elements would have different probabilities—those from big clusters would have much less chance of being selected than those from small clusters. This process would yield equal probabilites for elements only if all clusters were the same size.

2 Probability Proportionate to Size (PPS)   There is another method of obtaining equal element probabilities that is more statistically efficient than the equal-proportion method discussed above. In the equal-proportion method, a relatively small number of large clusters are selected, and thus the elements selected to represent all large clusters are selected from a few clusters. In response to this problem, the more recommended method of selecting first-stage clusters is the *probability proportionate to size* (PPS) method.

In a two-stage PPS the procedure would be as follows. In the first stage of the method, each cluster is assigned a chance of selection proportionate to the number of second-stage elements it contains, with the result that larger clusters have a better chance of selection than small ones. Then in the second stage the same number of sampling units are selected from each selected cluster. Thus a smaller proportion of elements will be selected from larger clusters than from small ones, with the result that the probability of all elements being selected at the second stage is the same. As an illustration, suppose we have 10 city blocks as follows:

Block number	Number of households
1	10
2	20
3	30
4	10
5	100
6	30
7	70
8	30
9	50
10	50
Total households	400

The relevant probability proportionate to size for block B is

$$PPS_B = \frac{\text{number of households in block B}}{\text{total number of households}}$$

For block 1,

$$PPS_1 = \frac{10}{400} = .025$$

For block 9,

$$PPS_9 = \frac{50}{400} = .125$$

We mechanically select a PPS block sample by calculating the cumulative number of households and assigning random numbers in proportion to this cumulative distribution.

Block number	Number of households	Cumulative number of households	Associated random numbers
1	10	10	001–010
2	20	30	011–030
3	30	60	031–060
4	10	70	061–070
5	100	170	071–170
6	30	200	171–200
7	70	270	201–270
8	30	300	271–300
9	50	350	301–350
10	50	400	351–400
Total	400		

If we wanted a sample of three blocks, we would obtain three 3-digit random numbers between 001 and 400. Suppose we obtained the numbers 124, 302, and 027; our sample would be blocks 5, 9, and 2. We then select five households from blocks 2, 5, and 9. The probabilities of selecting elements are:

Probability of element in
 block B
 = block probability × within-block element probability

For elements in block 2 = $\frac{20}{400} \times \frac{5}{20}$

= .05 × .25

= .0125

For elements in block 5 = $\frac{100}{400} \times \frac{5}{100}$

= .25 × .05

= .0125

For elements in block 9 $= {}^{50}\!/_{400} \times {}^{5}\!/_{50}$
$$= .125 \times .1$$
$$= .0125$$

The stage 1 and stage 2 probabilities balance each other to give equal probability of selection for all elements. The same result also holds for the unselected blocks.

In a multistage area sample we can use the PPS method for the first two stages to ensure equal probabilities to that point. Then we can select equal proportions from that point on to yield equal probabilities of all elements at the final stage. For example, if we really had a five-stage area sample and used PPS as in the example above, the element probability at the final stage might be:

Element probability = probability after 2 stages × probability at other stages
$$= .0125 \times .018 \times .50 \times .3$$
$$= .00003$$

PPS is used to help ensure that large clusters are represented in the sample. Alternatively, this may be done by stratifying the first-stage cluster by size and sampling within clusters. PPS and stratification on size would not be used together.

Unequal-Probability Area Sampling

In all the probability sampling methods discussed so far, except disproportionate stratified sampling, each population element had an equal chance of selection. Recall that in our orginal definition of probability sampling each element only needed a known chance of being selected to be a probability procedure. Often in area sampling, elements are selected disproportionately; that is, elements have different probabilities of being selected. The research may yield unequal probabilities for a number of reasons, including:

1 Wanting to do detailed subgroup analysis, the researcher purposely oversamples a small subgroup to have a large enough sample to do meaningful analysis for that group. Such a subgroup might be working women.

2 The researcher is doing disproportionate stratified sampling to reduce within-stratum and overall sampling error.

3 A sample yields a smaller proportion of a particular subgroup than the population proportion.

4 A PPS design requires knowledge of cluster sizes. If these sizes turn out to be incorrect, the result is that the cluster will be given a disproportionately high or low probability of being selected.

Thus, we may obtain unequal probabilities for element selection from a number of deliberate or accidental happenings. They present no problems as long as the researcher is interested in doing only within-subgroup analysis. Suppose, for example, we were estimating the weekly gasoline consumption among undergraduate and graduate students in our population of 50 students. If we took a sample of 10 from each subgroup, the graduate students would have a probability of selection of $^{10}/_{20} = .5$, and the undergraduates $^{10}/_{30} = .33$. Note that the overall sampling fraction $^{20}/_{50} = .4$ does not equal the probability of each element being selected. This relationship now holds only within the subgroups. Suppose we estimated the average gasoline consumption of graduate students as $^{100}/_{10} = 10$ gallons per week, and of undergraduates as $^{50}/_{10} = 5$ gallons per week. Those estimates are valid, and we can compare them with each other. However, if we combine the subgroups to make an overall estimate, the higher consumption of graduate students would be overrepresented, thus biasing the estimate upwards. This average is

$$\bar{X}_{\text{gasoline}} = .5(10) + .5(5)$$
$$= 5 + 2.5$$
$$= 7.5$$

What we want is to have the weights reflect the subpopulation sizes. So the unbiased estimate is

$$\bar{X}_{\text{gasoline}} = .4(10) + .6(5)$$
$$= 4 + 3$$
$$= 7$$

You will recognize these weights as the population proportions from the stratified sampling section. This example was easy because we knew all about the subpopulation sizes. More realistically, we are likely to know the probability of selecting an element from subgroups. Can we use element probabilities directly to obtain proper weights? The answer is yes.

The rule is that an element should be assigned a weighing factor *in proportion to the inverse of its probability of being selected.*

In our gasoline example,

1 For graduate students:

Probability of selection $= .5$

Inverse $= \dfrac{1}{.5} = 2.0$

2 For undergraduate students:

Probability of selection $= .33$

Inverse $= \dfrac{1}{.33} = 3.0$

With this information there are two ways to obtain our overall average of 7 gallons. The first is to multiply the total gallons in each subgroup and the number in the sample in each subgroup by their respective inverses, and then take the average. Here we get

Graduates:

$$100 \text{ gallons} \times 2 = 200$$
$$10 \text{ students} \times 2 = 20$$

Undergraduates:

$$50 \text{ gallons} \times 3 = 150$$
$$10 \text{ students} \times 3 = 30$$

$$\text{Total gallons} = 200 + 150 = 350$$
$$\text{Total students} = 20 + 30 = 50$$
$$\text{Average gallons} = \frac{350}{50} = 7$$

The 50 is called the *weighted sample size.*

The alternative is to convert the inverses to proportions with respect to each other, then take a weighted average:

$$\text{Graduate inverse} = 2$$
$$\text{Undergraduate inverse} = 3$$
$$\text{Total of inverses} = 5$$
$$\text{Proportion graduate} = \tfrac{2}{5} = .4$$
$$\text{Proportion undergraduate} = \tfrac{3}{5} = .6$$

You will recognize these as our population weighting factors.

The latter method is much preferred for large studies with small subgroup sampling fractions. For example, if three subgroups had probabilities of element selection of .00005, .000047, and .000052, the respective inverses are 20,000, 21,277, and 19,231. Multiplying by these weights is certainly more complicated than taking their proportions, which are .33, .35, and .31. Note that in equal-probability sampling each element would be assigned the same weight, as the inverses would be equal. This, of course, is as it should be.

Weighting can be handled in a number of ways. If we have our data on computer cards, we can simply duplicate cards for various subgroups to bring them up to the proper proportions. In our gasoline example, we would reproduce the graduate cards twice and the undergraduate ones three times. This method will do for small jobs but is impossible for large ones. Fortunately, most good computer data analysis packages have procedures where the researcher can specify weighting factors. The analysis program then automatically includes them as part of the analysis.

Statistical inference and Complex Sampling Procedures

Statistical inference was developed on the basis of simple random sampling. Can it be meaningfully applied to samples of the complexity we have seen in this chapter? The evidence leads us to believe that it can. Frankel's significant study in this area concluded that (1) the sample estimates were approximately unbiased, (2) the sample variances of these estimates were approximately unbiased, and (3) the calculated standard error allowed for the calculation of valid confidence intervals.[7]

You should now be able to outline the design of a sampling plan to meet your objectives. For the complexities of statistical inference in these complex designs, consult a technical specialist.

RANDOM-DIGIT DIALING

Within the context of all the probability sampling procedures discussed in Chapters 8 and 9, there is a very important procedure for actually selecting a sample element that needs to be understood. This procedure is *random-digit dialing*. It has become increasingly important with the growing dominance of telephone interviewing as a means of contacting respondents. Also, it allows contact with people who have unlisted numbers or who have moved since the directory was printed or whose number is in error in the telephone directory.

In a pure form, all seven digits of a telephone number can be generated randomly. However, this is both costly and inefficient, as many unused numbers are generated. What is more common in practice is that numbers are selected from a telephone directory using a systematic sampling procedure, and then the last one or two digits of these numbers are replaced with random numbers. This procedure gives a much higher percentage of used telephone numbers and has the properties of a true probability sample.

This procedure can be used with any of the probability sampling methods discussed so far. Let's use an area sampling context as an example. Looking back at Figure 9-1, we could use random-digit dialing in the context of a multistage area sample as follows: (1) proceed exactly as described in Figure 9-1 down as far as the sample location level which gives you a city or town, (2) obtain the telephone directories for the selected cities or towns and systematically select a sample of telephone numbers from the directories, (3) replace the last one or two digits of these selected numbers with random numbers, and (4) call the resultant numbers.

SAMPLE SIZE

The selection of a sample size in the more complex sampling procedures discussed in this chapter involves a tradeoff among the same factors discussed in Chapter 8. If we use the concept of statistically optimal sample size as part of this decision process, there is one modification that must be made. While we must make a precision and confidence level designation and apply the formula for size of standard error, the formula for standard error differs in stratified and area sampling from that of simple random sampling. Be careful to use the right formula.

[7] Martin R. Frankel, *Inference from Survey Samples: An Empirical Investigation* (Ann Arbor, Mich.: Survey Research Center, Institute for Social Research, the University of Michigan, 1971), pp. 104–116.

MANAGERIAL SUMMARY OF SAMPLING

To end this section on sampling, we shall present a brief summary of some of the dimensions of various sampling procedures. Table 9-3 is the heart of this summary. It presents comparisons among a census and various sampling procedures on a number of dimensions. The first is the ability of the procedure to generate a measure of sampling error, and the second is the related concept of statistical efficiency. The third dimension is the need for a list of population elements in order to draw the sample, the fourth is the cost of the procedure, and the fifth is the frequency of use in practice. A manager should consider all these aspects when choosing a sampling procedure.

SUMMARY

1 Stratified sampling allows for the reduction of the standard error over simple random sampling.

2 To select a stratified sample, divide the population into mutually exclusive and collectively exhaustive strata, and then select a probability sample from each stratum. The strata are designed to be more homogeneous than the total population.

3 A proportionate stratified sample is one where the sample size is allocated to strata in proportion to the number of population elements in the strata.

4 Sample elements may also be allocated on a basis disproportionate with the population size of strata. The objective here is to oversample the strata with the higher variability in order to reduce the standard error within the strata.

5 The overall mean in stratified sampling is the weighted average of the within-strata means. The weighting factor is the ratio of the stratum population size to total population size, $N_{\text{st}.j}/N$ or W_j.

6 The overall standard error is the square root of the weighted combination of the square of the standard error within each stratum. The weighting factor is the square of the W_j. The standard error is smaller than with simple random sampling because we use only within-stratum variation to calculate the overall standard error.

7 The number of possible stratified samples is the product of the number of all possible samples within each stratum.

8 For a stratification variable to be useful, it must be correlated with the variable we are measuring.

9 In cluster sampling we randomly select a cluster or group of sampling units at one time. To do this the population is divided into mutually exclusive and collectively exhaustive groups.

10 These groups are designed to be as heterogeneous as the population.

11 Statistical efficiency involves the comparison of the standard errors of different sampling procedures.

12 Overall efficiency involves the comparison of the standard error per dollar spent.

13 In systematic sampling, we select every kth element in the frame, after a random start somewhere within the first k elements.

14 The sampling interval equals N/n and is equal to the number of possible samples in a systematic procedure.

TABLE 9-3 MANAGERIAL SUMMARY ON SAMPLING

Dimensions	Nonprobability samples				Probability samples			
	Census	Convenience	Judgment	Quota	Simple random	Stratified	Systematic	Area
1. Generation of sampling error	No	No	No	No	Yes	Yes	Yes	Yes
2. Statistical efficiency		—No measurement—			The level compared to	High when stratification variables work	Somewhat low	Low
3. Need for population list	Yes	No	No	No	Yes	Yes	Not necessary in all applications	Only for selected clusters
4. Cost	Very high	Very low	Low	Moderate	High	High	Moderate	Moderate to high
5. Frequency of use in practice	Low	Extensive	Moderate	Very extensive	Low	Moderate	Moderate	Very extensive

Source: Adapted from Keith K. Cox and Ben M. Enis, *The Marketing Research Process* (Pacific Palisades, Calif.: Goodyear Publishing Co.), and the current authors' experience.

15 A frame with a cyclical pattern that coincides with a multiple of the size of the sampling interval will yield biased results in systematic sampling.

16 A systematic sample of a frame ordered on a stratification variable yields a proportionate stratified sample.

17 Area sampling involves selecting pieces of geography.

18 A multistage area sample involves the repeated process of listing sampling units and selecting a probability sample from this list.

19 A multistage sample will have equal probability of the selection of each element if the selection at each stage involves a given proportion of sampling units. The probability of element selection equals the product of the individual proportions.

20 Alternatively, equal element probability can be obtained by selecting the first-stage sampling units with probabilities proportionate to size, and then selecting the same number of second-stage sampling units in each selected first-stage unit.

21 Elements may be selected with unequal probabilities.

22 With disproportionate sampling, the elements must be weighted before meaningful total-sample analysis can be done.

23 An element should be assigned a weighting factor in proportion to the inverse of its probability of being selected.

24 Random-digit dialing is a method of drawing a probability sample for telephone interviewing. In practice, it usually involves drawing a systematic sample of telephone numbers from phone directories and then replacing the last one or two digits of these selected numbers with random numbers.

DISCUSSION QUESTIONS

1 How is a stratified sample selected?

2 What is the objective of stratified sampling?

3 What is proportionate stratified sampling?

4 What is disproportionate stratified sampling?

5 How are the whole-sample mean and standard error calculated from a stratified sample?

6 Under what circumstances does stratified sampling reduce the standard error?

7 Why does stratified sampling reduce the standard error?

8 What is cluster sampling?

9 What are statistical efficiency and overall efficiency?

10 How is a systematic sample selected?

11 What is periodicity? How is it caused and cured?

12 How does implicit stratification occur?

13 What is area sampling?

14 What is multistage area sampling?

15 How do you get equal probability of element selection using a multistage area sampling procedure?

16 Why do you sometimes get unequal probabilities of element selection?

17 How are whole-sample estimates made when elements have unequal selection probabilities?

18 Outline the steps in random-digit dialing.

CASES FOR PART THREE

CASE 3-1: Milan Food Cooperative (A)

Joyce Lauchner was the general manager of the Milan Food Cooperative (MFC). She had become concerned of late that she had lost touch with the buying patterns of the cooperative members. MFC just seemed so big now compared to the early days. She wondered whether she could make use of some data that were already available to her to increase her understanding of the members' purchasing habits. She hoped that she could use this knowledge to better plan the mix and quantity of goods that MFC carried.

Background of MFC

The MFC was founded in 1974 by Lauchner and a small group of volunteers. It had grown from 10 original members in January 1974 to 500 members in September 1986. It was located in an old warehouse on the northwest side of Milan, Michigan. Milan was a community of 7500 people located in southeast Michigan, about 40 miles southwest of Detroit. MFC drew membership from a number of communities around Milan, including Ann Arbor and Monroe.

The objective of MFC was to provide high-quality food products at a price below that available at local supermarkets. To accomplish this MFC used shipping cartons as shelves, required shoppers to mark their own prices on goods, carried only the best-selling brands, and generally did not offer the "luxuries" associated with traditional supermarkets. To shop at MFC one had to be a member. The membership fee was $25 per year. Any profits earned by MFC in a year were returned to the members as a credit against purchases. Lauchner thought that the members bought most of their food at MFC.

Lauchner's Concerns

In the early days of MFC Lauchner had prided herself on knowing all its members. She had spent a great deal of time in the store and felt she knew what people were buying and how much they were spending. As the membership grew, her administrative duties kept her in her office much more. She no longer knew all the members, nor did she have a good feel for their expenditure patterns. She wanted to develop a better understanding of these aspects of her business and thought that perhaps some of the data that had already been collected on the membership might provide answers.

The Available Data

In June 1986 a questionnaire was used to collect data on the membership. During the month all members came into the cooperative at least once. Thus, data were available on all members. The data consisted of demographic characteristics of the members plus their weekly food expenditures.

The data were available on the cards that were filled out by the members at the time of the interview. Lauchner had these cards in a filing cabinet in her office. A description of the contents of the cards is presented below. Actual card values are tabulated on the following pages.

As a first step in understanding the membership, Lauchner wanted to know their average weekly expenditure on food. Since time was short, she wanted to do this without having to look at all 500 cards. However, she also wanted the average she calculated to be an accurate one. She wondered how she could do this.

MFC DATA

Explanation of Items A–K on the Table (the Variables)

A = Household identification number; 1–500
B = Weekly food expenditure, actual; e.g., $37.50
C = Number of persons in household; 1–9
D = Annual income of household, actual; e.g., $17,500
E = Education of head of household; 1–5
F = Age of head of household, actual; e.g., 38
G = Weekly food expenditure, coded into seven categories; 1–7
H = Any children under 6 years in household; 1–2
I = Any children 6–18 years in household; 1–2
J = Annual income of household, coded in six categories; 1–6
K = Age of head of household, coded into seven categories; 1–7

Category Definitions for Variables

Variable C   (Total Number of Persons in Household)

1 = one person
2 = two persons

3 = three persons
4 = four persons
5 = five persons
6 = six persons
7 = seven persons
8 = eight persons
9 = nine or more persons

Variable E   (Education of Head of Household)

1 = less than grade 8
2 = grades 9–11
3 = high school graduate
4 = some college
5 = college graduate

Variable G   (Weekly Expenditures on Food)

1 = less than $15
2 = $15 29.99
3 = $30–44.99
4 = $45–59.99
5 = $60–74.99
6 = $75–89.99
7 = $90 or over

Variable H   (Any Children Under 6 Years Old in Household)

1 = no
2 = yes

Variable I   (Any Persons 6–18 Years Old in Household)

1 = no
2 = yes

Variable J   (Annual Income of Household)

1 = less than $3,000
2 = $3,000–5,999
3 = $6,000–9,999
4 = $10,000–14,999
5 = $15,000–24,999
6 = $25,000 or over

Variable K   (Age of Head of Household)

1 = less than 25
2 = 25–34

$3 = 35-44$
$4 = 45-54$
$5 = 55-64$
$6 = 65-74$
$7 = 75$ or older

A	B	C	D	E	F	G	H	I	J	K
1	12.00	1	2500	1	56	1	1	1	1	5
2	16.50	1	2800	1	70	2	1	1	1	6
3	18.00	1	2000	1	20	2	1	1	1	1
4	17.00	1	4500	1	60	2	1	1	2	5
5	46.50	1	8000	1	40	4	1	1	3	3
6	45.00	1	7000	1	51	4	1	1	3	4
7	15.00	1	3500	1	76	2	1	1	2	7
8	60.00	2	2800	1	20	5	1	1	1	1
9	15.00	2	2500	1	51	2	1	1	1	4
10	18.00	2	4000	1	32	2	1	1	2	2
11	22.50	2	5000	1	47	2	1	1	2	4
12	20.00	2	8000	1	35	2	1	1	3	3
13	97.00	2	5500	1	58	7	1	1	2	5
14	57.00	2	6000	1	27	4	1	1	3	2
15	39.00	2	3000	1	38	3	1	1	2	3
16	30.00	2	4000	1	40	3	1	1	2	3
17	42.00	2	3000	1	19	3	1	1	2	1
18	30.00	2	3000	1	50	3	1	1	2	4
19	30.00	2	6000	1	41	3	1	1	3	3
20	32.00	2	6500	1	34	3	1	1	3	2
21	33.00	2	13000	1	23	3	1	1	4	1
22	30.00	2	15000	1	34	3	1	1	5	2
23	37.50	2	22000	1	42	3	1	1	5	3
24	110.00	3	11000	1	43	7	1	2	4	3
25	53.00	3	6500	1	51	4	1	2	3	4
26	34.00	3	28000	1	50	3	1	2	6	4
27	27.00	4	4000	1	46	2	1	2	2	4
28	39.00	5	12000	1	56	3	1	2	4	5
29	67.50	7	11000	1	48	5	1	2	4	4
30	22.50	2	1900	1	40	2	2	1	1	3
31	7.50	3	2800	1	20	1	2	1	1	1
32	19.00	3	3200	1	24	2	2	1	2	1
33	22.50	4	5000	1	30	2	2	2	2	2
34	28.50	5	7000	1	33	2	2	2	3	2
35	34.50	5	10000	1	38	3	2	2	4	3
36	52.50	6	2500	1	37	4	2	2	1	3
37	58.00	8	10000	1	42	4	2	2	4	3
38	7.00	1	2500	1	19	1	1	1	1	1
39	26.00	1	500	1	68	2	1	1	1	6
40	15.00	1	2500	1	20	2	1	1	1	1
41	30.00	1	6000	1	34	3	1	1	3	2
42	25.50	1	6000	1	66	2	1	1	3	6
43	7.50	1	1500	1	67	1	1	1	1	6

A	B	C	D	E	F	G	H	I	J	K
44	12.00	1	1500	1	72	1	1	1	1	6
45	13.50	2	4000	1	28	1	1	1	2	2
46	18.00	2	2500	1	20	2	1	1	1	1
47	30.00	2	2500	1	21	3	1	1	1	1
48	12.00	2	500	1	26	1	1	1	1	2
49	15.00	2	1500	1	19	2	1	1	1	1
50	7.50	2	500	1	19	1	1	1	1	1
51	10.50	2	1500	1	33	1	1	1	1	2
52	12.00	2	1500	1	36	1	1	1	1	3
53	15.00	2	500	1	30	2	1	1	1	2
54	20.00	2	2500	1	45	2	1	1	1	4
55	16.00	2	500	1	54	2	1	1	1	4
56	15.00	2	500	1	56	2	1	1	1	5
57	26.00	2	6200	1	26	2	1	1	3	2
58	15.00	2	1500	1	39	2	1	1	1	3
59	30.00	2	2500	1	21	3	1	1	1	1
60	22.00	2	2500	1	40	2	1	1	1	3
61	22.50	2	2500	1	48	2	1	1	1	4
62	24.00	2	2500	1	60	2	1	1	1	5
63	20.00	2	3500	1	23	2	1	1	2	1
64	11.00	2	500	1	26	1	1	1	1	2
65	16.50	2	2500	1	64	2	1	1	1	5
66	15.00	2	500	1	70	2	1	1	1	6
67	15.00	2	2500	1	31	2	1	1	1	2
68	30.00	2	6300	1	32	3	1	1	3	2
69	28.00	2	4500	1	44	2	1	1	2	3
70	30.00	2	6000	1	49	3	1	1	3	4
71	37.50	2	3500	1	35	3	1	1	2	3
72	60.00	2	3500	1	22	5	1	1	2	1
73	24.00	2	2500	1	28	2	1	1	1	2
74	7.50	2	2500	1	51	1	1	1	1	4
75	87.00	3	11000	1	69	6	1	1	4	6
76	30.00	3	6300	1	43	3	1	1	3	3
77	21.00	3	2500	1	33	2	1	1	1	2
78	120.00	3	8000	1	39	7	1	1	3	3
79	20.00	3	8500	1	58	2	1	1	3	5
80	22.50	3	2500	1	19	2	1	1	1	1
81	30.00	3	10000	1	33	3	1	1	4	2
82	40.00	3	6000	1	41	3	1	1	3	3
83	37.50	3	6000	1	47	3	1	1	3	4
84	30.00	4	4500	1	48	3	1	2	2	4
85	38.00	4	2500	1	55	3	1	2	1	5
86	60.00	4	6400	1	36	5	1	2	3	3
87	37.50	5	6000	1	57	3	1	2	3	5
88	75.00	6	4500	1	49	6	1	2	2	4
89	37.50	6	3500	1	32	3	1	2	2	2
90	75.00	4	5000	1	32	6	2	1	2	2
91	51.00	4	6000	1	44	4	2	2	3	3
92	75.00	4	4500	1	40	6	2	2	2	3
93	50.00	5	2500	1	29	4	2	2	1	2
94	39.00	5	6000	1	47	3	2	2	3	4
95	60.00	5	9200	1	58	5	2	2	3	5
96	37.50	5	8000	1	51	3	2	2	3	4
97	80.00	6	12000	1	43	6	2	2	4	3

A	B	C	D	E	F	G	H	I	J	K
98	30.00	6	3500	1	39	3	2	2	2	3
99	40.00	6	14000	1	39	3	2	2	4	3
100	75.00	6	4500	1	33	6	2	2	2	2
101	15.00	7	1500	1	49	2	2	2	1	4
102	100.00	7	6000	1	53	7	2	2	3	4
103	30.00	9	2500	1	43	3	2	2	1	3
104	34.50	9	3500	1	60	3	2	2	2	5
105	60.00	1	8500	2	45	5	1	1	3	4
106	45.00	1	11000	2	45	4	1	1	4	4
107	51.00	1	15000	2	53	4	1	1	5	4
108	36.00	1	4000	2	42	3	1	1	2	3
109	37.50	1	4500	2	33	3	1	1	2	2
110	30.00	1	4200	2	59	3	1	1	2	5
111	15.00	1	2500	2	21	2	1	1	1	1
112	20.00	1	6000	2	64	2	1	1	3	5
113	7.50	1	500	2	69	1	1	1	1	6
114	10.00	1	1500	2	39	1	1	1	1	3
115	6.00	1	6000	2	26	1	1	1	3	2
116	15.00	2	2000	2	39	2	1	1	1	3
117	66.00	2	18000	2	62	5	1	1	5	5
118	20.00	2	10000	2	58	2	1	1	4	5
119	50.00	2	11000	2	38	4	1	1	4	3
120	57.00	2	13000	2	29	4	1	1	4	2
121	47.00	2	13000	2	60	4	1	1	4	5
122	48.00	2	12000	2	50	4	1	1	4	4
123	45.00	2	27000	2	40	4	1	1	6	3
124	15.00	2	4500	2	26	2	1	1	2	2
125	22.50	2	1500	2	24	2	1	1	1	1
126	52.50	2	2500	2	29	4	1	1	1	2
127	15.00	2	2500	2	31	2	1	1	1	2
128	20.00	2	8600	2	46	2	1	1	3	4
129	22.50	2	3500	2	30	2	1	1	2	2
130	30.00	2	6000	2	48	3	1	1	3	4
131	30.00	2	4500	2	36	3	1	1	2	3
132	37.50	2	6000	2	30	3	1	1	3	2
133	30.00	2	6000	2	70	3	1	1	3	6
134	30.00	2	3500	2	39	3	1	1	2	3
135	60.00	2	6200	2	44	5	1	1	3	3
136	50.00	2	6000	2	56	4	1	1	3	5
137	52.00	3	25000	2	59	4	1	1	6	5
138	15.00	3	4500	2	29	2	1	1	2	2
139	40.00	3	3500	2	46	3	1	1	2	4
140	50.00	3	17000	2	32	4	1	1	5	2
141	36.00	4	9000	2	73	3	1	1	3	6
142	30.00	4	6000	2	40	3	1	1	3	3
143	16.50	2	2800	2	59	2	1	2	1	5
144	40.00	2	3500	2	49	3	1	2	2	4
145	33.00	3	2500	2	47	3	1	2	1	4
146	40.00	3	3500	2	52	3	1	2	2	4
147	43.00	3	5000	2	48	3	1	2	2	4
148	44.00	3	6000	2	56	3	1	2	3	5
149	30.00	3	10000	2	24	3	1	2	4	1
150	68.00	4	9000	2	51	5	1	2	3	4
151	36.00	4	8000	2	38	3	1	2	3	3

A	B	C	D	E	F	G	H	I	J	K
152	45.00	4	6000	2	47	4	1	2	3	4
153	52.50	4	9900	2	58	4	1	2	3	5
154	75.00	5	12000	2	50	6	1	2	4	4
155	28.00	5	6500	2	49	2	1	2	3	4
156	39.00	5	6000	2	61	3	1	2	3	5
157	37.50	5	6000	2	53	3	1	2	3	4
158	50.00	5	6000	2	42	4	1	2	3	3
159	54.00	5	8500	2	39	4	1	2	3	3
160	21.00	6	12500	2	48	2	1	2	4	4
161	37.50	6	11500	2	47	3	1	2	4	4
162	39.00	6	16000	2	50	3	1	2	5	4
163	90.00	6	6000	2	46	7	1	2	3	4
164	11.00	3	5000	2	46	1	2	1	2	4
165	36.00	3	2800	2	31	3	2	1	1	2
166	35.00	3	3900	2	20	3	2	1	2	1
167	37.50	3	8000	2	29	3	2	1	3	2
168	24.00	3	2500	2	23	2	2	1	1	1
169	30.00	3	17000	2	41	3	2	1	5	3
170	30.00	3	4500	2	37	3	2	1	2	3
171	55.00	4	13000	2	30	4	2	1	4	2
172	23.00	4	2500	2	53	2	2	1	1	4
173	27.00	4	2500	2	31	2	2	1	1	2
174	45.00	6	2500	2	33	4	2	1	1	2
175	45.00	7	2500	2	35	4	2	1	1	3
176	52.00	3	9000	2	38	4	2	2	3	3
177	30.00	3	3500	2	37	3	2	2	2	3
178	45.00	4	12000	2	30	4	2	2	4	2
179	45.00	4	8000	2	41	4	2	2	3	3
180	37.50	4	6000	2	45	3	2	2	3	4
181	45.00	4	4500	2	30	4	2	2	2	2
182	55.00	4	17000	2	34	4	2	2	5	2
183	25.00	4	4500	2	29	2	2	2	2	2
184	80.00	5	13000	2	36	6	2	2	4	3
185	100.00	5	12500	2	30	7	2	2	4	2
186	60.00	5	8700	2	37	5	2	2	3	3
187	37.50	5	3500	2	36	3	2	2	2	3
188	65.00	5	21000	2	40	5	2	2	5	3
189	35.00	5	4500	2	39	3	2	2	2	3
190	37.50	5	7500	2	28	3	2	2	3	2
191	27.00	6	13000	2	38	2	2	2	4	3
192	58.00	6	11000	2	39	4	2	2	4	3
193	42.00	6	7000	2	33	3	2	2	3	2
194	37.50	6	4500	2	40	3	2	2	2	3
195	40.00	6	6000	2	48	3	2	2	3	4
196	45.00	6	6000	2	32	4	2	2	3	2
197	73.00	7	12000	2	30	5	2	2	4	2
198	39.00	7	12500	2	42	3	2	2	4	3
199	53.50	7	8500	2	36	4	2	2	3	3
200	57.00	8	20000	2	39	4	2	2	5	3
201	42.00	8	22000	2	39	3	2	2	5	3
202	38.00	8	9000	2	38	3	2	2	3	3
203	45.00	8	6000	2	41	4	2	2	3	3
204	52.50	9	6500	2	40	4	2	2	3	3
205	67.50	9	9500	2	45	5	2	2	3	4

A	B	C	D	E	F	G	H	I	J	K
206	75.00	9	500	2	35	6	2	2	1	3
207	63.00	1	4000	3	56	5	1	1	2	5
208	65.00	1	10000	3	59	5	1	1	4	5
209	45.00	1	2800	3	22	4	1	1	1	1
210	48.00	1	4500	3	24	4	1	1	2	1
211	57.00	1	5000	3	58	4	1	1	2	5
212	45.00	1	9000	3	36	4	1	1	3	3
213	45.00	1	25000	3	61	4	1	1	6	5
214	30.00	1	10000	3	36	3	1	1	4	3
215	37.50	1	14000	3	58	3	1	1	4	5
216	30.00	1	12000	3	29	3	1	1	4	2
217	30.00	1	12000	3	47	3	1	1	4	4
218	30.00	1	24000	3	32	3	1	1	5	2
219	60.00	1	3500	3	22	5	1	1	2	1
220	18.00	1	3500	3	29	2	1	1	2	2
221	20.00	1	4500	3	74	2	1	1	2	6
222	22.50	1	2500	3	20	2	1	1	1	1
223	30.00	1	6800	3	53	3	1	1	3	4
224	72.00	2	7000	3	30	5	1	1	3	2
225	67.50	2	10000	3	24	5	1	1	4	1
226	65.00	2	12000	3	54	5	1	1	4	4
227	60.00	2	17000	3	37	5	1	1	5	3
228	60.00	2	26000	3	66	5	1	1	6	6
229	45.00	2	18000	3	44	4	1	1	5	3
230	54.00	2	22000	3	42	4	1	1	5	3
231	48.00	2	18000	3	63	4	1	1	5	5
232	46.50	2	26000	3	50	4	1	1	6	4
233	42.00	2	13000	3	38	3	1	1	4	3
234	35.00	2	14000	3	59	3	1	1	4	5
235	37.50	2	10000	3	61	3	1	1	4	5
236	30.00	2	11500	3	44	3	1	1	4	3
237	45.00	2	30000	3	40	4	1	1	6	3
238	30.00	2	9000	3	29	3	1	1	3	2
239	38.00	2	4500	3	23	3	1	1	2	1
240	40.00	2	18000	3	57	3	1	1	5	5
241	20.00	2	6000	3	21	2	1	1	3	1
242	22.50	2	7000	3	27	2	1	1	3	2
243	25.00	2	18000	3	41	2	1	1	5	3
244	20.00	2	9000	3	34	2	1	1	3	2
245	30.00	2	24000	3	60	3	1	1	5	5
246	37.50	2	11000	3	23	3	1	1	4	1
247	60.00	2	9000	3	59	5	1	1	3	5
248	22.50	2	27000	3	46	2	1	1	6	4
249	15.00	2	3500	3	22	2	1	1	2	1
250	30.00	2	4500	3	63	3	1	1	2	5
251	37.50	2	7000	3	25	3	1	1	3	2
252	40.00	2	3500	3	68	3	1	1	2	6
253	45.00	2	15000	3	54	4	1	1	5	4
254	37.50	2	26000	3	34	3	1	1	6	2
255	45.00	2	17000	3	26	4	1	1	5	2
256	30.00	3	10000	3	50	3	1	1	4	4
257	45.00	3	14000	3	49	4	1	1	4	4
258	37.50	3	4500	3	62	3	1	1	2	5
259	18.00	3	7000	3	58	2	1	1	3	5

A	B	C	D	E	F	G	H	I	J	K
260	60.00	3	8000	3	31	5	1	1	3	2
261	45.00	3	8000	3	43	4	1	1	3	3
262	37.50	3	4500	3	27	3	1	1	2	2
263	37.00	3	6000	3	27	3	1	1	3	2
264	40.00	4	28000	3	39	3	1	1	6	3
265	45.00	4	19000	3	67	4	1	1	5	6
266	60.00	4	11000	3	59	5	1	1	4	5
267	30.00	4	6500	3	33	3	1	1	3	2
268	45.00	4	10000	3	68	4	1	1	4	6
269	50.00	4	6000	3	76	4	1	1	3	7
270	60.00	3	16000	3	40	5	1	2	5	3
271	20.00	3	2600	3	38	2	1	2	1	3
272	55.00	3	10000	3	45	4	1	2	4	4
273	50.00	3	10000	3	50	4	1	2	4	4
274	33.00	3	9000	3	40	3	1	2	3	3
275	33.00	3	11000	3	48	3	1	2	4	4
276	45.00	3	19000	3	49	4	1	2	5	4
277	18.00	3	6000	3	32	2	1	2	3	2
278	37.50	3	15000	3	50	3	1	2	5	4
279	45.00	3	8000	3	43	4	1	2	3	3
280	70.00	3	8800	3	58	5	1	2	3	5
281	67.50	4	10000	3	47	5	1	2	4	4
282	69.00	4	15000	3	34	5	1	2	5	2
283	120.00	4	13500	3	48	7	1	2	4	4
284	45.00	4	12000	3	33	4	1	2	4	2
285	42.00	4	10000	3	40	3	1	2	4	3
286	30.00	4	14000	3	49	3	1	2	4	4
287	39.00	4	10000	3	46	3	1	2	4	4
288	36.00	4	12000	3	57	3	1	2	4	5
289	39.00	4	12000	3	43	3	1	2	4	3
290	37.50	4	6000	3	28	3	1	2	3	2
291	45.00	4	18000	3	49	4	1	2	5	4
292	37.50	4	6000	3	31	3	1	2	3	2
293	45.00	4	6000	3	54	4	1	2	3	4
294	25.00	4	6000	3	29	2	1	2	3	2
295	50.00	4	8000	3	34	4	1	2	3	2
296	40.00	4	17000	3	38	3	1	2	5	3
297	54.00	4	20000	3	45	4	1	2	5	4
298	45.00	4	6000	3	39	4	1	2	3	3
299	60.00	4	8000	3	56	5	1	2	3	5
300	45.00	4	8000	3	49	4	1	2	3	4
301	45.00	4	15000	3	41	4	1	2	5	3
302	35.00	4	8000	3	33	3	1	2	3	2
303	80.00	5	11000	3	49	6	1	2	4	4
304	55.00	5	13000	3	48	4	1	2	4	4
305	37.50	5	10000	3	48	3	1	2	4	4
306	55.00	5	20000	3	42	4	1	2	5	3
307	35.00	5	2500	3	49	3	1	2	1	4
308	52.50	5	15500	3	34	4	1	2	5	2
309	80.00	6	14000	3	49	6	1	2	4	4
310	86.00	6	10000	3	56	6	1	2	4	5
311	110.00	6	13000	3	52	7	1	2	4	4
312	95.00	7	19000	3	39	7	1	2	5	3
313	45.00	7	6000	3	49	4	1	2	3	4

A	B	C	D	E	F	G	H	I	J	K
314	60.00	8	21000	3	44	5	1	2	5	3
315	67.50	9	15000	3	47	5	1	2	5	4
316	18.00	3	2500	3	27	2	2	1	1	2
317	47.00	3	11000	3	32	4	2	1	4	2
318	50.00	3	14000	3	29	4	2	1	4	2
319	45.00	3	16000	3	28	4	2	1	5	2
320	36.00	3	12000	3	28	3	2	1	4	2
321	30.00	3	6000	3	22	3	2	1	3	1
322	67.50	3	12000	3	24	5	2	1	4	1
323	22.50	3	6000	3	23	2	2	1	3	1
324	26.00	3	2500	3	32	2	2	1	1	2
325	27.00	3	3500	3	25	2	2	1	2	2
326	45.00	3	6000	3	35	4	2	1	3	3
327	30.00	3	10000	3	19	3	2	1	4	1
328	35.00	3	8000	3	30	3	2	1	3	2
329	52.50	3	8000	3	27	4	2	1	3	2
330	55.00	3	6000	3	20	4	2	1	3	1
331	35.00	3	20000	3	32	3	2	1	5	2
332	51.00	4	4000	3	24	4	2	1	2	1
333	37.50	4	12000	3	32	3	2	1	4	2
334	30.00	4	13000	3	30	3	2	1	4	2
335	75.00	4	8000	3	26	6	2	1	3	2
336	40.00	4	6000	3	22	3	2	1	3	1
337	37.50	4	4500	3	27	3	2	1	2	2
338	21.00	4	7000	3	30	2	2	1	3	2
339	30.00	4	6000	3	29	3	2	1	3	2
340	22.50	4	9500	3	28	2	2	1	3	2
341	67.50	4	14000	3	25	5	2	1	4	2
342	60.00	4	8000	3	33	5	2	1	3	2
343	87.00	5	14000	3	33	6	2	1	4	2
344	45.00	5	14000	3	29	4	2	1	4	2
345	50.00	5	9000	3	31	4	2	1	3	2
346	48.00	6	6000	3	38	4	2	1	3	3
347	60.00	7	4500	3	29	5	2	1	2	2
348	90.00	4	14000	3	34	7	2	2	4	2
349	45.00	4	14000	3	35	4	2	2	4	3
350	54.00	4	12500	3	30	4	2	2	4	2
351	37.50	4	17500	3	30	3	2	2	5	2
352	33.00	4	4500	3	29	3	2	2	2	2
353	72.00	5	14000	3	36	5	2	2	4	3
354	51.00	5	11000	3	35	4	2	2	4	3
355	36.00	5	14500	3	36	3	2	2	4	3
356	65.00	5	8000	3	32	5	2	2	3	2
357	60.00	5	16000	3	34	5	2	2	5	2
358	45.00	5	21000	3	40	4	2	2	5	3
359	45.00	5	7500	3	29	4	2	2	3	2
360	37.50	5	6000	3	31	3	2	2	3	2
361	67.50	5	6000	3	36	5	2	2	3	3
362	39.00	5	8000	3	40	3	2	2	3	3
363	45.00	5	3500	3	37	4	2	2	2	3
364	37.50	5	4500	3	46	3	2	2	2	4
365	24.00	6	8500	3	38	2	2	2	3	3
366	42.00	6	13000	3	39	3	2	2	4	3
367	60.00	6	6000	3	35	5	2	2	3	3

A	B	C	D	E	F	G	H	I	J	K
368	40.00	6	6000	3	41	3	2	2	3	3
369	37.50	6	6000	3	33	3	2	2	3	2
370	60.00	6	6000	3	38	5	2	2	3	3
371	73.50	7	12000	3	38	5	2	2	4	3
372	105.00	7	20000	3	38	7	2	2	5	3
373	52.50	7	6000	3	36	4	2	2	3	3
374	35.00	7	3500	3	37	3	2	2	2	3
375	37.50	7	6000	3	31	3	2	2	3	2
376	50.00	7	7000	3	47	4	2	2	3	4
377	49.00	7	8000	3	44	4	2	2	3	3
378	60.00	8	6000	3	41	5	2	2	3	3
379	67.50	8	6000	3	47	5	2	2	3	4
380	45.00	8	4500	3	51	4	2	2	2	4
381	75.00	8	18000	3	36	6	2	2	5	3
382	52.50	8	9000	3	46	4	2	2	3	4
383	54.00	9	20000	3	45	4	2	2	5	4
384	50.00	9	2500	3	50	4	2	2	1	4
385	75.00	9	18000	3	49	6	2	2	5	4
386	52.50	9	8000	3	44	4	2	2	3	3
387	35.00	1	4000	4	71	3	1	1	2	6
388	30.00	1	5000	4	28	3	1	1	2	2
389	36.00	1	5000	4	36	3	1	1	2	3
390	18.00	2	13000	4	56	2	1	1	4	5
391	52.00	2	5000	4	35	4	1	1	2	3
392	53.00	2	11000	4	40	4	1	1	4	3
393	45.00	2	10000	4	45	4	1	1	4	4
394	25.00	2	15000	4	24	2	1	1	5	1
395	27.00	2	18000	4	34	2	1	1	5	2
396	15.00	2	4500	4	26	2	1	1	2	2
397	75.00	2	22000	4	41	6	1	1	5	3
398	25.00	2	2500	4	69	2	1	1	1	6
399	22.00	2	17500	4	58	2	1	1	5	5
400	58.00	3	14000	4	40	4	1	1	4	3
401	40.00	3	30000	4	47	3	1	1	6	4
402	37.00	3	8000	4	45	3	1	1	3	4
403	27.00	3	20000	4	60	2	1	1	5	5
404	30.00	3	3500	4	59	3	1	1	2	5
405	50.00	3	4500	4	39	4	1	1	2	3
406	30.00	3	24000	4	62	3	1	1	5	5
407	75.00	3	6000	4	77	6	1	1	3	7
408	45.00	4	30000	4	52	4	1	1	6	4
409	55.00	3	28000	4	48	4	1	2	6	4
410	40.00	3	8000	4	23	3	1	2	3	1
411	60.00	3	22000	4	42	5	1	2	5	3
412	45.00	3	35000	4	44	4	1	2	6	3
413	60.00	4	14500	4	56	5	1	2	4	5
414	26.70	4	18000	4	54	2	1	2	5	4
415	51.00	4	11000	4	51	4	1	2	4	4
416	45.00	4	14500	4	56	4	1	2	4	5
417	57.00	4	10000	4	34	4	1	2	4	2
418	65.00	4	19000	4	47	5	1	2	5	4
419	115.00	4	3500	4	31	7	1	2	2	2
420	45.00	4	4500	4	55	4	1	2	2	5
421	60.00	4	9000	4	49	5	1	2	3	4

A	B	C	D	E	F	G	H	I	J	K
422	55.00	4	20000	4	41	4	1	2	5	3
423	75.00	4	22000	4	51	6	1	2	5	4
424	75.00	4	18000	4	33	6	1	2	5	2
425	48.00	4	17000	4	29	4	1	2	5	2
426	45.00	5	6000	4	31	4	1	2	3	2
427	52.50	5	8000	4	43	4	1	2	3	3
428	35.00	5	500	4	28	3	1	2	1	2
429	45.00	5	28000	4	36	4	1	2	6	3
430	52.50	5	4500	4	55	4	1	2	2	5
431	45.00	5	8000	4	48	4	1	2	3	4
432	135.00	6	22000	4	44	7	1	2	5	3
433	70.00	6	24000	4	44	5	1	2	5	3
434	60.00	6	24000	4	39	5	1	2	5	3
435	60.00	3	13000	4	33	5	2	1	4	2
436	51.00	3	10000	4	28	4	2	1	4	2
437	30.00	3	4000	4	32	3	2	1	2	2
438	53.00	3	8000	4	27	4	2	1	3	2
439	30.00	3	6000	4	23	3	2	1	3	1
440	70.00	4	14000	4	29	5	2	1	4	2
441	30.00	4	8000	4	28	3	2	1	3	2
442	37.50	4	4500	4	30	3	2	1	2	2
443	30.00	5	6000	4	32	3	2	1	3	2
444	48.00	4	13500	4	40	4	2	2	4	3
445	35.00	4	5500	4	29	3	2	2	2	2
446	55.00	4	20000	4	36	4	2	2	5	3
447	40.00	4	25000	4	41	3	2	2	6	3
448	27.00	5	12000	4	43	2	2	2	4	3
449	100.00	5	14000	4	36	7	2	2	4	3
450	57.00	5	9500	4	36	4	2	2	3	3
451	75.00	6	13000	4	40	6	2	2	4	3
452	45.00	6	8000	4	39	4	2	2	3	3
453	85.00	7	18000	4	38	6	2	2	5	3
454	100.00	7	20000	4	48	7	2	2	5	4
455	45.00	7	36000	4	43	4	2	2	6	3
456	50.00	7	4500	4	32	4	2	2	2	2
457	48.00	1	14000	5	24	4	1	1	4	1
458	52.50	1	12500	5	60	4	1	1	4	5
459	34.50	1	14000	5	28	3	1	1	4	2
460	9.00	1	2500	5	25	1	1	1	1	2
461	15.00	1	6000	5	28	2	1	1	3	2
462	13.00	2	13000	5	25	1	1	1	4	2
463	54.00	2	14500	5	47	4	1	1	4	4
464	25.00	2	8000	5	78	2	1	1	3	7
465	30.00	2	28000	5	64	3	1	1	6	5
466	35.00	2	3500	5	76	3	1	1	2	7
467	12.00	2	2500	5	23	1	1	1	1	1
468	39.00	3	13000	5	39	3	1	1	4	3
469	45.00	3	42000	5	54	4	1	1	6	4
470	37.50	3	17000	5	52	3	1	2	5	4
471	40.00	3	24000	5	40	3	1	2	5	3
472	52.50	3	17000	5	40	4	1	2	5	3
473	60.00	3	32000	5	48	5	1	2	6	4
474	37.50	4	17000	5	56	3	1	2	5	5
475	55.00	4	24000	5	44	4	1	2	5	3

A	B	C	D	E	F	G	H	I	J	K
476	56.00	4	16000	5	36	4	1	2	5	3
477	75.00	5	23000	5	48	6	1	2	5	4
478	45.00	5	6000	5	37	4	1	2	3	3
479	100.00	5	39000	5	44	7	1	2	6	3
480	72.00	2	14000	5	30	5	2	1	4	2
481	33.00	3	20000	5	36	3	2	1	5	3
482	30.00	3	22000	5	33	3	2	1	5	2
483	37.50	3	8000	5	28	3	2	1	3	2
484	30.00	3	9000	5	32	3	2	1	3	2
485	22.00	3	7000	5	30	2	2	1	3	2
486	60.00	4	5000	5	28	5	2	1	2	2
487	20.00	4	9000	5	30	2	2	1	3	2
488	25.50	4	4500	5	26	2	2	1	2	2
489	33.00	4	6000	5	32	3	2	1	3	2
490	51.00	4	9000	5	34	4	2	1	3	2
491	45.00	7	26000	5	39	4	2	1	6	3
492	75.00	4	14500	5	34	6	2	2	4	2
493	18.00	4	14000	5	36	2	2	2	4	3
494	40.00	4	15500	5	40	3	2	2	5	3
495	75.00	5	28000	5	42	6	2	2	6	3
496	24.00	5	24000	5	33	2	2	2	5	2
497	115.00	6	24000	5	36	7	2	2	5	3
498	75.00	7	28000	5	37	6	2	2	6	3
499	105.00	7	20000	5	39	7	2	2	5	3
500	75.00	8	33000	5	42	6	2	2	6	3

CASE QUESTIONS

1. What alternative sampling procedures are available to estimate weekly food expenditures?
2. Explain how each would be carried out.
3. Discuss the pros and cons of each.

CASE 3-2: Ellen Parsons, School Board Candidate*

Ellen Parsons is running for the school board in Davidson, Oregon. Davidson is a small town of about 8000 people, mostly middle-class adults aged 25–65. Davidson Community Schools are attended only by children who live in Davidson or in Davidson Township (population 2000). One week prior to the November 4, 1986 election, Ellen has hired you to determine her chances of defeating the other two candidates vying for the position.

Prepare a sampling plan. Be sure to designate a population definition, a sampling frame, a sampling procedure, and a method for determining the accuracy of the results.

* Coauthored by Sheryl Petras.

CASE 3-3: President's Council on Physical Fitness*

With excess weight becoming an ever-increasing problem among young adults, the President's Council on Physical Fitness is planning to create a brochure promoting the importance of physical fitness for high school students. To help determine the most effective way to "sell" fitness, the council chairperson wants to discover what factors motivate active students to engage in physical activity and what benefits they perceive resulting from it. You have been assigned by the council chairperson to design a sample for this study.

Prepare a sampling plan. Be sure to designate a population definition, a sampling frame, a sampling procedure, and a method for determining the accuracy of the results.

CASE 3-4: Ice Cream Castle†

Lynne Adams is the manager of Ice Cream Castle, an ice cream parlor located in Castle City, Arizona. She plans to place an advertisement in Sunday's *Castle City Chronicle*, the local newspaper, announcing "Silver Anniversary Savings Days" on the upcoming Monday and Tuesday. You have been retained to develop a sampling plan for the customers coming into the store on those two days. At that time a questionnaire will be administered to this sample to determine what influence the Sunday advertisement had on their coming to the store.

Prepare a sampling plan. Be sure to designate a population definition, a sampling frame, a sampling procedure, and a method for determining the accuracy of the results.

CASE 3-5: Polling Pole‡

United Press International and the Allen, Shapiro, and Keller marketing research firm (UPI ASK) have begun to market the Polling Pole, a computer-operated interviewing device, as an alternative to the typical interview methods. This 6-foot tall cylinder contains a computer, a color monitor, a keypad, a coupon dispenser, an audio speaker, and a videocassette recorder. The Polling Pole is generally placed in a high-traffic area, such as a mall, and uses a variety of techniques to draw people to it. At the Polling Pole, questions are displayed on the monitor and consumers are asked to enter their responses on the keypad.

According to Arthur Shapiro, president of UPI ASK, this technique is a less expensive way to test such things as new ad campaigns, new product concepts, and promotional incentives. Other benefits cited by Shapiro include: elimination of interviewer bias, confidentiality of questionnaires, quick tabulation of data, and ease in changing the program content. Furthermore, it costs 40 to 50 percent less than other forms of interviewing.

* Coauthored by Sheryl Petras.
† Coauthored by Sheryl Petras.
‡ Coauthored by Sheryl Petras.

"Tests have shown that it has high consumer acceptability and gives more candid responses and higher quality research," Shapiro said. Nonrandom sampling is a problem with the Polling Pole, but UPI ASK claims reliable samples can still be drawn using special techniques it has developed.*

John Trevda, a marketing manager at Gadgets, Inc., has just been given the results of a Polling Pole questionnaire. The survey measured consumer responses to a proposed new television advertisement for one of Gadget's products, a small household appliance. The Polling Pole kiosks had been set up in hotel lobbies, supermarkets, and office buildings throughout the U.S. The finished ad was displayed in color and with sound. Over 100,000 consumers took part in the computer interview, and John was ecstatic with the large sample size. Usually ad copy testing had a significantly smaller sample size—rarely more than 300—but was more academic in nature. Because of the sample size and the positive results that were generated, John has decided to use the ad in a national campaign.

CASE QUESTIONS

1 What is the population definition in this study? Does it differ from the study population?
2 What is the sampling frame used?
3 What sampling procedure was used?
4 Because of its large sample size, is the Polling Pole survey superior to more academic studies? How is sample size determined in these studies?
5 What nonsampling errors might be present in this study?

CASE 3-6: STP Corporation[†]

In February 1978, the STP Corporation signed a consent decree under which it agreed to discontinue certain advertising claims about its motor oil additive and to make a $700,000 settlement, including $200,000 to place a "public notice" advertisement in 14 periodicals.

The text of this advertisement began with the heading "FTC Notice" and stated that "as a result of an investigation by the Federal Trade Commission into certain allegedly inaccurate past advertisements for STP's oil additive, STP Corporation has agreed to a $700,000 settlement." This was then followed by a statement by STP indicating that STP had stopped making the claim when it was learned that their test data did not properly support the claim and that the agreement with the Federal Trade Commission did not constitute an admission by STP that the law had been violated.

The public notice advertisement first appeared in the financial sections of *The New York Times* and *The Wall Street Journal* on February 10, 1978. Over the next three weeks the advertisement appeared in six other periodicals. During the period the advertisement appeared, it was mentioned in various news media, including network television

* *Marketing News*, vol. 19, no. 1, p. 44, Jan. 4, 1985.
† Coauthored by Kenneth Bernhardt and Michael Mazis.

and major newspapers and magazines. An evaluation of the impact of these advertisements was undertaken by telephone interviews. One major issue in this evaluation was the selection of a sample for the study.

Using the Louis Harris national sample selection procedure, the sample was selected based upon the national population of the United States, excluding Alaska and Hawaii and those in prisons, hospitals, or religious and educational institutions. Figures are updated annually by intercensal estimates provided by the Bureau of Census, with sample locations selected biannually to reflect demographic changes.

Both geographic region and metropolitan (and nonmetropolitan) status were used as stratification variables for the national samples. Multistage cluster sampling was used to select the sampling units from each stratum. First states, then counties, and then minor civil divisions or towns or cities were selected with probability proportionate to census estimates of their respective household populations.

Within the geographic clusters so generated, respondents were then selected using a modified form of random-digit dialing. Phone numbers were drawn from randomly selected residential phone numbers that had previously been stratified by geographic location, and the final two digits were replaced with random digits to form a seven-digit phone number.

CASE QUESTIONS

1 What sampling units were defined by this procedure? What were the sampling frames?
2 Why was stratification used?
3 What purpose was there in selecting cities or towns with probability proportionate to census estimates of their respective household populations? How could this be accomplished?
4 What alternative sampling procedures could be used here?

MEASUREMENT AND CAUSALITY

THE MEASUREMENT PROCESS

The process of measurement is a commonplace occurrence for college students. Entrance examinations are measuring devices designed to assess the student's potential for college-level work. Once in college, the student is confronted with an array of examinations to measure achievement in courses such as marketing research. Measurement is involved when we count the number of students in a class, classify them as male or female, or judge which students are most attractive in appearance or personality. These are only a few examples of the use of measurement in our daily activities. Typically, the measurement process is taken for granted. Rarely do we stop to think about the differences in the type of measurements taken and the accuracy of the conclusions drawn. This chapter is designed to stimulate your thinking in this regard.

MEASUREMENT IN MARKETING

The process of measurement is a fundamental aspect of marketing research. It is often stated that the best way to really understand a thing is to try to measure it. For this reason, if for no other, the topic of measurement is of growing concern to those in the field of marketing.

Decision makers are interested in measuring many aspects of the marketing system; for example, they may want to measure the market potential for a new product; group buyers by demographic or psychographic characteristics; measure buyers' attitudes, perceptions, or preferences toward a new brand; or determine the effectiveness of a new advertising campaign. Consequently, the measurement of marketing phenomena is essential to the process of providing meaningful information for decision making.

Developing effective measures of marketing phenomena is not an easy task. In Chapter 1, measurement error was cited as being a substantial share of the total error in marketing research information. For many research projects, measurement error can be substantially greater than sampling error. Having a clear understanding of the measurement problem and how to control this error is an important aspect of designing an effective marketing research project.

The marketing manager rarely becomes directly involved in the actual measurement process. The task of selecting and designing measurement techniques is the responsibility of the research specialist. However, the decision maker must often approve the measurement techniques that are recommended and needs to be confident that these techniques are effective in controlling measurement error.

In order to control measurement error effectively, the marketing manager should be concerned with three issues. First, the specification of information needs should recognize the degree of difficulty in obtaining accurate measures. Second, the alternative measurement procedures for obtaining the information should be recognized. Third, the cost of measurement versus the accuracy of measurement should be evaluated. This chapter and many of the remaining chapters deal with these three issues.

The Measurement Process

In marketing research, the measurement process involves using numbers to represent the marketing phenomena under investigation. Stated formally, the *empirical system* includes marketing phenomena, such as buyer reactions to products or advertisements, while the *abstract system* includes the numbers used to represent the marketing phenomena. Figure 10-1 depicts the measurement process as one of developing a correspondence between the empirical system and the abstract system. The former is composed of the physical sciences (the study of physical things) and the social sciences (the study of people). Marketing is a member of the social sciences in that it involves "human activity directed at satisfying needs and wants through exchange processes."[1]

---

[1] Philip Kotler, *Marketing Management,* 3d ed. (Englewood Cliffs, N.J.: Prentice-Hall, 1977), p. 5.

FIGURE 10-1 The measurement process.

Definition of Measurement

The previous discussion suggests that measurement is concerned with developing a correspondence between the empirical system (e.g., preference) and the abstract system (e.g., numbers). Therefore, measurement may be defined as *the assignment of numbers to characteristics of objects or events according to rules.* Effective measurement is possible when the relationships existing among the objects or events in the empirical system directly correspond to the rules of the number system. If this correspondence is misrepresented, measurement error has occurred. More will be said about this shortly.

It is important to note that the definition of measurement suggests that it is the characteristics of objects or events that are measured and not the objects or events themselves. We do not measure a buyer or a product, but rather we measure some characteristic of a buyer or a product. For example, we can measure a buyer's preference, usage rate, income, or attitude. We can measure a product's speed, sweetness, size, or color.

The term "number" in the definition of measurement imposes certain restrictions on the type of numerical manipulations admissible. Numbers are being used as symbols to model the characteristics of interest in the empirical system. The nature of the relationships existing in the empirical system determines the type of numerical manipulations which are valid in the abstract system. There is a great temptation to use all the characteristics of the number system in our data analysis and to disregard the restrictions imposed by the empirical phenomena under study. We now turn to a discussion of the characteristics of the number system, which should provide a better understanding of this issue.

Number System Characteristics

Very early in our educational career we learned four characteristics of the number system 0, 1, 2, 3, 4, 5, 6, 7, 8, and 9. First, each number in the series is unique, and there are ten numbers. Second, the ordering of the numbers is given by convention, e.g., $2 > 1, 1 > 0$. Third, we can define equal differences, e.g., $3 - 2 = 7 - 6, 7 - 5 = 3 - 1$. Fourth, we can define equal ratios, e.g., $10 \div 5 = 6 \div 3$.

The manipulation of numbers using mathematics or statistics involves one or more of these four characteristics of the number system. There is a great temptation to use more of these characteristics in our data analysis than may actually exist in the empirical system being modeled. The problem is one of focusing clearly on determining how many of these four characteristics are present in the marketing phenomena under investigation, and then restricting our data analysis to using only appropriate characteristics in our manipulation of the numbers. Often, this restriction hampers the sophistication of data analysis that can properly be performed.

Types of Scales

Scales have been classified in terms of the four characteristics of the number system. These scales of measurement are *nominal, ordinal, interval,* and *ratio.* The characteristics

TABLE 10-1 CHARACTERISTICS OF MEASUREMENT SCALES

Scale	Number system	Marketing phenomena	Permissible statistics[*]
Nominal	Unique definition of numerals (0, 1, 2, . . ., 9)	Brands Male-female Store types Sale territories	Percentages Mode Binomial test Chi-square test
Ordinal	Order of numerals (0 < 1 < 2 ⋯ < 9)	Attitudes Preference Occupation Social class	Percentiles Median Rank-order correlation
Interval	Equality of differences (2 − 1 = 7 − 6)	Attitudes Opinions Index numbers	Range Mean Standard deviation Product-moment correlation
Ratio	Equality of ratios ($\frac{2}{4} = \frac{4}{8}$)	Age Costs Number of customers Sales (units/dollars)	Geometric mean Harmonic mean Coefficient of variation

[*]All statistics appropriate for nominal measurement are appropriate for higher scale measurement. The same is true for ordinal- and interval-scale measurement.
Source: Adapted from S. S. Stevens, "On the Theory of Scales of Measurement," *Science,* vol. 103, pp. 677–680, June 7, 1946.

of these scales are summarized in Table 10-1, and the following paragraphs discuss each of these scales and their characteristics in detail.

Nominal Scale   A nominal scale is one where numbers serve only as labels to identify or categorize objects or events. A familiar example is the use of numbers to identify football players. Assume that the quarterback for the blue team is 12, and the quarterback for the green team is 9. Numbers used in this manner serve only as a label to identify the players. The numbers assume equality with respect to the characteristics of the players. For example, we cannot infer that the quarterback of the blue team is superior in ability to the quarterback of the green team due to the higher number of 12. Therefore, the number 12 does not imply a superior characteristic compared to the number 9—it only serves as a unique label for identification of the player.

Nominal scales are used for the lowest form of measurement, namely classification and identification. Few restrictions are imposed in the assignment of numerals to the objects or events. The rule is simply: Do not assign the same number to different objects or events, or different numbers to the same object or event. For example, we could change the number of our blue-team quarterback from 12 to 56 or any other number desired. The only restriction is that within the blue team each player must have a unique number for purposes of identification. Consequently, many possible numbers can be used to identify the players, and we cannot argue that one number is better for our quarterback than another number. They all serve the purpose of identification equally.

TABLE 10-2   REASONS FOR PURCHASE BY SEX

Reason for purchase	Male		Female		Total	
	n	Percent	*n*	Percent	*n*	Percent
Weight	10	20	28	56	38	38
Speed	31	62	10	20	41	41
Miscellaneous	9	18	12	24	21	21
	50	100	50	100	100	100

A substantial proportion of marketing phenomena require nominal-scale measurement. Such nominal-level identification and classification are needed to measure brands, store types, sales territories, geographic locations, heavy versus light users, working versus nonworking women, and brand awareness versus nonawareness. It is a rare marketing research study that does not involve marketing data of this nature.

An illustration of the use of nominal measurement involves a bicycle manufacturer who wants to determine whether there are differences in the reasons why males and females purchase 10-speed bicycles. Former purchasers of the bicycle (50 males and 50 females) were randomly selected and interviewed over the telephone. Table 10-2 presents the results of the survey. It would appear that females are more concerned with the weight of the bicycle, while males are more concerned with speed.

The types of statistical analysis appropriate for nominally scaled data include the mode, percentages, the binomial test, and the chi-square test (see Table 10–1). The mode is the only measure of central tendency which can be used. A mean or median cannot be calculated since they involve higher-level properties of the number system than are present in nominally scaled data. (See Chapter 17 for a detailed discussion of these data analysis issues.)

Ordinal Scale   An ordinal scale defines the ordered relationship among objects or events. It involves the number system characteristic of the order of numerals. Ordinal scales measure whether an object or event has more or less of a characteristic than some other object or event. However, this scale does not provide information on how much more or less of the characteristic various objects or events possess.

Let's illustrate ordinal measurement by assuming that our previous bicycle manufacturer is interested in determining the preference ordering of males among the firm's 10-speed bicycle (A) and two leading competitors (B and C) with regard to the characteristic of speed. A survey was conducted of 200 male potential buyers. The results are reported in Table 10-3.

An ordinal scale can be developed by assigning numerals to the first-, second-, and third-order preference judgments. This involves the assignment of numerals such that the resulting numerical series properly maintains the ordered relationship of the preference judgments. But which set of numbers should be assigned? Obviously, a large number of sets of numbers might be assigned, the only restriction being that the numbers be assigned in such a manner that their order corresponds directly with the ordinal relationships present in the preference judgments. For example, the number 1 can be

TABLE 10-3   MALE PREFERENCE ORDERING OF BICYCLES A, B, AND C WITH
REGARD TO SPEED (n = 200)

Preference ordering	Proportion of preferences			
	A	B	C	Total
First	.15	.35	.50	1.00
Second	.50	.25	.25	1.00
Third	.35	.40	.25	1.00
Total	1.00	1.00	1.00	

used to represent the first-order preferences, number 2 for the second-order preferences, and number 3 for the third-order preferences. Alternatively, another set of permissible numerals would be to assign the number 1 to the first-order preferences, the
number 3 to the second-order preferences, and the number 30 to the third-order preferences. Other numerical sets include 5, 6, and 7; 1, 20, and 100; and so forth. All
these numerical sets form acceptable ordinal scales, and we cannot argue that one set is
better than the others.

A more restrictive rule for the assignment of numerals exists with ordinal measurement than with nominal measurement. An important characteristic of measurement is
its power to enable us to establish rules which define the domain of numerical sets that
can properly be assigned to the empirical system under investigation.

Ordinal measurement involves the rule that any series of numbers can be assigned
that preserves the ordered relationships present in the empirical system. This restriction
that the numbers be arranged in serial order substantially eliminates many numerical
series from consideration. It is equally true, however, that a great deal of freedom remains regarding which numerical set can be used. This domain of freedom can be
formally defined as any order-preserving (i.e., monotonic) transformation of the numerical
series chosen. Consequently, with an ordinal scale, the only restriction in the assignment of a new series of numbers is that an increasing monotonic transformation be
used. Such transformations are illustrated in Figure 10-2(a).

The overall ranking of the three bicycles based on the mode is presented in Table
10-4. The results are presented for both numerical sets 1 and 2. It is important to note
that the preference ordering of the three bicycles is identical for both numerical sets
1 and 2. Here, the overall preference ordering is bicycle C first, A second, and B third.
We can generalize these findings to all statistics appropriate for the analysis of ordinal
data. Consequently, regardless of which order-preserving numerical set is selected for
data analysis, the research findings will not change or be dependent upon the numerical set selected. More formally, we can state that for any increasing monotonic scale
transformation, the conclusions drawn from the data analysis using statistics appropriate
for ordinal data *will not change as a result of the assignment of alternative numerical sets*.
Some of the statistics appropriate for ordinal data are presented in Table 10-1.

Note that the mean is not an appropriate statistic for ordinal data. What happens
if we do calculate the mean? The means for numerical sets 1 and 2 have been calculated
to answer this question (see Table 10-4). The result is that the preference ordering of

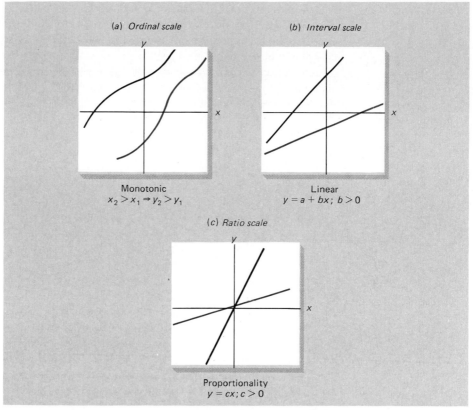

FIGURE 10-2 Permissible transformation by scale type. [*Adapted from Paul E. Green and Donald S. Tull, Research for Marketing Decisions, 3d ed. (Englewood Cliffs, N.J.: Prentice-Hall, 1975), p. 60.*]

the three bicycles is different for the two numerical assignments. For numerical set 1, bicycle C is first, B is second, and A is last. However, for numerical set 2, bicycle C is first, A is second, and B is third. Bicycles A and B have reversed positions because of the scale transformation. This result is not surprising when we realize that the calculation of a mean involves the equal-interval characteristic of the number system.

TABLE 10-4   OVERALL RANKING OF BICYCLES A, B, AND C

Descriptive statistic	Ranking		
	1st	2d	3d
Mode (numerical set 1) *	C (1)	A (2)	B (3)
Mode (numerical set 2) †	C (1)	A (3)	B (30)
Mean (numerical set 1)	C (1.75)‡	B (2.05)	A (2.20)
Mean (numerical set 2)	C (8.75)	A (12.15)	B (13.10)

* 1st = 1, 2d = 2, 3d = 3.
† 1st = 1, 2d = 3, 3d = 30.
‡ Mean = (1) (.50) + (2) (.25) + (3) (.25) ÷ 1 = 1.75.

Since the scale transformation maintained only a monotonic or ranked relationship rather than an equal-interval relationship, the results of our statistical analysis are dependent upon the number series selected. This is a clear example of measurement error occurring in our results.

An important segment of marketing data involves ordinal measurement. Most data collected by the process of interrogating people have ordinal properties. For example, the measurement of attitudes, opinions, preference, and perception frequently involves a "greater than" or "less than" judgment. In addition, many characteristics of buyers or purchasing units can involve a ranked characteristic (e.g., occupation, social class, or image). Consequently, a significant share of marketing research data involve ordinal judgments, and the analysis of these data should be subject to the restrictions discussed previously.

Interval Scale An interval scale involves the use of numbers to rank objects or events such that the distances between the numerals correspond to the distances between the objects or events on the characteristic being measured. Interval scales possess all the requirements of an ordinal scale plus the "equality of difference" characteristic of the number system. The remaining freedom in assigning numbers is reduced to the arbitrary selection of a unit of measurement (distance) and an origin (zero point). Suppose that we have measured four ordered objects A, B, C, and D and determined that the distance between adjacent objects is equal on some characteristic. In the assignment of numbers to the objects, we must arbitrarily decide how to represent the size of the distance between adjacent objects and where to assign the zero points. For example, the numbers 0, 1, 2, and 3 represent an arbitrary assignment of zero to one object and of a one-unit difference between adjacent objects. An alternative number assignment could be 7, 9, 11, and 13. Both numerical assignments are acceptable, and we cannot say that one is better than the other.

The most common examples of interval scales are the Fahrenheit and Celsius scales used to measure temperature. The freezing point of water is assigned a different numerical value on each scale, 32 on Fahrenheit and 0 on Celsius. The unit of measurement and the origin or zero point have been arbitrarily determined for these scales. Equal differences in the temperature are measured by equal-volume expansion in the mercury used in the thermometer.

The arbitrary assignment of the zero point on an interval scale places restrictions on the statements that can be made regarding comparisons of intervals. For example, you cannot say that $100°$ Celsius is twice as hot as $50°$ Celsius. A scale transformation to Fahrenheit demonstrates why. The formula is $C = (F - 32)(5/9)$. Using the formula, the previous Celsius temperatures of $100°$ and $50°$ correspond to $212°$ and $122°$ on the Fahrenheit scale. Our previous statement that $100°$ Celsius is twice as warm as $50°$ does not hold with our new numbers for the Fahrenheit scale. We cannot say that $212°$ is twice as warm as $122°$, because the zero point on each scale is arbitrary. Consequently, comparison of absolute magnitude or ratios is not possible.

The above example with a temperature scale applies to all interval scales. Assume that we have scaled brands A, B, and C on an interval scale regarding buyers' degree of liking of the brands. Brand A receives a 6, the highest liking score, B receives a 3, and C receives a 2. We cannot say that brand A is liked twice as much as brand B. Such a statement assumes that the absolute zero point or the absence of liking has been identified and assigned the value zero on the interval scale. What can we say about these interval-scaled data? First, the liking for brand A is more favorable than that for brand B (order of numerals). Second, the degree of liking between A and B is three times greater than the liking between B and C (equality of differences).

The area of freedom in assigning new numerical sets to an interval scale is more restricted than for an ordinal scale. This new numerical assignment involves a positive linear transformation of the form $y = a + bx$, where b is positive. Here, x is the original scale number and y is the new scale number. Figure 10-2(b) gives examples of two such transformations. Statements comparing intervals are valid with an interval scale because, by taking differences, the nature of the functional relationships is the same regardless of the constants chosen for a and b in the scale transformation formula.

A positive linear scale transformation of an interval scale will not change the research findings when appropriate statistical techniques are used. The majority of such techniques can be used to analyze interval data (see Table 10–1); they include the range, arithmetic mean, standard deviation, product-moment correlation, and so forth. Only a few statistical techniques (such as geometric mean, harmonic mean, and coefficient of variation) could lead to misleading results if applied to interval data.

In marketing, it is very common for attitudinal, opinion, and predisposition judgments to be treated as interval data. To be technically correct, these judgments are ordinal. Researchers disagree as to the amount of measurement error present in the results given by ordinal data treated as interval data. The magnitude of this error must be weighed against the data analysis advantages associated with the more sophisticated statistical techniques applicable to analysis of interval data. It is often argued that while the equality-of-interval characteristic may be violated, the degree of violation is typically small, and the results of most statistical techniques are not affected to the point that significant measurement error exists. In the final analysis, it is the responsibility of the researcher to determine (1) how closely the relationships existing in the marketing phenomena under study approximate an interval scale and (2) the appropriateness of treating the data as interval-scaled. Various data collection instruments for developing interval scales will be discussed in Chapter 11.

Ratio Scale   A ratio scale has all the properties of an interval scale plus an absolute zero point. With ratio measurement, only one number may be assigned arbitrarily, namely, the unit of measurement or distance. Once this is determined, the remaining numerical assignments are completely determined.

Absolute or natural zero point refers to the assignment of the number zero to the absence of the characteristic being measured. For example, in our discussion of the Fahrenheit and Celsius temperature scales, it was stated that the zero points were arbitrarily assigned on both scales. Consequently, the zero points on these scales do not correspond to the absence of heat and are not absolute zero points. The ratio measurement of temperature is known as the Kelvin scale. Here, the zero point is absolute and represents the absence of heat ($-273.15°C$).

A ratio scale implies that equal ratios among the scale values correspond to equal ratios among the marketing phenomena being measured. The statement that the sales of product A are twice as large as the sales of product B is perfectly legitimate with ratio scale data. The scale transformations for a ratio scale involve a positive proportionate transformation of the form $y = cx$; $c > 0$. Figure 10-2(c) presents two such transformations.

A great many very important marketing phenomena possess the properties of a ratio scale. These include sales, market share, costs, ages, and number of customers. In each case a natural or absolute zero exists.

The entire range of statistical techniques can be applied to the analysis of ratio-scaled data. However, the significance of the data analysis techniques gained by having a ratio scale is not great compared with those available for the analysis of interval-scaled data.

DIFFICULTY OF MEASUREMENT

When we discuss the measurement process, most people think in terms of their own experiences with weight, height, and distance, "Since I've been jogging two miles each day, my weight has dropped by five pounds." The measurement of weight, length, and height is typically an easy task involving the use of a ratio scale. The natural zero point and equality of differences are obvious. This type of measurement situation is more characteristic of the physical sciences than of the social sciences, of which marketing is a part. Consequently, the measurement task in marketing is typically more difficult and involves lower scales of measurement than those found in the physical sciences. Figure 10-3 illustrates this type of comparison.

Why is measurement so difficult in marketing? A key problem area relates to the domain of the phenomena studied, namely, the behavior of people. The typical measurement device is that of interrogating people regarding their behavior. The use of a questionnaire is a relatively crude technique which is subject to substantial measurement error.

The measurement task in marketing is complicated by the many concepts or constructs which pervade marketing thought. These concepts or constructs must be precisely defined and measured in a marketing research project if useful information is to be provided for management decision making.

The terms "concept" and "construct" have similar meanings and are used interchangeably in this book.[2] A construct is defined as *the mental abstraction formed by the perception of a phenomenon.* In marketing, we refer to constructs such as sales, product positioning, demand, attitudes, and brand loyalty. Constructs serve to simplify and synthesize the complex phenomena present in the marketing system.

Some constructs are directly related to aspects of physical reality. For example, the constructs of length and weight are closely related to observations regarding heavy or light and tall or short. The measurement of these constructs is commonplace and fairly easy.

[4] For a discussion of their distinction, see Fred N. Kerlinger, *Foundations of Behavior Research,* 2d ed. (New York: Holt, 1973), p. 28.

FIGURE 10-3 Difficulty of the measurement process.

In marketing there are many constructs which do not have observable physical references. Examples include constructs such as predisposition, attitude, preference, and image. These constructs exist in the minds of individuals and are not directly observable. Effective marketing research requires that constructs be defined precisely. This can be done in two general ways—by means of (1) a constitutive definition and (2) an operational definition.[3]

A *constitutive definition* defines a construct with other constructs. This approach is similar to that used in a dictionary where words are used to define other words. A constitutive definition should identify the main features of the construct such that it is clearly differentiated from other constructs. For example, how would you define brand loyalty? Engel et al. define it as "the preferential attitudinal and behavioral response toward one or more brands in a product category expressed over a period of time by a consumer."[4] In this definition, constructs such as preferential attitudes, behavior response, and consumer are used to define the construct "brand loyalty."

An *operational definition* specifies how a construct is to be measured. "An operational definition is a sort of manual of instructions to the investigator. It says, in effect, 'Do such-and-such in so-and-so manner.' In short, it defines or gives meaning to a variable by spelling out what the investigator must do to measure it."[5]

A constitutive definition directs the development of an operational definition. Consider our previous constitutive definition of brand loyalty by Engel et al., which clearly

[3] Ibid., p. 30.
[4] James Engel et al., *Consumer Behavior,* 2d ed. (New York: Holt, 1973), p. 552.
[5] Kerlinger, op. cit., p. 31.

rules out the measurement of brand loyalty solely in terms of consecutive purchases of the brand. For example, the pattern of consecutive purchase of brand B (BBBB) could result from convenience, lack of availability of substitutes, indifference, or lower price rather than from an intrinsic preferential attitude toward the brand. Consequently, an operational definition that is consistent with this constitutive definition of brand loyalty must specify how the preferential attitude is to be measured, what type of behavioral response is consistent with this loyalty state, and how the consumer is to be defined.[6]

Marketing has few examples of standardized constitutive and operational definitions of constructs. This has been a serious hindrance to the effectiveness of marketing research projects, largely reflecting the difficulty of the measurement process in this young field of study.

CONCEPTS OF VALIDITY AND RELIABILITY

Measurement error is minimized when a direct correspondence exists between the number system and the marketing phenomena being measured; in this case the numbers accurately represent the characteristics being measured and nothing else. Obviously, this is an idealized situation which rarely exists in practice. More typically our measurements possess some degree of error in that the numerical scale does not exactly represent the marketing phenomenon under investigation.

There are many ways to describe and classify potential sources of error. The following discussion outlines several of the more common sources.[7]

1 Short-term characteristics of the respondent—personal factors such as mood, fatigue, health, etc. may influence the measurements.

2 Situational factors—variations in the environment in which the measurements are reached.

3 Data collection factors—variations in how the questions are administered and the influence of the interviewing method, e.g., phone, personal, or mail.

4 Measuring instrument factors—the degree of ambiguity and difficulty of the questions and the ability of the respondent to answer them.

5 Data analysis factors—errors made in the coding and tabulation process.

The total error of measurement consists of two components. The first is *systematic error,* which is error that causes a constant bias in the measurements. For example, assume we are measuring the speed of events at a swimming meet using a stopwatch which systematically runs fast. To the disappointment of the swimmers, this will cause an upward bias in the measured swimming speeds for all events.

The second component of the total error of measurement is *random error,* which involves influences that bias the measurements but are not systematic. For example, in our swimming meet several stopwatches could be used to time the race. Assuming the absence of systematic error, you would find that the recorded times fall within a

---

[6] For an interesting discussion of this issue, see J. Jacoby and D. Kyner, "Brand Loyalty vs. Repeat Purchase Behavior," *Journal of Marketing Research,* vol. 10, pp. 1–9, February 1973.

[7] For a more complete discussion, see Claire Selltiz et al., *Research Methods in Social Relations,* rev. ed. (New York: Holt, 1959), pp. 150–154.

range around the true time. This random error has been discussed previously in the chapters dealing with sampling.

Returning to our swimming meet example, we can think of the stopwatch time or observed measurement O_m as composed of three elements, (1) the true speed or score T_s, (2) systematic error S_e, and (3) random error R_e. Formally we can state the relationship as

$$O_m = T_s + S_e + R_e$$

where O_m = observed measurement
$\quad\quad T_s$ = true score of the characteristic measured
$\quad\quad S_e$ = systematic error
$\quad\quad R_e$ = random error

Validity and Reliability Defined

The *validity of a measure* refers to the extent to which the measurement process is free from both systematic and random error. The *reliability of a measure* refers to the extent to which the measurement process is free from random errors. Reliability is concerned with the consistency, accuracy, and predictability of the research findings. Validity is concerned with the question: Are we measuring what we think we are measuring? Validity is a broader and more difficult issue than reliability.

Assume we are conducting a survey of buyers to estimate the market share for brand X. For purposes of illustration, assume the market share is actually 10 percent. Let us also assume that four potential conditions exist regarding the influence of systematic and random error on our observed measure of market share. Condition (a) is no systematic error and low random error; condition (b) is high systematic error and low random error; condition (c) is no systematic error and high random error; and condition (d) is high systematic error and high random error. These four conditions represent extremes, and the more typical situation would lie somewhere in the middle. Figure 10-4 illustrates these four conditions.

The figure also presents the influence of systematic and random error on the distribution of sample means for each of these four conditions. In condition (a), the expected value of the distribution of sample means is identical to the true market share of 10 percent. The low random error is reflected in a tight distribution of sample means. Here, repeated samples consistently produce means which are close to the true market share. In this condition, our survey results would be described as both valid and reliable. Condition (b) has the same tight distribution of sample means, but the influence of the high systematic error has biased the expected value 3 points above the true share of market. Repeated sampling would produce means which are close to the 13 percent result. In this situation, our survey results would be reliable but not valid.

In condition (c), the expected value of the distribution of sample means is identical to the true market share of 10 percent, but the high random error causes the distribution of sample means to be highly dispersed. Here, repeated sampling would find many sample means dramatically different from the true market share. In this condition,

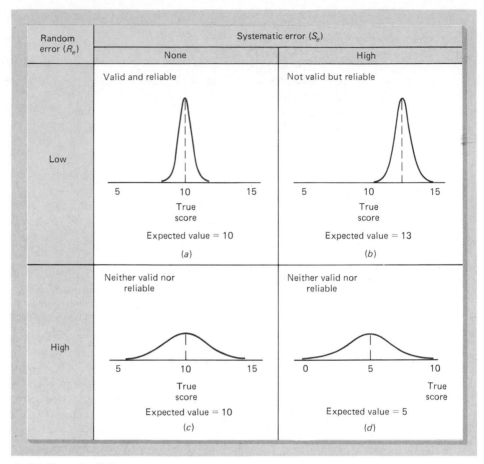

FIGURE 10-4 Reliability and validity.

our survey results would be described as neither valid nor reliable. Finally, condition (d) has the same high random error as condition (c), but here the systematic error is also high, causing the expected value of the sampling distribution to be 5 points below the true market share. In this situation, our survey results would again be described as neither valid nor reliable.

To summarize, for a measure to be valid it must be reliable. Here, systematic error S_e and random error R_e are small or zero. However, if a measure is not reliable, it cannot be valid, and if it is reliable, then it may or may not be valid. Reliability is a necessary but not a sufficient condition for validity. Consequently, the validity of a measure is of main concern since it deals with both systematic and random error. Reliability is a weaker concept since it involves only random error. The ease of measuring reliability compared with validity has given emphasis to the reporting of reliability scores in preference to validity scores in research studies.

Estimation of Validity and Reliability

It is rare to find a decision maker spending the money and taking the time to determine the validity and reliability of research results. The pressures and practical considerations of the typical decision-making situation leave the issue of validity and reliability to those concerned with basic research or academic research projects. Consequently, we will only overview the main methods for estimating validity and reliability. An in-depth discussion of this area can be found in Selltiz.[8]

An easy measure of validity would be to compare the observed measurement with the true measure. However, rarely do we know the true measure, and if we did there would be no reason to measure it in the first place. Consequently, what we do is to infer the validity of the observed measurement using one or more estimation methods. The major ways to estimate the validity of measurement are (1) construct validity, (2) content validity, (3) concurrent validity, and (4) predictive validity.

Construct Validity   Construct validity involves understanding the theoretical rationale underlying the obtained measurements. The approach is to relate the construct of interest to other constructs such that a theoretical framework is developed for the marketing phenomenon being measured. Construct validity increases as the correlation between the construct of interest and the related constructs increases in the predicted manner.

To illustrate construct validity, assume that a sales manager believes there is a relationship among job satisfaction, degree of extrovert personality, and job performance of a sales force. Construct validity could be assessed by developing measures of these three constructs and ascertaining the relationship among the measures for a group of sales personnel. Those who have high job satisfaction and extrovert personalities should exhibit high job performance scores; if they do not, we could question the construct validity of the measures and/or question the validity of the hypothesized relationship. If that relationship is sufficiently confirmed from previous research, the conclusion could be drawn that the measures do not measure what we think they measure.

Construct validity can be evaluated with other approaches. If a construct exists, it should be successfully measured by methods that are different or independent. *Convergent validity* involves the measurement of a construct with independent measurement techniques and the demonstration of a high correlation among the measures. Alternatively, if a construct exists, it should be distinguished from constructs which differ from it. *Discriminant validity* involves demonstrating a lack of correlation among differing constructs.

Content Validity   Content validity involves a subjective judgment by an expert as to the appropriateness of the measurement. This is a common method used in marketing research to determine the validity of measurements.

To illustrate content validity, assume we are going to measure the image of retail stores in a grocery chain. Rather than asking a simple question, a multi-item measuring technique is to be developed. Assume that 20 items or questions are proposed

---

[8] Ibid.

which, when combined in an index, represent the measure of store image. The content validity of these 20 items would be determined by having an expert or experts assess the representativeness of the items used to measure store image. The content validity could be challenged if items such as store cleanliness, friendly atmosphere, or price competitiveness were excluded from the list of items. Content validity is frequently called "face validity" because of the emphasis on the expert's critical eye in determining the relevance of the measurements to the underlying construct.

Concurrent Validity   Concurrent validity involves correlating two different measurements of the same marketing phenomenon which have been administered at the same point in time. It is primarily used to determine the validity of new measuring techniques by correlating them with established techniques.

To illustrate concurrent validity, assume that our previous 20-item measurement technique of store image is valid. Also, assume that an alternative and shorter technique is proposed. Concurrent validation would involve administering both techniques under similar or identical conditions and correlating the two measures of store image. A high correlation would establish the concurrent validity of the new technique.

Predictive Validity   Predictive validity involves the ability of a measured marketing phenomenon at one point in time to predict another marketing phenomenon at a future point in time. If the correlation among the two measures is high, the initial measure is said to have predictive validity, sometimes also called *pragmatic validity* or *criterion-related validity*. It is to be distinguished from concurrent validity, where the two correlated measures occur at the same point in time.

To illustrate predictive validity, consider the use of the Scholastic Aptitude Test to predict college performance. Here, the test measures the student's aptitude for college-level work, and this is used as a predictor of future performance at college. The wide use of this test by colleges attests to its predictive validity.

The major methods of estimating the reliability of measurement are the test-retest, the alternative-forms, and the split-half methods.

Test-Retest Reliability   Test-retest reliability involves repeated measurement of the same person or group using the same scaling device under conditions which are judged to be very similar. The results of these measurements are compared to determine their similarity. This approach assumes that the greater the discrepancy in scores the greater the random error present in the measurement process and the lower the reliability.

Let's return to our multi-item technique for measuring retail store image, discussed in reference to content validity. Test-retest reliability would involve administering our 20-item measuring technique to a group of store shoppers at two points in time. The results of the two measurements would then be correlated to determine the degree of correspondence. The lower the correlation, the lower the reliability.

There are a number of problems with this approach to measuring reliability. First, it may not be logical or possible to administer the measurement twice to the same subject. Second, the first measurement may change the subject's response to the second measurement. Third, situational factors may change, causing the second measurement to change. These types of problems can bias our measurement of reliability.

Alternative-Forms Reliability   Alternative-forms reliability involves giving the subject two forms which are judged equivalent but are not identical. The results of the two measurements are compared to determine the degree of discrepancy in scores, as in the test-retest approach.

Using this approach to determining reliability would require a second set of 20 items to be developed for our retail image–measuring instrument. The two equivalent forms would be administered to the same subjects and the degree of correspondence determined. The problems associated with the alternative-forms approach are the expense and delay associated with developing a second measuring instrument and the difficulty of making them equivalent.

Split-Half Reliability   Split-half reliability involves dividing a multi-item measurement device into equivalent groups and correlating the item responses to estimate reliability. This approach is really a version of the alternative-forms technique.

For example, if we believed that the retail image was composed of a single characteristic or dimension (e.g., favorable-unfavorable image dimension), we could use split-half reliability to measure the internal consistency or internal homogeneity of the 20 items forming the retail image–measuring instrument. Here, each item is assumed to measure this single characteristic independently. The approach would be to randomly divide the 20 items into two groups and determine the degree of correspondence. A high correlation coefficient means that the items are measuring the same characteristic.

SUMMARY

1 The process of measurement is a fundamental aspect of marketing research. It involves the use of numbers to represent the marketing phenomena under investigation.

2 Measurement is defined as the assignment of numbers to characteristics of objects or events according to rules. It is the characteristics of objects or events that are measured, not the items themselves. Measurement error is present when the characteristics of the number system do not represent the relationships present in the marketing phenomena being measured.

3 The four characteristics of the number system—equality of numerals, order of numerals, equality of differences, and equality of ratios—correspond to the four scales of measurement, i.e., nominal, ordinal, interval, and ratio. A nominal scale consists of identifying and categorizing, with no implications of "more or less." An ordinal scale involves the determination of more or less but with no indication as to the distance or interval. An interval scale involves the determination of distance, while a ratio scale involves the additional characteristic of an absolute zero point.

4 Each of these four types of measurement is important in marketing research. Significant marketing phenomena exist at each level of measurement. As we move from nominal to ratio measurement, the rules for assigning numerals to the marketing phenomena become increasingly more restrictive. However, as these rules become more restrictive, the range and sophistication of statistical techniques for data analysis increase.

5 The measurement task in marketing is typically more difficult and involves lower scales of measurement than found in the physical sciences. The problem lies in the measurement of the behavior of people. This often involves measuring concepts or constructs believed to exist in people's minds. The measurement process requires that the construct be operationally defined. Marketing has few examples of standardized operational definitions of constructs.

6 The total error of measurement consists of two components, systematic and random error. The validity of a measurement refers to the extent to which the measurement process is free from both systematic and random error. The reliability of a measure refers to the extent to which the measurement process is free from random error. Measurement can be valid and reliable; not valid, but reliable; or neither valid nor reliable. Reliability is a necessary but not a sufficient condition for validity.

7 The main methods for estimating validity and reliability are (a) construct validity, (b) content validity, (c) concurrent validity, (d) predictive validity, (e) test-retest reliability, (f) alternative-forms reliability, and (g) split-half reliability. Reliability is a weaker concept than validity since it involves only random error. Consequently, reliability is easier to measure than validity and is reported more frequently in research studies.

DISCUSSION QUESTIONS

1 What is measurement?

2 What is the objective of the measurement process?

3 What role does measurement play in marketing?

4 Why is measurement so difficult in marketing?

5 What are the four characteristics of the number system?

6 Distinguish among the four scales of measurement. Give examples of the types of marketing phenomena which each scale might be used to measure.

7 What is measurement error?

8 Distinguish between the validity and reliability of a measure.

9 Discuss the major ways in which the validity of measurement is assessed.

10 How may the reliability of a measure be evaluated?

11

ATTITUDE MEASUREMENT

The marketing manager for a leading hair shampoo aimed at the female market is listening to an exploratory research group discussion on women's reactions to the product. The following statements are typical of this discussion:

"I like the plastic bottle."

"It has lots of suds."

"I don't like the rose smell."

"This is a high-priced product."

"I don't buy it anymore."

"I always purchase that product."

After listening to this discussion for more than an hour, the marketing research manager is asked to comment on what this discussion means and why it is important. How would you respond? It would be important to characterize clearly the meaning of the attitudes expressed by the discussion group, establish why these attitudes are important to the successful marketing of the product, and point out how the significance of these attitudes can be established by formally measuring the attitudes in the context of a conclusive research study.

The objective of this chapter is to address the above issues by building on our discussion of the measurement process in the previous chapter. In the first section the importance of attitudes in marketing will be discussed. The second section provides a detailed discussion of the nature of attitudes, and the final section discusses the many approaches used to measure attitudes and the development of attitude scales.

IMPORTANCE OF ATTITUDES IN MARKETING

The measurement of attitudes is central to many marketing situations. The strategy of market segmentation is often based on attitudinal data. Determining the attitudes of different market segments toward a product can be essential to developing a "positioning" strategy. Attitude measurement is often the basis for evaluating the effectiveness of an advertising campaign. In addition, the assumed relationship between attitudes and behavior helps in the prediction of product acceptance and in the development of marketing programs.

NATURE OF ATTITUDES

An attitude is an individual's enduring perceptual, knowledge-based, evaluative, and action-oriented processes with respect to an object or phenomenon.[1]

Components of Attitude

Attitudes are generally considered to have three main components: (1) a *cognitive* component—a person's beliefs about the object of concern, such as its speed or durability; (2) an *affective* component—a person's feelings about the object, such as "good" or "bad"; and (3) a *behavioral* component—a person's readiness to respond behaviorally to the object.

Link between Attitude and Behavior

Attitudes are important in marketing decision making because of the assumed relationship between attitudes and behavior. Models which conceptualize the construct of attitude typically represent an attitude as a series of sequential components which lead to behavior.[2] Research evidence indicates that the link between attitudes and behavior is not simplistic, and the decision maker and researcher should be cautious in assuming that such a relationship exists in a decision situation. The prediction of future behavior for an aggregate of buyers does appear to be higher than the prediction of behavior regarding an individual buyer.[3] Since most decision situations are concerned with aggregate behavior rather than individual behavior, the attitude-behavior link does have some empirical support for many marketing decision situations. However, attitudes are only one influence on behavior, and in a particular decision situation other factors could be more influential than attitudes. An obvious example would be an individual who has a highly favorable attitude toward purchasing

---

[1] For alternative definitions see D. Krech and R. S. Crutchfield, *Theory and Problems in Social Psychology* (New York: McGraw-Hill, 1948), p. 152; and J. F. Engel, D. T. Kollat, and R. D. Blackwell, *Consumer Behavior* (New York: Holt, 1968), p. 165.

[2] See E. K. Strong, *The Psychology of Selling* (New York: McGraw-Hill, 1925), p. 9; Robert J. Lavidge and Gary A. Steiner, "A Model for Predictive Measurements of Advertising Effectiveness," *Journal of Marketing*, October 1961, p. 61; and Everett M. Rogers, *Diffusion of Innovations* (New York: Free Press, 1962), pp. 79–86.

[3] For a discussion of the research on this issue, see G. S. Day, *Buyer Attitudes and Brand Choice Behavior* (New York: Free Press, 1970).

a new sports car but, because of economic constraints, has to purchase a less desirable used compact.

The marketing implications of this attitude-behavior link relate to measuring the cognitive and affective components of the buyer's attitude and being able to predict future purchase behavior. Alternatively, by influencing the cognitive and affective components, purchase behavior could be influenced.

Model of Behavioral Response

The purpose of marketing activity is to bring about some response from the targeted market segment. The response may be at the cognitive, affective, or behavioral level. Figure 11-1 shows these three basic levels of response plus a more detailed classification called the *hierarchy-of-effects model*. This model hypothesizes that the buyer passes through the stages of awareness, knowledge, liking, preference, intention-to-

FIGURE 11-1   Model of behavioral response.

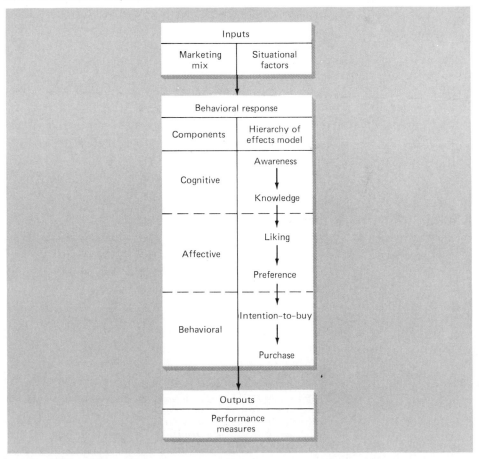

buy, and purchase in succession. Research by Ray suggests that these stages can occur in different sequences depending on the degree of buyer involvement with the purchase and the degree of differentiation among the alternatives.[4]

Cognitive Component   The cognitive component refers to the respondent's awareness of and knowledge about some object or phenomenon. This is sometimes called the *belief component*. It is expressed by statements such as: "I believe product A does . . ." or "I know that product B will . . . ."

The cognitive component is of considerable importance for many types of information needs. Many decision situations require information regarding the market's awareness/knowledge about product features, advertising campaigns, pricing, product availability, and so forth.

Affective Component   The affective component refers to the respondent's liking and preference for an object or phenomenon. Sometimes called the *feeling component,* it is expressed by such statements as: "I dislike product A," "Advertisement X is poor," and "I prefer product A to product B."

The affective component, like the cognitive component, is an important aspect of the information needs for many decision situations. Examples include determining buyers' positive and negative feelings and preferences regarding the organization's marketing program as well as those of competitors.

Behavior Component   The behavioral component refers to the respondent's intention-to-buy and actual purchase behavior. The intention-to-buy stage refers to the respondent's predisposition to action prior to the actual purchase decision. Marketers are interested in respondents' buying intentions as indicators of future purchase behavior. A well-known survey regarding purchase intentions is conducted by the Survey Research Center at the University of Michigan. The Center asks consumers about their buying intentions for durable goods such as automobiles and appliances during the next few months. The assumption is that the decision process for durable goods involves extensive planning and that purchase intentions should correlate with actual purchase behavior. Despite this logic, the predictive ability of data regarding intentions appears to be lower than many would anticipate.[5]

Behavior refers to what the respondents *have done or are doing*. In marketing, behavior refers to the buyer's purchase and use patterns for a product or service. Information needs typically focus on what is purchased, how much, where and when the purchase took place, the circumstances surrounding the purchase, and the characteristics of the buyer. The measurement of behavior involves the development of a comprehensive description of the purchase situation.

---

[4] Michael L. Ray, "Marketing Communication and the Hierarchy-of-Effects" (unpublished research paper No. 180, Stanford University, August 1973).

[5] F. Thomas Juster, "Durable Goods Purchase Intentions, Purchases, and the Consumer Planning Horizon," in Nelson Foote (ed.), *Household Decision Making, Consumer Behavior,* vol. 4 (New York: New York University Press, 1961), pp. 311–342.

Difficulty of Measuring Attitude

As discussed in Chapter 10, the measurement task in marketing is typically more difficult and involves lower scales of measurement than are used in the physical sciences. A prime example of this difficulty is the measurement of the construct of attitude, which exists in the minds of individuals and is not directly observable. Attitude scaling refers to the various operational definitions developed for the measurement of this construct.

In measuring attitudes, one must be sensitive to the scale-level assumptions and the restrictions these assumptions impose on data analysis. Typically, attitudes are measured at the nominal or ordinal level, although several more complex scaling procedures allow measurement at the interval level. There is always the temptation to assume that the attitude measurements have the more poweful properties of an interval scale. The researcher must always be sensitive to these questions: (1) What are the characteristics of the construct being measured? (2) What properties of the number system properly relate to this construct?

ATTITUDE-SCALING PROCEDURES

Attitude scaling is the term commonly used to refer to the process of measuring attitudes. Attitude scaling in marketing tends to focus on the measurement of the respondent's beliefs about a product's attributes (cognitive component) and the respondent's feelings regarding the desirability of these attributes (affective component). Some combination of beliefs and feelings typically is assumed to determine intention to buy (behavioral component).

General Methods of Attitude Measurement

Attitude measurement procedures rely on data from respondents. The measuring techniques can be grouped into those based on communicating with respondents and those based on observing respondents. [6]

Communication Techniques

1 Self-reports: Respondents are directly asked to report their beliefs or feelings by responding to one or more questions on a questionnaire. A number of scaling techniques have been developed to measure these beliefs and feelings.

2 Responses to unstructured or partially structured stimuli: The respondents are shown a picture of a product being purchased or used, or some other situation, and are asked to express their reaction. Other approaches include story telling, word-association tests, and sentence completion.

3 Performance of objective tasks: Respondents are asked to memorize and/or report factual information about products. These responses are analyzed and inferences drawn

---

[6] Stuart W. Cook and Claire Selltiz, "A Multiple-Indicator Approach to Attitude Measurement," *Psychological Bulletin* 62 (1964), pp. 36–55.

MARKETING RESEARCH IN ACTION

PHILIP MORRIS MARKETS GALAXY IN BRAZIL

"Properly conceived, conducted, and interpreted, attitude research findings played a vital role in the developmental thinking and implementation of our strategy to penetrate what seemed to be an impenetrable market: Brazil," said Edward J. Gray, director of marketing administration at Philip Morris International, New York. Philip Morris was attempting to introduce a new low-tar low-nicotine cigarette in Brazil at a time when the British Tobacco Co. had a virtual monopoly in the Brazilian tobacco market.

Philip Morris's research began with the consumer. The data revealed that more than 40 percent of Brazil's smokers were 35 or older, and they accounted for more than 48 percent of all cigarettes purchased. Consumers also expressed a preference for brands that didn't irritate their throats and had less nicotine. Furthermore, those consumers who had switched to low-tar cigarettes in other markets were in the 35-and-over age group and upwardly mobile. Brazil seemed the perfect place for Galaxy, a cigarette tailored by Philip Morris specifically for Brazilian smokers. Galaxy had significantly less tar and nicotine than any competing product.

Philip Morris established credibility for the new brand by hiring Nationwide Consumer Testing Institute, Inc. (NCTI) to verify the ad copy claims. Philip Morris was primarily touting Galaxy as a low-tar, low-nicotine cigarette, a new concept in Brazil.

Galaxy sales didn't take off as expected, and Philip Morris ran focus-group interviews to discover the problem. It was found that, because of its low-tar image, Galaxy was seen as a cigarette for those who were trying to quit smoking. To combat this, new Galaxy ads were created to educate consumers about the benefits of a low-tar cigarette. The ads also linked intelligence with switching to low-tar Galaxy.

Further attitude research was perfomed, and Galaxy found itself oddly positioned in comparison with its competition. On a two-dimensional map of brand image, Galaxy was seemingly perceived as low quality. In Latin America, price and quality were highly correlated, but the Brazilian government tightly controlled cigarette prices. They did allow price increases for new packaging, however. So, to increase the quality image of Galaxy, Philip Morris introduced a flip-top box and a 100-mm cigarette, both costing more than the original Galaxy. A second attitude survey was done after the changes were instituted, and it placed Galaxy where it was supposed to be, with the upper-class brands.

By the end of 1981, Galaxy had captured a 2.3 percent share of the total Brazil market and 5.4 percent of the market in Rio de Janeiro and São Paulo. Considering that one market share point was worth more than $2 million in marginal profits in the highly populated Brazil, Galaxy was considered a success.

Based on *Marketing News* vol. 16, no. 6, sec. 2, p. 74, Sept. 17, 1982.

regarding the nature of the respondents' beliefs and feelings. The assumption is that respondents are more likely to remember those things which are consistent with their beliefs and feelings.

Observation Techniques

1 Overt behavior: Individuals are put in a situation which allows behavior patterns to be exhibited and inferences to be drawn regarding the individuals' beliefs and feelings. This technique is based on the assumption that a person's behavior is dependent on beliefs and feelings.

2 Physiological reactions: Respondents are exposed to products or advertisements and their physiological reactions are measured. The measurement device typically is the galvanic skin response technique, which measures sweating of the hand, or the eye dilation technique, which measures changes in the diameter of the pupil of the eye. A limitation of the physiological response approach is that it measures only the intensity of feelings and not direction (positive or negative).

Of these general methods for measuring attitudes, the self-reporting technique is by far the most widely used, and the remainder of this chapter will focus on the various scaling procedures which use it. These procedures are most appropriate for conclusive research studies which require that attitudes be formally measured and quantified using a large sample of respondents. The remaining general methods for measuring attitudes are most appropriate for exploratory research designed to develop the nature of beliefs and feelings present in a decision situation. These remaining methods will be discussed in more detail in Chapter 13, which deals with data collection methods.

Self-Report Techniques

The most common tool of attitude measurement is the self-report method. Several such techniques will be discussed here, with emphasis on the development of unidimensional scales.

Nominal Scale   The simplest self-reporting scale is a nominal scale, where the respondent's beliefs are classified in two or more categories. For example, a nominal scale can be developed from responses to the question: "Does your automobile have radial tires—yes or no?" A third category of "don't know" might be included for those respondents who are not informed concerning this feature of their automobile. The result of this scaling is a three-category classification of respondents with respect to their responses—yes, no, and don't know. Here a nominal scale has been developed, and numbers can be assigned to the categories for data analysis purposes. Keep in mind that these numbers can be used only to identify the categories.

Rating Scales   Rating scales refer to measurement situations which involve ordinal, interval, and ratio scales. Typically, the focus of the measurement situation is on developing ordinal or interval scales of the affective component.

A rating scale requires the respondent to indicate the position on a continuum or among ordered categories which correspond to his or her attitude. Numerical values may be part of the scale or be assigned after the respondent completes the self-rating task.

An ordinal scale is formed when respondents order themselves by responding to a question such as: "Do you like, dislike, or are you indifferent to radial tires?" The result of this scaling is a three-category ordinal scale which ranks the respondents according to their feeling about radial tires, i.e., like—indifferent—dislike. Numbers can be assigned to these ordered categories for purposes of data analysis.

Graphic Rating Scales   A graphic rating scale requires the respondents to indicate their position on a continuum which ranges from one extreme of the attitude in question to the other extreme. The format of this graphic continuum is as varied as the imaginations of the researchers who devise such a scale.

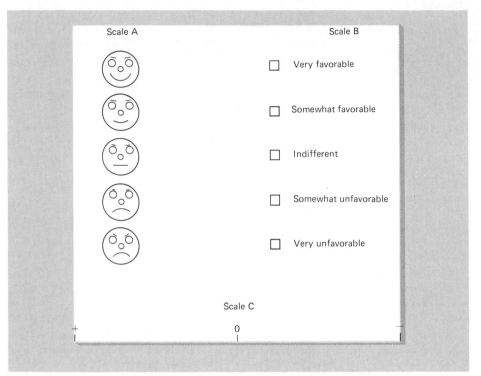

FIGURE 11-2 Graphic and verbal rating scales.

Figure 11-2 presents two different examples of graphic scales (scales A and C).[7] Let's assume that several respondents have sampled a new formulation of cake mix, and we want to measure their feelings about the sweetness of the cake mix. Scale A relies on a series of facial expressions to represent the varying degrees of like and dislike. The respondents are asked to indicate which of the facial expressions best represents their reaction to the sweetness level. A most favorable response means the sweetness level is "just right" (extreme smile) while a least favorable response (extreme frown) means the cake is either "too sweet" or "not sweet enough." Such an unfavorable response would require additional questioning of the respondent to determine what was wrong with the sweetness level. Graphic scales of this nature are especially useful when the respondents speak different languages or when the respondents are children.

Scale C presents a positive-negative continuum. The respondents are asked to indicate their position by checking a location on this continuum. Once the judgments are recorded, the researcher can subdivide the continuum into an appropriate set of categories and assign numerals to the judgments. It is argued that the advantage of this continuous scale is that the respondent is not confronted with a predetermined set of response categories. Rather, the categorization of the scale is left to the respondent,

[7] Jean Morton-Williams, "Questionnaire Design," in Robert M. Worchester (ed.), *Consumer Market Research Handbook* (London: McGraw-Hill, 1972), pp. 85–87.

who implicitly determines the number of categories during the judgment process. A disadvantage of this graphic scale is that it requires the respondent to deal with an abstract judgment situation. In addition, since the researcher does not know how the respondents subdivided the continuum, the comparison and grouping of responses across respondents are difficult to justify.

Verbal Rating Scales Verbal rating scales are probably the most frequently used scales in marketing research. These require the respondents to indicate their position by selecting among verbally identified categories. Scale B in Figure 11-2 is an example; here, the respondents are asked to check the box adjacent to the phrase which best corresponds to their reaction given the question at hand.

It is important to understand the issues surrounding the construction of verbal rating scales.[8] The major issues are: (1) number of categories, (2) odd or even number of categories, (3) balanced versus unbalanced scale, (4) extent of verbal description, (5) category numbering, (6) forced versus nonforced scales, and (7) comparative versus noncomparative scales.

While there is no established *number of categories* which is deemed optimal for a scale, in practice scales of five or six categories are typical.[9] Some researchers argue that more than five or six are needed in situations where small changes in attitude are to be measured.[10] Others argue that it is doubtful that the majority of respondents can distinguish between more than six to eight categories. Beyond this point, additional categories do not increase the precision with which the attitude is being measured.[11] Most researchers find that it is as easy to administer and analyze a scale with five or seven categories as it is to use one with, say, three categories. Consequently, researchers typically utilize at least a five-category scale unless special circumstances dictate fewer or more categories.

Should the scale have an *odd* or *even number of scale categories?* The answer to this is unclear. If an odd number of categories is selected, the middle category is typically identified as a neutral position. If an even number is selected, the scale does not have a neutral category, and the respondent is forced to take a position expressing some degree of feeling. The results of a research study comparing an odd (seven-category) scale with an even (six-category) scale concluded that there was no significant difference in the results between scales.[12]

Should the number of favorable and unfavorable categories be *balanced* or *unbalanced?* A balanced scale has the same number of favorable categories as unfavorable

[8] This discussion follows that in Donald S. Tull and Del I. Hawkins, *Marketing Research* (New York: Macmillan, 1976), pp. 336–339.

[9] D. R. Lehmann and J. Hulbert, "Are Three-Point Scales Always Good Enough?" *Journal of Marketing Research,* vol. 9, pp. 444–446, November 1972; see also M. S. Matell and J. Jacoby, "Is There an Optimal Number of Alternatives for Likert-Scales Items?" *Journal of Applied Psychology,* vol. 56, pp. 506–509, December 1972.

[10] G. D. Hughes, "Selecting Scales to Measure Attitude Change," *Journal of Marketing Research,* vol. 4, pp. 85–87, February 1967.

[11] P. E. Green and V. R. Rao, "Rating Scales and Information Recovery—How Many Scales and Response Categories to Use?" *Journal of Marketing,* vol. 34, pp. 33–39, July 1970.

[12] G. S. Albaum and G. Munsinger, "Methodological Questions Concerning the Use of the Semantic Differential," paper presented at the Spring 1973 meeting of the Southwestern Marketing Association.

categories. The argument for an unbalanced scale relates to the nature of the attitude distribution to be measured. If the distribution is predominantly favorable, an unbalanced scale with more favorable categories than unfavorable categories would be appropriate. The argument for balanced scales emphasizes the potential biasing of responses which can result from limiting the response categories on the favorable or unfavorable side of the scale.

How extensive should the *verbal description* of a category be? Some researchers believe that clearly defined response categories increase the reliability of the measurements.[13] It is argued that each category should have a verbal description and that these verbal descriptions should have a clear and precise wording such that each response category is differentiated.

In many situations the researcher believes that the respondent's judgments can be treated as interval data. Implicit in this decision is the assumption that the respondent views the differences between verbal descriptions to be equally spaced. When using the phrases "very good," "fairly good," and "neutral" as verbal descriptions for an interval scale, the researcher assumes that the distance between "very good" and "neutral" is twice the distance of that between "fairly good" and "neutral." A research study which measured the relative size of "very" and "fairly" found a respective weight of $+3.74$ and $+1.22$ rather than the assumed weight of $+2$ and $+1$, respectively.[14] In this situation, the assignment of the weights $+2$ and $+1$ for purposes of data analysis would obviously introduce measurement error in the research results. It is common practice to treat rating scales as interval scales and to compute means and standard deviations on such measurements. The researcher should be sensitive to this practice and remember the potential for measurement error in the research findings.[15]

Should *numbers* be assigned to the response categories? The argument is that they should be used when the researcher believes the respondent's judgments can be treated as interval data. The numbers 5, 4, 3, 2, and 1 could be used on a five-category scale to communicate to the respondent that the intervals between response categories are intended to be of equal distance.

Another issue in constructing a rating scale concerns the use of a *forced* versus a *nonforced scale*. A forced scale requires all respondents to indicate a position on the attitude scale. The argument for a forced scale is that those who are reluctant to reveal their attitude are encouraged to do so with the forced scale. Those respondents who have no opinion or no knowledge typically mark the "neutral" category on the scale. If a significant proportion of the respondents have no opinion, rather than a reluctance to reveal their feelings, it is best to have a category of "no opinion" or "no knowledge" rather than forcing their response in the "neutral category."[16]

[13] C. Selltiz, M. Jahoda, M. Deutsch, and S. W. Cook, *Research Methods in Social Relations* (New York: Holt, 1959), p. 349.

[14] Cliff Holmes, "A Statistical Evaluation of Rating Scales," *Journal of the Market Research Society*, 1974, vol. 16, p. 91.

[15] J. A. Martilla and D. W. Carvey, "Four Subtle Sins in Marketing Research," *Journal of Marketing*. vol. 39, pp. 8–10, January 1975.

[16] G. D. Hughes, "Some Confounding Effects of Forced-Choice Scales," *Journal of Marketing Research*, vol. 6, pp. 223–226, May 1969.

A final issue concerns the use of *comparative* and *noncomparative scales*. A comparative scale requires the respondents to express their attitude by making a direct comparison with a standard or reference point. This reference point could be the current brand used, an ideal product, or a competitive product. A comparative scale allows the researcher to report the respondents' attitudes relative to a standard that may be of importance in a decision situation. The argument for noncomparative scales is that they allow each respondent to choose his or her own reference point, and that consequently a more accurate measurement of the respondent's attitude is achieved. In practice, the selection of comparative and noncomparative scales is dependent on the specific information needs of the decision situation.

Rank-Order Scale   The rank-order technique involves having the respondent rank various objects with regard to the attitude in question. Thus, the respondent may be required to rank five print advertisements on the basis of either awareness of, liking for, preference for, or intention to buy the product advertised.

The rank-order technique is widely used in marketing research. It is comparative in nature and forms an ordinal scale of the objects evaluated.

This technique has important advantages. It is simple in concept, easy to administer, and less time-consuming to administer than other comparative techniques, such as paired comparison. The instructions for ranking objects are easy to comprehend; consequently, the technique can be used on self-administered questionnaires. In addition, it is argued that the technique is similar to the purchase decision process and forces respondents to discriminate among products in a realistic manner.

The limitations of rank-order techniques are important also. The forced-choice and comparative nature of the technique results in a ranking of objects regardless of the attitudinal position of the respondent to the objects as a group. It could be that the respondent "dislikes" all of the objects in the set. In this case, the object ranked first is the least "disliked" of the objects in the set. Obviously the researcher must be sensitive to the attitudinal position of the respondent and be confident that a realistic set of objects is being evaluated.

Another limitation of the rank-order technique is the fact that it produces only ordinal data. While there are scaling techniques which form higher-order scales based on ranked input data, these techniques bring a degree of complexity to the data collection and analysis phase which may be undesirable. Finally, several research studies have found that the ranking and rating-scale techniques yield similar results.[17] Other things being equal, in selecting between these two techniques researchers must weigh the pros and cons of each technique against the specific needs of the research project.

Paired-Comparison Scale   With the paired-comparison technique, respondents are presented with two objects from a set and required to pick one with regard to the attitude in question. Thus, the respondent is required to make a series of paired

---

[17] See Jack Abrams, "An Evaluation of Alternative Rating Devices for Consumer Research," *Journal of Marketing Research,* vol. 3, pp. 189–193, May 1966; and H. H. Kassarjian and M. Nakanishi, "Study of Selected Opinion Measurement Techniques," *Journal of Marketing Research,* vol. 4, pp. 148–153, May 1967.

judgments between objects regarding preference, amount of some attribute present, and so forth.

The data collection procedure typically requires the respondent to compare all possible pairs of the objects. If there are 5 objects ($n = 5$) to be evaluated, there will be 10 paired comparisons [$n(n - 1)/2$] required in the judgment task. The evaluation of 10 objects requires 45 paired comparisons. The geometric expansion in the number of paired comparisons limits the usefulness of this technique for the evaluation of large object sets.

In Table 11-1, matrix A presents paired-comparison data for five brands of cake mix, A, B, C, D, and E. The judgment task was to pick the cake mix sample which had the lightest and fluffiest texture. Each cell entry in matrix A represents the proportion of respondents who believed that the "column" brand has more of the attributes in question than the "row" brand. For example, in the brand A versus brand B comparison 90 percent of the respondents believed that brand B was lighter and fluffier than A. An inspection of the column proportions reveals that brand B dominates the other brands on this attribute.

How can an ordinal scale be developed given these paired-comparison data? The first step is to convert matrix A to 0-1 scores, which indicate whether the column brand dominates the row brand and vice versa (see matrix B in Table 11-1). Here, "1" is assigned to a cell if the column brand dominates the row brand (if the proportion $>.5$), and "0" is assigned to a cell if the column brand does not dominate the row brand (if the proportion $\leq.5$). The ordinal relationship among brands is determined by totaling the columns. Here, the ordinal scaling of the brands is $B > C > A > E > D$. Thus, brand B has the lightest and fluffiest texture, followed by C, A, E, and D.

If the researcher requires an interval scaling of the cake mix brands, the paired-comparison data in matrix A of Table 11-1 can be analyzed using a technique called

TABLE 11-1   PAIRED-COMPARISON DATA

	Matrix A				
	A	B	C	D	E
A	—	.90	.64	.14	.27
B	.10	—	.32	.02	.21
C	.36	.68	—	.15	.36
D	.86	.98	.85	—	.52
E	.73	.79	.64	.48	—

	Matrix B				
	A	B	C	D	E
A	—	1	1	0	0
B	0	—	0	0	0
C	0	1	—	0	0
D	1	1	1	—	1
E	1	1	1	0	—
Total	2	4	3	0	1

Thurstone's law of comparative judgment, which converts ordinal judgments into interval data. While the details are too extensive for the purposes of this book, several excellent explanations of the technique are available for those interested.[18]

The arguments in favor of the paired-comparison technique relate to the simplicity of the judgment task, the comparative nature of the task, and the availability of scaling methods which produce interval data. This interval-scaling feature can be important in assessing differences among competitive products and advertisements.

The paired-comparison technique has important limitations. As the number of objects to be evaluated increases arithmetically, the number of paired comparisons increases geometrically. Consequently, the technique is limited to a small number of objects in order to control respondent fatigue during the judgment process. In addition, research indicates that the order in which the objects are presented can bias the results,[19] that the paired-comparison task is not typical of the actual choice process present in the marketplace, and that simpler noncomparative rating scales provide results similar to those obtained from paired comparisons.[20]

Semantic Differential Scale   This is one of the most popular attitude measurement techniques in marketing research.[21] The main application of the semantic differential has been in connection with company and brand image studies.

An image can be defined as an average of many separate attitudes toward a company, brand, or concept. As discussed previously, each separate attitude has three components—cognitive, affective, and behavioral. Consequently, image measurement requires the respondents to express their position on many attitudes using a multiscale questionnaire.

The semantic differential typically requires the respondents to evaluate an object on a seven-point rating scale bounded at each end by bipolar adjectives. For example:

Retail Store X

Reliable	__ :	__ :	X :	__ :	__ :	__ :	__	Unreliable
Friendly	X :	__ :	__ :	__ :	__ :	__ :	__ :	Unfriendly
Modern	__ :	__ :	__ :	__ :	X :	__ :	__ :	Old-fashioned
Inexpensive	__ :	__ :	__ :	__ :	__ :	X :	__ :	Expensive
Progressive	__ :	__ :	__ :	X :	__ :	__ :	__ :	Not progressive

[18] See Allen L. Edwards, *Techniques of Attitude Scale Construction* (New York: Appleton-Century-Crofts, 1957), pp. 20–29; P. E. Green and D. S. Tull, *Research for Marketing Decisions* (Englewood Cliffs, N.J.: Prentice-Hall, 1974), pp. 184–191; H. A. David, *The Method of Paired Comparisons* (London: Charles Griffin & Co., 1963).

[19] P. Daniels and J. Lawford, "The Effect of Order in the Presentation of Samples in Paired Comparison Tests," *Journal of the Market Research Society,* vol. 16, pp. 127–133, April 1974.

[20] R. Seaton, "Why Ratings Are Better Than Comparisons," *Journal of Advertising Research,* vol. 14, pp. 45–48, February 1974.

[21] B. A. Greenberg, J. L. Goldstucker, and D. N. Bellenger, "What Techniques Are Used by Marketing Researchers in Business?" *Journal of Marketing,* vol. 41, pp. 62–68, April 1977.

Respondents are instructed to check the blank location which most accurately reflects their position regarding the object in connection with each of the bipolar adjectives.

The semantic differential was originally developed by Osgood.[22] He developed 50 bipolar adjectives which measured three basic dimensions of an object: (1) evaluative—good versus bad; (2) activity—active versus passive; and (3) potency—strong versus weak. Marketing researchers rarely use the semantic differential in the manner proposed by Osgood. Rather, the technique is typically adapted to fit the specific needs to the research project at hand, as the following examples demonstrate.[23]

1 The single-word adjectives are sometimes replaced with descriptive phrases tailored to a particular company, product, or concept. The following could be used, for example, to measure the brand image of a cola soft drink:

Very special drink—just another drink
Fun type of drink—kind of serious drink
Regular people drink it—snobs drink it

2 The polar opposites have been replaced with phrases that may not include extremes and may be eliminate the negative portion of the scale. The reason is that some respondents are unwilling to check the extremes of a scale, and some either are unwilling to express a negative view or do not have negative views toward the objects under investigation. The following phrases represent this adaptation:

High-quality product—so-so product
Modern company—somewhat old-fashioned company

3 Many researchers have the respondent evaluate an "ideal product" or "ideal company" in addition to the objects under investigation. This approach allows the objects under investigation to be compared to a norm or standard.

4 Each position on the scale can be assigned a numerical value, such as 7, 6, 5, 4, 3, 2, 1 or $+3$, $+2$, $+1$, 0, -1, -2, -3. The assumption is that the respondents' judgments can be treated as interval data, which makes possible the calculation of the arithmetic mean for an object on each scale. This approach is widely accepted by researchers who use the semantic differential.[24] However, there is a controversy as to whether these measurements can be treated as interval data. Critics argue that the median is the appropriate summary measure.

Semantic differential data are typically analyzed using the profile analysis approach. This involves calculating the arithmetic mean or median for each set of verbal phrases

[22] C. Osgood, G. Suci, and P. Tannenbaum, *The Measurement of Meaning* (Urbana: University of Illinois Press, 1957).

[23] William A. Mindak, "Fitting the Semantic Differential to the Marketing Problem," *Journal of Marketing,* vol. 25, pp. 28–33, April 1961.

[24] For a more detailed discussion see F. N. Kerlinger, *Foundations of Behavioral Research* (New York: Holt, 1973), pp. 566–581, or C. Holmes, "A Statistical Evaluation of Rating Scales," *Journal of the Marketing Research Society,* vol. 16, pp. 87–107, April 1974.

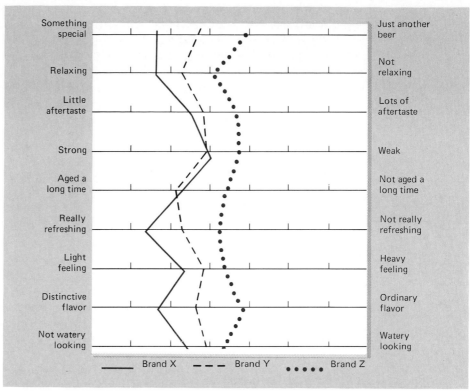

FIGURE 11-3 Profile analysis of beer brand images. *(Source: William A. Mindak, "Fitting the Semantic Differential to the Marketing Problem," Journal of Marketing, pp. 28–33, April 1961.)*

or polar opposites for each object evaluated. These summary measures are usually plotted on the scales such that the profiles of the objects can be compared. Figure 11-3 provides an illustration of the profiles for three brands of beer.[25] Brand X has the most favorable brand image, while brand Z has the least favorable image. All three brand images are on the positive side of the scales.

The popularity of the semantic differential is attributed to its versatility and simplicity. The technique is easy to develop and administer, and the results can be readily communicated to management. In addition, it has been found to be a discriminating and reliable research tool.[26]

The limitation of the semantic differential relates to the requirement that the scales be composed of true bipolar adjectives or phrases. It is argued that the pilot testing necessary to meet this requirement can be expensive and time-consuming. In practice, formal pilot testing is rarely done, and the bipolar adjectives or phrases are developed using the researcher's judgment.

[25] Mindak, op. cit.
[26] R. F. Carter, W. L. Ruggels, and S. H. Chaffee, "The Semantic Differential in Opinion Measurement," *Public Opinion Quarterly*, vol. 32, pp. 666–674, Winter 1968–69.

Stapel Scale The Stapel scale is a modification of the semantic differential scale. It is a unipolar 10-point nonverbal rating scale with values ranging from +5 to −5. The scaling technique is designed to measure the direction and intensity of attitudes simultaneously.[27] It differs from the semantic differential in that the scale values indicate how close the descriptor or adjective fits the object evaluated.

Table 11-2 presents the format of a Stapel scale. Respondents are instructed to evaluate how accurately the adjective or phrase describes the object to be evaluated. The following instructions are given to the respondent:

> You would select a *plus* number for words that you think describe (Bank A) accurately. The more accurately you think the word describes it, the larger the *plus* number you would choose. You would select a *minus* number for words you think do not describe it accurately. The less accurately you think a word describes it, the larger the *minus* number you would choose. Therefore, you can select any number from +5, for words that you think are very accurate, all the way to −5, for words that you think are very inaccurate.[28]

Unipolar judgments can be analyzed the same way that semantic differential data are treated. Figure 11-4 presents hypothetical results of a profile analysis of two banks based on Stapel-scale data.

The arguments in favor of the Stapel scale relate to its convenience of administration and the absence of the requirement that the scales be composed of truly bipolar adjectives or phrases.[29] Research indicates that the Stapel scale can produce results similar to those of the semantic differential.[30] In addition, the technique has

[27] I. Crespi, "Use of a Scaling Technique in Surveys," *Journal of Marketing,* vol. 25, pp. 69–72, July 1961.
[28] Ibid., p. 71.
[29] E. J. Lusk, "A Bipolar Adjective Screening Methodology," *Journal of Marketing Research,* vol. 10, pp. 202–203, May 1973.
[30] D. I. Hawkins, G. Albaum, and R. Best, "Stapel Scale or Semantic Differential in Marketing Research?" *Journal of Marketing Research,* vol. 11, pp. 318—322, August 1974; and J. J. Vidali, "Single-Anchor Stapel Scales Versus Double-Anchor Semantic Differential Scales," *Psychological Reports,* vol. 33, pp. 373–374, October 1973.

TABLE 11-2   STAPEL SCALE FORMAT

	Bank	
	+5	+5
	+4	+4
	+3	+3
	+2	+2
	+1	+1
Fast service	Friendly	
	−1	−1
	−2	−2
	−3	−3
	−4	−4
	−5	−5

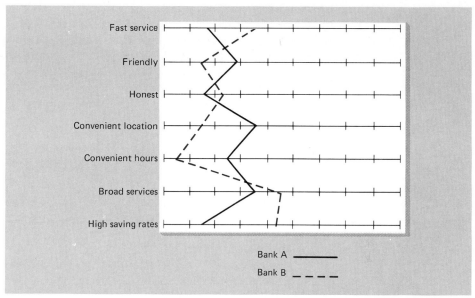

FIGURE 11-4 Stapel scale comparative profiles.

produced satisfactory results when administered over the telephone.[31] Despite these advantages, the Stapel scale has experienced limited use in marketing research in comparision with the semantic differential. It appears to be a useful technique which is growing in popularity with researchers.

Indirect Scales The self-report scaling techniques previously discussed require the respondents to report directly what their position is about the attitude in question. While this is a very efficient way to measure attitudes, it is argued that under certain circumstances (e.g., reluctance to express an attitude in regard to a controversial issue), respondents may not accurately report their position using direct measurement techniques. A respondent might not be directly aware of his or her position on an issue. Concern with the limitations of direct measurement techniques has resulted in the development of indirect self-reporting scaling techniques.[32] While these techniques have been developed to deal with attitude measurement problems present in the field of psychology, marketing researchers have applied them to similar problems in marketing.

Indirect scales combine the respondents' judgments on several questions in order to develop a measure of their position on the attitude in question. Indirect scales are commonly called *attitude scales* and *attitude batteries*.

To ensure that the questions included in the scaling technique contribute efficiently to the measurement of the attitude in question, it is usually necessary to try out a

[31] Hawkins et al., op. cit.
[32] Edwards, op. cit.

large number of items in a pilot study using 50 to 100 respondents and then apply various criteria for selecting those questions which are most appropriate for the actual scale. It is typical to phrase questions so that the respondent can indicate agreement or disagreement with them. Based on these responses, a score is developed for each respondent which represents his or her position with regard to the attitude in question.

There are four main types of indirect scaling techniques: (1) Likert's method of summated ratings; (2) Thurstone's method of "equal-appearing intervals"; (3) Guttman's cumulative scales; and (4) the Q-sort technique.

Indirect techniques in marketing have not been widely used because of the time and expense involved in developing them and the difficulty of administering the scales. In addition, most attitudes in marketing can be measured effectively using direct attitude measurement techniques. We will briefly discuss the Likert scale, since it is used more frequently than the other three. There are several excellent sources which thoroughly explain the mechanics of how to construct, analyze, and interpret these indirect scaling techniques.[33]

The Likert Scale This involves a series of statements related to the attitude in question. The respondent is required to indicate degree of agreement or disagreement with each of these statements, and responses are given a numerical score that will consistently reflect the direction of the person's attitude on each statement. The respondent's total score is computed by summing scores for all statements. The following example illustrates the use of the Likert scale.

A homemaker is given a card with the following verbal scale.[34]

___ Strongly agree
___ Agree
___ Neither agree nor disagree
___ Disagree
___ Strongly disagree

Next, the homemaker is read or shown a list of statements about the object under investigation. For each statement the homemaker is required to indicate the phrase which best represents his or her position concerning the statement. Assume that the following statements are used to determine the homemaker's attitude toward brand X chocolate cake mix:

1 Brand X is expensive.
2 Brand X is rich in taste.
3 Brand X is light and fluffy.
4 Brand X has real chocolate flavor.
5 Brand X has a moist texture.

The responses to these statements are scored from 5 to 1 (strongly agree through strongly disagree) for statements favorable to brand X (statements 2 through 5) and

---

[33] Edwards, op. cit., and Selltiz et al., op. cit.
[34] Several versions of this scale are used in practice. Some researchers prefer a 7-point scale, while others include a "don't know" category.

scored from 1 to 5 (strongly agree through strongly disagree) for statements unfavorable to brand X (statement 1). The sum of these scores represents the homemaker's total score on the attitude in question. In this example, the total score could range from a high of 25 (very favorable) to a low score of 5 (very unfavorable).

There are five steps in the construction of a Likert scale:[35]

1 The researcher collects a large number of statements considered relevant to the attitude being measured which can be clearly identified as either favorable or unfavorable.

2 These statements are given to a group of respondents representative of the respondent population of interest. The respondents indicate their position on each statement by checking a category on an agreement-disagreement scale.

3 The responses to the various statements are scored by summing the respondent's numerical score on each statement. The responses must be scored in such a manner that favorable responses toward the object consistently receive the same numerical scores. This will require the reversing of the numerical assignment depending on whether the statement is favorable or unfavorable.

4 The statements are analyzed to determine which of them discriminate most clearly between the high scorers and low scorers. Statements which do not indicate a substantial correlation with the total score or do not elicit different responses from those who score high and those who score low on the overall test are eliminated. This process increases the internal consistency or reliability of the measurement technique.

5 The remaining statements form the Likert scale, which can be used to measure the attitude in question.

The Likert scale has several advantages over other indirect scaling techniques. It is reasonably easy to construct and administer, and the simplicity of the instructions and the judgment task allow its use on mail surveys.

The arguments against the Likert scale are that it produces only an ordinal scale.[36] Many researchers believe that the Likert data closely resemble those of an interval scale, and so they prefer to use statistical techniques requiring interval data. On balance, most researchers find that the advantages of the Likert scale outweigh the disadvantages of other indirect scaling techniques.

SUMMARY

1 Attitude measurement is important in marketing because of the central role it plays in developing a segmentation/positioning strategy, evaluating the effectiveness of advertising, predicting product acceptance, and facilitating the development of marketing programs.

2 An attitude represents an individual's enduring perceptual, knowledge-based, evaluative, and action-oriented processes with respect to an object or phenomenon.

---

[35] Selltiz et al., op. cit., pp. 367–368.
[36] An improved Likert scale is presented in G. Kundu, "A Comparison of the Likert and a New Technique of Attitude Measurement," *Indian Journal of Psychology*, vol. 47, pp. 245–258, September 1972.

The three components of an attitude are (a) cognitive—relating to beliefs, (b) affective—relating to feelings, and (c) behavioral—relating to action tendency.

3 Marketing activities are designed to bring about some response from the targeted market segment. This response can be at the cognitive, affective, or behavioral level. The hierarchy-of-effects model hypothesizes a cognitive-affective-behavioral sequence resulting from the marketing effort. While the order of this sequence may vary depending on the specifics of the marketing situation, the measurement of an attitude component early in the sequence may allow predictions regarding the character of subsequent components.

4 An attitude is a construct which exists in the minds of individuals. Attitude scaling refers to operational definitions for the measurement of this construct. This is a difficult measurement task, and typically it results in a nominal or ordinal scale.

5 The general methods for measuring attitudes rely on communicating with respondents and on observing respondents. Communication techniques include (a) self-reports, (b) responses to unstructured or partially structured stimuli, and (c) performance of objective tasks. Observation techniques include (a) overt behavior, and (b) physiological reactions.

6 The self-reporting technique, the most widely used method of attitude measurement in marketing, is composed of many specific scaling approaches. Of these approaches, graphic and verbal rating scales are among the most frequently used. The major issues surrounding the construction of rating scales are (a) number of categories, (b) odd or even number of categories, (c) balanced versus unbalanced scale, (d) extent of verbal description, (e) category numbering, (f) forced versus nonforced scales, and (g) comparative versus noncomparative scales.

7 The rank-order scaling approach involves a ranking of objects with regard to the attitude in question. This popular approach results in an ordinal scaling of the objects.

8 The paired-comparison scaling approach involves a series of pairwise judgments among objects in a set. This more complex scaling approach results in an ordinal scale. However, the paired comparison data can be analysed using *Thurstone's law of comparative judgment* which converts the ordinal-judgements into interval data.

9 The semantic-differential scaling approach is a popular way to measure "image," which can be defined as an average of many separate attitudes toward a company, brand, or concept. With this method, an object is evaluated on several rating scales bounded at each end by bipolar adjectives or phrases. The data are analyzed using the profile analysis approach.

10 The Stapel scale is a modification of the semantic-differential scale. It uses a unipolar 10-point nonverbal rating scale to measure how closely the descriptor fits the object evaluated.

11 Indirect scales attempt to measure attitudes in situations where the respondent may not accurately report beliefs and feelings using direct scaling approaches. These more complex approaches include (a) Likert's method of summated ratings; (b) Thurstone's method of "equal-appearing intervals"; (c) Guttman's cumulative scales; and (d) the Q-sort technique. Of these scaling approaches, only the Likert scale has received much attention in the measurement of attitudes in marketing.

DISCUSSION QUESTIONS

1 What is an attitude?
2 What are the three main components of attitudes?
3 Describe the stages of the hierarchy-of-effects model.
4 What questions must the researcher always be concerned with when measuring attitudes?
5 What general methods of attitude measurement exist?
6 What self-report techniques are used in marketing research?
7 Discuss some of the issues involved in constructing a verbal rating scale.
8 What are the advantages and disadvantages of rank-order scales?
9 Describe the methods by which ordinal and interval scales can be derived from paired-comparison data.
10 What advantages and limitations exist for the paired-comparison technique?
11 Explain the profile analysis method of evaluating data from semantic-differential scales.
12 How does the Stapel scale differ from the semantic-differential scale?
13 When may an indirect scale offer advantages to the marketing researcher over other self-reporting methods?
14 What are the steps involved in constructing a Likert scale?

CHAPTER 12

CAUSAL DESIGNS

In Chapter 1, improper causal inferences were identified as one type of nonsampling error. In this chapter, we shall discuss this problem in the context of different types of research designs and their ability to distinguish causality. The chapter first describes the necessary conditions for causality to be inferred, then the principles of experimental and quasi-experimental design, the managerial aspects of these designs, and finally the basics of designed experiments.

THE SEARCH FOR CAUSALITY

Introduction

Marketing managers want to be able to make *causal statements* about the effects of their actions: "The new advertising campaign we developed has resulted in a 10 percent increase in sales." In similar fashion, a sales manager might boast: "The new sales training program has resulted in lower sales force turnover." In both of these examples the managers are making a causal statement. Are these statements valid, however? We cannot answer, because we do not have enough information about each situation. The brand manager has observed that sales increased after the change in the advertising campaign. Similarly, the sales manager has observed lower sales force turnover after the change in the sales training program. However, the fundamental question that should be asked in the presence of all causal statements has been neither asked nor answered: *"Are there some other possible factors that could have caused the changes you observed?"*

Our brand manager's increase in sales could have been caused by the increased product penetration in the distribution channel, a strike at a competitor's plant, a new package design, a decrease in price, etc. The decrease in sales force turnover that the sales manager boasted about could have been caused by a new quota payment system, a change in the type of people hired by the company, the fact that poor economic conditions have made job opportunities at other companies scarce, etc. Clearly, marketing managers and researchers must be able to know the conditions where proper causal statements may be applied. Also, it is the nature of marketing decision making that all the conditions allowing the most accurate causal statements are usually not present. In these circumstances, causal inference will still be made by marketing managers. In doing so, they should clearly understand the risk of error they are taking. This error possibility should be explicitly considered and not just ignored. The information in this chapter provides the framework for understanding the conditions necessary to make causal inferences.

The Necessary Conditions for Causality

Before outlining the conditions that allow causal statements to be made, we must first develop a more formal understanding of the concept of causality. The scientific concept of causality is complex and differs substantially from the one held by the average person-on-the-street. Selltiz et al.[1] identify some differences between the scientific and so-called "common-sense" concept of causality. The common-sense view holds that a single event (the "cause") always results in another event (the "effect") occurring. In science, we recognize that an event has a number of determining conditions or causes which act together to make the effect probable. Note that in the common-sense notion of causality, the effect always follows the cause. We refer to this as *deterministic causation*. In contrast, the scientific notion specifies the effect only as being probable. This is called *probabilistic causation*. The common-sense notion talks of proving that X causes Y; the scientific notion holds that we can only infer causality and never really prove it. This inference comes from analyzing data that we have generated. The chance of an incorrect inference is always thought to exist.

The world of marketing fits the scientific view of causality. Marketing effects are probabilistically caused by multiple factors, and we can only *infer* a causal relationship—we can never really prove it definitively. We must always live with the possibility that we have not identified the true causal relationship.

We now examine the conditions under which we can make causal inferences. These are (1) concomitant variation, (2) time order of occurrence of variables, and (3) elimination of other possible causal factors.

Concomitant Variation　Concomitant variation is the extent to which a cause, X, and an effect, Y, occur together or vary together in the way predicted by the hypothesis under consideration. Consider the example of a marketer of small foreign cars. This company has undertaken a new advertising campaign "to improve the attitudes people have towards our cars and therefore to increase sales." Suppose that in testing the results of this campaign they find that both aims have been achieved—attitudes have

---

[1] This section follows an excellent discussion in Claire Selltiz, Marie Jahoda, Morton Deutsch, and Stuart W. Cook, *Research Methods in Social Relations*, rev. ed. (New York Holt, 1959), pp. 80–88.

become more positive, and sales have increased. We can then say that there is concomitant variation between attitudes and sales. Note that the implied hypothesis here is that "improved attitudes cause sales to increase."

We can now conclude that the hypothesis of a causal relationship between attitudes and sales is tenable. However, it is not yet proved. There are other possible explanations of the observed relationship that are equally tenable. Two examples follow: (1) The increase in sales has resulted in more people becoming more experienced with these cars, which may have resulted in the observed improvement in attitudes. That is, the increase in sales has caused the attitude change. (2) Some other variables may have caused the observed relationship. For example, the company may have improved the quality of their cars during the period in question. Clearly, we must go beyond concomitant variation before making valid causal inferences.

Time Occurrence of Variables   The hypothesis that improved attitudes cause increases in sales can be examined further by collecting data about attitudes from people at various times in their purchase process, specifically (1) before exposure to the advertising campaign, (2) after exposure but before car purchase, and (3) after both exposure and car purchase. If attitudes improved only after exposure to the campaign but prior to car purchase, we would have more evidence that the hypothesis is tenable. If, however, attitudes improved only after car purchase, the hypothesis would be untenable. That sales increases caused improved attitudes would be a more tenable hypothesis in this situation.

The general statement of this very intuitive concept is that one event cannot cause another if it occurs after the other event. *The causing event must occur either before or simultaneously with the effect.*

There is one complication in this seemingly straightforward concept, namely, that it is possible for two events to be both a cause and an effect of each other. In our example, improved attitudes may cause increases in sales, *and* increased sales may cause improved attitudes. Thus, the relationship between attitudes and sales could be that of alternately "feeding" on each other. This type of relationship would be demonstrated in a purchase decision study if attitudes improved both before and after the increase in sales occurred.

If we now had demonstrated concomitant variation and proper time occurrence of variables, we would still be left with the fundamental question of causality noted earlier: "Are there some other factors that could have caused the observed relationship between X and Y?"

Elimination of Other Possible Causal Factors   Consider the case of a slightly mixed-up scientist who formulated the hypothesis that soda water caused intoxication. To test this hypothesis a randomly selected group of animals were given soda water mixed with scotch, rye, bourbon, and vodka. Intoxication was observed in each case. The scientist then reasoned: "I have observed concomitant variation between soda consumption and intoxication. Also, the proper time order of events to infer causality is present. My hypothesis is, therefore, correct." Well, we all know that another factor, the presence of alcohol, is the true cause of what he observed. The scientist had not searched for other possible causes. Also, the research design used did not allow for the identification of the true causal relationship. This ability of research design to assist in making proper causal inferences is the subject of the next section of this chapter. First, however, we should note that the brand manager and sales manager who made the causal statements we examined early in this chapter were making exactly the same type of causal statement as our mixed-up scientist; they were no less mixed-up than he.

EXPERIMENTATION

The Use of Experiments in Marketing

The fundamental research tool used to help identify causal relationships is the experiment. The objective of an experiment is to measure the effect of explanatory variables or independent variables on a dependent variable, while controlling for other variables that might confuse one's ability to make causal inferences.

As recently as 20 years ago experimental research was little used in marketing research, but this is no longer the case. Experimentation has been used successfully to reach conclusive answers to such questions as:

1 Can we increase profits by servicing small accounts by mail rather than from branch stores?

2 Can we increase supermarket sales of our product by obtaining additional shelf space?

3 Will the addition of stannous fluoride to our toothpaste reduce users' cavities?

4 Does the number of times that a salesperson calls on a particular account in a given time period affect the size of the order obtained from that account?

5 Is a given newspaper advertisement more effective in color than in black and white?

6 Which of several promotional techniques is most effective in selling a particular product?

7 Is it necessary for an advertisement to change the attitude of subjects in order to cause them to use more of the product?[2]

This list could be extended indefinitely, for experimental procedures are useful across the whole domain of marketing decision making. As Cox and Enis note:

The usefulness of experimental design in marketing extends across the functional areas of promotion, distribution, pricing and product policies. Wherever marketing management is interested in measuring the effects of alternative courses of action, experimentation may be a practical means of reducing the risk involved in deciding among the alternatives?[3]

Some Definitions and Concepts

To understand experimentation properly, we must first learn some basic definitions and concepts.

Experiment   An experiment is executed when one or more independent variables are consciously manipulated or controlled by the person running the experiment, and their effect on the dependent variable or variables is measured.

---

[2] These examples are from Keith K. Cox and Ben M. Enis, *Experimentation for Marketing Decisions* (Scranton, Pa.: International Textbook Company, 1969), p. 4.

[3] Ibid., p. 5.

In surveys and observational studies there is no manipulation of independent variables by the researchers. This is the fundamental difference between experimental and nonexperimental research. In searching for causal relationships in nonexperimental situations the researcher must proceed ex post facto—that is, observe the effect and then search for a cause. In these circumstances we can never completely be sure of the proper time order of occurrence of variables and the effects of other possible independent variables that have been excluded from consideration. The superiority of experiments in this regard is absolute.

Treatments Treatments are the alternatives or independent variables that are manipulated and whose effects are measured. Examples in marketing include product composition, advertising executions, price levels, etc. In a measurement sense, treatments need only form a nominal scale.

Test Units The test units are the entities to whom the treatments are presented and whose response to the treatments is measured. It is common in marketing for both people and physical entities, such as stores or geographic areas, to be used as test units. For example, people may be asked to try a product and then have their attitudes toward it measured. Here people are the test units. Alternatively, different end-aisle displays may be set up in supermarkets and sales levels measured. Here, supermarkets are the test units.

Dependent Variables These are the measures taken on the test units. Typical marketing examples include sales, preference, awareness, etc. In a measurement sense the dependent variables must form an interval scale.

Extraneous Variables These are all the variables other than the treatments that affect the response of the test units to the treatments. These variables can distort the dependent variable measures in such a way as to weaken or invalidate one's ability to make causal inferences. For example, a book publisher attempting to measure the response of buyers to two different cover designs would want to keep other aspects of the book the same for each buyer group. If the publisher allowed the extraneous variable, price, to vary between buyer groups, she could not be sure that she was measuring the effect of the cover. The price change would thus "confound" the experiment.

The researcher has three possible courses of action with respect to extraneous variables. First, you may physically control the variable. In our book example, we could hold constant the price of the book. Second, if physical control is not possible, you may randomize the assignment of treatments to test units. Our book publisher could randomly assign different prices to all buyers. In experiments with human test units, this usually takes the form of randomly assigning the test units to the different treatments. In this way it is hoped that an extraneous factor (such as IQ or age) is equally represented in each treatment group. Obviously we would prefer physical control, but unfortunately in marketing applications we must often rely on randomization.

A third way to control the effects of extraneous variables is through the use of specific experimental designs that accomplish this purpose. Much of the rest of this chapter discusses how specific designs can accomplish this task.

If physical control, randomization, and design features do not eliminate the differential effects of extraneous variables among treatment groups, the experiment is confounded, and no causal statements are possible. We call such an extraneous variable a *confounding variable*. For example, suppose we are using two cities as our test units, and it rains in one city and not the other. If rain affects the dependent variable (say, the number of car washes), our experiment is confounded, and rain is the confounding variable.

Actually we still have one line of defense against the confounding variable. We may statistically control the effects of this variable on the dependent variable with a technique called *analysis of covariance* (ANCOVA), which is discussed in Chapter 20. To make use of ANCOVA we must be aware of the confounding variable and be able to measure it. Therefore, the kind of extraneous variable that we are most worried about in experimentation is the one that operates differentially among treatment groups and is unknown to the experimenter.

Experimental Design An experimental design involves the specification of (1) treatments that are to be manipulated, (2) test units to be used, (3) dependent variables to be measured, and (4) procedures for dealing with extraneous variables.

Validity in Experimentation[4]

Two concepts of validity are relevant in experimentation, internal validity and external validity.

Internal Validity Internal validity is the basic minimum that must be present in an experiment before any conclusion about treatment effects can be made. It is concerned with the question of whether the observed effects on the test units could have been caused by variables other than the treatment. Without internal validity the experiment is confounded.

External Validity External validity is concerned with the "generalizability" of experimental results. To what populations, geographic areas, treatment variables, and measurement variables can the measured effects be projected?

The researcher, obviously, would like an experimental design to be strong in both kinds of validity. Unfortunately, it is sometimes necessary to trade off one type of validity for another. For example, in order to remove the effects of an extraneous variable, we may create a very artificial environment for an experiment. In doing this, we may have decreased the generalizability of the results to more realistic environments. For example, an advertiser may ask respondents to view advertisements in a

---

[4] This section follows the now classic presentation of this material in Donald T. Campbell and Julian C. Stanley, *Experimental and Quasi-Experimental Design for Research* (Chicago: Rand McNally, 1966), pp. 5–6.

trailer. Can the effects that are measured in this environment be generalized to a home viewing environment?

Symbols Defined

To facilitate our discussion of specific experimental designs, we will make use of a set of symbols that are now almost universally used in marketing research.[5]

X Represents the exposure of a test group to an experimental treatment, the effects of which are to be determined.

O Refers to processes of observation or measurement of the dependent variable on the test units

R Indicates that individuals have been assigned at random to separate treatment groups or that groups themselves have been allocated at random to separate treatments

- Movement from left to right indicates movement through time.
- All symbols in any one row refer to a specific treatment group.
- Symbols that are vertical to one another refer to activities or events that occur simultaneously.

A few examples should make this symbolic scheme clear. The symbols

$$O_1 X_1 O_2$$

indicate that one group received a measurement of the dependent variable both prior to (O_1) and after (O_2) the presentation of the treatment (X_1). Further the symbols

$$RX_1 O_1$$
$$RX_2 O_2$$

indicate that two groups of subjects were randomly assigned to two different treatment groups at the same time. Further, the groups received different experimental treatments at the same time, and the dependent variable were measured in the two groups at the same time.

Types of Extraneous Variables

Previously, we discussed the need for controlling extraneous variables in order to ensure that the experiment has not been confounded. That is, we want to be assured that the experiment is internally valid. In this section we shall classify these extraneous variables using the scheme suggested by Campbell and Stanley.[6]

History   History refers to the occurrence of specific events that are external to the experiment but occur at the same time as the experiment. These events may affect

---

[5] These symbols are from ibid., p. 6. The specific definitions used are adopted from Seymour Banks, *Experimentation in Marketing* (New York: McGraw-Hill, 1965), pp. 25–26.
[6] Campbell and Stanley, op. cit., p. 5.

the dependent variable. For example, consider the design

$$O_1 \quad X_1 \quad O_2$$

where O_1 and O_2 are measures of the dollar sales of sales personnel and X_1 represents a new sales training program. The difference $O_2 - O_1$ is the measurement of the treatment effect. However, the new sales training program is not the only possible explanation of a positive difference $O_2 - O_1$; an improvement in general business conditions between O_1 and O_2 is as plausible a hypothesis for explaining the observed increase in sales as is the new training program. The greater the length of time between observations, the greater the chance of history confounding an experiment of this type. What we need is a procedure to control the effects of history.

Maturation   Maturation is similar to history except that it is concerned with changes in the experimental units themselves that occur with the passage of time. Examples would include getting older, growing hungrier, and growing more tired. In our sales training design, sales may have increased because the sales force has become somewhat older and more experienced. Clearly, people change over time. However, so do stores, geographic regions, and organizations. The longer the time between O_1 and O_2 the greater the chance of maturation effects.

Testing   Testing is concerned with the possible effects on the experiment of taking a measure on the dependent variable before presentation of the treatment. There are two kinds of testing effects. The first could be called the *direct* or *main testing effect,* and it occurs when the first observation affects the second observation. For example, consider the case of respondents who have completed a pretreatment questionnaire. If they are asked to complete the same questionnaire after exposure to the treatment, they may respond differently just because they are now "experts" with that questionnaire. The internal validity of the experiment is then compromised.

The second testing effect affects external validity but is important enough to mention here. It is called the *reactive* or *interactive testing effect.* This is the situation where the test unit's pretreatment measurement affects the reaction to the treatment. For example, a pretreatment questionnaire that asks questions about shampoo brands may sensitize the respondent to the shampoo market and distort the awareness levels of a new introduction (the treatment). The measured effects are then not really generalizable to nonsensitized persons.

Instrumentation   Instrumentation refers to changes in the calibration of the measuring intrument used or changes in the observers or scorers used. In the sales training study mentioned previously, the dependent variable, sales, was measured in dollars. If there had been a price increase in the company's products between O_1 and O_2, the difference $O_2 - O_1$ could be explained by this change in instrumentation.

An interviewer presenting the pre- and posttreatment questionnaires in different fashions could also cause an intrumentation effect. Similarly, a difference in the presentation of the treatment itself to different test units could cause this effect.

Statistical Regression   Statistical-regression effects occur where test units have been selected for exposure to the treatment on the basis of an extreme pretreatment score. The effect is that such "outliers" tend to move toward a more average position with the passage of time. Suppose that in the sales training example above only poorly performing salespersons had been given the new training program. Subsequent sales increases might be attributed to the regression effect. This is because random occurrences such as weather, family problems, or luck helped define good and poor performance of salespersons in the pretreatment measurement. These same random occurrences will make some of the poor performers better performers in the next year, thus confounding the experiment.

Selection Bias   Selection bias refers to the assigning of test units to treatment groups in such a way that the groups differ on the dependent variable prior to the presentation of the treatments. If test units self-select their own groups or are assigned to groups on the basis of researcher judgment, the possibility of selection bias exists. Test units should be randomly assigned to treatment groups.

Test Unit Mortality   Test unit mortality refers to test units withdrawing from the experiment while it is in progress. What can we conclude if a number of salespersons quit the company between X_1 and O_2? It is possible that those who were not improving quit, or that just the opposite happened.

All these types of extraneous variables constitute alternative explanations of what is observed in an experiment. They are the rivals of the hypothesis that the researcher is testing. One objective of our research designs should be to eliminate the possibility of these effects confounding our results.

Three Preexperimental Designs

What follows is an examination of three preexperimental designs. They are considered preexperimental because inherent weaknesses in the designs make internal validity very questionable. This will highlight the sources of invalidity that may arise in non-true experiments.

The One-Shot Case Study   This design is presented symbolically as:

$$X \quad O$$

In words, a single group of test units is first exposed to a treatment X, and then a measurement is taken on the dependent variables. Note that the symbol R does not appear in the design, so there was no random assignment of test units to the treatment group. The test units were self-selected or arbitrarily selected by the experimenter.

An example of this design might be as follows. A sales manager requests volunteers to take part in a new sales training program, and a measure of their sales performance is taken some time after the training program is completed. The impossibility of drawing meaningful conclusions from such a design should be apparent. The level of O is the result of many uncontrolled factors, and it cannot be deemed to be good or bad in the absence of a pretreatment observation of sales performance. Thus history, maturation, selection, and mortality problems all serve to render this design internally invalid.

The One-Group Pretest-Posttest Design   This design is presented symbolically as

$$O_1 \quad X \quad O_2$$

Here, for example, we have added a pretest measurement of sales performance to the one-short case study design. If we then took the difference between O_2 and O_1 as our measure of experimental effect, would we have a valid measure of the effect of the sales training program? Clearly a number of extraneous variables could explain the difference $O_2 - O_1$, rendering this design useless for reaching conclusive answers.

Specifically, (1) the economic situation could have changed (history), (2) the salespersons could have matured (maturation), (3) the premeasure could have affected performance (testing), (4) prices of goods sold could have changed (instrumentation), (5) the test units could have been self-selected (selection), (6) some test units could have dropped out, with an unknown result on O_2 (mortality), and (7) test units could have selected themselves on the basis of the bad year they had just experienced, and they could have a better subsequent year just because of luck (regression). Even if this design had been

$$R \quad O_1 \quad X \quad O_2$$

all sources of invalidity except selection would still apply.

This latter design is the one used by the mixed-up scientist doing the experiment with soda water. He had not controlled for the extraneous variable, intake of alcohol (history).

The Static-Group Comparison   The static-group comparison design uses two treatment groups, one that has been exposed to the treatment and one that has not. Both groups are observed only after the treatment has been presented, and test units are not randomly assigned to the groups. Symbolically, this design is

$$\begin{array}{lll} \text{Group 1:} & X & O_1 \\ \text{Group 2:} & & O_2 \end{array}$$

Group 2 is called a control group because it has not received the treatment and so may serve as the baseline for comparison. In marketing we often define the control group treatment as the current level of marketing activity. This design would then be presented symbolically as

$$\begin{array}{lll} \text{Experimental group:} & X_1 & O_1 \\ \text{Control group:} & X_2 & O_2 \end{array}$$

where X_2 is the baseline marketing program that we wish to compare X_1 with. For example, in trying out the new sales training program on some salespersons, the sales manager would not be likely to drop all sales training for the other salespersons. The manager is interested in comparing one program with another, so the old program is the control group treatment.

The overwhelming source of invalidity in this design is selection. Test units have not been randomly assigned to treatment groups; therefore, the groups may differ on the dependent variable prior to the presentation of the treatment. The experimental result $O_1 - O_2$ could clearly be attributed to this pretest difference caused by selection procedures. Differential test unit mortality is also possible because of the nature of the treatment. More experimental-group test units may have withdrawn because of the offensive nature of the new sales training program, for example.

Three True Experimental Designs

A true experimental design is one where the researcher is able to eliminate all extraneous variables as competitive hypotheses to the treatment. Three true experimental designs follow.

The Pretest-Posttest Control Group Design   This design is presented symbolically as

$$
\begin{array}{lccccc}
\text{Experimental group:} & R & O_1 & X_1 & O_2 \\
\text{Control group:} & R & O_3 & & O_4
\end{array}
$$

where X_1 is the treatment of interest. Again the control group could have a baseline treatment applied to it. The random assignment of test units to the treatment groups eliminates selection bias as a potential confounding variable.

The premise here is that all extraneous variables operate equally on both the experimental and control groups. The only difference between the groups is the presentation of the treatment to the experimental group. Therefore, the difference $O_2 - O_1$ is the sum of the treatment effect plus the effects of the extraneous variables, whereas the difference $O_4 - O_3$ is the sum of the extraneous variables only. In symbols:

$$O_2 - O_1 = TE + H + M + T + I + R + TM \tag{12-1}$$
$$O_4 - O_3 = H + M + T + I + R + TM \tag{12-2}$$

where TE = treatment effect, H = history, M = maturation, T = testing, I = instrumentation, R = regression, and TM = test unit mortality.

If we subtract Equation 12-2 from 12-1, we find that

$$(O_2 - O_1) - (O_4 - O_3) = TE$$

the true treatment effect we sought. So we have found a way to identify the effect of an independent variable. All potential destroyers of internal validity are controlled by this design. Note the fundamental principle of experimental design that is operative here: The experimenter does not care what extraneous variables are operative *as long as they operate equally on all treatment and control groups.* Even with a control group design, the experiment is confounded if an extraneous variable operates differentially among treatment and control groups. The assumption must be that they operate equally.

A major difficulty with this design is the effect of the pretest measurement on the test units' reaction to the treatment (the interactive testing effect). Since this is a potential confounder of external validity, in the experimental group we must add another variable to the equation explaining the difference $O_2 - O_1$. This variable is *IT*, the interactive testing effect. If we also define *EXT* as the symbol indicating the sum of all other extraneous variables, then:

$$O_2 - O_1 = TE + EXT + IT$$
$$O_4 - O_3 = \qquad EXT$$

therefore

$$(O_2 - O_1) - (O_4 - O_3) = TE + IT$$

That is, we cannot separate the interactive testing effect from the treatment effect. We must always have some doubt about the generalizability of our treatment.

If the scientist doing the experiment with soda water had used this design, he would not have concluded that soda water causes intoxication, because the control group would have consumed the alcohol without the soda water. Clearly, their level of intoxication would have equaled that of the experimental group. The possibility of the interactive testing effect occurring here is quite small. We should be able to measure pretest levels of intoxication in animals without sensitizing them to the coming treatment. Other researchers may not be quite so fortunate, however. A shampoo marketer using this design to measure the effect of a new advertising campaign may generate an interactive testing effect. Specifically, the pretest may sensitize test units in the experimental group to advertisements in the shampoo product category, and the resultant posttest levels of advertising awareness would not be generalizable to a nonsensitized population. In this case, the researcher would look to other designs that control for this effect.

The Solomon Four-Group Design This design controls for all extraneous variable effects on internal validity, plus the interactive testing effect. Symbolically:

Experimental group 1:	R	O_1	X	O_2
Control group 1:	R	O_3		O_4
Experimental group 2:	R		X	O_5
Control group 2:	R			O_6

What we have done here is add another experimental group and another control group to the previous design. This second experimental group receives no pretest but otherwise is identical to the first experimental group. The second control group receives only a posttest measurement. What effects do the differences between the various pre- and post- measures give us?

Experimental group 1: $O_2 - O_1 = TE + EXT + IT$ (12-3)

Control group 1: $O_4 - O_3 = \quad\quad EXT$ (12-4)

Experimental group 2: $O_5 - O_1 = TE + EXT$ (12-5)

$O_5 - O_3 = TE + EXT$ (12-6)

Control group 2: $O_6 - O_1 = \quad\quad EXT$ (12-7)

$O_6 - O_3 = \quad\quad EXT$ (12-8)

Equations 12-5 and 12-6 are usually averaged to give

$$O_5 - \frac{O_1 + O_3}{2} = TE + EXT \tag{12-9}$$

Also, Equations 12-7 and 12-8 are averaged to give

$$O_6 - \frac{O_1 + O_3}{2} = EXT \tag{12-10}$$

The experimental treatment effect is then obtained by subtracting Equation 12-10 from 12-9. Thus,

$$\left(O_5 - \frac{O_1 + O_3}{2}\right) - \left(O_6 - \frac{O_1 + O_3}{2}\right) = TE + EXT - EXT = TE$$

which is the desired result.

This design also gives us a direct measure of the effect of extraneous variables, *EXT*, and allows us to calculate the interactive testing effect, *IT*. This effect is obtained by subtracting Equation 12-9 from Equation 12-3:

$$(O_2 - O_1) - \left(O_5 - \frac{O_1 + O_3}{2}\right) = TE + EXT + IT - TE - EXT = IT$$

i.e., the interactive testing effect.

We have now not only controlled all extraneous variables and the interactive testing effect, but we have also succeeded in measuring their effects. Unfortunately, these benefits come at the expense of increases in the time, cost, and effort needed to conduct the experiment, and consequently this design is little used in marketing practice. However, it does serve as a standard against which to compare other designs. What we would like is a smaller design that controls extraneous variables and the interactive testing effect. Such a design is the posttest-only control group design.

Posttest-Only Control Group Design This design is written as:

Experimental group: R X O_1
Control group: R O_2

It is essentially the last two groups of the Solomon four-group design. Here the O_1 and O_2 measurements are composed of the following parts:

$$O_1 = TE + EXT$$
$$O_2 =\quad EXT$$

Therefore

$$O_1 - O_2 = TE + EXT - EXT = TE$$

i.e., the treatment effect.

Since there is no pretest in this design, the interactive testing effect cannot occur. Also, the extraneous variables have been controlled, and we have a nonconfounded measure of the treatment effect. But wait: suppose the pretreatment measures on the dependent variable were different between the experimental and control group? Would not this confound the experiment? Indeed, it would. What we must assume is that the random assignment of test units to the groups has resulted in the groups being approximately equal on the dependent variable prior to the presentation of the treatment to the experimental group. We also must assume that test unit mortality affects each group in the same way. With large enough samples and proper randomization these assumptions are not unreasonable, a fact which, when combined with the reactive nature of a great deal of marketing research, helps explain why this design is probably the one used most often in marketing practice. The soda-testing scientist, the sales manager, and the shampoo manufacturer could all use this design to obtain a nonconfounded measure of their treatment effect.

QUASI EXPERIMENTATION

In designing a true experiment, the researcher often creates artificial environments in order to have control over independent and extraneous variables. As a result, serious questions are raised about the external validity of the experimental findings. One response to this problem has been the development and use of quasi-experimental designs.

A quasi-experimental design is one where the researcher has control over data collection procedures (i.e., the "when" and "to whom" of measurement) but lacks complete control over the scheduling of the treatments (i.e., the "when" and "to whom" of exposure) and also lacks the ability to randomize test units' exposure to treatments.[7]

[7] This definition and section draw heavily on Campbell and Stanley, op. cit., pp. 34–64; Banks, op. cit., pp. 37–45; and James Caporaso, "Quasi-Experimental Approaches to Social Science: Perspectives and Problems," in James A. Caporaso and Leslie L. Roos, Jr. (eds.), *Quasi-Experimental Approaches: Testing Theory and Evaluating Policy* (Evanston, Ill.: Northwestern University Press, 1973), pp. 3–38.

With loss of control of test unit assignments and treatment manipulations, the possibility of obtaining confounded results is great. The researcher must then be aware of what specific variables are not controlled. An attempt must be made to incorporate the possible effects of these uncontrolled variables into the interpretation of the findings. We now turn to an examination of selected quasi-experimental designs.[8]

Specific Designs

Time-Series Experiment   A time-series experiment may be presented symbolically as:

$$O_1 \quad O_2 \quad O_3 \quad O_4 \quad X \quad O_5 \quad O_6 \quad O_7 \quad O_8$$

The essence of this design is the undertaking of a periodic measurement on the dependent variables for some test units. The treatment is then introduced, or occurs naturally, and the periodic measurements are continued on the same test units in order to monitor the effects of the treatment.

Note how this design conforms to our definition of a quasi experiment. The researcher does have control over *when* measurements are taken and *on whom* they are taken. However, there is no randomization of test units to treatments, and the timing of treatment presentation, as well as exactly which test units are exposed to the treatment, may not be within the researcher's control. A common example of this type of design in marketing involves the use of consumer purchase panels. These panels provide periodic measures on their purchase activity (the O's). A marketer may undertake a new advertising campaign (the X) and examine the panel data to look for the effect. Here, the marketer has control over the timing of the advertising campaign but cannot be sure when the panel members were exposed to the campaign, or even whether they were exposed at all. Also, other consumers outside the panel would be exposed to the campaign. Attempting to make causal inferences from this type of situation is common in marketing.

This design is, of course, very similar to the preexperimental one-group pretest-posttest design, $O_1 \quad X \quad O_2$. Does not the time-series design suffer from all the same problems? The answer is no; the fact that we have taken many pretest and posttest measurements provides more control over extraneous variables. To illustrate this increase in control, let's examine some possible results of this type of design (see Figure 12-1). Assume that X represents a change in advertising campaign, and the O's represent the market share of the product in question. The following conclusions about the advertising campaign seem reasonable:

1 In situation A, the campaign has had both a short-run and a long-run positive effect.

2 In situation B, the campaign has had a short-run positive effect.

[8] Only a few simple possible quasi-experimental designs are discussed here. For other useful designs see Campbell and Stanley, op. cit., pp. 34–64; Banks, op. cit., pp. 37–45; and Caporaso and Roos, op. cit., pp. 11–31.

FIGURE 12-1 Some possible results of a time-series experiment. [*Adapted from Donald T. Campbell and Julian C. Stanley, Experimental and QuasiExperimental Design for Research (Chicago: Rand McNally, 1966), p. 38.*]

3 In situation C, the campaign may have had a longer-term effect. Since the reaction was delayed for a period, we cannot be as sure as we were in A and B.

4 In situations D, E, and F, the changes that occur after X are consistent with the pattern prior to X. Therefore, we cannot infer that the advertising campaign had an effect.

Note that the one-group pretest-posttest design would have measured only O_4 and O_5. With these measures only, we could easily infer an effect of the campaign, $O_5 - O_4$, in situations D, E, and F; we could also miss the effect in C and the nature of the effects in A and B.

The multiple observations in this design also provide additional control of extraneous variables. For example, the maturation effect on $O_5 - O_4$ can be ruled out as a cause, because this effect would also show up in other observations. It would not affect the O_4 to O_5 period alone. By similar reasoning, main testing, instrumentation, and statistical regression effects can be ruled out. If we then randomly or with good judgment select our test units and take strong measures to prevent test unit mortality (i.e., panel members dropping out), we can at least partially rule out the effects of selection bias and test unit mortality.

The fundamental weakness of this design is the experimenter's inability to control history. But all is not lost; the experimenter could maintain a careful log of all possible relevant external happenings that could have an effect. If this process failed to turn up any unusual competitive activity, economic changes, etc., the experimenter might reasonably conclude that the treatment has had an effect.

The other weakness of this design is the possibility of an interactive testing effect from the repeated measurements being made on test units. For example, panel members may become "expert" shoppers, thus making generalizations to other populations more difficult. This design is used a great deal, and it can provide meaningful information if used carefully.

Multiple Time-Series Design   In some studies utilizing the time-series design, it may be possible to find another group of test units to act as a control group. For example, an advertiser may try out a new campaign in a few cities only. Panel members in these cities would constitute the experimental group, while members from other cities would constitute a control group. In symbols, this design is:

Experimental group: O O O X O O O
Control group: O O O O O O

If the researcher is very careful in selecting the control group, this design can add more certainty to the interpretation of the treatment effect than is obtainable with the straight time-series experiment. This is so because the treatment effect is tested both in its own group and against the control group. The main problem with this design lies in the possibility of an interactive effect in the experimental group.

Equivalent Time-Sample Design   An alternative to finding a control group is to use the experimental group itself as its own control. In symbols this design might be:

$$O \quad X_1 \quad O \quad X_0 \quad OOO \quad X_1 \quad OO \quad X_0 \quad O$$

where X_1 is the experimental treatment and X_0 is the absence of the treatment. Here the treatment is repeatedly presented, measurements are repeatedly taken, and periods of treatment absence are spaced between. This design is best utilized when the effect of the treatment is transient or reversible.

An example of its use would be the testing of the effect of in-store conditions, such as music, on total purchases per customer.[9] Here we could use a single store, whose customers make up the test units, and utilize equivalent sets of days with and without music over a period of many months.

The biggest problem with this design is the possibility of the interactive testing effect occurring. It is basically a reactive design because of all the measurements taken, and therefore it is best used where the repeated measurements are nonreactive. In situations

[9] Adapted from Banks, op. cit., p. 39.

like the store example, we are able to measure per-customer sales without sensitizing customers to the treatment. If we did repeated interviewing of customers about in-store music, sensitization would no doubt be a problem.

Nonequivalent Control Group Design   This is the last quasi-experimental design to be examined in this chapter. Here, the experimental group and the control group are both given pretest and posttest measurements, but the two groups do not have pre-experimental test unit selection equivalence. Symbolically, this design is:

$$
\begin{array}{lccc}
\text{Experimental group:} & O_1 & X & O_2 \\
\text{Control group:} & O_3 & & O_4
\end{array}
$$

This is a quasi-experimental design because the groups were not created by the random assignment of test units from a single population. However, the existence of even a nonequivalent control group improves the ability of the researcher to interpret results in comparison with the one-group pretest-posttest design discussed previously. In this design the researcher has control over who is exposed to the treatment. Clearly, the more similar the experimental and control groups are in composition, and the closer the pretest measurements, the more useful the control group becomes. If these criteria are met, this design can effectively control the effects of history, maturation, main testing, instrumentation, selection, and test unit mortality. Regression may provide one major source of problems in this design, that is, if either group has been selected on the basis of extreme scores. In such cases some of the differences in pretest and posttest measures may result from regression effects. Care must be taken to avoid this problem. The possibility of an interactive testing effect is also present in this design.

MANAGERIAL ASPECTS OF EXPERIMENTATION AND QUASI EXPERIMENTATION

In this section, we shall discuss the types of issues that are important to managers in the use of experimental and quasi-experimental designs.

Comparison with Other Procedures

There are many procedures for collecting data in marketing research—for example, the use of secondary data, observation, survey, and simulation. They can all provide useful information for marketing decision making. However, since they are basically descriptive techniques, none of these procedures allows for the identification of causal relationships. Only experimental and quasi-experimental designs can identify such relationships; the other procedures can only find correlation. The cause and effect cannot be separated. Yet all too often descriptive studies are used to argue causal relationships. For example, the National Tourism Council does a survey. In this survey, the respondents are measured on what is assumed to be an effect variable, say, the amount of money spent on vacations in Georgia. Then, in the same survey, the respondents are measured on a series of hypothesized causal variables. If one of these "causal" variables, say, awareness of Georgia tourism advertisements, is found to be correlated with the effect, the advertising is assumed to have caused dollars to be spent on tourism in Georgia. Clearly, this is ex post facto reasoning. What is observed is concomitant variation only. The time order of the two variables is not establised, nor have other possible variables been eliminated. Only experimentation and quasi experimentation can do this.

This does not mean that a correct causal relationship cannot be established in descriptive studies, for the researcher may be absolutely correct with a causal guess. The point is that we can never be sure. Descriptive studies are the most frequently used type of study in marketing research practice, and they will continue to be used to state causal relationships. Constraints of time, money, and so on may make this the only type of study available to a manager. In using them for causal purposes the manager should be aware of the risk of error that is being taken.

Laboratory versus Field Environments

There are two types of environments in which an experiment may be conducted. The first is a laboratory environment, that is, one where the experimenter conducts the experiment in an artificial environment constructed expressly for the purpose of the experiment. The field environment is the alternative. Here, the experiment is conducted in actual market situations, and no attempts are made to change the real-life nature of the environment. An example of a laboratory experiment would be the showing of test commercials to test units in a theater. This same experiment could be conducted in the field by having test commercials run on actual television programs.

Validity   Laboratory environments provide the researcher with maximum control over possible confounding variables. They have higher internal validity. A consequence of the artificial nature of a laboratory, however, is the loss of generalizability to more realistic situations. Thus, they have lower external validity. Experiments conducted in the field have lower internal validity and higher external validity. Often a field experiment provides so little control over extraneous variables that we must be content to conduct a quasi experiment.

Cost   Laboratory experiments are generally less expensive than field experiments. They tend to be smaller in size (i.e., with a smaller number of test units), shorter in duration, more tightly defined geographically, and therefore much easier to administer.

Time   The simpler nature of laboratory experiments also means that they require less time to execute.

The researcher must trade off these factors in selecting an environment for an experiment. Table 12-1 presents a summary of these factors.

Control of Invalidity

In presenting alternative experimental and quasi-experimental designs, we discussed possible sources of invalidity in detail; this section contains a managerial summary of these points. Table 12-2 presents the sources of invalidity of preexperimental and

TABLE 12-1 LABORATORY VERSUS FIELD EXPERIMENTATION

Factor	Laboratory	Field
Internal validity	High	Low
External validity	Low	High
Cost	Low	High
Time	Low	High

TABLE 12-2 SOURCES OF INVALIDITY OF PREEXPERIMENTAL AND EXPERIMENTAL DESIGNS

Design	Source of invalidity							
	Internal							External
	History	Maturation	Testing	Instrumentation	Regression	Selection	Mortality	Interaction of testing and X
Preexperimental designs:								
One-shot case study X O	−	−				−	−	
One-group pretest-posttest design O X O	−	−	−	−	?			−
Static-group comparison X O O	+	?	+	+	+	−	−	
True experimental designs:								
Pretest-posttest control group design R O X O R O O	+	+	+	+	+	+	+	−
Solomon four-group design R O X O R O O R X O R O	+	+	+	+	+	+	+	+
Posttest-only control group design R X O R O	+	+	+	+	+	+	+	+

Adapted from Donald T. Campbell and Julian C. Stanley, *Experimental and Quasi-Experimental Design for Research* (Chicago: Rand McNally, 1966), p. 8.

TABLE 12-3   SOURCES OF INVALIDITY OF QUASI-EXPERIMENTAL DESIGNS

| | Source of invalidity | | | | | | | |
| | Internal | | | | | | | External |
Design	History	Maturation	Testing	Instrument decay	Regression	Selection	Mortality	Interaction of testing and X
Times series O O O X O O O	−	+	+	?	+	+	+	−
Multiple time series O O O X O O O O O O O O O	+	+	+	+	+	+	+	−
Equivalent time sample O X_1O X_0O X_1O	+	+	+	+	+	+	+	−
Nonequivalent control group O X O O O	+	+	+	+	−?	+	+	−

Adapted from Seymour Banks, *Experimentation in Marketing* (New York: McGraw-Hill, 1965), p. 44.

experimental designs, and Table 12-3 presents the same information for quasi-experimental designs. In these tables, a minus sign indicates a definite weakness in that design in controlling the relevant sources of invalidity; a plus sign indicates that the factor is controlled; a question mark indicates a possible source of concern; and a blank indicates that the factor is not relevant. Use these tables only when you are sure that you understand why each design is classified as it is.

Limitations of Experimentation

The manager should recognize the following limitations of experimentation:[10]

1 It is not always possible to control the effects of extraneous variables. Differential effects among treatment groups can easily occur in field experiments.

2 In field experiments, lack of cooperation from wholesalers and retailers can limit experimental activity.

3 Lack of knowledge about experimental procedures on the part of marketing personnel may limit the use of experimentation, and in addition it may lead to experimental conclusions being discarded as not meaningful.

4 Experiments can be costly and time-consuming.

---

[10] Adapted from Cox and Enis, op. cit., pp. 108–109.

5 In using people as test units, care must be taken that the experimenter does not say and do things that bias test unit responses.

Stages in Executing an Experiment

Once the researcher has a firm understanding of procedures alternative to experimentation, has considered what environment might be used, has a good understanding of how to control sources of invalidity, and has recognized the limitations of experimental procedures, he or she is ready to begin the necessary steps for the proper execution of an experiment. These steps are:[11]

1 State the problem.

2 Formulate a hypothesis.

3 Construct an experimental design.

4 Formulate made-up results and check to see that these results are the type required by the problem statement. In other words, be sure that the design answers the question at hand.

5 Check that the types of results that are possible can be analyzed by available statistical procedures. (See Chapter 20.)

6 Perform the experiment.

7 Apply statistical-analysis procedures to the results to see whether effects are real or just error or noise in the experiment.

8 Draw conclusions with concern for both internal and external validity.

Once again the emphasis is on a meaningful statement of a problem and the provision of information relevant to this problem. Then and only then are the technical aspects of design and analysis useful to the marketer.

The Future of Experimentation and Quasi Experimentation

Marketing research textbooks written 25 years ago contained little or no mention of the use of experimental and quasi-experimental procedures in marketing research. This accurately reflected the practice of the day. Since then these procedures have gained substantially in use and are now considered viable alternatives to other types of studies. Cox and Enis[12] identified four reasons why this trend continues:

1 Experimentation works. Meaningful marketing results are generated by the procedures.

2 The costs of making wrong causal inferences in marketing are increasing.

3 Educational levels are rising, with an associated increase in the understanding of these procedures.

4 The capabilities of computerized analysis procedures have eliminated the tedium of hand analysis of results.

The modern marketing manager should understand what can be accomplished by experimental and quasi-experimental designs.

---

[11] Adapted from Oscar Kempthorne, *The Design and Analysis of Experiments* (New York: Wiley, 1952), p. 10.
[12] Cox and Enis, op. cit., pp. 109–110.

FOUR DESIGN PROCEDURES: AN OVERVIEW

We have just examined the design procedures that allow us to make proper causal inferences. Now we address the issue of statistical significance in experimentation. Specifically, we shall describe procedures that allow us to determine when a measured effect is greater than that due to sampling error. We shall do this in the context of some specific design procedures. This section presents only an overview of four experimental design procedures: (1) completely randomized design, (2) randomized block design, (3) Latin square design, and (4) factorial design. The detailed statistical calculations for these procedures are presented in the appendix to Chapter 20 dealing with analysis of variance (ANOVA).

Completely Randomized Design

A completely randomized design is the simplest type of designed experiment. It is useful when the researcher is investigating *the effect of one independent variable*. This independent variable need only be a nominal scale, so that it may have many categories. Each category of the nominal independent variable is a treatment. As an example, suppose that the independent variable of interest is "type of sales training program," and it has three categories:

1 No sales training
2 Head office lectures for sales training
3 On-the-job sales training

So we have one independent variable, type of sales training program, with three categories. Each category represents a treatment, with category 1 representing the control group treatment.

In a completely randomized design the experimental treatments are assigned to test units on a completely random basis. In our sales training example, salespersons would randomly receive the three treatments without any regard for external factors such as their previous experience, age, size of sales territory to which they will be assigned, etc. If sales were our dependent variable, we would then compare the average sales level of each of the three treatment groups to see which treatment was best.

Randomized Block Design

In the completely randomized design, all extraneous variables were assumed to be constant over all treatment groups. But what if this were not true? What if those receiving on-the-job sales training tended to be assigned to larger territories than those in other treatment groups? Would not the results obtained be misleading? Indeed they would. The size-of-territory effect would be obscuring the measurement of the treatment effect. What we would like to do is "block out" this extraneous effect. One procedure for doing this is the randomized block design.

This design is built upon the principle of combining test units into blocks based on some external criterion variable. For example, size of sales territory could be such a criterion variable. These blocks are formed[13] with the anticipation that the test units' scores on the dependent variable within each block will be more homogeneous, in the absence of treatment, than those of test units selected at random from all test units.

For example, let's divide our sales territories into three blocks based upon sales potential as follows:

Block number	Sales potential per year
Block 1	$200,000–$999,999
Block 2	$1,000,000–$1,999,999
Block 3	$2,000,000–$2,999,999

The sales levels we would expect test units to have within these blocks would be more homogeneous than sales levels we would expect if we ignored the blocking and selected test units at random. Note that the assumption here is that the blocking factor, sales potential per year, is correlated with the dependent variable, salesperson sales level. Note also that the blocking is done prior to the presentation of the treatment.

Once the blocks have been established and test units identified by block, we are ready to assign treatments. In this design each treatment must appear at least once in each block. Thus each block must have, at a minimum, a number of test units equal to the number of treatments. In our example, we would need at least three salespersons in each sales potential block, each receiving a different sales training treatment.

The fundamental reason for doing blocking is to allow the researcher to obtain a measure of sampling error smaller than that which would result from a completely randomized design. This occurs because some of the variation in the dependent variable is assigned to the blocking factor, leaving a smaller sampling error.

The parallel between blocking in experimentation and stratification in sampling should be apparent. In both situations, we form subgroups so that *the variable of interest is more homogeneous within the groups than it would be across all groups.* The result of this process is a smaller measure of sampling error.

In the randomized block design the researcher can make use of only one blocking factor. However, we can define the blocking factor by using more than one external variable. For example, in our sales training situation we could have defined our blocking factor using both sales potential in territories and age of salespersons. Assume that the sales potential categories were defined as before and age was categorized as:

Category 1   18–30
Category 2   Over 30

---

[13] Allen L. Edwards, *Experimental Design in Psychological Research,* 3d ed. (New York: Holt, 1968), p. 155.

Then with three sales potential categories and two age categories, we would have a blocking factor composed of $3 \times 2 = 6$ blocks as follows:

Block number	Description
Block 1	$200,000–$999,999 potential and age 18–30
Block 2	$1,000,000–$1,999,999 potential and age 18–30
Block 3	$2,000,000–$2,999,999 potential and age 18–30
Block 4	$200,000–$999,999 potential and age over 30
Block 5	$1,000,000–$1,999,999 potential and age over 30
Block 6	$2,000,000–$2,999,999 potential and age over 30

Note that blocks, like independent variables in experimentation, are nominally scaled.

The number of variables used to create a blocking factor can be extended beyond two. The problem is that the number of blocks required in the blocking factor increases as a multiplicative function of the number of categories in the external variables used. The other problem with blocking by using more than one external variable is that the researcher can measure only the overall effect of the blocking factor. You cannot isolate the separate effects of the variables defining the blocking factor. A possible partial solution to this problem is the Latin square design.

Latin Square Design

In situations where the researcher wishes to control and measure the effects of two extraneous variables, the Latin square design may be used. Table 12-4 illustrates the layout of a Latin square design applied to our sales training example. The rows and columns of Table 12-4 designate the extraneous variables that are to be controlled and measured. In our example, we have identified three categories for the row variable, age of salesperson, and three categories for the column variable, sales potential per year. The three treatments are identified by the letters A, B, and C, where A = no sales training, B = head office lectures for sales training, and C = on-the-job sales training. The number of categories of each variable to be controlled exactly equals the number of treatments. This is a necessary condition for using the Latin square design, and it is the reason why we have three age categories in this situation while there were only

TABLE 12-4   LATIN SQUARE DESIGN FOR SALES TRAINING EXPERIMENT

Age of salespersons	Sales potential per year (in thousands)		
	$200–$999	$1000–$1999	$2000–$2999
18–25	A	B	C
26–30	B	C	A
Over 30	C	A	B

A = no sales training, B = head office lectures, for sales training, and C = on-the-job sales training.

two in the randomized block design discussed previously. Without this condition we would not have a square design. Our example yields a 3×3 Latin square. If we had four treatments, we would have to designate four categories for the row and column variables. This would be a 4×4 Latin square.

Another necessary condition for the use of the Latin square design relates to the way in which the treatments are assigned to cells of the square; they are assigned to cells randomly, subject to the restriction that each treatment occurs once with each blocking situation. Since each row and column category defines a blocking situation, each treatment must appear once in each row and once in each column. The treatments in Table 12-4 conform to this restriction.

Factorial Design

In marketing we are often interested in the *simultaneous effects of two or more independent variables*. The three design procedures discussed so far allow for the use of only one independent variable. If we wish to examine two or more independent variables in an experimental situation, we must use a factorial design. Suppose that, in our sales training example, the interest was in measuring the effects of the sales training procedure and the compensation scheme used. Suppose that there were two categories of compensation schemes to be tested, as follows:

Category number	Compensation type
Category 1	Straight salary
Category 2	Straight commission

So we have two independent variables: (1) type of sales training and (2) compensation scheme. Both form a nominal scale. The first has three categories, the second two. In a factorial design the categories of the independent variables are called *levels*. In the design each level of each independent variable appears with each level of all other independent variables. In our example, we would say that we have a 3×2 factorial design. This design would yield $3 \times 2 = 6$ cells in a design matrix. Table 12-5 shows the layout of our 3×2 factorial experiment. If we were running an experiment with four independent variables, with 2, 3, 3, and 4 levels, respectively, we would have

TABLE 12-5 3×2 FACTORIAL DESIGN FOR SALES TRAINING AND COMPENSATION EXPERIMENT

		B	
		B_1 Straight salary	B_2 Straight commission
A	A_1 No sales training	A_1B_1	A_1B_2
	A_2 Head office lectures	A_2B_1	A_2B_2
	A_3 On-the-job training	A_3B_1	A_3B_2

TABLE 12-6   AN ILLUSTRATION OF MAIN EFFECTS

		Compensation scheme	
		B_1	B_2
Training program	A_1	$200,000	$150,000
	A_2	$190,000	$140,000

$2 \times 3 \times 3 \times 4 = 72$ cells in our design matrix. Obviously, one adds independent variables and levels with great care.

Note that we no longer call the individual independent variable categories "treatments." They are called levels. The treatments are now the various combinations of levels that occur. In Table 12-5 we have six treatments defined by the combinations of training and compensation, $A_1B_2, \ldots, A_3B_2$.

A factorial design allows us to measure the separate effects of each variable working alone. Thus the sales training effect calculated from a factorial design would be exactly the same as that calculated from a completely randomized design, but the factorial design would also give us the individual effect of the compensation schemes. These individual effects of each independent variable are called the *main effects*.

There is one other type of effect that is important in factorial designs. This effect is used to recognize that a number of independent variables working together often have a total effect greater than the straight sum of their main effects. This extra effect is called an *interaction effect*. More formally, interaction occurs when the relationship between an independent variable and the dependent variable is different for different categories of another independent variable. In our example, the relationship between sales level (the dependent variable) and type of sales training program (the first independent variable) may vary depending upon which compensation scheme was used (the second independent variable). If this were so, we would say that the two independent variables, type of training and compensation scheme, interact.

Tables 12-6 and 12-7 illustrate the meaning of main and interaction effects. Table 12-6 presents a simplified version of our sales experiment. Here we have just two training programs, A_1 and A_2, and two compensation schemes, B_1 and B_2. The entries in the cells represent average salesperson sales in thousands of dollars during the experiment. We note that, regardless of the compensation scheme used, training program A_1 yields $10,000 more sales on average than A_2. The main effect of A_1 is then $10,000. Note also that, regardless of the sales training program used, compensation

TABLE 12-7   AN ILLUSTRATION OF INTERACTION EFFECTS

		Compensation scheme	
		B_1	B_2
Training program	A_1	$200,000	$180,000
	A_2	$190,000	$140,000

scheme B_1 yields $50,000 more sales than B_2 on average. The main effect of B_1 is then $50,000. The total effect of treatment A_1B_1 is $10,000 + $50,000 = $60,000.[14] There is no interaction between sales training and compensation.

Table 12-7 presents the same design matrix with different results. Here the effect of the training program depends on the compensation scheme used. Specifically, A_1 is $10,000 better than A_2 when B_1 is used and $40,000 better when B_2 is used. Similarly, B_1 is $20,000 better than B_2 when A_1 is used and $50,000 better when A_2 is used. Here the effect of one independent variable on the dependent variable is different for different levels of the other independent variable. We have interaction. Statistical analysis procedures for factorial experiments can separate both the main effects and the interaction effect.

We should note that the number of interactions rises as the number of independent variables increases. For example, a listing of main and interaction effects for two and three independent variables follows:

Number of independent variables and description	Main effects	Interaction effects
2: *A* and *B*	*A, B*	*AB*
3: *A, B,* and *C*	*A, B, C*	*AB*
		AC
		BC
		ABC

In marketing, interaction among marketing variables is likely to be the rule rather than the exception. The factorial design is thus a very important one given its ability to identify and measure interaction. It may be used in a completely randomized design, with randomized blocks, or with a Latin square. These latter two refinements are beyond the scope of this book.[15] We will examine the statistical analysis of a completely randomized factorial design later in Chapter 20.

A final noteworthy aspect about interaction: The randomized block design assumes that there is no interaction between the blocking factor and the independent variable, and the Latin square design assumes that there is no interaction between the two blocking factors.

Usage in Practice

Almost all real marketing problems involve the need for the control of extraneous variables or the simultaneous application of more than one marketing variable. Thus randomized block, Latin square, and factorial designs are the most used in practice.

Commonly used blocking factors in marketing include store size, days of the week,

---

[14] "Main effect" and "total effect" are used here to illustrate these concepts and are not technically correct in a statistical sense. More formal definitions are presented in Chapter 20.

[15] If interested, consult a book on experimental design—for example, Edwards, op. cit.

time of the year, and geographical regions, all of which often contribute extraneous variation in the dependent variables that interest marketers. For example, you might be interested in measuring the effects of different prices on coffee sales. Suppose that these sales are measured in food stores on each day of the week and in different regions of the country. The actual sales of coffee that we observe might be affected by the different prices plus the different sizes of stores, the day of the week, and the region of the country. What we do is control the effects of these extraneous variables to get a clear measure of the price effect.

SUMMARY

1 Causality may be inferred when concomitant variation, the proper time order of occurrence of variables, and the elimination of other possible causal factors have all occurred.

2 An experiment is executed when one or more independent variables are consciously manipulated and controlled by the person running the experiment, and their effect on the dependent variable is measured.

3 Treatments are the alternatives which are manipulated and whose effects are measured.

4 Test units are the entities to whom the treatments are presented and whose response to the treatments is measured.

5 Dependent variables are the measures taken on the test units.

6 Extraneous variables are all the variables other than the treatments that affect the response of the test units to the treatments. They may be physically controlled, or randomization may be used to obtain control of them.

7 Internal validity is concerned with the question of whether the observed effects could have been caused by variables other than the treatments.

8 External validity is concerned with the generalizability of experimental results.

9 Categories of extraneous variables are history, maturation, testing, instrumentation, statistical regression, selection bias, and test unit mortality.

10 Specific designs differ in their ability to control extraneous variables. These specifics are summarized in Tables 12-2 and 12-3.

11 Experimental and quasi-experimental procedures are the only ones that allow proper causal inferences to be made. All other study types proceed ex post facto.

12 In a completely randomized design, treatments are assigned to test units on a completely random basis.

13 In a randomized block design (RBD), test units are combined into blocks based on some external criterion variable. Treatments are then randomly assigned within blocks of test units.

14 RBD allows the measurement and control of one blocking factor.

15 In a Latin square design (LS), test units are combined into blocks based on two external criterion variables. Treatments are then randomly assigned to blocks subject to the restriction that each treatment occurs once within each blocking situation.

16 LS design allows the measurement and control of two blocking factors.

17 A factorial design allows for the analysis of the main effects of more than one independent variable, plus the effect of the interaction among independent variables.

18 Interaction occurs when the relationship between an independent variable and the dependent variable is different for different categories of another independent variable.

DISCUSSION QUESTIONS

1 What is the fundamental question that should be asked when searching for causality?

2 What are the necessary conditions to infer causality?

3 What is an experiment?

4 How does an experiment differ from surveys or observational studies?

5 What scale of measurement must the independent and dependent variables form in an experiment?

6 How may you control the effects of extraneous variables?

7 What are internal and external validity?

8 Describe seven different types of extraneous variables.

9 What is the interactive testing effect?

10 How can a design described as $R \quad O_1 \quad X \quad O_2$ be confounded?

11 What design could control the confounding variables in question 10?

12 Under what circumstances is it impossible for even the best design to control an extraneous variable?

13 What is a quasi experiment?

14 How does a time-series experiment allow for the control of extraneous variables?

15 Compare laboratory and field experiments.

16 How do you choose between laboratory and field environments?

17 Outline the limitations of experimentation in marketing.

18 What steps should be taken in executing an experiment?

19 What is a CRD (completely randomized design)?

20 How does an RBD (randomized block design) aid the experimenter?

21 Why are LS (Latin square) designs so utilized in marketing field experiments?

22 What is a factorial design?

CASES FOR PART FOUR

CASE 4-1: New England Soup Company

On January 11, 1987, William Kolander, president of the New England Soup Company of Boston, Massachusetts, was reviewing a research report he had received from a Boston-based research house. The report presented the findings of a study on the firm's new formulation of Kolander's Chowder brand of canned soup. The study had also been sent to the firm's sales manager, Kirk George, and the production manager, Edward Corey. A meeting was scheduled for January 12 with the research firm and the New England Soup Company management. The purpose of the meeting was to discuss the research findings and to make decisions concerning Kolander's product offerings.

THE COMPANY

The New England Soup Company was a small firm which produced and distributed a line of specialty canned soup products to both the institutional and retail markets. Approximately 62 percent of their 1986 sales volume went to the institutional market ($68,526), and 38 percent went to the retail market ($42,102).

The company was founded by William Kolander in 1957. Kolander's father was a successful owner of several restaurants in the Boston area which were famous for their chowder soup. The young Kolander convinced his father in 1956 that there was a market to sell the chowder to local institutions (restaurant, hospitals, etc.) in the New England area, and he developed a canned chowder under his father's supervison. Production facilities were acquired in the same year.

After losses in the first few years, the business turned profitable in 1960. At this time, Kolander decided to enter the retail market with Kolander's Chowder brand. Both the institutional and retail business grew rapidly during the 1960s, as did the firm's profitability. Expanded production facilities were built in 1968, and two additional specialty soup lines were introduced in 1970. These lines experienced limited success at retail but were reasonably profitable in the institutional market.

CURRENT SITUATION

The last five years had been a period of level and then declining sales for Kolander's Chowder (1983—6943 cases, 1984—5676 cases, 1985—5105 cases, and 1986[1]—4900 cases). Kolander attributed this decline in sales to the market entry of two new canned chowders in 1982 and 1983 (see Appendix A). The new competitors were Fisherman's Delight Chowder and Cape Cod Chowder. Both brands were produced locally and appeared very similar in formulation to Kolander's Chowder.

Both of the new competitors had entered the market with a somewhat lower selling price than the Kolander's brand. Distributors were also attracted by the slightly higher margins plus the desire to carry a competitive alternative to Kolander's Chowder. Several large retailers had advertised the Fisherman's Delight brand as a "weekly special" at 43 cents per can.

MANAGEMENT OBJECTIVE

Kolander recognized that the firm faced a serious competitive threat from the two new brand entries. While there were several long-term issues he was considering, his immediate concern was one of developing a competitive strategy to counter the sales decline of Kolander's Chowder. Specifically, he wanted to recover the lost distribution of the brand and switch customers from competitive brands back to the Kolander's brand. This was to be accomplished within the next 12 months. While increased distribution outside the current market area was a possibility, Kolander's immediate objective was to improve the market position of Kolander's Chowder at retail within the New England area.

THE RESEARCH PROJECT

In October 1985, Kolander contacted a local research firm. After a number of meetings, the research firm recommended that a series of group interviews be conducted with current users of the two competitive chowder brands in order to explore reasons for product usage, reactions to the brands, and perceived product differences. Through group sessions of this nature, the research firm believed that the cause of declining sales of Kolander's Chowder could be established and potential solutions identified.

The results of the group sessions suggested that an important proportion of the competitive canned chowder users preferred a chowder that was thicker and creamier than the current Kolander's Chowder brand formulation. Of the former Kolander's Chowder users, the desire for a creamier formulation was the predominant reason for

---

[1] Estimated from 1985 company records.

switching. Many of these chowder users had switched to either Fisherman's Delight or Cape Cod Chowder.

Based on these findings, the research firm recommended that further research be conducted to evaluate changing Kolander's Chowder to a creamier formulation. For purposes of the test, it was recommended that two creamier formulations be developed, a "creamy" version and an "extra creamy" version. These two new formulations would be evaluated in a taste test along with Kolander's current chowder plus the two competitive brands.

After several meetings on specific aspects of the proposed research design, Kolander decided to approve the project. Appendix B presents the results of this study.

CASE QUESTION

What action should Kolander take based on the research findings)

APPENDIX A: New England Soup Company, Audit of Retail Food Outlets (Selected Tables from the Report)

Fifty retail food outlets in the New England market area have been audited annually since 1975. These are deemed representative of the potential distribution outlets for the New England Soup Company of canned soups.

PERCENTAGE OF STORES STOCKING CANNED CHOWDER BRANDS

Brand	1983	1984	1985
Kolander	94	86	82
Cape Cod	20	36	42
Fisherman's Delight	4	18	24

NUMBER OF BRANDS OF CANNED CHOWDER STOCKED

Brand	1983	1984	1985
None	3	1	0
One	34	25	23
Two	10	20	24
Three	2	3	2
Four or more	1	1	1
Total stores	50	50	50

RANGE OF RETAIL PRICES OF CANNED CHOWDER SOUP (IN CENTS)

Brand	1983	1984	1985
Kolander	49–53	48–55	47–54
Cape Cod	48–51	49–53	48–51
Fisherman's Delight	46–50	47–51	47–49

APPENDIX B: Research Report: Evaluation of Two New Formulations of Kolander's Canned Chowder

Research Objectives   To evaluate the preference for two new chowder formulations among users of Kolander's Chowder, Cape Cod Chowder, and Fisherman's Delight Chowder.

Research Design and Procedure   Two hundred male ($n = 100$) and female ($n = 100$) canned chowder users were selected from four geographic locations representative of the New England market area. The subjects were selected using a probability sampling procedure involving a telephone-administered qualifying questionnaire. Each subject was paid $5 for participating in the test.

The subjects came to one of four test locations (local churches). They were tested individually in 30-minute sessions. Subjects were brought into the testing room and seated at stalls. An instruction sheet explained that the subject was to evaluate several samples of chowder, that the test would consist of three parts, and that they would be required to taste a total of 15 cups of chowder. Normal taste-testing procedures were followed.

TABLE 1   PREFERENCE ORDERINGS OF FIVE CANNED CHOWDERS

Subject	Kolander's regular	Fisherman's Delight	Kolander's creamy	Cape Cod	Kolander's extra creamy
1	1	2	3	4	5
2	2	1	3	4	5
3	1	2	3	4	5
4	5	4	3	2	1
5	5	4	3	2	1
6	5	4	1	2	3
7	1	2	3	4	5
8	5	4	3	2	1
9	1	2	3	4	5
10	5	4	3	2	1
11	3	1	2	4	5
12	5	2	1	3	4
13	5	4	3	1	2
14	5	3	1	2	4
15	1	2	3	4	5
16	1	2	3	4	5
17	5	4	2	1	3
18	3	2	1	4	5
19	5	4	3	2	1
20*	4	2	1	3	5
.	.	.	.	.	.
.	.	.	.	.	.
.	.	.	.	.	.
200	.	.	.	.	.
Total =	685	550	482	588	712
n =	200	200	200	200	200
Mean =	3.4	2.8	2.4	2.9	3.6

*The first 20 preference orderings are representatives of the total sample of 200 subjects.

The first part involved tasting five samples of chowder and ranking them from "most pre-ferred" to "least preferred." The five chowders were Kolander's regular chowder, Fisherman's Delight, Kolander's creamy (version 1), Cape Cod, and Kolander's extra creamy (version 2).

The second and third parts of the test involved tasting five samples again. The samples had different code letters and the subjects were not told the samples were identical to the previous five. After tasting the five samples, the subjects were again asked to rank-order the five samples.

For each subject, the test procedure resulted in three preference orderings of the five chowder samples. The preference orderings were combined to form a composite ordering for each subject, a procedure that resulted in a more reliable measure of each subject's true preference ordering.

Results   The data set consisted of 200 preference orderings of the five chowders. Table 1 presents 20 preference orderings which are representative of the entire data set. The difference between male and female preference orderings was not statistically significant.

The data set was analyzed by calculating the average rank order of each chowder and scaling the chowders on a five-point scale ranging from most preferred (1) to least preferred (5). Table 2 presents the results of this analysis.

Recommendation and Discussion   Recommendation: Change the current Kolander's Chow-der formulation to the version 1—"creamy"—formulation and develop a new label which makes this change conspicuous at point of purchase.

The Table 2 results clearly indicate that the current Kolander's Chowder formulation and the "extra creamy" formulation ranked significantly (.05 level of significance) lower than the two competitors' brands and the "creamy" formulation. These findings suggest that the market posi-tion of Kolander's Chowder can be improved by a formulation change to the "creamy" version, which ranks higher than the two competitors and should recapture a significant share of sales lost to the Cape Cod and Fisherman's Delight brands.

TABLE 2   PREFERENCE SCALE (n = 200)

Most preferred	1.00	
	1.25	
	1.50	
	1.75	
	2.00	
	2.25	
	2.50	← Kolander's Creamy (2.4)
	2.75	← Fisherman's Delight (2.8)
	3.00	← Cape Cod (2.9)
	3.25	
	3.50	← Kolander's Regular (3.4)
	3.75	← Kolander's Extra Creamy (3.6)
	4.00	
	4.25	
	4.50	
	4.75	
Least preferred	5.00	

CASE 4-2: Federal Trade Commission— Corrective Advertising[2]

Dr. William Kranz had recently joined the Federal Trade Commission (FTC) staff as a consumer behavior consultant. He was on leave from a leading midwestern graduate school of business administration and was especially interested in the application of consumer behavior concepts and research to legal issues involving advertising.

In his first few months at the FTC, Kranz became interested in the area of corrective advertising, specifically in the way information from consumers could be utilized in the legal process involving corrective advertising.

CORRECTIVE ADVERTISING

Corrective advertising may be defined an advertising run by a commercial sponsor for the purpose of correcting consumer misimpressions resulting from the sponsor's earlier ads. Corrective advertisements are clearly "remedial" in nature, are run by a private concern in response to earlier commercials of that same firm, and are the outcome of a specific regulatory procedure of the Federal Trade Commission.

Corrective advertising was developed by the FTC as a mechanism for more efficient regulation of false or deceptive advertising. The concept was originally advanced by a group of law students (Students Opposed to Unfair Practices, or SOUP) who sought to intervene in an FTC complaint against Campbell's Soup advertising in 1970. SOUP contented that traditional use of cease and desist orders (under which the company simply withdraws the particular advertisement and does not run it again) would not adequately protect the public interest. Their reasoning was that consumers who may have relied upon the hypothesized deceptions should be informed of such deception in future advertisements run by the company.

From Kranz's viewpoint, the general framework of FTC's corrective advertising program was reasonably well developed. However, there was no decision system to help determine when corrective advertising was needed and how it should be implemented. For this reason, he believed consumer research could offer significant benefits for both FTC and businesses responding to the program.

DECISION MAKING IN CORRECTIVE ADVERTISING

The primary objective of a corrective advertisement is to dispel "residual effects" of a deceptive advertisement. Robert Pitofsky, the chief architect of the FTC's program, described three benefits expected from successful corrective advertising:

1 Misleading effects on consumer are dissipated.
2 Adverse competitive effects are dissipated.
3 The wrongdoer is denied the fruits of his violation.[3]

---

[2] This case was prepared by James R. Taylor and William L. Wilkie. Sections of the case are based on the research report by William Wilkie, "Consumer Research and Corrective Advertising: A New Approach," Marketing Science Institute, Cambridge, Mass., Oct. 1973.

[3] Stanley Cohen, "Enforcer Pitofsky Explains FTC's New Get Tough Policy," *Advertising Age*, p. 2, Jan. 18, 1971.

An additional administrative benefit—increased deterrence of deceptive advertising through threat of this stronger remedy—should not be overlooked.

Note, however, that a corrective-advertising order cannot be punitive in intent. While "wrongdoers" may legitimately be denied ill-gotten gains, they cannot be punished beyond this point. This suggests a need for precision in the development of specific remedial orders.

After studying the corrective-advertising cases, Kranz identified three rather distinct stages, shown in Figure 1, which characterize the FTC's decision process for corrective advertising. Stage 1 determines whether an advertisement has the "tendency or capacity to mislead." This often involves lengthy hearings in which various forms of evidence and expert witnesses are introduced. The five FTC Commissioners are then endowed with sufficient expertise to determine whether there has been deception or not. A judgment that deception has or could have occurred provides a necessary but not sufficient condition for corrective advertising.

Stage 2 reflects a decision as to the appropriateness of a corrective remedy as opposed to the more typical "cease and desist" order. The hearing record is examined for evidence on the existence of residual effects from the deceptive advertisement. Corrective advertising may be ordered when it appears that significant residual effects have been felt at either the consumer or competitive level.

Stage 3 requires a specification of all aspects of the corrective remedy. Note that there is not a "yes-no" decision for this stage; a detailed corrective campaign must be developed whether or not the lawyers know how to precisely dispel residual effects.

It appeared to Kranz that stages 2 and 3 were additions to FTC's traditional regulatory decision process. These new decisions represent a shift from legal reaction to marketing action; FTC is in effect adopting the role of a public advertising agency which designs communications mixes for offending advertisers.

The shift of focus meant that the FTC had to deal with a number of complex issues involved in developing a corrective-communications mix. For example, should companies be required to run corrective ads whether or not future promotional advertising is continued? How long should the corrections be run? Which media should be selected and scheduled? What budget is correct? Should the company be permitted to promote the brand actively during this period? If so, can the promotion be in the same insertion as the corrective message? What characteristics should be built into the copy of the corrective advertisement?

Kranz believed that the FTC lacked the necessary skills to deal adequately with these complex questions and that it should seriously consider an alternative option. This option was outlined in a report prepared by Kranz and sent to various members of the FTC.

A NEW APPROACH TO CORRECTIVE ADVERTISING

Kranz identified three areas of concern in corrective advertising: (1) message, (2) audience, and (3) response. The message (M) represents an advertisement which is transmitted to and received by members of an audience (A), who then respond (R) in some fashion.

FTC has traditionally stressed M and A factors in advertising. "Capacity to mislead or deceive" has often been judged from overt characteristics of the message, especially when statements were literally untrue. Special attention has been given to advertisements aimed at certain susceptible audiences such as children and elderly or low-income consumers.

Kranz believed that corrective-advertising cases should focus on the R factor, namely, behavioral response. The primary objective of corrective advertising is to remove certain residual effects of deception. Residual effects are simply responses (R) which have continued over time. Specification of the particular R variables to be remedied is needed in order to clarify the objectives of corrective advertising. Measurement of this response level can then be used for stages 2 and 3 of the decision process (Figure 1).

A major issue presented by Kranz's proposal was the appropriate specification and measurement of behavioral response. Should the behavioral response be specified at the cognitive level (awareness and knowledge), at the affective level (liking and preference), or at the behavioral level (intention-to-buy and purchase)?

Kranz's suggested criteria for selection of an appropriate level of behavioral response include:

1 That it follow as directly as possible from exposure to an advertisement
2 That it reflect claims (deceptive or corrective) made in the advertisement
3 That it reflect the meaning or salience of impact of exposure to such claims in terms of consumer injury or benefit
4 That it offer an opportunity for precision in remedy

HAWAIIAN PUNCH COMPLAINT AND ORDER

In the fall of 1972, Kranz was asked to consult with the FTC staff investigating RJR Foods' advertising for Hawaiian Punch beverages. Since many of the staff members were familiar with Kranz's evaluation of the FTC's approach to corrective advertising, it was believed that this case offered an opportunity for him to put his recommendations into operation.

The proposed complaint contended that RJR Foods' advertising misrepresented the proportion of natural fruit juice as greater than the actual proportion of 11 percent. Consequently, the complaint implied that there were "residual effects" of the deception. This raised the issue of how these "residual effects" could be corrected (see Figure 1).

The issue before Kranz was how to measure the "residual effects" such that the FTC could determine when corrective action had dispelled the effects of the deception. Once it was demonstrated that the "residual effects" were dispelled, the corrective advertising could be terminated by RJR Foods.

In a subsequent meeting with the investigating staff, Kranz proposed that a follow-up consumer survey be used to measure the effect of any corrective action taken by RJR Foods. The details of the survey would have to be negotiated with RJR Foods as a part of the final decision and order. The reaction of the staff was favorable to this approach, and he was asked to participate in future meetings with RJR Foods regarding the proposed complaint.

In the meeting with RJR Foods and its advertising agency, William Esty Company, the proposed complaint was debated along with the staff recommendations as to corrective action and the proposed consumer survey. After several lengthy sessions, RJR Foods tentatively agreed to the FTC consent order requiring "affirmative disclosure"[4] of product content. This order meant that any Hawaiian Punch label or ad which depicted fruits or juice, visually or verbally, would have to clearly and conspicuously disclose the total percentage of fruit juice concentrate in a single serving. RJR Foods complied with the consent order by inserting the statement that Hawaiian Punch "has not less than 10 percent natural fruit juices" in all of its future advertising of Hawaiian Punch. The details of the consumer survey were to be worked out at future meetings once each side had an opportunity to formulate specific proposals as to the nature of the consumer survey and how it would be implemented.

Kranz was very pleased with the tentative agreement regarding the consumer survey. While the rationale for the survey was clearly understood by both parties, the specific issues involved in implementing the survey were still subject to difficult negotiation.

The investigating staff had requested that Kranz develop a consumer research proposal for in-house discussion before the next meeting with RJR Foods. Kranz felt that the data should be collected by a telephone survey. The remaining issues in developing the research proposal were less clear. Of immediate concern was the development of a question or series of questions to measure whether residual effects of the Hawaiian Punch advertising had been dispelled by the corrective advertising. In addition, what criterion should be set for determining whether the effects of the deception had been dispelled? How should the population be defined? Should the same criteria be applied to all segments of the population? If not, how should they be varied? Should statistical concepts such as tests of significance be used in deciding whether the residual effects had been dispelled? How big should the sample be? Kranz immediately began to tackle these questions in preparation for the meeting with staff members.

CASE QUESTION

Design a telephone survey which addresses the specific measurement and sampling issues of concern to Kranz.

---

[4] This "affirmative disclosure" consent order represents a partial application of the corrective-advertising approach. It did not require reference to prior advertising.

CASE 4-3: Mainline Package Goods*

Ken Gibbs was the recently promoted product manager for Ice-Away, a windshield deicer marketed by Mainline Package Goods. Windshield deicers are sprayed on car windows to instantly melt ice and frost. As brand manager, Gibbs was responsible for all marketing decisions related to Ice-Away. He was currently preparing Ice-Away's marketing plan for the next fiscal year and had to submit the finalized version to his boss in 2 weeks. Two major changes in package design had been test-marketed by Research Design, Inc. (RDI), and Gibbs was in the process of reviewing the results. The field experiment was designed to measure the effects of different packaging on consumer attitudes and on sales of Ice-Away.

Mainline was one of the largest American package goods companies, marketing everything from floor wax to over-the-counter drugs. Ice-Away was the leader in its product category, windshield deicers, with annual sales of $10 million and profits of $1.25 million. Ice-Away first entered the market in 1970, and by 1975 it was the number one brand, mostly due to intensive advertising and retail promotion. Ice-Away's main competition came from the other major brands on the market—Snowflake, No-Frost, and Melt It!. All of these brands were about the same price as Ice-Away and had equivalent distribution at retail. For the last 3 years, Ice-Away had been losing market share to the competition, and Gibbs was convinced that poor packaging was the reason.

Ice-Away's package, a metal aerosol can, had not materially changed since 1970. When the competition changed to nonaerosol containers, Ice-Away retained the same packaging, and it was then that Ice-Away's market share began to decline. Mainline's R&D department had come up with two alternatives to the metal aerosol can. First, a nonaerosol plastic container which utilized a pump mechanism to expel the deicer, and second, a nonaerosol metal can that had an aerosol-like spray. On the front of the metal version, the words "NEW NONAEROSOL FORMULA" were printed in large letters to ensure that consumers would note the difference between new and old packages. The $25,000 RDI study examined the effects of the two new package designs on sales and consumer attitudes. The research report submitted by RDI appears below.

THE RESEARCH REPORT

Objectives

1. To test the relative effectiveness of alternative package designs for Ice-Away.
2. To recommend the best design.

Packaging Tested

1. Metal aerosol can (control market)
2. Plastic nonaerosol pump
3. Metal nonaerosol can

The price was the same for all three alternatives.

* Coauthored by Sheryl Petras.

Test Markets Used   The three cities used were selected to be as similar as possible with respect to (1) the distribution penetration of Ice-Away and its three major competitors, and (2) the following economic characteristics:

	Newark	Cleveland	Denver
Population	1,870,000	1,840,000	1,580,000
Households	661,000	704,000	619,000
Effective buying income per household	$30,000	$25,000	$28,000
Retail sales index*	105	99	106

* National base of 100.

The metal aerosol can was tested in Newark, the metal nonaerosol can in Denver, and the plastic pump in Cleveland.

Data Collection Method   The data were collected by means of telephone interviews. Samples were chosen randomly from phone books in each of the three cities. To qualify for the questionnaire, a respondent had to be a user of windshield deicer. The realized sample sizes were: Newark, 300; Cleveland, 297; and Denver 501. The following purchase measures were taken:

1. Brand of deicer usually purchased
2. Brand of deicer last purchased
3. Brand of deicer the respondent intended to purchase next

Attitude measures were taken on (1) convenience (vs. scraping the windows), (2) effectiveness in melting ice, (3) speed in deicing, (4) aesthetic appeal of the package, (5) ease in using the package, and (6) frequency of use. Respondents were asked to rate each attribute on a 7-point scale, with a 1 indicating the lowest attitude measure and a 7 the highest.

Timing   The new package designs were introduced in December, and interviewing was done in March.

Results   Selected tables from the report appear below.

BRAND USUALLY PURCHASED

	Newark, %	Denver, %	Cleveland, %
Ice-Away	12	17*	10
Snowflake	11	10	9
No-Frost	14	9	11
Melt It!	9	12*	8

* Significant difference from control at $p < .05$.

BRAND LAST PURCHASED

	Newark, %	Denver, %	Cleveland, %
Ice-Away	11	15*	11
Snowflake	11	9	9
No-Frost	12	10	10
Melt It!	7	13*	10*

* Significant difference from control at $p < .05$.

ATTITUDE MEASURES

Attributes	Ice-Away			Snowflake			No-Frost			Melt It!		
	N	C	D	N	C	D	N	C	D	N	C	D
Convenience	5.4	5.6	5.5	5.5	5.8	5.6	5.8	5.1	5.4	5.5	4.9	4.6
Effectiveness melting ice	6.0	6.5*	6.0	5.9	6.0	5.8	5.7	5.8	5.6	5.2	5.0	5.7*
Speed in deicing	5.9	6.1	5.8	6.0	5.8	6.1	5.4	5.8	5.1	5.7	5.9	6.0
Package appeal	6.2	6.1	6.4	6.0	6.0	6.0	5.2	5.0	4.9	5.1	5.2	5.0
Ease in using package	4.2	5.1*	4.6	4.1	4.4	4.2	4.0	3.9	4.1	3.7	3.6	4.1
Frequency of use	4.5	4.0*	5.1*	4.9	4.9	4.8	4.7	4.9	4.7	4.9	4.5	4.6

Note: N = Newark (metal aerosol)
    C = Cleveland (plastic pump)
    D = Denver (metal nonaerosol)
* Significant difference from control at $p < .05$.

Recommendations   Ken Gibbs wanted to analyze the data himself before initiating a packaging change. If his analysis of the data did not lead to the same conclusions as the RDI analysis, Gibbs planned to adopt the package he felt was best, and to this end he began to review the data.

CASE QUESTIONS

1 Evaluate the experimental design used by Mainline Package Goods. Be sure to discuss the validity of the experiment.
2 Do you feel the design can be improved? If yes, indicate how you would do so. Be specific!
3 What conclusions can be drawn from the study? What action would you recommend if you were in Ken Gibbs's position?

CASE 4-4: Crest Toothpaste

Crest toothpaste, at the time of its national introduction in 1955, was the first fluoride dentifrice with clinical proof of effectiveness against caries. This proof was based upon a series of experiments on human subjects that resulted in Crest being the first dentifrice accepted (in 1960) by the American Dental Association (ADA). That acceptance and strong Crest advertising featuring its cavity reduction properties have allowed Crest to take and hold the number one share of the toothpaste market from 1960 to the present.

In the late 1970s, an advanced formula Crest (AFC) was developed at Procter & Gamble. Crest management believed that AFC was a superior product to the previous formulation. Improving Crest was important as a number of other toothpastes had introduced fluoride formulations and were accepted by the ADA, including Colgate and Aim. Also, Crest's market share had fallen somewhat in recent years.

Crest management knew that the effectiveness of AFC would have to be clinically documented by experimental procedures. They intended to use the results of these tests as the cornerstone of an advertising campaign introducing AFC to the market place.

CASE QUESTIONS

1 Prepare an experimental design that would allow for the effectiveness of AFC to be measured. Be sure to identify clearly: test units, dependent variable(s), independent variable(s), treatments, possible sources of extraneous variation on the dependent variable, methods of control of extraneous variables, timing of measurements taken, selection of test units, and assignment of test units to treatments.
2 Display your design using the R, O, X symbols of design.

CASE 4-5: New Coca-Cola Taste Test*

Coca-Cola: the "sublimated essence of all America stands for—a decent thing, honestly made, universally distributed, conscientiously improved with years."

The late William Allen White, Pulitzer Prize winning editor of the *Emporia Gazette* (Kansas), 1938.

April 23, 1985: "New Coke"   In a bold strategic move to counter its declining popularity among America's youth, the Coca-Cola Co. announced the reformulation of its flagship brand, Coke. Except for the elimination of $\frac{1}{400}$ of a percent of cocaine in 1903, previous formula changes had involved only minor modifications in caffeine or sugar content. Then came New Coke—a noticeably sweeter version of America's number one

* Coauthored by Sheryl Petras.

soft drink. With this reformulation, Coke had positioned itself closer to archrival Pepsi in taste (much to the delight of PepsiCo's executives and advertising managers). But, given its declining performance in taste tests against Pepsi, Coke executives felt that major reformulation was the best way to counter the "Pepsi Challenge."

Before beginning mass production, the company did marketing research to test New Coke. According to top Coca-Cola executives, 180,000–200,000 secret blind taste tests pitted the new formula against the old, and the majority of people preferred New Coke. In fact, widely reported results gave New Coke a 61 to 39 percent edge over Old Coke. Thus, the decision to go ahead with the new formula was made.

April 24–July 10, 1985: "Mutiny" Coke drinkers revolted. Old Coke clubs sprang up everywhere; 1500 calls a day poured into Coca-Cola's toll-free customer service line; Coke loyalists all over the country began to stockpile the "real thing." Ironically, though, even the founder of Old Cola Drinkers of America (Gay Mullins) did not consistently identify—or prefer—Old Coke in taste tests.

July 11, 1985: "Coca-Cola Classic" or "Coke Are It!" "We did not read the deep emotional ties that people had to the whole concept of Coca-Cola," said Brian G. Dyson, senior vice president of Coca-Cola Co. He made this statement at the July 11 press conference held to reintroduce Old Coke. The company decided to bring it back as Coca-Cola Classic, while keeping the brand name "Coke" for the new formula.

CASE QUESTIONS

1 Marketing research showed New Coke to be favored over both Old Coke and Pepsi. Why then did New Coke meet with such resistance among consumers? What (if anything) was wrong with the research?

2 a Design and carry out an experimental taste test for two or three cola beverages (you could use Coke, Coca-Cola Classic, and Pepsi-Cola, for example). There are numerous colas on the market—any of them could be used in this experiment.

   Run two separate taste tests. In one, let the subjects know which cola they are drinking. Let them see the container while you pour from it, then ask them which taste they prefer. (If three colas are used, have them rank order the data 1–2–3.) The other test should be "blind." Pour the beverages from behind a screen so the subjects don't know which colas they are tasting. Then have them rank the soft drinks. Identify clearly:

   Test units
   Dependent variable(s)
   Independent variable(s)
   Treatments
   Possible sources of extraneous variation on the dependent variable
   Ways to control these extraneous variables
   Timing of the measurements taken
   Selection of test units
   Assignment of test units to treatments

b Suppose the results of your taste test are to be used in a national advertising campaign. How would you change your design to account for this? (Be aware that your experiment results could be challenged in court by the competition!)

3 Analyze the data you gathered from the experiment. Do equal numbers of people prefer each brand? Does it make a difference whether or not they see the can before they taste the beverage (i.e., is there interaction between knowledge of brand and brand preference)?

OBTAINING INFORMATION FROM RESPONDENTS

CHAPTER 13

DATA COLLECTION METHODS

Previous chapters have emphasized the role of exploratory research both in formulating problems and in stimulating the creative process involved in identifying alternative courses of action. It was stressed that the decision problem must be clearly stated and the alternative courses of action specified before the conclusive research project can be initiated.

Once the need for conclusive research is established, the researcher must clearly state the objectives of the proposed research and develop a specific list of information needs. The next step in the formal research project is to determine whether the desired data are currently available from secondary data sources. These sources can be internal or external to the organization. Typically, secondary data sources do not completely meet the information needs of the study, and the researcher turns to formulating a research design based on primary data sources. These include (1) respondents, (2) analogous situations, and (3) experiments. Previous chapters have discussed the data sources of analogous situations and experimentation. This chapter focuses on the remaining primary data source, namely, respondents.

Respondents are a major source of marketing data. There are two methods of acquiring data from respondents—communication and observation. Communication requires the respondent to actively provide data through verbal response, while observation involves the recording of the respondent's behavior.

Before turning to a discussion of the data collection issues that arise in connection with respondent data, let us first overview the types of data that can be collected from respondents.

TYPES OF RESPONDENT DATA

In a fundamental sense, all marketing decision making is concerned with taking action today so that future objectives can be accomplished. In this context, marketing research can be viewed as a forecasting technique designed to facilitate the process of predicting market behavior. The types of data that can be obtained from respondents for use in forecasting market behavior are (1) past behavior, (2) attitudes, and (3) respondent characteristics.

Past Behavior

Evidence regarding the respondent's past behavior has wide usage as a predictor of future behavior. In our personal activities we all use evidence of past behavior to predict the future behavior of our friends and relatives. In similar fashion, a marketing research study can gather evidence on a respondent's behavior regarding purchase and use of some product or brand to predict future behavior. The specific evidence gathered about this past behavior can be as follows: (1) What was purchased/used? (2) How much was purchased/used? (3) How was it purchased/used? (4) Where was it purchased/used? (5) When was it purchased/used? and (6) Who purchased/used it?[1] Consequently, there are many dimensions to understanding past behavior. The researcher must be sensitive to the key behavioral dimensions relevant to predicting future behavior when specifying the data required to meet the information needs of a study.

Attitudes

Attitudes are important in marketing because of the assumed relationship between attitudes and behavior. Attitudinal data are used to identify market segments, to develop a "positioning" strategy, and to evaluate advertising programs.

An attitude is generally considered to have three main components: (1) a *cognitive* component—a person's beliefs about the object of concern, such as its speed or durability; (2) an *affective* component—a person's feelings about the object, such as "good" or "bad"; and (3) a *behavioral* component—a person's readiness to respond behaviorally to the object.

The measurement of attitudes was discussed extensively in Chapter 11. The emphasis was on the quantification of attitudes, using self-report scaling techniques. This chapter will discuss additional techniques for identifying the nature of attitudes and their measurement.

Respondent Characteristics

"Respondent characteristics" describe respondents on particular variables of interest. These include demographic, socioeconomic, and psychological characteristics. For many products, variables of this nature have been found to be correlates of purchase behavior. In addition, variables such as age, sex, marital status, family size, income, occupation, and education level have been found useful in sample stratification and validation.

---

[1] Fred T. Schreier, *Modern Marketing Research—A Behavioral Science Approach* (Belmont, Calif.: Wadsworth, 1963), p. 251.

TABLE 13-1 LIFE-STYLE CHARACTERISTICS

Activities	Interests	Opinions
Work	Family	Themselves
Hobbies	Home	Social issues
Social events	Job	Politics
Vacation	Community	Business
Entertainment	Recreation	Economics
Club membership	Fashion	Education
Community	Food	Products
Shopping	Media	Future
Sports	Achievements	Culture

Source: Adapted from J. T. Plummer, "The Concept and Application of Life-Style Segmentation," *Journal of Marketing*, vol. 38, p. 34, January 1974.

A popular way of describing respondents is in terms of their life-style, defined as *a distinctive mode of living of a society or segment thereof.*[2] Life-style focuses on respondent activities, interests, opinions, and demographic characteristics as determinants of style of living. The first three of these, listed in more detail in Table 13-1, are called A-I-O items, which stands for activities, interests, and opinions.

The term *psychographics* is closely related to the concept of life-style. It is a broader term which includes the life-style concept. One definition is as follows:

Psychographics is a quantitative research procedure which seeks to explain why people behave as they do and why they hold their current attitudes. It seeks to take quantitative research beyond demographic, socioeconomic and user/non-user analysis, but also employs these variables in the research. Psychographics looks into three classes of variables, of which life-style is one. The others are psychological and product benefits.[3]

METHODS OF COLLECTING RESPONDENT DATA

As stated earlier, the two basic methods of collecting data from respondents are communication and observation. We shall examine the communication method first. Discussion of the observation method will follow.

Communication Method

The communication method of data collection is based on the questioning of respondents. It is logical to ask respondents questions if you want to know what brand of soup they buy, which television programs are viewed, or why they shop at a particular store. Such questions may be asked verbally or in writing, and the responses may

[2] W. Lazer, "Life-Style Concepts and Marketing," in S. A. Greyser (ed.), *Toward Scientific Marketing* (Chicago: American Marketing Association, 1964), p. 130.
[3] Emanuel Demby, "Psychographics and from Whence It Came," in William D. Wells (ed.), *Life Style and Psychographics* (Chicago: American Marketing Association, 1974), p. 28.

be in either form. The data collection instrument used in this process is called a *questionnaire*. The questionnaire has come to be the predominant data collection instrument in marketing research. It is estimated that over half of the United States public has participated in one or more research studies of this nature.[4]

Advantages of the Communication Method   The main advantage of the communication method is its *versatility*. Versatility refers to the ability of the method to collect data on a wide range of information needs. The vast majority of marketing decision problems involve people. Consequently, the information needs focus on people's past behavior, attitudes, and characteristics. The communication method can gather data in all three of these areas.

Additional advantages relate to the *speed* and *cost* of the communication method as compared with the observation method. The speed and cost advantages are highly interdependent. The communication method is a faster means of data collection than observation in that it provides more control over the data collection process. The researcher does not have to predict when and where the behavior will occur or wait for it to occur. For example, it would be much faster and cheaper to ask the respondent about the purchase of a dishwasher than to try to anticipate and observe the purchase.

Disadvantages of the Communication Method   There are several important limitations of the communication method. The first relates to the respondent's *unwillingness to provide the desired data*. The respondent may refuse to take the time to be interviewed or refuse to respond to particular questions. The second limitation concerns the respondent's *inability to provide the data*. The respondent may not recall the facts in question or may never have known them to begin with. The final limitation involves the *influence of the questioning process* on the responses. The respondents may bias their responses in order to give a socially acceptable answer or in order to please the interviewer. While the limitations can seriously reduce the validity of the communication method, they can also be controlled by properly designing the data collection instrument. More will be said about this in the following chapter on designing data collection forms.

Communication Techniques Classified by Structure and Directness

There are various ways to classify the data collection techniques which utilize the method of communication. A useful classification scheme is to categorize techniques by their degree of structure and their degree of directness.[5] Figure 13-1 presents the four classes which emerge from this classification scheme: (1) structured, direct; (2) unstructured, direct; (3) unstructured, indirect; and (4) structured, indirect.

---

[4] Frank D. Walker, "Their Opinion Counts," in W. S. Hale (ed.), *Proceedings: 20th Annual Conference* (New York: Advertising Research Foundation, 1974), p. 14.

[5] This classification scheme was first suggested by Donald T. Campbell, "The Indirect Assessment of Social Attitudes," *Psychological Bulletin,* vol. 47, p. 15, January 1950.

	Structured	Unstructured
Direct	Survey questionnaire	Focus–group interview Depth interview
Indirect	Performance of objective task technique	Thematic apperception test Role playing Cartoon completion Word association Sentence completion

FIGURE 13-1   Communication techniques classified by structure and directness.

Structure refers to the degree of standardization imposed on the data collection process. A formal questionnaire is typically used to bring structure to the data collection process. With a highly structured approach, the questions asked and the responses permitted are completely predetermined. A multiple-choice examination in a marketing research course would be an example of a questionnaire with a high degree of structure. With a highly unstructured data collection approach, the questions to be asked are loosely predetermined and the respondents are encouraged to express their views freely. An intermediate degree of structure would involve standardized questions but an "open-ended" response format.

A direct data collection approach is one where the objective of the study is obvious to the respondent from the nature of the questions asked. In contrast, an indirect approach asks questions in a manner that disguises the objective of the study.

Structured-Direct   The most common data collection technique is the structured-direct questionnaire, which requires that the questions be asked with exactly the same wording and in exactly the same sequence for all respondents. This standardization is designed to control response bias by ensuring that the respondents are responding to exactly the same question. The response to a standardized question may require the selection of an alternative from a predetermined set of responses

Conclusive research projects typically require a structured-direct questionnaire. The standardized questions and fixed-response alternatives can evolve from previous research which used less structured techniques. In addition, the structured question-

and-response categories usually require extensive pretesting to ensure that the questions measure what they are designed to measure. The structured-direct questionnaire requires extensive time and skill to develop. More will be said in this regard in the following chapter.

There are several advantages of the structured-direct approach,[6] the greatest being administrative simplicity and ease of data processing, analysis, and interpretation. The structured question format is designed to control response bias and increase the reliability of the data. In addition, it can be administered over the telephone, through the mail, and by personal interview.

The disadvantages of the structured-direct approach are the same as the limitations of the communication method: the respondents may not be able to provide the desired data, they may not be willing to provide the data, and the questioning process may bias their responses. In addition, structured questions and fixed-response alternatives may result in loss of validity for certain types of data. If the data required from the respondent are clear-cut, limited in scope, and well known, the structured-fixed alternative question may be very appropriate. However, when the information needs involve exploring the nature of recently formed or evolving beliefs and feelings, the structured approach could seriously influence the validity of the data.

Unstructured-Direct   With the unstructured-direct approach the purpose of the research study is clear to the respondent. There is a great degree of flexibility in how the questions are asked and in the degree of probing. The response format is open-ended, and respondents are encouraged to freely express their beliefs and feeling on the issues presented by the interviewer.

There are two techniques that use the unstructured-direct approach: (1) the focus group interview and (2) the depth interview.[7]

Focus Group Interview   The focus group interview, or group depth interview, is one of the most frequently used techniques in marketing research. It can be defined as a *loosely structured interview conducted by a trained moderator among a small number of respondents simultaneously.* This technique has its origins in the group therapy methods used by psychiatrists. While the interview does require a preinterview organization of topics or interviewer guide, the setting emphasizes flexibility, and the value of the technique lies in discovering the unexpected which results from a free-flowing group discussion. Exhibit 13-1 presents an example of a focus group interviewer guide.

Focus group interviews can be used for a number of different purposes. Interviews with researchers suggest the following uses.[8]

1 To generate hypotheses that can be further tested quantitatively
2 To generate information helpful in structuring consumer questionnaires
3 To provide overall background information on a product category

---

[6] Claire Selltiz et al., *Research Methods in Social Relations,* rev. ed. (New York: Holt, 1959), pp. 257–263.
[7] The discussion of these two techniques follows the presentation in D. N. Bellenger, K. L. Bernhardt, and J. L. Goldstucker, *Qualitative Research in Marketing,* Monograph Series No. 3 (Chicago: American Marketing Association, 1976), pp. 7–33.
[8] Ibid., pp. 18–19.

EXHIBIT 13-1

GUIDE FOR FOCUS GROUP INTERVIEWS ON AUTOMOBILE INSURANCE

1 Do you have insurance on your automobile now?
  a (for those who do have it) Why?
  What are the most important reasons why you have automobile insurance?
  What are some other reasons?
  What reasons have you heard—for instance, advertising—that you think are *not* important?
  Have you ever driven without insurance?
  How did that happen?
  Would you do it again?
  What do the others in the group think? Would they do it?
  b (for those not carrying insurance) Why not?
  Have you ever had it?
  Why did you drop it?
  Do you expect to get some? When?
2 Turn the discussion to types of auto insurance coverage.
  a What is collision insurance? (Try to get the group to define it, but make sure they know that it means insurance that pays for damage to the owner's car as a result of an accident, no matter whose fault.)
  Do you have collision insurance?
  Why? (probe)—Have you ever had it? (if yes) Why did you drop it?
  Do you expect to get it again?
  (Encourage discussion between those who do have it and those who don't on the merits of this type of insurance.)
  b (repeat the preceding discussion for):
  Liability Insurance (Bodily Injury and Property Damage)—that which pays for damage done by a driver to other cars or property or to other people. Comprehensive Insurance (Fire, Theft, etc.)—that which pays for loss or damage to a car as a result of fire, theft, natural hazards, vandalism, etc. Medical Payments Insurance—that which pays medical expenses of guests in the car.

Source: J. W. Newman, *Motivation Research and Marketing Management* (Boston: Harvard Business School, Division of Research, 1957), p. 130. Used with permission of the Harvard Business School, Division of Research.

---

4 To get impressions on new product concepts for which there is little information available
5 To stimulate new ideas about older products
6 To generate ideas for new creative concepts
7 To interpret previously obtained quantitative results

The respondent group should be composed of people with fairly homogeneous characteristics. One organization, which conducts approximately 600 focus groups per year, avoids combining full-time married homemakers with children at home and unmarried working women, because their life-styles and objectives are substantially different. They also avoid grouping men and women together as well as teenagers and younger children.[9] Thus, it is important to maintain as much homogeneity or commonality among group members as possible. This avoids interactions and conflicts among group members on issues not relevant to the study objectives.

The size of the group can be as many as 10 or 12 people for consumer goods research. Experience suggests that a group with less than 8 people results in the discussion being dominated by a few respondents, and having more than 12 people tends to diminish the opportunity for some respondents to participate. It is argued that for nonconsumer goods research (architects, doctors, industrial purchasers, engineers, investors, contractors, etc.), 6 or 7 people may be best for maximum interaction among participants.

When selecting respondents, most researchers believe that careful screening is essential to the success of the focus group interview. First, the group members must have had adequate experience with the object or issue being discussed. Second, those respondents who have previously participated in a group session should not be included a second time. Some research organizations allow the respondents to participate a second time if they have not participated in a session within the last year. The reason for this rule is that former participants often play the role of expert by dominating the discussion and trying to "show off" for the first-time participants.

Another issue in respondent selection relates to allowing people to participate in a group which contains a relative, neighbor, or friend. Since friends sometimes tend to talk to each other and not to the whole group, many researchers will not select respondents from church groups or other organizations where participants have established relationships.

Most researchers believe the physical setting to be very important to the effectiveness of the group session. The atmosphere should encourage a relaxed feeling, one where informal and spontaneous comments are encouraged. It is best to establish a "coffee klatsch" or "bull session" atmosphere in this regard.

A living room environment is considered more appropriate than a conference boardroom setting, since the latter can inhibit many of the respondents or encourage them to play the role of expert. While a living room in a private home is ideal, most research organizations have participants come to a central facility which has a specially designed laboratory furnished like a comfortable, but not elaborate, living room. The advantage of a laboratory lies in the availability of facilities for recording the session and for allowing the client to indirectly observe the group session in process.

How long is a group session? The typical focus group interview lasts $1\frac{1}{2}$ to 2 hours. This period of time is needed to establish rapport with the respondents and explore in depth their beliefs, feelings, ideas, and insights regarding the discussion topic.

The number of group sessions to be conducted depends on the nature of the issue at hand, the number of market segments involved, and the time and cost constraints of the project. Typically the researcher must concentrate the group session on those segments most critical to the topic being considered. It is very desirable to replicate the focus group session for each market segment being studied.

---

[9] Myril D. Axelrod, "10 Essentials for Good Qualitative Research," *Marketing News*, March 14, 1975, p. 10.

Clients frequently observe the focus group session, and it is better to have them behind a two-way mirror rather than present in the room with the participants. The client can let the moderator know during short breaks in the session if certain areas need more exploration. This detached location of the client avoids the danger of disrupting the group session by having the participants observe the client's reactions or note taking.

The moderator's role is of prime importance to the success of the focus group technique. Highly skilled moderators can ensure that proper respondent rapport is established, that the discussion is directed along relevant dimensions, and that the degree of probing and depth of insight are sufficient to accomplish the research objectives. In addition, the moderator is central to the analysis and interpretation of the data. Great skill, experience, knowledge of the discussion topic, and intuitive insights about the nature of group dynamics are required to accomplish this task. Consequently, the moderator is often a trained psychologist who has developed special moderator skills through intensive study and practice.

The moderator's skill is clearly demonstrated by the ability to maintain a high degree of interaction among group members. Unskilled moderators typically find themselves conducting individual interviews with each of the participants rather than stimulating interaction within the group. Only with interaction can the group interview (1) provide the desired spontaneity of response by participants, (2) produce the degree of emotional involvement essential to produce "depth"-level responses, and (3) produce the kind and degree of rapport which facilitates a "give-and-take" exchange of attitudinal and behavioral information.[10]

The key qualifications for moderator are:[11]

1 *Kindness with firmness*—In order to elicit necessary interaction, the moderator must combine a disciplined detachment with understanding empathy.

2 *Permissiveness*—While an atmosphere of permissiveness is desirable, the moderator must be at all times alert to indications that the group atmosphere of cordiality is disintegrating.

3 *Involvement*—Since a principal reason for the group interview is to expose feelings and to obtain reactions indicative of deeper feelings, the moderator must encourage and stimulate intensive personal involvement.

4 *Incomplete understanding*—A most useful skill of the group moderator is his or her ability to convey lack of complete understanding of the information being presented.

5 *Encouragement*—Although the dynamics of the group situation facilitate the participation of all members in the interaction, there may be individuals who resist contributing.

6 *Flexibility*—The moderator should be equipped prior to the session with a topic outline of the subject matter to be covered. By committing the topics to memory before the interview, the moderator may use the outline only as a reminder of content areas omitted or covered incompletely.

7 *Sensitivity*—The moderator must be able to identify, as the group interview progresses, the informational level on which it is being conducted, and determined if it is appropriate for the subject under discussion. Sensitive areas will frequently produce superficial rather than deep responses. Depth is achieved when there is a substantial amount of emotional response, as opposed to intellectual information. Indications of depth are provided when participants begin to indicate how they feel about the subject, rather than what they think about it.

[10] Bellenger et al., op. cit., pp. 12–16.
[11] Donald A. Chase, "The Intensive Group Interview in Marketing," *MRA Viewpoints,* 1973.

Does the sex of the moderator influence the effectiveness of the group session? There are two views about this. The first holds that the sex of the moderator should be the same as that of the group members to ensure proper rapport. The second view is that the sex of the moderator should be different from that of the group members. The argument is that the participants will not assume that the moderator knows what they are talking about and will be more explanatory in their responses.

What special techniques can the moderator use in running a group session? When one person tries to dominate the discussion, the moderator can stop the proceedings and poll each participant regarding the issue at hand. This technique is also useful to encourage the shy person to express a viewpoint and participate in the discussion. At the close of the session, each person can be asked to summarize what the group has resolved. Another useful technique is to call each of the participants a day or so after the completed session and have them express their viewpoints again. Many times viewpoints change due to passage of time or more reflective thinking on the issues.

Should the same moderator be involved in all group sessions on the topic? Most researchers believe so. With each session the moderator becomes more effective and gains additional insights as to the analysis and interpretation of the sessions.

The major advantage of the focus group interview rests on the premise that if you want to understand your consumers, you have to listen to them. There is much to be gained from listening to consumers describe a product in their own vernacular, and from having them portray how they buy products and how they perceive product benefits and limitations, using highly personalized terms. Data such as these can bring insight to potential problems and opportunities and can identify possible marketing program strategies that have not occurred to the manager.

When compared with other data collection techniques, the focus group interview has these specific advantages:[12]

1 *Synergism:* The combined effect of the group will produce a wider range of information, insight, and ideas than will the cumulation of the responses of a number of individuals when these replies are secured privately.

2 *Snowballing:* A bandwagon effect often operates in a group interview situation in that a comment by one individual often triggers a chain of responses from the other participants.

3 *Stimulation:* Usually after a brief introductory period the respondents get "turned on" in that they want to express their ideas and expose their feelings as the general level of excitement over the topic increases in the group.

4 *Security:* The participants can usually find comfort in the group in that their feelings are not greatly different from other participants and they are more willing to express their ideas and feelings.

5 *Spontaneity:* Since individuals aren't required to answer any question in a group interview, their responses can be more spontaneous and less conventional, and should provide a more accurate picture of their position on some issues.

6 *Serendipity:* It is more often the case in a group rather than individual interview that some idea will "drop out of the blue."

[12] John M. Hess, "Grouping Interviewing," in R. L. King (ed.), *New Science of Planning* (Chicago: American Marketing Association, 1968), p. 194.

7 *Specialization:* The group interview allows the use of a more highly trained, but more expensive, interviewer since a number of individuals are being "interviewed" simultaneously.

8 *Scientific scrutiny:* The group interview allows closer scrutiny of the data collection process in that several observers can witness the session and it can be recorded for later playback and analysis.

9 *Structure:* The group interview affords more flexibility than the individual interview with regard to the topics covered and the depth with which they are treated.

10 *Speed:* Since a number of individuals are being interviewed at the same time, the group interview speeds up the data collection and analysis process.

The focus group interview is an exploratory research technique which can be extremely valuable in developing hypotheses regarding problems and opportunities, facilitating the development of a clear statement of the decision problem, and stimulating the creative process designed to formulate alternative courses of action. Conclusive research is the next logical step in the testing of these hypotheses and the evaluation of the courses of action. In special circumstances, the decision maker's experience and judgment may be sufficient for a course of action to be selected without gathering conclusive research evidence. Most typically, however, such evidence is required, and the decision maker would be making a serious error to assume that the focus group interview could provide evidence of a conclusive nature.

We have just touched upon a major disadvantage of the focus group interview, namely, that the decision maker cannot use the evidence in a conclusive research manner. The evidence is not projectable to a target segment for two reasons. First, the sample is not representative of the target segment in the sense that quantitative statements can be made regarding the significance of the research findings. Second, the evidence itself is highly dependent upon the experience and perception of the moderator and other observers. The danger is that the decision maker may use the exploratory findings as conclusive evidence to support preconceived notions about the decision situation.

As in any area of human endeavor, there are individuals who will compromise proper research procedures for personal gain. With the focus group interview, these improper procedures involve poor recruitment of participants, poor physical environment, and an unskilled moderator.

Depth Interview   The depth interview may be defined as an *unstructured personal interview which uses extensive probing to get a single respondent to talk freely and to express detailed beliefs and feelings on a topic.* The purpose of this technique is to get below the respondent's surface reactions and discover the more fundamental reasons underlying the respondent's attitudes and behavior.

The depth interview can extend over an hour or more with the interviewer typically committing to memory the outline of topics to be covered. The actual wording of questions and their sequencing are left to the discretion of the interviewer, who tries to identify general areas for discussion and then encourages the respondent to discuss freely, in depth, the topic of interest. The interviewer will probe responses that are of interest by asking such questions as "That's interesting, can you tell me more?" and "Why do you say that?"

While not an active participant in the discussion, the interviewer has a critical role in the success of the depth interview technique. It is the interviewer's responsibility to create an environment where the respondent is relaxed and free to present beliefs and feelings without fear of criticism or lack of understanding. As in the focus group interview, the interviewer's role is central to the success of this technique.

The advantage of the depth interview over the focus group interview relates to the greater depth of insight that can be uncovered and the ability to associate the response directly with the respondent. With the focus group interview it is difficult to determine which respondent made a particular response. In addition, the interviewer can develop a high level of rapport with the respondent, which results in a freer exchange of responses than may be possible with the focus group technique.

As with the focus group interview, the primary use of the depth interview is exploratory research. The technique is useful in developing hypotheses, defining decision problems, and formulating courses of action.

The depth interview is seldom used in marketing research. The disadvantages of the technique contribute to its limited use, and its success rests entirely with the skills and experience of the interviewer. Since there are few adequately qualified interviewers and those who are qualified are highly paid, the technique has not experienced wide acceptance as a regular research tool. The length of the interview combined with the high interviewer cost means that the number of persons interviewed in a project is small. The small sample size and the complete reliance on the interviewer for analysis and interpretation are important limitations that restrict this technique's use to special problem situations.

Unstructured-Indirect Unstructured-indirect data collection techniques are called *projective techniques*. They come from clinical psychology and are designed to obtain data indirectly about respondents' beliefs and feelings. Structured-direct data collection techniques presume that the respondents clearly understand their beliefs and feelings and are willing to communicate these data directly. However, in certain situations, this may not be the case. Projective techniques are designed to explore the "whys" of behavior. A projective technique can be defined as any indirect form of questioning in which an environment is created which encourages the respondent to freely project beliefs and feelings regarding the topic of interest.

Projective techniques require the respondents to interpret the behavior of others, rather than directly asking them to report their beliefs and feelings. In interpreting the behavior of others, the respondents are indirectly projecting their own beliefs and feelings into the situation.

While the majority of projective techniques are easily administered and interpreted, their use in marketing research has been limited to special situations where attitudes cannot be directly measured. The most commonly found in marketing research are (1) the Thematic Apperception Test, (2) role playing, (3) cartoon completion, (4) word association, and (5) sentence completion.

Thematic Apperception Test The Thematic Apperception Test (TAT)[13] is the most frequently used projective technique in marketing research. TAT involves use of one or

---

[13] "Thematic" stands for themes that are elicited, and "apperception" stands for the perceptual-interpretive use of pictures.

more pictures or cartoons which depict a situation relating to the product or topic under investigation. The cartoon format is most frequently used. The pictures or cartoons are neutral, in that few clues as to positive or negative feelings are present in the situation. The respondent is presented with this ambiguous situation and asked to describe what has happened or what will happen as a result of the situation. This leaves the respondent free to indirectly project personal beliefs and feelings into the interpretation of what is happening.

Role Playing   Role playing, or the third-person technique, presents the respondent with either a verbal or visual situation. Rather than directly expressing personal beliefs and feelings regarding the situation, the respondent is asked to relate the beliefs and feelings of another person to the situation. This third person can be a friend, a neighbor, or a "typical" person. In describing the reaction of others, it is believed, the respondent will reveal personal beliefs and feelings regarding the situation.

A popular version of this technique is to provide the respondent with a description of what a person has purchased and ask the respondent to characterize that person. It is assumed that the respondent's beliefs and feelings toward the products on the list will be reflected in the description of the purchaser.[14]

Cartoon Completion   The cartoon completion technique presents the respondent with a cartoon drawing containing one or more people in a particular situation. The respondent is asked to complete a cartoon in response to the comment of another cartoon character. The cartoon captions are typically depicted with a bubble next to the cartoon character. Examples are: "My friend bought a digital watch," "We are planning to purchase a microwave oven," "Our neighbors purchased a foreign car," and the like.

Word Association   The word association technique consists of presenting a series of words to a respondent, then recording thoughts that come to the respondent as a result of exposure to a word.

The words read to the respondent are carefully selected and sequenced to reveal his or her beliefs and feelings. A version of this procedure is to ask the respondent to quickly give as many single words as possible in response to each word presented by the interviewer.

Word association tests are analyzed by the frequency with which a response is given, by the amount of hesitation in responding, and by the number of respondents who cannot respond to a test word after a reasonable time period. The common responses are analyzed to reveal patterns of beliefs and feelings. Respondents who hesitate are assumed to be sufficiently emotionally involved that an immediate response is delayed. Nonresponse is assumed to indicate a very high level of emotional involvement.

Sentence Completion   The sentence completion test is similar to the word association test and requires the respondent to finish an incomplete sentence. The beginning phrase is read to the respondent, who is asked to complete the sentence. The meaning of the beginning phrase is disguised such that there is no correct response. The respondent is instructed to reply with the first thoughts that come to mind, and the responses are analyzed for their content. Since this test requires more thought in the

[14] Mason Haire, "Projective Techniques in Marketing Research," *Journal of Marketing*, vol. 14, pp. 649–656, April 1950; see also C. R. Hill, "Haire's Classic Instant Coffee Study—18 Years Later," *Journalism Quarterly*, vol. 45, pp. 466–472, August 1968.

responses, it is argued that it provides better results than the word association test.

Projective techniques, like the depth interview, have significant disadvantages which contribute to their limited use in marketing research. Since they typically require personal interviews using highly skilled interviewers and interpreters to analyze the data, they tend to be a very expensive research tool. The high cost per respondent interviewed has resulted in the use of small nonprobability sample sizes, which result in high sampling errors. Projective techniques are complex and can be highly misleading in the hands of an amateur.[15]

Despite these limitations, projective techniques have been found to be useful in many situations.[16] Their proper use still lies in exploratory research designed to discover hypotheses to be tested using more structured and direct research techniques.

Structured-Indirect   The structured-indirect approach is often called the *performance of objective task technique*. Respondents are asked to memorize and/or report factual information about the topic of interest. These responses are analyzed and inferences are drawn about the nature of the respondents' underlying beliefs and feelings regarding the topic.

The central assumption of this technique is that respondents are more likely to recall those things which are consistent with their beliefs and feelings. Presumably greater knowledge reflects the strength and direction of the other attitude components. This contention is based on research findings on selective information processing, findings which indicate that people tend (1) to selectively expose themselves to information, (2) to selectively perceive the information, and (3) to selectively retain information which is consistent with their attitudes. Consequently, asking respondents to recall factual information about a topic is a way to indirectly measure the direction and strength of their attitudes. Those respondents who possess the most knowledge regarding product X are assumed to have highly positive attitudes toward the product.

The structured-indirect approach is rarely used in marketing research. It represents an attempt to gain the advantages of indirect attitude measurement with the data collection and processing advantages of structured approaches. Whether the measurement of factual information is a valid indicator of the direction and strength of the underlying attitude structure is a subject of concern to many researchers.

Communication Media

The previous section classified communication techniques on the basis of a combination of structure and directness. Another classification scheme focuses on the types of communication media available for obtaining data from respondents. Three communication media are available: (1) personal interview, (2) telephone interview, and (3) mail interview.

---

[15] P. Sampson, "Qualitative Research and Motivation Research," in R. M. Worcester (ed.), *Consumer Market Research Handbook* [London: McGraw-Hill (U.K.), 1972], pp. 7–28.
[16] H. L. Steck, "On the Validity of Projective Questions," *Journal of Marketing Research*, vol. 1, pp. 48–49, August 1964.

Structured communication techniques can use all three of these. Nonstructured techniques typically require the personal interview. The telephone interview has been used successfully with the focus group technique, using a conference call arrangement with, say, doctors at various geographic locations. Telephone and mail interviews do not usually lend themselves well to unstructured techniques.

Personal Interview The personal interview consists of an interviewer asking questions of one or more respondents in a face-to-face situation. The interviewer's task is to contact the respondent(s), ask the questions, and record the responses. The questions must be asked in a clear manner and recorded accurately. The recording of responses can take place either during or after the interview.

The face-to-face interviewing process may cause the respondents to bias their responses (for example, because of desire to please or impress the interviewer).[17] This potential for social motives to bias personal interview data will be discussed in more detail in the section on criteria for selecting a communication medium.

Telephone Interview The telephone interview consists of an interviewer asking questions of one or more respondents via the telephone instead of by direct personal contact. Telephone interviewing is the most widely used of the three communication media.[18] The reasons for its popularity are its efficient and economical procedures and its application to a wide range of information needs.

With the telephone interview, the lower degree of social interaction between the interviewer and respondent reduces the potential for bias in comparison with the personal interview. The basic limitations of the telephone interview relate to the limited amount of data that can be obtained and the potential bias that can result from an incomplete listing of the target population (i.e., unlisted telephones and non-phone ownership).

Mail Interview The mail interview consists of a questionnaire mailed to the respondent and the return by mail of the complete questionnaire to the research organization. It is as popular as the personal interview but less so than the telephone interview.[19]

Mail interviews are flexible in their application and relatively low in cost, and they lack the potential for bias resulting from the interview-respondent interaction. The major disadvantage relates to the problem of nonresponse error.

Many approaches can be used to distribute and collect the questionnaire. It can be left and/or retrieved by an individual rather than using the mail.[20] It can be distributed in magazines and newspapers. Warranty cards can be attached to products and data collected regarding the characteristics of the purchaser and the purchase decision process.

---

[17] J. B. Lansing and J. N Morgan, *Economic Survey Methods* (Ann Arbor: The University of Michigan Press, 1971), p. 160.

[18] T. T. Tyebjee, "Telephone Survey Methods: The State of the Art," *Journal of Marketing,* vol. 43, p. 68, Summer 1979.

[19] Ibid.

[20] R. V. Stover and W. J. Stone, "Hand Delivery of Self-Administered Questionnaires," *Public Opinion Quarterly,* vol. 38, pp. 284–287, Summer 1974.

Criteria for Selecting Communication Media

Several criteria are relevant for evaluating which communication media best meet the needs of a research project, namely: (1) versatility, (2) cost, (3) time, (4) sample control, (5) quantity of data, (6) quality of data, and (7) response rate. The importance assigned these criteria will vary with the specific needs of the research project.

Versatility   Versatility refers to the ability of the medium to adapt the data collection process to the special needs of the study or the respondent. The personal interview is the most versatile of the three communication media. Telephone interviews are less versatile than personal interviews, while the mail interview is the least versatile.

The personal interview has high versatility in that the interviewing process involves a face-to-face relationship between the respondent and interviewer. The latter can explain and clarify complex questions, administer complex questionnaires, utilize unstructured techniques, and present visual cues such as advertisements and product concepts to the respondent as part of the questioning process. The telephone interview is not as versatile as the personal interview in that the interviewer is not in a face-to-face relationship with the respondent. Consequently, it is more difficult to use unstructured techniques, to include complex questions, and to require in-depth answers to open-ended questions. When the research design involves structured questions with simple instructions which can be answered easily by the respondent, the interviewer's role can often be eliminated, and the mail interview may be the more appropriate medium for the study.

The researcher must determine the degree of versatility required in a research project and select the communication media which best meet the needs of the study. In practice, most research projects do not require the high versatility that the personal interview provides.

Cost   The number of hours of labor tends to determine the relative cost of the three communication media. Labor costs include the salaries of the interviewers and the supervisory costs associated with controlling the quality of the data collection process.

The personal interview is typically the most expensive medium per completed interview. Telephone interviews are usually more expensive than those conducted by mail. When the questionnaire is short, the cost of the telephone interview usually compares with that of the mail interview.

While the cost of a communication medium is highly dependent upon the specific details of the research design, a general estimate of data collection cost per completed interview would be as follows: (1) personal interview—$10 to $30, (2) telephone interview—$5 to $15, and (3) mail interview—$5 to $12.[21]

Time   Among the three communication media, the telephone interview is the fastest way to obtain data. With a short questionnaire, an interviewer can complete perhaps 10 or more interviews per hour. Using the same questionnaire, a personal interviewer

---

[21] The cost per interview, which includes data collection, analysis, and report, would be: (1) personal interview—$25 to $55, (2) telephone interview—$10 to $25, and (3) mail interview—$10 to $22.

would be fortunate to complete two or three interviews per hour. Obviously the travel time between interviews represents a serious time constraint on the personal interviewer's completion rate. Consequently, personal interview studies are typically longer in elapsed time from the beginning of field work to project completion than telephone or mail interview studies.

The total project completion time can be shortened by increasing the number of interviewers working on the study when the personal or telephone interview is used. With the telephone interview it is reasonably easy to train, coordinate, and control the staff of interviewers.[22] Since the interviewing staff can phone from a central location, the project supervisor can easily monitor the interviews and control the quality of the interviewing. Consequently, a large interviewing force can be efficiently used with telephone interviewing to meet the time constraint placed on a research project.

While the number of personal interviewers can also be increased to meet the time constraints placed on a project, the problems associated with training, coordinating, and controlling a large interviewing staff are compounded very quickly, to a point where it is neither feasible nor economical to increase the number of interviewers on the project. Consequently, personal interview studies are typically longer in elapsed time than mail or telephone studies.

It is very difficult to shorten the elapsed time for completing a mail study. Once the questionnaires are mailed, there is little the researcher can do to speed their completion and return. Typically, it takes two or three weeks to secure the bulk of the replies. A series of follow-up mailings may be required to stimulate the return of the remaining questionnaires. Each follow-up mailing may require two or more weeks to determine whether an acceptable response rate is going to be achieved. While several months could be required to complete a mail study, if the number of interviews to be completed is large, the elapsed time may not be as great as that required to conduct a similar study using personal interviews.

Sample Control   Sample control refers to the ability of the communication media *to reach the designated units in the sampling plan effectively and efficiently.* The three communication media differ significantly in this regard.

The personal interview offers the best degree of sample control. As discussed in Chapter 9, area sampling procedures exist which overcome the problems created by the absence of a complete listing of the sampling frame. The sampling frame is the list of population units from which the sample will be drawn. Sampling procedures which do not require a list of the sampling units rely heavily upon the personal interviewer in the process of selecting the sample. Working through the personal interviewer, the researcher can control which sampling units are interviewed, who is interviewed, the degree of participation of other members of the unit in the interview, and many other aspects of the data collection process.

The telephone interview is highly dependent upon a sampling frame. One or more telephone directories usually serve as the sampling frame, with respondents being

---

[22] J. O. Eastlack, Jr., and H. Assael, "Better Telephone Surveys through Centralized Interviewing," *Journal of Advertising Research,* vol. 6, pp. 2–7, March 1966.

selected from directories serving the population of interest using probabilistic selection procedures.

Telephone directories are often poor sampling frames in that they are an incomplete listing of persons in an area for the following reasons: (1) not everyone has a phone, (2) phone directories are old and do not reflect new phones in service since the directory was published, and (3) some people have unlisted phones.

Telephone ownership in the United States is very high. In 1971 it was estimated that 93 percent of households had telephones.[23] Today telephone ownership is near 100 percent in most areas of the country. Consequently, phone ownership is typically not a serious problem for most telephone studies.

In some areas, estimates as to the percentage of phones not listed in new phone directories run as high as 30 percent.[24] This can be a serious source of bias, since research indicates that persons with voluntary unlisted numbers differ from persons with listed phone numbers on a number of important demographic characteristics.[25]

As telephone directories grow older, an increasing proportion of persons who have moved to the area do not have an opportunity to list their phone in the current directory. Since persons who move frequently differ from less mobile persons on a number of demographic characteristics, older phone directories become less representative of the population of phone owners.

Because of unrepresentative phone directories, the telephone interview permits only limited control over the sample. The procedure designed to overcome this problem is *random-digit dialing.*[26] As we discussed in Chapter 12, this procedure involves the random generation of at least some of the digits used in the sampling plan. A central interviewing facility can be used to place calls, using the Wide Area Telephone Service (WATS).[27] This allows a geographically wide sampling plan. However, even with these improvements, telephone surveys still rely on simple random sampling or systematic sampling. As discussed in the sampling chapters, alternative sampling procedures exist which are more efficient than either of these.

The mail interview, like the telephone interview, requires a listing of the population elements. Ideally, this frame is composed of both names and addresses. Typically, telephone street directories are used for a listing of the general population. The problems in the use of this type of list have already been discussed.

Several commercial research firms have panels of respondents who have agreed to answer mail questionnaires sent to them. One such organization is National Family Opinion (NFO). This form maintains a panel of over 150,000 U.S. families who have agreed to cooperate without compensation in completing questionnaires mailed to them on a variety of subjects. A current demographic profile is maintained for each

[23] *Statistical Abstract of the United States,* 1973, 94th ed. (U.S. Bureau of the Census, 1973), p. 496.

[24] G. J. Glasser and G. D. Metzger, "Random-Digit Dialing As a Method of Telephone Sampling," *Journal of Marketing Research,* vol. 9, pp. 59–64, February 1972.

[25] J. A. Brunner and G. A. Brunner, "Are Voluntary Unlisted Telephone Subscribers Really Different?" *Journal of Marketing Research,* vol. 8, pp. 121–124, February 1971; S. Roslow and L. Roslow, "Unlisted Phone Subscribers Are Different," *Journal of Advertising Research,* vol. 12, pp. 25–38, August 1972.

[26] S. Sudman, "The Uses of Telephone Directories for Survey Sampling," *Journal of Marketing Research,* vol. 10, pp. 204–207, May 1973; M. Hauck and M. Cox, "Locating a Sample by Random Digit Dialing," *Public Opinion Quarterly,* vol. 38, pp. 253–260, Summer 1974.

[27] Eastlack and Assael, op. cit.

family. Other organizations which maintain mail panels are the Home Testing Institute and Market Facts, Inc.

Mailing lists for specialized groups of respondents can be purchased from firms that specialize in this area. Catalogs are available which contain thousands of lists, many of which can be segmented in various ways.[28] Even with a mailing list that contains the target population, the researcher still has the problem of limited control over the person or persons at the mailing address who complete the questionnaire, as well as whether it will be returned.

Quantity of Data   An established rule is that the largest amount of data can be collected using the personal interview, followed by the mail interview, and then the telephone interview. There is growing evidence that the mail and telephone interview can collect more data than previously assumed. In situations where the respondents are emotionally involved in the topic, all three media can provide substantial amounts of data. At normal involvement levels, however, the personal interview can collect substantially more data than the other two.

The main advantage of the personal interview stems from the social relationship between the interviewer and the respondent. This social setting typically motivates the respondent to spend more time in the interview setting. The University of Michigan Survey Research Center finds that a 75-minute interview is feasible with the personal interview, while the telephone interviews must be limited to 30 or 40 minutes.[29] It is much easier for the respondent to terminate the telephone or mail interview, because of its impersonal nature, than to terminate the personal interview.

An advantage of the personal and telephone interview over the mail interview is that less effort is required of the respondent in the data collection process. Here, the interviewer asks the questions, probes the responses, and records the answers. The personal interview has the added advantage of allowing the visual presentation of rating scale categories and other support material that can facilitate the respondent's comprehension of the questions asked. These advantages all contribute to the respondent's willingness to provide a greater quantity of data.

Quality of Data   Quality of data refers to the degree to which the data are *free from potential bias resulting from the use of a particular communication medium*. When the subject matter is unemotional and the questionnaire is properly designed and administered, quality data will generally result regardless of which medium is used.

Researchers have found substantial differences among the three media when sensitive or embarrassing questions are involved, e.g., bank loans, income, or sexual behavior. For sensitive topics, there is evidence that mail surveys collect better-quality data than personal interviews.[30] Telephone interviews most likely would lie between these two media.

---

[28] *1973–1974 Catalog of Mailing Lists* (New York: Fritz S. Hofheimer, Inc., 1972).

[29] Personal communication with Richard T. Curtin, Director, Surveys of Consumer Attitudes, Survey Research Center, University of Michigan.

[30] B. Dunning and D. Cahalan, "By Mail versus Field Self-Administered Questionnaires: An Armed Forces Survey," *Public Opinion Quarterly*, vol. 34, pp. 618–624, Winter 1973–74; F. Wiseman, "Methodological Bias in Public Opinion Surveys," *Public Opinion Quarterly*, vol. 36, pp. 105–108, Spring 1972.

Another source of bias can result from respondent confusion regarding the question asked. Since the respondent cannot seek clarification from the interviewer with the mail interview, it offers the greatest chance for inaccurate results resulting from confusion. The telephone interview would offer more potential for bias from confusion than the personal interview because of the lack of an interviewer's physical presence.

The mail interview has another potential bias which can result from the respondent's reading through the questions before answering them or changing answers earlier in the questionnaire as a result of responses given later in the questionnaire. Both the personal and telephone interview are free from this type of bias.

The quality of data obtained in telephone interviews tends to be better than that from personal interviews because the data collection process can be better supervised and controlled. Fewer interviewers are needed for the telephone survey, and they can be trained and supervised at a central location.

Both the telephone and personal interview have an important advantage over the mail interview in that they can be used to collect data near the time the behavior occurs. This reduces the bias associated with failure to recall events accurately.

A final consideration regarding the quality of data obtained concerns cheating by the interviewer. Cheating is easier with the personal interview, since the phone interview can be directly monitored and the former cannot. Since the mail interview does not have an interviewer, it is not subject to bias resulting from cheating. Properly designed personal interview studies have procedures for controlling cheating which can be effective in minimizing this source of bias.

Response Rate   Response rate refers to the percentage of the original sample that is actually interviewed. A low response rate can result in a high nonresponse error, which can invalidate the research findings. Nonresponse error is the difference between those who respond to a survey and those who do not respond.

Nonresponse error is one of the most serious sources of error confronting the researcher.[31] Table 13-2 illustrates the type of difference that can exist between those who respond and those who do not respond. The median income of respondents for each of a series of callback interviews is shown. A policy of no callbacks (median income of $4188) would have produced an estimate of income 25 percent below that found after extensive callbacks (median income of $5598). This finding represents a clear example of nonresponse error.

The probability of nonresponse error increases as the survey response rate decreases. However, it is important to recognize that a low response rate in itself does not imply that a high nonresponse error is present in the data. It is only when there is a difference between respondents and nonrespondents on the variables of interest that nonresponse error occurs. If the reason for nonresponse is independent of the key variables of interest, there should be little difference between the respondent and nonrespondent groups.

[31] P. Ognibene, "Traits Affecting Questionnaire Response," *Journal of Advertising Research*, vol. 10, pp. 18–20, June 1970; R. L. Day and J. B. Wilcox, "A Simulation Analysis of Nonresponse Error in Survey Sampling," in F. C. Allvine (ed.), *Relevance in Marketing: Marketing in Motion* (Chicago: American Marketing Association, 1971), pp. 478–483.

TABLE 13-2   MEDIAN INCOME VARIATION BY NUMBER OF CALLBACKS

Number of call at which interviewed	Median income	Number of interviews
1	$4188	427
2	5880	391
3	6010	232
4	6200	123
5	6010	77
6+	7443	59
All	$5598	1309

Source: J. B. Lansing and J. N. Morgan, *Economic Survey Methods* (Ann Arbor: The University of Michigan Press, 1971), p. 161. Used with permission of the University of Michigan Press.

Nonresponse can result from two sources: (1) not-at-homes and (2) refusals. Nonresponse caused by the respondent not being at home can seriously affect telephone and personal interviews, but it has limited influence on mail surveys. Since respondents are more likely to answer a phone than to answer the door when a stranger is present, the telephone interview has less of a not-at-home problem than the personal interview.

Once a potential respondent has informed the interviewer of an unwillingness to be interviewed, there is little that can be done to reverse the respondent's position. While the offer to call at another time may be favorably received by some respondents, the majority still refuse the interview.

While the mail interview avoids the nonresponse caused by not-at-homes, it is seriously influenced by the refusal to respond. However, the failure to complete and return the questionnaire on time does not imply a strong unwillingness to respond. Many respondents may be influenced to respond if reminded.

The major emphasis on reducing nonresponse in personal and telephone interviews centers on establishing contact with the potential respondent. A series of callbacks is required to reduce the proportion of not-at-homes.[32] Most situations require a minimum of three callbacks. The callback schedule should be varied by time of day and by day of the week. An excellent guide for the scheduling of telephone and personal interviews is provided by the Bureau of the Census.[33] This study provides estimates of the proportion of people at home between 8:00 A.M. and 9:00 P.M. on an hourly basis.

The reduction of nonresponse in mail surveys focuses on motivating the respondent to answer the questionnaire and return it. The response rate of the mail interview is directly related to the respondent's interest in the survey topic.[34] If the target

---

[32] W. C. Dunkelberg and G. S. Day, "Nonresponse Bias and Callbacks in Sample Surveys," *Journal of Marketing Research*, vol. 10, p. 160, May 1973.

[33] Bureau of the Census, *Who's Home When* (Government Printing Office, 1973).

[34] R. F. Mautz and F. L. Neumann, "The Effective Corporate Audit Committee," *Harvard Business Review*, vol. 48, p. 58, November–December 1970.

population's interest in the survey topic varies, a serious source of nonresponse error can be introduced to the results.

Some of the more successful ways to increase the response rate of mail surveys are as follows.[35]

1 Use an advance letter or telephone call notifying the respondent of the study and requesting cooperation.

2 Use first-class postage in mailing to the respondent and provide handstamped return envelopes.

3 Consider the use of a monetary incentive in those situations where motivation needs to be stimulated.

4 Use a postcard or letter in follow-up contacts requesting completion and return of the questionnaire. Other follow-ups include phone contacts, telegraph, a new questionnaire, and personal contact.

A five-step procedure for securing returns to mail surveys was proposed by Robin.[36] These steps include (1) a prequestionnaire letter, (2) a questionnaire with cover letter, (3) a follow-up letter, (4) a second questionnaire, and (5) a third follow-up letter. A seven-day interval between mailings is recommended.[37] A 77.8 percent response rate was achieved using this five-step procedure in a mail survey of dentists.[38]

Mail surveys conducted by experienced researchers should achieve response rates of over 50 percent, and some surveys achieve rates as high as 80 percent. An 80 percent response rate is suggested as the standard for mail surveys by the Advertising Research Foundation.[39] In practice, most fall substantially below this rate. A mail survey which achieves an 80 percent return rate is comparable to many personal and telephone interview studies in the proportion of completed interviews.

For all three communication media, the decision regarding the number of callbacks involves weighing the benefits of reduced nonresponse error against the additional cost of the callback campaign. The central issue is: "How different is the nonrespondent group from the respondent group?" Several methods for estimating the degree of nonresponse error have been proposed and will be briefly discussed.[40]

1 *Sensitivity analysis.* Determine how different each successive callback group is from the previous respondent group. If the management decision is insensitive to this difference, cease future callbacks.

[35] For an expanded discussion of this topic which includes an extensive series of references, see Donald S. Tull and Del I. Hawkins, *Marketing Research* (New York: Macmillan, 1976), pp. 391–394.

[36] S. S. Robin, "A Procedure for Securing Returns to Mail Questionnaires," *Sociology and Social Research*, vol. 50, pp. 24–35, October 1965.

[37] R. C. Nichols and M. A. Meyer, "Timing Postcard Follow-ups in Mail Questionnaire Surveys," *Public Opinion Quarterly*, vol. 30, pp. 306–307, Summer 1966.

[38] A. F. Williams and H. Wechsler, "The Mail Survey: Methods to Minimize Bias Owing to Incomplete Response," *Sociology and Social Research*; vol. 54, pp. 553–535, July 1970.

[39] Paul L. Erdos, "Data Collection Methods: Mail Surveys," in Robert Ferber (ed.), *Handbook of Marketing Research* (New York: McGraw-Hill, 1974), p. 2-102.

[40] For an expanded discussion of this topic, see Tull and Hawkins, op. cit., pp. 394–396.

2 *Trend projection.* Based on the results of successive waves of callbacks, if a trend develops on the variables of interest, it can be used to estimate the characteristics of the nonrespondent group.

3 *Subsample measurement.* A specially designed telephone or personal interview is used to estimate the results of the nonrespondent group. This estimate is then incorporated into the data set of those who responded to the survey.

4 *Subjective estimate.* The researcher, given the nature of the survey topic, uses experience and judgment to estimate the degree of nonresponse error.

Selection of Communication Medium   Which communication medium should be selected for a study? The answer is the medium which is best capable of meeting the information needs of the study given the time and cost constraints. It should be emphasized that the three communication media are not mutually exclusive. Various combinations of media can be used in the research design; this allows the researcher to design a study which builds on the strengths of all three media.

Observation Method

Observation involves the recording of the respondent's behavior; it is the process of *recognizing and recording the behavior of people, objects, and events.*

Informal observation is used extensively by decision makers. All marketers take special note of customer buying patterns, competitive advertising and pricing, product availability, and so forth. The danger in drawing conclusions from informal observation, as in the case of informal communication, is that the potential for both sampling and nonsampling errors is very large. Consequently, techniques for formal observation are designed to control these errors and provide valid data for decision making. This section presents the techniques used in formal observation.

It is rare for a research design to rely entirely on the observational method. Estimates suggest that no more than 1 percent of research projects are of this nature.[41] Consequently, the observational method has major weaknesses when compared with other data collection methods. In practice, observational techniques are used in conjunction with other data collection techniques. It is important to understand the advantages and disadvantages of the observational method to position its role in the array of data collection tools available to the researcher.

Advantages of the Observation Method   The observation method has several advantages when compared with the communication method. First, it does not rely on the respondent's willingness to provide the desired data. Second, the potential bias caused by the interviewer and the interviewing process is reduced or eliminated. Therefore, observational data should be more accurate. Third, certain types of data can be collected only by observation. Obviously, those behavior patterns of which the respondent is not aware can be recorded only by observation.

---

[41] Michael L. Ray, *Unobtrusive Marketing Research Techniques* (Cambridge, Mass.: Marketing Science Institute, 1973), p. 13.

Disadvantages of the Observation Method   The observation method has two major weaknesses which significantly limit its use. First is the inability to observe such things as awareness, beliefs, feelings, and preferences. In addition, it is difficult to observe a host of personal and intimate activities such as applying makeup and deodorant, eating, family games with the children, and late-evening TV watching. Second, the observed behavior patterns must be of a short duration, occur frequently, or be reasonably predictable if the data collection costs and time requirements are to be competitive with other data collection techniques. This requirement limits the observation method to a unique set of circumstances.

Observational Techniques Classified

Observational techniques can be classified five ways: (1) natural or contrived observation, (2) disguised or undisguised observation, (3) structured or unstructured observation, (4) direct or indirect observation, and (5) human or mechanical observation. Observational techniques will typically possess degrees of these characteristics rather than the dichotomous distinction as presented.

Natural versus Contrived Observation   Natural observation involves observing behavior as it takes place normally in the environment, e.g., shopping in a grocery store. Contrived observation involves creating an artificial environment and observing the behavior patterns exhibited by persons put in this environment, e.g., having people shop in a simulated grocery store.

The advantage of a more natural environmental setting is the increased probability that the exhibited behavior will more accurately reflect true behavior patterns. Against this must be weighed the added costs of waiting for the behavior to occur and the difficulty of measuring behavior in a natural setting.

Disguised versus Undisguised Observation   Disguise refers to whether or not the respondents are aware they are being observed. The role of the observer should be disguised in situations where people would behave differently if they knew they were being observed. Various approaches such as two-way mirrors, hidden cameras, and observers dressed as sales clerks can be used to disguise the observations.

Researchers disagree as to how much the presence of the observer will affect people's behavior patterns. One position is that the observer effect is small and short-term,[42] and the other is that the observer can introduce serious bias in the observed behavior patterns.[43]

Structured versus Unstructured Observation   Structured observation is appropriate when the decision problem has been clearly defined and the specification of

---

[42] F. Kerlinger, *Foundations of Behavioral Research*, 2d ed.(New York: Holt, 1973), p. 538.
[43] E. J. Webb, D. T. Campbell, K. D. Schwartz, and L. Sechrest, *Unobtrusive Measures: Nonreactive Research in the Social Sciences* (Chicago: Rand McNally, 1966), pp. 113–114.

information needs permits a clear identification of the behavior patterns to be observed and measured. Unstructured observation is appropriate in situations where the decision problem has yet to be formulated and a great deal of flexibility is needed in the observation to develop hypotheses useful in defining the problem and in identifying opportunities. This distinction is similar to that observed in the discussion of communication methods.

Structured observation is more appropriate for conclusive research studies. When using the structured approach the researcher must specify in detail what is to be observed and how the measurements are to be recorded. The structuring of the observation reduces the potential for observer bias and increases the reliability of the data.

Unstructured observation is more appropriate for exploratory research studies. Here, the observer is free to monitor those behavior patterns which seem relevant to the decision situation. Since there is great opportunity for observer bias, the research findings should be treated as hypotheses to be tested with a conclusive research design.

Direct versus Indirect Observation   Direct observation refers to observing behavior as it actually occurs. Indirect observation refers to observing some record of past behavior. Here, the effects of behavior are observed rather than the behavior itself. This involves the examination of *physical traces*, a process which includes such things as counting the number of empty liquor containers in trash cans to estimate the liquor consumption of households.[44] A *pantry audit* is an example of the use of physical traces. Here, the observer asks the respondent if the pantry can be inspected for certain types of products. The successful use of the indirect observation approach rests with the ability of the researcher to identify creatively those physical traces which can provide useful data for the problem at hand.

Human versus Mechanical Observation   In some situations it is appropriate to supplement or replace the human observer with some form of mechanical observer. The reason could be increased accuracy, lower costs, or special measurement requirements. The major mechanical devices used in observation include the (1) motion picture camera, (2) Audimeter, (3) psychogalvanometer, (4) eye-camera, and (5) pupilometer.

The *motion picture camera* can be used to record shopping behavior in supermarkets, drugstores, and the like. Here, the observer evaluates the film and measures the desired behavior. The use of several observers plus repeated viewing allows more accurate measurement of behavior.

The *Audimeter* is a device developed by the A. C. Nielsen Company to record when radio and television sets are turned on and the station to which they are tuned. The observations made from a sample of households are important in determining which programs are aired and which are canceled.

---

[44] H. G. Sawyer, "The Meaning of Numbers," speech before the American Association of Advertising Agencies, 1961. Reported by Webb et al., op. cit., pp. 41–42.

The *psychogalvanometer* measures changes in perspiration rate from which inferences are drawn regarding a person's emotional reaction to stimuli present at the time of the measurement. The stimuli presented might include brand names, copy slogans, or advertisements. It is assumed that the stronger the reaction, the more favorable the person's attitude.

The *eye-camera* measures the movements of the eye. It is used to determine how a person reads a magazine, newspaper, advertisement, package, and the like. Measurements are taken on the sequence of what is observed and the time spent looking at various sections.

The *pupilometer* measures changes in the diameter of the pupil of the eye. An increase in pupil diameter is assumed to reflect the person's favorable reaction to the stimuli being observed.

Children

With children today spending more than $2 billion a year on personal purchases, it's no wonder that marketers are anxious to understand their wants and needs. This is no simple task, though. Some children are reluctant to respond to any type of questioning. Others do their best to resist giving accurate responses to the interviewer. Children often give what they feel is the "right answer," rather than divulging their true feelings. Researchers have come up with several techniques to help overcome these problems.

First, marketing information can be collected by observing children's play. Small groups are placed in structured lab settings, where products of possible interest to the kids are scattered throughout the lab. The manufacturers or advertisers can then observe their reactions to the various products. Other methods of analyzing play include having one researcher play games with the children while a psychologist observes and analyzes their reactions. "Games" can include charades, word associations, pretending to be Mom or Dad, and acting out favorite commercials.

It is also possible to use structured methods in researching children. A short questionnaire specifically for children has been developed by John R. Rossiter.[45] It can be self-administered by the child in 5 to 10 minutes. Furthermore, it is very reliable, having both statistically high internal consistency and test-retest reliability. Variations of the Rossiter questionnaire have been used extensively by researchers because of its ease in scoring and its proven reliability.

When depth interviews are used, it often behooves an interviewer to ask for nonverbal, rather than verbal responses, especially in younger children. Children are more likely to point to a picture or a smile-face to indicate their degree of product liking than they are to tell the interviewer their feelings. Asking young children to verbalize responses is more a test of their verbal capabilities than of their opinions about the question posed.

[45] *Marketing News*, vol. 17, no. 2, sec. 2 pp. 21–20, Jan. 21, 1983.

These techniques are among the many employed by marketing researchers to discover the wants and needs of children. Their increasing importance in the family decision-making process has made children a valuable source of marketing information.

SUMMARY

1 Respondents are a major primary source of marketing data. Data can be collected from respondents by means of communication and observation. Communication requires the respondent to provide data actively through verbal response, while observation involves the recording of the respondent's behavior. There are three types of respondent data: (1) past behavior, (2) attitudes, and (3) respondent characteristics.

2 The advantages of the communication method are (1) versatility, (2) speed, and (3) cost, and the possible disadvantages are (1) the respondent's unwillingness to provide data, (2) the respondent's inability to provide data, and (3) the influence of the questioning process.

3 The structured-direct questionnaire is the most common data collection technique. Here, the questions asked and the possible responses are predetermined. In addition, the objective of the study is obvious to the respondent from the questions asked. This technique is used for conclusive research purposes.

4 The unstructured-direct approach involves a high degree of flexibility in how the questions are asked and in the degree of probing. The techniques which use this approach are (1) the focus group interview and (2) the depth interview. The former is the more popular of the two, and the primary use of the both techniques is for exploratory research.

5 The unstructured-indirect approach uses projective techniques designed to obtain data indirectly about respondent's beliefs and feelings. The most common techniques used in marketing research are (1) the Thematic Apperception Test, (2) role playing, (3) cartoon completion, (4) word association, and (5) sentence completion. These techniques have experienced limited use in marketing research, their primary use being for exploratory research purposes.

6 The structured-indirect approach assumes that asking respondents to recall factual information about a topic is a way to indirectly measure their attitudes. This approach is rarely used in marketing research.

7 Three communication media are available: (1) personal interviews, (2) telephone interviews, and (3) mail interviews. All three can be used with structured techniques, while the personal interview is typically required for unstructured techniques. The criteria for selecting among these media are (1) versatility, (2) cost, (3) time, (4) sample control, (5) quantity of data, (6) quality of data, and (7) response rate.

8 The advantages of the observation method are: (1)·it does not rely on the respondent's willingness to provide the data, (2) the potential for bias from the interviewer and interviewing process is reduced, and (3) certain types of data can be collected only with this method. The disadvantages are: (1) one cannot observe constructs and certain behavior patterns, and (2) cost and time constraints limit observation to behavior patterns which are short in duration, occur frequently, or are predictable. These disadvantages seriously limit the use of the observation method.

9 Observational techniques can be classified as (1) natural or contrived, (2) disguised or undisguised, (3) structured or unstructured, (4) direct or indirect, (5) human or mechanical.

DISCUSSION QUESTIONS

1 What major types of respondent data exist?

2 List the advantages and disadvantages of communication methods.

3 Discuss two major unstructured, direct communication techniques.

4 What uses in marketing can focus group interviews serve?

5 Discuss some of the issues involved in carrying out focus group interviews.

6 What are some of the desirable characteristics for focus group moderators?

7 Discuss the advantages and disadvantages of focus groups.

8 How does the depth interview differ from the focus group method?

9 What unstructured, indirect techniques are most often used in marketing?

10 List the communication media commonly used in respondent data collection; what criteria are used to select among them?

11 Identify the techniques used for estimating nonresponse error when communication media are used.

12 What are the advantages and disadvantages of observation methods?

13 Discuss the classification of observational techniques.

14 What major mechanical devices are employed in observation techniques in marketing?

CHAPTER 14

DESIGNING DATA COLLECTION FORMS

Previous chapters have discussed the types of primary and secondary marketing data, and now we consider the issues involved in designing data collection forms for primary data collection. The emphasis is on constructing forms appropriate for conclusive research, where the research design requires a structured data collection method capable of providing valid and relevant data for decision making.

The last chapter emphasized that there are various unstructured data collection techniques which require the use of forms. The nature of these forms can range from fairly structured questionnaires to rough topical outlines. The discussion presented in this chapter will apply only indirectly to the construction of forms for unstructured data collection.

Data collection forms are a central component of most research studies. All three communication media—personal, telephone, and mail interviews—rely on a questionnaire. Since questionnaire studies are far more prevalent than observational studies, the bulk of this chapter will be devoted to issues involved in questionnaire construction. While much of this discussion will be relevant to the issues involved in developing data collection forms for observation, the final section of this chapter will be specifically devoted to observational forms.

IMPORTANCE OF QUESTIONNAIRE

A questionnaire is a *formalized schedule for collecting data from respondents*. The function of the questionnaire is that of measurement. Questionnaires can be used to measure (1) past behavior, (2) attitudes, and (3) respondent characteristics.

The measurement of attitudes has grown in importance, and so has the number of attitude measurement techniques, several of which have been discussed in Chapters 11 and 13. These techniques are typically incorporated into a questionnaire. The issues involved in questionnaire design directly relate to developing and administering these attitude measurement techniques.

Measurement error is a serious problem in questionnaire construction. For example, the Survey Research Center at the University of Michigan asked half of the sample in their May 1977 consumer survey this question on attitudes toward a gasoline price increase: "Are you in favor of the proposed standby gasoline tax, starting with 5 cents and rising to 50 cents, which will be imposed if we do not meet conservation goals?" The results were that 27 percent favored the additional taxes while 65 percent opposed them. The other half of the sample was asked: "If the United States had to choose between becoming dependent on uncertain foreign oil supplies or curbing gasoline use with rising taxes, which would you favor?" In contrast to the previous finding, 71 percent favored the higher tax alternative, with only 13 percent opting for uncertain oil sources.[1] What could cause such a marked difference in responses? The answer lies in the question wording. The first question does not pose an explicit alternative to the consumer. Rather, the consumer is offered the implicit alternative of higher gasoline prices versus lower gasoline prices. It is not hard to see that consumers would prefer lower prices. The second question poses the alternative of higher prices now versus more dependence on foreign oil supplies. The lesson to be learned from this example is that when a preference question is asked without posing realistic alternatives, the results can be meaningless.

Let's consider another example. Two rather similar ways of posing a question to a sample of nonworking women have been developed. The first question is: "Would you like to have a job, if this were possible?" The second question is: "Would you prefer to have a job, or do you prefer just to do your housework?" The second question makes explicit the implied choice in the first question. Each question was put to half of a sample of nonworking women. The first question resulted in 19 percent stating they would not like to have a job, while the second question resulted in 68 percent who would not like to have a job.[2] This dramatic difference again emphasizes the importance of questionnaire wording. The researcher must ask: "Do the questions measure what they are supposed to measure?" If the answer is no, measurement error is present.

Both of the previous examples illustrate the importance of controlling measurement error in questionnaire construction. Rarely will sampling error result in outcomes of the magnitude observed in these examples. This point is expressed by one of the leading researchers in marketing research as follows:

> . . . error or bias attributable to sampling and to methods of questionnaire administration were relatively small as compared with other types of variation—especially variation attributable to different ways of wording questions.[3]

---

[1] F. Thomas Juster, "A Note on Energy Policy and Automobile Demand," *Economic Outlook USA*, Summer vol. 4, no. 3 (Ann Arbor: Survey Research Center, The University of Michigan, 1977), p. 43.

[2] E. Noelle-Neumann, "Wanted: Rules for Wording Structured Questionnaires," *Public Opinion Quarterly*, vol. 34, p. 200, Summer 1970.

[3] Samuel A. Stouffer et al., *Measurement and Prediction, Studies in Social Psychology in World War II*, vol. 4 (Princeton, N.J.: Princeton University Press, 1950), p. 709.

Consequently, a skilled researcher is needed to design the questionnaire such that the questions asked measure what they are supposed to measure.

QUESTIONNAIRE COMPONENTS

A questionnaire typically has five sections: (1) identification data, (2) request for cooperation, (3) instructions, (4) information sought, and (5) classification data.

Identification data typically occupy the first section on a questionnaire—data regarding the respondent's name, address, and phone number. Additional data would include items such as the time and date of the interview plus the interviewer's name or code number.

The *request for cooperation* is an opening statement designed to enlist the respondent's help regarding the interview. This statement typically first identifies the interviewer and/or the interviewing organization. Next, the purpose of the study is explained, and the time required to complete the interview is given.

The *instructions* refer to comments to the interviewer or respondent about how to use the questionnaire. These comments appear directly on the questionnaire when using a mail survey. With the personal and telephone survey, a separate sheet titled "Interviewer Instructions" would explain the purpose of the study, the sampling plan, and other aspects of the data collection process. In addition, the questionnaire may contain special instructions regarding the use of specific questions, e.g., attitude scaling technique.

The *information sought* forms the major portion of the questionnaire. The remainder of this chapter deals with designing this aspect of the questionnaire.

The *classification data* concern the characteristics of the respondent. These data are provided directly by the respondent in the case of a mail survey. With the personal and telephone interview surveys the data are collected from the respondent by the interviewer, or in some cases the personal interviewer may estimate more sensitive types of data based on observation, e.g., income. Classification data are typically collected at the end of the interview. However, some sampling procedures require that classification data be collected at the beginning of the interview to determine whether the person qualifies as part of the sampling plan.

QUESTIONNAIRE DESIGN

The design of a questionnaire is more of an art form than a scientific undertaking. There are no series of steps, principles, or guidelines which guarantee an effective and efficient questionnaire. Questionnaire design is a skill which the researcher learns through experience rather than by reading a series of guidelines. The only way to develop this skill is to write a questionnaire, use it in a series of interviews, analyze its weaknesses, and revise it.

What we do know about questionnaire design comes from the experience of researchers who have specialized in this area. From this accumulated experience have emerged a series of rules or guidelines which can be useful to the beginning researcher confronted with the task of designing a questionnaire. While these rules are useful in avoiding serious errors, the fine tuning of questionnaire design comes from the creative inspiration of the skilled researcher. Consequently, while the guidelines discussed in this section lay the foundation for questionnaire design, ultimately the quality of the questionnaire depends on the skill and judgment of the researcher, a clear understanding of the information needed, a sensitivity to the role of the respondent, and extensive pretesting.

The discussion of questionnaire design will be organized as a series of seven steps. At each of these steps, various guidelines for questionnaire construction will be presented. While these rules are presented as part of a step-by-step approach to questionnaire development, in practice the steps are highly interrelated. Decisions made early in the sequence will often influence choices later in the sequence, and vice versa. The seven steps, as presented in Figure 14-1, are (1) review preliminary considerations, (2) decide on question content, (3) decide on response format, (4) decide on question wording, (5) decide on question sequence, (6) decide on physical characteristics, and (7) carry out pretest, revision, and final draft.

Review Preliminary Considerations

The preliminary considerations for conducting conclusive research were discussed in Chapter 4, which focused on methods of establishing an effective link between the decision-making process and the research process. Central to this process is the development of research objectives and the listing of information needs. The research design must be formulated and the steps in the research process visualized and

FIGURE 14-1   Steps in questionnaire design.

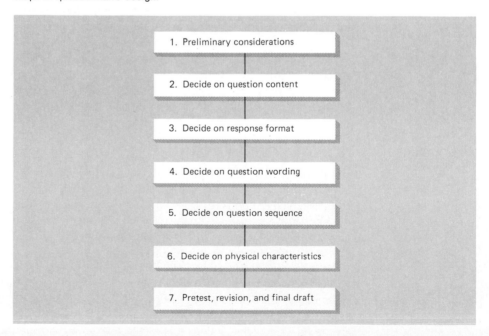

planned. Consequently, many decisions must be made before the questionnaire can be designed.

Previous Decisions   The questionnaire design stage presumes that the research project is well under way and that many decisions have already been made. Decisions regarding questionnaire design must build upon and be consistent with decisions relating to other aspects of the research project.

Previous decisions regarding the type of research design and the sources of data directly influence the character and the role of the questionnaire in the research project (see Chapters 5 and 6). It is essential to have a clear picture of the target population and to know the details of the sampling plan (see Chapters 7, 8, and 9). Questionnaire design is highly influenced by the characteristics of the respondent group. The more heterogeneous the respondent group, the more difficult it is to design a single questionnaire which is appropriate for everyone. Typically, the questionnaire must be designed to be comprehensible to the least able respondent. The measurement scales and communication media that will be used must be specified (Chapters 11 and 13). The data processing and analysis stages must be visualized, as well as the nature of the research findings. The tactical aspects of questionnaire design are closely related to these final stages of the research process. A review of Chapter 3 would illustrate the nature of these decisions in the context of an actual research project.

Link between Information Needs and Data to Be Collected   Before designing the questionnaire, the researcher must have a detailed listing of the information needs as well as a clear definition of the respondent group. The questionnaire is the link between the information needed and the data to be collected. Figure 14-2 illustrates the nature of this linkage.

The questions on the questionnaire should flow logically from the list of information needs. It would seem obvious that no question should be included on the questionnaire unless it relates to a specific information need.[4] In practice, however, there is a strong tendency to include questions which appear "interesting" but have

---

[4] Unnecessary questions can be justified if they facilitate gaining the respondent's cooperation or add continuity to the questioning process.

FIGURE 14-2   Information needs—data linkage.

no specific link to the information needs. Unnecessary questions add expense to the survey and increase the demands placed on the respondent.

Decide on Question Content

The content of the questions is influenced by the respondent's ability and/or willingness to respond accurately.

Ability to Answer Accurately   Assuming the desired data are relevant to the decision problem, the researcher must be sensitive to the respondent's ability to provide the data. Many types of data cannot be accurately collected from respondents. Inaccurate data can result from two sources: (1) the respondent is uninformed, and (2) the respondent is forgetful.

Respondent Is Uninformed   We are frequently asked questions on issues we do not have the answers to. As students, we confront this situation far too often. Questions on a questionnaire may confront respondents with the same situation. They could be asked to provide data about their spouse's monthly gross income or credit card purchases when they do not possess accurate data. They could be asked questions about advertisements, products, brands, or retail outlets of which they are unaware.

Researchers have discovered that respondents, like students, will often answer questions even though they have no knowledge of the topic, perhaps because of unwillingness to admit this lack of knowledge. This situation represents a serious source of measurement error.

Often the phrasing of the question will encourage the respondent to answer it by implying that the answer should be known. Consider the question: "What is the current interest rate you receive on your savings account?" It implies that the respondent should know the answer. An alternative would be: "Do you know the current interest rate on you savings account?" This question implies that some people do not know the interest rate, which makes it easier for the respondent to admit a lack of knowledge. If the respondent answers this question affirmatively, the first question could then be asked.

Respondent Is Forgetful   We are frequently asked questions which we were able to answer at one time, but now we have forgotten. As students, we are continually confronted with this situation.

Research studies have shown that we forget most events fairly rapidly after we learn about them.[5] The rate of forgetting is very rapid over the first few days. Consequently, the farther in the past the learning took place, the higher the chance of forgetting.

The probability of forgetting is influenced by the importance of the event and the repetition of the event. It is easier to remember important events such as the first person we kissed, the first person on the moon, the first car we purchased, and the like. In contrast, how many of us remember the second person kissed, the second person on the moon, and the second car we purchased? It is also easier to remember events that are repeated frequently, e.g., frequently purchased products or frequently viewed advertisements.

When the information needs of a study require questions asking the respondent to

---

[5] J. F. Engel, D. T. Kollat, and R. D. Blackwell, *Consumer Behavior*, 2d ed. (New York: Holt, 1973), pp. 340–341.

recall unimportant or infrequently occurring events, the researcher has a potentially serious problem in designing the questionnaire. He or she must not overestimate the ability of the respondent to recall the event and the surrounding circumstances accurately. This is an easy mistake to make when the topic of the questionnaire is personally important to the researcher or decision maker.

When faced with collecting data about unimportant or infrequent events, there are several options available. First, the researcher can try to interview those respondents most likely to remember, e.g., recent purchasers. Second, the questionnaire can include techniques which stimulate the respondent's recall of the event.

Several studies suggest that questions which rely on unaided recall—questions that do not give cues as to the event—can underestimate the actual occurrence of the event.[6] The aided-recall approach is an attempt to overcome the memory problem; it provides the respondent with cues regarding the event of interest. Students should be familiar with the distinction between aided and unaided recall. An essay question is an example of unaided recall, while a multiple-choice question is an example of aided recall.

An unaided question designed to measure the respondent's awareness of a commercial could be: "What products do you recall were advertised last night on television?" The aided-recall approach would list a number of products for the respondent and then ask: "Which of these products were advertised on television last night?"

The advantage of the aided recall comes from the cue used to stimulate the respondent's memory. The degree of stimulation can vary from limited hints to the presentation of the actual event. This latter approach to aided recall is called the *recognition method*. With increased attempts to stimulate the respondent's memory comes the possibility of suggestion bias resulting from the presentation of the cues. When using the aided-recall approach, researchers often recommend that it is useful to have several levels of successive stimulation. This allows the researcher to analyze the influence of the question sequence and select a level of stimulation most appropriate for the study.

Willingness to Respond Accurately   Assuming that the respondent can accurately answer the question, the next issue is to determine his or her willingness to do so. Unwillingness to respond accurately could be reflected in (1) refusing to respond to a question or a series of questions, i.e., item nonresponse error, and (2) deliberately providing an incorrect or distorted response to a question, i.e., measurement error.

There are three reasons for unwillingness to respond accurately: (1) the situation is not appropriate for disclosing the data, (2) disclosure of the data would be embarrassing, and (3) disclosure is a potential threat to the respondents' prestige or normative views.

It is important to remember that the respondent has limited motivation to respond accurately to the questions. With the personal and telephone interview, the interviewer's presence can cause the respondent to be more concerned with how the interviewer may react to the responses than with the accuracy of responses. This is especially the situation if the questions are embarrassing or a threat to prestige and normative viewpoints. The result can be item nonresponse or, worse yet, inaccurate responses.

---

[6] J. H. Myers and W. H. Reynolds, *Consumer Behavior and Marketing Management* (Boston: Houghton Mifflin, 1967), pp. 65–67.

The respondent's willingness to answer questions is conditioned by the interviewing context. A question regarding personal hygiene habits may be appropriate when asked by a nurse or doctor as part of a physical examination but may be inappropriate when asked by an interviewer conducting a study for a pharmaceutical manufacturer.

The respondent's willingness to answer a question is also a function of his or her understanding of whether the data are needed for a legitimate purpose. The collection of classification data can be a serious problem in this regard. The respondent may be hesitant to provide accurate data when abruptly faced with personal questions regarding age, occupation, and income. The following request for personal data does not explain to respondent how the data are to be used: "Next, I would like to ask you some questions about yourself. What is your . . . ?" Even a brief explanation such as the following can make such a request legitimate for most respondents: "To better understand how the reactions to this new product differ among people with different age, income, and occupational characteristics, we need to know your . . ."

Questions which embarrass the respondent or have an element of prestige or adherence to social norms can result in a biased response. This is especially the situation when the personal or telephone interview is employed. Researchers have found that questions on topics such as sexual behavior and attitudes, number of automobile accidents, or purchase of personal hygiene products and alcoholic beverages can embarrass the respondent and result in a refusal to answer or the distortion of the response.

Questions which have an element of prestige or adherence to social norms include level of education, income earned, and amount of time spent reading or watching educational television. The answers to these types of questions typically result in an upward response bias.

Various approaches have been developed to deal with the bias resulting from the respondent's unwillingness to respond accurately.

1 *Counterbiasing statement:* Begin the question with a statement which suggests that the behavior in question is rather common and then ask the respondent the question.[7]

2 *Indirect statement:* Present the respondent with the sensitive question phrased to refer to "other people." It is assumed that the respondent's own behavior or attitude will be reflected in the response.

3 *Labeled response categories:* Present the respondent with a card which lists the sensitive response alternatives and has them identified by letters or numbers. The respondent uses the letter or number to indicate a response to the sensitive question.

4 *Randomized response technique:* Present the respondent with two questions, either of which can be answered "yes" or "no." One question is the sensitive issue (e.g., "Have you shoplifted in the last month?"), while the other question is the insensitive issue (e.g., "Were you born in January?"). A random procedure (e.g., flipping a coin) is used to determine which of the two questions the respondent will answer. Since the response format of the two questions is identical (i.e., yes or no), the interviewer does not know which question the respondent has answered.

[7] Donald S. Tull and Del I. Hawkins, *Marketing Research* (New York: Macmillan, 1976), p. 261.

The following formula is used to estimate the proportion of respondents who answered "yes" to the sensitive question.[8]

$$P(\text{yes}|\text{sens. quest.}) = \frac{P(\text{yes}) - P(\text{insens. quest.})P(\text{yes}|\text{insens. quest.})}{P(\text{sens. quest.})}$$

In the shoplifting study, if the proportion of respondents who answered "yes" is .10, the proportion born in January is .05 (census of population), and the probability of answering each question is .5, the estimate of the proportion of respondents answering "yes" to the shoplifting question is:

$$P(\text{yes}|\text{shoplifting}) = \frac{.10 - (.5)(.05)}{.5} = .15$$

Decide on Response Format

Once the problems related to the content of the questions have been analyzed, the next issue concerns the type of questions to use. The concern here involves the degree of structure imposed on the person's responses. The three types of questions range from unstructured to structured response formats: (1) open-ended questions, (2) multiple-choice questions, and (3) dichotomous questions.

Open-Ended Questions   An open-ended question requires the respondents to provide their own answer to the question. This is often referred to as a free-response or free-answer question. For example, the respondent could be asked, "What is your reaction to this new cake mix?" With the mail interview, space would be provided for the respondent to write the answer. With the personal and telephone interview, the respondent would verbally report the answer to the interviewer, who would then record the answer on the questionnaire.

Advantages of Open-Ended Questions   Open-ended questions serve as an excellent first question to a topic. They allow general attitudes to be expressed which can aid in interpreting the more structured questions. In addition, they establish rapport and gain the respondent's cooperation in answering more specific and structured questions. Introductory open-ended questions are especially important in mail surveys.

Open-ended questions influence responses less than multiple-choice or dichotomous questions. Respondents are not influenced by a predetermined set of response alternatives and can freely express views divergent from the researcher's expectations. This characteristic makes open-ended questions useful for exploratory research purposes.

Finally, open-ended questions can provide the researcher with insights, side comments, and explanations which are useful in developing a "feel" for the research

---

[8] C. Campbell and B. L. Joiner, "How to Get the Answer Without Being Sure You've Asked the Question," *The American Statistician,* vol. 27, pp. 299–231, December 1973.

findings. The final report may include quotations from open-ended questions to bring realism and life to the more structured research findings.

Disadvantages of Open-Ended Questions A major disadvantage of open-ended questions is the high potential for interviewer bias. Interviewers rarely record the respondent's answers verbatim. This results in the interviewer summarizing the respondent's answers or deleting those aspects of the answer deemed unimportant. In addition, those interviewers who write slowly or do not take shorthand typically fail to record parts of the answer due to time constraints. The more the interviewer summarizes and edits the respondent's answers, the more the recorded responses will vary from the actual responses. A tape recorder should be used if verbatim responses are required.

A second major disadvantage of open-ended questions lies in the time and cost associated with coding the responses. For a large survey, extensive coding procedures are required to summarize the divergent responses in a format useful for data analysis and presentation. The time and cost of this coding process can be a significant portion of the total cost of the research project.

Sometimes, in order to gain the advantages of open-ended questions yet avoid some of the time and cost associated with the editing and coding process, precoded questions are used. A precoded question is a multiple-choice question which is presented to the respondent as open-ended. The response alternatives are not read to the respondent. Rather, the interviewer selects the appropriate response alternative based on the respondent's reply to the open-ended question.

This approach works well when the response is easily formulated in the respondent's mind and the possible answers are limited in variety, e.g., number of household members, age of the refrigerator, or monthly grocery expenditures. However, questions which are not well formulated in the respondent's mind and result in a variety of answers have a high probability of interviewer bias.

Other disadvantages include the implicit extra weight given to respondents who are more articulate and tend to raise more points in their answers. Also, open-ended questions are less suited for self-administered questionnaires. The reason is that respondents tend to write more briefly than they speak, and there is also the problem of illegible handwriting. Finally, compared with questions that have structured response formats, open-ended questions are three to five times as costly because of the complexity associated with the data processing.[9]

In general, open-ended questions are most appropriate for exploratory research purposes and research designed to develop more structured questions.[10] While the cost of developing effective structured questions can be high, it must be weighed against the disadvantages of open-ended questions.

Multiple-Choice Questions A multiple-choice question requires the respondent to choose an answer from among a list provided in the question proper or following

[9] Jeffrey L. Pope, "12 Ways to Cut Marketing Research Costs," *Marketing News*, p. 6, June 6, 1975.
[10] This conclusion is consistent with S. L. Paayne, "Are Open-Ended Questions Worth the Effort?" *Journal of Marketing Research*, vol. 2, pp. 417–418, November 1965.

the question. The respondent may be asked to choose one or more of the alternatives presented.

Advantages of Multiple-Choice Questions Multiple-choice questions overcome many of the disadvantages associated with open-ended questions. Most important, they reduce interviewer bias and the cost and time associated with data processing. Typically, the interviewer will find this type of question easier and faster to administer. Finally, self-administered questionnaires have a difficult time maintaining respondent cooperation unless the bulk of the questions have a structured-response format.

Disadvantages of Multiple-Choice Questions Against these advantages must be weighed several disadvantages. First, the design of effective multiple-choice questions requires considerable time and cost. Typically, an exploratory study using open-ended questions is required to formulate the response alternatives. If the latter do not include one or more of the predominant responses, substantial bias can be introduced into the results. Even with an alternative of "other (specify)," there is a tendency for the respondent to choose from among the alternatives specified rather than using the "other" alternative. Second, multiple-choice questions tend to bias the data by the order in which the response alternatives are given the respondent.

Issues in Multiple-Choice Question Design There are two issues in the design of multiple-choice questions: (1) number of alternatives and (2) position bias.

The *number of alternatives* to include in a question is typically influenced by the following two guidelines. First, the response alternatives should be *collectively exhaustive*, that is, they should include all the possible response alternatives. The inclusion of the alternative labeled "other (please specify)" accompanied by a space to record the answer is an attempt to comply with this guideline. It is hoped that those major response alternatives which were excluded will be identified in the "other" alternative. Second, the response alternatives should be *mutually exclusive*, that is, the respondents should be able to identify one alternative which clearly represents their response. In some situations the researcher may desire to have the respondent make two or more choices, but multiple responses create special data processing problems.

If the set of response alternatives is reasonably short, they may be included in the question proper. In most cases there are too many alternatives to be included here, and they are listed at the end of the question. With a long list of alternatives, the choices should be listed on a card and given the respondent for inspection.

Another important issue concerns *position bias*. With a list of numbers, such as prices or number of store visits, there is a bias toward the central position of the number array. When ideas are involved, the first alternative on the list has a greater chance of choice. To control position bias, the researcher should alternate the order in which alternatives are listed. This procedure will average out the response bias. Unfortunately it is not easy to rotate most numbers, since they logically should appear as a sequence, for example, 5, 6, 7, 8, and 9. Even if they are presented out of order, the respondent may sort them into sequence before making a choice.

Dichotomous Questions A dichotomous question is an extreme form of the multiple-choice question which allows the respondent only two responses, such as yes—no, did—did not, agree—disagree, and so on. Typically the two alternatives of interest are combined with a neutral alternative, such as "no opinion" or "don't know."

Advantages of Dichotomous Questions   The advantages of the dichotomous question are essentially the same as those mentioned for multiple-choice questions. The interviewers find the questions quick and easy to administer. There is less chance of interviewer bias, and the responses are easy to code, process, and analyze.

Disadvantages of Dichotomous Questions   There is a risk of assuming that the respondent group approaches the topic of interest in dichotomous terms when, in reality, there may be many grades of feeling present or indecision may predominate. Forcing respondents to express their views in a dichotomous manner when they are not thus polarized can produce results which contain substantial measurement error. Dichotomous questions are especially susceptible to error resulting from how the question is worded. For example, early in this chapter, error in our illustrations resulted from implied versus explicit alternatives. In addition, the positive or negative posture of the question can have a strong effect on the nature of the response.

Issues in Dichotomous Question Design   The central issue concerns whether to include a neutral response alternative in the question. If it is not included, the respondent is forced to select between the two positions presented. If a neutral alternative is available, and especially if it is shown to the respondent, the latter can avoid taking a position on the topic by selecting the neutral alternative. When the neutral alternative is included, the number of nonresponses should decline and the number of neutral responses increase. If a significant group of respondents are truly neutral, the inclusion of the neutral alternative should increase the accuracy of the results. However, a source of bias can enter when respondents who are not neutral select the neutral alternative for reasons of convenience, embarrassment, or the like. If the proportion of respondents who are truly neutral is large, it is best to include the neutral alternative. If it is believed that the proportion of neutral respondents is small, it is best to force the respondents to select between the two positions of interest.

Decide on Question Wording

The heart of the questionnaire consists of the questions asked. These questions represent the link between the data and the information needs of the study. It is critical that the researcher and the respondent assign the same meaning to the questions asked. If not, serious measurement error will be present in the research results.

You should never be misled into believing that there is a "right" and "wrong" way of asking questions. In a real sense, survey data are created rather than unobtrusively collected. The manner in which data are collected determines to a large degree the character of the data. Consequently, you must be very sensitive to the effect of the question wording on the character of the results to be obtained.

Since no single wording of a question is correct, it is important for you to understand clearly what effect a particular wording can have on the results. The split ballot technique, which splits the questionnaires into groups and assigns alternative questions to each group, can be used for this purpose. The comparison of alternative questions determines how question wording affects the results. This technique allows

MARKETING RESEARCH IN ACTION

BURGER KING QUESTIONNAIRE BIASED?

The race was on. What was number 1, flame-broiling or frying? Or should it have been "cooked over an open gas flame" vs. "grilled"? According to independent researcher Leo Shapiro, the wording of Burger King's questionnaire may very well have influenced the outcome of its survey, where it claimed that consumers liked flame-broiling better than frying.

Although keeping its actual survey details under close wraps, in comparative advertising with McDonald's, Burger King said that its flame-broiled burger was preferred to McDonald's fried burger by a 3 to 1 margin. The actual question Burger King used to secure this data was, "Do you prefer your hamburgers flame-broiled or fried?"

When Shapiro substituted for that question: "Do you prefer a hamburger that is grilled on a hot stainless steel grill or cooked by passing the raw meat through an open gas flame?", the results were (not surprisingly) reversed. Fifty-three percent of the people polled chose McDonald's cooking process over Burger King's. When Shapiro further enlightened consumers that flame-broiled burgers were kept in a microwave oven before serving, the preference for fried burgers increased to 85 percent.

In effect, what the Burger King survey did was to pit the most appealing word it could find to describe its cooking process against the most unappealing word it could use to portray the cooking of McDonald's burgers. Semantics rather than the actual product determined the preference for cooking methods.

Based on *Advertising Age*, p. 16, April 4, 1983

a better interpretation of the survey results than is possible when a single version of the question is used.

The following are nine general guidelines which you should consider in designing the wording of a question: (1) use simple words, (2) use clear words, (3) avoid leading questions, (4) avoid biasing questions, (5) avoid implicit alternatives, (6) avoid implicit assumptions, (7) avoid estimates, (8) avoid double-barreled questions, and (9) consider the frame of reference.

Use Simple Words The words used in the questionnaire should be consistent with the vocabulary level of the respondents. If in doubt, it is best to err on the side of simplicity.

Questions designed for children obviously must have a simpler vocabulary than those designed for, say, medical doctors. When designing a questionnaire for the general public, keep in mind the often surprising fact that the vocabulary skills of most seventh graders (12 years of age) are greater than those of many adults. For example, a significant proportion of the general population does not understand the word "Caucasian."[11] Consequently, when designing a questionnaire, be certain that it is comprehensible to persons with minimal vocabulary skills.

Use Clear Words Words which are "clear" have a single meaning which is known to all the respondents. Unfortunately, identifying words which are clear or unambiguous

[11] Alan E. Bayer, "Construction of a Race Item for Survey Research," *Public Opinion Quarterly*, Winter 1972–73, p. 596.

is more difficult than one might expect. Many words which appear to be clear to everyone can have different meanings among population groups and geographic locations.

Consider the words "dinner" and "lunch." Studies indicate that middle- and upper-class families use "dinner" to refer to the evening meal and "lunch" to refer to the noon meal. In contrast, many working-class families refer to the evening meal as "supper" and the noon meal as "dinner." In designing a question which refers to mealtime, it would be better to use "noon meal" and "evening meal" rather than "lunch" and "dinner." Since comparable responses cannot be expected from respondents who assign different meanings to a word, serious measurement error would be present if the words "lunch" and "dinner" were used in the question.

In a study of soup usage in the home, the question "How often do you serve soup at home?" resulted in responses which suggested that soup usage was lower than believed by the management. Additional research indicated that to many respondents the word "served" meant a special occasion, such as when entertaining. Soup eating by the family alone was not considered to be "served." A revised question with better wording was: "How often do you use soup at home?"[12]

Researchers have found that words such as "usually," "regularly," "kind," "normally," and "frequently" are ambiguous. It is difficult to be sensitive to all of the commonly used words which some respondents interpret one way, others another way. In this regard, Payne advises that the researcher consult a leading dictionary and thesaurus and ask the following six questions of each word in the question:

1 Does it mean what we intended?
2 Does it have any other meanings?
3 If so, does the context make the intended meaning clear?
4 Does the word have more than one pronunciation?
5 Is there any word of similar pronunciation that might be confused?
6 Is a simpler word or phrase suggested?[13]

Avoid Leading Questions A leading question is one where the respondent is given a cue as to what the answer should be to the question. Leading questions often reflect the researcher's or decision maker's viewpoint regarding the question's answer. A leading question causes a constant measurement error in the research findings.

In a question to measure the claim service of automobile insurance companies, the following statement preceded the question on claim service: "It has been alleged that some low-rate companies are much tougher in adjusting claims than standard-rate companies, and that you are more likely to have to go to court to collect the sum due you."[14] This statement would probably influence the response to the questions

---

[12] J. M. Bowen, "Questionnaire Design for the Personal Interview," in *Fieldwork, Sampling and Questionnaire Design* (Amsterdam: European Society for Opinion Surveys and Market Research, 1973), pt. 1, p. 88.

[13] S. L. Payne, *The Art of Asking Questions* (Princeton, N.J.: Princeton University Press, 1951), p. 41.

[14] J. Stevens Stock and Barbara K. Auerback, "How Not to Do Consumer Research," *Journal of Marketing,* vol. 27, p. 21, July 1963.

on the companies' claim service which followed. Consequently, statements designed to clarify a question can have an influence on the responses to the questions they clarify. Be sensitive to this source of measurement error.

Consider the question: "Do you own a Zenith television set?" This would be a leading question if the reported ownership of Zenith television sets were higher in this case than when the question simply asked: "What brand of television set do you own?" The use of a brand or company name in a question can cause the respondent to believe that this company is the sponsor of the survey. There is a tendency for the respondent to express positive feelings toward the survey sponsor, which can result in measurement error.

Avoid Biasing Questions   A biasing question includes words or phrases which are emotionally colored and suggest a feeling of approval or disapproval.[15] Most researchers would recognize the biasing effect of a question that began, "Don't you agree with Ralph Nader in the belief that . . ." or "Do you believe that the oil monopolies should be . . .?" No reputable researcher would phrase questions in this manner. Unfortunately, the biasing effect of words and phrases is far more subtle than these examples suggest.

The mere suggestion of an attitude or position associated with a prestigious or nonprestigious person or organization can seriously bias the respondent's reply. The question, "Do you agree or disagree with the American Dental Association's position that advertising presweetened cereal to children is . . ." would have such an effect. The nature of the bias would be increased support reported for the position held by the prestigious person or organization over that reported when the person or organization is not included in the question.

It is difficult to avoid leading questions because those words or phrases that bias one respondent group can be neutral with another group. A pretest of the questionnaire is one way to identify which respondent groups find the question biased.

Avoid Implicit Alternatives   In a previous section of this chapter, examples were presented which indicated a marked difference in the answers to questions which pose implicit and explicit alternatives to the respondents.[16] Other research has demonstrated equally dramatic results.[17] As a rule, it is best to state clearly all relevant alternatives to a question unless there is a special reason for not doing so.

When using explicit alternatives, research indicates that the order in which the alternatives are presented can affect the response. When the number of alternatives is long and complex or close in preference, the alternatives presented at the end of the list have a higher chance of being selected.[18] Consequently, the split-ballot technique should be used to ensure that each alternative appears at each location on the alternative listing.

[15] A. N. Oppenheim, *Questionnaire Design and Attitude Measurement* (London: Heinemann Educational Books, Ltd., 1966), p. 59.

[16] See the section on the importance of the questionnaire.

[17] E. Noelle-Neumann, op. cit., pp. 200–201, and S. L. Payne, op. cit., pp. 55–74.

[18] M. Parten, *Surveys, Polls, and Samples* (New York: Harper & Row, 1950), p. 211.

Avoid Implicit Assumptions   It is easy to design a question where the answer is dependent upon a number of implicit assumptions. Consider the question, "Are you in favor of curtailing the amount of sugar allowed in children's cereals?" Implicit in this question is that this action will result in some favorable outcome, e.g., lower rate of tooth decay. An improved wording would be: "Are you in favor of curtailing the amount of sugar allowed in children's cereal if it would result in . . . ?" The failure to make explicit the assumptions in a question often results in overestimating the respondent's support for the issue at hand.

Avoid Estimates   The questions should be designed in such a way that the respondent does not have to answer by giving an estimate or making a generalization. Consider the question: "How many boxes of powdered soap do you purchase in a year?" This question requires the respondent to determine the number of boxes of powdered soap purchased in a month and multiply by 12. The survey results would be more accurate if the question were, "How many boxes of powdered soap do you purchase in a month?" The yearly figure can be determined by multiplying by 12.

Avoid Double-Barreled Questions   A double-barreled question occurs when the wording calls for two responses. Consider the question, "What is your evaluation of the snowmobile's ride and acceleration?" Here, two questions have been asked under the guise of a single question. As a rule, when the question includes "and," review it to see whether two responses are required.

Consider Frame of Reference   By frame of reference we refer to the respondent's viewpoint in responding to the question. Consider these two questions: "Are automobile manufacturers making satisfactory progress in controlling automobile emissions?" and "Are you satisfied with the progress automobile manufacturers are making in controlling automobile emissions?" The viewpoint of the first question is that of an objective evaluation based on how people in general would react to this question. The second question is oriented to the respondent's personal feeling regarding the issue of automobile emissions and is more subjective in this respect. The objectives of the research study will determine which frame of reference is more appropriate. The point is that you must be aware that the respondent's viewpoint can seriously influence the study results.

Decide on Question Sequence

Once the wording of the questions has been determined, the next step is to establish their sequence, i.e., the order or flow of the questions in the questionnaire. The sequencing of the questions can influence the nature of the respondents's answers and be the cause of serious error in the survey findings. While this aspect of questionnaire design draws heavily on the skills of an experienced researcher, several guidelines are presented which the beginning researcher should find useful.

Use a Simple and Interesting Opening Question   The opening question must capture the respondent's interest and curiosity immediately, or the respondent may terminate the interview. Often, the opening question does not relate to the information needs of the study; its sole purpose is to gain the respondent's cooperation and establish rapport. In this regard, a simple question which asks the respondent to express an attitude is a good starter, since most people like to express their feelings and can do so easily. This approach gives respondents confidence that they can answer the remaining questions in the interview.

Ask General Questions First   Within a topic, general questions should precede specific questions. Consider the following two questions: "What considerations are important to you in buying cereal?" and "When buying cereal, is the sugar content important to you?" If these questions were asked in reverse order, sugar content would appear more frequently in the answer to the first question than if the questions were asked in the order given here. Consequently, asking general questions first and specific questions second reduces the chance of sequence bias.

Place Uninteresting and Difficult Questions Late in Sequence   Sequence any questions which are embarrassing, sensitive, complex, or dull well down in the questionnaire. After rapport has been established by the interviewer and the questioning process, the respondent is less apt to object to more demanding and personal questions.

Arrange Questions in Logical Order   The flow of the questioning process must be logical from the respondent's perspective. A question sequence designed to facilitate data processing or established from the perspective of the researcher can cause respondent confusion, frustration, and indecision, and it can seriously influence cooperation and rapport.

When the information needs of a study are extensive and different groups within the sample need to be asked different questions, it is helpful to "flowchart" the question sequence. Figure 14-3 presents a flowchart plan for a questionnaire. Flowcharting can be very helpful in visualizing the structure of the questionnaire and in ensuring that the questions asked flow logically.

Decide on Physical Characteristics

The physical appearance of the questionnaire can be influential in securing the cooperation of the respondent. This is particularly the case with mail surveys. The quality of the paper and printing often determines the respondent's first reaction to the questionnaire. It is important that the name of the organization sponsoring the survey (often fictitious to avoid bias) and the project name should appear clearly on the first page.

With the personal and telephone interview, the questionnaires should be numbered serially. This facilitates control of the questionnaire in field operations and during data processing. Mail questionnaires may not be identified numerically when respondent anonymity is important.

FIGURE 14-3 Example of a flowchart plan for a draft questionnaire.

Finally, the format of a question can influence the response. For both self-administered and interviewer-administered questionnaires, researchers have discovered that the more lines or space left for recording the response to open-ended questions, the more extensive the the reply.

Carry Out Pretest, Revision, and Final Draft

Before the questionnaire is ready for field operations, it needs to be pretested and revised. Pretesting refers to the initial testing of one or more aspects of the research design. We are concerned here with pretesting the questionnaire design, for regardless of the researcher's skill a pretest is needed to search out areas for improvement. Most questionnaires require at least one pretest and revision before they are ready for field operations.

Preferably, the questionnaire should be pretested in the manner intended for the final study. However, with an early draft of the questionnaire it is best to pretest using personal interviewers, even though the survey is to be administered by mail or telephone. It is important that only the best interviewers be used for pretest work. A skilled interviewer can respond to requests for explanation, detect areas of confusion, and probe the nature of this confusion. The interviewer should be sensitive to words which are not understood by all respondents, should test question sequence, and should note mechanical difficulties and the like. Ultimately, the revised questionnaire should be pretested in the manner intended for the final survey.

The open-ended response format can be used in the pretest to determine appropriate response categories for what will become a multiple-choice question in the final questionnaire. A new pretest should be conducted to uncover any problems with the standardized response categories created.

The number of people interviewed in a pretest can range from 15 to 30. The sample should be similar to those interviewed in the main study.

Whenever significant changes are made in the questionnaire, another pretest should be conducted. If the pretest results suggest minor changes, the questionnaire is ready for the final draft and distribution to field operators.

OBSERVATIONAL FORMS

Observational forms are easier to design than questionnaires, since the question-asking process is eliminated and design problems related to controlling nonsampling error are reduced. Even so, there are still important issues in the construction of observational forms. The researcher needs to make very explicit the types of observations to be made and how they are to be measured. The measurement process can involve an observer with observational forms, a mechanical recording device, or a combination of both.

The design of observational forms should flow logically from the listing of information needs, which must clearly specify those aspects of the behavior to be observed. It is often useful to characterize the information needs as the "who, what, when, and where" of behavior. Consider the information needs for a study designed to observe shoppers purchasing cereal. They should specify in detail:

1 Who is to be observed?—Purchasers, lookers, males, females, couples, couples with children, children alone.

2 What is to be observed?—Brands purchased, size, brands considered, influence of children and adults, price of product package inspected.

3 When is observation to be made?—Days of week, hours, date and time of purchase recorded.

4 Where should observations be made?—Type of store, location, how selected.

Observation forms should be simple to use. They should be designed so that they logically follow the behavior observed. They should permit the observer to record the behavior in detail, rather than requiring a summary regarding a number of behavior patterns. The physical characteristics of the form should follow the same rules given for questionnaires. Finally, observational forms need the same degree of pretesting and revision as questionnaires.

SUMMARY

1 A questionnaire is a formalized schedule for collecting data from respondents. It can collect data on past behavior, attitudes, and respondent characteristics. The questionnaire is a critical component of the research project in that a poorly designed questionnaire can be a major source of error in the research results.

2 The five sections to a questionnaire are (1) identification data, (2) request for cooperation, (3) instructions, (4) information sought, and (5) classification data.

3 While a number of guidelines are useful in designing a questionnaire, its quality depends on the skill and judgment of the researcher. The steps in questionnaire design are (1) review preliminary considerations, (2) decide on question content, (3) decide on response format, (4) decide on question wording, (5) decide on question sequence, (6) decide on physical characteristics, and (7) carry out pretest, revision, and final draft.

4 The design of the questionnaire is dependent upon previous decisions regarding the nature of the research design, sources of data, target population, sampling plan, communication media, measurement techniques, and the data processing and analysis plan. The questionnaire is the link between the information needed and the data to be collected.

5 Question content is influenced by the respondent's ability and willingness to respond accurately. The question response format can be open-ended, multiple-choice, or dichotomous.

6 The guidelines for designing the question wording are (1) use simple words, (2) use clear words, (3) avoid leading questions, (4) avoid biased questions, (5) avoid implicit alternatives, (6) avoid implicit assumptions, (7) avoid estimates, (8) avoid double-barreled questions, and (9) consider the frame of reference.

7 The guidelines for determining the question sequences are (1) use simple and interesting opening questions, (2) ask general questions first, (3) place uninteresting and difficult questions late in the sequence, and (4) arrange questions in logical order.

8 The physical characteristics of the questionnaire can influence the degree of respondent cooperation and the character of the responses. The questionnaire needs to be pretested and revised before it is ready for use in the field.

9. Observational forms are easier to design than questionaires, since the design problems associated with the question-asking process have been eliminated. The data collection forms should flow logically from a clear specification of the types of observations to be made and how they are to be measured.

DISCUSSION QUESTIONS

1 What role does the questionnaire play in the research project?

2 What are the typical components of a questionnaire?

3 What decisions precede the questionnaire design stage?

4 What criterion governs the inclusion of questions in the questionnaire?

5 How does the respondent affect the content of the questions?

6 How can a researcher overcome the problems associated with collecting data about unimportant or infrequent events?

7 Why may a respondent be unwilling to respond accurately to a given question?

8 What approaches are available for dealing with the bias resulting from a respondent's unwillingness to respond accurately?

9 What are the advantages and disadvantages of open-ended questions?

10 List the advantages and disadvantages associated with multiple-choice questions.

11 What guidelines govern the design of responses to multiple-choice questions?

12 Under what conditions would dichotomous questions be inappropriate?

13 What general guidelines should one utilize in designing the wording of a question?

CHAPTER 15

FIELD OPERATIONS

The methods of collecting data and the design of data collection forms have been discussed in the previous two chapters. This chapter completes the section on collecting data from respondents by discussing field operations.

The field operation is that phase of the project during which researchers make contact with the respondents, administer the data collection instruments, record the data, and return the data to a central location for processing. The wisdom behind the research design and the skill involved in developing the data collection instrument will be wasted if the field operation is poorly administered. An important source of error in the research process can be identified with the field operation.

The planning of the field operation is highly influenced by the data collection method employed; for example, the field operation for a personal interview study is substantially different from that for a mail interview study. However, given these differences, there are some basic issues which are common to all field operations.

This chapter will first discuss the common issues in planning and controlling field operations. Next, the more specific aspects of field operations associated with alternative data collection methods will be introduced. The last part of the chapter will be devoted to the sources of error in field operations and the presentation of various guidelines for controlling these errors.

PLANNING FIELD OPERATIONS

Four aspects of planning are common to all field operations: (1) time schedule, (2) budget, (3) personnel, and (4) performance measurement.[1]

---

[1] This section follows closely the discussion presented by Mathew Hauck, "Planning Field Operations," in Robert Ferber (ed.), *Handbook of Marketing Research* (New York: McGraw-Hill, 1975), pp. 2-147 to 2-154.

Time Schedule

Every project must have a time schedule specifying (1) when the project is to begin and end and (2) the sequencing of activities within this time frame. The number of days needed to complete various activities must be estimated and the degree of overlap among activities determined. It is very important that realistic time periods be established so that the project can be completed in a reasonable amount of time. Often target completion dates are set which do not realistically reflect the time required to carry out field operations properly. Attempts to cut corners to reach unreasonable completion dates can be costly and decrease the accuracy of the results.

Figure 15-1 presents a detailed time schedule for a personal interview study. Experience suggests that those activities for which time requirements are most likely to be underestimated are the final approval and printing of the questionnaire, the selection of interviewers, the evaluation of the pretest, and the cleanup in the field. It is best to leave room in the schedule for inaccurate time estimates and unforeseen events.

Budget

The budget involves the assignment of costs to specific activities identified in the field time schedule. The budget and the time schedule are closely interrelated. In most cases they are prepared together, since changes in one can result in changes in the other.

FIGURE 15-1   Field time schedule flow diagram [*Source: Matthew Hauck, "Planning Field Operations," in Robert Ferber (ed)., Handbook of Marketing Research (New York: McGraw-Hill, 1975), pp. 2–149.*]

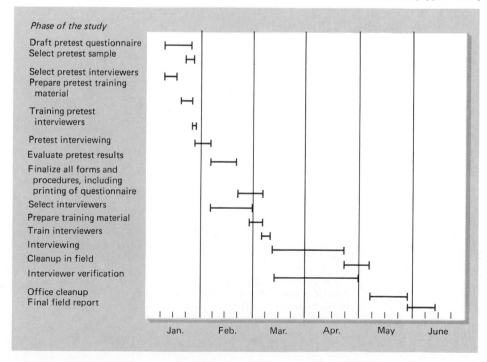

The main cost categories for a personal interview study are (1) office wages and salaries, (2) materials and supplies, (3) telephone, (4) field supervisors or interviewing services, (5) interviewers' compensation, and (6) reproduction of questionnaires and other field forms. These cost categories can be further segmented and assigned to the stages of the data collection process: (1) pretest, (2) selection and hiring of interviewers, (3) interviewer training, (4) final field reports, and (5) data collection.

Effective budgeting and cost control requires a detailed breakdown of the major cost categories into their smallest components.[2] Specific categories need to be reviewed to see whether the costs have been underestimated, and a reserve fund is needed for unforeseen contingencies. Finally, the budget should be reviewed and possibly approved by those individuals responsible for carrying out the activities associated with the cost category.

Personnel

The success of the field operation depends on the quality of the personnel used to execute the plans. Skilled personnel are required, along with the clear assignment of responsibility for all aspects of the plan, if completion dates are to be met and costs controlled. Finally, the personnel must clearly understand what is expected of them and how this performance will be measured.

Performance Measurement

To control activities and accomplish objectives, clear performance measures are required. Too often, the number of interviews to be completed is the only measure

---

[2] Seymour Sudman, *Reducing the Costs of Surveys* (Chicago: Aldine, 1968).

TABLE 15-1   STUDY PERFORMANCE MEASURES: EXPECTED AND ACTUAL

Performance Measure	Expected	Actual
1 Total eligible respondents	____	____
1.1 Interviews	____	____
1.2 Refusals	____	____
1.3 Noncontacts (assumed eligible)	____	____
1.4 Other (specify)		
2 Total ineligible respondents	____	____
2.1 Moved	____	____
2.2 Other (specify)	____	____
3 Total sample	____	____
Response rate (1.1 ÷ 1)	____%	____%
Refusal rate (1.2) ÷ (1.1 + 1.2)	____%	____%
Contact rate ((1 − 1.3) ÷ 1)	____%	____%
Eligibility rate (1 ÷ 3)	____%	

Source: Adapted from Mathew Hauck, "Planning Field Operations," in Robert Ferber (ed.), *Handbook of Marketing Research* (New York: McGraw-Hill, 1975), p. 2-151.

clearly specified for a study, yet it is just as important to specify the number of expected refusals, noncontacts, and other noninterviewing situations. Table 15-1 presents these performance measures in a format where expected results can be compared with actual results. The ratios presented at the bottom of the table are used to derive the figures in the body of the table. These ratios can be determined by pretest results and/or the past experience of the researcher.

The totals in Table 15-1 should be broken down by region, interviewing agency, supervisor, and other categories useful for control purposes. The personnel responsible for accomplishing the expected results should participate in determining whether they are reasonable.

Most research projects exceed their initial research budgets. The causes are changes in the research design, poor time scheduling, and inaccurate budget estimates. Upon the completion of a study, the final costs should be compared with the budget so that future budget estimates can be more accurate.

DATA COLLECTION METHODS

This section presents those aspects of field operations which differ according to whether personal interview, telephone interview, mail interview, or observation is used to collect the data.

Personal Interview

The use of interviewers in a face-to-face setting presents special problems relating to their selection, training, and supervision. Researchers have three options in this regard—they can use their own research organization, contract with an outside field work agency, or do both. No matter which option is chosen, sufficient time and money must be assigned to this very expensive and complicated aspect of the field operation.

Finding qualified interviewers is a difficult task. First, the researcher must specify the job qualifications needed for the project. Next, applicants must be located, screened, and hired in those geographic locations required by the sampling plan. Typically, outside field work organizations are hired to conduct the interviewing. These organizations maintain contact with interviewers and have files on their qualifications.

Once the interviewers are selected, they must be trained. The objective of training is to establish a high degree of commonality in the data collection process among interviewers. Because of time constraints and geographic dispersion in the sampling plan, most training programs consist of written instructions to the interviewer covering areas such as the purpose of the study, how to carry out the sampling plan, and how to approach the respondent, establish rapport, ask the questions, and the like. For complex studies, the training may be conducted by supervisors in person at one or more central locations.

The pretest results should provide valuable insights as to the nature and extent of the training required. It is important to allot enough time in the schedule for adequate training.

Following the training program, the interviewer begins the interviewing process. During this process there should be constant monitoring to determine whether the interviewing is adhering to plans. Completed interviews need to be inspected for completeness, accuracy, neatness, and so forth. If the work of an interviewer is unsatisfactory, retraining or dismissal may be required.

How should the interviewer be compensated—hourly or by the interview? The common answer is to pay by the hour, since an incentive pay scheme may cause the interviewer to rush through the interview and seriously reduce the quality of the data gathered. This could be reflected in cheating or falsification of interviews, failure to ask all the questions, and failure to probe answers adequately.

The argument for an incentive pay scheme, where personnel are paid per interview, is that the interviewers can earn more money by planning their activities more efficiently. It is argued that target completion dates are reached more often and that the quality of data collected can be higher if only those interviews which meet specified standards are acceptable for payment. The important element in the successful use of the incentive pay scheme appears to be the extensive use of controls.

Finally, the success of the field work is dependent on the skill and experience of the field supervisor. The competence of a new supervisor should be checked by contacting previous clients, and only the highest-quality supervisors should be used in field work.

Telephone Interview

Most of the issues involved in the selection, training, and supervision of personal interviewers apply equally well to telephone interviewers. This is particularly the case if the telephone interviews are to be conducted from several geographic locations. However, if they are to be conducted from a central location, the ability to control the field work closely becomes an important distinguishing factor. The entire interviewing process can be directly monitored and the quality of the interview evaluated. Poor-quality interviewing can be detected early and corrected. In addition, problems resulting in a delay in the interviewing time schedule can be detected immediately and, one hopes, corrected.

Delays in the interviewing time schedule usually are attributed to (1) an inadequate population list, (2) a higher rate of callbacks required than planned, and (3) interviews taking longer than expected because of questionnaire length and/or complexity. Problems of this nature typically result from inadequate pretesting of the questionnaire and the data collection process.

A major budget item is the phone calls, especially if WATS lines are not available.

Mail Interview

The mail interview is distinguished from other data collection methods in that more aspects of the data collection process are under the central control of the researcher. This is because of the elimination of the interviewer from the field operation.

Consequently, mail surveys are more likely to meet time schedules and stay within budgets than other data collection methods.

The time schedule should classify activities into phases, such as (1) drafting the questionnaire, (2) pretesting, (3) questionnaire finalization and production, (4) first mailing, (5) second or third mailing if used, (6) check of nonrespondents, and (7) data collection from a subsample of nonrespondents. The experience of the researcher is the key to developing realistic time schedules for mail surveys.

Observation

The nature of the plans for observation field operations depends on the complexity of the research design and whether personal or mechanical recording is to be used. When field personnel are to be used, the previous discussion regarding personal interviews applies here. When mechanical recording is to be used, special problems are presented. The budget and time schedule must consider the equipment costs, set-up time, maintenance, breakdown, and the like.

ERRORS IN FIELD OPERATIONS

The validity of the research results is directly related to the number and size of sampling and nonsampling errors. This section describes sources of error connected with field operations. Previous sections of the book have discussed sampling and nonsampling errors as they relate to other aspects of the research process.

The main sources of error to be discussed here are (1) sample selection errors, (2) nonresponse errors, and (3) interviewing errors.

Sample Selection Errors

The chapters on sampling have discussed the quota sampling procedure. It was noted that this nonprobability sampling procedure is very common in marketing research and requires the interviewer to select the individuals to be included in the study, subject to various quotas specified in the sampling plan. This interviewer control of the sample selection process is likely to result in respondent selection error.

Despite formal quotas and procedures for sample selection, interviewers will sometimes try to bend or falsify rules and select respondents who are most convenient or offer the least resistance. For quotas on economic levels, interviewers tend to focus on the middle-income levels and to avoid high- and low-income respondents.

Probability sampling procedures which appear to eliminate interviewer sample selection errors still contain the potential for error. The interviewer usually participates in the probability procedure used to identify the list of dwelling units, select the dwelling unit, and select the individual to be interviewed in the unit. In listing dwelling units, interviewers tend to underlist low-income blocks. Random selection procedures for selecting from the list are typically biased by the interviewer in favor of middle-income dwellings. Within the dwelling unit, interviewers tend to select the more accessible persons in the unit.

Nonresponse Errors

Nonresponse error, described in detail in Chapter 13, refers to the difference between those who respond to a survey and those who do not respond. It can be one of the most serious sources of error confronting the researcher. We will briefly build on the earlier discussion of the topic and emphasize its importance to field operations.

Nonresponse can result from two sources: (1) not-at-homes and (2) refusals. The nonresponse problem appears to be increasing. In the 1960s, researchers obtained response rates of 80 to 85 percent using three or four callbacks, but in the 1970s response rates dropped to 60 to 65 percent. The nonresponse is equally divided between not-at-homes and refusals.[3]

The most common procedure for increasing the response rate is to make callbacks. The cost of a callback program can be reduced by the use of the telephone and/or the self-administered questionnaire. The telephone can be used to contact respondents and make appointments for the personal interview. When appropriate, a self-administered questionnaire with a stamped, self-addressed evelope can be left at the dwelling of all not-at-homes.

Interviewing Errors

With the personal and telephone interview, the interviewer can be a serious source of errors. These errors are related to (1) interviewer-respondent rapport, (2) asking the questions, (3) recording responses, and (4) cheating.

Interviewer-Respondent Rapport   An interview involves a social interaction between two people. During this interaction, the respondent's perception of the interviewer can directly affect the latter's ability to establish proper rapport. Interviewers who can establish effective relationships with respondents are able to collect more complete and accurate data.

With the personal interview, the interviewer's style of dress should resemble that of the respondent. The interviewer's dress and grooming are important in establishing rapport in that they are regarded by most people as indications of a person's attitudes and orientation. The demeanor of the interviewer should be pleasant, if nothing else.

As a general rule, the more the interviewer and respondent have in common, the greater the opportunity for rapport. Basically, the respondent should see the interviewer as capable of understanding his or her viewpoint.

Asking the Questions   Guidelines appropriate for most interviewing situations have been developed and are briefly outlined in this section.[4]

(1) *Be thoroughly familiar with the questionnaire*. The interviewer must study the questionnaire carefully, question by question, and practice reading it aloud. Each ques-

---

[3] *Report on the ASA Conference on Surveys of Human Populations* (Washington, D.C.: American Statistical Association, 1973), p. 3.

[4] This section follows closely the material in *Interviewer's Manual*, rev. ed., Survey Research Center, Institute for Social Research, University of Michigan, Ann Arbor, 1976, pp. 11–13.

tion must be read without error or stumbling over words and phrases. The interviewer's role resembles that of an actor reading lines in a play or motion picture. The questions must be read naturally and conversationally.

(2) *Ask the questions exactly as they are worded in the questionnaire.* Researchers have found that even a slight change in wording can distort results. The interviewer must be sensitive to inadvertent changes in a question, such as leaving out part of a question, changing a word, or adding a few words at the end of the question for conversational purposes.

(3) *Ask the questions in the order in which they are presented in the questionnaire.* In the design of the questionnaire, the question sequence was established to ensure that questions early in the sequence will not bias the answers to questions later in the sequence. In addition, the question sequence was designed from the respondent's perspective to create a sense of continuity in the topic covered.

(4) *Ask every question specified in the questionnaire.* The respondent's answer to one question may answer another question later in the questionnaire. In this situation, the interviewer should never skip the question which appears to have been answered earlier. It is the interviewer's responsibility to ask every question, even when it has clearly been answered previously. This can be done by letting the respondent know that the interviewer is aware of the earlier response and is asking the respondent's cooperation in answering again. The interviewer might say, for example: "We have already touched on this, but let me ask you . . ."

(5) *Use probing techniques to get the respondent to answer the question.* The questions have been designed to be understood by all respondents in the sampling plan. However, at times the interviewer may find respondents who misunderstand or misinterpret what is asked, who are reluctant to give a complete answer, or who get sidetracked on another topic in answering the question. The quality of the data collected depends upon the interviewer's skill in overcoming these problems through the use of *neutral* probing techniques.

Probing techniques are intended to perform the following two functions without introducing bias: (1) motivate the respondents to communicate more fully so that they can enlarge on, clarify, or explain the reasons behind what is said and (2) help the respondent focus on the specific content of the interview so that irrelevant or unnecessary data can be avoided.[5]

There are several kinds of neutral probing techniques which may be used to stimulate a fuller, clearer response:

1 *Repeating the question.* A very effective approach is to repeat the question just as it is written in the questionnaire. Typically, further probes are unnecessary.

2 *An expectant pause.* The interviewer's silence or pause is an effective cue to the respondent that a more complete response is expected. This is often difficult for new interviewers to do.

3 *Repeating the respondent's reply.* Respondents often are stimulated to further comments on hearing their thoughts repeated. This can be done while the interviewer is recording the comments on the questionnaire.

[5] Ibid, p. 15.

TABLE 15-2   COMMONLY USED PROBES

Interviewer's probe	Standard abbreviation
Repeat question	(RQ)
Anything else?	(AE or Else?)
Any other reason?	(AO?)
How do you mean?	(How mean?)
Could you tell me more about your thinking on that?	(Tell more)
Would you tell me what you have in mind?	(What in mind?)
What do you mean?	(What mean?)
Why do you feel that way?	(Why?)
Which would be closer to the way you feel?	(Which closer?)

Source: Interviewer's Manual, rev. ed., Survey Research Center, Institute for Social Research, University of Michigan, Ann Arbor, 1976, p. 16.

4 *Reassure the respondent.* If the respondent appears hesitant to respond, it may be helpful to use a comment such as: "We're just trying to get people's ideas on this," or "There are no right or wrong answers, just your ideas on it," If the respondent needs an explanation of a word or phrase, the interviewer should not offer a definition, rather the responsibility for the definition should be returned to the respondent. This might be done as follows: "Just whatever it means to you—anything you would call . . ."

5 *Neutral questions or comments.* Several examples of the most commonly used probes and their "key word" phrases or abbreviations are presented in Table 15-2. The standard abbreviations are to be recorded on the questionnaire in parentheses next to the question asked. The new interviewer will find it useful to have a copy of Table 15-2 available for easy reference during the interview.

6 *Asking for further clarification.* Asking the question: "I'm not quite sure I know what you mean by that—could you tell me a little more?" can arouse the respondent's desire to cooperate with the interviewer who appears to be trying to do a good job. It is often effective to appear somewhat bewildered by the respondent's answer when asking this question.[6]

In summary, effective probing requires that the interviewer recognize immediately just how the respondent's answer has failed to meet the objectives of the specific question. Next, the interviewer must be able to select an appropriate probing technique to elicit the data required by the question. Each question should have instructions indicating how forcefully the interviewer should probe.

(6) *Keep track of changes made in the questionnaire.* If the interviewer makes any changes—even inadvertent ones—in the wording, phrasing, or order of questions, they should be clearly noted on the questionnaire. This allows the researcher to analyze the potential bias and decide how the data should be coded.

(7) *Provide a logical reason for collecting personal data.* If the respondent asks why the interviewer needs to know age, religion, income, and the like, the following explanation could be used:

Well, as I was saying earlier, we are talking with people of different ages and various occupations in all parts of the country. We put all of the interviews together, and then count them up to see whether men feel differently from women, whether young people feel differently

[6] Ibid., pp. 15–16.

from older people, and so on. To do this we need to know a few things about the people we talk to. So I have just a few questions on that type of thing.[7]

Recording Responses   Even though an error-free job of asking questions has been accomplished, the next concern is recording the data in an unbiased form which can be interpreted accurately by the coders. Each interviewer must use the same format and conventions in recording the interviews and in editing each completed interview.

Rules for Recording Responses   The interviewer should record not only what was said but also how it was said. It should transmit a picture of the respondent's personality and the interview situation. The following six rules are designed to aid in accomplishing this type of recording:

1 Record responses during the interview.
2 Use the respondent's own words.
3 Do not summarize or paraphrase the respondent's answers.
4 Include everything that pertains to the question objectives.
5 Include all probes and comments by entering them next to the question in parentheses.
6 Hold the respondent's interest by repeating the response as it is written down.[8]

Tips on Note Taking   The skill of note taking is developed with practice. Practice recording the comments of friends or a news broadcast.[9] Keep in mind the following:

1 When starting the interview, try to find a place where you will be able to write comfortably.
2 When the respondent starts to talk, begin to write immediately.
3 Abbreviate words and sentences. During the editing process, put these in along with punctuation.

Mechanics of Recording and Editing Interviews   These procedures are suggested to facilitate the recording and editing process.[10]

1 Use a pencil to record.
2 Writing must be legible.
3 Use parentheses to indicate the interviewer's words or observations.
4 Do not put anything the respondent says in parentheses.
5 During editing, cross-reference the responses to one question that also apply to other questions.
6 Each question must have an answer or an explanation as to why it was not answered.
7 Check to see that the identification data are complete—name, date, interviewer number, project number, and the like.

Cheating   What is cheating? In practice, it is hard to define. Obviously, the personal interviewer who sits at home and fills out the questionnaire is cheating. More frequently, cheating is defined as the falsification of a question or questions within the questionnaire. This type of cheating is extremely difficult to detect. Phone calls to respondents to determine whether the personal interview took place will not detect the

---

[7] Ibid., p. 13.
[8] Ibid., pp. 20–21.
[9] Ibid., pp. 21–22.
[10] Ibid., pp. 22–23.

partial falsification of the questionnaire. The monitoring of phone interviews is an effective way to control cheating with the telephone interview.

SUMMARY

1 Four areas are common to planning all field operations: (1) time schedules, (2) budgets, (3) personnel, and (4) performance measurement. The time schedule specifies when the project is to begin and end, and also the sequencing of activities within this time period. The budget involves the assignment of costs to the specific activities identified in the time schedule. Skilled personnel are required, along with the clear assignment of responsibility for activities, if completion dates are to be met and costs controlled. Finally, clear performance measures are required if activities are to be controlled and objectives met.

2 Field operations differ according to whether personal interview, telephone interview, mail interview, or observation is used to collect data. When interviewers are used to collect the data, they must be selected, trained, and supervised, which involves time-consuming and expensive activities. When telephone interviews are conducted from a central location, the ability to control the interviewing activity closely is an important distinction from personal interviewing. With the mail interview, the elimination of the interviewer from the data collection process allows the centralization of the field operation directly under the researcher's control. When observers are used in observational studies, the nature of the field operation is similar to that of the personal interview study. If mechanical recording is to be used, special problems are presented for field operations.

3 The main sources of error in field operations relate to (1) sample selection errors, (2) nonresponse errors, and (3) interviewing errors. The more control the interviewer has over who will be interviewed, the greater the opportunity for sample selection error. Nonresponse error refers to the difference between those who respond and those who do not. Nonresponse can result from (1) not-at-homes and (2) refusals. The callback procedure is most commonly used to increase the response rate.

4 The major sources of interviewing error occur in the areas of (1) interviewer-respondent rapport, (2) asking the questions, (3) recording errors, and (4) cheating.

5 For the new interviewer, a series of guidelines are available regarding the process of asking questions and recording answers. These guidelines, combined with practice sessions, will be useful in improving the new interviewer's skills and reducing interviewing errors.

DISCUSSION QUESTIONS

1 What four areas are important in the planning of field operations?
2 What are the problems peculiar to the use of the personal interview in field operations?
3 Evaluate the use of the telephone interview in field operations.
4 What are the main sources of error in field operations?
5 What is nonresponse error?
6 How can the interviewer contribute to measurement error?
7 What guidelines should an interviewer be given regarding the asking of questions?

CASES FOR PART FIVE

CASE 5-1: Parkside Corporation

In early January 1987, Barbra Lott, vice president of marketing for Parkside Corporation, a leading manufacturer in the recreational vehicle (RV) market, was approached by Paul Ransom, Parkside's president and chief executive officer. Ransom, sensitive to continuing developments in the RV market, was concerned with whether Parkside's strategy of concentrating on the motor home segment of the RV market was still sound.[1]

Given the company's strong cash position, Ransom told Lott that she should analyze from a marketing perspective whether Parkside should expand into other RV markets and/or vertically integrate forward or backward in the RV supplier-manufacturer-distributor chain. If so, Ransom said that he knew of two companies that could be purchased. The first company, Travelall, was a respected, medium-sized manufacturer of travel trailers. The second company, Flushaway, was a small and expanding regional manufacturer of toilets for RVs, boats, and aircraft.

Lott recognized the need for marketing research as part of the process of addressing these strategic questions. She first talked with her assistant, Joel Christopherson, about the situation. Christopherson was a recent graduate of a leading business school and had specific training in the area of marketing research. After thoroughly discussing the decision situation, they formulated the following statement:

Management objective: To expand Parkside's long-term profitability by entering new market segments within the RV market and/or by integrating forward or backward in the RV business.

---

[1] The RV market is composed of motor homes (motor vehicle combined with living unit), travel trailers (living unit pulled by car or truck), campers (living unit sits in bed of truck), and accessories (sundry items purchased for RV vehicles).

The RV market segments were clearly defined as those of (1) travel trailers, (2) motor homes, (3) slide-in campers, and (4) RV accessories. Given the current alternatives of purchasing Travelall and/or Flushaway, it was decided to concentrate initial effort on the travel trailer segment (Travelall) and backward integration to a toilet supplier (Flushaway). Christopherson was directed to develop a written proposal for research directed at evaluating this issue within three days.

Returning to his office, Christopherson decided that his first steps were to formulate clear research objectives and to specify in detail the information needed. The more he investigated the situation, the more he recognized that very little was known about the travel trailer segment or the toilet aspect of the RV business in general.

Christopherson believed that a two-stage research program was needed. The first stage would be exploratory research designed to better understand the travel trailer owner and reactions to RV toilets. Is the reason for buying a travel trailer different from that for buying a motor home? What are the problems with travel trailers? What are the important considerations in purchasing a travel trailer? Is the toilet an important feature in buying an RV? Are there opportunities for product improvement? It seemed important to find out about questions of this nature before a more formal research program could be formulated. The second stage could involve large-scale telephone or personal interviews with RV owners.

Focus group interviews appeared to be the best choice for the exploratory research phase. Of immediate concern were the many details involved in designing a focus group study. How should the respondents be selected? Male or female? Age? Families or individuals? How experienced should the respondents be? Recent or lifetime owners? How many people should be in a session? How many sessions? Where should they be held? Who should conduct (moderate) the sessions? How long should the sessions run? Should the sessions be taped? What questions needed to be included on the interviewer's question guide?

CASE QUESTION

Design the focus group study and develop the interviewer's guide.

CASE 5-2: Mayfield Health and Racquet Club*

The Mayfield Health and Racquet Club was located in a small suburb of Milwaukee, Wisconsin. Established in 1972, the club had grown to 2000 members by 1986—mostly young professionals in the $25,000 + income bracket. Mayfield's 12 indoor tennis courts provided year-round tennis, and its $\frac{1}{8}$-mile indoor track was the only one in the area.

Margaret Searns, manager of Mayfield, was concerned about the lack of growth in new memberships. Despite the escalating population and the American public's increased interest in health clubs, Mayfield's membership had stagnated at 2000. An

_____

* Coauthored by Sheryl Petras.

outdoor swimming pool was installed in 1984, but that hadn't sparked any added interest in the club. By 1986, the revenues from membership fees barely covered Mayfield's high fixed costs. Searns, though, feared an increase in dues might result in a decrease in revenues because current patrons might leave the club.

To provide a needed boost in revenues, Searns was considering the installation of a weight room—with both free weights and Nautilus machines. She also wanted to hire a trainer to come in 4 days a week. She thought this would prompt new memberships, since the closest gym with this type of equipment was more than 20 miles away. Previous management had been opposed to the idea, insisting that the interest in body building and weight lifting was a fad. Their judgment proved to be wrong—by 1986 weight lifting had become more popular than ever, and Searns was sure this popularity would continue. To ascertain consumer attitudes about weight lifting, Searns hired a marketing research firm to conduct an inexpensive study. She was currently in the process of evaluating their proposed questionnaire, which was to be administered over the telephone.

QUESTIONNAIRE

Part I
1. Are you familiar with weight lifting or weight-lifting equipment?
   Yes _____   No _____
   (If they answer "no," tell them they don't qualify for the study, and thank them for their time.)

2. Do you currently weight lift?
   Yes _____   No _____   (If "yes," skip to question 4.)

3. Have you ever lifted weights?
   Yes _____   No _____   (If "no," skip to question 8.)

4. Where do (did) you usually lift?
   Home   _____
   Private club _____
   Public gym   _____

5. How often do (did) you lift?
   Every day   _____
   Twice weekly   _____
   Once a week   _____
   Less than once a week _____

6. What type of equipment do (did) you use?
   Nautilus   _____
   Universal   _____
   Free weights _____
   Other   _____

7. What influenced you to begin lifting weights?
   _____
   _____

Part II

8. Do you belong to a health club? If "no," skip to question 9.

Yes _____   No _____

Which club? _____

What are the membership dues? _____

Does it offer a weight room?

Yes _____   No _____

Would you change clubs if you were offered an extensive weight room equipped with free weights and Nautilus machines?

Yes _____   No _____

Skip to question 10.

9. Would the presence of an extensive weight room, equipped with both free weights and a complete Nautilus setup, induce you to join a club?

Yes _____   No _____

Part III

10. Which of the following statements best describes you?
    a. To keep in shape I have a regular exercise program.
    b. I exercise occasionally when I feel that I really need to.
    c. I exercise as a social activity.
    d. I get enough exercise at work, so I don't need an exercise program.
    e. I don't have an exercise program, but would like one.
    f. I don't have an exercise program.

11. Do you see weight lifting as a passing fad, or a form of exercise which will be around for a while?

_____

_____

12. What is your opinion about Nautilus and free-weight workouts as an exercise regimen?
    a. Adequate by themselves.
    b. Can be integrated into a current exercise program without having to increase the total exercise time.
    c. Are good as an addition to other exercise, but the total exercise time should be increased to include weight lifting.
    d. Weight lifting is not a good form of exercise.

13. Would you lift weights if they were available to you?

Yes _____   No _____

Part IV

14. Could you please give us the following statistical information?
    a. Male _____   Female _____
    b. Your age _____
    c. Your occupation _____
    d. Into which category does your income fall?

    Under $5,000   _____
    $5,000– $8,000   _____
    $8,000–$12,000   _____
    $12,000–$16,000   _____

$16,000–$20,000 _____

$20,000 and over _____

Thank you very much for helping us out.

Respondent's Name _____

Telephone _____

CASE QUESTION

Evaluate and revise the proposed questionnaire. Explain thoroughly the reasons for your proposed changes.

CASE 5-3: A Day in the Careers of Pamela Palmers and Sandy Sanders—Professional Interviewers

Pamela Palmers and Sandy Sanders, professional interviewers for Tri-State Interviewing, were working on a project involving in-store interviews with female supermarket shoppers. The study was to determine homemakers' reactions to two brownie mix formulations. One version (Sample R) was the formula used in the client's current brownie mix, which had achieved a substantial market share. The second version (Sample G) was a new R&D formulation. The client was concerned with homemakers' preferences for the two formulations and their comments/reactions in depth.

Palmers and Sanders had spent the previous afternoon in a briefing session with the client concerning the study procedure and questionnaire execution. Both women were to interview as many female shoppers as possible in the period from 9 A.M. to 9 P.M. The two brownie samples would be prepared locally by a home economist from the client's R&D facilities.

The questionnaire and "contact sheets" are reprinted at the end of the case.

The following interviews are representative of those conducted by Palmers and Sanders during the one-day brownie taste test.

TYPICAL INTERVIEWS: PAMELA PALMERS (*PP*)

(Kroger Supermarket, Saturday, July 14th)

Contact No. 1 (9:08 A.M.)

A middle-aged woman approaches the test area with a few items in her cart from the entry displays.

PP: Good morning! I am Pamela Palmers, and we are having a brownie taste this morning. I would like to have you try our two brownie samples and give us your reaction.

Resp.: Why yes, I love brownies.

RR: Please sit down at our test table and try the brownies.

(The respondent sits down and proceeds to taste each of the brownies marked "G" and "R.")

PP: After you have had time to try each brownie, I'd like to ask you a few questions. It will only take a few minutes. Can I get you a cup of coffee?

Resp.: Yes—black, please.

PP: Which of the two brownie samples did you prefer?

Resp.: Sample "G."

PP: What did you particularly like about the brownies?

Resp.: I liked the taste of "G."

PP: What was there about the taste of "G" that you liked?

Resp.: The chocolate taste was good.

PP: In what way was the chocolate taste good?

Resp.: It wasn't too bitter and it wasn't too sweet-tasting, it was just the right taste.

PP: Sorry for the delay—I am writing this down, and I want to be sure I am writing it just as you are telling it to me. What else did you like about Sample "G"?

Resp.: Well, I like the color; it's a nice light brown, just a perfect chocolate color for a brownie.

PP: What else did you like?

Resp.: I guess I've told you everything I like about Sample "G."

PP: What did you like about Sample "R"?

Resp.: There wasn't anything I liked about it.

PP: What did you particularly dislike about the brownies?

Resp.: Well, Sample "R" was sweet, and the texture was terrible.

PP: In what ways was the texture terrible?

Resp.: It's too fluffy: I hate cake brownies.

PP: What else didn't you like about Sample "R"?

Resp.: That's about it.

PP: What did you dislike about Sample "G"?

Resp.: It's a little crumbly.

PP: What else didn't you like?

Resp.: Nothing, it is really an excellent brownie.

Recorded Answer—Question 2

(Sample G), I liked the taste (taste), the chocolate taste was good (good). It wasn't too bitter and it wasn't too sweet-tasting, it was just the right taste (P). Well, I liked the color, it's a nice light brown, just a perfect chocolate color for a brownie. (P) I guess I've told you everything I liked about Sample L. (Sample R) There wasn't anything I liked about it.

Recorded Answer—Question 3

(Sample R) Well, sample R was sweet and the texture was terrible (texture). It's too fluffy, I hate cake brownies (P) That is about it. (Sample L) It is a little crumbly (P) nothing, it is really an excellent brownie.

Contact No. 4 (10:43 A.M.)

A family with two children, aged approximately four and seven, enters the test area. The woman is pushing the cart, with the four-year-old riding.

PP: Good morning, sir. I'm Pamela Palmers, and we are having a brownie taste test. Won't you try one? Coffee is available on the table.

(The man picks up the brownie and proceeds to the table for a cup of coffee.)

PP: I would like to have your wife try two samples of our brownies and answer a few brief questions. Do you mind watching the children while she tries the brownies? It will just take a minute.

(The man smiles at Ms. Palmers and suggests to his wife that she try brownies. The interview is then completed.)

Contact No. 7 (11:32 A.M.)

A middle-aged woman enters the test area pushing the cart at a brisk pace.

PP: Good morning! I'm Pamela Palmers, and we are conducting a brownie taste test this morning. I would like to have you try our brownies and answer a few questions.

Resp.: Sorry, honey, I'm in a hurry.

(She proceeds down the aisle, stopping briefly to grab a loaf of bread. Interview was not completed.)

Contact No. 18 (3:32 P.M.)

A young woman enters the test area and smiles as she sees Pamela.

PP: Mary, how good to see you. I didn't know you shopped at Kroger.

Resp.: Sometimes they have good specials. What are you doing here, running one of those surveys?

PP: How about helping me out and trying our brownies?

Resp.: Love to.

(Mary sits down and tastes the two samples.)

PP: Which of the two brownie samples did you prefer?

Resp.: "G."

PP: What did you particularly like about the brownies?

Resp.: They taste homemade, especially "G."

PP: In what way does Sample "G" taste like homemade?

Resp.: It's very chewy and not too sweet.

PP: What else did you like about Sample "G"?

Resp.: Nothing.

PP: What did you particularly like about Sample "R"?

Resp.: It's very light.

PP: What do you mean by light?

Resp.: The weight of the sample, it is more like a cake in its texture.

PP: What else did you like about Sample "R"?

Resp.: That's about it.

PP: What did you particularly dislike about the brownies?

Resp.: Sample "R" had a strong chocolate flavor.

PP: What do you mean by strong chocolate flavor?

Resp.: Rather sweet chocolate taste.

PP: What else didn't you like about sample "R"?

Resp.: Nothing else, I guess.

PP: What did you particularly dislike about sample "G"?

Resp.: Could be somewhat more chewy.

PP: What else didn't you like?

Resp.: That's it; it is really a good brownie, like I make at home.

(The rest of the interview is completed, and Pamela and Mary discuss personal matters for a few minutes.)

Contact No. 24 (8:03 P.M.)

A middle-aged couple enter the test area. Pamela approaches their cart, smiles at both, and addresses the woman:

PP: Good evening. I am Pamela Palmers, and we are conducting a brownie taste test this evening. I would like to have you try our brownies and answer a few brief questions. It will only take a minute or so.

(Turning to the man, and smiling.)

PP: We have coffee available on the table, and you are free to try brownies yourself while I talk with your wife.

(The woman looks at her husband. He nods his head in approval. The woman sits down and tries the brownies. The interview is completed.)

TYPICAL INTERVIEWS: SANDY SANDERS (*SS*)

(A&P Supermarket, Saturday, July 14th)

Contact No. 1 (9:22 A.M.)

A young woman and a year-old child approach the test area. The young child is riding quietly in the chart.

SS: Hi, we are testing brownies this morning—please try some.

Resp.: Okay.

SS: Please sit down at the table and taste the two samples I have labeled "R" and "G." Would you like some coffee?

Resp.: Yes, cream and sugar.

(The woman tries each of the brownies.)

SS: How did you like the brownies?

Resp.: They were good.

SS: Which of the two brownie samples did you prefer?

Resp.: Sample "G."

SS: What did you like about Sample "G"?

Resp.: The nice flavor. The texture of "G" was good; I like a moist brownie.

SS: By moist, do you mean chewy?

Resp.: Yes, I like a chewy brownie.

SS: How about Sample "R"? You said they were both good.

Resp.: I like "R," but it didn't have the flavor of "G."

SS: Is there anything else?

Resp.: No.

SS: What didn't you like about the brownies?

Resp.: I like my brownies warm.

SS: Anything about Sample "G" you didn't like?

Resp.: It was a little heavy.

SS: Anything else?

Resp.: No.

SS: How about Sample "R"?

Resp.: Rather sweet.

SS: Anything else?

Resp.: No.

Recorded Answer—Question 2

> Both good (L) nice flavor, texture good, moist
> (moist), chewy (R / ok, flavor not as good
> (P) No.

Recorded Answer—Question 3

> Not warm enough (L) heavy (P) no (R)
> sweet (P) no

Contact No. 3 (10:24 A.M.)

An elderly couple slowly push their cart to the test area.

> *SS:* Hello, would you like to try some brownies this morning?
> *Resp.:* (male) No, can't eat that stuff—dentures.
> (The couple passes through the test area. Interview not completed.)

Contact No. 4 (10:27 A.M.)

A middle-aged couple enters the test area. They have with them two girls aged five and eight. The eight-year-old is pushing the cart, while the husband and wife are talking about the grocery list.

> *SS:* How are you this morning? We are testing brownies; would you be interested?
> *Resp.:* (female) No, not today.
> (Interview not completed.)

Contact No. 14 (2:13 P.M.)

A middle-aged woman briskly pushes her cart toward the test area.

> *SS:* Hi, we are testing brownies this morning. Would you care to try our two versions and answer some questions?
> *Resp.:* How long will it take?
> *SS:* Just two or three minutes. We have coffee also.
> *Resp.:* I don't drink coffee—do you have tea?

SS: No.
Resp.: How about milk?
SS: No.
Resp.: Well, I'll try them quickly.
SS: Please sit down at the table. Here are the two samples. I think you will like them.
(The woman quickly tastes each sample.)
SS: Which did you prefer?
Resp.: Sample "R."
SS: What did you like about "R"?
Resp.: It was tasty, more like homemade.
SS: Anything else?
Resp.: It was light; the other one was too chewy.
SS: Anything else?
Resp: No.
SS: How about "G," what did you like about it?
Resp.: Nothing.
SS: What did you particularly dislike about the brownies?
Resp.: "G" was too chewy, and the flavor was poor.
SS: What do you mean—poor?
Resp.: It was flat.
SS: Anything else?
Resp.: No.
SS: How about "R"?
Resp.: It was great.
(The rest of the interview is completed.)

Contact No. 21 (4:30 P.M.)

A young teenage couple enters the test area. The male is pushing the cart.

SS: Hi, we are having women try brownies this afternoon. Do you have time to try them and answer some questions?
Resp.: (female) No.
Resp.: (male) They look good—you don't mind if I try one?
(He picks up three brownies, and the couple proceeds. Interview not completed.)

Contact No. 27 (7:42 P.M.)

A young couple enters the test area. A boy, about five, is trying to push the cart while his father guides it from the front.

SS: Hello, we are having women taste two versions of brownies this evening. Would you please try them for us? We have coffee if you would like some.
Resp.: (Man) Go ahead, honey, I'll grab a cup of coffee and meet you in the cereal section.

SS: Please be seated at our test table and try the two samples marked "R" and "G."
(The woman tastes each sample.)
SS: Which sample did you like best?
Resp.: They were both good.
SS: You must have liked one better than the other.
Resp.: Well, "G" was a little better, but not much.
SS: What did you like about "G"?
Resp.: It was light and mild.
SS: Do you mean its weight?
Resp.: No, its color.
SS: Anything else?
Resp.: Not really.
SS: What did you like about "R"?
Resp.: It had a rich flavor.
SS: What do you mean by rich?
Resp.: The texture was light and delicate.
SS: Anything else?
Resp.: No, that's it.
SS: What did you particularly dislike about the brownies?
Resp.: As I said before, I liked them equally well. They're both excellent.
SS: There must be something you didn't like—was the color too dark on "R"?
Resp.: No, it was fine.
(The interview is completed.)

At 9:32, Sandy meets Pamela at a nearby cocktail lounge. They both order drinks and proceed to check their completed questionnaires for completeness and legibility. By 11:03 they have completed their work and proceed to the local post office to mail the questionnaires to the client's home office.

CASE QUESTION

How would you evaluate the interviewing skills of Pamela Palmers and Sandy Sanders? What specific suggestions would improve their effectiveness?

QUESTIONNAIRE

Store _____   Date _____
Interviewer _____   Time _____

BROWNIE STUDY

1. Which of the two brownie samples did you prefer?
   Sample R (   )   Sample G (   )   No preference (   )

2. What did you particularly like about the brownies? (Probe and clarify fully)

_____
_____
_____

3. What did you particularly dislike about the brownies? (Probe and clarify fully)

_____
_____
_____

4. How frequently do you serve brownies to your family?
   Once a week ( )   Every two weeks ( )   Once a month ( )   Less frequently ( )

5. Do you make your brownies from a mix or from scratch?
   Mix ( )   Scratch ( )   Both ( )

6. If mix, or both, what brand of mix do you usually buy?
   Brand name(s) _____ , _____

(7 through 11: demographic information)

CONTACT SHEET

Interviewer _Pamela Palmer_   Firm _Tri-State_

Place _Kroger_   Address _1436 Maple_

City/State _St. Louis, Mo._   Date _Sat. July 14th_

	Contact Time	Couple	Female	Completed Yes	Completed No
1	9:08 A.M		✓	✓	
2	9:20 A.M.		✓		✓
3	9:31 A.M	✓		✓	
4	10:43 A.M.	✓	✓	✓	
5	11:14 A.M		✓		✓
Total	28	15	13	16	12

CONTACT SHEET

Interviewer _Sandy Sanders_   Firm _Tri-State_

Place _A & P_   Address _1592 Maple_

City/State _St. Louis, Mo._   Date _Sat. July 14th_

	Contact Time	Couple	Female	Completed Yes	Completed No
1	9:22 am		✓	✓	
2	9:50 am	✓		✓	
3	10:24 am	✓			✓
4					
.					
.					
.					
.					
Total	39	18	21	12	27

CASE 5-4: Plastics Company of America*

Anne Marre was the president of the Dallas-based Plastics Company of America (PCA), a large manufacturer of plastic and plastic-based products. PCA was very diverse, producing everything from plastic bottles to furniture components. It had been a product innovator in both these markets by utilizing plastic production technologies in new and unique ways. But a slumping economy, coupled with poor strategic marketing planning, caused PCA's profits to plunge 36 percent—from $30.3 million in 1983 to $19.4 million in 1985. Marre was convinced that PCA could reverse this trend by exploiting new product opportunities that were present in its existing markets. She thought that the automative sound deadener market would be well suited to PCA's entry.

Sound deadeners are devices which limit engine noise from entering the passenger compartment of an automobile. The typical materials used include PVC (a hard-rubber material), mastic (a gluelike substance), and resinated fibers (such as fiberglass). Marre saw potential for the use of polyurethane rubber (PUR) as an alternative to these materials. Currently it was used in very limited sound-deadener applications, and Marre hoped that the use of PUR could be expanded enough to provide a profitable market for PCA. PUR had several advantages over other sound deadeners—it was very effective, and at the same time extremely lightweight. Since lighter cars were more fuel-

* Coauthored by Sheryl Petras.

efficient, automakers took weight into consideration when choosing a sound-deadener package.

On the negative side, PUR was more expensive than PVC, mastic, or fibers, and its use would require auto companies to allocate more money to sound deadening. Marre, though, felt that PCA's current research and development project would enable it to cut the costs of producing PUR. Another disadvantage was that PUR could only be used in cars sporting new designs because other sound-deadening materials had already been engineered into existing models.

Marre wanted to determine how automakers felt about the use of PUR as a sound-deadening material. Her marketing director suggested that a questionnaire would be the best method of determining automakers' acceptance of PUR. The marketing director subsequently designed a questionnaire and presented it to Marre. After reviewing the questionnaire, she began to design the rest of the marketing research project. A limited budget forced her to keep the project very small.

CASE QUESTIONS

1. What type of communication structure—structured vs. unstructured, direct vs. indirect—seems most appropriate? Why? Is this questionnaire appropriate for that type of structure?
2. Give the advantages and disadvantages of each of the various communications media. Which one should Marre choose?
3. Evaluate the proposed questionnaire, suggesting changes if they are necessary.
4. What are potential problems in the field operations associated with this study? Suggest ways to overcome these problems.

QUESTIONNAIRE

Sound-Deadener Study

Name of respondent _____
Title of respondent _____

1. Please estimate what percentage of your total sound-deadening package the following materials represent.
   PVC _____%
   Mastic _____%
   Resinated fibers _____%
   Polyurethane rubber _____%
   Other (please specify) _____   _____%

2. How much per vehicle does [insert company name] spend on sound-deadening materials?
   $_____

3. How much importance is attached to sound deadening?
   Very little _____   Little _____   Some _____   Great _____   Very Great _____

4. Concerning sound deadeners, please rank the importance [insert company name] gives the following attributes. Use the scale appearing above the attribute list on the next page.

Not much importance						Much importance
1	2	3	4	5	6	7

Weight _____
Cost of material _____
Durability _____
Availability _____
Cost of installation _____
Effectiveness in sound deadening _____
Amount of wasted material _____
Storage considerations _____
Skill required to install _____
Ease of installation _____

5. Now rank the same attributes with respect to the degree of satisfaction your current sound-deadening package delivers. Use the scale presented below.

Low satisfaction						High satisfaction
1	2	3	4	5	6	7

Weight _____
Cost of material _____
Durability _____
Availability _____
Cost of installation _____
Effectiveness in sound deadening _____
Amount of wasted material _____
Storage considerations _____
Skill required to install _____
Ease of installation _____

6. Have you investigated the use of polyurethane rubber as an alternative to your present sound-deadening packages?

    Yes _____   No _____

If not, please tell us why:

7. What are your current information sources regarding PUR, and how would you rank them?

Source	Not very useful	Useful	Very useful
Trade publications	_____	_____	_____
Manufacturer's representative	_____	_____	_____
Contact with present user	_____	_____	_____
Trade shows	_____	_____	_____
Other (please specify)	_____	_____	_____

8. If you are currently using PUR, which of the above sources was the most influential in helping you make your decision? _____

9. Why did you decide to use PUR? Please rank the following items in order of their importance.
   Supplier _____   Effectiveness _____
   Customer satisfaction _____   Weight   _____
   Ease in use   _____

10. Are you presently satisfied with your sound-deadening materials?
    Yes _____   No _____   If not, state your reasons why.

11. If you are not currently using polyurethane rubber, have you done a feasibility study into its possible use?   Yes _____   No _____

12. If you decided to utilize a greater percentage of polyurethane rubber in your future sound-deadening packages, what emphasis would you place on the following factors?

	Emphasis				
Factor	**Very little**	**Little**	**Some**	**Great**	**Very great**
Environmental concerns (biodegradability, etc.)	_____	_____	_____	_____	_____
Number of PUR suppliers	_____	_____	_____	_____	_____
Materials cost	_____	_____	_____	_____	_____
Possibility that PUR costs will decline	_____	_____	_____	_____	_____
Ease in installing PUR	_____	_____	_____	_____	_____
Material employees prefer to install	_____	_____	_____	_____	_____
Amount of sound deadening per lb	_____	_____	_____	_____	_____
Material used by competition	_____	_____	_____	_____	_____
Other (please specify)	_____	_____	_____	_____	_____

Which of the above factors would be the most important?

13. In your opinion, how much effect will the supply and cost of fuel have on the type of sound deadeners used?
    None _____
    Little _____
    Some _____
    Much _____
    Great _____
    Very great _____

Anne: I can modify this questionnaire to make it appropriate for phone interviews. Just let me know of any changes you'd like made. Thanks.

Manuel Lopez
Marketing Director

FINAL STAGES OF THE RESEARCH PROCESS

CHAPTER 16

DATA PROCESSING

Picture yourself as a marketing research analyst. You are sitting in your office when a delivery service drops two large boxes of questionnaires on your desk, the results of six weeks of field interviewing done by a research supply house that you hired to do the interviewing for your study. You decided earlier that you would directly supervise all the work for this study yourself, except for the field work. Now you have to get these questionnaires into a form that allows you to analyze the data they contain. Just what must you do to accomplish this task?

A description of the functions necessary to prepare raw data collection forms, called *instruments,* for data analysis constitutes the topic of this chapter. We begin with a description of some of the basic terms and concepts of data processing as applied to marketing research. Next we discuss the decision concerning whether a particular respondent's instrument should be prepared for data analysis. It may not be filled out properly, and thus we may not want to use it. Other sections will cover the editing of data collection instruments, coding, data cleaning, creation of new variables, and data weighting.

SOME BASIC CONCEPTS

Our basic task in data processing is to *convert the raw data in the data collection instrument into a computer-readable form.* We can then make use of computerized data analysis procedures to extract information from the data. Before we see how this is done, there are some concepts and terms that we need to understand.[1]

[1] This section follows an excellent discussion in Earl Babbie, *Survey Research Methods* (Belmont, Calif.: Wadsworth, 1973), pp. 187–191.

Case A case refers to *a specific unit of analysis* for the study. Quite often the unit of analysis is the respondent to a questionnaire, so each respondent would be considered a case, and the total number of cases would equal the sample size.

The Computer Card The data provided by a research instrument must be converted into a computer-readable form, and the computer card is the basic device used for this purpose. Quite often now the data are entered directly into the computer at the time of data collection. These computer-based interviewing systems make the use of computer cards unnecessary. They are described in detail later in the chapter. However, these systems store data under the same basic logic as the computer card. Also, a significant amount of marketing research still does use card-based data entry. Thus, we will begin by understanding the computer card system and evolve the discussion to computer-direct methods.

A computer card is divided into 80 vertical columns. Data are put on the card by punching holes within the columns. Within each vertical column there are 12 spaces available for punches. Ten of these spaces are designated by the numbers 0, 1, 2, 3, 4, 5, 6, 7, 8, 9 running from the top to the bottom of each column. The other two spaces for punches are located above the zero space. They are unnumbered but are sometimes called the 11 and 12 punch, counting from the zero space. By means of a keypunch machine, you can use combinations of punches within a column to form letters or special characters. These types of letters and characters will not be used in the data processing discussed in this chapter. Our interest here is in having only one numeric punch (0–9) within each column, as most computer data analysis programs can handle only numeric data.

How is information on a questionnaire converted into punches in a computer card? One or more specific columns of the computer card are assigned to a variable, and then numeric punches are assigned within that column to represent the available responses for that variable. For example, the respondent's year in college might be assigned to column 20 of the computer card. If the respondent is a senior, a 1 could be punched in column 20. If the respondent is a junior, a 2 could be punched in column 20, and so on. If a variable contains more than 10 categories or requires two or more digits to represent the data, the specific variable in question would be assigned as many columns as needed to present the data. For example, the respondent's scores on the Scholastic Aptitude Test (SAT) would require three columns, as each score is out of 800. Columns 71–73 might be assigned for this variable, and the exact score would be punched in the columns. If the score was 625, the 6 would be punched in column 71, the 2 in column 72, and the 5 in column 73. The data collection instrument for a study may require far more than 80 columns to punch the data properly, but this presents no problem. Each respondent can have as many computer cards as are necessary to represent the data. All that is required is that specific columns within a specific card represent a variable. For example, columns 56–57 of card 3 might represent the respondent's age. The data on the computer cards are read into a computer by a card reader. This device is able to locate the columns on the card and identify the specific punch within each column. The computer can then make use of the data.

Data Deck   The data deck is made up of all the computer cards necessary to represent the data on all the questionnaires. For example, if we had used a questionnaire that needed three cards to represent the data on it, and had a sample size of 400, we would have 3 × 400 = 1200 cards in our data deck. It is this data deck that is read into the computer.

Data Storage   Once the data are read into the computer, the researcher may use the computer capabilities to store the data from the data deck in either a computer disk file or on a computer tape. The problems of dropping or losing the data deck are thus removed. Also, data stored in a computer disk file or on tape are much easier for the computer to access for later data analysis. All the physical problems of carrying the data deck to the computer for each data analysis run are eliminated; for a data deck running into thousands of cards, this is a must. Tape storage has the advantage over the disk file of allowing the researcher to transport the data. You can easily carry

FIGURE 16-1   The concept of a data matrix.

			Variables (1 to m)			
			Column numbers			
		1	2	. . .		m
	1	2	625			4
	2	3	710			1
	3	1	521			3
	4	1	601			2
	5	4	706			1
Cases (1 to n)	Row Numbers 6	3	507			5
	7	2	429			1
	.					
	.					
	.					
	n	1	764			2

Variable 1 = Year in college
         (1 = 1st year, 2 = 2nd year, 3 = 3rd year, 4 = 4th year)
Variable 2 = SAT score (out of 800)
Variable m = Region of the country parents live in
         (1 = Northeast, 2 = Southwest, 3 = Southwest
         4 = Northwest, 5 = Midwest)

in one hand a large data set that is stored on tape, whereas a disk file cannot be transported. Also, tape storage is cheaper than disk storage. In practice, data from old studies are usually saved on tape.

Data Matrix The data storage on disk file or tape may be thought of as forming a data matrix (see Figure 16-1). Each row of the matrix represents a case, and each column represents a variable. Note that the total number of rows equals the number of cases, n, and the total number of columns equals the number of variables, m. We refer to this as an $n \times m$ (n by m) data matrix. The data presented in this sample matrix are the values associated with the specific cases for three variables—year in college, SAT score, and region of the country parents live in. Note that each variable, no matter how many digits it requires, occupies only one column of the data matrix. The number of cases and variables in a data matrix is limited only by the capacity of the computer. It is not uncommon in practice to have a data matrix that is 2500×200 or even larger. It is on this data matrix that computer programs perform data analysis.

With these basic concepts in hand, we now examine the individual steps in the flow of data processing.

DATA PROCESSING FLOW

Figure 16-2 presents an overview of the traditional sequence of functions to be performed in data processing. These include (1) deciding whether to use the data collection instrument for analysis, (2) editing it, (3) coding it, (4) keypunching and verifying the data, (5) converting the data deck into a computer-readable form, (6) cleaning the dataset, (7) generating new variables as necessary, (8) weighting the data in accordance with the sampling plan and results, and (9) storing the dataset on disk or tape. The following section presents a discussion of each of these functions.

Identification of Acceptable Instruments

Upon receiving a data collection instrument from the field, the researcher should examine it to determine whether it is acceptable for use in the study. The exact criteria for judging an instrument unacceptable vary from study to study, but those listed below are typical:

1 A significant portion of the instrument is left unanswered, or key elements are left unanswered.

2 It is clear from the answers given that the respondent did not understand the task required in filling out the instrument.

3 The answers show too little variance. For example, the answers to a series of attitude questions are all 3s on a 7-point scale. This is evidence that the respondent is not taking the task seriously.

4 The wrong sample element has filled out the instrument. For example, the study calls for respondents to be working women, and a man has completed the instrument.

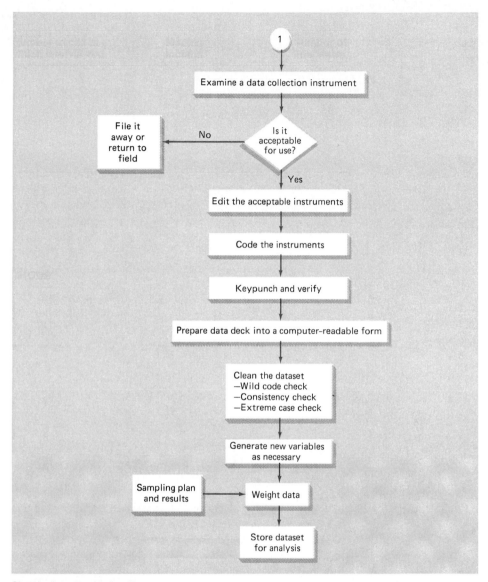

FIGURE 16-2   Classic data processing flow.

5 The instrument is physically incomplete. For example, a page may not have been included or may have been taken off in the field.

6 The instrument is received after an established cutoff date. If you wait for all instruments to be returned from the field, the study likely would not be completed on time.

If the researcher thinks that the particular defect in question could be corrected within reasonable time and cost constraints, the data collection instrument may be returned to the field. Otherwise, the instrument is filed away.

All data collection instruments should be subjected to this type of preliminary examination before being sent through the rest of the data processing flow. Above all, the criteria for accepting or rejecting an instrument should be established before the instruments are received.

Editing

Editing means reviewing the data collection instruments to ensure maximum accuracy and unambiguity.[2] It is important that editing be done consistently. In a small study, one person may perform the editing function, and consistency is likely to be high. In a large study that requires many editors, an editing supervisor is necessary to ensure that consistency is maintained among editors. This person would have to sample-check different editors on different sections of the instrument. Alternatively, each editor could be made responsible for a different section of the instrument and edit all instruments for this section.

In performing the editing function, be concerned with:

1 Legibility To be properly coded later, the data must be legible. Sometimes an illegible response can be corrected by contacting the person who recorded it, and sometimes the correct response can be inferred from other parts of the instrument. If no definitive answer is available, the response should be designated as missing data. To sum up, the editor takes the ambiguity out of the recorded data, so that the coder knows exactly what to do.

2 Completeness Questions that are not answered may be treated in one of three ways. First, the editor may contact the interviewer to try to determine whether the respondent did not answer the question or whether the interviewer just failed to record the response. In doing this, there is a risk that the interviewer will not remember this particular interview correctly. Alternatively, the respondent may be contacted again for a response to a specific question. The second approach is to designate this particular piece of data as missing data. Finally, if the editor deems that too many data items are missing, the whole instrument may be sent back to the field or removed from the study.

3 Consistency At this point, a preliminary check is made on the consistency of the data. (A more detailed check will be performed later by the computer.) For example, the editor might verify that respondents who claim to buy gasoline by credit card do hold credit cards. The editor may ask the interviewer to resolve any inconsistencies, designate the responses to these questions as missing data, or remove the instrument from the study.

[2] Donald S. Tull and Gerald S. Albaum, *Survey Research: A Decisional Approach* (New York: Intext Educational Publishers, 1973), p. 168.

4 Accuracy   The editor needs to be attentive to evidence of inaccuracy in the data. The most important area here relates to possible interviewer bias or cheating. Such activities may be spotted by looking for a common pattern of responses in the instruments of a particular interviewer or recorder.

5 Response Clarification   Sometimes the responses to open-ended questions are difficult to interpret clearly. The recorder's words may have abbreviated the answer too much, or some words may be ambiguous. The editor may designate a meaning to the response or ask the interviewer what was meant. The risk of error is high in both instances. Obviously, good field work in the first place can prevent many problems from arising.

Difficulties also occur when questions are not answered in the way the instructions to the instrument required. This is especially a problem in mail surveys. For example, a respondent may be asked to underline a number on a 7-point rating scale. Suppose he or she underlines the numbers 4 and 5. Does this mean that 4.5 is intended as the response? The editor must decide whether to designate the response as a 4 or as a 5, or record it as missing data.

Coding

Coding involves the assignment of a designated numeric symbol into a designated computer card column, to represent a specific response on a data collection instrument. We saw examples of this earlier in the chapter in our discussion of the computer card and how it is used.[3]

Closed and Open-Ended Questions   For structured or closed questions, the coding scheme is usually designated prior to the undertaking of field work. This may go as far as having the actual codes printed on the data collection instruments. For example, a designation of sex may appear on the instrument as:

```
2/31     What is your sex?
  1      Female
  2      Male
```

The numbers on the left side of the question indicate the coding scheme. Here 2/31 indicates that the response to this question will appear in the 31st column of the 2d card for this respondent. A 1 in this column designates a female and a 2 designates a male. This same approach can be used for coding numeric data that either are not to be coded into categories or have had their relevant categories specified. A respondent's age may be requested and coded as:

```
1/6–7     What is your age?____
```

---

[3] For a detailed discussion of coding, see Philip S. Sidel, "Coding," in Robert Ferber (ed.), *Handbook of Marketing Research* (New York: McGraw-Hill, 1974), pp. 2-178 to 2-199.

or as:

1/6	What is your age?
1	0–18
2	19–35
3	36–50
4	over 50

In both cases the codes can be specified prior to the field work. If the codes are written on all questions on the questionnaire, it is said to be wholly precoded.

Open-ended questions present a more complex problem for coding. Here the verbatim responses of respondents are recorded by the interviewer. How do you convert data like these into a punch in a computer card? There are two general approaches to this problem. The first is the preparation of a relatively well-developed coding scheme prior to the completion of the field work. To be able to do this, the researcher must be guided by the results of previous studies or by some overriding theoretical considerations. The major task of the researcher is then to train coders so that they will convert the verbatim response into the correct code category.

The second approach involves waiting until the instruments return from the field before developing the coding scheme. Here the researcher lists, say, 50 to 100 of the responses to the specific question. He or she then examines this list and decides what categories are appropriate to summarize the data. The researcher then trains the coders in this scheme and also alerts them to watch for other responses that occur with some frequency. If this happens, it may be necessary to go back and revise the coding scheme and thus have to recode all instruments on this question.

Rules and Conventions for Code Construction   There are a number of rules or conventions that make the coding function work well. They are:

1 *Establish mutually exclusive and collectively exhaustive code categories.* It is easy to make categories collectively exhaustive by adding, for example, the code category "other," "no information," or "none" to the major categories for the variable in question.[4] By "mutually exclusive" is meant that every response must fit into one and only one code category. Categories must not overlap; this is the one hard and fast rule of all coding. The other items in this section are best described as useful conventions, not rules.
2 If uncertainty exists about possible uses for a particular variable in analysis, the data should be coded so as to *retain a great deal of detail.* It is possible to combine code categories at the time of analysis if such detail is not required. However, it is impossible to "expand" codes for analysis if they have been recorded with too little detail. We may therefore want to code in more detail than we intend to use in analysis. An example of this would be to code the respondent's exact age, and then combine ages into categories at the time of analysis.

[4]Ibid., p. 2-181.

3 Follow the following card layout conventions:[5]

   a Use only one punch per column, as most computer programs cannot read multi-punched cards.

   b Use only numeric codes, not special characters or blanks.

   c The card position for a variable may consist of as many columns as are necessary, but no more than one variable may be assigned to a single column.

   d Use standard codes for missing data, if at all possible. For example, some researchers always use 9 for a one-column variable and 99 for a two-column variable, etc., for designating missing data. The researcher may have a number of different types of missing data such as "don't know," "does not apply," "refused to answer," etc. If this detail is to be preserved, a standard code should be set for each one. This facilitates coding and later interpretation of data analysis.

4 In choosing breakpoints for continuous variables, consider the following questions.[6]

   a Into how many categories should the variable be cast given the plan of analysis that has been developed?

   b Should the categories be equal-interval (0–9, 10–19, 20–29, etc.), or should they be constructed so that each category has about the same number of cases?

   c Should the extreme categories be open (under $9000; $60,000 and over) to take in a wide range of extreme scores, or should the intervals be fixed?

In making these decisions the researcher must recognize that the use of equal intervals allows for easier statistical analysis later and that the number of categories selected affects the detail of the information retained from the instruments. The more categories you have, the greater the detail. In the end, the number and definition of categories selected must satisfy the user of the research. The researcher must consult with the manager on this issue.

5 Put a respondent and card identification number on each card in the data deck. Figure 16-3 illustrates part of a data deck in which each respondent has three computer cards. Column 1 of each card presents the card identification number. Since there are three cards for each respondent, we see the numbers 1, 2, 3 repeating in column 1 for each of the *n* respondents. Columns 2 to 4 of each card present the case number. Obviously, we expect a sample size of less than 1000. With the cards arranged in this manner, we can instruct the computer to check to see that the required number of cases are in the data deck and that the sequence of cards within each case is the same. If the cards are not in the same order within each case, correct data analysis is impossible, because the computer expects to find a given variable in the same card and column location for each case. Case identification numbers also facilitate data cleaning later.

Multiple Responses[7]   The problem of multiple responses arises in two contexts. The first is where the researcher expects to receive a single answer. In this case the decision may be to select one of the answers on some established priority basis—for

[5]Ibid., pp. 2-128 to 2-184.
[6]Ibid., p. 2-183.
[7] See Babbie, op. cit., p. 193.

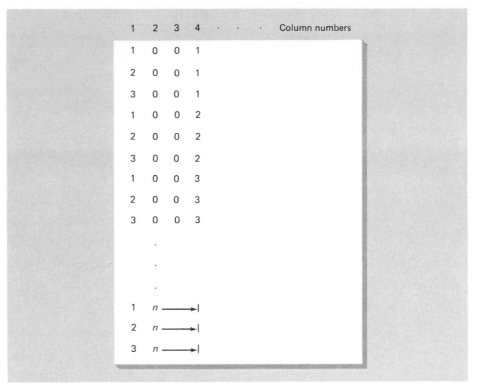

	1	2	3	4	·	·	·	Column numbers
1	0	0	1					
2	0	0	1					
3	0	0	1					
1	0	0	2					
2	0	0	2					
3	0	0	2					
1	0	0	3					
2	0	0	3					
3	0	0	3					

FIGURE 16-3 Illustrative data deck with respondent and card identification numbers.

example, the answer written down first. Alternatively, you may develop code categories to represent combinations of responses. For example, a "7" punch may represent those respondents who said that flavor and baking time were important cake mix attributes. Finally, you may designate this response as missing data.

In situations where the researcher expects more than one answer, two procedures are available. The first is to treat each possible response as a separate variable, with a separate card column. For example, a question may ask what sports a respondent plays. Each sport would be answered "yes" or "no" and assigned to a unique column. The second option is available where the researcher has a specific number of responses expected. The researcher could assign a separate column for "first responses," another for "second responses," and so on. The codes within each column would be the same, representing the available options. For example, a "1" in the first response column could indicate that flavor was the first response for this respondent as an important attribute for cake mix. A "1" in the second response column would indicate that flavor was the second response as an important attribute for cake mix. In analysis, the researcher could examine each response column separately or combine them to get total responses. Care should be taken in combining data of this type; it is possible that an attribute placed second or third, etc., by a great many respondents could have more total mentions than another attribute that had more first mentions. A simple sum of mentions across the columns could confuse managers. They should be consulted as to the importance they place on second- or third-mention levels, etc., before a combining scheme is developed.

It should be recognized that coding is a potentially boring task. After working hard and creatively to develop the coding scheme, the actual coding process may seem very tedious. In addition, this function is often not a highly paid job, which results in problems with quality of personnel. Coding errors often occur unless the researcher maintains close supervision over the coding. You can keep the coders on their toes by asking to see how a sample of instruments were coded. You will also get a better feel for the report that is going to emerge later.

The detail of the coding scheme needs to be documented, and this documentation is placed in what is called a *codebook*.

Codebook   A codebook is the place where all the needed information about variables in the data set is documented. It has three functions. First, it serves as a guide to the coders; second, it helps researchers locate the variables they desire to use in a particular data analysis run; and third, it allows for the proper identification of variable categories as computer output is interpreted. The researcher would literally be lost without a good codebook.

The contents of the codebook vary. For a very simple study, you may just write the relevant column number and punch number on the instrument itself. A completely precoded questionnaire could serve as its own codebook.

In more complex studies, it is useful to have a codebook that contains more information. The researcher often wants the details of open-ended questions documented, or wishes to refer to variables by number for designation in a computer run. So a codebook might contain (1) the question number, (2) the variable number, (3) the relevant card columns, (4) the format (any implied decimal places), (5) the variable name, and (6) the category definitions. Table 16-1 presents a portion of an illustrative codebook. A quick look at the codebook informs us exactly how the variables (sex, age, and grade point average or GPA) appear in the data deck and how we will refer to them in later analysis. For example, GPA will be called variable 121, is in card columns 21–23 of card 3, and has an implied decimal place two places to the left of the end of the field, i.e., between columns 21 and 22. We never punch the decimal place; we need only tell the computer with the formal statement. The GPA was obtained in question 74 on the instrument. For a complex open-ended question, the description of the code categories may be quite lengthy.

Actual Coding   Once the code categories are established, the actual coding can take place. Here, the coders write the proper codes in the designated location on 80-column paper or on some special "code sheet." These sheets may be thought of as a paper version of a computer card. Once this is done, the coding is completed.

TABLE 16-1   AN ILLUSTRATIVE CODEBOOK

Question number	Variable number	Card column	Format*	Variable name	Category definitions
35	46	1/52	I1	Sex	1 = Female 2 = Male 9 = Missing data
36	47	1/53–54	I2	Age	Two-digit number 00–98 99 = Missing data
.	.	.	.	.	
.	.	.	.	.	
.	.	.	.	.	
74	121	3/21–23	F3.2	Grade point average	Three-digit number 000–400 with decimal place two places to left in field given by format

*The use of "I" refers to an integer value in card column(s). The number after the "I" indicates the number of digits in the variable. For example, I1 indicates a one-digit integer variable, I6 a six-digit integer variable, and so on.

The use of "F" indicates that other variables in the card column(s) can take on real values. That is, the variable with an F can have a decimal place. The position of the decimal is given by the number after the decimal place, and the number of digits is given by the number before the decimal For example, F3.2 indicates a real variable containing three digits with the decimal place position before the second digit. That is, the decimal is two places from the end of the field.

Keypunching and Verifying

The completed coding sheets are delivered to keypunchers, who punch the exact number on the sheets into computer cards. We have now converted the data in the data collection instrument into holes in computer cards. However, we must be careful here, as it is very easy for a keypunch operator to make a mistake. It is therefore wise to have the data deck verified after it has been punched. It is put into a verifier (a machine that compares the key that an operator punches with the hole already in a card), and an operator keys from the coding sheets again. If the key pressed by the operator differs from the one on the previously punched card, the operator is signaled that an error has occurred. He or she may then check to see whether the original punch was incorrect. If the punch was in error, this fact is noted with a notch in that column, and correction is made later. The result of this process should be an accurate data deck.

Convert Data Deck Into a Computer-Readable Form

The data deck must now be presented to the computer in such a way that data analysis computer programs can make use of it. Most programs that a researcher is likely to use are contained within a package of programs. One such package of programs is called SPSS (the Statistical Package for the Social Sciences).[8] There are many others, but we shall use SPSS to illustrate the structure of these packages. Figure 16-4 gives an overview of what is done to make an SPSS data file out of the raw data deck. The data deck is read into the computer along with a number of descriptors, including

[8] N. H. Nie, D. H. Bent, and C. H. Hull, *SPSS*, 2d ed. (New York: McGraw-Hill, 1975).

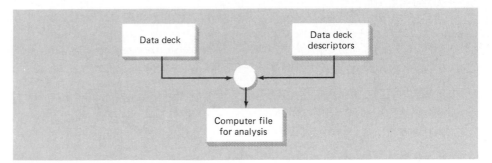

FIGURE 16-4   Creation of a computer file for analysis.

(1) variable numbers and names, (2) variable format, (3) missing-data codes, and (4) variable-category descriptors (if the user desires to have them on computer printouts). The result of this is an SPSS datafile ready for analysis. It has in essence made an SPSS-readable data matrix out of the data deck, and all SPSS analysis programs can make use of this one datafile. We can do an analysis run without worrying about properly locating and defining missing-data codes for the variables of interest in our data deck. All we need to do is refer to the desired variable numbers in the SPSS datafile. This leads to great efficiencies in data analysis.

An item that *must* be included as a variable in the datafile is the case identification number. This will help expedite the data cleaning that is to follow.

Clean the Dataset

We now have a dataset structured as a computer datafile, but we must still attempt to clean the dataset of possible errors. Three types of checks are run on the dataset, namely, (1) a wild code check, (2) a consistency check, and (3) an extreme-case check.

Wild Code Check   The first items we want to get out of our dataset are so-called "wild codes," i.e., codes that are not defined in the codebook for a particular variable. For example, the variable "sex" may have three legitimate codes (the third being for missing data). A number 4 or greater for this variable would be a wild code, probably the result of an error in coding or punching. This check can be done by having the computer list the numbers of responses in each category of each variable, which will tell us whether a wild code exists. But in which case does it occur? This represents no problem if we have made case number a variable. All we do is command the computer to print out the case numbers for those cases that have a wild code, then examine the data collection instruments for these cases and make the appropriate correction in the datafile. Most computer analysis packages allow us to do this easily.

Consistency Check   The next step is to check the consistency of responses within each case. During the editing task we did a preliminary consistency check, but the one performed by the computer can be much more complete. For example, we might check to see that those who have a mortgage also own a house. There are two types of consistency checks: one-way and two-way.[9] In a one-way consistency situation A is true if B is true, but the reverse need not hold. In a two-way consistency situation A is true if and only if B is true, and vice versa. The house and mortgage example above would be an example of a one-way consistency check. That is, those having a mortgage must own a house, but some homeowners may not have a mortgage. A two-way consistency check could be done in a study of university students. A check could be made between credit hours obtained and year of standing in school (senior, junior, etc.). If a junior is someone with between 60 and 90 credit hours, a two-way check could be made between credit hours and year of standing. That is, people with between 60 and 90 credit hours would be checked to see that they were classified as juniors, and junior-classified people would be checked to see that they have the proper number of credit hours. A good data analysis package should have the commands necessary to do this type of checking. Again, once an error is found, the case number is printed out, the data collection instrument is examined, and the correction is made.

Extreme-Case Check An extreme case is defined as a response on a variable that is well out of the ordinary. For example, an SAT score recorded as 796 in the datafile may be substantially higher than all other scores. We could command the computer to print out the case numbers of all cases with SAT scores above 775. We would then check to see whether these scores were correct. This is another way of identifying possible coding or punching errors.

Generating New Variables

Once the originally coded dataset is cleansed, we can proceed to add new variables to this dataset that will be used later in analysis. Again, the computer's capabilities make this task simple. There are a number of circumstances where we might generate new variables:[10]

1 We may want to add data not collected in the interview. For example, we may want to add census information about the area in which a respondent lives.

2 We may want to collapse an interval variable, such as income, into categories, or combine the categories of some variables to give a variable with fewer categories.

3 We may want to form a variable to be defined by combinations of other variables. For example, the variable "stage of family life cycle" is formed using age, marital status, presence of children, etc.

4 We may want to create an index to represent a number of variables. For example, we may simply add a set of scaled measures about a product to form an index related to interest in the product. More complex indices are also possible.

These new variables are placed in the dataset for each case and assigned a variable number. They must also be entered in the codebook with a detailed description as to how they were formed.

---

[9] See John B. Lansing and James N. Morgan, *Economic Survey Methods* (Ann Arbor: Institute for Social Research, The University of Michigan, 1971), p. 237, for a more detailed discussion.
[10] Ibid., pp. 238–240.

Weighting

There is one last task that may need to be performed on the datafile, namely, weighting the data in accordance with the sampling plan or because of unexpected sampling results. (Weighting was discussed in detail in Chapter 9.) Basically, we need to weight if the probability of element selection varies across subgroups, and if we wish to do analysis with the whole sample. We command the computer to assign the appropriate weights to cases. If we desire to do subgroup analysis, we simply command the analysis program to ignore the weighting.

Storing

We now have a dataset completely ready for analysis. It is generally stored on disk file or tape, with a copy made on another tape to be put away for safekeeping. We are ready to do data analysis.

ALTERNATIVE PROCESSING FLOWS

Although the data processing flow presented in the previous section represents the classic approach, there are alternative ways of getting the data from acceptable data collection instruments into the computer. Babbie calls these alternatives *data processing tracks*.[11] We shall use his terminology here in describing these tracks.

Track One Processing: Traditional   This is the method that we have just presented. In review, its steps are (1) coding of instruments, (2) transferring of codes to coding sheets, and (3) keypunching and verifying of a data deck.

Track Two Processing: Edge Coding   It is possible to eliminate the step requiring the transferring of codes to coding sheets by doing what is called *edge coding*. The outside margin of each page of the data collection instrument is marked with spaces representing the columns of a computer card. The coder writes the relevant codes in these spaces instead of on the coding sheets. The edge-coded instruments are then delivered to keypunchers for punching and verifying.

Track Three Processing: Direct Punching   It may be possible to eliminate both the coding step and the transferring of codes to coding sheets. That is, we may be able to have the keypunchers directly punch and verify the data from the edited data collection instrument itself. To do this, we need an instrument that is made up of closed-ended questions that are wholly precoded. Also, the instrument must be laid out in such a way that the keypuncher can easily follow the flow of responses.

Track Four Processing: Mark-Sensed Entry   It is possible to eliminate the manual keypunching and verifying of the data by having coders use special mark-sensed coding sheets to record the data codes. These sheets can then be read into the computer by

[11] Babbie, op. cit., pp. 197–200.

an optical scanner. The computer can then store the data in a disk file or punch out a data deck of computer cards. Here the coder does not write the code number but fills in appropriate spaces on the mark-sensed sheets with a special pencil. Most coders find this a more difficult task than recording the number themselves. The marks must be made with care, as the optical scanner has tight tolerances and errors can easily result. Also, if the mark-sensed sheets are damaged, the scanner may be unable to read them.

Track Five Processing: Respondent Mark-Sensed Entry   In order to get around the coding problems inherent in track four processing, the respondents could be asked to indicate their responses by filling our the mark-sensed sheet themselves. Students completing a multiple-choice examination are often asked to do this. Both coding and keypunching are thus eliminated in the flow. For this technique to work properly, the respondents must have the proper pencil and must understand exactly how to record their responses on the sheets. Close supervision by the researcher is a necessity. Thus, mail instruments are not compatible with this approach. Also, closed-ended questions are the only type possible here.

Track Six Processing: CRT Systems[12]   This track is appropriate for telephone interviewing only. Here the questionnaire is programmed into a computer with cathode ray tubes (CRT) for display.[13] The interviewer sits in front of the CRT and commands the computer to display the questions one at a time. Precoded answers are also displayed on the CRT. The respondent indicates a response, and the interviewer types this response directly into a computer file. Thus editing, coding, keypunching, and verifying of written questionnaires are eliminated. The data are ready for instant cleaning and analysis. Also, the computer will remember phone numbers that need to be called back; take the correct branching and skip patterns in the questionnaire based upon a respondent's answers; rotate alternative parts of questions (for example, use random order of brand names in a question); and inform the interviewer if an illegal code is entered. The major historical drawbacks of this system were its costs in equipment, software, and staff. One company put this figure at $200,000.[14] Very large, well-structured studies make the most effective use of this system. As telephone interviewing increases in marketing research, CRT systems become ever more important in data processing and interviewing. Virtually all major marketing research suppliers have such systems.

Also the increasing power of personal computers has opened new opportunities for these types of systems. It is now possible to do questionnaire development, data collection, and basic data analysis using software packages specially developed for an IBM-PC. Such software sells for less than $1000.[15]

---

[12] Babbie does not discuss this option, but we continue to use his terminology.

[13] Jack J. Honomichl, "Computers Speed Up Interviewing Process, Also Can Supply Instant Survey Results," *Advertising Age,* Feb. 14, 1977, pp. 14 and 76.

[14] Ibid.

[15] For example see Paul E. Green, Pradeep K. Kedia, and Rishiyur S. Nikhil, *Electronic Questionnaire Design and Analysis with CAPPA* (Palo Alto, Calif.: The Scientific Press, 1985).

Selection of a Track Your choice of a data processing track depends on the availability of computer hardware, optical scanners, etc. It also depends on the time and cost constraints imposed on the study and the degree of complexity in the data collection instrument. Generally, the more complex the instrument, the more you would tend to do traditional track one processing. Other tracks can be used as the instrument becomes more structured and as time and cost constraints put pressure on the researcher. If we can get the respondent to fill out a mark-sensed card, we obviously save time and money. The CRT track saves time but costs more money. The researcher must pick a data processing track that fits the type of study being undertaken and the constraints imposed upon its execution.

We now know exactly what the research analyst described earlier in the chapter must do to get data collection instruments ready for analysis. Data processing is not the most exciting area of marketing research, but it is very important. Since a significant proportion of nonsampling errors occur in data processing, the researcher and manager must be attentive to this area.

SUMMARY

1 Data processing is the conversion of raw data in a data collection instrument into a computer-readable form.

2 A traditional approach to data processing includes the functions of (a) deciding whether to use the data collection instrument, (b) editing, (c) coding to coding sheets, (d) keypunching and verifying, (e) putting the resultant data deck into a computer-readable form, (f) cleaning the data, (g) generating new variables, (h) weighting, and (i) storing the dataset on disk or tape.

3 It is possible to eliminate some of these functions by using edge coding, by keypunching directly from the data collection instruments, by using mark-sensed coding sheets, or by recording respondent answers directly into the computer.

DISCUSSION QUESTIONS

1 How are responses to a questionnaire represented on a computer card?
2 How do you identify data collection instruments that are unacceptable for data processing?
3 What should an editor do in examining an instrument?
4 What are the fundamental rules of code construction?
5 How should multiple responses be handled?
6 What is a codebook? What should it contain?
7 How is a dataset cleaned?
8 Why would you want to create new variables?
9 What are the alternative data processing tracks?
10 How do you select a track?

17

UNIVARIATE DATA ANALYSIS

Once the collected data have been properly converted to a computer file, as described in the previous chapter, we are ready to turn our attention to data analysis. Improper data analysis can be a significant source of nonsampling error. The primary objective of the data analysis chapters in this book is to provide an overview of when specific analysis techniques may properly be used. In order to reach this objective we shall identify a number of data analysis techniques, list the circumstances where they may be used, and give examples of their use. We shall not attempt to list all techniques or to explain their computational aspects in any detail, because we believe that the purpose of data analysis is to provide meaningful information for decision making and that much valuable information can be provided by means of relatively simple data analysis procedures.

Some marketers and others mistakenly think that data analysis is the most important aspect of marketing research. Our premise is that the most sophisticated data analysis available cannot make up for poor problem definition, bad study design, improper sampling, poor measurement, bad field work, or sloppy data processing. Data analysis is just one of many activities that must be done correctly to yield relevant information for decision making. However, it too must be done properly.

We shall begin this first chapter on data analysis by distinguishing among univariate, bivariate, and multivariate data analysis procedures. Then we shall distinguish between procedures whose objective is description of the sample-based dataset at hand and procedures whose objective is inference about the population from which the dataset was selected. Finally, we shall discuss a number of descriptive and inferential techniques appropriate for univariate analysis.

OVERVIEW OF DATA ANALYSIS PROCEDURES

The fundamental data analysis question facing a marketing manager or researcher is: "What data analysis technique should be used?" The answer is provided by outlining specifics about the situation faced by the marketer. There are three overview questions that help the marketer begin to identify the appropriate technique: (1) How many variables are to be analyzed at the same time? (2) Do we want description or inference questions answered? and (3) What level of measurement (nominal, ordinal, interval) is available in the variable or variables of interest?

Number of Variables to Analyze

The first specific aspect of the situation that must be clarified relates to the objectives of the analysis. This is *the number of variables the marketer wishes to have analyzed at the same time.* Figure 17-1 shows this decision question, the possible outcomes to the question, and where in this book the relevant techniques are discussed.

If you wish to examine the analysis of one variable at a time, this is called *univariate data analysis,* and it constitutes the topic of this chapter. The relationship of two variables at a time is examined by means of *bivariate data analysis,* the subject of Chapter 18. The relationships of more than two variables at a time call for *multivariate data analysis,* to be covered in Chapters 19 and 20.

Description versus Inference

The second question that must be answered is whether you are interested in the *description of the sample* or in making *inferences about the population* from which

FIGURE 17-1   Overview of data analysis techniques.

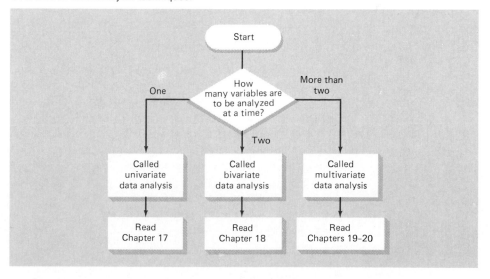

the sample was drawn. Descriptive statistics is a branch of statistics that provides researchers with summary measures for the data in their samples. It provides answers to such questions as: (1) What is the average age in the sample? (2) What is the dispersion of ages in the sample? and (3) What is the level of association between age and income in the sample? Inferential statistics is a branch of statistics that allows researchers to make judgments about the whole population based upon the results generated by samples. It is based upon probability theory. It provides answers to such questions as: (1) Is the average age of the population 25? (2) Is the level of association between age and income in the population greater than zero? (3) Are the population treatment means in an experiment equal to each other? Both descriptive and inferential statistics have important applications in marketing research. Marketers must know which type of analysis they are interested in.

Level of Measurement

The third question that must be answered is whether the variable or variables to be analyzed have been measured at a nominal-, ordinal-, or interval-scale level.[1] Both descriptive and inferential techniques vary by the scale level inherent in the variable or variables being analyzed.

If marketers know the number of variables to be analyzed at a time, whether the interest is in description or inference, and the scale level of the variable or variables, they are then in a position to select the appropriate statistical procedure. The rest of this chapter identifies and describes the relevant techniques for the analysis of one variable at a time. In presenting this material we recognize that a computer will be doing the calculations. This does not negate the need for us to know when to use what procedure, because the computer will calculate any statistic we ask it to, even if that statistic is not appropriate for the data.

OVERVIEW OF UNIVARIATE DATA ANALYSIS PROCEDURES

Figure 17-2 presents an overview of statistical techniques available for univariate data analysis.[2] It is often important in studies to do a univariate analysis on some variables. For example, the manager might want a description of the sample's demographic characteristics, of the usage of the company's product, or of respondent attitudes toward a competitive activity. In each situation, you can gain useful information by examining statistics related to one variable at a time. To make sure we are looking for the right procedure, we begin the process described in Figure 17-2 by asking if we want to ana-

---

[1] There are procedures available for ratio data only. However, they have little relevance to real marketing research problems. Any ratio data in marketing research are usually analyzed by procedures relevant to interval data.

[2] For a complete classification scheme for univariate, bivariate, and multivariate analysis see Frank M. Andrews, Laura Klem, Terrence N. Davidson, Patrick M. O'Malley, and Willard L. Rogers, *A Guide for Selecting Statistical Techniques for Analyzing Social Science Data* (Ann Arbor: Institute for Social Research, the University of Michigan, 1974).

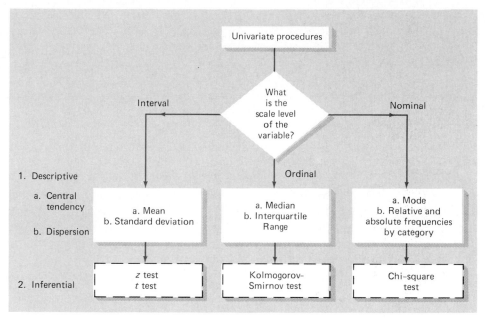

FIGURE 17-2   Overview of univariate data analysis procedures.

lyze one variable at a time. Only if this question is answered positively does Figure 17-2 provide us with a guide to the correct procedure. Our next question concerns the scale level of the variable to be analyzed. It may be nominal, ordinal, or interval. Below each of these possible answers to the scale-level question on Figure 17-2, two sets of boxes are shown. The first set presents the relevant descriptive statistics. The top part of these boxes presents the appropriate measure of central tendency, while the bottom part presents the appropriate measure of dispersion. The boxes defined by dashed lines, positioned below the descriptive statistics boxes, show the appropriate tests of statistical inference for each data type. Note that statistics appropriate for lower scales can be applied to higher scales. For example, a mode and median can properly be calculated for interval data. However, the opposite is not true; the mean is not an appropriate statistic for ordinal or nominal data.

It is not our purpose here to give details of every descriptive statistic and every test of interference for every measurement level. This task would take too long. The discussion presented in these chapters will deal with only those techniques that are most relevant to marketing research practice. Thus in this chapter we will not discuss the interquartile range statistic or the Kolmogorov-Smirnov test, for these are not in the mainstream of marketing research practice.[3] What follows, then, is a discussion of those statistical procedures with which we feel a practicing marketing researcher should be familiar.

[3] If you need this set, see Sidney Siegel, *Nonparametric Statistics for the Behavioral Sciences* (New York: McGraw-Hill, 1956), pp. 47–52.

DESCRIPTIVE STATISTICS

The objective of descriptive statistics is to provide summary measures of the data contained in all the elements of a sample. In doing so the marketing researcher is usually concerned with measures of central tendency and measures of dispersion. We now turn our attention to identifying these measures by measurement scale level.

Measures of Central Tendency

Three measures of central tendency are often used in marketing research: the mean, the median, and the mode.

Interval Data—The Mean   The mean is the appropriate measure of central tendency for interval data. The reader should be familiar with the concept of a mean, since we made use of it for both a continuous variable and a proportion in Chapter 8, when discussing simple random sampling. To review, the mean is *the sum of the values divided by the sample size*. In formula,

$$\overline{X} = \frac{\sum\limits_{i=1}^{n} X_i}{n}$$

Thus, if our sample yielded the values, 22, 26, 25, 21, and 19, the mean would be 113/5 = 22.6.

It is also possible to calculate a mean when interval data are grouped into categories or classes. Here the formula for the mean is

$$\overline{X} = \frac{\sum\limits_{i=1}^{k} f_i X_i}{n}$$

where f_i = frequency of the ith class
X_i = midpoint of the ith class
k = number of classes

Table 17-1 illustrates such a calculation.

TABLE 17-1   CALCULATION OF THE MEAN USING GROUPED INTERVAL DATA

Age classes	Number in class, f_i	Mid point, X_i	$f_i X_i$
15 to under 20	10	17.5	175
20 to under 25	20	22.5	450
25 to under 30	30	27.5	825
30 to under 35	20	32.5	650
$k = 4$	$\Sigma f_i = 80 = n$		$\Sigma f_i X_i = 2100$
$\overline{X} = 2100/80 = 26.25$			

TABLE 17-2   IDENTIFICATION OF THE MEDIAN FOR
UNGROUPED DATA

Observation, X_i	Score or value of X_i
X_1	10
X_2	20
X_3	70 ← median
X_4	140
X_5	. 500

Ordinal Data—The Median   If our data form an ordinal or interval scale, we may legitimately make use of the median as a measure of central tendency. The median for ungrouped data is defined as *the midvalue when the data are arranged in order of magnitude*. Table 17-2 presents an ordered set of observations and identifies the median. The median may also be calculated for grouped data. The formula for doing so is complex and would add little to our understanding of the concept here.[4] What is important is that the median can be applied to either ordinal or interval data.

Nominal Data—The Mode   The mode is a measure of central tendency appropriate for nominal or higher-order scales. It is *the category of a nominal variable that occurs with greatest frequency*. It should not be applied to ordinal or interval data unless these data have been grouped first. For example, in Table 17-1 the modal class is formed by the ages 25 to under 30.

Sometimes a variable is bimodal. That is, two classes have relatively similar frequencies. This should be a tip-off to the researcher to look for some other variable in the situation that may be causing this situation. For example, coffee sales recorded at both large and small stores could yield a bimodal distribution. The researcher should have been aware of this. Also, if the distribution is bimodal, the mean and median do not describe the variable well. They are simply some "midpoints" between the modes. It is therefore a good idea to look at measures of dispersion.

Measures of Dispersion

Measures of central tendency do not provide enough information for researchers to fully understand the distribution they are examining. For example, the numbers 10, 15, 20 and 5, 10, 30 both have a mean of 15. Clearly, we need a measure of the spread of the distribution of the variable, i.e., a measure of dispersion.

Interval Data—The Standard Deviation   The appropriate measure of dispersion for interval data is the standard deviation, the measure we calculated for a continuous

---

[4] If interested, consult almost any basic statistics book. For example, see Morris Hamburg, *Statistical Analysis for Decision Making* (New York: Harcourt Brace Jovanovich, 1977), p. 28.

variable and a proportion in Chapter 8. In formula, the standard deviation of a sample is

$$s = \sqrt{\frac{\sum_{i=1}^{n} (X_i - \bar{X})^2}{n - 1}}$$

We calculated this value in detail in Chapter 8 and will therefore not repeat the calculation here.

Whether or not a particular size of standard deviation constitutes a large or small dispersion depends on the size of the mean with which it is associated. For example, to be told that a standard deviation is 100 does not help us much. However, if we are told that in this case the mean is 200, we can conclude that the variable has a large dispersion. If the mean were instead 2000, we could conclude that the variable had a small dispersion. We formalize this type of conclusion by calculating what is called the coefficient of variation. In formula:

$$CV = \frac{s}{\bar{X}}$$

where CV is the coefficient of variation. Thus CV is the standard deviation expressed as a percentage of the mean. In our example above,

$$CV_1 = \frac{100}{200} = .5 \quad \text{and} \quad CV_2 = \frac{100}{2000} = .05$$

Nominal Data—Relative and Absolute Frequencies   For nominal data or better, we may legitimately calculate relative and absolute frequencies as measures of dispersion. Table 17-3 illustrates such a calculation for the nominal variable "region of the country." Absolute frequencies are just the numbers in the sample that appear in each category of the nominal variable. Thus, in our example in Table 17-3, 210 elements were found to have come from the East. Relative frequencies are the percentages of the total elements that appear in each category; thus 20.2 percent (210/1040) of the elements are from the East.

TABLE 17-3   PRESENTATION OF RELATIVE AND ABSOLUTE FREQUENCIES FOR NOMINAL VARIABLE

Region of the country	Absolute frequency (number)	Relative frequencies (percentage)
East	210	20.2
West	405	38.9
North	109	10.5
South	316	30.4
Total	1040	100.0

Often, just describing what is in the sample is not enough. We may also want to make inferences from the sample to the population from which it was drawn. It is to this issue that we now turn our attention. In order to understand properly the following discussion on inference, you must understand the basics of hypothesis testing, which we present first.

HYPOTHESIS TESTING

Hypothesis testing is a procedure that is familiar to those who have had a basic statistics course. We assume that you have had such a course but would benefit from the review which follows.

The Concept of a Null Hypothesis

Hypothesis testing begins with the statement of a hypothesis in a *null form,* i.e., a form which *supposes that a population parameter takes on a particular value or set of values.* For example, we might wish to test to see whether the mean age of a class was 25 years. The null hypothesis (H_0) is:

$$H_0: \mu = 25$$

It is the null hypothesis that we evaluate in hypothesis testing. A null hypothesis may be rejected and some alternative hypothesis accepted. Alternatively, the null hypothesis may not be rejected in the test. In this situation, we do not conclude that the null hypothesis is valid. We do not accept a null hypothesis. All we can say is that we do not have the evidence to reject it. It may later be proved incorrect with the collection of new sample data. Note that we test the value of a population parameter with data generated by a sample; thus, the sample value might differ from the population value simply because of sampling error. By examining the sampling distribution of a statistic we can determine whether the sample value is different enough from the proposed null hypothesis value to have occurred just by sampling error. If this difference were greater than that due to sampling error, we would reject the null hypothesis. Stating the null hypothesis as we did above implies a number of *alternative hypotheses.* One such hypothesis is that the mean age is not 25. We can write the null and alternative hypotheses as:

$$H_0: \mu = 25$$
$$H_1: \mu \neq 25$$

In testing this null hypothesis, we would reject it if the mean age were either greater or less than 25. We are thus interested in the sampling distribution of mean ages on both sides of 25. This type of test is called a "two-tailed" test since we will examine both ends of the sampling distribution to see at what level of chance the mean value our sample generated could have occurred just because of sampling error.

Another alternative hypothesis in this situation is that the mean age is greater than 25. We write:

$$H_0: \mu = 25$$
$$H_1: \mu > 25$$

Here, our interest is only in the upper part of the sampling distribution of means. A hypothesis test applied here is called a "one-tailed" test since we have a specific direction in mind for the alternative hypothesis. The final alternative hypothesis here is that the mean age is less than 25. Again this would be a one-tailed test.

It is possible to phrase the null hypothesis to cover a range of values. For example,

$$H_0: \mu \leq 25$$

implies an alternative hypothesis

$$H_1: \mu > 25$$

With a direction given to the alternative hypothesis, a one-tailed test applies. Take care to phrase the null hypothesis in such a way as to accept the alternative hypothesis that is really of interest if the null hypothesis is rejected.

Possible Errors

In hypothesis testing the decision maker either rejects or does not reject H_0. The decision may or may not be correct. If H_0 is true and is not rejected, the decision is correct. Also, if H_0 is false and is rejected, the decision is correct. Alternatively, the rejection of a true H_0 or the nonrejection of a false H_0 would indicate that an error had been made. These errors are named *type I* and *type II errors,* respectively. They are also referred to as α error and β error, respectively. Table 17-4 presents a summary of sample conclusions and their possible outcomes.

TABLE 17-4 SUMMARY OF HYPOTHESIS TESTING ERRORS

	True condition	
Sample conclusions	H_0 is true	H_0 is false
Do not reject H_0	(1) Correct decision (2) Confidence level (3) Probability $= 1 - \alpha$	(1) Type II error (2) Probability $= \beta$
Reject H_0	(1) Type I error (2) Significance level (3) Probability $= \alpha$	(1) Correct decision (2) Power of the test (3) Probability $= 1 - \beta$

Also summarized in Table 17-4 are the probabilities of being correct and of making each type of error. The usual beginning point in testing a null hypothesis is to specify the level of type I error the researcher is willing to tolerate. You know that a null hypothesis is tested with sample data, so you expect some sampling error to be in the data. The farther the sample result is from the null hypothesis, the more likely that H_0 is not true. However, you recognize that the sample estimate you have generated may have come from the tail of the sampling distribution of the statistic about the true value H_0. It may be an outlier. In specifying an α error level, the researcher indicates that an α proportion of the outlying part of the sampling distribution of the statistic will be assumed to be too far from H_0 not to reject H_0. In doing so, you recognize the probability equal to α of making a type I error. This designation of α is referred to as the *significance level* of the hypothesis test. For example, a researcher may specify $\alpha = .05$, indicating that there is a probability of .05 that a type I error has been made. We say *the test is performed at the .05 significance level*.

Instead of looking at the probability of making an α error, we could also consider the probability of not rejecting H_0 when it is true. This probability is $1 - \alpha$ and is referred to as the *confidence level* of the test. The more confidence we want in the test, the smaller we make α. A test performed at the .05 significance level is thus performed at the $1 - .05 = .95$ confidence level. The confidence level discussed here is exactly the same concept as the confidence level we discussed in connection with calculating confidence intervals in Chapter 8 (which dealt with simple random sampling). It relates to the proportion of the sampling distribution of a statistic that is within a certain distance from the true population value.

Now we examine the possible outcomes when H_0 is false. If we do not reject H_0 when it is false, we have made a type II or β error. This occurs when we observe what we think is an outlier of the sampling distribution of the statistic about H_0, when we really are looking at a value drawn from a sampling distribution about a value other than H_0. The farther an observed value of a statistic is from H_0, the more likely it is that it comes from another sampling distribution. Thus, the smaller we set α, the larger the probability of a type II error. We call this probability of a type II error β.

If H_0 is false and we reject it, we have made a correct decision. We describe the probability of rejecting a false null hypothesis as the *power of the test*. The measure of this probability is $1 - \beta$. β and therefore $1 - \beta$ take on a specific value only when a specific alternative hypothesis value for a statistic is given. For now, it is enough to recognize that β increases as α decreases for a given sample size. In practice β is often determined only after the sample has been selected, or it is just ignored. The problem with this approach in marketing is that the cost of a type II error to an organization may be much greater than the cost of a type I error. Consider this example presented by Cox and Enis:

> In the case of making a type I error in the choice of the best promotional strategy for a new product introduction, suppose that we reject the true hypothesis (conclude that one promotional strategy was better than the others) even though all were, in fact, equally effective. Since we have to select one of the equally effective alternatives, there is actually little risk associated with our choice of strategies.

On the other hand, we might accept the hypothesis (conclude that there is no difference in the effectiveness of the three promotional strategies) when one promotional strategy is, in fact, more effective than the others. This type II error could be very expensive, in terms of opportunity costs, if we select one of the less effective strategies.[5]

Obviously, then, there are compelling managerial reasons for choosing a level of significance (α) in the .10 to .25 range instead of the traditional .01 or .05 levels used in social science research.

Steps in Hypothesis Testing

The steps we will use in hypothesis testing are:

1 Formulate a null and alternative hypothesis.
2 Select the appropriate statistical test given the type of data the researcher has.
3 Specify the significance level, α.
4 Look up the value of the test statistic in a set of tables (see Appendix A) for the given α; these tables give points on the sampling distribution of the statistic in question that occur with different α probabilities.
5 Perform the statistical test chosen in (2) on the data available; this yields a value of the relevant statistic.
6 Compare the value of the statistic calculated in (5) with the value looked up in (4). If (5) is greater than (4), we reject the null hypothesis, because the value of (5) has come too far out on the sampling distribution to be considered by us a part of the sampling distribution about H_0.

In the next sections of this chapter, we will apply these steps.

INFERENTIAL STATISTICS

The appropriate test of statistical inferences also varies by the scale level of the data available.

Interval Data

Two different tests, the z test and the t test, are appropriate for interval data. The choice between the two depends on the researcher's knowledge of the population standard deviation and the sample size used. These tests are tests about the size of the population mean.

z Test The z test allows researchers to compare the mean generated from a sample with a mean hypothesized to exist in the population, and to decide whether the sample mean allows them to conclude that the hypothesized population mean is true. The z test is appropriate for interval data in situations where (1) the sample size is any

---

[5] Keith K. Cox and Ben M. Enis, *Experimentation for Marketing Decisions* (Scranton, Pa.: International Textbook Company, 1969), p. 11.

size and the population standard deviation σ is known or (2) the sample size is greater than 30 and the population standard deviation σ is unknown. In situations where $n <$ 30 and σ is unknown, the t test should be used. It will be discussed shortly.

Let us illustrate the z test for the continuous variable "age," using the following steps in hypothesis testing. Also, let us assume that a sample of university students taking marketing research has yielded the following information: $\bar{X} = 24$, $s = 5$, and $n = 100$.

Step 1: Formulate null and alternative hypotheses. In this situation the null and alternative hypotheses are:

$$H_0: \mu = 23$$
$$H_1: \mu \neq 23$$

So the researcher wants to know whether the sample mean age of 24 will allow the conclusion that the population mean age is 23. The alternative hypothesis, H_1, is phrased so that we know that a sample value too far above or below 23 will allow us to reject H_0. Thus, we will be using a two-tailed test. If $H_1: \mu < 23$ were the alternative hypothesis, we would reject H_0 only if the mean age were far below H_0. This would be a one-tailed test. It is important to know which test you are doing, because the number of tails affects the position in a statistical table that you consult to find the critical value of the statistic involved.

Step 2: Select the appropriate statistical tests. The appropriate test here is the z test because $n > 30$ and we are testing a hypothesis about means. This test is based on the nature of the sampling distribution of the mean as discussed in Chapter 8. We know by the central-limit theorem that the mean value we generated from our sample comes from a sampling distribution of means that forms a normal curve. Also, we know the area under a normal curve and thus the number of sampling means located within a certain number of standard errors of the mean of this distribution. Because of this we can determine the probability that any sample mean could have come from a sampling distribution of means that lies about the hypothesized population mean. This was essentially what we were doing in Chapter 8 when we calculated confidence intervals.

The critical values of the z statistic are given in Table A-2 of Appendix A for a two-tailed test and in Table A-3 for a one-tailed test. The values in these tables are given for a mean of zero and a standard deviation of 1. Thus to use these tables we will have to convert data from a sample to remove the effects of the unit of measurement. The values in the first column and first row of the table are combined to give the z values (i.e., the number of standard deviations about the mean that interest the researcher). The values in the body of the table give the area contained in the tail or tails of the distribution. This provides a measure of the probability of rejecting a true null hypothesis. In other words, these values are α, the probability of making a type I error.

For example, in Table A-2 for $\alpha = .05$, we find that this is 1.96 (1.9 from column 1 + .06 from row 1) standard deviations from the mean. We note that this represents the 95 percent confidence level. In Chapter 8 it was stated that the 95 percent confidence interval was $\bar{X} \pm 2$ times the standard error; in truth it is $\bar{X} \pm 1.96$ times the standard error, but we simply rounded it off to facilitate the discussion in that chapter.

What the 1.96 tells us is that the probability of getting a value of z greater than 1.96 is less than .05. In Table A-3 we note that the probability of getting a value of z greater than 1.96 is less than .025. Thus, here we would be using a test with $\alpha = .025$. For $\alpha = .05$ in a one-tailed test, we note that $z = 1.64$. Thus the probability of getting a z value greater than 1.64 in a one-tailed test is less than .05.

Step 3: Specify the significance level. The researcher must specify a significance level, α. In doing so you must recognize that the smaller you set α, the bigger β will be for any given sample size. In our example we shall use $\alpha = .1$.

Step 4: Look up the z value for $\alpha = .1$. We note in Table A-2 that $z = 1.64$ for $\alpha = .1$. This is our critical value of z. If the z calculated from the data exceeds 1.64, we will reject the null hypothessis.

Step 5: Perform the statistical test. If the population standard deviation is known,

$$z = \frac{\bar{X} - \mu}{\sigma_{\bar{X}}} = \frac{\bar{X} - \mu}{\sigma/\sqrt{n}}$$

If σ is not known,

$$z = \frac{\bar{X} - \mu}{s_{\bar{X}}} = \frac{\bar{X} - \mu}{s/\sqrt{n}}$$

In our example σ is not known, so we use the latter formula. What the formula does is express the difference between the observed mean $\bar{X}$ and the hypothesized mean μ as a measure expressed as a number of standard errors. The question is: Is the difference $\bar{X} - \mu$ expressed in standard error (the calculated z value) large enough to be likely to occur by sampling error less than .1 of the time?

In our example,

$$z = \frac{24 - 23}{5/\sqrt{100}} = \frac{1}{.5}$$
$$= 2.0$$

Thus the difference $24 - 23$ is equal to 2 standard errors.

Step 6: Compare z values. The calculated z value exceeds the z value for $\alpha = .1$ $(2.0 > 1.64)$, and thus we reject the null hypothesis. We may not conclude that the average age in the population is 23.

The z test may also be applied to a proportion. Here, for a situation where $n > 30$ and σ_p is known,[6]

$$z = \frac{p - \pi}{s_p} = \frac{p - \pi}{\sqrt{pq/n}}$$

---

[6] For small n the binomial distribution must be used. This is so atypical of real marketing research problems that it is not discussed here.

where p = sample proportion

π = hypothesized proportion

s_p = standard error of the proportion

In a situation designed to measure market share, a sample might generate an estimate of market share p. We might wish to compare this with a target market share of over π. If $p = .3$, $n = 30$, H_0: $\pi \leq .25$, H_1: $\pi > .25$,

$$z = \frac{.3 - .25}{\sqrt{(.3)(.7)/30}} = \frac{.05}{.084} = .60$$

The difference between the observed and hypothesized proportions, is .60 standard error. At $\alpha = .01$ in the one-tailed test, $z = 2.32$. Therefore, because the calculated z is less than the critical z from the table, we cannot reject the null hypothesis that $\pi \leq .25$. Therefore, we cannot conclude in a managerial sense that we have reached our target market share of over 25 percent. Note that this is true even though the sample market share was 30 percent.[7]

***t* Test** The t test is appropriately used in hypothesis testing about means for all sample sizes when σ is unknown. The reason we use z when $n > 30$ is that the t distribution and the z distribution are virtually identical when $n > 30$, and the values of the t distribution have not been calculated for large sample sizes. In a t test we estimate σ by using s. The critical values of the t statistics are presented in Table A-4 of Appendix A. The critical value of t varies by the α level selected, the number of degrees of freedom in the sample, and whether a one- or two-tailed test is needed. For example, we note that for $\alpha = .05$ in a one-tailed test with 10 degrees of freedom, $t = 1.812$. There are always $n - 1$ degrees of freedom in a t test of the mean, because we are using s as an estimate of σ, and s has $n - 1$ degrees of freedom. The t table gives values of t that can occur simply as a result of sampling error.

Let us quickly illustrate a t test. Suppose that in attempting to estimate yearly rates of cola consumption per capita,

$$H_0: \mu = 100 \text{ gallons}$$
$$H_1: \mu > 100 \text{ gallons}$$

and a sample has yielded the following:

$$\bar{X} = 120, \qquad s = 15, \qquad n = 7$$

---

[7] For any given α, n, and related sample results, it is possible to calculate the probability of making a type II error, β, and the resultant power of the test, $1 - \beta$. However, these are complex statistical topics which are almost never calculated in real marketing research problems. Thus, we have omitted their calculation from the current discussion. If you are interested, you should consult any good basic statistics book. For example, see Hamburg, op. cit., pp. 271–280.

Here

$$t = \frac{\bar{X} - \mu}{s_{\bar{X}}} = \frac{\bar{X} - \mu}{s/\sqrt{n}}$$

$$= \frac{120 - 100}{15/\sqrt{7}} = \frac{20}{5.67}$$

$$= 3.53$$

The critical value of t at $\alpha = .1$ for a one-tailed test at 6 df is 1.44. Since our calculated t exceeds the critical t, we reject the null hypothesis and accept the alternative that per capita cola consumption in the population exceeds 100 gallons.

Nominal Data

Researchers are interested in more than just hypotheses about the mean. Often they wish to make inferences about how respondents are distributed across the possible categories of a nominal variable. For example, in a sample of families who purchase re-turnable bottles, the researcher might want to know whether these respondents are distributed equally in all occupational categories. The chi-square test is a procedure for comparing a hypothesized population distribution across categories against an observed distribution.

Chi-Square Test   In a chi-square test, a hypothesized population distribution is compared with a distribution generated by a sample. The formula for chi square is

$$\chi^2 = \sum_{i=1}^{k} \frac{(O_i - E_i)^2}{E_i}$$

where k = number of categories of the variable
O_i = observed number of respondents in category i
E_i = hypothesized number of respondents in category i

Table A-6 of Appendix A gives the critical values of the chi-square distribution. These are the values of chi square that can occur by chance (due to sampling error) for various degrees of freedom and various α levels. The number of degrees of freedom is given in the left-hand column of Table A-6. It is referred to as n on the table. In a univariate chi-square test, the degrees of freedom equal $k - 1$, since for a given sample size, once the number of respondents in $k - 1$ categories is known, the number in the k category is automatically determined. The top row in Table A-6 gives the value of $1 - \alpha$. So if we want $\alpha = .05$, we look in the column for $1 - \alpha = .95$. Let's see how to find a critical value of chi square. Suppose that we have a variable with 7 df and have specified that $\alpha = .05$. Then we look down the $1 - \alpha = .95$ column until it intersects with the row representing 7 df. The critical chi square would be 14.1.

Column 1 of Table 17-5 gives the observed distribution of returnable-bottle users across occupational categories. The null hypothesis here is that there is no difference

TABLE 17-5   CALCULATION OF CHI SQUARE FOR OCCUPATIONAL CATEGORIES

Occupational category	O_i	E_i	$O_i - E_i$	$(O_i - E_i)^2$	$(O_i - E_i)^2/E_i$
Labor	15	25	-10	100	4
Clerical	20	25	-5	25	1
Managerial	30	25	5	25	1
Student	35	25	10	100	4
Total	100	100			10

$df = k - 1 = 3$; calculated $\chi^2 = 10$; critical χ^2 at 3 df and $\alpha = .1 = 6.25$.

in the population of returnable-bottle users across occupational categories. Thus we would expect an equal number of respondents in each occupational category. These expected numbers are given in column 2 of Table 17-5. The remaining columns of the table present the steps necessary to calculate chi square in this situation. We see that the calculated chi square equals 10. If we set $\alpha = .1$, the critical chi square from Table A-6 at 3 df is 6.25. Since the calculated chi square exceeds the critical chi square, we reject the null hypothesis and conclude that users of returnable bottles differ in occupational category. Note that the chi-square test merely tells us that there is a significant relationship. We must then go back and look at the distribution itself to see the nature of the relationship. Here we see that students form the modal category.

It is not necessary to have the null hypothesis that all categories have an equal number of respondents; the chi-square test may be used to compare observed results with any hypothesized distribution.

Of course, a good computer data analysis package would provide all the procedures presented in this chapter. The purpose of this chapter has been to let you know which statistics to ask the computer to generate in a univariate context.

SUMMARY

1 The choice of data analysis procedure depends upon the number of variables to be analyzed at the same time, whether the interest is in description or inference, and the level of measurement of the variable or variables.

2 Descriptive statistics provide summary measures of the data contained in the sample.

3 Inferential statistics allow the researcher to make judgments about the population based upon the sample results.

4 The mean and standard deviation are the relevant descriptive measures of central tendency and dispersion, respectively, for interval data.

5 The median is the relevant descriptive measure of central tendency for ordinal data.

6 The mode and relative and absolute frequencies are the relevant descriptive measures of central tendency and dispersion, respectively, for nominal data.

7 A null hypothesis is a statement that a population parameter takes on a particular value or set of values.

8 A null hypothesis may be rejected or not rejected. If it is rejected, the alternative hypothesis is accepted. A null hypothesis is never accepted.

9 Type I error occurs when you reject a true null hypothesis. It occurs with a probability of α, where α is called the significance level of the hypothesis test.

10 $1 - \alpha$ is the probability of not rejecting a true null hypothesis. It is called the level of confidence.

11 Type II error occurs when one does not reject a false null hypothesis. It occurs with a probability of β.

12 $1 - \beta$ is the probability of rejecting a false null hypothesis. It is called the power of the test.

13 From a management point of view, the cost of a type II error may be greater than that of a type I error.

14 The steps in hypothesis testing are: (1) Formulate null and alternative hypotheses, (2) select the appropriate statistical test, (3) specify the significance level, (4) find the critical value of the test statistic in tables, (5) calculate the statistic using the sample data, and (6) compare the statistic values. If (5) is greater than (4), reject the null hypothesis.

15 The z test is the appropriate inferential test about means for interval data when σ is known for any sample size, or for situations where σ is unknown and $n > 30$.

16 The t test is the appropriate inferential test about means for interval data when σ is unknown.

17 The chi-square test is the appropriate inferential test for the distribution of subjects across a nominal variable.

DISCUSSION QUESTIONS

1 What is univariate data analysis?

2 Distinguish between descriptive and inferential statistics.

3 Why are (1) measures of central tendency and (2) measures of dispersion both necessary to describe a variable?

4 Describe the steps in hypothesis testing in general.

5 Distinguish between significance level and confidence level.

6 What are type I and type II errors?

7 What is the power of the test?

8 From a sample of Tide users, the following frequency count was generated for the categories of the variable age:

Age	Frequency
55 and over	100
40–54	120
25–39	80
18–24	60
	$n = 360$

Is Tide usage spread evenly across the population in terms of age?

9 The manager of a movie theater hypothesized that twice as many of the theater's patrons were under 30 as were 30 and over. A sample of patrons yielded the following results:

Age	Frequency
under 30	220
30 and over	120
	$n = 340$

Is the theater manager's hypothesis about the population of patrons correct?

10 A sales manager had promised the entire sales force a special trip if average daily sales per salesperson were $1000 or more. A sample of 10 salespersons yielded the following results: Average daily sales per salesperson = $1050; standard deviation = $150. Can the sales manager conclude that the entire sales force has reached the goal?

11 A political research firm undertook a sample of registered voters in a small community to see whether a particular candidate would win the election. The sample size was 50, and the result was that 51 percent of the sample favored this candidate. If people vote as they say they will, do the results indicate that this candidate will win the election?

12 A company had adopted the following decision rule with respect to introducing a new product: If average monthly consumption is 100 ounces or more, we will enter into test market. An in-home placement test of $n = 50$ yielded the following results: Average monthly consumption = 96 ounces; standard deviation = 15. Given their decision rule, what decision should they make?

13 The Lake City chief of police wanted to discover how fast the average car traveled on a particular stretch of highway. To get this information, he placed a hidden radar device beside the highway and clocked speeds for an hour. The following data were recorded by the device:

73	49	70	63
55	61	60	68
52	56	69	60
65	66	59	62

Questions:
a Calculate the appropriate statistics for central tendency and dispersion.
b What are the problems with this design?

CHAPTER 18

BIVARIATE DATA ANALYSIS

In most marketing research studies the interests of the researcher and manager go beyond the univariate data analysis discussed in Chapter 17. They are often interested in the relationship between variables taken two at a time. Typical questions for which bivariate analysis can provide answers include: (1) What is the relationship between using our brand and media viewing habits? (2) What is the relationship between sales force turnover and sales manager age? (3) Is there a difference between attitudes toward our brand and toward other brands?

This chapter presents those data analysis procedures that are appropriate for bivariate relationships. Again, the appropriate technique depends upon the scale level of the variables involved and whether the researcher wants a descriptive statistic or an inferential test. We shall also discuss some issues related to the interpretation of cross-tabulation tables.

OVERVIEW OF BIVARIATE PROCEDURES

Figure 18-1 presents an overview of some bivariate descriptive statistics and inferential tests. Here we must be sure that we want to analyze two variables at a time. If this is the case, the scale level of the variables involved then guides us to the appropriate statistic. Not all possible combinations of bivariate relationships are presented in Figure 18-1. For example, it is possible to analyze an interval and an ordinal variable together, or a nominal and an ordinal variable, etc. These types of bivariate relationships are not discussed here, as they have little application in marketing research. Further, some of the procedures presented in Figure 18-1 do not as yet have wide application in marketing research and will not be discussed here. Instead, this chapter will be devoted to the

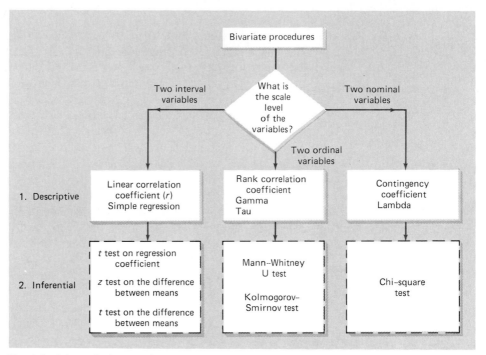

FIGURE 18-1   Bivariate data analysis procedures.

bivariate procedures that are most relevant to real marketing research problems. Specifically, from descriptive statistics for interval variables we shall discuss (1) the linear correlation coefficient, r, and (2) simple regression. Also, from inferential statistics for interval variables we shall discuss (1) the t test on the regression coefficient, (2) the z test on the difference between means, and (3) the t test on the difference between means. Finally, from inferential statistics for nominal variables, we shall discuss the chi-square test.[1]

DESCRIPTIVE STATISTICS

Often the interest of the researcher is in describing the nature of bivariate relationships generated from a sample. This section presents a description of two relevant descriptive statistical procedures appropriate for use with two interval variables. They are (1) the linear correlation coefficient and (2) simple regression.

[1] If you are interested in the other statistics presented in Figure 18-1, or in bivariate statistics for variables of different scales, you should consult Sidney Siegel, *Nonparametric Statistics for The Behavioral Sciences* (New York: McGraw-Hill, 1956), pp. 63–156, and Frank M. Andrews et al., *A Guide for Selecting Statistical Techniques for Analyzing Social Science Data* (Ann Arbor: Institute for Social Research, The University of Michigan, 1974), pp. 5–13.

Linear Correlation Coefficient

Linear correlation is a measure of the degree to which two interval variables are associated. For example, suppose we have data giving grades on a marketing management course, X, and data on grades in a marketing research course, Y. Our interest is in determining the level and direction of relationship between these two variables—for example, are high grades on X associated with high grades on Y, or vice versa, or is there no relationship between the two? The linear correlation coefficient, r_{XY}, is a measure of the linear relationship between X and Y.

In examining the relationship between two interval variables, a useful beginning is to plot the data on a scatter diagram. Figure 18-2 is an example of a plot for two variables, X and Y. If we draw the means of the two variables, $\bar{X}$ and $\bar{Y}$, on the scatter diagram, a first impression of possible relationships can be obtained. Drawing in the mean values divides the scatter diagram into four quadrants, labeled 1, 2, 3, and 4 in Figure 18-2. For data points in quadrant 1, both the X and Y values are above their respective means; i.e., they have positive deviations from their means. For quadrant 2, X values have negative deviations and Y values positive deviations; for quadrant 3, both have negative deviations; and for quadrant 4, X values have positive deviations and Y values have negative deviations. If the data points tend to be in diagonal quadrants, this would be evidence of a relationship between the two variables. For example, if most points were in quadrants 1 and 3, positive deviations on X would be associated with positive deviations in Y (quadrant 1), and negative deviations in X would be associated with negative deviations in Y (quadrant 3); i.e., as X increases, Y increases. X and Y would be positively related.

On the other hand, if data points tend to be in quadrants 2 and 4, negative deviations in X are associated with positive deviations in Y (quadrant 2), and vice versa (quadrant 4). This situation would indicate a negative relationship between X and Y. The intent of the correlation coefficient, r_{XY}, is to quantify the relationship between the variables.

FIGURE 18-2   An example of a scatter diagram and associated quadrants.

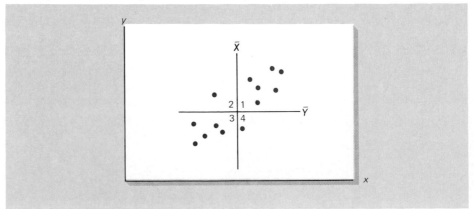

We begin this process by developing a distance measure between each point's X and Y values and the means of X and Y. We define:

$$x = (X_i - \bar{X}) \qquad (18\text{-}1)$$

and

$$y = (Y_i - \bar{Y}) \qquad (18\text{-}2)$$

These measures are deviations from their respective means, as discussed above. Each deviation calculated in the equations above has a sign attached. If the value of X_i or Y_i is greater than the mean, the sign is positive. If the value X_i or Y_i is less than the mean, the sign is negative. By multiplying the two deviations together we get a signed value. The sign of this number tells us something about the quadrant a data point falls into. We define:

$$xy = (X_i - \bar{X})(Y_i - \bar{Y}) \qquad (18\text{-}3)$$

Thus:

1 If x is positive and y is positive, xy is positive, and the data point falls in quadrant 1.
2 If x is negative and y is positive, xy is negative, and the data point falls in quadrant 2.
3 If x is negative and y is negative, xy is positive, and the data point falls in quadrant 3.
4 If x is positive and y is negative, xy is negative, and the data point falls in quadrant 4.

We see that xy is positive in quadrants 1 and 3 and negative in 2 and 4. Data points in quadrants 1 and 3 indicate a positive relationship between X and Y, as noted previously, and data points in quadrants 2 and 4 indicate a negative relationship between X and Y. Therefore, the sign of xy indicates the direction of relationship.

If we add up all the xy's for each data point, to get $\sum_{i=1}^{n} xy$, the sign of this number will indicate the overall direction of relationship. For example, if the data come mostly from quadrants 1 and 3, positive values of xy will outweigh negative values, and $\sum_{i=1}^{n} xy$ will be positive, indicating a positive relationship between X and Y. The opposite is true if the data come mostly from quadrants 2 and 4. If the data are evenly split among all four quadrants, positive and negative values of xy will tend to cancel, and $\sum_{i=1}^{n} xy$ will be zero.

The value of $\sum_{i=1}^{n} xy$ is an improvement over visual examination of the scatter diagram. However, it has two significant weaknesses. First, the value of $\sum_{i=1}^{n} xy$ is partially dependent on the number of data points, n. As n increases, the value of $\sum_{i=1}^{n} xy$ also increases.

Comparison of relationships involving different numbers of observations would then not be meaningful. Second, the value of $\sum_{i=1}^{n} xy$ depends in part on the unit of measurement being used on X and Y. For example, if an exam is marked out of 25 we would get a smaller value for $\sum_{i=1}^{n} xy$ than if the exam was marked out of 50, and a smaller value if it was out of 50 than if out of 100, and so forth.

We must then eliminate the effects of sample size and units from our measure of association $\sum_{i=1}^{n} xy$. We may eliminate the effects of sample size by dividing through $\sum_{i=1}^{n} xy$ by the degrees of freedom in the sample size, $n - 1$. This gives us a measure of the covariance of X and Y:

$$\text{Cov } (X, Y) = \frac{\Sigma(X_i - \bar{X})(Y_i - \bar{Y})}{n - 1}$$

Note that we will use Σ by itself to indicate addition across all n cases.

Covariance is positive if the values of X_i and Y_i tend to deviate from their respective means in the same direction. It is negative if they tend to deviate in the opposite direction. If X and Y are statistically independent, $\text{Cov } (X, Y) = 0$. We eliminate the effect of units by dividing $\text{Cov } (X, Y)$ through by the standard deviations of X and Y. We define this value as the correlation coefficient, r_{XY}. Thus,

$$r_{XY} = \frac{\Sigma(X_i - \bar{X})(Y_i - \bar{Y})}{(n - 1)s_X s_Y}$$

This formula may be simplified to yield

$$r_{XY} = \frac{\Sigma(X_i - \bar{X})(Y_i - \bar{Y})}{\sqrt{\Sigma(X_i - \bar{X})^2 \Sigma(Y_i - \bar{Y})^2}} \tag{18-4}$$

or alternatively

$$r_{XY} = \frac{\Sigma xy}{\sqrt{\Sigma x^2 \Sigma y^2}} \tag{18-5}$$

We see then that correlation is just a standardized measure of covariation. This standardization allows two correlations to be compared independently of the units in which observations are measured. The correlation coefficient may take on any value between -1.00 and $+1.00$. When $r = 1.00$, this indicates a perfect positive correlation. When $r = -1.00$, this indicates a perfect negative correlation. If $r = 0$, there is no relationship between the variables. Thus correlation provides a measure of the direction and strength of the relationship between two variables.

TABLE 18-1   MARKETING MANAGEMENT (X) AND MARKETING RESEARCH (Y) GRADES FOR 10 STUDENTS

X	Y	$x = (X - \bar{X})$	$y = (Y - \bar{Y})$	xy	x^2	y^2
75	85	1	10	10	1	100
80	85	6	10	60	36	100
60	65	−14	−10	140	196	100
55	60	−19	−15	285	361	225
85	80	11	5	55	121	25
95	95	21	20	420	441	400
70	60	−4	−15	60	16	225
75	80	1	5	5	1	25
80	80	6	5	30	36	25
65	60	−9	−15	135	81	225
$\Sigma X = 740$	$\Sigma Y = 750$	$\Sigma x = 0$	$\Sigma y = 0$	$\Sigma xy = 1200$	$\Sigma x^2 = 1290$	$\Sigma y^2 = 1450$
$\bar{X} = 74.0$	$\bar{Y} = 75.0$					

Correlation is a measure of the extent to which two variables share variation between them. The exact percentage of variation shared by two variables is calculated by squaring r. This r^2 is called the *coefficient of determination*.

In general, if r is bigger than 0.8 (sign of relationship ignored), the relationship between the variables is very strong; if r is between 0.4 and 0.8, the relationship is a moderate to strong one; and if r is less than 0.4, the relationship is a weak one.

A Numerical Example   The first two columns of Table 18-1 present the grades of 10 students in a course in marketing management, X, and in marketing research, Y. Figure 18-3 shows a scatter plot of the grades in the two courses. What we want to

FIGURE 18-3   Scatter diagram of course grades.

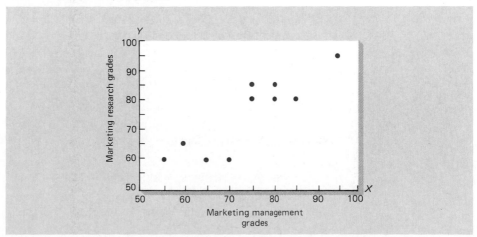

know is the correlation coefficient between the grades in the two courses. We have calculated the necessary values for Equation 18-5 on Table 18-1. Thus,

$$r_{XY} = \frac{1200}{\sqrt{1290 \times 1450}}$$
$$= \frac{1200}{1368}$$
$$= .88$$

The percentage of variation shared by these two variables is given by the coefficient of determination:

$$r^2 = (.88)^2 = .77$$

This represents the amount of variation in one of the variables we can explain by knowledge of the other variable.

Often the interests of the research go beyond the direction and strength of association between two variables. In this circumstance, simple regression is often useful.

Simple Regression

Regression is a method of analysis that applies when the research is dealing with one intervally scaled dependent variable and a number of intervally scaled independent variables. The purposes of regression are to show *how* the independent variables in the analysis are related to the dependent variable, and to make *predictions* about scores on the dependent variable based upon knowledge of independent variable scores. We begin our study of regression by examining the special case where we have one dependent variable and only one independent variable. Regression used in this context is called *simple regression*. The data on course grades presented in Table 18-1 will again be used. The marketing management grade, X, will be designated as the independent variable, and the marketing research grade, Y, will be designated as the dependent variable. We could fit a linear relationship to these data by drawing an eye-fitted line through the middle of the scatter plot in Figure 18-3. However, we want to be more precise than this, so we look for a mathematical procedure to define the required straight line.

Partitioning the Sum of Squares   We begin this process by defining:

Y_i = the ith observation on the dependent variable
$\bar{Y}$ = the mean of all the Y's
$\hat{Y}_i$ = the predicted value of the ith observation of the dependent variable

We can write any observation as a deviation from the mean value, $\bar{Y}$.

$$\text{Total deviation for } i\text{th observation} = (Y_i - \bar{Y})$$

This represents the total deviation of Y_i, because if we know nothing about X values, we can still guess $\bar{Y}$ as our estimate of Y. Total deviation must then be expressed as deviation from $\bar{Y}$. We can partition this deviation into components:

$$\text{Total deviation} = \text{deviation due to } X's + \text{deviation due to error}$$

$$(Y_i - \bar{Y}) \quad = \quad (\hat{Y}_i - \bar{Y}) \quad + \quad (Y_i - \hat{Y}_i) \tag{18-6}$$

$$\text{Total variation} = \begin{array}{c} \text{variation explained} \\ \text{by regression} \end{array} + \begin{array}{c} \text{variation unexplained} \\ \text{by regression} \end{array}$$

Figure 18-4 graphically shows this partitioning of total deviation. Note that the explained deviation is the amount the total deviation is reduced by our knowledge of the regression line from the level of deviation present by knowledge of $\bar{Y}$. If we add the deviation in Equation 18-6 across all observations and square this equation, we can partition the sums of squares into the part explained by the regression equation and

FIGURE 18-4   Partioning of deviations in regression.

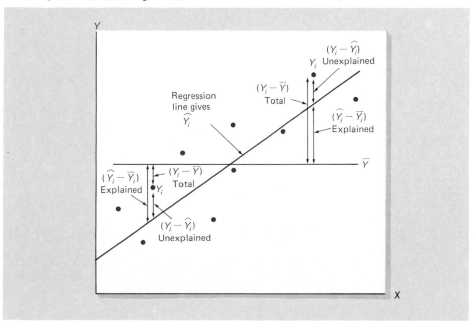

the part that is unexplained, as follows:

$$\Sigma(Y_i - \bar{Y})^2 = \Sigma(\hat{Y}_i - \bar{Y})^2 + \Sigma(Y_i - \hat{Y}_i)^2$$

$$SS_{\text{total}} = SS_{\substack{\text{explained} \\ \text{by regression}}} + SS_{\substack{\text{unexplained} \\ \text{by regression}}}$$

| Total | = | explained | + unexplained |
| variation | | variation | variation |

Presenting the deviations in this fashion provides a conceptual understanding of how a regression aids our understanding of the dependent variable. However, we still have not developed a procedure to fit a line to the data.

Fitting the Regression Line   We want to be able to predict a Y value based on knowledge of an X value and to note the direction of relationship (positive or negative) and rate of change (slope level) between X and Y. These tasks require us to fit a mathematical linear equation to the data. Of course, we want an equation that fits the data well. A good fit could be one that minimizes the error or unexplained deviation. The criterion usually used is to minimize the sum of the squares of the errors. The "least squares" solution has desirable statistical properties that are well dealt with in texts on regression. Intuitively, we can see that large errors are avoided as much as possible, thereby providing a good fit; thus, we want to fit a line of the form

$$Y = a + bX$$

where a = the value of the intercept on the Y axis
$\quad\quad b$ = the slope of the line

Using our knowledge of the X and Y values, we solve for a and b. One way to do this is to first cast the X values as deviations from their mean: $x = X - \bar{X}$. Now we are solving for an equation of the form $Y = a + bx$. We want to find the values of a and b that minimize the sum of squared errors $\Sigma(Y_i - \hat{Y}_i)^2$.

The mathematical knowledge necessary to develop the formulas for the a and b values is beyond the scope of this book. The resultant formulas are

$$a = \bar{Y}$$

$$b = \frac{\sum\limits_{i=1}^{n} Y_i x_i}{\sum\limits_{i=1}^{n} x_i^2}$$

A Numerical Example   Let us do a regression with the data on grades that we used to calculate the correlation coefficient. The basic data and calculations are presented in Table 18-2. The resultant equation is

$$\hat{Y}_i = 75.0 + .93x_i \tag{18-7}$$

TABLE 18-2 REGRESSION CALCULATIONS FOR DATA IN TABLE 18-1

X_i	Y_i	$x_i = (X_i - \bar{X})$	$Y_i x_i$	x_i^2	$\hat{Y}_i = 75 + .93X_i$	$(Y_i - \hat{Y}_i)$	$(Y_i - \hat{Y}_i)^2$
75	85	1	85	1	75.9	9.1	82.81
80	85	6	510	36	80.6	4.4	19.36
60	65	-14	-910	196	62.0	3.0	9.00
55	60	-19	-1140	361	57.3	2.7	7.29
85	80	11	880	121	85.2	-5.2	27.04
95	95	21	1995	441	94.5	0.5	0.25
70	60	-4	-240	16	71.3	-11.3	127.69
75	80	1	80	1	75.9	4.1	16.81
80	80	6	480	36	80.6	-.6	0.36
65	60	-9	-540	81	66.6	-6.6	43.56
$\Sigma X_i = 740$ $\bar{X} = 74.0$	$\Sigma Y_i = 750$ $\bar{Y} = 75.0$	$\Sigma x_i = 0$	$\Sigma Y_i x_i = 1200$	$\Sigma x_i^2 = 1290$		$\Sigma(Y_i - \hat{Y}_i) = 0$	$\Sigma(Y_i - \hat{Y}_i)^2 = 334.17$

$$a = \bar{Y} = 75.0$$

$$b = \frac{\Sigma Y_i x_i}{\Sigma x_i^2} = \frac{1200}{1290} = .93$$

$$\hat{Y}_i = 75.0 + .93x_i$$

In making predictions it is sometimes easier to deal with X_i values and not the deviations x_i. Thus Equation 18-7 becomes

$$\hat{Y}_i = 75.0 + .93(X_i - \bar{X})$$
$$= 75.0 + .93(X_i - 74.0)$$
$$= (75.0 - 68.8) + .93X_i$$
$$= 6.2 + .93X_i \tag{18-8}$$

We note in Equation 18-8 that the b value or slope remains the same. The intercept only has shifted.

The Meaning of the Coefficients   What exactly do the coefficients we calculated mean? The a tells us the predicted value of Y when X is zero. In our example we would predict a score of 6.2 in the marketing research course even if the grade in marketing management were zero. Obviously, such a person should not even be allowed to take marketing research. This points up a general comment, namely, that the a coefficient is generally of less interest to us than the b coefficient.

The b represents *the amount of change we would predict in Y for a one-unit change in X*. Thus, in our example we would predict a .93 increase in the grade in marketing research for each increase of one grade point obtained in marketing management. A negative sign on a b coefficient would indicate that as X increases, Y decreases. Graphically, b is the slope of the regression line.

We may use the regression equation to generate predicted values of Y. These $\hat{Y}_i$'s are presented for the given X_i's in Table 18-2. We can then calculate the difference between the observed and predicted values, $Y_i - \hat{Y}_i$. If we square these values and add them across all observations, we get the sum of squares error, $\Sigma(Y_i - \hat{Y}_i)^2$. These values are calculated in Table 18-2. The sum of squares error here is 334.17. No other values of a and b would give this small an SS_{error}. This is the meaning of a "least squares" solution.

Explained Variation   The question naturally arises as to how much of the variation in Y was explained by our knowledge of X. This question is answered by calculating the ratio of explained variation to total variation. Previously we defined the coefficient of determination, r^2, as the amount of variation explained in a correlation context. The same concept applies here, except that in simple regression

$$r_{XY}^2 = \frac{\text{explained variation}}{\text{total variation}}$$
$$= \frac{\Sigma(\hat{Y}_i - \bar{Y})^2}{\Sigma(Y_i - \bar{Y})^2}$$
$$= \frac{SS_{explained}}{SS_{total}}$$

r_{XY}^2 is again called the coefficient of determination, and it represents the proportion of the total variation in Y explained by fitting the regression line.

From Table 18-1, we note that for our grades example

$$SS_{\text{total}} = \Sigma(Y_i - \bar{Y})^2 = \Sigma y^2 = 1450$$

Also from Table 18-2, we note that

$$SS_{\text{error}} = \Sigma(\hat{Y}_i - Y_i)^2 = 334.17$$

Thus,

$$
\begin{aligned}
SS_{\text{explained}} &= \Sigma(\hat{Y}_i - \bar{Y})^2 \\
&= SS_{\text{total}} - SS_{\text{error}} \\
&= 1450 - 334.17 \\
&= 1115.83
\end{aligned}
$$

Therefore,

$$r_{XY}^2 = \frac{1115.83}{1450} = .77$$

This is exactly the value of r^2 we obtained by squaring the correlation coefficient, as we would expect.

In practice, the size of r^2's obtained from regression vary greatly. In forecasting applications where the environment is quite stable, r^2's may be as high as .8 or .9. In situations where the environment changes a great deal, or where we are trying to predict individual attitudes or behavior, r^2's may be in the .15 to .3 range. These latter small r^2's indicate the lack of ability of marketers to fully understand the world in which they are working. However, all is not lost. Individual coefficients may still provide useful information even though the total r^2 is small.

Correlation and simple regression allow the researcher to describe the relationship between two individual variables. For example, we could describe the relationship between (1) age and amount of credit card usage, (2) income and wine consumption per year, (3) advertising expenditures and attitudes toward a brand, (4) years of education and expenditures on housing per year, or (5) number of advertising insertions and brand awareness. These are but a few examples of possible situations where correlation and simple regression could be useful.

It should be recognized that correlation and regression provide measures of association, not causation. However, marketing managers may use these procedures to help them better understand the nature of the implicit or explicit causal model they are using.

INFERENTIAL STATISTICS

As with univariate analysis, the interest of the researcher often goes beyond describing sample relationships to making judgments about population parameters. In theory it is possible to test a hypothesis about any descriptive statistic. Thus, for example, we could test hypotheses about the size of the population correlation coefficient. However, in this chapter we will restrict our attention to a few bivariate inferential tests. Specifically, for interval data we shall discuss (1) the t test on the regression coefficient, (2) the z test on the difference between means, and (3) the t test on the difference between means. These tests are somewhat mathematically detailed, and for some readers they will constitute a restatement of material already covered in a basic statistics course. Thus, the discussion of these tests is continued in the appendix at the end of this chapter.

One bivariate inference test will be discussed, namely, the chi-square test, which is appropriate for examining the relationship between two nominal variables. It is discussed here because of its usefulness in analyzing cross-tabulation tables, and because it is often not covered in basic statistics courses.

The Chi-Square Test

Perhaps the most common type of bivariate analysis in practice is the cross tabulation of two nominal variables. In truth we need not have nominal variables to do this; interval or ordinal variables can be analyzed in this fashion if we first group them into classes or categories. Typical questions addressed by cross tabulation might be: (1) Is there a relationship between age and media habits? (2) Is there a relationship between region of the country and brand preference? (3) Is there a relationship between lifestyle types and car ownership?

As we see from the examples, the objective of cross tabulation is to identify a relationship between variables. In data from a sample we might observe what appears to be a relationship between two nominal variables. A question naturally arises as to whether this observed relationship is simply the result of sampling error, and the chi-square test is designed to answer this question. The null hypothesis for a chi-square test is that the two variables are *independent* of each other. The alternative hypothesis is that they are not independent, that is, that there is a relationship between the two variables.

Let's illustrate the chi-square test. Table 18-3 presents the cross tabulation of an income measure and a measure of brand purchased last. The cell entries indicate the numbers in the sample that form the various combinations of income and brand categories. For example, we note that there were 50 people earning less than $10,000 who purchased brand 1 last. The expected number in each cell is not the same, as it was with the univariate chi square. This is so because the totals for each category of each variable are not the same. For example, with 650 people earning $10,000–$20,000, we should certainly not expect the cells to be equal. What then should be the expected cell values? To answer this question we turn to one of the elementary rules of probability theory.

TABLE 18-3 CROSS TABULATION OF INCOME AND BRAND PURCHASED LAST

		B Brand purchased last			
	Income	B_1 Brand 1	B_2 Brand 2	B_3 Brand 3	Total
A	A_1 Less than \$10,000	50	200	125	375
	A_2 \$10,000–\$20,000	200	100	350	650
	A_3 Over \$20,000	100	25	50	175
	Total	350	325	525	1200

Note in Table 18-3 that we have defined income as variable A and the categories of income as A_1, A_2, and A_3. "Brand purchased last" is defined as variable B, and the categories as B_1, B_2, and B_3. The various combinations of A_iB_i's are the occurrences of various events. Let us use A_1B_1 to illustrate the required theory.

If A and B are independent, the probability of A_1 and B_1 occurring is the product of the probability of A_1 times the probability of B_1. This is the multiplication theorem of statistics. In symbols,

$$P(A_1 \text{ and } B_1) = P(A_1)P(B_1)$$

Also we note that

$$P(A_1) = \text{relative frequency of } A_1 \text{ over all } A\text{'s}$$

$$= \frac{A_1}{A} = \frac{375}{1200}$$

$$P(B_1) = \text{relative frequency of } B_1 \text{ over all } B\text{'s}$$

$$= \frac{B_1}{B} = \frac{350}{1200}$$

$$P(A_1 \text{ and } B_1) = \frac{375}{1200} \times \frac{350}{1200} = .091$$

The expected number in cell A_1B_1 is then

$$n[P(A_1 \text{ and } B_1) = 1200\left(\frac{375}{1200} \times \frac{350}{1200}\right)$$

$$= 109.38$$

In general, the formula for expected value is

$$E_{ij} = \frac{n_{A_i}n_{B_j}}{n}$$

where E_{ij} = expected number in cell ij
$\quad n_{A_i}$ = number of elements in category A_i
$\quad n_{B_j}$ = number of elements in category B_j

For $A_1 B_1$ the expected number is

$$E_{11} = \frac{(375)(350)}{1200} = 109.38$$

We can repeat this process for all cells.

Table 18-4 presents the observed and expected numbers for each cell and the calculation of the associated chi square. The relevant formula is

$$\chi^2 = \sum_{i=1}^{R} \sum_{j=1}^{C} \frac{(O_{ij} - E_{ij})^2}{E_{ij}}$$

where R = number of categories of the row variable
$\quad C$ = number of categories of the column variable
$\quad O_{ij}$ = observed number in cell ij
$\quad E_{ij}$ = expected number in cell ij

The calculated chi square is 252.2. The number of degrees of freedom is $(R - 1)(C - 1)$, since once the number of elements in $R - 1$ row categories and the total are known, the number in the last category is determined. A similar argument holds for column degrees of freedom. In our example there are $(3 - 1)(3 - 1) = 4$ degrees of freedom. If $\alpha = .01$, the critical value of chi square at 4 df is 13.3 (see Table A-6 of Appendix A). Since the calculated chi square exceeds the critical value, we reject the null hypothesis that income and brand purchased last are independent.

TABLE 18-4 CALCULATION OF BIVARIATE CHI SQUARE

Cell number	O_{ij}	E_{ij}	$O_{ij} - E_{ij}$	$(O_{ij} - E_{ij})^2$	$(O_{ij} - E_{ij})^2 / E_{ij}$
1,1	50	109.38	−59.38	3526.0	32.2
1,2	200	101.56	98.44	9690.4	95.4
1,3	125	164.06	−39.06	1525.7	9.3
2,1	200	189.58	10.42	108.6	0.6
2,2	100	176.04	−76.04	5782.1	32.8
2,3	350	284.38	65.62	4306.0	15.1
3,1	100	51.04	48.96	2397.1	47.0
3,2	25	47.40	−22.40	501.8	10.6
3,3	50	76.56	−26.56	705.4	9.2
Total	1200	1200.00			252.2

$\chi^2 = 252.2$

In using the chi square, we should have all the expected cell sizes equal to at least 5. If this is not the case, it is generally recommended that cells be combined to give an expected frequency of at least 5. It is also important to have the two measurements independent of each other. That is, we should not use the chi square to compare repeated measures on the same variable.

The chi-square test may tell us that two variables are not independent. However, it does not tell anything about the nature of the relationship. To determine this, we must look back into the table of interest. In Table 18-3, we see that as income increases, "brand last purchased" shifts from brand 2 to brand 3 and then to brand 1. A researcher often confronts many cross-tabulation tables. A good strategy to use in evaluating these tables is first to examine the chi square for significance, then examine closely those tables with significant chi squares. Fortunately, all good data analysis programs offer the chi-square test as part of a cross-tabulation output. There are a number of other issues related to interpreting cross-tabulation tables that will be addressed.

INTERPRETATION OF CROSS-TABULATION TABLES

The position of crosstab tables in marketing research practice is so important that we must go beyond the mere concern about significance discussed previously in our examination of the chi-square test. Certain fundamental issues related to the interpretation of these tables must be clarified: (1) the use of percentages and (2) the elaborations of discovered relationships with the introduction of additional variables.

Use of Percentages

In doing the chi-square test we use the raw frequency counts in each cell. This is fine for this test, but raw frequencies are often difficult to interpret. To aid in the interpretation of significant relationships it usually helps to cast the data in the crosstab table in percentage form. The problem is that the researcher has three alternative ways to calculate percentage: (1) row percentages, such that the percentages in each row add to 100 percent; (2) column percentages, such that the percentages in each column add to 100 percent; or (3) cell percentages, such that the percentages added across all cells equal 100 percent. Table 18-5 presents four tables. The first is a set of raw frequencies in a crosstab between income and consumption of types of wines. The other three tables present the raw frequencies presented in row, column, and cell percentage form.

Which of these percentages is most useful to the researcher? We may try to determine a general rule by examining Table 18-5. Clearly, cell percentages tell us little about the relationship between income and type of wine consumed. They are generally useful only in identifying the size of particular segments, not for assisting one in understanding relationships. If we looked at the column percentages, we would make conclusions such as the following: 65.2 percent of those consuming cheap wine earn less than $15,000, while only 34.8 percent of those consuming cheap wine earn $15,000 and over. This sort

TABLE 18-5 ALTERNATIVE WAY OF PRESENTING CROSS-TABULAR RESULTS

A. Raw frequencies

Income	Type of wine consumed		Total
	Cheap	Premium	
Less than $15,000	75	10	85
$15,000 and over	40	80	120
Total	115	90	205

B. Row Percentages

Income	Type of wine consumed		Total
	Cheap	Premium	
Less than $15,000	88.2%	11.8%	100.0
$15,000 and over	33.3	66.7	100.0

C. Column percentages

Income	Type of wine consumed	
	Cheap	Premium
Less than $15,000	65.2%	11.1%
$15,000 and over	34.8	88.9
Total	100.0%	100.0%

D. Cell percentages

Income	Type of wine consumed	
	Cheap	Premium
Less than $15,000	36.6%	4.9%
$15,000 and over	19.5	39.0
	Total 100.0%	

of conclusion seems to imply that type of wine consumed is having an effect on income earned. This is obviously not what we mean in this case. Clearly, we expect that income is having the effect on type of wine consumed and not the other way around. Examination of the row percentages shows us the type of relationship we were looking for. Here we could make conclusions such as: 88.2 percent of those earning less than $15,000 consume cheap wine, while only 11.8 percent of these people consume premium wine. This conclusion implies that income is affecting the type of wine consumed.

The rule, then, is to *cast percentages in the direction of the causal factor*. Thus, if the causal factor is the row factor, calculate (by computer) row percentages, and vice versa.

Elaboration of Relationships[2]

Care must be taken in the use of crosstab tables. It is possible that the true relationship is more complex than one that can be properly identified by looking at the cross tabulation of two variables. This is especially true if the user believes that there is a causal relationship between the variables. You might ask: Does this relationship hold when other variables are considered? For example, how are type of wine consumed and income related for different age groups, or different regions of the country, or different sexes, etc.? What we need to do is elaborate on the relationship that was discovered in two-way tables. We do this by obtaining the cross tabulation of the same variables as before, except that now we get one cross tabulation of these variables for each category of some other variable or variables. Thus, we could see whether there was a different relationship for males and females, etc.

The original association between the two variables is called the *total or zero-order association*. The tables showing the association between the two variables within categories of other variables are called *conditional tables* and reveal *conditional associations*.[3] The variables on which the crosstab is conditional are called *control variables*. Therefore, we might ask for the crosstab of income and type of wine consumed, controlling on age. When conditional tables are developed on the basis of one control variable, they are called *first-order conditional tables*. It is also possible to control on more than one variable. Here conditional tables are developed for elements within the various combinations of control categories. For example, one control combination might be "females from California" in the use of the two control variables, sex and region of the country. We would then obtain a table for each combination of sex and region. When two controls are present, the tables are called *second-order conditional tables;* if three control variables are present, they are called *third-order conditional tables,* and so on. The more control variables we add, the more tables we will obtain, and the harder will be the interpretation of the results. For example, if we had three control variables with 2, 3, and 4 categories, respectively, we would then get $2 \times 3 \times 4 = 24$ conditional tables. Thus, we add control variables with care, usually being guided by some theory of the underlying relationship in doing so. Our discussion of this elaboration process will be limited to first-order conditional tables.

The possible outcomes of elaboration depend on the original conclusion. Suppose the original zero-order table leads to the conclusion of a relationship between the variables. Then from the conditional tables we might (1) retain the original conclusion that a relationship exists, (2) specify a different relationship by control categories, or (3) identify the original relationship as spurious. On the other hand, the original table may have led to the conclusion of no relationship. Then from the conditional tables we might (1) retain the original conclusion that there was no relationship or (2) identify a relationship. The next two sections of this chapter illustrate these outcomes.

---

[2] For a more detailed treatment of this subject see Herman J. Loether and Donald G. McTavish, *Descriptive Statistics for Sociologists* (Boston: Allyn and Bacon, 1974), pp. 264–305. A good discussion is also given in Gilbert A. Churchill, Jr., *Marketing Research: Methodological Foundations* (Hinsdale, Ill.: Dryden Press, 1976), pp. 367–375.

[3] Loether and McTavish, op. cit., pp. 266–267.

Zero-Order Relationship Found

This section presents illustrations of the various possible outcomes of conditional table analysis when a zero-order relationship is found.

Retain Original Conclusion of a Relationship Existing   Table 18-6 illustrates a situation where the original conclusion that a relationship exists is retained. The numbers in parentheses in the table indicate the frequency counts for the cells. Part A of the table shows the relationship between income and credit card usage, obtained using the whole sample. Clearly, higher income is associated with greater use of credit cards. Part B of the table shows this same crosstab presented for two age categories. Note that the conclusion about income and credit card usage is retained.

Specification of Original Relationship   A good question to ask about a crosstab relationship is: Under what conditions does this relationship hold? For example, it is possible that the relationship between credit card usage and income could have been different for the different age categories. If the relationship between the dependent variable (credit card usage) and the independent variable (income) is different for differ-

TABLE 18-6   RETAIN ORIGINAL CONCLUSION OF A RELATIONSHIP EXISTING

A.   Total Sample (n = 1000)

	Income			
Use credit cards	Under $15,000		$15,000 and over	
Yes	(100)	25.0%	(500)	83.3%
No	(300)	75.0	(100)	16.7
Total	(400)	100.0%	(600)	100.0%

B.   Conditional on Age

B-1. For ages 18–35 (n = 350)

	Income			
Use credit cards	Under $15,000		$15,000 and over	
Yes	(34)	29.6%	(199)	84.7%
No	(81)	70.4	(36)	15.3
Total	(115)	100.0%	(235)	100.0%

B-2. For ages over 35 (n = 650)

	Income			
Use credit cards	Under $15,000		$15,000 and over	
Yes	(66)	23.2%	(301)	82.5%
No	(219)	76.8	(64)	17.5
Total	(285)	100.0%	(365)	100.0%

TABLE 18-7 SPECIFICATION OF RELATIONSHIP

A. Total Sample (n = 1000)

Use credit cards	Income			
	Under $15,000		$15,000 and over	
Yes	(175)	43.8%	(350)	58.3%
No	(225)	56.2	(250)	41.7
Total	(400)	100.0%	(600)	100.0%

B. Conditional on Age

B-1. For ages 18–35 (n = 350)

Use credit cards	Income			
	Under $15,000		$15,000 and over	
Yes	(100)	76.9%	(150)	68.2%
No	(30)	23.1	(70)	31.8
Total	(130)	100.0%	(220)	100.0%

B-2. For ages over 35 (n = 650)

Use credit cards	Income			
	Under $15,000		$15,000 and over	
Yes	(75)	27.8%	(230)	60.5%
No	(195)	72.2	(150)	39.5
Total	(270)	100.0%	(380)	100.0%

ent categories of the control variable (age), we say that the independent variable and control variables are interacting. The search for this type of statistical interaction is called *specification of the relationship*. Table 18-7 illustrates a situation where interaction is present. Again we present the whole sample and conditional tables. In this instance, the same initial relationship between income and credit usage is present, except that it is not as strong as before. The conditional tables reveal two different relationships between income and credit card usage. Conditional table B-1 (of Table 18-7) gives one picture. Here, lower income is slightly more associated with credit card usage. B-2 shows a different pattern. It shows a stronger positive relationship between income and credit card usage than that found in the whole sample table. It appears that younger people earning less than $15,000 are more likely to use credit cards than older people of the same income. Age and income are interacting to affect credit card usage.

Identification of a Spurious Relationship Table 18-8 illustrates the situation where the zero-order table reveals a relationship between two variables, while the conditional tables reveal that the relationship was spurious. That is, the original relationship *disappears* when a control variable is present. In this example, the cross tabulation is between attendance at theater movies and ownership of a television set. The whole-sample table reveals that those owning television sets are more likely to attend theater movies.

TABLE 18-8   IDENTIFICATION OF A SPURIOUS RELATIONSHIP

A. Total Sample ($n = 1430$)

Attendance at theater movies	Television ownership			
	No		Yes	
Yes	(240)	36.4%	(610)	79.2%
No	(420)	63.6	(160)	20.8
Total	(660)	100.0%	(770)	100.0%

B. Conditional on Income

B-1. For income under $15,000 ($n = 550$)

Attendance at theater movies				
	No		Yes	
Yes	(40)	9.1%	(10)	9.1%
No	(400)	90.9	(100)	90.9
Total	(440)	100.0%	(110)	100.0%

B-2. For income $15,000 and over ($n = 880$)

Attendance at theater movies	Television ownership			
	No		Yes	
Yes	(200)	90.9%	(600)	90.9%
No	(20)	9.1	(60)	9.1
Total	(220)	100.0%	(660)	100.0%

Source: Adapted from Herman J. Loether and Donald G. McTavish, *Descriptive Statistics for Sociologists* (Boston: Allyn and Bacon, 1974), pp. 276–287.

Graphically, this hypothesis can be represented as:

This result seems somewhat illogical, since it is not clear how television ownership is causing attendance at theater movies. We might hypothesize that a third variable is operative that is causing both television ownership and attendance at movie theaters. This variable might be income. Graphically, this hypothesis can be represented as:

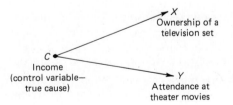

Here income is hypothesized to be causing both X and Y. If the original relationship between X and Y is indeed a causal one, we would expect it to be maintained within categories of the control variable. Part B of Table 18-8 reveals that this is not true. For those earning less than $15,000, the pattern of attendance at theater movies is the same whether the individual owns a television set or not. Specifically, both television ownership and attendance are low. For those earning $15,000 and over, the pattern of attendance is the same for both categories of television ownership. Here, both television ownership and attendance are high. Thus, the original relationship was spurious.

No Zero-Order Relationship Found

This section presents illustrations of the various possible outcomes of conditional-table analysis when no zero-order relationship is found.

Retain Original Conclusion of No Relationship   Table 18-9 illustrates the situation where the whole-sample table revealed no relationship between two variables and the

TABLE 18-9   RETAIN ORIGINAL CONCLUSION OF NO RELATIONSHIP

A. Total Sample ($n = 1000$)

Home ownership	Region of the country			
	East		West	
Yes	(205)	41.0%	(201)	40.2%
No	(295)	59.0	(299)	59.8
Total	(500)	100.0%	(500)	100.0%

B. Conditional on Income

B-1. For income under $15,000 ($n = 300$)

Home ownership	Region of the country			
	East		West	
Yes	(60)	40.0%	(63)	42.0%
No	(90)	60.0	(87)	58.0
Total	(150)	100.0%	(150)	100.0%

B-2. For income $15,000 and over ($n = 700$)

Home ownership	Region of the country			
	East		West	
Yes	(145)	41.4%	(138)	39.4%
No	(205)	58.6	(212)	60.6
Total	(350)	100.0%	(350)	100.0%

conditional tables show no relationship. The crosstab is between home ownership and region of the country. The control variable is income.

Identify a Relationship Table 18-10 illustrates the possibility of a control variable assisting the researcher in identifying a relationship where none seems to exist on the basis of examining zero-order results. In this context the control variable is acting to suppress the observed relationship between two variables, and it is called a *suppressor variable*. This can happen when a relationship in one conditional table is equally sized but in the opposite direction of the other conditional table. The result is that the relationships cancel each other when presented in the zero-order situation.

Table 18-10 presents the cross tabulation of income and credit card usage, controlling for sex. The total-sample table shows no relationship between income and credit card usage. On the other hand, the conditional tables for male and female show strong but opposite relationships. Males earning $15,000 and over are much more likely to use credit cards than those males earning under $15,000. Exactly the opposite is true for females. Note that this is a special case of interaction. Here sex and income are interacting to hide the effect on credit card usage.

TABLE 18-10 IDENTIFICATION OF A RELATIONSHIP

A. Total Sample (n = 1000)

	Income			
Use credit cards	Under $15,000		$15,000 and over	
Yes	(160)	40.0%	(240)	40.0%
No	(240)	60.0	(360)	60.0
Total	(400)	100.0%	(600)	100.0%

B. Conditional on Sex

B-1. For males (n = 500)

	Income			
Use credit cards	Under $15,000		$15,000 and over	
Yes	(30)	15.0%	(200)	66.7%
No	(170)	85.0	(100)	33.3
Total	(200)	100.0%	(300)	100.0%

B-2. For females (n = 500)

	Income			
Use credit cards	Under $15,000		$15,000 and over	
Yes	(130)	65.0%	(40)	13.3%
No	(70)	35.0	(260)	86.7
Total	(200)	100.0%	(300)	100.0%

Concluding Comment on Cross Tabulation

In any dataset containing even a small number of variables, there are a great many possible crosstab tables. If one attempts to elaborate on these, the number of possible tables becomes huge. Obviously, researchers cannot just go on a "shopping trip" to find relationships, for they would be overwhelmed with computer output. They must have a model of the problem that focuses on the interrelationships among relevant variables to do proper cross-tabulation analysis. A good definition of the problem at hand combined with the specification of information needs can go a long way in guiding the data analysis process.

BANNER FORMAT

In the past few years, the presentation of data in banner form has gained in popularity as an alternative to the crosstab format. In a banner format typically one row variable is cross tabulated with a series of column variables. Table 18-11 presents an example of a banner. Here the row variable, income, is simultaneously cross tabulated with the variables: persons in the household, head of household occupation, and rooms in the house. In standard crosstabs, percentages can be cast in either direction. In banner format, percentages are cast in one direction only, limiting the information generated Also, the direction of the percentages must be by column even when the causal direction is really by row. This is true in the data given in Table 18-11. Income is the causal variable, yet banner format requires percentages cast the other way.

Crosstab tables are probably the most popular method of presenting in-house data, while banners are favored among marketing research vendors due to their ability to simplify data presentation. The popularity of crosstabs can be attributed to many factors: (1) They are easily presented and understood by management; (2) they allow for statistical hypothesis tests on nominal data (generally chi-square tests); (3) the categories are flexible and can be easily redefined; and (4) they are helpful in exposing hidden and spurious relationships that may otherwise go unnoticed.

Crosstabs and banners are not a marketing research panacea, though. Crosstabs have several disadvantages.[4] First, each cell must have at least five pieces of data in order to have reliable chi-square estimates. Second, crosstabs can result in a deluge of worthless data in the hands of an inexperienced researcher. For example, 40 pieces of data would yield 780 two-way crosstabs. Third, the commonly used chi-square test only indicates the existence, not the strength, of crosstab relationships. Fourth, and perhaps the biggest disadvantage, is the difficulty they present in discovering covariation in a hidden variable.

Banners are basically a variation of the two-way crosstab with the percentages cast in only one direction. Thus, many of the advantages and disadvantages are the same for banners as for crosstabs. Banners, though, unlike crosstabs, allow many variables to be presented at once. But because the percentages are cast in only one direction, banners do not allow the reader of the tables to look for alternative conclusions. Oftentimes banners collapse several categories, making it difficult to infer accurate results

---

[4] For an excellent discussion of banners, see Roseann Maguire and Terry C. Wilson, *Marketing News,* Vol. 17, no. 10, sec. 1, pp. 10–11, May 13, 1983.

TABLE 18-11 EXAMPLE OF BANNER FORMAT: FAMILY INCOME FOR 1986

| Income group | Sample | Total persons in household | | | | Head of household occupation | | | | | | | | Rooms | |
| | | Children | | Teenagers | | Prof., tech. | Managers | Sales clerical | Craft, operators, Lab. tech. | Service workers | Students, home-makers | Retired | Unemployed | 5 or less | 6 or more |
		None	1+	None	1+										
$5,999 or less	243	81	38	93	20	4	3	11	11	14	45	83	33	136	98
	9%	9	5	9	4	1	1	5	2	10	38	18	35	16	6
$6,000–$9,999	280	112	44	116	39	8	8	21	28	24	29	116	25	129	144
	11%	13	6	11	8	2	2	10	4	18	25	25	27	15	8
$10,000–$14,999	328	115	72	134	33	16	22	55	69	25	15	98	13	150	170
	12%	13	9	13	7	3	6	25	11	18	13	21	14	18	10
$15,000–$19,999	340	121	102	147	58	47	24	42	127	17	9	58	7	117	218
	13%	14	13	14	11	10	7	19	20	12	8	12	8	14	13
$20,000–$24,999	351	110	126	155	73	65	46	29	138	22	6	35	4	104	243
	13%	13	17	15	14	14	13	13	22	16	5	7	4	12	14
$25,000–$29,999	269	80	109	115	59	62	49	9	117	12	1	15	1	60	205
	10%	9	14	11	12	14	14	4	18	9	1	3	1	7	12
$30,000–$34,999	218	71	88	94	49	62	45	19	64	9	1	13	1	32	184
	8%	8	12	9	10	14	13	9	10	7	1	3	1	4	11
$35,000 or more	434	144	146	151	146	176	141	23	51	9	4	21		52	375
	16%	16	19	14	29	38	39	11	8	7	3	4		6	22
Refused/no answer	172	39	34	42	30	19	20	8	36	5	8	28	9	63	77
	.7%	4	4	4	6	4	6	4	6	4	7	6	10	7	4
Total	2635	873	759	1047	507	459	358	217	641	137	118	467	93	843	1714
	100%	100	100	100	100	100	100	100	100	100	100	100	100	100	100

Source: Adapted for *Marketing News*, vol. 13, pp. 11, (May 13, 1983.)

from the data. The probability of obtaining a spurious relationship increases. Also, the chance of discovering hidden variables decreases, as does the possibility of detecting covariation.

Because banners prevent the researcher from discovering misleading relationships and inhibit the exploration of alternative conditions where a relationship may or may not exist, banners should not be used as a substitute for crosstabs. They can be used, however, to complement crosstabs as a way of simplifying the presentation of results.

SUMMARY

1 Bivariate analysis involves analyzing two variables at a time.

2 The choice of which statistical procedure to use depends on the scale level of the variables and on whether the researcher wants a descriptive statistic or an inferential test.

3 Linear correlation (r) is a measure of the degree to which two interval variables are linearly associated.

4 The coefficient of determination (r^2) is the amount of variation in one variable that can be explained by knowledge of the other.

5 Simple regression is appropriate for one intervally scaled dependent variable and one intervally scaled independent variable.

6 Simple regression shows how the independent variable is related to the dependent variable.

7 The simple regression model can be presented as

$$SS_{total} = SS_{explained} + SS_{unexplained}$$

8 The simple regression equation is

$$\hat{Y}_i = a + bX_i$$

where a is the intercept and b is the slope or the amount of increase in $\hat{Y}$ predicted to occur with a one-unit increase in X.

9 A t test on the b coefficient provides a measure of the null hypothesis that the population regression coefficient is zero. (See appendix.)

10 The coefficient of determination in regression (r^2) equals

$$\frac{\text{Explained variation}}{\text{Total variation}} = \frac{SS_{explained}}{SS_{total}}$$

11 The difference between two sample means may be tested to see whether the population means are really different. This may be done with a z or t test, depending on the circumstances. (See appendix.)

12 The chi-square test evaluates the null hypothesis that two nominal variables are independent.

13 Cast percentages in cross-tabulation tables in the direction of causation.

14 Total-sample cross-tabulation tables may be elaborated by using control variables.

15 If a total-sample relationship is found, this elaboration may find the same relationship, interaction, or spuriousness.

16 If no total-sample relationship is found, this elaboration may find no relationship again or identify a relationship.

17 Banners provide benefits in data presentation but have limitations related to complex causal structures in data.

DISCUSSION QUESTIONS

1 What questions must you answer in order to select the appropriate bivariate statistical procedure?

2 What is linear correlation?

3 What is the coefficient of determination?

4 When can simple regression be used?

5 How do you test to see whether a simple regression has explained a significant portion of the variation in the dependent variable?

6 When should the z and t tests on the difference between means be used?

7 What is the chi-square test a test for?

8 In what alternative ways may percentages be calculated in a crosstab table? Which way is the best?

9 What is elaboration?

10 What may be found in elaboration?

11 A marketing manager was given the following table of frequency counts to show the nature of the relationship between age and attendance at NFL games. What conclusion should be drawn?

	Age		
Attend NFL games	**Under 40**	**40 and over**	**Total**
Yes	66	31	97
No	24	23	47
Total	90	54	144

12 The same marketing manager also had a table of frequency counts between age and attendance at college football games. What conclusion should be drawn?

	Age		
Attend college football games	**Under 40**	**40 and over**	**Total**
Yes	42	71	113
No	51	65	116
Total	93	136	229

13 In a study of advertising effects, two waves of consumers were interviewed. Wave 1 took place before a new campaign was introduced, and wave 2 a few months after the new campaign had started. As part of the analysis of the data, a comparison was made between the demographic characteristics of the consumers in wave 1 and wave 2. The hope was that the demographics would be the same. Typical of the reported results is the following:

	Sex	
	Male	**Female**
Wave 1	52%	47%
Wave 2	48	53
(chi-square = 4.16)		

What conclusion can be drawn from this result?

14 The same study used in questions 11 and 12 yielded the following data concerning the number of NFL home games attended in a year and the number of years the person has lived in the city:

Case	Number of home games attended	Years lived in city
1	7	30
2	2	6
3	1	2
4	3	12
5	7	20
6	4	23

What is the relationship between the two variables?

15 Mark Schwinn and Jennifer Grier were resident advisors assigned to the first coed hall at Montana College. A welcome party was scheduled to take place the weekend after classes started, and the RAs had the responsibility of ordering the soft drinks. They couldn't, however, agree on kinds of soft drinks they should order (diet cola vs. regular cola vs. other assorted flavors). A total of 30–40 cases was to be ordered, and any unopened cans could be returned. Mark wanted 16 cases of regular cola, 6 diet cola, 6 regular noncola, and 2 diet noncola. Jennifer wanted to order, respectively, 11, 6, 9, and 4 cases. To avoid running out of anything, they decided to get the highest estimate of each kind, making a 35-case order (16 cases regular cola, 6 diet cola, 9 regular noncola, and 4 diet noncola). The actual consumption at the party was 12 cases of regular cola, 4 diet cola, 8 regular noncola, and 1 diet noncola.
Questions:
(a) Is there a difference in preferences between regular vs. diet pop? Cola vs. noncolas? Are the two variables independent?

16. In a recent study on American travel habits, the following data were obtained:

Case	Sex	Children at home?	Respondent's age	Vacations per year
1	M	Y	25	1
2	M	N	52	16
3	F	N	34	8
4	F	Y	33	1
5	F	Y	51	5
6	F	Y	29	0
7	M	Y	35	2
8	F	N	27	8
9	M	Y	46	4
10	M	N	30	10
11	F	N	45	14
12	M	Y	38	3

Questions:

a Is there a relationship between the presence of children at home and the sex of the respondent?

b What is the relationship between age and the presence of children at home? (*Hint:* Create nominal age categories.)

c What is the relationship between age and number of vacations taken per year? Calculate *r*-squared. (*Hint:* Plot the data points before doing a regression analysis. Look for the interaction of an extraneous variable, and calculate your least-squares regression line(s) accordingly. Is one equation appropriate? Would two explain the data better?)

d Is (are) your answer(s) to question c significant? (i.e., was a significant proportion of the variance in the dependent variable explained by the regression?) (See chapter appendix, Bivariate Inference Tests.)

e Using the equation(s) you computed in the previous problem, complete the following data set:

Case	Sex	Children at home?	Respondent's age	Vacations per year
a	M	Y	40	?
b	F	N	40	?
c	M	Y	65	?
d	F	N	18	?

APPENDIX: Bivariate Inference Tests

This appendix contains a description of a number of bivariate inference tests, specifically (1) the *t* test on the simple regression coefficient, (2) the *F* test on the explained sum of squares in regression, (3) the *z* test on the difference between means, and (4) the *t* test on the difference between means. All tests presented here assume that the variables of interest are intervally scaled.

The *t* Test on the Regression Coefficient

The null hypothesis that interests the researcher with respect to simple regression is that the slope is zero. In formula, the null and alternative hypotheses are:

$$H_0: \beta = 0$$
$$H_1: \beta \neq 0$$

where β is the population regression coefficient. In essence, we are testing to see whether the X values make a significant contribution to the explanation of the Y values. We begin the *t* test by first calculating the standard error of the estimate.

Standard Error of the Estimate   The measure of the scatter of the actual Y_i values about the regression line, $\hat{Y}_i$, is called the standard error of the estimate. It is the standard deviation of Y_i about $\hat{Y}_i$.

$$\text{Standard error of the estimate} = s_{YX} = \sqrt{\frac{\Sigma(Y_i - \hat{Y}_i)^2}{n - 2}}$$

We divide by $n - 2$ to adjust for sample bias effect on this estimator because one degree of freedom is used up in fitting the regression line, and there are $n - 1$ degrees of freedom in the sample. The slope of the regression line requires one degree of freedom. A small standard error of the estimate indicates a tight scatter of observations about the regression line, and vice versa. We could use this value to calculate a confidence interval about the regression line. However, this is not our interest here. For our purposes the standard error of the estimate will be used as an intermediate step in testing the null hypothesis that $\beta = 0$.

From the data in Table 18-2,

$$\Sigma(Y_i - \hat{Y}_i)^2 = 334.17$$

thus

$$s_{YX} = \sqrt{\frac{334.17}{10 - 2}}$$
$$= \sqrt{41.77125}$$
$$= 6.5$$

Standard Error to the Regression Coefficient   We may also calculate the standard error or standard deviation of the sampling distribution of the regression coefficient. It is a measure of the amount of sampling error present in the determination of b:

$$s_b = \frac{s_{YX}}{\sqrt{\Sigma x^2}}$$

or, since $x = X_i - \bar{X}$,

$$s_b = \frac{s_{YX}}{\sqrt{\Sigma(X_i - \bar{X})^2}}$$

In our example,

$$s_b = \frac{6.5}{\sqrt{1290}}$$

$$= \frac{6.5}{35.9}$$

$$= .18$$

The t Test   The standard error of the regression coefficient can be used to test the statistical significance of the b coefficient. We do this by use of the knowledge that

$$t = \frac{b}{s_b}$$

We then compare this computed t value with the value in the t distribution given in Table A-4 of Appendix A, at $n - 2$ degrees of freedom.

In our example,

$$b = .93 \qquad \text{and} \qquad s_b = .18$$

then

$$t = \frac{.93}{.18}$$

$$= 5.17$$

At 8 degrees of freedom and $\alpha = .05$, for a two-tailed test, the critical value of t is 2.306. Therefore our b coefficient is statistically significant. We conclude that the population regression coefficient is not zero. Thus, knowledge of grades in marketing management is significantly helping us explain grades in marketing research. For $n > 30$, the value of t calculated is compared with z values of the normal distribution given in Table A-2 of Appendix A.

F Test on the Explained Sum of Squares

Since we have calculated SS associated with the regression and SS error, we are in a position to convert these SS to variances (or mean squares, as they are called) by dividing by the relevant number of degrees of freedom. We could then compare the regression-associated variance with the error variance and determine whether the regression has explained a statistically significant portion of the variance in Y. Here the F statistic is the appropriate test. Specifically,

$$F = \frac{\text{variance explained by regression}}{\text{variance unexplained}}$$

$$= \frac{SS_{\text{explained}}/df}{SS_{\text{unexplained}}/df}$$

Table A18-1 presents the calculation of the F value for our grades data. As always, there are $n - 1$ degrees of freedom in the sample. The b coefficient requires one degree of freedom, thus leaving $n - 2$ for the error term. The calculated F is 26.71. The critical F (given in Table A-5 of Appendix A) at $\alpha = .05$, and at 1 and 8 degrees of freedom, is 5.32. Thus we conclude that the regression has explained a significant proportion of the variance in Y.

TABLE A18-1   SIGNIFICANCE TABLE FOR GRADES DATA

Source of variation	SS	Df	Mean square (MS)	F
$SS_{explained}$ $\Sigma(Y_i - \overline{Y})^2$	1115.83	1	1115.83	26.71
$SS_{unexplained\ (error)}$ $\Sigma(Y_i - \hat{Y}_i)^2$	334.17	$n - 2 = 8$	41.77	
SS_{total} $\Sigma(Y_i - \overline{Y})^2$	1450.00	$n - 1 = 9$		

Previously, we calculated $t = 5.17$ for the b coefficient. This value is the square root of the F value we just calculated. We then note the fundamental relationship between the F and t distributions:

$$F = t^2$$

A t test on the b coefficient or an F test on the variance will lead to similar conclusions with regard to statistical significance in simple regression. In regression with more than one independent variable, the difference between the t and F tests will become important. This will be discussed in Chapter 20; for now, we merely note the two procedures.

The z Test on the Difference between Means

A question that often arises in marketing research is whether or not an observed difference between two means generated by a sample is large enough to be a significant difference. That is, are the population means really different from each other? For example, we might want to know whether the mean consumption levels of two brands of cola are the same, or whether the mean attitude scores of male and female salespersons about their jobs are the same, or whether the mean sales levels generated by two coupon plans are equal. To do this we may use either the z or t test on the difference between the mean values. The choice between a z and t test is made on essentially the same basis as in univariate analysis. Specifically, we use z when the population standard deviation, σ, is known for both measures under consideration, or if $n > 30$ for both measures. We use t when the population standard deviation is unknown for either measure when $n \leq 30$.

The null hypothesis is usually that the two population means are equal. However, it is possible to test that the difference between two means is some specific value. The relevant formula if σ is known is

$$z = \frac{(\overline{X}_1 - \overline{X}_2) - (\mu_1 - \mu_2)}{\sigma_{\overline{X}_1 - \overline{X}_2}}$$

where $\overline{X}_1$ = sample mean for the first variable
$\overline{X}_2$ = sample mean for the second variable
μ_1 and μ_2 = hypothesized population means for the two variables
$\sigma_{\overline{X}_1 - \overline{X}_2}$ = standard error of the difference between the means (standard deviation of the sampling distribution of the difference between means)

The central-limit theorem applies to this sampling distribution of the difference between means, except that the formula for the standard error is different. Specifically,

$$\sigma_{\bar{X}_1 - \bar{X}_2} = \sqrt{\sigma_{\bar{X}_1}^2 + \sigma_{\bar{X}_1}^2} = \sqrt{\frac{\sigma_1^2}{n_1} + \frac{\sigma_2^2}{n_2}}$$

where σ_1^2 and σ_2^2 are the population variances for the two variables of interest and n_1 and n_2 are the respective sample sizes.

Suppose that we knew the following related to the average weekly consumption of two cola brands.

$$\text{Brand A:} \quad \bar{X}_1 = 50 \text{ ounces per week; } \sigma_1 = 12; \, n_1 = 40$$
$$\text{Brand B:} \quad \bar{X}_2 = 60 \text{ ounces per week; } \sigma_2 = 16; \, n_2 = 40$$

Here the null and alternative hypotheses are

$$H_0: \mu_1 = \mu_2 \quad \text{or} \quad (\mu_1 - \mu_2) = 0$$
$$H_1: \mu_1 \neq \mu_2 \quad \text{or} \quad (\mu_1 - \mu_2) \neq 0$$

The standard error is

$$\sigma_{\bar{X}_1 - \bar{X}_2} = \sqrt{\frac{(12)^2}{40} + \frac{(16)^2}{40}} = \sqrt{10} = 3.16$$

and so the calculated z value is

$$z = \frac{(50 - 60) - (\mu_1 - \mu_2)}{3.16} = \frac{-10 - 0}{3.16}$$
$$= -3.16$$

The calculated z value exceeds the critical z value of -1.96 at $\alpha = .05$ for a two-tailed test. Therefore, we reject the null hypothesis and conclude that brand B has significantly more consumption than brand A.

If σ_1 and σ_2 are unknown and not assumed to be equal, we use s_1 and s_2 to estimate $s_{\bar{X}_1 - \bar{X}_2}$ as follows:

$$s_{\bar{X}_1 - \bar{X}_2} = \sqrt{s_{\bar{X}_1}^2 + s_{\bar{X}_2}^2} = \sqrt{\frac{s_1^2}{n_1} + \frac{s_2^2}{n_2}} \tag{A18-1}$$

If σ_1 and σ_2 are unknown but assumed to be equal, we can pool our sample results to estimate $s_{\bar{X}_1 - \bar{X}_2}$ using this formula:

$$s_{\bar{X}_1 - \bar{X}_2} = \sqrt{\left(\frac{n_1 s_1^2 + n_2 s_2^2}{n_1 + n_2 - 2}\right)\left(\frac{n_1 + n_2}{n_1 n_2}\right)} \tag{A18-2}$$

It is just a matter of plugging the value of n_1, s_1, etc., into the relevant formula and getting $s_{\bar{X}_1 - \bar{X}_2}$. If n_1 and $n_2 > 30$, we can calculate z as follows:

$$z = \frac{(\bar{X}_1 - \bar{X}_2) - (\mu_1 - \mu_2)}{s_{\bar{X}_1 - \bar{X}_2}}$$

The *t* Test on the Difference between Means

The *t* statistic can be calculated when σ_1 and σ_2 are unknown in a manner parallel to the calculation for *z*:

$$t = \frac{(\bar{X}_1 - \bar{X}_2) - (\mu_1 - \mu_2)}{s_{\bar{X}_1 - \bar{X}_2}}$$

where *t* has $n_1 + n_2 - 2$ degrees of freedom. The value of $s_{\bar{X}_1 - \bar{X}_2}$ can be calculated using either Equation A18-1 or A18-2, depending on whether the researcher assumes that the population variances are equal or not. Suppose a sample yielded the following results:

Coupon plan *A*: $\bar{X}_1 = 20$ sales per day; $s_1 = 3$; $n_1 = 10$
Coupon plan *B*: $\bar{X}_2 = 16$ sales per day; $s_2 = 2$; $n_2 = 5$

and the researcher assumes that $\sigma_1^2 = \sigma_2^2$. Thus, the formula in Equation A18-2 should be used, and

$$s_{\bar{X}_1 - \bar{X}_2} = \sqrt{\left(\frac{(10)(3)^2 + (5)(2)^2}{10 + 5 - 2}\right)\left(\frac{10 + 5}{(10)(5)}\right)}$$

$$= \sqrt{(8.46)(.3)} = \sqrt{2.54} = 1.59$$

then

$$t = \frac{(20 - 16) - (\mu_1 - \mu_2)}{1.59} = \frac{4 - 0}{1.59} = 2.52$$

At $\alpha = .1$ and 13 *df*, the critical *t* value from Table A-4 of Appendix A for a two-tailed test is 1.77. Since the calculated *t* is greater than the critical *t*, we reject the null hypothesis that the means are equal.

Difference between Proportions

We may apply the same type of hypothesis-testing procedures to the difference between two proportions when $n > 30$.[1] If σ_1 and σ_2 are known (i.e., if π_1 and π_2 are known), we use the formula

$$z = \frac{(p_1 - p_2) - (\pi_1 - \pi_2)}{\sigma_{p_1 - p_2}}$$

where p_1 and p_2 are the two observed sample proportions, and

$$\sigma_{p_1 - p_2} = \sqrt{\sigma_{p_1}^2 + \sigma_{p_2}^2} = \sqrt{\frac{\pi_1(1 - \pi_1)}{n_1} + \frac{\pi_2(1 - \pi_2)}{n_2}}$$

---

[1] When $n < 30$, the binomial distribution should be used. This situation will not be discussed in this book.

When π_1 and π_2 are not known (and therefore σ_1 and σ_2 are not known), we use the formula

$$z = \frac{(p_1 - p_2) - (\pi_1 - \pi_2)}{s_{p_1 - p_2}}$$

Since the null hypothesis is that $\pi_1 = \pi_2$, we are assuming that $\sigma_1 = \sigma_2$, and so we can pool our sample results to estimate $s_{p_1 - p_2}$ using the formula

$$s_{p_1 - p_2} = \sqrt{(p^* q^*)\left(\frac{n_1 + n_2}{n_1 n_2}\right)}$$

where

$$p^* = \frac{n_1 p_1 + n_2 p_2}{n_1 + n_2} = \frac{\text{total number of yes answers in the two samples}}{\text{total number of answers in the two samples}}$$

and

$$q^* = 1 - p^*$$

That is, p^* is a pooled estimate of p.

Let us illustrate the latter situation where π_1 and π_2 are not known. Suppose that the two different product concepts are tested with the following results:

$$\text{Concept A:} \quad p_1 = .20; \, n_1 = 40$$
$$\text{Concept B:} \quad p_2 = .24; \, n_2 = 60$$

where p_i = the number of people who indicated they would buy the ith product concept. Here:

$$H_0: \pi_1 = \pi_2$$
$$H_1: \pi_1 \neq \pi_2$$

$$p^* = \frac{(40)(.20) + (60)(.24)}{40 + 60} = .224$$

and

$$s_{p_1 - p_2} = \sqrt{(.224)(.776)\left(\frac{40 + 60}{(40)(60)}\right)}$$
$$= .085$$

then

$$z = \frac{(.20 - .24) - (\pi_1 - \pi_2)}{.085} = \frac{.04 - 0}{.085}$$
$$= -.47$$

That is, the difference between the two proportions is equal to .47 of a standard error. For $\alpha = .05$ and a two-tailed test, the critical $z = 1.96$. Since the calculated z is less than the critical z, we cannot reject the null hypothesis that the two population proportions are equal.

CHAPTER 19

MULTIVARIATE DATA ANALYSIS I: INTERDEPENDENCE METHODS

In Chapters 17 and 18 we examined data analysis as it relates to univariate and bivariate situations. These analysis types are the heart of current data analysis in marketing research practice. As a result, we presented the appropriate univariate and bivariate procedures in some detail.

The next two chapters are a brief overview of a number of *multivariate data analysis procedures,* which involve the simultaneous analysis of more than two variables. The objectives of our discussion of these techniques are (1) to make you aware of the existence of the techniques, (2) to position each technique in terms of the type of input data required, and (3) to discuss the type of output generated by each technique.

Great care should be taken in applying the techniques presented in this and the next chapter. There are a number of problems and statistical assumptions related to each technique that we do not discuss at all. You should recognize that these techniques are extremely dangerous *when used by unskilled people*. Unfortunately, a proper step-by-step description of how each procedure works, the assumptions made, and the problems in using them would at least double the size of this book. We leave it to a more advanced course in marketing research to cover this material in the required depth.

Emanuel Demby perhaps explained it best in an article where he described the factors that make a successful marketing researcher. He noted that most successful marketing researchers have certain common traits, including these:

They rarely go to multivariate analysis until they have tested hypotheses through crosstabulation.

If multivariate findings run counter to what was learned in bivariate analysis, they tend to trust the latter. (Once, an excellent statistician brought me a factor analysis I had challenged, giving me a fascinating explanation for the solution. Just as he finished, the computer house called to say that they had made a mistake in running the program. The researcher walked out of my office, mumbling, "But I had it all worked out. . . .")

The smartest marketing researcher I know asks such naive questions of his statistical consultant that he is later able to communicate complex analyses to his non-statistician management. Apparently, you don't have to be a great statistician to be a success in marketing research, but you do have to know how to use statisticians.[1]

Despite this there is a growing understanding in marketing research of the need for, and usefulness of, multivariate data analysis procedures. There are a number of reasons for this trend. First, marketing problems are usually not completely described by one or two variables. Many variables combine to yield marketing outcomes. Second, the advent of high-speed computers and associated analysis software has made the solution of multivariate statistical procedures relatively easy. Problems that were virtually impossible to solve by human calculation twenty years ago can now be solved in less than a second with a computer. The mid-1980s technology of the personal computer allows virtually all these multivariate techniques to be run at one desk. Packages such as SPSS-PC and SYSTAT are powerful and readily available. Third, improved understanding of statistical concepts among marketing researchers and managers has increased the likelihood of multivariate procedures being used to make decisions.

This chapter begins by distinguishing multivariate procedures that do not specify a dependent variable from those that do specify a dependent variable. Then three procedures are discussed which do not require that a dependent variable be specified. These procedures are factor analysis, cluster analysis, and multidimensional scaling.

INTERDEPENDENCE VERSUS DEPENDENCE METHODS

The multivariate analysis chapters in this book are organized around a scheme suggested by Kendall.[2] This scheme divides procedures into interdependence and dependence procedures. The fundamental differentiating aspect between the two is whether or not one or more variables have been designated as dependent on other variables. In *dependence methods,* one or more variables are designated as being predicted by (dependent on) a set of independent variables. Regression is an example of this type of analysis. In *interdependence methods,* no variable or variables are designated as being predicted by others. It is the interrelationship among all the variables taken together that interests the researcher. Factor analysis is an example of this type of procedure. Figure 19-1 illustrates this fundamental distinction and notes where in this book the various methods are presented.

This chapter discusses three interdependence methods: factor analysis, cluster analysis, and multidimensional scaling.

[1] Emanuel H. Demby, "Success in Marketing Research? Here are 15 Key Factors That Will Help You Achieve It," *Marketing News,* Jan. 28, 1977, p. 5.

[2] Maurice G. Kendall, "Factor Analysis As a Statistical Technique," *Journal of the Royal Statistical Society,* vol. 121, 1950, pp. 60–73

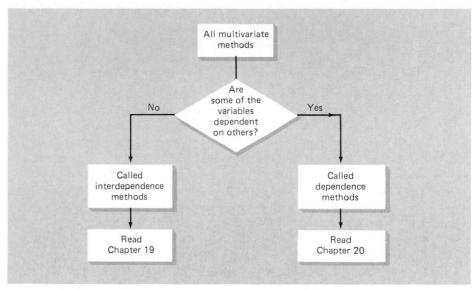

FIGURE 19-1   Interdependence versus dependence methods.

FACTOR ANALYSIS

Factor analysis is a procedure that takes a large number of variables or objects and searches to see whether they have a small number of factors in common which account for their intercorrelation.[3] For example, we might attribute the high association between grades in business administration courses to the factor of intelligence, or the association between certain chemical attributes of coffee to the factor of acidity (pH level).

Marketing Applications

Factor analysis has a number of possible applications in marketing research. These include data reduction, structure identification, scaling, and data transformation.

Data Reduction   Factor analysis can be used for reducing a mass of data to a manageable level. For example, the researcher may have collected data on 50 attributes of a product. The analysis and understanding of these data may be aided by reducing the attributes to a minimum number of factors that underlie the 50 attributes. These factors may then be used in further analysis in place of the original attributes.

Structure Identification   Factor analysis may be used to discover the basic structure underlying a set of measures. For example, the above 50 attributes may reduce

[3] Karl Schuessler, *Analyzing Social Data* (Boston: Houghton Mifflin, 1971), p. 4.

to two factors identified by the researcher as (1) sweetness/bitterness and (2) degree of freshness. The assumption is that at least some of the measures taken are redundant. The factor analysis then finds the underlying structure of the redundancy by placing the measures on underlying factors or dimensions.

Scaling A researcher may wish to develop a scale on which subjects can be compared. A problem in developing any scale is in weighting the variables being combined to form the scale. Factor analysis helps the process by dividing the variables into independent factors. Each factor represents a scale measure of some underlying dimension. Further, factor analysis gives the weights to use for each variable when combining them into a scale.

Data Transformation A number of dependence analysis techniques require independent variables that are themselves uncorrelated (e.g., multiple regression). Factor analysis can be used to identify factors that are uncorrelated. These factors can then be used as input in the relevant dependence method.

Thus, the following have all made use of factor analysis: the development of personality scales, market segments based upon psychographic data, the identification of key product attributes, similarities among magazines, and uncorrelated factors for regression analysis.[4]

Steps in Factor Analysis

There are essentially three steps in a factor analysis solution. The first is to develop a set of correlations between all combinations of the variables of interest. Since we are using correlations, we must then be assuming that the input variables are intervally scaled.[5] The second step is to extract a set of initial factors from the correlation matrix developed in the first step. The third step is to "rotate" the initial factors to find a final solution. The concept of rotation will be discussed later in the chapter. There are a number of decisions that a researcher must make at each of these steps that determine the type of factor analysis that will take place.

Calculation of Correlations With respect to the calculation of the correlation matrix, two broad classes of factor analysis may be distinguished. These are (1) R-factor analysis and (2) Q-factor analysis. In R-factor analysis, these correlations are calculated *between variables;* in Q-factor analysis, they are calculated *between cases.* Cases could be people, products, or whatever else the variables have been measured on, so a Q-factor analysis would group cases on specific factors. Such a procedure could then be used to find similar products or people who belong to different segments. For example, Levi Strauss makes use of Q-analysis to identify and profile segments within the male and female clothing market.

---

[4] For a more detailed review see Gilbert A. Churchill, Jr., *Marketing Research: Methodological Foundations* (Hillsdale, Ill.: Dryden Press, 1976), pp. 561–564.

[5] There are some advanced factor-analysis procedures that do not require interval variables as input. These techniques are beyond the scope of this book.

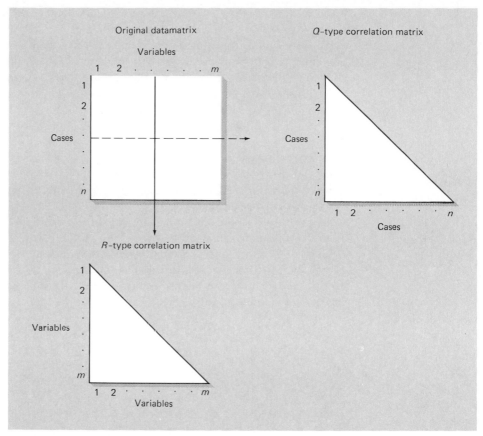

FIGURE 19-2   Development of *R*-type and *Q*-type correlation matrices.

Figure 19-2 shows how *R*- and *Q*-type correlations are developed from the basic data matrix. The solid arrow going down indicates that *R*-type correlations are calculated between variables by using data from all cases. With *m* variables in the data matrix, the result of this process is an *m* by *m* correlation matrix among variables. The dashed arrow going horizontally to the right indicates that *Q*-type correlations are calculated between cases by using data from all variables. With *n* cases in the data matrix, the result of this process is an *n* by *n* correlation matrix among cases. The calculation of correlation coefficients has been discussed in detail in Chapter 18, where the example given is of an *R*-type correlation coefficient, since it shows the relationship between two variables. To calculate a *Q*-type correlation coefficient we simply treat the cases as if they were variables, and vice versa.

Extraction of Initial Factors   There are many methods for extracting the initial factors from the correlation matrix. In general, these methods are far too numerically complex to even begin to discuss here, but one of them is worthy of our consideration.

It is used extensively in practice and will serve to illustrate the nature of factor extraction. It is called the *principal factors method.*

The object of factor extraction is to find a set of factors that are formed as a linear combination of the variables in the correlation matrix. Thus, if the variables X_1, X_2, and X_3 were highly correlated with each other, they would be combined together to form one factor. A linear combination could be defined as follows:

$$z = b_1 X_1 + b_2 X_2 + \cdots + b_m X_m$$

Here z is the linear combination, and it is called a *principal component* or a *principal factor.* The principal-factors methodology involves searching for the values of the b's above which form a linear combination that explains more variance in the correlation matrix than any other set of b's. This is called the first principal factor. This explained variance is then subtracted from the original input matrix to yield a residual matrix. Then a second principal factor is extracted from this residual matrix. This factor explains more of the variance in the residual matrix than any other. The procedure is then repeated until there is very little variance remaining to be explained. The nature of this procedure is such that the factors extracted are uncorrelated with each other. The factors are said to be *orthogonal.*

Rotation   The initial factors are often very difficult to interpret. Thus the initial solution is rotated to yield a solution that is more amenable to interpretation. There are two broad classes of rotation—(1) *orthogonal rotation,* which maintains the factors as uncorrelated with each other, and (2) *oblique rotation,* which allows the factors to be correlated with each other. The basic idea of rotation is to yield factors that each have some variables that correlate highly and some that correlate poorly. This avoids the problem of having factors with all variables having midrange correlations, and thus it allows for easier interpretation.

An Example[6]

Factor analysis is best understood by looking at an example. This one is designed to reduce a set of coffee attributes to a set of underlying factors. Table 19-1 shows the set of 14 coffee attributes on which data were collected on a 10-point semantic differential scale. This table also gives the correlation matrix between the various combinations of attributes. Table 19-2 presents the principal factors extracted from the correlation matrix, plus the orthogonally rotated factors (varimax rotation) and the obliquely rotated factors.

Let us first examine the unrotated principal-factor matrix. Note that there are four factors underlying the 14 attributes. The elements in this matrix listed under the factors are called unrotated factor loadings. The loadings measure which variables are involved in which factor pattern, to what degree and in what direction. They can be interpreted

[6] This example is adapted from Bishwa Nath Mukherjee, "A Factor Analysis of Some Qualitative Attributes of Coffee," *Journal of Advertising Research,* vol. 5, pp. 35–38, March 1965.

TABLE 19-1 COFFEE ATTRIBUTES AND INTERCORRELATIONS AMONG ATTRIBUTE RATINGS

14 coffee attributes investigated

Pleasant flavor—Unpleasant flavor
Stagnant, muggy taste—Sparkling, refreshing taste
Mellow taste—Bitter taste
Cheap taste—Expensive taste
Comforting, harmonious, smooth, friendly taste—Irritating, discordant, rough, hostile taste
Dead, lifeless, dull taste—Alive, lively, peppy taste
Tastes artificial—Tastes like real coffee
Deep, distinct flavor—Shallow, indistinct flavor
Tastes warmed over—Tastes just brewed
Hearty, full-bodied, full flavor—Watery, thin, empty flavor
Pure, clear taste—Muddy, swampy taste
Raw taste—Roasted taste
Fresh taste—Stale taste
Overall preference
Excellent quality—Very poor quality

Note. Ten blank boxes separated each set of opposing statements. Subjects checked the position which came closest to describing how they felt toward the product.

Intercorrelations among attribute ratings

	1	2	3	4	5	6	7	8	9	10	11	12	13	14
1. Pleasant flavor	1.00	.76	.81	.79	.83	.81	.74	.66	.65	.71	.76	.65	.71	75
2. Sparkling taste		1.00	.78	.85	.77	.87	.83	.65	.70	.78	.85	.69	.74	.83
3. Mellow taste			1.00	.77	.85	.81	.77	.60	.65	.64	.75	.69	.69	.74
4. Expensive taste				1.00	.78	.87	.83	.76	.69	.81	.81	.64	.71	.87
5. Comforting taste					1.00	.82	.77	.66	.60	.69	.82	.69	.69	.74
6. Alive taste						1.00	.88	.70	74	.80	.81	.65	.77	.87
7. Tastes like real coffee							1.00	.67	.76	.75	.79	.62	.76	.87
8. Deep distinct flavor								1.00	.51	.84	.70	.54	.59	.70
9. Tastes just brewed									1.00	.67	.65	.67	.80	.75
10. Hearty flavor										1.00	.83	.65	.72	.76
11. Pure clear taste											1.00	.66	.73	.76
12. Roasted taste												1.00	.78	.61
13. Fresh taste													1.00	.73
14. Overall preference														1.00
Mean rating*	4.5	4.3	4.4	4.6	4.4	4.2	4.2	4.3	4.3	4.2	4.3	4.4	4.6	6.9
Standard deviation	1.6	1.3	1.4	1.4	1.3	1.4	1.6	1.5	1.5	1.5	1.4	1.2	1.4	2.7

*The ten scale categories were assigned successive integers beginning with one at the favorable side of the scale. Thus ratings could vary from one (very "good") to ten (very "bad") on an attribute.

Source: Bishwa Nath Mukherjee, "A Factor Analysis of Some Qualitative Attributes of Coffee," *Journal of Advertising Research*, vol. 5, p. 36, March 1965. Used with permission.

TABLE 19-2 FACTOR LOADINGS

	Principal factor matrix					Rotated (varimax) matrix				Oblique factor matrix			
	I	II	III	IV	h^2	A	B	C	D	A	B	C	D
1.	.86	−.01	−.20	.04	.78	.63	.38	.36	.34	.34	.01	.07	−.03
2.	.91	−.01	−.01	−.09	.83	.48	.43	.53	.38	.14	.04	.23	.04
3.	.86	.11	.28	.002	.83	.70	.26	.38	.36	.36	.13	−.003	−.01
4.	.91	.15	−.001	−.10	.87	.46	.53	.54	.29	.16	−.05	.34	−.07
5.	.87	−.002	−.31	.10	.87	.74	.38	.30	.32	.47	.01	−.004	−.08
6.	.93	.03	−.02	−.16	.90	.49	.43	.59	.35	.12	.07	.30	−.01
7.	.90	−.02	.04	−.21	.86	.42	.38	.64	.37	.03	.11	.33	.04
8.	.77	.36	.11	.16	.77	.31	.74	.27	.22	.24	−.40	.32	−.10
9.	.79	−.28	.24	−.09	.76	.23	.24	.52	.62	−.15	.11	.14	.37
10.	.87	.25	.22	.17	.89	.28	.75	.33	.39	.14	.38	.31	.07
11.	.89	.11	.05	.10	.82	.51	.55	.36	.36	.28	−.15	.17	−.01
12.	.76	−.29	.04	.27	.74	.43	.28	.16	.67	.18	−.08	−.18	.38
13.	.84	−.27	.19	.12	.83	.33	.32	.36	.70	.01	−.03	−.001	.41
14.	.90	.04	.08	−.23	.86	.38	.43	.65	.34	.002	.08	.39	.01
Percent common variance	90.0	4.1	3.3	2.6									
Percent total variance	74.4	3.4	2.7	2.6									

Source: Adapted from Bishwa Nath Mukherjee, "A Factor Analysis of Some Qualitative Attributes of Coffee," *Journal of Advertising Research*, vol. 5, p. 37, March 1965. Used with permission.

like correlation coefficients. The square of the loading equals the proportion of the variation that a variable has in common with an unrotated factor.

Another way to conceptualize this relationship is to remember that a loading is a correlation coefficient between a variable and a factor. In essence, when we square a loading we are calculating a coefficient of determination, r^2, between a variable and a factor. Thus, the squared loading represents the amount of shared variation between a variable and a factor.

The h^2 measures are called *communalities*. Communality is the proportion of a variable's total variation that is involved in the factors. Mathematically h^2 equals the sum of the squared loading of a variable on all factors. For example, for attribute 1:

$$h^2 = (.86)^2 + (-.01)^2 + (-.20)^2 + (0.4)^2 = .78$$

Communality may be interpreted as a measure of uniqueness. By subtracting h^2 from 1.0, the degree to which a variable is unrelated to the others may be calculated. Here we note that 78 percent of the variation in scores on attribute 1 can be predicted from the other variables, leaving 22 percent uniquely related to this attribute.

To get the percentage of total variance in the data explained by the four factors, we simply calculate H, where

$$H = \frac{\text{sum of all } h^2\text{'s}}{\text{number of variables}} \times 100$$

$$= \frac{11.61}{14} \times 100$$

$$= 83\%$$

This value is called the *common variance* explained by the factors.

To calculate the amount of variation in the data accounted for by a factor, we square each loading for a factor, add, and then divide the result by the number of variables. For example, for factor 1 the value is

$$(.86)^2 + (.91)^2 + (.86)^2 + \cdots + (.90)^2 = 10.42$$

This value is called an *eigenvalue* in the vocabulary of factor analysis. Thus, the percentage of total variance explained by factor 1 is $10.42/14 = 74.4$ percent. The percentage of common variance explained by this factor is then $10.42/11.61 = 90$ percent. We note that the percentages of both common variance and total variance are presented in Table 19-2.

In order to obtain an interpretation of the results we examine the rotated factors. Table 19-3 presents one such interpretation. There the factors have been placed with high-loading variables and each given a "creative" name by the author of the study. Note that there is no unique definition of the meaning of any factor; it is up to the creativity of the researcher. Unfortunately, researchers can all too easily fool themselves with wonderful-sounding interpretations. Great care must be taken in this regard.

TABLE 19-3 INTERPRETATION OF FACTORS

Factor A (comforting quality)

Variable	Attribute	Varimax	Oblique
1.	Pleasant flavor	.625	.340
3.	Mellow taste	.698	.359
5.	Comforting taste	.736	.465
11.	Pure clear taste	.512	.283

Factor B (heartiness)

Variable	Attribute	Varimax	Oblique
8.	Deep distinct flavor	.742	.396
10.	Hearty flavor	.745	.380

Factor C (genuineness)

Variable	Attribute	Varimax	Oblique
2.	Sparkling taste	.524	.232
4.	Expensive taste	.541	.334
6.	Alive taste	.594	.301
7.	Tastes like real coffee	.636	.328
8.	Deep distinct flavor	.268	.323
10.	Hearty flavor	.332	.310
14.	Overall preference	.653	.387

Factor D (freshness)

Variable	Attribute	Varimax	Oblique
9.	Tastes just brewed	.621	.359
12.	Roasted taste	.670	.465
13.	Fresh taste	.698	.238

Source: Bishwa Nath Mukherjee. "A Factor Analysis of Some Qualitative Attributes of Coffee." *Journal of Advertising Research,* vol. 5, p. 37, March 1965. Used with permission.

The presentation of factor anaylsis has concentrated on the nature of the input and output. There are many more issues on all aspects of factor analysis not covered here. You should consult a more advanced reference if interested.

CLUSTER ANALYSIS

Factor analysis allows the researcher to study the structure of a set of variables or objects in relation to how their variance is explained by a set of underlying factors. Cluster analysis allows the researcher *to place variables or objects into subgroups or clusters.* These clusters *are not defined a priori* by the researcher but are formed by the cluster analysis procedure itself. In actuality, cluster analysis is a group of ad hoc computational procedures. Their common dimensions are:

1 They form subgroupings and assign variables or objects to these groups.

2 They take as input a matrix of associations between variables or objects; a correlation matrix is an example of one such matrix. There are clustering algorithms available that take nominal, ordinal, interval, or ratio measures in this matrix of associations as input.

3 They assume that natural clusters exist within the data.

The number and diversity of these algorithms make a detailed presentation of cluster analysis procedures impossible in anything except a long book.

We noted that cluster analysis can be applied to either variables or objects (people, products, places, etc.). However, its major application is in the placement of objects into clusters, based upon the values these objects have for a set of variables. Thus, our input matrix will contain the measures of association between objects. This was basically the approach used in Q-type factor analysis. In fact, some researchers consider Q-factor analysis to be a form of cluster analysis.

In general, an object is assigned to a cluster in such a way that it is more associated (as measured by the appropriate measure of association in the input matrix) with the other objects in its cluster than with objects in any other cluster. At a minimum, the computer output of a cluster analysis run identifies the objects of interest by cluster. Sometimes a number of alternative groupings of objects into clusters are presented. These alternative clusters differ in the level of association within the cluster. The researcher then selects the solution for the level of association that seems appropriate. This type of solution is called *hierarchical* because solutions are presented at many different levels of within-cluster association. For example, you may want clusters that have $r = .5$ to .6 for the objects within the clusters. You would then be considering r's of less than .5 to be too weak, and r's over .6 to be too stringent a requirement. Of course, once clusters are formed it is up to the researcher to give them a marketing interpretation. This, like naming factors in factor analysis, is an art and must be done with great care.

Cluster analysis has been used in marketing to do such things as develop consumer segments based upon demographic and psychographic profiles, identify test market cities, determine similar markets in various countries, and find similar groups of magazine readers to aid in media selection.

MULTIDIMENSIONAL SCALING

Overview

Multidimensional scaling encompasses a set of computational procedures that can summarize an input matrix of associations between variables or objects. Generally, its main thrust in marketing has been to examine relationships among objects—usually brands of a particular product group. These techniques take as input a matrix of relationships between objects that have an unknown underlying dimensionality. Then they determine *the minimum dimensionality of the relationships between the objects and the position of each object on each dimension.*

Although multidimensional scaling can be used to analyze virtually any matrix of associations, its fundamental applications in marketing have been to analyze (1) consumer perceptions of the similarity of brands and (2) consumer preferences for brands. In this context, multidimensional scaling is really an extension of the unidimensional attitude scales discussed in Chapter 11 (e.g., semantic differential). Instead of positioning attitudes about brands on unidimensional scales, we can use multidimensional scaling to position brands in an *n*-dimensional space, where *n* is the minimum underlying dimensionality of the relationship. Thus, we can speak of positioning brands and preferences related to brands in a perceptual space.

There are in general three types of multidimensional scaling. These types, which relate to the nature of the input and output data, are as follows:[7]

1 *Fully metric.* These methods require intervally or ratio-scaled input measures and generate a set of relationships among objects that is also interval or ratio.

2 *Fully nonmetric.* These methods take ordinally scaled input measures and generate the rank order of each object on each dimension.

3 *Nonmetric.* These methods take ordinally scaled input measures and generate a set of relationships among the objects that is interval. That is, the distances between objects in the perceptual space have useful meaning. It is nonmetric multidimensional scaling that has obtained the most frequent marketing application.

The mathematics of nonmetric multidimensional scaling are far too complex to discuss here. What follows is an example of this technique in which the nature of the input and output will be discussed.

An Example[8]

Suppose that we wanted to measure consumer perceptions of the similarity of, and their preference for, 11 car models: (1) Ford Taurus, (2) Mercury Sable, (3) Lincoln Continental, (4) Ford Thunderbird, (5) Ford Escort, (6) Cadillac Eldorado, (7) Jaguar XJ Sedan, (8) AMC Alliance, (9) Plymouth Reliant, (10) Buick Le Sabre, and (11) Chevrolet Cavalier.

For similarities we need to obtain from the consumers the rank order of the similarity of all 55 combinations of car models taken two at a time. In general, there are $n(n-1)/2$ rank orders to obtain, where *n* is the number of objects of interest. One way to do this is to put each of the 55 combinations on a separate card. The respondents are then asked to rank-order the cards in terms of the most similar pair to the least similar pair.[9] One consumer's possible ranking of the pairs of models is given in Table 19-4. Here, for example, the consumer considered cars 1 and 2 (Taurus and Sable) to be the eighth most similar pair, and the Lincoln (car 3) and Cadillac (car 6) to be the most

---

[7] Paul E. Green and Frank J. Carmone, *Multidimensional Scaling* (Boston: Allyn & Bacon, 1970), pp. 10–11.

[8] This example is adapted from one presented in Green and Carmone, pp. 23–33. Basically we have updated some of the car names to reflect the 1980s, replacing 1968 car names used in their study.

[9] This task can become difficult as the number of objects increases. A number of other procedures are available, but they are not discussed here.

TABLE 19-4   RANK ORDER OF SIMILARITIES BETWEEN PAIRS OF CAR MODELS

Stimuli	1	2	3	4	5	6	7	8	9	10	11
1	—	8	50	31	12	48	36	2	5	39	10
2		—	38	9	33	37	22	6	4	14	32
3			—	11	55	1	23	46	41	17	52
4				—	44	13	16	19	25	18	42
5					—	54	53	30	28	45	7
6						—	26	47	40	24	51
7							—	29	35	34	49
8								—	3	27	15
9									—	20	21
10										—	43
11											—

The rank number "1" represents the most similar pair.
Source: Paul E. Green and Frank J. Carmone, *Multidimensional Scaling* (Boston: Allyn & Bacon, 1970), p. 34.

similar. Preference data could be collected by asking each consumer to simply rank-order the eleven cars from most preferred to least preferred.

Figure 19-3 illustrates the type of output generated by analyzing the similarities matrix given in Table 19-4. In this case a two-dimensional perceptual space was deemed appropriate to represent the data. We note that the positioning of the car models with respect to each other seems to give us competitive segments. For example, the Taurus, Sable, Alliance, and Reliant are positioned close to each other.

FIGURE 19-3   Perceptual space solution based on data in Table 19-4. *[Adapted from Paul E. Green and Frank J. Carmore, Multidimensional Scaling (Boston: Allyn & Bacon, 1970), p. 34.]*

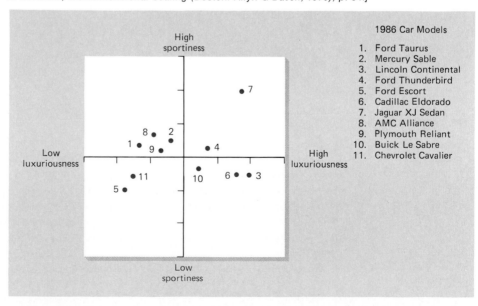

The preference data can be analyzed so that they are positioned within the similarities space in Figure 19-3. Each consumer would be positioned within this space. These positions are referred to as "ideal points." For example, consumer A, who likes big luxury cars, may have an ideal point near Lincoln and Cadillac. When each consumer's ideal point is positioned in the space, we can determine the size of ideal point locations. That is, we may get clusterings of ideal points in particular locations, and this can be used to predict market shares. On Figure 19-3 the two dimensions were labeled "sportiness" and "luxuriousness." These labels, like factor labels in factor analysis, are based upon research judgment.

The questions naturally arise: (1) How do we get interval output from ordered input? (2) How do we determine the required dimensionality? We get interval output because the large number of rank-order pairs in the input matrix puts so many constraints on the positioning of objects that we find an underlying interval relationship. The dimensionality of the space is determined by calculating a goodness-of-fit measure between the input rank order and the output. This measure is called *stress*. Stress gets smaller as the number of dimensions increases. When a rule-of-thumb acceptable level is reached, the dimensionality is determined.

Marketing Applications

There are a number of possible applications of nonmetric multidimensional scaling in marketing. These include:[10]

1 The identification of salient product attributes perceived by buyers in a market
2 The combination of attributes most preferred
3 The products that are viewed as substitutes and those that are differentiated from one another
4 The viable segments that exist in a market
5 Those "holes" in a market that can support a new product venture

The method also appears applicable to problems of product life-cycle analysis, market segmentation, vendor evaluations, advertising evaluation, test marketing, salesperson and store image, brand switching research, and attitude scaling.[11]

Final Comment

This presentation of multidimensional scaling has ignored many computational issues, and it has not discussed the limitations of the technique; this is also true for our discussion of factor analysis and cluster analysis. If interested, you should consult a more advanced source. We must also leave you with a final word of warning. All three techniques discussed in this chapter leave the researcher with major interpretation difficulties after the output is generated, and different computer programs for a technique often yield different results. Great care and skill are required in their application.

[10] James R. Taylor, "Management Experience with Applications of Multidimensional Scaling Methods," unpublished working paper, Marketing Science Institute, Cambridge, Mass., 1970, p. 15.
[11] Green and Carmone, op. cit., pp. 14–19.

SUMMARY

1 Dependence methods designate one or more variables as being predicted by a set of independent variables.

2 Interdependence methods do not designate any variables as being predicted by others. The interest is in the interrelationship among all the variables taken together.

3 Interdependence methods include factor analysis, cluster analysis, and multidimensional scaling.

4 Factor analysis is a procedure that takes a large number of variables or objects and searches to see whether they have a small number of factors in common which account for their intercorrelations.

5 Applications of factor analysis include data reduction, structure identification, scaling, and data transformation.

6 Factor analysis takes a correlation matrix as input. In R-factor analysis these correlations are between variables, and in Q-factor analysis these correlations are between cases or objects.

7 The factor analysis output gives the loading of each variable on each underlying factor. This output may be rotated to give either uncorrelated or correlated factors.

8 Cluster analysis places variables or objects into subgroups or clusters that are defined by the procedure. It is generally used for objects.

9 The cluster analysis input is a matrix of associations between variables or objects. These measures can be for different scale levels depending on the computer procedure.

10 The output of cluster analysis places objects in clusters or a set of alternative clusters at different levels of association.

11 Multidimensional scaling takes a matrix of relationships between objects as input, then determines the underlying dimensionality and places each object on each dimension.

12 Multidimensional scaling is generally used in marketing to measure the perception of brand similarities and preferences.

13 Nonmetric multidimensional scaling takes ordinal input measures and generates a set of relationships among the objects that is interval.

DISCUSSION QUESTIONS

1 Why is multivariate analysis becoming more used in marketing research?
2 Distinguish between dependence and interdependence methods.
3 What is the overall objective of factor analysis?
4 Describe the nature of the input and output of factor analysis.
5 What are R- and Q-type factor analyses?
6 What is the objective of cluster analysis?
7 Describe the nature of the input and output of cluster analysis.
8 What is the objective of multidimensional scaling?
9 What is nonmetric multidimensional scaling?
10 Describe the nature of the input and output of nonmetric multidimensional scaling.
11 How do you name factors, clusters, and dimensions for interdependence methods?

CHAPTER 20

MULTIVARIATE DATA ANALYSIS II: DEPENDENCE METHODS

This chapter is a direct follow-up to the previous one. Here we present an elementary discussion of a number of dependence methods of multivariate analysis. Again the mathematical complexities are omitted, with the emphasis being on the nature of input and output of the procedures. Each of the techniques discussed in this chapter has a number of important statistical assumptions and limitations associated with it. These assumptions and limitations are not included here because of their complexity. Our approach is simply to present a brief overview of each technique. Again, if you are interested in using these techniques, you should consult a technical specialist or a more advanced book. *The techniques are extremely dangerous when used by unskilled people.* Don't just let SPSS-PC run wild.

The specific techniques we will touch on are multiple regression, analysis of variance, analysis of covariance, dummy-variable multiple regression, automatic interaction detector, discriminant analysis, conjoint measurement, canonical correlation, and multivariate analysis of variance.

CLASSIFICATION OF PROCEDURES

The selection of the appropriate dependence procedure depends on (1) the number of variables that have been designated as dependent and (2) the scale levels of the dependent and independent variables. Figure 20-1 presents a flowchart that will guide you to the appropriate procedure. It is based on decision points related to the number of dependent variables designated, and on the scale level of the dependent and independent variables. Find the appropriate technique by following the flow of questions in the

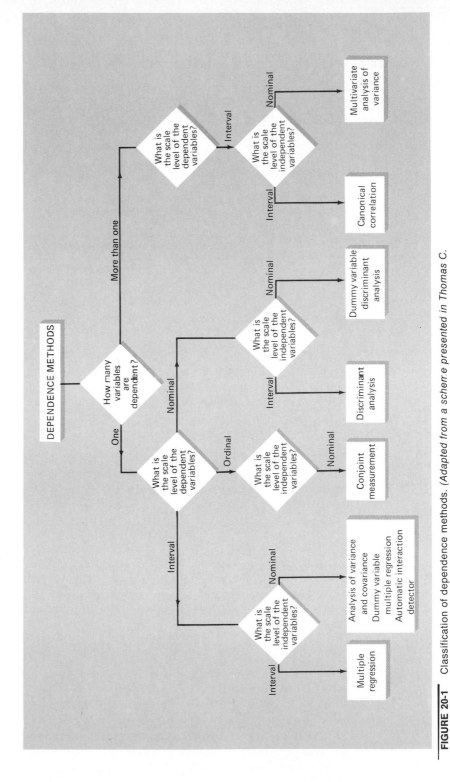

FIGURE 20-1 Classification of dependence methods. *(Adapted from a scheme presented in Thomas C. Kinnear and James R. Taylor, "Multivariate Methods in Marketing Research: A Further Attempt at Classification," Journal of Marketing, vol. 35, pp. 56–59, October 1971.)*

TABLE 20-1 SITUATION WHERE DEPENDENCE METHODS ARE APPROPRIATE

A. One dependent variable

Technique	Dependent variable scale level	Independent variables scale level
1 Multiple regression	Interval	Interval
2 Analysis of variance and covariance	Interval	Nominal
3 Dummy-variable multiple regression	Interval	Nominal
4 Automatic interaction detector	Interval	Nominal
5 Discriminant analysis	Nominal	Interval
6 Dummy-variable discriminant analysis	Nominal	Nominal
7 Conjoint measurement	Ordinal	Nominal

B. More than one dependent variable

Technique	Dependent variables scale level	Independent variables scale level
8 Canonical correlation	Interval	Interval
9 Multivariate analysis of variance	Interval	Nominal

figure. Table 20-1 summarizes the situation where each technique is appropriate. It should be recognized that each technique has some additional statistical assumptions.

The rest of this chapter discusses each of these procedures.

MULTIPLE REGRESSION

Multiple regression is a straightforward extension of simple regression as discussed in Chapter 18. The difference is that in multiple regression the analysis is done with *more than one independent variable*. The predictive equation for a two-independent variable situation would be

$$\hat{Y}_i = a + b_1 X_1 + b_2 X_2$$

where X_1 and X_2 are the independent variables and a, b_1, and b_2 are the regression coefficients generated from our sample data. Again, we recognize that these coefficients are statistics that estimate the population parameters of the regression. We can easily generalize the equation to m independent variables. Here

$$\hat{Y}_i = a + b_1 X_1 + b_2 X_2 + \cdots + b_m X_m$$

The formulas for the coefficients are too complex to present, even for a two-independent-variable situation.

Multiple regression requires that both the dependent and independent variables be intervally scaled. Also, it assumes that the underlying relationship is linear, although data transformations can overcome this latter problem. Finally, our sample size must be large enough to give many observations per independent variable. The more independent variables, the larger should be the sample size.

The total variation in the dependent variable may be partitioned in exactly the same fashion as with simple regression. Specifically,

$$SS_{\text{total}} = SS_{\text{explained}} + SS_{\text{unexplained}}$$
$$\sum (Y_i - \bar{Y})^2 \quad \sum (\hat{Y}_i - \bar{Y}_i)^2 \quad \sum (Y_i - \hat{Y}_i)^2$$

We can convert these SS to variances by dividing them by the appropriate degrees of freedom. We could then compare the explained variance with the error variance to see whether the regression as a whole has explained a significant amount of the variance in Y. We would use an F test, a detailed description of which is presented in the appendix to this chapter. (The use of the F test for simple regression was discussed in the appendix to Chapter 18.)

The only difference in doing this in multiple regression as opposed to simple regression is that the degrees of freedom are different. Each independent variable requires one degree of freedom. Thus, with $n - 1$ degrees of freedom in the whole sample, the error degrees of freedom will be $n - 1 - m$, where m is the number of independent variables. The number of explained degrees of freedom is simply m. We may also calculate the standard error and thus the significance of each regression coefficient. Here we use a t test. In simple regression an F test on SS and a t test on the coefficient yielded identical results; in multiple regression the F test tells us whether the regression as a whole is significant, and the t tests tell us which coefficients are statistically significantly different from zero.

An Example

An example should help clarify the nature of results generated by a multiple regression program. Table 20-2 presents regression results for the following situation: (1) The

TABLE 20-2   REGRESSION RESULTS

Source	SS	Df	Mean square	F
Regression	15,552	2	7,776	162
Error	574	12	48	
Total	16,126	14		

Variable	Coefficient	Standard error	t statistic
Constant	−1305.2		
Income	2.3	.13	18.03
Family size	−2620.8	1320.6	−1.98

Multiple R = .98205   Multiple R^2 = .96441

Source: Adapted from an example prepared by Prof. William Wrobleski, the University of Michigan.

dependent variable is the dollar amount of life insurance owned, (2) the independent variables are income and family size, and (3) the sample size is 15.

We see that with two independent variables the regression degrees of freedom equals 2, and within 15 cases the error degrees of freedom is $n - 1 - m = 15 - 1 - 2 = 12$. The calculated F is 162. The critical F at $\alpha = .01$ and 2 and 12 degrees of freedom is 6.93 (see Table A-5 of Appendix A). The regression clearly explains a significant amount of the variation in Y. Similarly, the critical t value for the coefficients at $\alpha = .01$ and 12 degrees of freedom is 3.055. Thus we can reject the null hypothesis that the income coefficient is zero, while we cannot do so for the family size coefficient. Note that if we had set $\alpha = .1$, the critical t would be 1.782, and we would have concluded that the family size coefficient is significant.

The *size* and *direction* of the coefficients also have meaning. In general, a positive coefficient indicates a direct relationship between that independent variable and the dependent variable. A negative coefficient indicates an inverse relationship. The size of the coefficient indicates the amount of change in the dependent variable associated with a one-unit increase in that independent variable, given that all other independent variables remain constant. In our example, the amount of life insurance will increase by $2.30 for every $1.00 increase in income, given that family size is held constant.

The computer is also likely to generate the *multiple correlation coefficient, R.* This is the correlation coefficient between the observed Y_i and the estimated $\hat{Y}_i$'s. The closer the regression equation predictions are to the actual observations, the higher will be R. We may also calculate the *coefficient of multiple determination,* which is R^2. It is the proportion of the variation in Y explained by the regression. Alternatively, the coefficient of multiple determination may be obtained by taking the ratio $SS_{explained}$ over SS_{total}. In our example,

$$R^2 = \frac{15,552}{16,126} = .96441$$

The type of regression in our example is called *total regression;* with this type, all the independent variables are entered into the regression equation in one step. An alternative type is called *stepwise regression;* here the independent variables enter the regression equation one at a time. The variable selected to enter first is the one that explains the most variation in Y. The next variable to enter is the one that explains the greatest amount of the variation in Y after the effect of the first variable has been removed. This process continues until no significant variation remains or no variable is left that explains a significant amount of the variation.

Another point about the regression coefficients is important: The size of the coefficient does not provide a measure of its importance in the regression. In the case being studied, the smaller coefficient is the better one because the independent variables are measured in different units (people and dollars). It is possible to take the effects of units used out of the regression. We do this by means of the same principle with which we obtained unit-free measures in correlation calculations. That is, we divide the observed values' deviations from the mean by their standard deviation. We define x° and y° as measures of X and Y that have the units removed. In formula,

$$x^\circ = \frac{X - \bar{X}}{s} \quad \text{and} \quad y^\circ = \frac{Y - \bar{Y}}{s}$$

This expresses values of X and Y as a number of standard deviations. We can then directly compare regression coefficients to see their relative importance.

The applications of multiple regression in marketing are the same as for simple regression, except that the use of more independent variables allows one to specify the relationship more precisely.

ANALYSIS OF VARIANCE

Analysis of variance (ANOVA) is a statistical procedure most used in the analysis of experimental data. It requires an intervally scaled dependent variable and a nominally scaled independent variable or variables. The details of ANOVA are important but also complex. Thus it is discussed in the appendix at the end of this chapter.

ANALYSIS OF COVARIANCE

Analysis of covariance (ANCOVA) is appropriate in experimental situations where it is discovered after the experiment that some extraneous source of variation is contributing to the values of the dependent variable. For example, we may discover that store size has contributed to sales in an experiment we ran to test the effect of alternative coupon plans; that is, large stores automatically sell more than small stores.

A detailed example of ANCOVA would take too much space. What follows here, then, is a conceptual overview of how ANCOVA works. To use ANCOVA we must have an intervally scaled dependent variable and nominally scaled independent variables, and the variables to be controlled must be measured at an interval level. These latter variables are called *covariates*. ANCOVA essentially undertakes the following:

1 A regression is run with the covariates as independent variables (e.g., store size) and the dependent variable from the experiment as the dependent variable (sales).

2 The regression estimates, the $\hat{Y}_i$'s, are calculated for each covariate observation.

3 The estimated $\hat{Y}_i$'s are subtracted from the observed experimental data Y_i; the result of this is a set of experimental data that has the effect of the covariates removed; we define $Y_i' = Y_i - \hat{Y}_i$, where Y_i' is a covariate-free observation.

4 ANOVA is then undertaken on the Y_i''s in a regular fashion.

In doing this, be careful to keep the degrees of freedom straight. Since we are using regression, each covariate uses one degree of freedom. Thus if we have k covariates, the total degrees of freedom left to do the ANOVA is $n - 1 - k$. From this adjusted number of degrees of freedom, the treatment and error degrees of freedom for ANOVA are calculated in the usual manner; if we had two covariates, one treatment with four categories, and 50 test units, the total degrees of freedom for ANOVA would be $50 - 1 - 2 = 47$. The treatment degrees of freedom would be $t - 1 = 4 - 1 = 3$, and the error would be $47 - 3 = 44$. (See the appendix to this chapter for details.)

DUMMY-VARIABLE MULTIPLE REGRESSION

The use of regression in marketing research could be severely hampered by the fact that the independent variables must be intervally scaled. Fortunately there is a way to use nominal independent variables in a regression context. The procedure that we use is called *dummy-variable multiple regression* (DVMR). Basically, DVMR converts nominal variables into a series of binary variables that are coded 0-1. For example, suppose we wish to use the nominal variable "sex" in a regression. We could code it as follows:

Category	Code
Male	0
Female	1

The interval 0 to 1 is equal and thus acceptable to regression. Note that we have converted a two-category nominal variable into one 0-1 variable. We may extend this approach to a multicategory nominal variable. The four-category nominal variable "region of the country" could be converted to three dummy variables, X_1, X_2, and X_3 as follows:

Category	X_1	X_2	X_3
East	1	0	0
West	0	1	0
North	0	0	1
South	0	0	0

This four-category nominal variable is now converted to three 0-1 variables. In general, a k-category nominal variable converts to $k - 1$ dummy variables, because once we know whether the first $k - 1$ categories are 0 or 1, the kth category is automatically determined as 0 or 1. To create a kth dummy variable would be redundant, and in fact it would invalidate the whole regression. The choice of the category that will have all zeros is arbitrary.

To illustrate DVMR, suppose that sales of Japanese cars represents the dependent variable. The regression equation might be:

$$\hat{Y}_i = 250{,}000 + 50{,}000X_1 + 80{,}000X_2 - 6{,}000X_3$$

Note that only one of either X_1, X_2, or X_3 will take on the value 1 for any one subject, and the other two X's will be zero. The coefficients provide a measure of the effect of being from a particular region. The equations by region are:

$$\text{East:} \quad \hat{Y}_i = 250{,}000 + 50{,}000(1) = 300{,}000$$
$$\text{West:} \quad \hat{Y}_i = 250{,}000 + 80{,}000(1) = 330{,}000$$
$$\text{North:} \quad \hat{Y}_i = 250{,}000 - 6{,}000(1) = 244{,}000$$
$$\text{South:} \quad \hat{Y}_i = 250{,}000$$

We can have as many dummy variables as we need in a regression, subject to the constraint that each dummy variable uses a degree of freedom. Thus, we must have an adequate sample size.

There is a special computational version of DVMR called *multiple classification analysis* (MCA) that has attained significant marketing application. The specific nature of this procedure, however, lies beyond the scope of this book.[1]

AUTOMATIC INTERACTION DETECTOR

The *automatic interaction detector* (AID) is another technique that is used with an interval dependent variable and a set of nominal independent variables. Its basic objective is to break down a total sample into a number of subgroups that are more homogeneous on the dependent variable than the sample as a whole. It does this by the repeated application of one-way ANOVA. Specifically, AID does the following:

1 It calculates the explained SS ($SS_{\text{between}}/SS_{\text{total}}$) on the dependent variable for each combination of categories for the independent variables.

2 It splits the sample into two groups based on the categories of that independent variable that explain the most SS.

3 It then repeats steps 1 and 2 for the two new groups, then splits these groups, and so on.

AID is primarily used in marketing to help identify market segments and to identify variables that seem to be importantly related to the dependent variable. These variables could then be used in a DVMR analysis.

Figure 20-2 illustrates AID output.[2] This output is called an *AID tree*. The top number in each box is the sample size for that group. The lower number is the probability of a subject purchasing a nonphosphate detergent. Here the dependent variable is the likelihood of someone using a nonphosphate detergent, and the independent variables are a set of attitude measures. Group 1 is the whole sample size of 1499. Note that:

> The overall probability of a subject drawn at random from the sample using a nonphosphate laundry product was .37 (group 1's mean probability). We note that the subgroup that stated an extreme self-interest in the pollution aspects of products and who were willing to accept a moderately or more or less clean wash (group 5) had a mean probability of purchasing a nonphosphate product of .75. At the other extreme, we note that those who stated that they were less than extremely interested, and who perceived consumers to be less than very highly effective against pollution, and who thought that urging one's friends to purchase nonpollution products was not a good idea, and who were not willing to accept clothes that were any less clean (group 12), had a mean probability of purchase of .06.[3]

---

[1] If interested, see Frank M. Andrews, James N. Morgan, and John A. Sonquist, *Multiple Classification Analysis* (Ann Arbor: Institute for Social Research, The University of Michigan, 1967).
[2] This example is adapted from Thomas C. Kinnear and James R. Taylor, "Identifying Ecological Buying Segments through Attitude Measurement," *Journal of Business Administration*, vol. 5, pp. 33–43, Spring 1974.
[3] Ibid., p. 49.

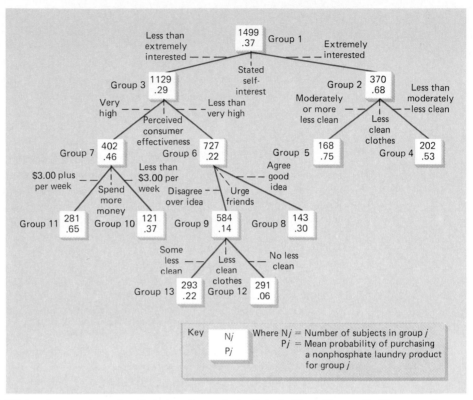

FIGURE 20-2 AID tree for use of nonphosphate laundry products. *(Adapted from Thomas C. Kinnear and James R. Taylor, "Identifying Ecological Buying Segments through Attitude Measurement," Journal of Business Administration, vol. 5, p. 41, Spring 1974.)*

The major constraint for use of AID is that a large sample size (1000 plus) is needed; otherwise the subgroups become too small too soon.

DISCRIMINANT ANALYSIS

Discriminant analysis (DA) is a technique that is appropriate with a nominal dependent variable and interval independent variables. Nominal dependent variables are very common in marketing; for example, good versus bad credit risks, brand-loyal versus nonloyal consumers, different brand users, and successful versus unsuccessful salespersons. As a result of this, DA has received extensive application in marketing research.

The basic idea of DA is to find a linear combination of the independent variables that makes the mean scores across categories of the dependent variable on this linear combination maximally different. This linear combination is called the *discriminant function* (DF). In symbols,

$$DF = v_1X_1 + v_2X_2 + \cdots + v_mX_m$$

TABLE 20-3   CONFUSION MATRIX FOR CREDIT RISKS

Actual category	Predicted category	
	Good	Bad
Good	800	40
Bad	60	100

where X_m is the mth independent variable. The objective is to find the values for the v's that give us the required DF. The criterion used to decide when group means are maximally different is the familiar ANOVA F test for the differences among means. Thus, the v's are derived such that

$$F = \frac{SS_{\text{between}}}{SS_{\text{within}}}$$

is maximized.

The output of DA usually includes the values of the v's, plus what is called a *confusion matrix.* This matrix compares the category of the dependent variable that the discriminant function predicts a subject will be in with the category that the subject is actually in. Table 20-3 presents a confusion matrix for good and bad credit risks based upon a set of demographic independent variables (e.g., age, income, years in same house, etc.). Note that it is the elements on the diagonal running from top left to bottom right that give those subjects that are correctly classified by the DA. Ninety percent of subjects in this example are correctly classified. This example is for a two-category dependent variable (often called two-group). It can easily be extended to a k-group dependent variable.

The constraint of having to have interval independent variables is really no problem. As we did with regression, we can convert nominal independent variables to dummy variables in order to yield dummy-variable discriminant analysis (DVDA).

CONJOINT MEASUREMENT

A set of procedures that has attracted much attention in marketing research is *conjoint measurement* (CM), or *conjoint analysis.* CM is concerned with the joint effects of two or more nominal independent variables on the ordering of a dependent variable. Thus, CM is appropriate for nominal independent variables and an ordinal dependent variable. It is in essence an analysis of variance of rank-order data. The benefit of CM is that it generates interval-level measures of the effects of the categories of the independent variables.

Its primary marketing application has been to measure the trade-offs that consumers make on product attributes, as the following example shows. Suppose we are concerned with the attributes of an airplane and that (for simplicity) only two attributes are noteworthy—price and cruising speed. Table 20-4 presents an input matrix to CM for the

TABLE 20-4   RANK-ORDER JOINT-EFFECT INPUT MATRIX

Cruising speed, mph	Price levels		
	$400,000	**$600,000**	**$800,000**
300	7	8	9
400	3	4	6
500	1	2	5

two attributes for one individual. Three different prices and cruising speeds are given. The entries in the matrix are the rank order of the preferences for the attribute combinations for one consumer. You can follow the trade-offs this consumer will make by following the rank order.

We shall illustrate the nature of CM by discussing how an additive version of CM could utilize the input data from Table 20-4. The basic idea is that CM develops measures of the effect of each level of each attribute such that the additive combination of these effects optimally maintains the rank order of the input preferences. Table 20-5 gives a possible result of a CM analysis of Table 20-4. Here the interval-level effects are given in parentheses. The numbers in the matrix are the various sums of the effect combinations. For example, the combination of 300 mph and $400,000 is valued at .20 + .52 = .72. Note that the interval values in the matrix perfectly maintain the input rank order. This is not always possible, but CM finds the effect measures that achieve it best.

The effect measures may be interpreted as the utility the consumer places on a particular attribute. The number of independent variables can easily be extended to more than two. Thus we can realistically use this technique to measure the total utility a consumer places on various possible attribute combinations for a product. If we did this for a sample of consumers, we could use CM to predict market share, profitability, etc., of a product offering various attribute combinations.[4] The Marketing Research in Action in this section shows AT&T's use of conjoint measurement in the data communications terminal market.

[4]For a discussion of this and other possible applications, see Paul E. Green and Vithala R. Rao, "Conjoint Measurement for Quantifying Judgmental Data," *Journal of Marketing Research*, vol. 8, pp. 355–363, August 1971.

TABLE 20-5   INTERVALLY SCALED EFFECT MEASURES FOR ATTRIBUTE LEVELS

Cruising speed, mph	Price levels		
	$400,000 (.52)	**$600,000 (.45)**	**$800,000 (.30)**
300 (.20)	.72	.65	.50
400 (.61)	1.13	1.06	.91
500 (.75)	1.27	1.20	1.05

MARKETING RESEARCH IN ACTION

AT&T USES CONJOINT ANALYSIS

Conjoint analysis, coupled with attitude research, was a major influence in AT&T's decision to enter the data communications terminal market. These techniques even allowed AT&T to predict what their market share would be 4 years down the road.

According to Rochelle L. Benbenisty, research manager at AT&T, Parsipany, New Jersey, the primary objectives of AT&T's data terminal research were to discover the key product attributes, determine the total market share, and come up with an estimate for AT&T's potential market.

First, AT&T did a virtual survey of all firms that used a significant number of data communication terminals. From these interviews, attribute performance and purchase intent were determined. Second, AT&T selected a probability sample of U.S. firms having 100 or more employees. Interviews were then conducted with those persons having influence over the data terminal purchase decision.

To facilitate data collection and analysis, marketing personnel reduced the 140 product attributes identified in the first survey down to 16. Respondents from the probability sample were presented with a table and asked which attribute pair corresponded to their first choice, their second choice, and so on. This would determine the trade-offs potential buyers were willing to make on each attribute. An individual respondent was asked to rate only 24 of the possible 120 pairs of attributes.

Conjoint analysis was then used to determine the relative utility scores of the 16 attributes. These utility scores were considered along with the total market demand, estimated from the first survey, to get an expected AT&T market share.

A simulation model designed to maximize share was used. Competitive products and AT&T's proposed product were entered into the model in terms of the 16 product attributes used in the interviews. The model compared the actual products' benefits with the consumers' wants in order to help determine future market shares.

The first result (4.7 percent market share, $114/month rental fee), proved too low to be profitable. So AT&T identified four possible product changes which might improve their projected share. When these modifications were run on the simulator, AT&T found that a $150/month rental price would be optimal, and that market share would be 8 percent in four years after introduction.

Benbenisty said, "We waited and waited and counted and counted to see how well our predictions had done. Believe it or not, the simulator's estimate of the [AT&T] share was achieved and demand reached a level just under 8 percent by the fourth year.

"This is but one way attitude research can be used in making marketing decisions. Through the conjoint analysis approach, you can identify how respondent attitudes on a myriad of variables interact and lead to buyer preferences and purchase decisions."

Based on *Marketing News*, vol. 17, no. 10, sec. 1, p. 12, May 13, 1983.

CANONICAL CORRELATION

Canonical correlation (CC) is a technique that is occasionally used in marketing research. It is appropriate when you have both a set of intervally scaled dependent and independent variables. For example, an organization might want to know how a set of attitude measures relates to a set of behaviors. Basically, CC forms one linear combination of the dependent variables and one of the independent variables. It finds the values of the coefficients of these combinations that yield the maximum correlation between the combinations.

MULTIVARIATE ANALYSIS OF VARIANCE

Multivariate analysis of variance (MANOVA) is appropriate when you have two or more intervally scaled dependent variables and one or more nominally scaled independent variables. A straightforward extension of ANOVA, it is used when the researcher wishes to test the effects of the independent variables on a series of dependent variables. For example, sales and attitude measures may be deemed appropriate dependent variables in an experiment. MANOVA allows you to judge whether the treatments were significant on the set of dependent variables as a group, and in addition it gives an ordinary ANOVA on each one individually.

SUMMARY

1 The choice of dependence method depends on the number of variables that have been designated as dependent and on the scale level of the dependent and independent variables.

2 Multiple regression is used with one intervally scaled dependent variable and a set of intervally scaled independent variables.

3 Analysis of variance, dummy-variable multiple regression, and the automatic interaction detector are used with one intervally scaled dependent variable and a set of nominally scaled independent variables.

4 Discriminant analysis is used with one nominally scaled dependent variable and a set of intervally scaled independent variables.

5 Dummy-variable discriminant analysis is used with one nominally scaled dependent variable and a set of nominally scaled independent variables.

6 Conjoint measurement is used with one ordinally scaled dependent variable and a set of nominally scaled independent variables.

7 Canonical correlation is used with a set of intervally scaled dependent variables and a set of intervally scaled independent variables.

8 Multivariate analysis of variance is used with a set of intervally scaled dependent variables and a set of nominally scaled independent variables.

9 All the techniques discussed in this chapter are very complex, and in most cases a marketing research generalist would consult with a technical specialist when using them.

DISCUSSION QUESTIONS

1 How are dependence methods classified?

2 What is the coefficient of multiple determination? How is it calculated from a regression printout?

3 What does a coefficient mean in multiple regression?

4 How does ANCOVA work?

5 How are nominal independent variables handled in a regression?

6 How is AID related to ANOVA?

7 What is a discriminant function? What criterion is used to derive its coefficients?

8 How could conjoint measurements be used to predict market share?

APPENDIX: Analysis of Variance

STATISTICAL ANALYSIS OF EXPERIMENTS

We are now ready to develop an understanding of the ANOVA procedure. ANOVA is a method of analysis that applies when the researcher is dealing with *one intervally scaled dependent variable and one or more nominally scaled independent variables.*[1] ANOVA is related to a number of other data analysis procedures that were discussed in Chapter 20. An understanding of the basics of ANOVA will add greatly to our understanding of these other techniques. The procedures discussed here can be applied to any of the designs presented in Chapter 12; what we are adding now is the flesh that goes with the bones given in Chapter 12. Again, all that the statistics allow us to do is to identify when an effect is greater than we could expect by chance.

There are actually three different ANOVA procedures.[2] They are:

Model I: Fixed Effects   In this model the researcher makes inferences only about differences among the *j* treatments actually administered, and about no other treatment that might have been included. In other words, no interpolation between treatments is made. For example, if the treatments were high, medium, and low advertising expenditures, no inferences are drawn about advertising expenditures between these points.

Model II: Random Effects   In the second model, the researcher assumes that only a random sample of the treatments about which one wants to make inferences has been used. Here, one would be prepared to interpolate results between treatments.

Model III: Mixed Effects   In the third model, the researcher has independent variables that are both fixed and random types.

The major differences among these models relate to the formulas used to calculate sampling error and to some data assumptions. We shall only show the calculations for the fixed effects model, since the basic approach and the principles to be established are the same for the other models.[3] Also, in marketing research most experiments fit the fixed effects model, as the experiments usually include all treatments which are important in relation to the decision to be made.

In applying the fixed effects model the researcher makes assumptions about the data. Specifically:[4]

1 For each treatment population *j*, the experimental errors are independent and normally distributed about a mean of zero with an identical variance.
2 The sum of all treatment effects is zero.
3 In the calculations presented here, each treatment group has the same number of observations. This assumption is not generally necessary, but it makes the calculations easier.

In experimentation, the null hypothesis is that *the treatment effects, and any interaction effects that might apply, equal zero.* If τ_j represents the effect of treatment *j*, we can write the

---

[1] There are statistical techniques that can be applied to ordinal dependent variables in experimentation. These techniques are more advanced than the approach taken in this book, and so they are not addressed here.
[2] This section draws on William L. Hayes, *Statistics* (New York: Holt, 1963), pp. 356–358 and 439.
[3] If interested, consult a more advanced book; for example, see ibid., pp. 356–457.
[4] Ibid., pp. 364–365.

null hypothesis as

$$\tau_1 = \tau_2 \cdots = \tau_j = 0$$

or
$$\tau_j = 0 \quad (j = 1, 2, \ldots, j)$$

where j = a specific treatment. The alternative hypothesis is that

$$\tau_j > 0 \quad (j = 1, 2, \ldots, j)$$

If the treatments have had no effect, we would expect the scores on the dependent variable to be the same in each group. Thus, the mean values would be the same in each group. So our null hypothesis is equivalent to the statement that

$$\mu_1 = \mu_2 \cdots = \mu_j = \mu$$

where $1, 2, \ldots, j$ represent treatment groups, and μ represents the whole population mean without regard to groups. ANOVA is the hypothesis-testing procedure used in experimentation. It is essentially a procedure for simultaneously testing for the equality of two or more means.

Completely Randomized Design (CRD)

ANOVA applied to a CRD is called "one-way" ANOVA because it is being applied to categories of one independent variable. Table A20-1 presents results generated by a CRD. The measures on the dependent variable, Y, are taken on the test units. Here there are four test units in each of three treatments. We have $4 \times 3 = 12$ test units. The units are stores in the relevant geographic region where each of three coupon plans was applied. The dependent variable is the number of cases of cola sold the day after the different coupons were run in the local papers. The treatments are the three categories of the independent variable, T.

T_1 Coupon plan 1
T_2 Coupon plan 2
T_3 Coupon plan 3

So we have 3 treatments, 12 test units, and an interval-dependent variable measure on each test unit.

In Table A20-1, we define the mean of each treatment group as

$$\bar{Y}_{.j} = M_{.j} = \frac{\Sigma Y_{.j}}{n}$$

The use of the period (.) in front of the j implies that we are calculating the mean by adding all i's in the jth treatment group. Note also that $\Sigma Y_{i.}$ would indicate the sum of all j's for a given i, and $\Sigma Y_{..}$ would indicate the sum of all i's and all j's. In our example,

$$\bar{Y}_{.1} = M_{.1} = \frac{64}{4} = 16$$

$$\bar{Y}_{.2} = M_{.2} = \frac{52}{4} = 13$$

$$\bar{Y}_{.3} = M_{.3} = \frac{36}{4} = 9$$

TABLE A20-1   COMPLETELY RANDOMIZED DESIGN WITH THREE TREATMENTS (Coupon Plans)

	Treatments (j)		
	Coupon plan 1	**Coupon plan 2**	**Coupon plan 3**
Test units (i)	20	17	14
	18	14	10
	15	13	7
	11	8	5
Treatment totals	$\Sigma Y_{.1} = 64$	$\Sigma Y_{.2} = 52$	$\Sigma Y_{.3} = 36$
Treatment means	$\overline{Y}_{.1} = M_1$ $= \Sigma Y_{.1}/n_1$ $= 64/4 = 16$	$\overline{Y}_{.2} = M_2$ $= \Sigma Y_{.2}/n_2$ $= 52/4 = 13$	$\overline{Y}_{.3} = M_3$ $= \Sigma Y_{.3}/n_3$ $= 36/4 = 9$
		Grand total	$\Sigma Y_{..} = 64 + 52 + 36 = 152$
		Grand mean	$\overline{Y}_{..} = M = \Sigma Y_{..}/n_1 + n_2 + n_3)$ $= 152/12 = 12.7$

Note: $n_1 = n_2 = n_3 = n_j = 4$.

We also define the *grand mean* of all observations across all treatment groups as $\overline{Y}..$ or M. Here

$$M = \frac{64 + 52 + 36}{12} = 12.7$$

These various means will be used in order to understand the meaning of ANOVA. In an experimental context, we want to determine whether the treatments have had an effect on the dependent variable. (By "effect" we mean a functional relationship between the treatment T_j and the dependent variable Y.) That is, do different treatments give systematically different scores on the dependent variable? For example, in our coupon plan situation, if the plans have had differing effects on sales, we would expect the amount of sales in the stores in treatment T_1 to differ systematically from T_2 and T_3. If in fact they do, the mean of each treatment group would also differ. In ANOVA an effect is defined as *a difference in treatment means from the grand mean*. What we are doing in ANOVA is determining whether differences in treatment means are large enough to have occurred other than just by chance.

Some Notation and Definitions   Let Y_{ij} be the score of the ith test unit on the jth treatment. For example, in Table A20-1,

$$Y_{11} = 20, \qquad Y_{42} = 8, \text{ etc.}$$

We define any individual test unit's scores as equal to

$$Y_{ij} = \text{grand mean} + \text{treatment effect} + \text{error}$$

or

$$Y_{ij} = \mu + \tau_j + \epsilon_{ij}$$

This is a simple linear, additive model with values specified in terms of population parameters. Since we are going to be using sample results to make our inferences, we can rewrite this model as

$$Y_{ij} = M + T_j + E_{ij} \tag{A20-1}$$

where M = the grand mean
   T_j = the effect of the jth treatment
   E_{ij} = the statistical error of the ith test unit in the jth treatment

In this model the treatment effect is defined as the difference between the treatment mean and the grand mean:

$$T_j = M_{.j} - M$$

The reason we use M as the base from which to compare the various M_j's is that even if we did not know from which treatment a test unit came, we could still guess the grand mean as their score on the dependent variable. Knowledge of treatment group memberships improves our ability to predict scores as an improvement over M.

The error for an individual unit, E_{ij}, is estimated by the difference between an individual score and the treatment group mean to which the score belongs.

$$E_{ij} = Y_{ij} - M_{.j}$$

It is a measure of the difference in scores that occur which are not explained by treatments. This is the measure of sampling error in the experiment. It is also called experimental error. For example, if all scores within a treatment are close together, the individual scores will be close to the treatment mean and the error will be small, and vice versa. This deviation is a measure of the random variation within each treatment in an experiment.

We can rewrite Equation A20-1 as

$$
\begin{array}{ccccccc}
Y_{ij} & = & M & + (M_{.j} - M) & + (Y_{ij} - M_{.j}) \\
\downarrow & & \downarrow & \downarrow & \downarrow \\
\text{Individual} & = & \text{grand} & + \text{treatment} & + \text{error} \\
\text{score} & & \text{mean} & \text{effect} &
\end{array}
\tag{A20-2}
$$

Alternatively, we can write any observation as a deviation from the grand mean. We do this by moving M to the left side of Equation A20-2:

$$
\begin{array}{ccccc}
(Y_{ij} - M) & = & (M_{.j} - M) & + & (Y_{ij} - M_{.j}) \\
\downarrow & & \downarrow & & \downarrow \\
\text{Individual score} & & \text{deviation of group} & & \text{individual score} \\
\text{deviation from} & = & \text{mean from grand} & + & \text{deviation from} \\
\text{grand mean} & & \text{mean, i.e., treatment} & & \text{group mean, i.e.,} \\
& & \text{effect} & & \text{error}
\end{array}
\tag{A20-3}
$$

Partitioning the Sum of Squares   The idea of ANOVA is built around the concept of the sum of squared deviations from the grand mean and from group means. We partition the total sum of squares into components. Begin by squaring the deviation from the grand mean, M, for each score in the sample and then sum these squared deviations across all test units, i, in all groups, j. Do this by squaring Equation A20-3 for all individuals in all groups, which becomes

$$\sum_{i=1}^{n} \sum_{j=1}^{t} (Y_{ij} - M)^2 = \sum_{i=1}^{n} \sum_{j=1}^{t} [(M_{.j} - M) + (Y_{ij} - M_{.j})]^2 \qquad \text{(A20-4)}$$

All the $\sum_{i=1}^{n}$ means is that we are adding across all individuals in a treatment and all $\sum_{j=1}^{t}$ means is that we are doing this for all treatments. Equation A20-4 expanded becomes

$$\sum_{i=1}^{n} \sum_{j=1}^{t} (Y_{ij} - M)^2 = \sum_{i=1}^{n} \sum_{j=1}^{t} (M_{.j} - M)^2 + \sum_{i=1}^{n} \sum_{j=1}^{t} (Y_{ij} - M_{.j})^2$$
$$+ 2 \sum_{i=1}^{n} \sum_{j=1}^{t} (M_{.j} - M)(Y_{ij} - M_{.j}) \qquad \text{(A20-5)}$$

This is simply squaring an equation of the form

$$A = B + C$$

to get

$$A^2 = B^2 + C^2 + 2BC$$

The sum of deviations about any mean equals zero.[5] Therefore the

$$2 \sum_{i=1}^{n} \sum_{j=1}^{t} (M_{.j} - M)(Y_{ij} - M_{.j})$$

part of Equation A20-5 is zero, as

$$\sum_{i=1}^{n} (Y_{ij} - M_{.j}) = 0$$

and

$$\sum_{j=1}^{t} (M_{.j} - M) = 0$$

Also note that

$$\sum_{i=1}^{n} \sum_{j=1}^{t} (M_{.j} - M)^2 = \sum_{j=1}^{t} n_j (M_{.j} - M)^2$$

where n_j is the number of subjects in group j. This is so because $M_{.j} - M$ is a constant (as we are dealing with means only) for each individual i in a particular group j. We can then multiply this constant by the number in the group to yield an equivalent number. Equation A20-5 then

---

[5] This basic finding of statistics is easily illustrated. $10 + 5 + 15 = 30$ and the mean is $30/3 = 10$. The sum of deviations $= (10 - 10) + (5 - 10) + (15 - 10) = 0 + (-5) + 5 = 0$.

becomes

$$\sum_{i=1}^{n} \sum_{j=1}^{t} (Y_{ij} - M)^2 = \sum_{j=1}^{t} n_j(M_{.j} - M)^2 + \sum_{i=1}^{n} \sum_{j=1}^{t} (Y_{ij} - M_{.j})^2 \qquad \text{(A20-6)}$$

↓	↓	↓
Total sum of squared deviations from the grand mean	= weighted sum of squared deviations of group means from grand mean	+ sum of squared deviations within groups
↓	↓	↓
Total sum of squares (SS_T)	= sum of squares between groups	+ sum of squares within groups
	↓	↓
	treatment effect sum of squares + (SS_{TR})	error sum of squares (SS_E)

What we have done is divide the total sum of squares into two components. These components are the sum of squares *within* groups and the sum of squares *between* groups. These are measures of variation. If the treatments have had no effect, the scores in all treatment groups should be similar. If this were so, the variance of the sample calculated using all test unit scores, without regard to treatment groups, would equal the variance calculated within treatment groups. That is, the *between*-group variance would equal the *within*-group variance. If the treatments *have* had an effect, however, the scores within groups would be more similar than scores selected from the whole sample at random. Thus, the variance taken within groups would be smaller than the variance between groups. Therefore, we could compare the variance between groups with the variance within groups as a way of measuring for the presence of an effect. This is exactly what is done.

But how do we get variance from the sum-of-squares terms we have in Equation A20-6? Since variance equals SS/df, all we need to do is divide each component of Equation A20-6 by its appropriate df, and we will have the necessary variance terms. To obtain the required degrees of freedom we apply the rule we learned in Chapter 8. For the sample as a whole we used up one degree of freedom to calculate the grand mean; therefore, the relevant number of degrees of freedom for the SS_T is the total number of test units minus one. For the SS_{TR} the number of degrees of freedom is always one less than the number of treatments, because once we have determined $t - 1$ group means and the grand mean, the last group mean can only take on one value. The degrees of freedom for the error term equals the number of test units minus the number of treatment groups, because we only use the t within-group means to calculate the error sum of squares. In summary:

	General formula	Our example
df for SS_T =	$tn - 1$	$(3 \times 4) - 1 = 11$
df for SS_{TR} =	$t - 1$	$3 - 1 = 2$
df for SS_E =	$tn - t$	$(3 \times 4) - 3 = 9$

Note: df for $SS_{TR} + SS_E = df$ for SS_T.

TABLE A20-2   ANOVA TABLE FOR COMPLETELY RANDOMIZED DESIGN

Source of variation	Sum of squares, SS	Degrees of freedom, df	Mean square, MS	F ratio
Treatments (between groups)	SS_{TR}	$t - 1$	$MS_{TR} = \dfrac{SS_{TR}}{t - 1}$	$\dfrac{MS_{TR}}{MS_E}$
Error (within groups)	SS_E	$tn - t$	$MS_E = \dfrac{SS_E}{tn - t}$	
Total	SS_T	$tn - 1$		

Knowledge of the SS_{TR} and SS_E, plus their relevant degrees of freedom, allows us to calculate an estimate of the associated treatment and error variances. These estimates of population variances are called *mean squares* (MS) in experimental situations. This term recognizes the fact that they are estimates of population variances.

One more piece of information is needed before we can determine the significance of an effect. Since our test of effect involves taking the ratio of MS_{TR} to MS_E, we need to know the sampling distribution of this ratio under the null hypothesis (that there is no effect). It can be shown that this ratio is distributed as the F statistic with $t - 1$ df for the numerator and $tn - t$ df for the denominator. (The critical values of the F distribution are given in Table A-5 of Appendix A.) If the treatments have had no effect, the scores in all treatments should be similar, and so the treatment and error mean squares should be almost identical. The calculated F would then equal 1, or nearly so. The larger the treatment effect, the larger the ratio MS_{TR} to MS_E will be. The calculated F value will then get larger. The F distribution in Table A-5 of Appendix A gives the F values that can occur at various type I error levels given the null hypothesis of no effect. What we do is compare the calculated F against the table value for F at a designed α. If the calculated F exceeds the table F, we reject the null hypothesis. Table A20-2 presents the various components of the calculation of the experimental F value in formula form.

A Calculated Example   We now apply what has been developed to see whether there is a significant treatment effect in the data presented in Table A20-1.

Total Sum of Squares[6]

$$SS_T = \sum_{i=1}^{n} \sum_{j=1}^{t} (Y_{ij} - M)^2$$
$$= (20 - 12.7)^2 + (17 - 12.7)^2 + \cdots + (5 - 12.7)^2$$
$$= 232.7$$

Treatment Sum of Squares

$$SS_{TR} = n_j \sum_{j=1}^{n} (M_{\cdot j} - M)^2$$
$$= 4[(16 - 12.7)^2 + (13 - 12.7)^2 + (9 - 12.7)^2]$$
$$= 98.7$$

---

[6] We could, of course, use the computational formula for SS that was presented in Chapter 8.

TABLE A20-3   ANOVA FOR COUPON EXPERIMENT WITH COMPLETELY RANDOMIZED DESIGN

Source of variation	Sum of squares, SS	Degrees of freedom, df	Mean square, MS	F ratio
Treatments	98.7	2	49.4	3.3
Error	134.0	9	14.9	
Total	232.7	11		

Error Sum of Squares

$$SS_E = \sum_{i=1}^{n} \sum_{j=1}^{t} (Y_{ij} - M_{.j})^2$$
$$= (20 - 16)^2 + (17 - 13)^2 + \cdots + (5 - 9)^2$$
$$= 134$$

Note that once we have obtained SS_T and SS_{TR} we can calculate SS_E by subtracting SS_{TR} from SS_T. However, we can double-check our calculations by using the formula for SS_E.

By applying the appropriate df to these SS, we can obtain the mean squares necessary to calculate F. Table A20-3 presents the calculations of F for these data.

The calculated F value is

$$F = \frac{49.4}{14.9} = 3.3$$

at 2 and 9 df. Now look up the critical value of F in Table A-5. In this table, degrees of freedom for the numerator are the column headings, and degrees of freedom for the denominator are the row headings. The table gives critical values at different levels of confidence $(1 - \alpha)$. The intersection of a given row and column at a given $1 - \alpha$ gives the critical values at the α level of significance. In our example, the critical F value at $\alpha = .1$ for 2 and 9 df is 3.01. Our calculated F was 3.3, so our F value could have occurred by chance less than 10 percent of the time, and we reject the null hypothesis of no treatment effect.

Our result would not be significant if we had set $\alpha = .05$, as the critical value is 4.26. Given our choice of $\alpha = .1$, we conclude that the choice of coupon plan does make a difference in sales. We would then examine the data to see which plan was best. In this case, it is obviously plan 1.[7] Note that all an F test does is tell us that there has been a significant effect. We must dig back into the data to see which treatment is causing the effect.

We have now established the procedure for determining the significance of an effect in a completely randomized design. The procedures for other designs apply exactly the same principles; the only difference relates to some extra computations.

RANDOMIZED BLOCK DESIGN

ANOVA for a *randomized block design* (RBD) involves only one more step than that for a CRD. Table A20-4 presents the data for our CRD coupon experiment as if the experiment had

---

[7] It is not always as easy as this to see which treatment is the best; there may be a large number of treatments, or results may be less clear-cut. More advanced procedures are available to determine which treatment is best—for example, in Hayes, *Statistics*, pp. 459–489.

TABLE A20-4   RANDOMIZED BLOCK DESIGN WITH THREE TREATMENTS AND FOUR BLOCKS

Blocks (i) store sizes	Treatments (j)			Block totals	Block means
	Coupon plan 1	Coupon plan 2	Coupon plan 3		
1	20	17	14	$\Sigma Y_{1.} = 51$	$\overline{Y}_{1.} = M_{1.} = 51/3 = 17$
2	18	14	10	$\Sigma Y_{2.} = 42$	$\overline{Y}_{2.} = M_{3.} = 42/3 = 14$
3	15	13	7	$\Sigma Y_{3.} = 35$	$\overline{Y}_{3.} = M_{3.} = 35/3 = 11.7$
4	11	8	5	$\Sigma Y_{4.} = 24$	$\overline{Y}_{4.} = M_{4.} = 24/3 = 8$
Treatment totals	$\Sigma Y_{.1} = 64$	$\Sigma Y_{.2} = 52$	$\Sigma Y_{.3} = 36$		
Treatment means	$\overline{Y}_{.1} = M_{1}$ $= \Sigma Y_{.1}/n_1$ $= 64/4$ $= 16$	$\overline{Y}_{.2} = M_{2}$ $= \Sigma Y_{.2}/n_2$ $= 52/4$ $= 13$	$\overline{Y}_{.3} = M_{3}$ $= \Sigma Y_{.3}/n_3$ $= 36/4$ $= 9$		
			Grand total		$\Sigma Y_{..} = 64 + 52 + 36 = 152$
			Grand mean		$\overline{Y}_{..} = M = \Sigma Y_{..}/(n_1 + n_2 + n_3)$ $= 152/12 = 12.7$

been blocked. Note that the table is the same as Table A20-1, except that the i's now represent blocks instead of test units, and we have calculated row totals and means in addition to column totals and means. Let's assume that the blocks represent different store sizes. In essence, we are saying that we expect some variation in cola sales just due to the differences in the size of the test unit stores. Block 1 represents the largest stores, block 2 the next largest, and so on. We must also assume that treatments were randomly assigned to test units within blocks to apply the RBD.

Partitioning the Sum of Squares   In the RBD we define an individual observation as

$$Y_{ij} = \text{grand mean} + \text{treatment effect} + \text{block effect} + \text{error}$$

or, in population parameter terms,

$$Y_{ij} = \mu + \tau_j + \beta_i + \epsilon_{ij}$$

Again, we will be estimating this model with sample results, so we state the model as

$$Y_{ij} = M + T_j + B_i + E_{ij} \tag{A20-7}$$

where B_i is the effect of the ith block and the other terms are defined as in the CRD. We have previously defined the M and T_j items in this model. We must define the blocking effect and also redefine the error term. We define blocking effect in a parallel manner to the treatment effect, the only difference being that the blocking effect is stated in terms of row means instead of column means.

$$B_i = (M_{i.} - M)$$

Here knowledge of blocking group membership *improves our ability to predict scores as an improvement over the grand mean.* We assume that $\sum_{i=1}^{n} B_i = 0$. That is, the net block effect is zero. We can rewrite Equation A20-7 as

$$
\begin{array}{ccccccccc}
Y_{ij} & = & M & + (M_{.j} - M) & + & (M_{i.} - M) & + & E_{ij} \\
\downarrow & & \downarrow & \downarrow & & \downarrow & & \downarrow \\
\text{Individual} & = & \text{grand} & \text{treatment} & + & \text{blocking} & + & \text{error} \\
\text{score} & & \text{mean} & \text{effect} & & \text{effect} & &
\end{array}
\tag{A20-8}
$$

We can then solve this equation for E_{ij} to get the measurement of error effect.

$$
\begin{aligned}
E_{ij} &= Y_{ij} - M - (M_{.j} - M) - (M_{i.} - M) \\
&= Y_{ij} - M - M_{.j} + M - M_{i.} + M \\
&= Y_{ij} - M_{.j} - M_{i.} + M \quad \text{or} \quad Y_{ij} + (M - M_{.j} - M_{i.})
\end{aligned}
$$

The error terms thus represent the difference between an individual score, Y_{ij}, and the net difference between the grand mean and the sum of the treatment and block means. If the blocking effect is significant, this error will be smaller than an error defined without blocking. As an illustration, look at score Y_{21} in Table A20-4. This score is 18. The error without blocking is

$$
Y_{ij} - M_{.j} = 18 - 16 = 2
$$

With blocking, the error is

$$
Y_{ij} + M - M_{.j} - M_{i.} = 18 + 12.7 - 16 - 14 = .7
$$

A similar pattern would be found with the other scores. Thus blocking reduces the size of experimental error. We may rewrite Equation A20-8 as

$$
Y_{ij} = M + (M_{.j} - M) + (M_{i.} - M) + (Y_{ij} - M_{.j} - M_{i.} + M)
\tag{A20-9}
$$

If we move M to the left side of Equation A20-9, sum the resultant deviations across all blocks and all treatments, and square both sides, we get

$$
\sum_{i=1}^{n} \sum_{j=1}^{t} (Y_{ij} - M)^2 = n \sum_{j=1}^{t} (M_{.j} - M)^2 + t \sum_{i=1}^{n} (M_{i.} - M)^2 + \sum_{i=1}^{n} \sum_{j=1}^{t} (Y_{ij} + M - M_{.j} - M_{i.})^2
$$

You should recognize this result as

$$
SS_T = SS_{TR} + SS_B + SS_E
$$

It follows from the fact that all the cross products again become zero because each involves a sum of individual deviations about a mean. Also, we may write

$$
t \sum_{i=1}^{n} (M_{i.} - M)^2 \qquad \text{instead of} \qquad \sum_{i=1}^{n} \sum_{j=1}^{t} (M_{i.} - M)^2
$$

because we are again adding constant means over the t treatments. It is just simpler to multiply by t than to add the same thing t times. Note that this result was obtained by exactly the same principle as that used in a CRD.

TABLE A20-5 ANOVA TABLE FOR RANDOMIZED BLOCK DESIGN

Source of variation	Sum of squares, SS	Degrees of freedom, df	Mean square, MS	F ratio
Treatments (between columns)	SS_{TR}	$t - 1$	$MS_{TR} = \dfrac{SS_{TR}}{t - 1}$	$\dfrac{MS_{TR}}{MS_E}$
Blocks (between rows)	SS_B	$n - 1$	$MS_B = \dfrac{SS_B}{n - 1}$	$\dfrac{MS_B}{MS_E}$
Error	SS_E	$(t - 1)(n - 1)$	$MS_E = \dfrac{SS_E}{(t - 1)(n - 1)}$	
Total	SS_T	$tn - 1$		

The relevant df for the block is $n - 1$, because once this number of block means are determined, the other is automatically fixed given the grand mean value. If we subtract the treatment and block degrees of freedom from the total degrees of freedom, we get the error degrees of freedom as

$$\text{Error } df = \text{total } df - \text{treatment } df - \text{block } df$$
$$= (tn - 1) - (t - 1) - (n - 1)$$
$$= tn + 1 - t - n$$

In our example, the error $df = (3 \times 4) + 1 - 3 - 4 = 6$. More generally, the same result may be obtained by applying the formula

$$\text{Error } df = (t - 1)(n - 1)$$

Table A20-5 presents the ANOVA table for an RBD.

A Calculated Example We shall now apply the RBD ANOVA procedure to the data in Table A20-4.

Total Sum of Squares

$$SS_T = \sum_{i=1}^{n} \sum_{j=1}^{t} (Y_{ij} - M)^2$$
$$= (20 - 12.7)^2 + (17 - 12.7)^2 + \cdots + (5 - 12.7)^2$$
$$= 232.7$$

Thus SS_T is exactly the same here as with the CRD, as we would expect.

Treatment Sum of Squares

$$SS_{TR} = n \sum_{j=1}^{t} (M._j - M)^2$$
$$= 4[(16 - 12.7)^2 + (13 - 12.7)^2 + (9 - 12.7)^2]$$
$$= 98.7$$

Note that the SS_{TR} is exactly the same as with the CRD.

TABLE A20-6 ANOVA TABLE FOR COUPON EXPERIMENT WITH BLOCKING FOR STORE SIZE

Source of variation	Sum of squares, SS	Degrees of freedom, df	Mean square, MS	F ratio
Treatment	98.7	2	49.4	70.6
Block	129.8	3	43.3	61.9
Error	4.2	6	0.7	
Total	232.7	11		

Block Sum of Squares

$$SS_B = t \sum_{i=1}^{n} (M_{i.} - M)^2$$
$$= 3[(17 - 12.7)^2 + (14 - 12.7)^2 + (11.7 - 12.7)^2 + (8 - 12.7)^2]$$
$$= 129.8$$

Error Sum of Squares

$$SS_E = SS_T - SS_{TR} - SS_B$$
$$= 232.7 - 98.7 - 129.8$$
$$= 4.2$$

Table A20-6 presents the calculated F values for the treatment and block effect.

For the treatment effect, the critical value of F for $\alpha = .1$ at 2 and 6 df is 3.46. For the blocking factor, the critical value of F for $\alpha = .1$ at 3 and 6 df is 3.29. Both the treatment and the block effects are statistically significant, but in this case even at $\alpha = .01$ the treatment effect is now significant (critical $F = 10.9$). By blocking we have obtained a smaller measure of error and thus a more reliable measure of the treatment effect. All the SS_B comes out of the SS_E for the CRD; that is,

$$SS_E \text{ (with blocking)} = SS_E \text{ (without blocking)} - SS_B$$

In our example,

$$SS_E \text{ (with blocking)} = 134.0 - 129.8 = 4.2$$

LATIN SQUARE DESIGN

If we wanted to block out and measure the effects of two extraneous variables, we could use the *Latin square* (LS) design. In an LS design the number of categories of each blocking variable must equal the number of treatment categories, and each treatment must appear once and only once in each row and column of the design. Table A20-7 shows selected LS designs of different sizes. The letters A, B, etc. represent treatments. To generate the treatment assignment pattern for a particular study, pick the appropriately sized layout from Table A20-7 and randomize the column order. For example, a 3 × 3 LS might yield the following treatment pattern when the columns are randomized with the random numbers 3, 1, 2:

C A B
A B C
B C A

TABLE A20-7   ILLUSTRATIVE LATIN SQUARE LAYOUT

3×3	4×4
A B C	A B C D
B C A	B C D A
C A B	C D A B
	D A B C

5×5	6×6
A B C D E	A B C D E F
B C D E A	B C D E F A
C D E A B	C D E F A B
D E A B C	D E F A B C
E A B C D	E F A B C D
	F A B C D E

Now randomize the row assignments within columns, subject to the constraint that each treatment may appear only once in each row. One such result of this process could be the following LS:

$$B C A$$
$$C A B$$
$$A B C$$

We can now illustrate the LS design with a numerical example. Suppose we ran our coupon experiment again to see whether the results could be replicated in other areas. The only difference is that this time we want to block out and measure the effect on sales of both store size and day of the week. In doing so, we must expect significant variation in cola sales simply because of these factors. For one reason or another, we have been unable to measure sales on the same day of the week for each test unit. Since there are three treatments (coupon plans), we must have three categories of store size and three categories of days of the week to use the LS design. Table A20-8 presents the data generated from this LS design experiment. The pattern of treatment assignments is the one generated previously by randomization with these three plans:

A   Coupon plan 1
B   Coupon plan 2
C   Coupon plan 3

The treatment designation is noted next to the cola sales on Table A20-8.

Partitioning the Sum of Squares   In the LS design we define an individual observation as

$$Y_{ijk} = \text{grand mean} + \text{row effect} + \text{column effect} + \text{treatment effect} + \text{error}$$

where Y_{ijk} = the measured result when the kth treatment is applied to the ith row and the jth column. In population parameter terms, the model is

$$Y_{ijk} = \mu + \alpha_i + \beta_j + \tau_k + \epsilon_{ijk}$$

Again we will be estimating this model with sample results, so we state the model as

$$Y_{ijk} = M + R_i + C_j + T_k + E_{ijk} \tag{A20-10}$$

TABLE A20-8   LATIN SQUARE DESIGN WITH THREE TREATMENTS

Rows (i)	Columns (j)			Row totals	Row means
	1 Mon.–Tues.	**2** Wed.–Thurs.	**3** Fri.–Sun.		
1 Large stores	25 *(B)*	15 *(C)*	50 *(A)*	$\Sigma Y_{1..} = 90$	$M_{1..}$ = 90/3 = 30.0
2 Medium stores	5 *(C)*	25 *(A)*	25 *(B)*	$\Sigma Y_{2..} = 55$	$M_{2..}$ = 55/3 = 18.3
3 Small stores	15 *(A)*	15 *(B)*	14 *(C)*	$\Sigma Y_{3..} = 44$	$M_{3..}$ = 44/3 = 14.7
Column totals	$\Sigma Y_{.1.} = 45$	$\Sigma Y_{.2.} = 55$	$\Sigma Y_{.3.} = 89$	$\Sigma Y_{...} = 189$	
Column means	$M_{.1.}$ = 45/3 = 15.0	$M_{.2.}$ = 55/3 = 18.3	$M_{.3.}$ = 89/3 = 29.7		M = 189/9 = 21.0

Treatments (k)	A*	B	C
Treatment totals	$\Sigma Y_{..1} = 90$	$\Sigma Y_{..2} = 65$	$\Sigma Y_{..3} = 34$
Treatment means	$M_{..1}$ = 90/3 = 30.0	$M_{..2}$ = 65/3 = 21.7	$M_{..3}$ = 34/3 = 11.3

*For example, $\Sigma Y_{..1} = 15 + 25 + 50 = 90$; i.e., we add the scores at all the places where A appears.

where R_i = the effect of the *i*th row block (i.e., store size)
  C_j = the effect of the *j*th column block (i.e., day of the week)
  T_k = the effect of the *k*th treatment (i.e., coupon plan)
  E_{ijk} = the experimental error of the *ijk* observation
  $i, j, k = 1, 2, \ldots, t$ where t = the number of treatments

The three effects of interest are:

1 Row effect (i.e., effect of store size) = $(M_{i..} - M)$, the difference between the row mean and the grand mean, adding across all *j*'s and *k*'s.
2 Column effect (i.e., effect of the day of the week) = $(M_{.j.} - M)$, the difference between the column mean and the grand mean, adding across all *i*'s and *k*'s.
3 Treatment effect (i.e., effect of coupon plan) = $(M_{..k} - M)$, the difference between the treatment mean and the grand mean, adding across all *i*'s and *j*'s.

We assume that the net effect of each effect is zero. That is,

$$\sum_{i=1}^{t} R_i = 0 \qquad \sum_{j=1}^{t} C_j = 0 \qquad \text{and} \qquad \sum_{k=1}^{t} T_k = 0$$

We can then rewrite Equation A20-10 as

$$Y_{ijk} = M + (M_{i..} - M) + (M_{.j.} - M) + (M_{..k} - M) + E_{ijk}$$

$$\begin{array}{ccccccccccc} \downarrow & & \downarrow & & \downarrow & & \downarrow & & \downarrow & & \downarrow \\ \text{Individual} & = & \text{grand} & + & \text{row} & + & \text{column} & + & \text{treatment} & + & \text{error} \\ \text{score} & & \text{mean} & & \text{effect} & & \text{effect} & & \text{effect} & & \end{array}$$

TABLE A20-9 ANOVA TABLE FOR LATIN SQUARE DESIGN

Source of variation	Sum of squares, SS	Degrees of freedom, df	Mean square, MS	F ratio
Between rows	SS_R	$t-1$	$MS_R = \dfrac{SS_R}{t-1}$	$\dfrac{MS_R}{MS_E}$
Between columns	SS_C	$t-1$	$MS_C = \dfrac{SS_C}{t-1}$	$\dfrac{MS_C}{MS_E}$
Between treatments	SS_{TR}	$t-1$	$MS_{TR} = \dfrac{SS_{TR}}{t-1}$	$\dfrac{MS_{TR}}{MS_E}$
Error	SS_E	$(t-1)(t-2)$	$MS_E = \dfrac{SSE}{(t-1)(t-2)}$	
Total	SS_T	t^2-1		

We can solve this equation for E_{ijk} to get the measurement of error:

$$E_{ijk} = Y_{ijk} - M - (M_{i..} - M) - (M_{.j.} - M) - (M_{..k} - M)$$
$$= Y_{ijk} + 2M - M_{i..} - M_{.j.} - M_{..k}$$

If both blocking factors are correlated with the dependent variable, this error measure will be smaller than that obtained with a CRD or RBD that uses only one blocking factor.

If we moved M to the left side, added all these deviations across all rows and columns, and squared the equation, we would obtain the required SS. The model would then be

$$SS_T = SS_R + SS_C + SS_{TR} + SS_E$$

as again all the cross products fall out to zero. Table A20-9 shows the ANOVA layout for an LS design. SS_R, SS_C, and SS_{TR} each have $t-1$ df. With $(t)(t) - 1$ or $t^2 - 1$ df in the whole sample, this leaves $(t-1)(t-2)$ df for the error term.

A Calculated Example We shall now apply the LS design ANOVA to the data in Table A20-8.

Total Sum of Squares

$$SS_T = \sum_{i=1}^{t} \sum_{j=1}^{t} (Y_{ijk} - M)^2$$
$$= (25 - 21)^2 + (15 - 21)^2 + \cdots + (14 - 21)^2$$
$$= 1302$$

Row Sum of Squares

$$SS_R = t \sum_{i=1}^{t} (M_{i..} - M)^2$$
$$= 3[(30 - 21)^2 + (18.3 - 21)^2 + (14.7 - 21)^2]$$
$$= 383.9$$

Column Sum of Squares

$$SS_C = t \sum_{j=1}^{t} (M_{\cdot j \cdot} - M)^2$$
$$= 3[(15 - 21)^2 + (18.3 - 21)^2 + (29.7 - 21)^2]$$
$$= 356.9$$

Treatment Sum of Squares

$$SS_{TR} = t \sum_{k=1}^{t} (M_{\cdot\cdot k} - M)^2$$
$$= 3[(30 - 21)^2 + (21.7 - 21)^2 + (11.3 - 21)^2]$$
$$= 526.7$$

Error Sum of Squares

$$SS_E = SS_T - SS_R - SS_C - SS_{TR}$$
$$= 1302 - 383.9 - 356.9 - 526.7$$
$$= 34.5$$

Table A20-10 presents the calculated F values for the treatment and the two blocks. For the treatment and blocking factors, the critical value of F for $\alpha = .1$ at 2 and 2 df is 9.0. Therefore, both blocking factors and the treatment are significant. Note that none of these effects would have been significant at $\alpha = .05$, as the critical F is 19.0. If we had used a CRD or blocked with just one of our two blocking factors in an RBD, the treatment effect would not have been significant at $\alpha = .1$. This is so because the SS_R and SS_C would be added back into the LS design SS_E to give the SS_E for the CRD. As for the RBD, either SS_R or SS_C would be added back to the LS design SS_E to give the SS_E for the RBD. In either instance, the SS_R or SS_C is large enough to render the calculated F ratio nonsignificant at $\alpha = .1$. Here we needed two blocking factors to find a significant treatment effect. The value of blocking in marketing experiments should be clear. Again note that we must look into the data to see that treatment A is the best coupon plan.

TABLE A20-10   ANOVA TABLE FOR COUPON EXPERIMENT WITH 3 × 3 LATIN SQUARE DESIGN

Source of variation	Sum of squares, *SS*	Degrees of freedom, *df*	Mean square, *MS*	*F* ratio
Row effect (store size)	383.9	2	192.0	11.1
Column effect (days of week)	356.9	2	178.5	10.3
Treatment	526.7	2	263.4	15.2
Error	34.5	2	17.3	
Total	1302.0	8		

FACTORIAL DESIGN

In a *factorial design* (FD) we measure the effects of two or more independent variables and their interactions. Suppose that in our coupon experiment we are interested not only in the effect of coupon plans, but also in the effect of the media plans that support the coupon plans. Table A20-11 presents data generated from such an experiment. You should recognize these as the data we used in Table A20-1 for our CRD. All we have done here is regroup the data and present them as if they came from an FD.

Partitioning the Sum of Squares   In the FD with two independent variables, we define an individual observation as

Y_{ijk} = grand mean + effect of treatment A

+ effect of treatment B + interaction effect AB + error

where Y_{ijk} = the kth observation on the ith level of A and the jth level of B.
For example, here

$$Y_{111} = 20, \qquad Y_{231} = 7$$

In population parameter terms, the model is

$$Y_{ijk} = \mu + \alpha_i + \beta_j + (\alpha\beta)_{ij} + \epsilon_{ijk}$$

Again, we will be estimating this model with sample results, as we write

$$Y_{ijk} = M + A_i + B_j + (AB)_{ij} + E_{ijk} \tag{A20-11}$$

where A_i = the effect of the ith level of A (media plan), $i = 1, \ldots, a$, where a is the number of levels in A
B_j = the effect of the jth level of B (coupon plan), $j = 1, \ldots, b$, where b is the number of levels in B
$(AB)_{ij}$ = the effect of the interaction of the ith level of A and the jth level of B
E_{ijk} = the error of the kth observation in the ith level of A and the jth level of B, i.e., the ij cell

In our example $n_{ij} = 2$ for all ij cells.
The four effects of interest are:

1 A_i effect (i.e., media plan) = $(M_{i..} - M)$, the difference between the row mean and the grand mean.
2 B_j effect (i.e., coupon plan) = $(M_{.j.} - M)$, the difference between the column mean and the grand mean.
3 Error = $(Y_{ijk} - M_{ij})$, the difference between an individual observation and the cell mean to which it belongs. That is, the only difference within a cell should be random chance.
4 Interaction effect $(AB)_{ij}$ = any remaining variation in the data after main effects and error have been removed.

TABLE A20-11 A 2 × 3 FACTORIAL DESIGN WITH MEDIA PLANS AND COUPON PLANS AS INDEPENDENT VARIABLES

Media plans (i)		Coupon plans (j)			Media totals	Media means
		B_1	B_2	B_3		
	A_1	20 18	17 14	14 10	$\Sigma Y_{1..} = 93$	$M_{1..} = 93/6 = 15.5$
	A_2	15 11	13 8	7 5	$\Sigma Y_{2..} = 59$	$M_{2..} = 59/6 = 9.8$
Coupon totals		$\Sigma Y_{.1.} = 64$	$\Sigma Y_{.2.} = 52$	$\Sigma Y_{.3.} = 36$	$\Sigma Y_{...} = 152$	
Coupon means		$M_{.1.} = 64/4 = 16$	$M_{.2.} = 52/4 = 13$	$M_{.3.} = 36/4 = 9$		$M = 12.7$

Treatment cell (ij)	A_1B_1	A_1B_2	A_1B_3	A_2B_1	A_2B_2	A_2B_3
Cell total	$\Sigma Y_{11.} = 38$	$\Sigma Y_{12.} = 31$	$\Sigma Y_{13.} = 24$	$\Sigma Y_{21.} = 26$	$\Sigma Y_{22.} = 21$	$\Sigma Y_{23.} = 12$
Cell mean	$M_{11.} = 38/2$ $= 19$	$M_{12.} = 31/2$ $= 15.5$	$M_{13.} = 24/2$ $= 12$	$M_{21.} = 26/2$ $= 13$	$M_{22.} = 21/2$ $= 10.5$	$M_{23.} = 12/2$ $= 6$

Note: $n_{ij} = 2$ for all i's and j's.

We can rewrite Equation A20-11 as

$$Y_{ijk} = M + (M_{i..} - M) + (M_{.j.} - M) + (AB)_{ij} + (Y_{ijk} - M_{ij.})$$

and solve for the interaction term, $(AB)_{ij}$:

$$
\begin{aligned}
(AB)_{ij} &= Y_{ijk} - M - (M_{i..} - M) - (M_{.j.} - M) - (Y_{ijk} - M_{ij.}) \\
&= Y_{ijk} - M - M_{i..} + M - M_{.j.} + M - Y_{ijk} + M_{ij.} \\
&= M + M_{ij.} - M_{i..} - M_{.j.}
\end{aligned}
$$

In our example,

$$(AB)_{11} = 12.7 + 19 - 15.5 - 16 = 0.2$$

and

$$(AB)_{23} = 12.7 + 6 - 9.8 - 9 = -0.1$$

Results like this suggest that there is little interaction in the data. We may now rewrite Equation A20-11 as

$$Y_{ijk} = M + (M_{i..} - M) + (M_{.j.} - M) + (M + M_{ij.} - M_{i..} - M_{.j.}) + (Y_{ijk} - M_{ij.}) \quad \text{(A20-12)}$$

If we moved M to the left side, added all the deviations across all scores k in all ij cells, and squared the equation, we would obtain the required SS. The model would then be

$$SS_T = SS_{TRA} + SS_{TRB} + SS_{INT(AB)} + SS_E$$

where SS_{TRA} = sum of squares of treatment A
$\quad\quad SS_{TRB}$ = sum of squares of treatment B
$\quad SS_{INT(AB)}$ = sum of squares for interaction of A and B

This result occurs because all the cross products fall out to zero, as we would now expect. Table A20-12 shows the ANOVA layout for a two-factor FD. Each factor has one degree of

TABLE A20-12   ANOVA TABLE FOR A TWO-FACTOR FACTORIAL DESIGN

Source of variation	Sum of squares, SS	Degrees of freedom, df	Mean square, MS	F ratio
Treatment A	SS_{TRA}	$a - 1$	$MS_{TRA} = \dfrac{SS_{TRA}}{a-1}$	$\dfrac{MS_{TRA}}{MS_E}$
Treatment B	SS_{TRB}	$b - 1$	$MS_{TRB} = \dfrac{SS_{TRB}}{b-1}$	$\dfrac{MS_{TRB}}{MS_E}$
Interaction AB	$SS_{INT(AB)}$	$(a-1)(b-1)$	$MS_{INT(AB)} = \dfrac{SS_{INT(AB)}}{(a-1)(b-1)}$	$\dfrac{MS_{INT(AB)}}{MS_E}$
Error	SS_E	$ab(n-1)$	$MS_E = \dfrac{SS_E}{ab(n-1)}$	
Total	SS_T	$abn - 1$		

freedom less than its number of categories, and the interaction term has $(a - 1)(b - 1)$ df. With $abn - 1$ df in the whole sample, this leaves $ab(n - 1)$ for the error term.

A Calculated Example Now let us apply the FD to the data in Table A20-11.

Total Sum of Squares

$$SS_T = \sum_{i=1}^{a} \sum_{j=1}^{b} \sum_{k=1}^{n} (Y_{ijk} - M)^2$$
$$= (20 - 12.7)^2 + (17 - 12.7)^2 + \cdots + (5 - 12.7)^2$$
$$= 232.7$$

Again note that the SS_T is the same as in the CRD and RBD, as it must be.

Treatment A Sum of Squares

$$SS_{TRA} = bn \sum_{i=1}^{a} (M_{i..} - M)^2$$
$$= (3)(2)[(15.5 - 12.7)^2 + (9.8 - 12.7)^2]$$
$$= 97.5$$

Treatment B Sum of Squares

$$SS_{TRB} = an \sum_{j=1}^{b} (M_{.j.} - M)^2$$
$$= (2)(2)[(16 - 12.7)^2 + (13 - 12.7)^2 + (9 - 12.7)^2]$$
$$= 98.7$$

Note that this is the SS_{TR} we found for the CRD. In other words, the main effect of the coupon plan is identical under both analysis procedures, as we would expect.

Interaction Sum of Squares

$$SS_{INT(AB)} = n \sum_{i=1}^{a} \sum_{j=1}^{b} (M + M_{ij.} - M_{i..} - M_{.j.})^2$$
$$= 2[(12.7 + 19 - 15.5 - 16)^2]$$
$$+ (12.7 + 15.5 - 15.5 - 13)^2 + (12.7 + 12 - 15.5 - 9)^2$$
$$+ (12.7 + 13 - 9.8 - 16)^2 + (12.7 + 10.5 - 9.8 - 13)^2$$
$$+ (12.8 + 6 - 9.8 - 9)^2$$
$$= 0.7$$

Error Sum of Squares

$$SS_E = \sum_{i=1}^{a} \sum_{j=1}^{b} \sum_{k=1}^{n} (Y_{ijk} - M_{ij.})^2$$
$$= SS_T - SS_{TRA} - SS_{TRB} - SS_{INT(AB)}$$
$$= 232.7 - 97.5 - 98.7 - 0.7$$
$$= 35.8$$

TABLE A20-13 ANOVA TABLE FOR MEDIA AND COUPON EXPERIMENT USING A TWO-FACTOR 2 × 3 FACTORIAL DESIGN

Source of variation	Sum of squares, SS	Degrees of freedom, df	Mean square, MS	F ratio
Treatment A (media)	97.5	1	97.5	16.3
Treatment B (coupon)	98.7	2	49.4	8.2
Interaction (AB)	0.7	2	.4	.1
Error	35.8	6	6.0	
Total	232.7	11		

Table A20-13 presents the calculated F values for the two treatments and the interaction. For treatment A, the critical F for $\alpha = .05$ at 1 and 6 df is 5.99. Therefore, the media effect is significant. For treatment B, for $\alpha = .05$ at 2 and 6 df the critical F is 5.14. Thus, the coupon effect is also significant. Since the calculated interaction F is less than 1, we know it is not significant without even using the F table. We can now go back to the data to see that it is media plan A_1 and coupon plan B_1 that yield the best results.

This two-factor ANOVA is called "two-way" ANOVA. The factorial procedure can be extended to N independent variables. This is called "N-way" ANOVA. The calculations for an ANOVA greater than two-way are too complex to present here. The analysis of such an experiment is, however, easily handled by computer programs. In any event, the principle of these more advanced calculations is exactly the same as you have just learned.

SUMMARY OF APPENDIX

1 ANOVA is simply the calculation of different variances, SS/df.

2 The fixed effects model allows inferences only about the different treatments actually used. It is most relevant in marketing.

3 In ANOVA an effect is defined as a difference in treatment means from the grand mean.

4 Experimental error is the difference between an individual score and the treatment group mean to which the score belongs.

5 ANOVA is calculated by partitioning the SS_T into SS_{TR} and SS_E and dividing each of these by their relevant degrees of freedom to yield an estimate of treatment and error variances called the mean squares (MS_{TR} and MS_E). That is, the one-way ANOVA model is partitioned as follows: $SS_T = SS_{TR} + SS_E$.

6 The relevant statistic for a significance test is the F statistic, where $F = MS_{TR}/MS_E$.

7 The CRD measures the effect of one independent variable without statistical control of extraneous variation. Its basic composition is $SS_T = SS_{TR} + SS_E$.

8 The RBD design measures the effect of one independent variable with statistical control of one extraneous factor. Its basic composition is $SS_T = SS_{TR} + SS_B + SS_E$.

9 The LS design measures the effect of one independent variable with statistical control of two extraneous factors. Its basic composition is $SS_T = SS_R + SS_C + SS_{TR} + SS_E$.

10 The FD measures the main and interaction effects of two or more independent variables. Its basic composition for a two-way ANOVA is $SS_T = SS_{TRA} + SS_{TRB} + SS_{INT(AB)} + SS_E$.

CHAPTER 21

REPORTING RESEARCH FINDINGS

The final step in the research process is the preparation and presentation of the research report.[1] This could very well be the most important part of the research process. If the report is confusing or poorly written, all the time and effort spent gathering and analyzing data was for naught. The purpose of this chapter is to give you guidance in preparing a research report—which is simply the presentation of research findings to a specific audience. We shall cover written and oral reports, since both are usually prepared at the completion of a research project.

For many executives, the only aspect of a research project they perceive is an oral or written report. Their evaluation of weeks (or months!) of research rests solely upon this presentation. The best research methodology in the world will be useless to managers and executives if they can't wade through the research report. This chapter will offer advice on how to present research findings in a clear, interesting manner.

WRITTEN REPORT GUIDELINES

Researchers who are effective in report writing agree that there are a series of guidelines which should be followed.

Consider the Audience Make the report clear; use only words familiar to the readers, and define all technical terms. To make the comparison of figures easier, use percentages, rounded-off figures, ranks, or ratios; put the exact data in a table within

[1] We wish to acknowledge the assistance of Sheryl R. Petras, Ph.D student in marketing, University of Michigan, in preparing this chapter.

the text or in the appendix. Use graphic aids (charts, graphs, pictures, etc.) whenever they help clarify the presentation of data.

Address the Information Needs Remember—the research report is designed to communicate information to decision makers. Make sure it clearly relates the research findings to the objectives of management.

Be Concise, Yet Complete Most managers will not want to read about the details of a research project. Knowing what to include and what to leave out is a difficult task. It is up to you, the researcher, to take into account the information needs of the decision maker when writing your report.

Be Objective You will probably face at least one situation in which you know that the results will not be easily accepted by the client. The findings may conflict with the decision maker's experience and judgment, or they may reflect unfavorably on the wisdom of previous decisions. In these circumstances, there is a strong temptation to slant the report, making the results seem more acceptable to management. A professional researcher, however, will present the research findings in a objective manner (i.e., without bias) and will defend their validity if they are challenged by the client.

Style Writing style is a topic for an English or communications course, but here are a few tips to help you write a report that is easy to read.

- Write in brisk, businesslike English.
- Use short words and sentences.
- Be concise.
- Consider appearance. White space (portions of the page that are blank) makes a long report easier to read. Graphs and charts, used primarily to visually illustrate statistical ideas, are also useful for creating white space.
- Avoid clichés.
- Write in the present tense.
- Use the active voice.
- Placing short quotes from respondents throughout the report makes it more interesting and readable, and may provide insight or spark new ideas.

REPORT FORMAT

While there is no single format which is appropriate for all situations, the following outline is generally accepted as the basic format for most research projects:

1 Title page
2 Table of contents
3 Table of tables (or figures, graphs, etc.)

4 Management summary
  a Objectives
  b Results
  c Conclusions
  d Recommendations
5 Body
  a Introduction
  b Methodology
  c Results
  d Limitations
6 Conclusions and recommendations
7 Appendix
  a Sampling plan
  b Data collection forms
  c Supporting tables not included in the body

Title Page

The title page should contain a title which conveys the essence of the study, the date, the name of the organization submitting the report, and the name of the recipient organization. If the report is confidential, the individuals to receive the report should be named on the title page.

Table of Contents

The table of contents lists sequentially the topics covered in the report, along with their page references. Its purpose is to help readers find the particular sections of the report that are of most concern to them. See Exhibit 1 for an example of the table of contents used in reports written by the General Foods Corporation Marketing Research Department.

Table of Tables (or Table of Figures, Illustrations, etc.)

This table lists the titles and page numbers of all visual aids. This table can be placed either on the same page with the table of contents or on a separate page.

Management Summary

The management summary is a condensed, accurate statement of what is important in the report. This one- to two-page synopsis is a must for most research reports. Since many executives read only the management summary, it is extremely important that this section be both accurate and well written.

The management summary is not a miniature of the main report. Rather, it provides the decision maker with those research findings having the most impact on the decision to be made. The management summary is written specifically for decision makers and should enable them to take action.

EXHIBIT 1

TABLE OF CONTENTS

Your management summary should include:

1 Objectives of the research project
2 Nature of the decision problem
3 Key results
4 Conclusions (opinions and interpretations based on the research)
5 Recommendations for action

Body of Report

The details of the research project are found in the body of the report. This section includes (1) introduction, (2) methodology, (3) results, and (4) limitations.

Introduction   The purpose of the introduction is to provide the reader with background information needed to understand the remainder of the report. The nature of the introduction is conditioned by the diversity of the audience and their familiarity with the research project. The more diverse the audience, the more extensive the introduction.

The introduction must clearly explain the nature of the decision problem and the research objective. Background information should be provided on the product or service involved and the circumstances surrounding the decision problem. The nature of any previous research on the problem should be reviewed.

Methodology   The purpose of the methodology section is to describe the nature of the research design, the sampling plan, and the data collection and analysis procedure. This is a very difficult section to write. Enough detail must be conveyed so that the reader can appreciate the nature of the methodology used, yet the presentation must not be boring or overpowering. The use of technical jargon must be avoided.

The methodology section should tell the reader whether the design was exploratory or conclusive. The sources of data—secondary or primary—should be explained. The nature of the data collection method—communication or observation—must be specified. The reader needs to know who was included in the sample, the size of the sample, and the nature of the sampling procedure.

The methodology section is designed (1) to summarize the technical aspects of the research project in a style which is comprehensible to the nontechnician and (2) to develop confidence in the quality of the procedures used. The technical details should be minimized in this section and placed in an appendix for those who desire a more detailed methodological discussion.

Results   The bulk of the report is composed of the research findings, which should be organized around the research objectives and information needs. This presentation should involve a logical unfolding of information—as if you were telling a story. The reporting of findings must have a definite point of view and fit together into a logical whole; it is not just the presentation of an endless series of tables. Rather, it requires the organization of the data into a logical flow of information for decision-making purposes.

Limitations   Every research project has weaknesses which need to be communicated in a clear and concise manner. In this process, the researcher should avoid belaboring minor study weaknesses. The purpose of this section is not to disparage the quality of the research project, but rather to enable the reader to judge the validity of the study results.

The limitations in a marketing research project generally involve sampling and nonresponse inadequacies and methodological weaknesses. The writing of the conclusions and recommendations section is naturally affected by the recognized and acknowledged study limitations. It is the researcher's professional responsibility to clearly inform the reader of these limitations.

Conclusions and Recommendations

The conclusions and recommendations must flow logically from the presentation of the results. The conclusions should clearly link the research findings with the information needs, and based on this linkage recommendations for action can be formulated.

Many executives and researchers feel that the researcher shouldn't make recommendations. They argue that the recommendations for action must reflect a blend of the decision maker's experience and judgment with the findings from the research study. Since few researchers possess this degree of experience and judgment, the researcher's recommendations may be weighed more heavily in favor of the research findings.

Alternatively, many others feel strongly that the research report should include recommendations. They argue that as long as the decision maker recognizes the context in which recommendations are made, there are clear benefits from having them in the research report. First, the researcher must focus on the decision problem and think in terms of action. Second, the researcher must appreciate the broader management issues and the role of research in the decision-making process. Finally, the researcher may identify recommendations not otherwise considered by the decision maker. In the final analysis, however, the action taken is the responsibility of the decision maker, and the recommendations put forth in the research report may or may not be followed.

Appendix

The purpose of the appendix is to provide a place for material which is not absolutely essential to the body of the report. This material is typically more specialized and complex than material presented in the main report, and it is designed to serve the needs of the technically oriented reader. The appendix will frequently contain copies of the data collection forms, details of the sampling plan, estimates of statistical error, interviewer instructions, and detailed statistical tables associated with the data analysis process.

PRESENTATION OF DATA

Whenever you must present numerous figures or describe a technical process or procedure, graphic aids can help communicate this information to your audience more quickly. The two graphic aids most used in research reports are tables and graphs. Besides making the report easier to read and understand, graphic aids improve its physical appearance. This section will illustrate the various ways to present quantitative data by using tables and graphs.

General Guidelines for Presenting Graphic Aids

Usually it is best to place an illustration within the text if the reader will need to refer to it while reading the report. It should be placed as close to the discussion as possible. If the information is supplemental or extremely lengthy, it can be placed in the appendix.

Always introduce the reader to the illustration before you present it; a couple of sentences will usually suffice. You can highlight the extremes, averages, or other aspects of the data which are significant to your report development. Don't, however, discuss minute details of the illustration—readers will find it redundant and boring.

All graphic aids should contain the following elements:

1 *Table or figure number.* This permits easy location in the report.
2 *Title.* The title should clearly indicate the contents of the table or figure.
3 *Boxhead and stub head.* The boxhead contains the captions or labels to the columns in a table, while the stub head contains the labels for the rows.
4 *Footnotes.* Footnotes explain or qualify a particular section or item in the table or figure.

TABLE 21-1 WEEKLY TRAFFIC COUNT BY STORE LOCATION
(August 8–14, 1983)

Store	Number of persons entering	Percentage of total
West	4,731	25
North	4,821	26
East	3,514	19
South	3,534	19
Central	2,210	11
Total	18,810	100

Data can be presented in tabular or graphic form. The tabular form (tables) consists of the numerical presentation of data. Table 21-1 presents an illustration.

The graphical form (figures) involves the presentation of data in terms of visually interpreted sizes. The key to good presentation of graphics is simplicity. Graphics can dress up a presentation by calling attention to important points that can't be explained clearly in tables or words. They are a quick and attractive means of conveying numbers, trends, and relationships.

Once your data are in hand, you must select the best graphic format for your situation. This sounds easy, but deciding which format is most appropriate can be an arduous task. Pie, bar, and line charts are the formats used most frequently in business communication because they provide direct visual representation of complex data.

FIGURE 21-1 Pie chart of weekly traffic count by retail stores (August 8–14, 1983).

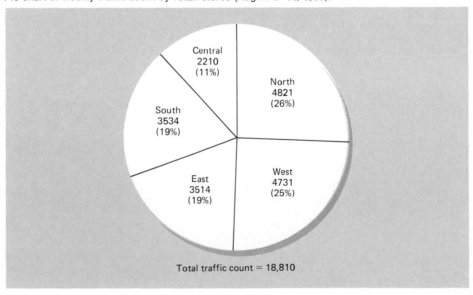

Pie Chart   The pie chart, which really looks like a pie, is one of the simplest and most effective ways to dramatize proportional relationships. It is a circle divided into sections such that the size of each section corresponds to a portion of the total. Figure 21-1 presents the data shown in Table 21-1 in the form of a pie chart. Notice how clearly the figure depicts the relative difference in weekly traffic counts by retail store.

Be wary of the tendency to pack excessive information into a single pie. Too many divisions will make the resulting portions too small to label. Stick to five or six segments, and group segments representing very small percentages (usually less than 5 percent) into a collective "other" category.

One dressy technique that has become popular in business presentations is the practice of exploding, or separating, segments of the pie from the rest of the drawing (see Figure 21-2). This technique directs attention to the most important pieces of information, but it may make the chart more complicated for the viewer. Limit the number of segments you explode to one or two. An alternative to using the exploding pie chart is to highlight the important segments with bright, solid colors.

Pie charts do not lend themselves to illustrating the passage of time, nor do they allow you to compare more than one group of data within a single chart. Comparing multiple entities requires multiple pie charts. If you find yourself using more than four pies, you may want to consider a bar chart instead.

Bar Chart   A bar chart depicts magnitudes of the data by the length of various bars which have been laid out with reference to a horizontal or vertical scale. When carefully designed, a bar (or column) chart is the easiest graphic image to understand. It's a tried-and-true business graphics standard. Figure 21-3 presents a bar chart depicting differences in retail store traffic count by day of the week.

FIGURE 21-2   Exploding pie chart.

FIGURE 21-3   Bar chart of traffic count of retail stores by day of week (August 8–14, 1983).

Bar charts are best at illustrating multiple comparisons and complex relationships. To compare several distinct sets of data in one chart, use a clustered bar graph. Clustered bars are like an outline for a report: they group general subjects together and then divide the information into specific categories. They are used for comparing different but related types of data within a group and over a period of time.

For simplicity, cluster bar charts should be limited to four groups and four types of data within each group (see Figure 21-4). It is very important to label a clustered chart clearly. Each cluster should have a label, and each bar within a cluster should be identified. Since there is usually insufficient room for all those labels, draw each bar in a different pattern or color and describe the bars in a legend under the graph.

FIGURE 21-4   Cluster bar chart.

FIGURE 21-5   Line chart of traffic count of retail stores by day of week (August 8–14, 1983).

Line Chart   Line charts effectively illustrate trends over a period of time. Such charts use a continuous line to trace the relationship between data points. The data presented in Figure 21-3 (bar chart) can be presented in the form of a line chart. Figure 21-5 presents a line chart depicting differences in retail store traffic count by day of the week.

A line chart is preferred over a bar chart in the following situations: (1) when the data involve a long time period, (2) when several series are compared on the same chart, (3) when the emphasis is on the movement rather than the actual amount, (4) when trends of frequency distribution are presented, (5) when a multiple-amount scale is used, or (6) when estimates, forecasts, interpolation, or extrapolation are to be shown.[2]

Computer graphics is a rapidly evolving method for conveniently displaying research data in the form of pie, bar, and line charts.[3] Special computer graphics software packages have been developed which complement popular data analysis software packages.[4] These new software packages allow the researcher to operate directly from large amounts of data to produce an array of graphs, preview them on a graphics terminal, decide which to use, and have the graphs drawn on a hard copy device—all in short order.

As companies become more market-oriented, they are increasingly swamped with data on their markets, their competition, and their marketing programs' effectiveness. A computer has the ability to spew out more data than a researcher can examine, interpret, and present in a manageable format, and computer graphics has the potential to redress this imbalance resulting from the overflow of market information and the overload on human resources charged with its analysis and reporting.

[2] M. E. Spear, *Practical Charting Techniques* (New York: McGraw-Hill, 1969), p. 74.
[3] H. Takeuchi and A. H. Schmidt, "New Promise of Computer Graphics," *Harvard Business Review*, pp. 122–131, January–February 1980.
[4] A leading supplier of computer graphics software is SPSS, Inc., 444 N. Michigan Avenue, Chicago, IL 60611.

ORAL PRESENTATION

Many companies require oral presentations of research reports. Before the presentation:[5]

1 Check all equipment (e.g., lights, microphones, projectors, and other visual aid equipment) thoroughly before the presentation.

2 Have a contingency plan for equipment failure.

3 Analyze your audience. How will they react to the research findings? Will they be in agreement? Hostile? Indifferent? Gauge your opening statements accordingly. It's usually wise to begin a presentation with ideas about which there is agreement.

4 Practice the presentation several times. If possible, have someone comment on how to improve its effectiveness.

During the presentation:

5 Start the presentation with an overview—tell the audience what you are going to tell them.

6 Face the audience at all times.

7 Talk to the audience or decision maker, rather than read from a script or a projection screen. Use notes only to make sure you don't forget any important points and to keep the presentation flowing in an organized manner.

8 Use visual aids effectively—charts and tables should be simple and easy to read.

9 Avoid distracting mannerisms while speaking. Constant or unnecessary motion is bothersome—make certain your movements have purpose. Also refrain from adding "fillers" such as "uh," "um," "y'know," "OK," etc., between words or sentences.

10 Remember to ask the audience if they have questions after your report is concluded. During the question period you should:

- Concentrate on the question. Don't think about the answer until the speaker has completed his or her question.
- Repeat the question. If it's a tough one, rephrase it. This assures that everyone in the audience has heard the question, and gives you the time to formulate an answer.
- Don't fake an answer. Admit that you don't know the answer, then tell the speaker that you will try to find it. After the presentation, find out where that person can be reached when you do in fact get the answer to the question. (Make sure you follow through on your promise!)
- Answer questions briefly and support your answers with evidence whenever possible.

SUMMARY

1 A research report is the presentation of the research findings to a specific audience for a specific purpose. The presentation can be written or given orally, or both.

---

[5] This section draws upon H. A. Murphy and H. W. Hildebrandt, *Effective Business Communications* (New York: McGraw-Hill, 1984), p. 595.

2 The guidelines for the written and oral reports are: (1) Consider the audience, (2) be concise yet complete, and (3) be objective yet effective.

3 The main elements of the written report are (1) the title page, (2) the table of contents, (3) the management summary, (4) the body of the report, (5) the conclusions and recommendations, and (6) the appendix.

4 The research data can be presented in tabular or graphic form. Three types of graphic forms are (1) the pie chart, (2) the bar chart, and (3) the line chart.

DISCUSSION QUESTIONS

1 Why is the research report important?
2 What general guidelines exist for the preparation of written research reports?
3 How might an oral presentation supplement a written research report?
4 What components are typically included in a research report?
5 What are the alternative means of displaying data graphically?

CASE 6-1: Detroit Public Library (B)[1]

In Case 1-3, we presented a proposal for research for the Detroit Public Library system. As part of the research that was actually done, a phone interview was administered to a sample of Detroit residents. Exhibit 1 shows selected questions from the 18-page, 47-question questionnaire. (Actual question numbers are used.)

CASE QUESTION

Prepare a coding scheme for the selected parts of the questionnaire.

EXHIBIT 1

DPL SURVEY

1b In what year were you born?_____
5b Why don't you go to the library more often? [Record as *many* responses as apply.]
- Not interested, no need, don't read books
- Use another library
- Located too far away
- Too noisy, uncomfortable
- Prefer to buy my own books
- Poor hours at the library

[1] This case was coauthored by Cynthia Frey.

EXHIBIT 1 (*Continued*)

Inadequate supply of books, magazines, other materials [Specify]:

_____

Other reasons [Specify]: _____

6 How many blocks away would you say the nearest branch of the public library is to your home? [Read choices. Circle *one* response.]
  1 Less than one block
  2 One to two blocks
  3 Two to four blocks
  4 Four to six blocks
  5 More than six blocks
  8 (Don't know)

33 What, if anything, bugs you about the people who work at the library? [Probe thoroughly.]

_____

45 What was the last grade you completed in school? [Do *not* read choices. Circle *one* response.]
  ● Eighth grade or less
  ● Ninth grade but not a high school graduate
  ● High school graduate
  ● Some college
  ● College graduate
  ● Post graduate
  ● Vocational school
  ● Still in high school
  ● Still in college
  ● Refused to answer
  ● Didn't know

CASE 6-2: Milan Food Cooperative (B)

The data presented in the Milan Food Cooperative (A) (Case 3-1) was subjected to correlation and regression analysis with three objectives in mind:

  1 Determination of the strength of association between families' food spending and demographic characteristics (correlation and regression)
  2 Determination of a function by which we can estimate a family's spending from its demographic data (regression)
  3 Determination of the statistical "confidence" in the above tests

The variables included in this analysis were:

  1 Weekly food expenditures ($)
  2 Number of persons in household

EXHIBIT 1   CORRELATION RESULTS

	Expenditures	Persons	Income	Kids 6–18	Kids <6	Education	Age
Expenditures	—						
Persons	.43	—					
Income	.38	.15	—				
Kids 6–18	.40	.70	.19	—			
Kids <6	.16	.56	−.01	.24	—		
Education	.23	.11	.48	.11	.11	—	
Age	.08	.00	.16	.11	−.32	−.06	—

3 Total annual income of household ($)
4 Children, 6–18 years old (0 or 1)
5 Children, <6 years old (0 or 1)
6 Education of head of household (5 levels)
7 Age of head of household (years)

Assume for the purposes of interpreting the results of this analysis, presented in Exhibits 1 and 2, that the 500 households used are randomly selected from a much larger population of households.

CASE QUESTIONS

1 For the correlation results:
   a What interpretation can you give to the results shown?
   b What assumptions underlie your interpretations?
   c How could these assumptions be tested?
2 For the regression results:
   a What interpretation can you give to these results?
   b What assumptions underlie your interpretations?
   c How could these assumptions be tested?
   d Does the low R^2 imply that our independent variables are poor predictors of food expenditures?
   e Support your position.

EXHIBIT 2   REGRESSION RESULTS
Six-Variable Regression: Weekly Food Expenditures in Dollars

Variable	Coefficient	Standard error	t	Significance level
Constant	17.21	4.95	2.78	.0056
Persons	3.51	.71	4.94	.0000
Kids <6	−1.87	2.23	−.84	.3998
Kids 6–18	5.30	2.30	2.31	.0215
Education	1.11	.76	1.47	.1431
Income	.768	.25	5.99	.0000
Age	.025	.069	.37	.7088

$R^2 = 0.296$ Error = 17.65

CASE 6-3: Bernie's Student Cafeteria[2]

James Burnett was head of Southwest University (SU) food services. SU had a student population of 25,000 and a faculty of 1800. In the fall of 1984, SU food service had opened a 24-hour cafeteria on central campus for SU students and faculty. "Bernie's" offered breakfast from 4:30 A.M. until noon, and complete hot meals between 10:00 A.M. and 10:00 P.M. It also served deli sandwiches, pizza, and burgers around the clock. The food was high quality (better than the typical dormitory fare), yet priced lower than comparable food at other restaurants. Students who had meal plans through their dormitories could get, as compensation for missed meals, deductions from their bills when they ate at Bernie's. In addition to food, Bernie's carried morning newspapers and the "essential" school supplies—pens, pencils, paper, and blue books.

One year after the opening of Bernie's, the president of Southwest commissioned Burnett to conduct a study to find out students' opinions about the new 24-hour cafeteria. The university was in dire need of office space, and if students weren't satisfied with Bernie's, the president was going to have it remodeled into offices. The president was most particularly interested in: (1) student awareness of Bernie's, (2) student use of the 24-hour cafeteria, and (3) overall student satisfaction with Bernie's. Since Burnett was fairly certain that the study results would favor keeping Bernie's, he decided to include questions in the survey which would help him to improve the existing services. Burnett wanted to know what specific things the students liked and disliked about Bernie's, and what they felt could be added or improved upon.

The questionnaire for the study was designed, pretested, and finalized by the University Research Center (URC). The version that was finally administered to students appears in Exhibit 1. A URC computer generated a simple random sample of 1300 students for the purposes of the study. In January 1986 these students were mailed a copy of the questionnaire. Burnett purposely chose January because it was long enough after the initial opening and far enough into the school year for an optimal number of students to have been exposed to Bernie's. The questionnaire was mailed with a cover letter and a return envelope. A copy of Bernie's menu and two coupons for $1.00 off any $5.00 purchase at Bernie's were included as incentives. The cover letter contained a request for cooperation and assured the students of anonymity. It requested that the student complete the questionnaire and return it within 7 days. Due to time constraints, questionnaires returned after 2 weeks were not included in the study.

Forty-nine percent (637) of the questionnaires were returned within 2 weeks after the mailing. Twenty of those were not usable, leaving 47 percent suitable for analysis. This was unusually high—the last university-conducted mail survey had only a 28 percent return rate. Burnett was extremely pleased with the success of the study. He had to give a presentation to the president in 2 days, so he sat down to begin analyzing the results. Exhibit 2 is a copy of the results as presented to Burnett by URC.

---

[2] This case was coauthored by Sheryl Petras.

EXHIBIT 1

QUESTIONNAIRE

1. How often do you eat out?
   _____ Less than once a month
   _____ One to three times a month
   _____ Once a week
   _____ Two to three times a week
   _____ More than three times a week

2. Please rank the following characteristics in order of their importance to you when you dine out. (1 = most important)
   _____ Food
   _____ Service
   _____ Atmosphere
   _____ Price

3. What type of food do you usually eat when you dine out?
   _____ Breakfast
   _____ Deli sandwiches
   _____ Salad bar
   _____ Typical "fast food" (burgers, fries, hot dogs, etc.)
   _____ Pizza
   _____ Complete meals (i.e., hot entrees)
   _____ Other (please specify) _____

4. Are you aware that the University Food Service has a 24-hour cafeteria, Bernie's, located on central campus? Yes _____ No _____

5. Have you ever eaten at Bernie's? Yes _____ No _____
   If you have never been to Bernie's, please skip to question number 9.

6. How many times since its opening in September 1984 have you eaten at Bernie's?
   _____ One
   _____ Two–five
   _____ Six–ten
   _____ Eleven–fifteen
   _____ More than fifteen

7. Based on your experience with Bernie's, we would like you to rank the following list of items as excellent (E), good (G), fair (F), or poor (P).

Item	E	G	F	P
Service				
Friendly	_____	_____	_____	_____
Courteous	_____	_____	_____	_____
Quick	_____	_____	_____	_____
Order taken correctly	_____	_____	_____	_____
Other _____	_____	_____	_____	_____
Overall service	_____	_____	_____	_____
Food				
Appearance	_____	_____	_____	_____
Taste	_____	_____	_____	_____
Variety	_____	_____	_____	_____
Portion size	_____	_____	_____	_____
Other _____	_____	_____	_____	_____
Overall service	_____	_____	_____	_____
Atmosphere				
Cleanliness	_____	_____	_____	_____
Noise level	_____	_____	_____	_____
Adequate seating	_____	_____	_____	_____
Other _____	_____	_____	_____	_____
Overall atmosphere	_____	_____	_____	_____
Overall experience	_____	_____	_____	_____

8. How do Bernie's prices compare with the prices of similar foods at other restaurants?

	Bernie's price:					
	Not sure	Much higher	Somewhat higher	About the same	Somewhat lower	Much lower
Food item						
Breakfast	_____	_____	_____	_____	_____	_____
Burgers	_____	_____	_____	_____	_____	_____
Fries	_____	_____	_____	_____	_____	_____
Hot entrees	_____	_____	_____	_____	_____	_____
Deli sandwiches	_____	_____	_____	_____	_____	_____
Pizza	_____	_____	_____	_____	_____	_____
Salad bar	_____	_____	_____	_____	_____	_____
Desserts	_____	_____	_____	_____	_____	_____
Beverages	_____	_____	_____	_____	_____	_____

Overall, Bernie's prices are:

_____ Much higher
_____ Somewhat higher
_____ About the same
_____ Somewhat lower
_____ Much lower
_____ I'm not sure

9. Do you plan to eat at Bernie's within the next month?
   Yes _____   No _____   Don't know _____

10. Personal Information:
    a. What is your age? _____
    b. Male/female? _____
    c. Married or single? _____
    d. Are you a full-time or part-time student? _____
    f. If you do not live in university housing, about how many miles are you from central campus?
       _____ Less than one-half mile
       _____ One-half mile up to (but not including) one mile
       _____ One mile up to (but not including) two miles
       _____ Two miles or more
    g. Do you have a meal contract through the university? _____
    h. Please indicate number of years you have attended Southwest (as of May 1986).
       _____ Less than one
       _____ One
       _____ Two
       _____ Three
       _____ Four
       _____ More than four
    i. Please list the first three digits of your hometown ZIP code _____

Additional comments: Please feel free to make any complaints or suggestions regarding Bernie's in the space provided below.

Thank you for your cooperation in responding to this survey. Please mail your completed questionnaire within seven days. A postage paid envelope has been provided for your convenience.

EXHIBIT 2

RESULTS

TABLE 1 HOW OFTEN DO YOU EAT OUT?
($n = 617$)

Less than once a month	21.1%
One to three times a month	34.5
Once a week	27.5
Two to three times a week	10.5
More than three times a week	6.3

TABLE 2 IMPORTANCE OF RESTAURANT CHARACTERISTICS
WHEN DINING OUT
[1 = Most important ($n = 617$)]

Characteristic	Rating			
	1	2	3	4
Food	47.2%	38.2%	14.4%	0.2%
Service	5.2	9.4	36.3	49.1
Atmosphere	15.9	21.2	24.1	38.7
Price	31.8	31.1	25.1	12.0

TABLE 3 ARE YOU AWARE OF BERNIE'S EXISTENCE?
($n = 617$)

Yes	97.1%
No	2.9

TABLE 4 HAVE YOU EATEN AT BERNIE'S?
($n = 617$)

Yes	82.2%
No	17.8

TABLE 5 HOW MANY TIMES HAVE YOU EATEN AT BERNIE'S?
($n = 488$)

One	37.1%
Two–five	24.2
Six–ten	19.3
Eleven–fifteen	15.6
More than fifteen	3.8

EXHIBIT 2 *(continued)*

TABLE 6 RATINGS OF SERVICE, FOOD, ATMOSPHERE, AND OVERALL
EXPERIENCE AT BERNIE'S
($n = 507$)

Characteristic	Avg. score
Overall food	3.5
Overall service	3.7
Overall atmosphere	2.4
Overall experience	3.1

Respondents rated the items on an "excellent, good, fair, poor" scale.
For data analysis, this has been converted into a 4-point numeric scale,
with 4 being excellent and 1 being poor. This table presents the average
of the respondents' scores.

TABLE 7 DO YOU PLAN TO EAT AT BERNIE'S
WITHIN THE NEXT MONTH?
($n = 617$)

Yes	20.3%
No	23.7
Don't know	56.1

TABLE 8 KNOWLEDGE OF BERNIE'S BY YEAR ON CAMPUS
($n = 617$)

	Years on campus						
Knowledge	Less than 1	1	2	3	4	More	Total
Yes	0%	29.7%	24.4%	18.9%	17.4%	9.7%	100.1%
No	16.7	27.8	22.2	16.7	5.6	11.1	100.1

$p < .005$. (All test are chi square.)

TABLE 9 NUMBER OF TIMES HAVING EATEN AT BERNIE'S BY HOW OFTEN EATEN OUT
($n = 488$)

	Eating out frequency					
Number times eaten at Bernie's	Less than once a month	1–3 times a month	Once a week	2–3 times a week	More than 3 times a week	Total
Once	32.0%	33.1%	29.3%	3.3%	2.2%	99.9%
2–5	26.3	36.4	26.3	4.2	6.8	100.0
6–10	10.6	39.4	24.5	19.1	6.4	100.0
11–15	0	38.2	28.9	22.4	10.5	100.0
More	0	5.3	26.3	26.3	42.1	100.0

$p < .005$.

EXHIBIT 2 *(continued)*

TABLE 10   UNIVERSITY MEAL CONTRACT BY NUMBER OF TIMES EATEN AT BERNIE'S
($n = 488$)

Meal Contract?	Times eaten at Bernie's					
	1	2–5	6–10	11–15	More	Total
Yes	13.8%	32.4%	35.7%	10.0%	8.1%	100.0%
No	22.3	30.6	33.5	9.7	4.0	100.1

$p < .1.$

TABLE 11   DISTANCE FROM CENTRAL CAMPUS BY HAVING EATEN AT BERNIE'S
($n = 545$)

Eaten at Bernie's	Distance from campus				
	In dorm	Less than 1 mi	1 mi	1–2 mi	2+ mi
Yes	90.0%	84.5%	85.6%	65.6%	15.0%
No	10.0	15.5	14.4	34.4	85.0
Total	100.0	100.0	100.0	100.0	100.0

$p < .005.$

TABLE 12   OVERALL EXPERIENCE BY INTENT TO EAT AT BERNIE'S IN THE NEXT MONTH
($n = 507$)

Rating of overall experience	Intend to eat at Bernie's in next month (% of those who gave yes/no responses)			
	Yes	No	Don't know	Total
Excellent	70.7%	29.3%	57	100%
Good	63.2	36.8	000	100
Fair	6.4	93.6	000	100
Poor	0	100.0	000	100

$p < .005.$

TABLE 13   HAVING EATEN AT BERNIE'S BY SEX
($n = 617$)

Eaten at Bernie's	Male	Female
Yes	42.0%	58.0%
No	26.4	73.6

$p < .005.$

EXHIBIT 2 *(continued)*

TABLE 14   TYPE OF FOOD USUALLY EATEN WHEN DINING
OUT BY SEX
($n = 617$)

Food Type	Male	Female
Breakfast	14.0%	4.0%
Deli sandwiches	12.0	10.1
Salad bar	7.9	18.9
Typical "fast food" (burgers, fries, hot dogs, etc.)	19.0	13.1
Pizza	26.0	29.9
Complete meals (i.e., hot entrees)	21.1	24.0
Other (please specify)	0	0
Totals	100.0	100.0

$p < .005$.
Note: Totals may not add to 100% due to rounding error.

CASE QUESTIONS

1 What conclusions can be drawn on the basis of the univariate analysis?
2 What conclusions can be drawn on the basis of the bivariate analysis? Be sure to write down the relevant conclusion for each crosstab table. Are all the percentages cast in the correct direction to aid in your interpretation?
3 Indicate which bivariate tables should be elaborated. Be specific with respect to the control variables you would use and to what effect the elaboration might have on the conclusions drawn from the bivariate table.
4 Write a management summary of the major findings of this study.

APPLICATIONS

CHAPTER 22

DEMAND MEASUREMENT AND FORECASTING

The measurement of demand is an essential activity for an organization. Based on the 1978 American Marketing Association (AMA) survey,[1] over 80 percent of the companies surveyed did research in the following areas:

1 Determining market characteristics
2 Measuring market potential
3 Short- and long-range forecasting

These areas showed a 34 percent or greater increase over the 1973 AMA survey. In this chapter we will define the major concepts and terms in demand measurement and present the methods for measuring demand potential as well as the methods for forecasting demand.

CONCEPTS AND TERMINOLOGY

Demand measurement involves developing a quantitative estimate of demand. Demand can be measured on four dimensions: (1) product, (2) geographic location, (3) time period, and (4) customer. Table 22-1 shows the many levels of measurement possible. Be aware that there are many combinations of these four dimensions (5 × 4 × 3 × 3 = 180), each representing a potential demand measurement and forecasting situation. Each can pose a different type of problem where the purpose, data availability, and techniques for measurement differ substantially. Let's discuss in detail the concepts and terminology used in measuring these demand situations.

[1] Dik W. Twedt, *1978 Survey of Marketing Research* (Chicago: American Marketing Association, 1978), Table 1-1.

TABLE 22-1 FOUR DIMENSIONS OF DEMAND MEASUREMENT AND FORECASTING

Product	Geographic location	Time period	Customer
Industry	World	Current	Consumer
Company	U.S.A.	Short-range	Business
Product line	Region	Long-range	Government
Product class	Territory		
Product item			

Market Demand

The market demand for a product is a concept that requires careful specification of several elements. For example, consider the following definition of market demand for automobiles. *The 1983 U.S. market demand for automobiles is the total unit volume that was sold by all manufacturers (domestic and foreign) in the United States to all buyers (consumer, business, and government).*

This definition stipulates that the market demand for a *product* is the total volume that would be purchased by a defined *customer group* in a defined *time period* and *geography* given the 1983 *environment* and *marketing programs*. Here, market demand refers to a single number, say, 10 million automobiles. If the definition of market demand is expanded to include alternative environments and marketing programs, it becomes apparent that market demand could have been higher or lower than 10 million automobiles, depending on the nature of the marketing programs employed and the state of the environment. Consequently, given alternative environments and marketing programs, market demand can be expressed as series of numbers or functions rather than a single number.

The importance of recognizing that market demand is a function becomes clear when it is related to the concepts of *market potential* and *market forecast*. Figure 22-1 illustrates the relationship between market potential, market forecast, and market demand function. Market demand is shown to be a function of the level of industry marketing effort plus a given environment. A market forecast is shown to be the level of market demand given an *expected* level of industry marketing effort and an *assumed* environment. Market potential then becomes the *limit* approached by market demand within an assumed environment as industry marketing effort approaches infinity. Market potential therefore establishes an upper limit to market demand, while a market forecast specifies the expected level of market demand for a particular time period.

Company Demand

Company demand is the company's share of the market demand. For example, consider the following definition of company demand: *The 1983 company demand for General Motors is 40 percent of market demand, or 4 million automobiles.* Company demand, like market demand, is a function. This function is called the company demand function or sales response function. It describes estimated company sales at alternative

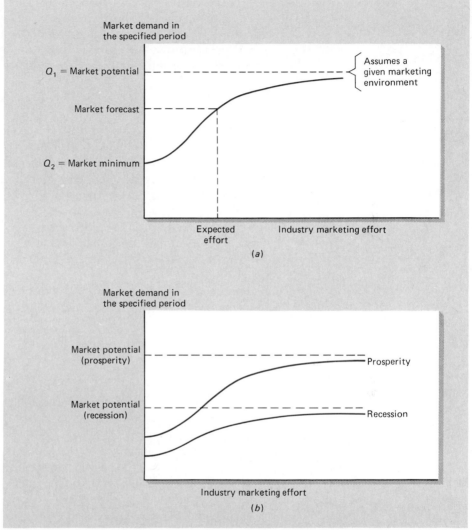

FIGURE 22-1 Market demand concepts and terminology. *(a)* Market demand as a function of industry marketing effort (assumes a particular marketing environment). *(b)* Market demand as a function of industry marketing effort (two different environments assumed). *[Source: Philip Kotler, Marketing Management, 4th ed. (Englewood Cliffs, N.J.: Prentice-Hall, 1980), p. 216]*

levels of company marketing effort. *Company sales potential* is the limit approached by company demand as company marketing effort increases relative to competitors.

The *company sales forecast* is the expected level of company sales based on a chosen marketing plan and assumed environment. It is important to recognize that this definition implies that the company sales forecast *does not* establish a basis for deciding on the amount and composition of marketing effort. Rather, this forecast is the *result* of a chosen marketing program and assumed environment.

Two additional concepts are used in relation to the company forecast. A *sales quota* is the sales goal set for a product line, company division, or sales representative. A *sales budget* is a conservative estimate of the expected volume of sales. A sales budget is lower than the company forecast in order to avoid excessive investment in purchasing, production, and cash flow in case the forecast is not realized.

ESTIMATION OF CURRENT DEMAND

Marketing researchers are frequently asked to measure the current market and sales potential for a new product or existing product. Such information is essential for designing sales territories, determining sales quotas, allocating salesforce effort, allocating advertising and sales promotion budgets, determining sales compensation levels, finding prospect accounts, dropping products, and making new product go–no go decisions.

It should be recognized that different methods are required for new versus established products or services. The distinction between new and established products is based on whether the product is new to the industry, rather than the individual seller. The research methods for new products tend to be more subjective than those for established products.[2]

The focus of this section will be on methods for estimating potential for established products. These methods may be classified into two groups: breakdown method and buildup method.

Breakdown Method

The breakdown method begins with aggregate industry or market data and breaks down the data into units of interest to the firm. Two approaches are used with the breakdown method—the direct data method and the indirect data method.

Direct Data Method   The direct data method relies on total industry or market data (usually shipments or consumption) as the basis for estimating market and sales potentials. The typical approach is to establish a sales or consumption index based on total industry or market data. If these data are reasonably accurate and timely, potentials based on them are "theoretically the most accurate."[3]

Table 22-2 exemplifies the direct data method. A manufacturer of cutting tools needs a market potential index for each of its exclusive industrial distributors. Since trade associations are a primary source of total industry shipments data, the company contacted the American Supply and Machinery Manufacturers Association, which issues a yearly report on sales made through industrial distributors by its members. Total shipments are classified by product categories, one of which is "Cutting Tools." This information is broken down by states and Metropolitan Statistical Areas (MSAs).

For example, in Table 22-2, territory number 3 includes the Chicago MSA plus 10 percent of the Illinois sales volume outside the Chicago MSA. The market potential

---

[2] For a discussion of methods to evaluate the market potential for new products, see Chap. 23.
[3] Frances E. Hummel, *Market and Sales Potentials* (New York: Ronald Press, 1961) p. 126.

TABLE 22-2   EXAMPLE OF DIRECT DATA METHOD

Exclusive distribution territories	Market potential index: cutting tools	Company sales potential	Actual company sales
1	.009	$ 165,131	$ 159,421
2	.004	73,392	10,734
3	.073	1,339,397	804,793
4	.031	568,785	501,732
Etc.	—	—	—
Total sales	$91,739,531	$18,347,906	$12,784,701

index of .073 for territory number 3 would be determined as follows:

Total cutting tool sales $91,739,531

Illinois sales   12,741,237

Chicago MSA sales   6,025,402

$$\text{Market potential index for territory 3} = \frac{(\$12,741,237 - \$6,025,402).1 + \$6,025,402}{\$91,739,531}$$

$$= .073$$

Company sales potential can be derived by estimating the share of market potential available to the firm. The usual approach is: (1) determine the market shares held by the firm in territories or segments where performance is judged to be superior under relevant business conditions and (2) use these shares to establish sales potentials.

Using this approach, assume that the company has determined that it holds a 20 percent share of the cutting tool business with well-established and effective distributors. Applying the 20 percent share to the market potential of $91,739,531 yields a potential of $18,347,906. Multiplying this sales potential by the market potential index for each distributor yields a distributor sales potential estimate.

Comparison of potential sales with actual sales indicates that distributors 1 and 4 are close to potential while distributors 2 and 3 are weak. The weak distributors could be investigated to determine why they are not achieving a higher share of potential sales. The cost of exploiting additional sales or the local competitive environment could explain such a deficit.

There are several sources of industry sales data available for this type of analysis. Sales data are recorded by federal and state agencies because of licensing and taxation. Trade associations compile industry sales data for an array of business organizations. A useful guide to many such sources of market potential data is the federal government publication *Measuring Markets*.[4]

---

[4] *Measuring Markets: A Guide to the Use of Federal and State Data,* U.S. Department of Commerce, Industry, and Trade Administration, August 1979.

TABLE 22-3   EXAMPLE OF INDIRECT DATA METHOD

States	Population (000)	Population percent	Drug market potential[1]	Company potential[2]
Michigan	8,073	.035	$ 350,000	$ 17,500
New York	15,529	.067	$ 670,000	$ 33,500
Florida	7,151	.031	$ 310,000	$ 15,500
Etc.	—	—	—	—
Total	230,667	1.00	$10,000,000	$500,000

[1]Determined by multiplying the population percent by $10 million—total competitive product sales in 1982.
[2]Determined by multiplying market potential by 5 percent—company estimated potential share of market.

The main advantage of using total industry sales to measure market potential is the validity of the data, given it is current and accurate. The direct data method is fairly simple and requires a few basic calculations to determine market and sales potentials.

The direct data method is not used frequently for two reasons. First, detailed industry and sales data are not available for many products and services. Second, when data are available, they may not reflect current market potential due to their historical nature.

Indirect Data Method   The indirect data method for determining market and sales potentials is based on the development of an index of potential from one or more statistical series related to the consumption or purchasing power of the product or service in question. The concept is to logically relate a series of data, such as number of employed persons, to industry sales for the product or service. This second series of data, being more detailed by market segments, may be used to indicate the distribution of industry sales in the market segments of concern. It is important to note that, in order to determine the market potential for an area or segment, it is necessary to have an estimate of total potential in dollars or units.

Table 22-3 illustrates this approach using a *single factor index* to determine the market and sales potential for a drug item. It assumes that the market potential for drugs is directly related to a single factor, such as population. Since population data are available by states, a simple calculation determines drug market potential by state. Assuming that this drug should achieve a 5 percent share of market, the company sales potential can easily be determined by state.

The limitation of this example is that rarely will a single factor such as population correlate highly with the sales of a product or service. Obviously, drug sales by state can be influenced by additional factors such as age distribution, disposable income, and number of physicians per thousand people. This leads to developing a *multiple-factor index,* each factor given a specific weight in the index.

A widely used multiple-factor index of area demand is the *Annual Survey of Buying Power* published by *Sales and Marketing Management.*[5] This index is designed to reflect the relative buying power in the different regions, states, and metropolitan areas of the nation. It is constructed from three factors—income, retail sales, and population.

[5] *1981 Survey of Buying Power* issue of *Sales Management,* July 27, 1981.

Income is weighted 5, sales 3, and population 2. For each county in the United States, income, retail sales, and population are determined as a percent of the total. These percentages are weighted as indicated above, then summed, and the total is divided by the sum of weights, which is 10.

A major limitation of such a *general multiple-factor index* is that it assumes the relative market potential in a given area is the same for an array of products. This is a weak assumption for most products. The market potential for powdered soft drinks and hot chocolate mix differ substantially in a market depending upon the season of the year. Thus, while general multiple-factor indexes may be useful for certain products or certain circumstances, more accurate market potentials may be found by developing special indexes.

The development of *special multiple-factor indexes* is not easy. In preparing the index, factor selection and weighting can be very judgmental. Whether this judgment is sound or not is difficult to demonstrate since such judgments are based on how close the indexes obtained correspond to actual sales results. But remember that actual sales results are not available for purpose of comparison; if they were, there would be no need to develop the index.

For industrial goods, a widely used general single-factor index is *Sales and Marketing Management*'s "Survey of Industrial Purchasing Power."[6] This annual survey provides data on the value of shipments of manufactured products by the Standard Industrial Classification (SIC) industry groups and geographic areas. When using this index, it is assumed that the value of shipments of an industry is an accurate indicator of the purchasing power of the industry and thus suitable as a single-factor index of market potential.

Buildup Method

This approach for estimating market and sales potentials involves the aggregation, or buildup, of data from the customer or account level to the industry or market level. Data are collected on customer past purchases or probable requirements for future purchases, and data are classified on the principal products/services produced, number of employees, and other relevant statistical series.

These data may be obtained from customers by mail, telephone, or personal interviews. Personal interviewers are required for highly technical products or services. Telephone and mail surveys are appropriate when factual data on past purchases and classification data are sought. If a mail survey is to be used, the researcher should be sensitive to the many sources of *error* possible with this approach.[7]

The buildup method, like the breakdown indirect method, seeks to establish a relationship between the purchases of a given product or service by firms within market groups (e.g., SIC classification) and one or more statistical series (e.g., number of employees). The following example will illustrate the steps in this approach.[8]

[6] "Survey of Industrial Purchasing Power 1981," *Sales and Marketing Management,* April 27, 1981.

[7] William E. Cox, Jr., and George N. Havens, "Determination of Sales Potentials and Performance for an Industrial Goods Manufacturer," *Journal of Marketing Research,* vol. 14, pp. 574–578, November 1977.

[8] This discussion follows that presented in William E. Cox, Jr., *Industrial Marketing Research* (New York: Ronald Press Publication, John Wiley and Sons, 1979) p. 161.

TABLE 22-4 EXAMPLE OF THE BUILDUP METHOD

SIC Code	Industry	Market survey data			U.S. total production employees	Estimated U.S. market potentials
		Product purchases	Number of production employees	Average purchases per employee		
3573	Computers and related equipment	$201,627	8,736	$23.08	78,000	$1,800,240
3585	Refrigeration and heating equipment	851,552	15,270	54.17	120,000	6,500,400
3721	Aircraft industry	292,692	20,020	14.62	130,000	1,900,600
3811	Engineering and scientific inst.	178,200	4,950	36.00	25,000	900,000

Notes: "Market survey data" are based on personal interviews with known users of roller bearings. "Product purchases" are totals purchased from all suppliers in previous calendar year. "Number of production employees" is the average employment during previous calendar year in user sample firms. "Average purchases per employee" is obtained from product purchases by the number of production employees. "U.S. total, production employees" data are estimated from the latest U.S. Bureau of the Census, *Annual Survey of Manufactures—General Statistics for Industry Groups and Industries.* "Estimated U.S. market potentials" are derived by multiplying "U.S. total production employees" by "average purchases per employee."

Source: Adapted and updated from Francis E. Hummel, "Market Potentials in the Machine Tool Industry—A Case Study," *Journal of Marketing,* vol. 19, pp. 34–41, July 1954.

Timken, the largest producer of tapered roller bearings, was interested in determining the market and sales potential for its products. Major users and potential users were identified using internal sales records and management expertise. A sample of firms was drawn from this prospect-user list and personally interviewed. The buildup method was used to determine market and sales potentials.

Table 22-4 presents the results of the buildup method for four market segments. The firms surveyed produced both data on their total purchases of tapered roller bearings from all sources for the preceding calendar year and data on the average number of production employees in the firm during the year. The average purchases per employee was calculated from these data for each of the market segments or user industries. The latest data from the *Annual Survey of Manufacturers* were used to estimate the total employment for each user industry. (The employment data represent all firms in the population from which the sample survey is drawn.) In Table 22-4 the market potential for SIC Code 3573 was determined by multiplying the average purchases per employee ($23.08) by total number of production employees (78,000) in all firms in the market segment or user industry. Market potentials for states, counties, and smaller geographic areas were similarly derived by substituting the employment data for these areas in place of the U.S. figures. Each market segment's sales potential was determined by estimating Timken's market share in each sample account and calculating a weighted average market share for each segment. Timken's sales potential in each market segment was determined by multiplying this weighted market share by the market potential.

The buildup method relies on valid published market data through which the survey results can be projected. As we saw, the SIC provides the market data on industrial products for such projections of market and sales potential. It is important enough for us to examine the system a little more closely.

The Standard Industrial Classification   The SIC system was developed by the federal government and is by far the most widely used system of industrial classification.[9] (See Chapter 6.) Most economic data published by U.S. government agencies are organized on the basis of the SIC system. In addition, a growing proportion of data from state and local governments, trade associations, publishing firms, and other private organizations uses the SIC system.

The SIC system covers all economic activities within our society and classifies them into: agriculture; forestry and fisheries; mining; construction; manufacturing; transportation; communication; electricity, gas, and sanitary services; wholesale and retail trade; finance, insurance, and real estate; service; and public administration. Within each economic classification, there is a further breakdown into industries and products.

Each firm or business entity is classified within this scheme on the basis of its principal product or business activity and given a four-digit code. Related four-digit industries are combined into three-digit groups; in turn these are combined into two-digit major groups.

Products are classified on the basis of five or more digits: the first four digits are based on the industries in which the products are primarily produced. Based on the SIC system, the Commerce Bureau publishes the *Census of Manufacturers,* which contains key manufacturing and sales data.

While the SIC system is a valuable tool, it is not without its drawbacks.[10]

1 *Multiproduct establishments.* If an establishment produces two or more products that are classified into more than one four-digit industry, the establishment will be assigned to a single industry, based on its primary activity. This practice leads to a tendency to overstate statistics for principal products and understate statistics for secondary products.

2 *Captive plants.* An establishment may have a "captive" operation that produces components for its primary and secondary products, although the components are also produced by other firms as a final product.

3 *Varying production and purchasing methods.* This situation makes it difficult to identify potential customers and to estimate market size.

4 *Need for finer classification.* The four-digit classification system results in aggregation of data that is sometimes dysfunctional for firms interested in specific product markets within the industry.

METHODS FOR FORECASTING DEMAND

In this section we examine forecasting the future demand for a product or service. The topics covered are: (1) importance of sales forecasting; (2) accuracy of sales fore-

---

[9] For a detailed presentation of the SIC system, see the Office of Management and Budget, *Standard Industrial Classification Manual* (Washington, D.C.: U.S. Government Printing Office, 1972).

[10] Francis E. Hummel, *Market and Sales Potentials* (New York: Ronald Press, 1961), pp. 74–76.

casting; (3) forecaster qualifications; (4) procedural guidelines for preparing a forecast; (5) management requirements for the forecasting report; and (6) forecasting techniques.

Importance of Forecasting

The forecasting of sales is a critical input to marketing decision making as well as that of other functional areas such as production, finance, and personnel. Poor forecasting can result in excessive inventory, inefficient salesforce expenditures, costly price reductions, lost sales, inefficient scheduling of production, and inadequate planning for cash flow and capital investments.

The importance of forecasting has increased because of the dynamic and hostile environment of the past decade. The shortages and high inflation of the early 1970s, followed by major recessions and high interest rates, have focused renewed attention on forecasting and the benefits it can provide.

Accuracy of Sales Forecasts

Sales forecasts are numerical estimates of the future sales of products or services of a company or industry. You should realize that sales forecasting is always wrong; that is, the numerical estimates always differ from actual sales results. Consequently, the issue of accuracy is one of how close the forecast is to actual reported sales. But this measure of accuracy is always too late; that is, it comes after the sales have been recorded. Therefore, there is no direct measure of forecasting accuracy ahead of the forecasting period.

If the accuracy of a forecast cannot be determined until after the forecast time period has expired, how can the quality of a forecast be judged beforehand? The answer lies in evaluating the characteristics of the forecasting process. Accurate forecasting, like any marketing research project, should (1) utilize systematic and objective procedures which are sensitive to statistical and nonstatistical sources of error and (2) employ valid data sources which provide timely information of adequate detail to meet the needs of the decision maker.

Forecaster Qualifications

Forecasters should have the level of training and experience appropriate for the requirements of the forecasting task. They could range from persons with bachelor's and master's degrees to highly trained statisticians or econometricians with advanced graduate degrees. The last section of this chapter reviews an array of forecasting techniques. Several require that the forecaster have special knowledge and skills if the techniques are to be used properly. Sophisticated techniques in the hands of unqualified persons can result in inaccurate forecasting.

Another perspective on forecaster qualifications relates to who should be discouraged from sales forecasting despite having the appropriate credentials. There are three types:[11] those who believe that the future is only a straight-line extrapolation of the past; those who substitute arithmetic for sense; and those who think they have the only magic formula.

Procedural Guidelines for Forecasting

The following guidelines have been suggested when starting a forecasting project:[12]

1 *Define the purpose for which the forecast is intended.* Will the forecast be used to determine sales quotas, set production levels, or establish promotion budgets? How accurate must the forecast be for various purposes?

2 *Define the products and product segments.* Is a separate forecast needed for each product? How detailed or segmented should the forecast be?

3 *Prepare an initial forecast.* Recognize there are various stages to developing a forecast. The first stage is relatively crude and simple but serves the purpose of defining data needs and the formation of hypotheses to be tested.

4 *Relate the forecast to company capabilities and objectives.* The final forecast should be consistent with corporate objectives as well as production, financial, and marketing capabilities.

5 *Review trends in the environment.* The forecast should reflect new variables or changes in the rates of historical variables. Areas such as competition, economic climate, and market trends should be analyzed carefully and incorporated into the forecasting model.

Management Requirements for Forecasting

There are several requirements that the forecaster should be sensitive to in preparing the forecast. From the manager's perspective, the forecast should meet the following requirements:[13]

1 Management should be given an industry (or all-company) forecast as an essential element in the company forecast package.

2 Management should expect a clear, brief statement of the assumptions underlying the forecast.

3 Forecasts should not be unduly qualified.

4 Management should require a clear statement of the period covered.

5 Management is entitled to a forecast that is not changed too often.

6 Details and techniques should be omitted from the forecast unless specifically requested. Most managers prefer this.

7 Management has a right to expect that forecasts be checked against what actually took place.

[11] William Copulsky, *Practical Sales Forecasting* (New York: American Management Association, 1970), pp. 13–14.

[12] Richard D. Crisp, "Objectives and Techniques of Sales Forecasting," in *Sales Forecasting: Uses, Techniques, Trends, Special Report No. 16* (New York: American Management Association, 1956), pp. 25–31.

[13] Ibid., pp. 13–16.

TABLE 22-5   FORECASTING METHODS

Qualitative methods	Time-series methods	Causal methods
Executive opinion	Moving average	Leading indicators
Salesforce-distributor estimates	Exponential smoothing	Regression models
Buyer or consumer surveys	Time-series decomposition	

Sales Forecasting Techniques

Table 22-5 groups eight forecasting techniques into three classifications:

1 *Qualitative methods.* These methods involve collecting judgments or opinions from knowledgeable individuals. These individuals may have access to quantitative or factual information about markets, products, and economic trends, but their judgments represent subjective conclusions on all the knowledge that they deem relevant to the forecasting situation. Such forecasts can use inputs from company management, salesforce personnel, and customers.

2 *Time-series methods.* These methods apply statistical techniques to historical sales data over time to make numerical sales forecasts.

3 *Causal models.* These methods apply statistical models to historical sales data plus measures of the underlying causes of sales dynamics.

Qualitative Methods   Judgment- or opinion-based forecasting techniques are the most popular methods of forecasting. Table 22-6 shows the frequency of use of these methods (executive consensus, aggregate of salesforce, and buyer or consumer surveys) compared to time-series analysis and causal models. Qualitative methods maintain their high usage levels across consumer, industrial, and service industries.

Executive Opinion   This qualitative method involves tapping the judgments of a group of managers regarding the forecast. The method is based on the assumption that several experts can arrive at a better forecast than one expert.

TABLE 22-6   USAGE LEVEL OF MAJOR SALES FORECASTING METHODS
Percentage of Firms' Rating Techniques as First or Second Most Valued

	Category			
Method	All firms	Industrial product	Consumer product	Service
Executive consensus	54	50	64	72
Aggregate of salesforce	56	62	40	42
Buyer or consumer surveys	29	35	13	7
Time-series analysis	30	35	46	34
Causal models	15	14	20	36
Number of firms	161	93	39	29

Source: S. J. P. Kempner and Earl L. Bailey, *Sales Forecasting Practices: An Appraisal* (*New York: The Conference Board*, 1970) p. 14.

There are a number of ways of combining the judgments of a group of executives.[14] The *group discussion method* involves meeting as a committee and coming up with a group consensus forecast. There is no secrecy among respondents, and communication is encouraged. However, the forecast may not reflect a true consensus in that individual judgments can be influenced by group pressure. A second approach is the *pooled individual estimates method*. Here, each executive separately submits estimates to a project leader who combines them into a single forecast. This procedure overcomes the potential group pressure bias of the open discussion approach. The third approach is called the *Delphi method,* which has become a popular market and technological forecasting approach.[15] Group members are asked to make individual judgments about a forecast. The group judgments are recorded and resubmitted to each group member. After comparing the anonymous judgments with their own, the executives can revise their judgments. In so doing, each person can justify the logic of the forecast that will be communicated to other members. After several iterations, group members typically reach a consensus. The assumption underlying this method is that a forecast developed in this manner is more accurate than the previous two methods.

Salesforce/Distributor Estimates   A common method of sales forecasting, especially among industrial firms (see Table 22-6), is to aggregate individual forecasts of salespeople or distributors. An advantage of this method is that a salesperson or distributor is close to the market and hence a fairly good judge of the peculiarities of demand in a sales region. Such forecasts are fairly accurate in the short run, i.e., the next month, quarter, or perhaps year, but become increasingly unreliable and even meaningless over longer time periods.

One problem with this method is of an administrative nature—getting a salesperson to make a conscientious forecast and turn it in on time. The other problem is one of reliability. Forecasts may be biased upward or downward depending on the motivations of the salesperson or distributor. For example, a sales representative paid on a commission basis may feel that a conservative forecast results in lower sales quotas. A distributor, fearful of potential out-of-stock problems, may project an optimistic forecast. An additional source of bias is salesperson-distributor ignorance of broad economic trends which would affect sales in that particular region.

Short-term forecasts based on this method can be very helpful if properly conducted using valid data collection procedures. Even when more sophisticated methods are adopted, a salesperson/distributor estimate could always be carried out to serve as a second forecast for comparison purposes.

Buyer or Consumer Surveys   Forecasts can be based on buyer judgments as to their intended purchase of goods and services. It is most appropriate when there are a limited number of buyers who have clear purchase intentions and are willing to disclose their intentions. Consequently, this method is used more for industrial products than for consumer products or services. (See Table 22-6.)

[14] Philip Kotler, *Marketing Management,* 4th ed. (Englewood Cliffs, N.J.: Prentice-Hall, 1980), p. 232.

[15] See Norman Dalkey and Olaf Helmer, "An Experimental Application of the Delphi Method to the Use of Experts," *Management Science,* pp. 458–467, April 1963. Also, see Roger J. Best, "An Experiment in Delphi Estimation in Marketing Decision Making," *Journal of Marketing Research,* pp. 447–452, November 1974.

For many companies, an alternative to going directly to consumers is to subscribe to publications of consumer surveys which reveal broad information of buyer intentions. One such service is the quarterly survey of consumer finances carried out by the Institute for Social Research at the University of Michigan. Other surveys of planned business plant and equipment expenditures are conducted and published by the Securities and Exchange Commission, McGraw-Hill Publishing Company (in *Business Week*), the National Industrial Conference Board, and *Fortune* magazine. Information from these sources can be used as input for the executive opinion method.

Time-Series Methods   The time-series approach to forecasting involves the extrapolation of historical sales data forward as a linear or curvilinear trend. This can be done by visual examination or by using statistical techniques. For short-term forecasting, time-series extrapolation can be a very effective tool.

Several conditions are necessary for time-series forecasting to be appropriate. First, it is best suited to rather stable situations where the future will be mainly an extension of the past. In other words, a time-series forecast is inappropriate for forecasting "turning points." Second, the historical sales data must have clear patterns or trends which are distinctive from the random-error component in the data.

Time-series forecasting raises a number of issues. First, how far back should the historical data go? Do older data represent conditions that have changed and therefore would more likely detract from the accuracy of the forecast? Second, given a time series, how should the data be weighted? Should each time period be given equal weight, or should most recent observations be given more weight? Third, should the data be decomposed into trend, cycle, season, and error? The following time-series methods differ in how to deal with these issues.

Moving Average   This method uses the average of the last *n* data points as the basis for trend extrapolation. In developing a short-term forecast, the random element in the data set is of major concern. One way to minimize the impact of random error is to average several of the past data points. This consists of weighting *n* of the recently observed data points by 1/*n*.

For example, if a marketing manager desired a monthly forecast of product shipments to key accounts, a 12-month moving average could be used. Next month's forecast would be based on data points for the past 12 months. Each month's product shipment data would be given a weight of 1/12, and the summed weighted values would form the forecast.

This method becomes a "moving" average when new data points become available and they are incorporated in the calculation for the next forecasting period. In addition, when a moving average period is selected which corresponds to a complete seasonal pattern (e.g., 12 months of data cover an annual seasonal sales pattern), the effect of seasonality is removed from the forecast since data points for each period of the season are included in the moving average.

Exponential Smoothing   This approach differs from the moving average method in that it does not use a constant set of weights for the data points. Rather, an exponentially decreasing set of weights is used. Here, the more recent data points receive more weight than older data points. The logic of this approach is that the more recent data are given greater weight, which should result in a more accurate forecast.

There are several different variations of exponential smoothing which build on the application of decreasing weights to older data points. These higher forms of exponential smoothing make adjustments for such things as trend and seasonal patterns.

Time-Series Decomposition   This widely used method consists of measuring four temporal components of a time series: (1) trend, (2) cycle, (3) season, and (4) error.

The trend component results from basic drivers of sales, such as disposable income, population, and technology. It is typically found to be a straight line or a gradually curved line when fitted to the data points.

The cycle component results from fairly systematic changes in the amplitude and periodicity of general economic activity. It is found by fitting a wavelike curve to the sales data.

The seasonal component results from changes in sales levels due to weather, holidays, and so on. It is represented in the data by a consistent pattern of sales for periods within a year (quarters, months, or weeks).

The error component results from such erratic events as price wars, blizzards, and strikes. The analytical problem in time-series decomposition is to separate the error component from the underlying systematic components of trend, cycle, and season.

Causal Methods   Causal models involve statistical techniques relating historical sales data to the economic forces that cause sales to rise or fall. These methods represent the most sophisticated sales forecasting tools. They are most accurate when relevant historical data are available on the major variables causing changes in sales.

The attraction of causal methods lies in three areas. First, they can predict turning points more accurately than time-series methods. Second, causal models have the potential to explain more of the variation in sales data and thus reduce the random-error component to a greater degree than may be possible with time-series methods. Third, an understanding of causal relationships in a market has more relevance to marketing decision making than is possible with isolated sales projections.

Leading Indicators   This approach involves the identification of leading indicators whose movement up or down usually precedes the sales variation of a good or service. By monitoring changes in indicators, it may be possible to forecast turning points in sales. The following are examples of leading indicators: (1) new housing starts lead major appliance sales, (2) number of births leads the sale of infant-related goods and services, and (3) disposable income leads demand for many durable goods. Frequently, leading indicators can be included in regression models.

Regression Models   Simple regression refers to two variables, where the explanatory or causal (independent) variable is considered to have a causal effect on the dependent variable of sales. As discussed in Chapter 18, the regression equation would be

$$\text{Sales forecast} = Y = a + bX$$

where Y = the dependent variable of sales
X = the independent variable
a = the value of the intercept on the Y axis
b = the slope of the line

As we saw in Chapter 20, multiple regression allows us to determine the causal relationship between several independent variables and the item being forecast, i.e., sales. The multiple regression model extends the simple regression theory to a predicting equation like

$$Y = a + b_1 X_1 + b_2 X_2 + b_3 X_3$$

This equation is fitted by the least-squares criterion and has three independent variables, X_1, X_2, and X_3, which are the assumed causes for past sales variations Y.

The regression model has a wide variety of applications to sales forecasting situations. The method is used extensively in practice and can be a very accurate sales forecasting technique. Of course, regression only shows the association among variables. The causal interpretation of these relationships is one added by the marketer based upon a good understanding of the world from which it comes.

SUMMARY

1 The development of quantitative measures of demand, present and future, is an essential activity in every organization.

2 Demand can be measured on four dimensions: (1) degree of product aggregation, (2) geographic location, (3) time horizon, and (4) customer type.

3 Essential demand measurement concepts distinguish between market demand and company demand, both of which have corollary concepts of potential and forecast.

4 The approaches for measuring current demand are the breakdown and buildup methods. Breakdown methods can be classified as the direct data and indirect data approaches.

5 When estimating future demand, the firm may use one or a combination of methods. These methods can be classified as: (1) qualitative methods, (2) time-series extrapolation, and (3) causal models.

6 Qualitative methods of forecasting include (1) executive opinion, (2) salesforce/distributor estimation, and (3) buyer or consumer surveys. These approaches are frequently used in consumer, industrial, and service organizations. Inexpensive and fast, they integrate the diverse information available to knowledgeable persons in the business. Qualitative methods are limited by the degree to which subjective judgments are biased and/or uninformed regarding key forecasting variables.

7 Time-series methods of forecasting include (1) moving average, (2) exponential smoothing, and (3) time-series decomposition. These methods are well suited to short-term forecasts when the historical data contain clear trend, seasonal, or cyclical patterns. They are ineffective in forecasting turning points.

8 Causal methods of forecasting include: (1) leading indicators and (2) regression models. These approaches require a thorough understanding of market dynamics, specifically those factors that influence sales. Causal methods can be used to help predict turning points.

DISCUSSION QUESTIONS

1 Develop four alternative definitions of market demand for television sets.

2 What is the difference between market potential and market forecast? Why is this difference important?

3 What is the difference between market forecast and company sales forecast?

4 Compare and contrast the breakdown and buildup methods of estimating current demand.

5 Why is accurate sales forecasting important to an organization?

6 How would you determine the accuracy of a proposed forecast?

7 Compare and contrast the three classifications of sales forecasting techniques: (a) qualitative methods, (b) time-series methods, and (c) causal models. Why is this distinction important?

CHAPTER 23

PRODUCT RESEARCH
AND TEST MARKETING

One of the major application areas of marketing research is in product research. A 1983 American Marketing Association study indicated that 92 percent of both industrial and consumer firms undertake some form of product research. In addition, 96 percent of financial service organizations, 83 percent of advertising agencies, and 76 percent of publishers and broadcasters surveyed undertake such research.[1] The increased use of marketing research in product decisions is easily understood when we consider the importance of those decisions. For many organizations, product decisions are the single most important set of decisions made by managers since they form the basis of the firm's marketing strategy. Additionally, expenditures on product development can run into the millions of dollars for a single product. For example, the average consumer product costs over $7 million to develop, and the average industrial product costs almost $3 million to develop.[2] Many products cost much more than this. And new product failure rates are estimated to be quite high—from about 30 percent to as high as 80 percent.[3] The power of marketing research to aid the product development process is clearly illustrated in the bank design Marketing Research In Action in this section.

Procedures used in product research include concept generation and testing techniques, laboratory testing, and test marketing. All of these will be discussed in this chapter. Test marketing (or market testing, as others call it) in particular has major ap-

---

[1] Dik W. Twedt, 1983 *Survey of Marketing Research* (Chicago: American Marketing Association, 1978), pp. 41–44.

[2] Glen L. Urban and John R. Hauser, *Design and Marketing of New Products* (Englewood Cliffs, N.J.: Prentice-Hall, 1980), pp. 56–57.

[3] David S. Hopkins and Carl L. Bailey ("New Product Pressures," *The Conference Board Record.* pp. 16–24, June 1971) give the high estimate, whereas David Hopkins ("Survey Finds 60 Percent of New Products Succeed," *Marketing News*, vol. XIII, p. 1, Feb. 8, 1980) gives the low estimate.

MARKETING RESEARCH IN ACTION

MARKETING RESEARCH USED IN DESIGNING BANKS

Southwest Bancshares, a large bank headquartered near Houston, Texas, was going to build two new branches. Following the creation of the drive-up teller windows, bank customers demanded both convenience in making transactions and closer interaction with bank personnel. Those banks who refused to keep up with the desires of the customer faced an early demise. Golemon & Rolfe Associates, Inc., architects, relied heavily on marketing research findings when drawing the plans for the two branches. Each bank was designed to meet the particular wants and needs of its customers.

The first, Westchase Bank, was to be located in Houston's southwest quadrant. This area was experiencing high growth in both the residential and commercial segments. Research identified the primary market as commercial, with a mix of upscale retail. Thus, the bank had to be large enough to service its customers quickly, as commercial clients were generally averse to waiting. The client mix was found to be very image conscious, mostly professionals between 25 and 40 years of age. Golemon & Rolfe designed Westchase's interior to augment its patrons' image—it was to be very sophisticated, without being overly stark. Thus, English oak was de-signated for the furnishings and the wood trim in the lobby area. Marble was used throughout the bank for tellers' counters and check-writing stands.

Woodlands Bank, on the other hand, was the prototypical neighborhood bank. It was to be located on the outskirts of Houston, in a wooded area adjacent to a newly built community. Woodlands' customers would be almost exclusively residential, so its design had to be different from that of the more "modern" Westchase Bank. Residential patrons preferred a building that blended in with its surroundings; thus, the bank's exterior was planned to complement its natural setting. They also favored an "open" interior design. To create this effect, windows were used extensively. Also, work stations separated by mahogany dividers replaced enclosed offices.

With the competition among banks at an all-time high, it was essential that Southwest Bancshares design each branch to suit its clients' personalities as well as their banking needs. It was a buyer's market—if customers didn't like a bank, they could and would go elsewhere. Since the architecture of any bank was a factor in its popularity, conducting marketing research before creating the final blueprints was very beneficial. It allowed each new branch to mesh its atmosphere and decor with its clients' tastes.

Source: Adapted from Robert Kester, "Market Research Invaluable to Bank Architectural Design," *The Magazine of Bank Administration,* February 1984.

plications not only for product research but also for other elements of the marketing mix. It will be covered extensively in this chapter.

The stages in the development of new products are: (1) idea generation, (2) concept development and testing, (3) business analysis, and (4) commercialization. Marketing research techniques can be applied in all these stages, although the specific techniques used are different at each stage.

IDEA GENERATION

The first stage in the product development process is *idea generation.* Here the objective is to come up with completely new ideas for products, or new attributes for current products, or new uses for current products. At this stage of the product development process, a great deal of flexibility and creativity is needed in the research procedures used. Two exploratory research procedures can be useful: the repertory grid technique and various types of focus-group interviews.

Repertory Grid

The repertory grid technique helps to generate a list of attributes which consumers can use to describe similarities and differences among products. The intention is to identify those attributes that will be important to consumers in their evaluation of new products in the product category or to identify an attribute that was previously not associated with a particular product.

The steps in the repertory grid technique are:

1 The products being tested are selected and printed on a set of cards; for example, if ten snacks were being examined, one snack would appear on each card.

2 The respondent sorts through the cards and removes cards for products that are unfamiliar.

3 Three cards are selected as directed by a prespecified plan, and the respondent is asked "to think of a way in which any two of the three items are similar to each other and different from the third." This identifies one attribute used by consumers in their perceptions of this product group.

4 The process is repeated with another group of three cards, but this time the respondent is asked for some new way in which two products differ from the third. This identifies a second attribute.

5 The process is repeated until the respondent can no longer identify additional product attributes. The average consumer can generate between 15 and 20 attributes in this way.

If the products are established ones, the researcher seeks new dimensions of consumer perception. For example, a major motorcycle firm identified a previously unrecognized dimension, "power image at a standing-still position," using the repertory grid procedure; it has since been incorporated in their product design and advertising. This procedure can also be used with a product concept statement included with established products or even with a group of concept statements. For example, the concept of an "electric car" could be teamed in the repertory grid procedure with a car already established in the "second car of the family" category.

Focus Groups

Consumer focus groups, described in Chapter 13, are used extensively in idea generation for new products. Additionally, a special type of focus group using experts as respondents, called a *synectic session,* or brainstorming session, may be used. Here the moderator carefully directs the discussion from general to increasingly specific issues. The idea is to generate as many ideas as possible without being critical, allowing the group activity to refine and improve them. Brainstorming is looser and less evaluative than a standard focus group.

CONCEPT DEVELOPMENT AND TESTING

Many new product ideas are eliminated if they can't be undertaken by the company. This can be because of lack of fit with production or marketing skills, technical impossibility, and so on. Ideas that do survive this kind of screening are then taken to consumers for testing.

The major objectives of concept testing are (1) to get first-cut reaction as to consumers' views of the product idea, (2) to give direction to future development of the project, (3) to select the most promising concepts for further development, and (4) to get an initial evaluation of potential commercialization prospects for the product. The research is exploratory in nature and thus tends to use small samples selected in nonprobability fashion—usually a judgment or quota sample.

The questions you want to answer with a concept test include: Do consumers understand the concept? Does the concept have a crucial flaw? Does the product meet the needs of some segment? and What alternate concepts would be preferred?

Relevant marketing research techniques used in concept testing are focus-group interviews, monadic ratings, paired comparison ratings, conjoint analysis, and usage tests. Before examining these techniques we will first address the issue of the nature of concept to be tested.

The Nature of the Concept Tested

The nature of the concept presented to consumers depends on the position in the product development process that has been reached. In the very early stages of the process, the concept description may be a few sentences or short paragraphs. For example, a major food marketer tested and refined its concept for a diet gravy product based solely on verbal descriptions. As the process advances, the concept may also include drawings or even roughed-out advertisements. Chatham Supermarkets, a large midwestern chain, tests advertising concepts using such ads. At a later stage, mock-ups of the product or even prototypes of the product may be presented. Automobile companies test car designs with consumers using full-scale clay models of their cars.

At some point it is important for the concept to include the essence of the marketing program that will support it. This is because consumers react to all marketing aspects of a product offering, including its price, name, advertising position, and even type of store in which it is sold.

Focus-Group Interviews

Given the exploratory nature of most concept testing, focus-group interviews are frequently used.

The moderator directs the group discussion much more specifically than in an idea-generating session. The objective is to address the specific concepts being evaluated by the firm, always seeking insights for further refinements.

Monadic Ratings

In a monadic rating session respondents are divided into as many groups as there are product concepts to test. Each respondent examines only one product concept and evaluates it on explicitly identified dimensions such as intention to purchase or level of liking. The scale used for recording the evaluations could be any of the attitude rating scales discussed in Chapter 11. It is common to use numeric rating scales.

The scores on the scale are averaged for each product concept, and comparisons are made across groups. The highest scoring concepts are subjected to further evaluation. Note that the comparison is an absolute one as each respondent does the rating without reference to other concepts. Because this is so, it is important to control sample differences across the groups of concept evaluators. For example, if age profiles in the groups were quite different, and the product concepts in question had age-related dynamics, then biased scores could result, depending on which age group received which concept.

Paired Comparison Ratings

Sample group differences and a lack of alternative product concepts to compare against may make monadic ratings somewhat unreliable. An alternative is the paired comparison test. Each respondent tests a set of product concepts two at a time and states which of the two is preferred. (The nature of paired comparison tests was discussed in detail in Chapter 11.)

An alternative with some characteristics of both monadic and paired comparison tests is a *sequential monadic,* or nondirect comparison, test. The subject is exposed to a product concept, waits some prescribed time period, and then is exposed to another concept. After a number of products have been exposed to the respondents, ratings of the products on a scale are taken. The order of presentation of product concepts to respondents may bias results so that randomization of the order across subjects is necessary. Proponents of this method argue that the sequential order of presentation reflects the way consumers actually evaluate products in the marketplace, and it avoids the artificial forced-choice situation that paired comparison tests make. In these latter tests, respondents may select one product over another just because they have to and do so using some trivial attribute.

Conjoint Analysis

Conjoint analysis, already introduced in Chapter 20, is another technique that can be used in concept testing. The researcher wants to measure the utility that respondents assign to each level of each explicitly defined attribute of a product concept. For example, the Canadian government in conjunction with Air Canada tested 13 attributes of a proposed new plane and associated services using verbal descriptions of such attributes as speed, food service, ticket prices, and seating arrangements. This procedure gives insight into the relative importance of product attributes and how they relate to each other, and allows us to determine the best combination of attributes.

Usage Tests

Once the marketer has a physical version of the product, it is possible to have it tested in various types of usage situations. The product may be tested in the *"laboratory."*

The Betty Crocker kitchens at General Mills are continuously trying new formulations of their products, and automobile companies test drive vehicles on their test tracks. Laboratory testers of products usually are more careful to follow instructions than actual consumers, who may evaluate the product on attributes not deemed important by research and development people. In the early development of Gaines•burgers dog food, for example, General Foods management found that it tested well in the laboratory, but in actual consumer use dog owners tended to overfeed their dogs and the dogs became ill. Clearly, consumer tests are also necessary.

In a *consumer usage test,* the product is given to a small sample of end consumers who are instructed to use it in a normal fashion. Typically, it is placed in the user's home (or company in the case of industrial products). For example, a small computer company placed their new desk-top computer and software system in five east coast companies. They were then able to identify problems in their instruction manual and to pinpoint some mechanical malfunctions. Respondents for a use test may be recruited by phone, mail, or even personal contacts in shopping malls.

One variation on the consumer usage test is the *blind usage test.* It is most typically used immediately after laboratory testing has been completed. The product is given to the consumer without its brand name or any supporting advertising copy. The intention is to get a reaction to the physical product without other marketing program variables affecting reactions. Firms frequently test a new formulation of an established brand in this fashion. Often the consumer will test more than one product in a specified sequence.

In usage tests the researcher must try to make sure that respondents follow instructions, actually use the product, and do not give biased responses just because they were given a free product. Usage tests do not measure acceptance of the product over the long run, and they tend to furnish inflated estimates if respondents are asked to state whether they intend to purchase the product. However, the main objective of this method is to test the acceptance of the physical product and not to predict sales.

BUSINESS ANALYSIS AND COMMERCIALIZATION

Product ideas that survive the concept testing process are often then subjected to a more conclusive business analysis. If this analysis indicates that the product's sales level and profitability are good enough, the product is then commercialized—taken to the marketplace. The research objective of business analysis is to estimate the sales level and profitability of the product. Two important techniques used for this purpose are test marketing and simulated test marketing, usually conducted in a laboratory environment.

Both of these procedures involve the application of experimental and quasi-experimental designs. A survey[4] by Bellenger et al. estimated that 36 percent of consumer

---

[4] Danny N. Bellenger, Jac L. Goldstucker, and Barnett A. Greenberg, "What Techniques Are Used by Marketing Researchers in Business?" *Journal of Marketing,* vol. 41, pp. 64–65, April 1977. Although this study suffers from serious nonresponse error, it still provides a feel for the use of various procedures in marketing research practice.

product companies use formal experimental designs, and 67 percent of them use informal (quasi) experimental designs. For industrial products companies and those marketing both consumer and industrial products, these usage rates are considerably lower. However, the fundamental point remains, namely that experimental and quasi-experimental procedures are extensively used in practice. They are used because they work.

TEST MARKETING

Test marketing is a field-oriented testing activity that may be either an experiment or a quasi experiment depending on how it is structured. In most cases it attains only quasi-experimental status. Our reason for dedicating a signficant portion of this chapter to test marketing relates to our underlying philosophy for this book, which is that we want you to get beyond technical concepts and into the flavor of the real world of marketing research. Test marketing is a very real activity that allows you to observe the use of experimental and quasi-experimental procedures, and it allows us to tie in of some of the syndicated data services discussed in Chapter 5. Also, since test marketing is heavily used in marketing research, it merits presentation here. The Bellenger study estimated that test marketing is used by 62 percent of consumer goods companies, 34 percent of industrial goods companies, and 40 percent of those companies marketing both types of products.

This section first describes the possible uses of test marketing, then discusses when test marketing should be undertaken as well as noting its limitations. A number of implementation decisions in test marketing will be covered, specifically the choice of the number of cities to use, the criteria for selecting test cities, the distinction between standard test cities and control test cities, and the length of time a test should run.

You should be aware that test marketing is as important as it is controversial in the marketing research community. The marketing research director of a major consumer goods company once described test marketing as "an archaic device." Still others have put forward the proposition that new forecasting techniques may make test marketing obsolete.[5] We shall discuss the reasons for some of the negative attitudes toward test marketing later. Yet, despite all the negatives, the use of test marketing remains high, and it is in fact growing. One article noted:

> A few years ago, some marketers were forecasting the imminent demise of test marketing. Growing sophistication of pre-market testing and computer modeling would make costly tryouts of new products unnecessary, they predicted. Somehow it just hasn't worked out that way. Contrary to the experts' opinion, test marketing has become more important in today's slow-growth, high-cost business environment.[6]

---

[5] "New Product Forecasting Techniques May Make Test Markets Obsolete," *Marketing News*, vol. 10, no. 10, Nov. 19, 1976, pp. 1 and 4.

[6] Sally Scanlon, "Calling the Shots More Closely," *Sales and Marketing Management*, May 10, 1976, p. 43.

Test Marketing Defined

Before proceeding further, we need a formal definition of test marketing. Achenbaum defines test marketing from the research-oriented person's point of view as follows:

> It is a controlled experiment, done in a limited but carefully selected part of the marketplace, whose aim is to predict the sales or profit consequences, either in absolute or relative terms, of one or more proposed marketing actions.[7]

Achenbaum goes on to explain that, at the other extreme, some people define test marketing loosely as "trying something out in the marketplace."[8] He recognizes that most test marketing activity falls between these two extremes. Cost and time pressures are the main reasons why the research-oriented extreme is not often used. But Achenbaum notes that "no matter what choice is made, one thing is common to all such tests: the results are used as if they were predictive"[9] of the whole marketplace. It should not be surprising that, with so much test marketing activity positioned toward the loose end of the definitional spectrum, it is easy to find examples of test market failures.

In our definition of test marketing, we shall take account of the practice of this activity. Specifically we define test marketing as *the implementation and monitoring of a marketing program in a small subset of the target market areas for the product in question.* This definition takes in designs that are not even good quasi experiments, let alone experiments, but this is the nature of this activity.

The Selection of Alternatives to Test

A product manager was overheard to say to a researcher in discussing the introduction of a new product: "I want to test at least two price levels, three different advertising executions, two coupon alternatives, two package designs, three point-of-purchase presentations, and two product formulas." This test could be designed as a controlled experiment, using a factorial design; but look how many test cities we would need to conduct this experiment! At a minimum it would require:

2 (prices) × 3 (advertising executions) × 2 (coupons) × 2 (packages)

× 3 (point-of-purchase presentations) × 2 (product formulas) = 144 cities

Obviously, the cost of such a test would be unreasonably high. This points out that true field experiments can test only a few levels of a few variables.

What the product manager must do in this situation is eliminate some combinations of variables prior to undertaking the test market. Basically, all the possible combinations of marketing variables must be reduced to a few alternative strategies. For

---

[7] Alvin R. Achenbaum, "Market Testing: Using the Marketplace as a Laboratory," in Robert Ferber (ed.), *Handbook of Marketing Research* (New York: McGraw-Hill, 1974), p. 4-32.

[8] Ibid.

[9] Ibid.

example, two strategies might be:

1 Price $1.15, advertising which depicts a hidden-camera interview, 10-cents-off coupon, plastic package, end-aisle display, and strong product formula.
2 Price $0.98, advertising using "slice of life" execution, 15-cents-off coupon, cardboard packages, middle-aisle display, and medium-strength product formula.

This test could be conducted in two cities (at a minimum). However, it does not allow the measurement of separate main effects or interaction effects. We can only grossly measure the effect of the two strategies. Hence, most test marketing would be best described as a quasi experiment.

How do researchers reduce to a few strategies the number of possible combinations they are interested in? They use personal judgment, based on the experience of both the manager and the company, and they also undertake research on each aspect of the strategy prior to the test market. For example, a researcher could (1) test the product formula in a home placement test, (2) do copy testing on the advertising executions, and (3) consult previous company experience with similar products to compare end-aisle displays with middle-aisle displays and to study the results of various coupon plans. A great many judgments must be made, and a great deal of research undertaken, prior to the test market.

THE USES OF TEST MARKETING

No matter how formal or informal the design of a test market, there are two fundamental uses for it:[10]

1 Test marketing can serve a *managerial control function*. That is, it can allow an organization to gain needed information or experience before undertaking a project on a grand scale.
2 Test marketing can serve a *predictive research function*. That is, it can predict the outcome of alternative courses of action. This input can be used to decide whether or not to undertake a course of action.

Test Marketing as a Managerial Control Tool

In undertaking any new marketing activity there is risk that something will go wrong. This is especially true in the marketing of new products or brands, but it is also true in established product categories where some innovation is being introduced. A test market here would be designed as a pilot operation for later larger-scale national introduction. It would give us needed experience in many areas, including the following:

1 We could gain experience in physically handling the product—i.e., shelf life, breakage, storage, shipping, etc. We could identify costly mistakes and thereby avoid

---

[10] This section follows an excellent discussion in ibid., pp. 4-33 to 4-38.

them on a national basis. In the case of Nabisco's "Legendary Pastries,"[11] a few months after the product was introduced in a test market, the cans of cherry topping began exploding. It seems that an apparently innocuous ingredient in the mix was fermenting the cherries. Consider the problem if Nabisco had put this product into national distribution.

2 It could give us experience in simply learning how things get done in marketing this product. We could learn the difficulties of gaining distribution, of producing a new commercial, of making our price hold at retail, etc. This experience would be used later in our national roll-out.

In designing test marketing programs for managerial control purposes we need not worry about having a correct experimental design. We are simply gaining experience, not making sales or profit projections, and therefore not making go—no—go decisions.

Test Marketing as a Predictive Research Tool

Of more interest to marketing researchers is test marketing as a predictive device. In fact, most test markets are used in this manner, no matter how badly designed. There are two situations in which test marketing is used as a predictive device: (1) in new-product or new-brand introductions, and (2) in the evaluation of alternative marketing programs for existing brands—i.e., to evaluate either individual marketing variables or programs. These two uses require reasonably tight experimental or quasi-experimental executions in order to generate reasonable predictions. Their only real difference from each other, from a methodological point of view, is that the testing of alternative marketing programs requires a control group (i.e., the present program).

In new-product or new-brand tests management wants to know how its new product or brand will do in terms of sales and profits in a national introduction. You may well wonder how one projects from test market results to a national performance, and indeed this is a very difficult problem. Projections are often made with what turns out to be a very large error when the national results are compared with the projection. Gold has suggested an approach to this problem,[12] offering three different methods for making this projection.

1 Buying Income Method   Here sales of the test brands are expanded by the ratio of the test area's buying income to the buying income of the country. In formula:

$$\text{National sales estimate} = \frac{\text{total U.S. income}}{\text{test area income}} \times \text{test area sales}$$

---

[11] Sally Scanlon, "Is the Chemistry Changing?" *Sales Management, The Marketing Magazine,* Apr. 16, 1973, p. 33.
[12] Jack A. Gold, "Testing Test Marketing Predictions," *Journal of Marketing Research,* vol. 1, p. 10, August 1964.

2 Sales Ratio Method Here sales of the test brand are compared with the sales of another brand where a logical sales relationship may be expected. That is:

$$\text{National sales estimate} = \frac{\text{national sales of other product}}{\text{test area sales of this other product}}$$

$$\times \text{ test area sales of test product}$$

The firm may have related experience with other brands that they assume to be similar to the new brand.

3 The Share-of-Market Method Here sales of a test brand are related to sales of the product category as a whole in the area where the new brand is being tested. In formula:

$$\text{National sales estimate} = \frac{\text{test area sales of new brand}}{\text{test area sales of this whole product category}}$$

$$\times \text{ national sales of this whole product category}$$

In Gold's study, the share-of-market method was found to be the most accurate,[13] but it also is the most expensive, as it requires the auditing of all the competitive brands in the product category. It also assumes that the test product will not expand sales of the product category.

More recently, a number of new procedures for projecting test market results have been proposed which are more sophisticated mathematically than Gold's approach. Our intention here is not to present the details of the mathematics of these approaches, but rather to give a brief overview of the similarities among them. Basically, these approaches have the following steps:

1 In undertaking a test market, collect purchase data from a panel in the test market area.

2 Obtain measures from the panel on the cumulative growth in the number of new buyers of the brand under study and the rate of repurchase activity for this brand over a number of purchase cycles.

3 Formulate a mathematical model to describe the demand for this brand. The model is expressed in terms of the measures taken in step 2, that is, cumulative growth rate and repurchase rate, plus the size of the panel relative to the national population.

4 Use this model, and the growth and repurchase rates obtained from the consumer panel in the test market, to project national sales levels.

---

[13] For a more detailed discussion of Gold's approach, see Edwin M. Berdy, "Testing Test Market Predictions: Comments," *Journal of Marketing Research*, pp. 196–198, May 1965. Also see Gold's reply, *Journal of Marketing Research*, pp. 198–200, May 1965.

Proponents of this type of method have reported very accurate projections from panel results to national outcomes.[14] Note that the Gold approach takes only gross measures of test market results, whereas the latter approaches measure purchase activity on an individual household basis by using a panel. An individual firm should develop projection formulas of its own to fit its own circumstances. The advent of scanner panels (see Chapter 5) enhanced the ability of panels to be useful to marketers in test marketing situations. Of course, the test must then be run in cities where scanner services are available. As yet, the cities available for scanner test markets are limited and are very atypical.

Some of the specific types of information a test market might provide for a company are:[15]

1 Sales in units and dollars

2 Market share

3 Profitability and return on investment

4 Consumer behavior and attitudes with respect to the product, i.e., who does and doesn't buy; who makes the buying decision; how the product is used; repurchase patterns; perceptions of the product, etc.

5 Effectiveness of alternative marketing strategies, and possibly of the various components such as coupon plans, advertising executions, etc.

6 Reaction of the trade to the product and its marketing program, i.e., willingness to stock it, location on shelf, use of point-of-purchase materials, assessment of the salesforce's presentation, etc.

In obtaining this information the company can make use of any of a number of syndicated test marketing services, some of which are discussed later in this chapter. Also, the firm is likely to need customized studies to measure some of the variables of interest. The power of test marketing to aid in decision making is illustrated in the Marketing Research In Action on Cyanamid in this section.

THE DECISION TO UNDERTAKE TEST MARKETING

The decision to undertake test marketing involves the examination of the costs of the test market against the expected benefit. This section examines some of the specific areas of costs that are related to test marketing, the potential benefits having been discussed in the previous section. The problems associated with test marketing will also be discussed here.

---

[14] Those who are interested in the details of these newer approaches should consult a number of excellent references, including J. H. Parfitt and B. J. K. Collins, "Use of Consumer Panels for Brand-Share Prediction," *Journal of Marketing Research,* vol. 5, pp. 131–145, May 1968; David H. Ahl, "New Product Forecasting Using Consumer Panels," *Journal of Marketing Research,* vol. 7, pp. 160–167, May 1970; Gerald J. Eskin, "Dynamic Forecasts of New Product Demand Using a Depth of Repeat Model," *Journal of Marketing Research,* vol. 10, pp. 115–129, May 1973; Benjamin Lipstein, "Modelling and New Product Birth," *Journal of Advertising Research,* vol. 10, pp. 3–11, October 1970.

[15] This list is adapted from F. Ladik, L. Kent, and P. C. Nahl, "Test Marketing of New Consumer Products," *Journal of Marketing,* vol. 24, pp. 29–34, April 1960.

MARKETING RESEARCH IN ACTION

CYANAMID TEST COMBAT

"It looked like a pretty good opportunity for us," says Dr. Ted Shapas, group leader for insecticide research at the Shulton Research Division, who explains that Americans spend about $400 million a year on household insecticides targeted for controlling roaches. Yet most people are unhappy with the products they use for three reasons: (1) sprays and foggers are smelly and messy; (2) they're toxic to humans and pets; and (3) one application is effective for only a few days. Sticky traps, although easy to use, have the highest consumer dissatisfaction rate (70 percent), says Shapas, because they make no appreciable dent in the roach population of a house or apartment.

Shulton expected Combat to test well because, enthuses Shapas, "it addresses the frustrations people have been having. It's childsafe, and there's no odor or mess. Efficacy results are so positive we're able to offer a moneyback guarantee for three months of roach control."

Although Cyanamid researchers were convinced of the superiority of Combat, they braced themselves for skepticism on the part of test market consumers who had learned to mistrust glowing claims for household insecticides. "Combat is different from sprays and foggers," explains Jim Janis, Shulton's strategic business unit manager for new ventures. "We knew we had to educate consumers about the hi-tech nature of the product, tell them why it was so revolutionary." As a result, he says, "Our whole test market campaign took an educational approach to the cockroach problem."

The three-pronged attack included: (1) Public relations, relying heavily on radio and TV talk show interviews with leading entomologists who talked about cockroach behavior and control; (2) advertising, which, unlike most entrants in the field, is neither flippant nor cartoonlike; and (3) use of an 800 number on package inserts and advertising to position the company as an authority on cockroach control.

The test was conducted in Kansas City and New Orleans, and ran for 2 years, ending last spring. "As you might expect," explains Shapas, "sales of insecticides are really skewed depending on the part of the country you're in. We wanted to test Combat in an average area, but also in a city where things are about as bad as they can get roachwise. The 100 line on the category development index for ant and roach insecticides goes right through Kansas City; south of that it gets increasingly higher: New Orleans is in the 300s, making it serious roach country."

Combat was sold primarily in food stores, but also in some drug chains, explains product manager Maria Miller. The test was heavily supported with advertising and consumer promotion dollars "approximately equal to what we are getting ready to introduce nationally," she says. (Combat's national rollout this spring will be backed by a first-year $16 million advertising and promotion budget.) "It was a full plan both years," reports Miller, "including TV and print advertising; consumer promotion events like Sunday inserts, as well as onpackage promotional coupons, prepacked display shippers, and discounts to dealers."

Results were tracked through Nielsen and SAMI reports of warehouse withdrawals. However, says product manager Miller, "We want to do our own research with consumers, not just rely on share data, so we conducted consumer tracking studies and attitude and usage studies."

One result of the research, says Miller, was a change in emphasis for the ad campaign during the test market that will be carried through in the national rollout. "The initial advertising focused on three-month kill," she says, "but we found out from consumers that a real attribute of the brand from their point of view was that it didn't have any mess or odor and was childsafe. All the benefits were being played back in the attitude and usage studies. That was a hot button we could definitely push, so we broadened the ads to say that Combat provided a superior combination of efficacy, aesthetic benefits, and safety vs. the competition."

Shulton keeps all its test marketing data secret, but Miller claims that the product met or exceeded all its objectives. "Test market success," she says, "gives a margin of comfort for the national plan. We anticipate being the no. 2 or 3 competitor in the ant and roach insecticide category within a year."

Source: Sales and Marketing Management, pp. 92–96, March 11, 1985.

Costs of Test Marketing

There are both direct and indirect costs of test marketing. The direct costs include:[16]

1 A pilot plant to make the product (if the test is for a new product)
2 Commercials
3 Payments to advertising agency for services
4 Media time at a higher rate because of low volume
5 Syndicated research information
6 Customized research information and associated data analysis costs
7 Point-of-purchase materials
8 Couponing and sampling
9 Higher trade allowances to obtain distribution

The typical two-city test market in 1986 had direct costs of $450,000, and a four-city test cost $900,000. Long-running, complex tests can have direct costs of over $1 million.

To these costs we must also add the indirect costs of the test to the company, which include:

1 Opportunity cost of lost sales that would have occurred in a successful national introduction
2 Cost of management time spent on the test market
3 Diversion of salesforce activity from money-making products
4 Possible negative impact on other products carrying the same family brand
5 Possible negative trade reactions to your products if you develop a reputation of "bombing"
6 Cost of letting your competitors know what you are doing, allowing them to develop a better strategy or beat you to the national market with a new product like yours.

These costs are indeed high. In deciding whether or not to undertake a test market we must also consider some of the problems associated with test marketing.

Problems of Test Marketing

A number of problems occur with test marketing, and they will be listed later in this section. All of them, however, give rise to one overriding negative consequence—the lack of projectivity of the test market results to the national roll-out of the product. *Printer's Ink—Consumer Advertising* undertook a review of test marketing and noted:

> Says the marketing chief of a large company: "Why? We never got clear answers (from test marketing). We never got accurate predictions on sales and profits."
>
> Leaders of the marketing research community themselves are among the first to admit this. Says Bart Panitierre, GF Corporate Marketing Research Director, "Life would be wonderfully simple if the so-called national sales picture were one smooth canvas. It's not. It's really

[16] Adapted from Jay E. Klompmaker, G. David Hughes, and Russell I. Haley, "Test Marketing in New Product Development," *Harvard Business Review*, p. 129, May–June 1976.

a mosaic—a rather uneven one—made up of hundreds of local markets each having a different shape and color. Test markets are only sample chips. Their results are difficult to project now to a national pattern, though the better the choice of sample chips, the better the odds on an accurate prediction—providing, of course, you are fair in handling the chip and running the market tests."

One research director—Arthur Koponen, then at Colgate-Palmolive—said, "Projectivity is a myth."[17]

There are a number of reasons for this poor projectivity in test marketing:[18]

1 The salespersons in the selected area are stimulated beyond normal activity levels by just the mere awareness that a test is being conducted in their market.

2 The trade is made aware of the test and gives artificially high distribution and retailer support.

3 Special introductory offers and promotions are often made to the trade and to consumers because it is so important to get and maintain distribution during the test to measure repurchase activity. Their offers are then not available at the scale of the test for a national roll-out.

4 Competitive efforts, both deliberate and coincidental, have profound effects on the test market results. These efforts are then different on a national basis. At an extreme, competitors can attempt to destroy your ability to make judgments from a test by increasing their efforts in your test cities out of proportion with their national effort. In 1957, Purex began a test of a liquid bleach in Erie, Pennsylvania. In response, Procter & Gamble increased its advertising efforts in Erie and also went into a heavy cents-off campaign for its Clorox brand. Purex had to cancel the test, as no meaningful results were possible.[19] Today it is sometimes possible to get court orders to restrain these actions.

5 Measurement accuracy can yield ambiguous data. Auditing store sales can often give inaccurate data because of poor store records or incomplete knowledge of the store's billing and handling systems. Also, only a sample of stores is used, with a resultant sampling error occurring. These sample results must also be weighted properly to take account of large versus small stores in the population of stores. This is especially a problem when the measurements are made on a temporary basis for this one test.

6 Competitors may use your test market to learn of your activities and monitor your results. They may then beat you to the national market with this type of product. Having this competitor in the national market would obviously make the test results less projectable. This happened to Lever Brothers in testing their "Mrs. Butterworth" syrup, and also to Procter & Gamble in testing "Bounce" fabric softener. Calgon used P&G's test to beat P&G to the national market with its "Cling Free" brand. P&G rushed its Crest pump to market without test in 1985 when it lost significant market share to the Colgate pump.

---

[17] Ford, "Management Guide: Test Marketing," *Printer's Ink*, Aug. 27, 1965, as quoted in Achenbaum, op. cit., p. 4-33.

[18] Adapted from David H. Hardin, "A New Approach to Test Marketing," *Journal of Marketing*, vol. 30, pp. 28–31, October 1966.

[19] U.S. Federal Trade Commission 1963, *United States of America before Federal Trade Commission in the Matter of Procter & Gamble Company*, Corporation Docket No. 6901.

When to Test Market

With a firm understanding of the costs and limitations of test marketing in mind, we are ready to turn to a checklist of points to consider in deciding when to test market:

1 Consider the cost and risk of failure versus the profit and probability of success. A product with low costs and low risk of failure may not need testing.

2 Consider the plant investment to go national versus that required for the test. Lean toward a direct national roll-out if little extra plant investment is necessary, and vice versa.

3 Consider the likelihood and speed with which the competition will copy and/or preempt your product or campaign. The faster they will respond, and the more likely they are to do so, the more reason there is for skipping the test.

4 Consider the effects of a national failure on the trade and on consumers. Will the company's reputation and other products suffer?

Thus, if the costs and risk are low, little incremental plant investment is needed for a national roll-out, competitors are likely to be able to copy your program quickly, and a failure is not likely to have major long-term consequences on the company's reputation, you would probably not do test marketing before a national launch. A company may consider one of these factors important and decisive enough on its own. For example,[20] Pillsbury developed a powdered soft drink to compete with Kool-Aid (General Foods), Wyler's (Borden), and Hawaiian Punch (R.J.R. Foods), all well-established competitors. Pillsbury's product, called "Squoze," had half the sugar and half the calories of the other mixes. Pillsbury reasoned that they would lose out if they gave their product a test market, because the competitors would easily match them and preempt the national market; so they skipped the test market.

DESIGNING TEST MARKETS

Three design issues will be covered in this section: (1) the choice of how many cities to use in the test, (2) the criteria to be used for selecting cities, and (3) the length of time the test should run.

The Number of Cities

Ladik et al.[21] offer the following guidelines:

1 Select at least two cities for each program variation to be tested.

2 Where projectivity is important, at least four geographic areas should be used.

We would of course consider the cost of adding more cities against the expected benefits. In general, the greater the risk of loss on a national basis, the more alternative programs should be considered; and the greater the regional differences in relation to your product, the more cities should be used.

---

[20] Scanlon, "Calling the Shots More Closely," p. 48.
[21] Ladik et al., "Test Marketing of New Consumer Products."

Criteria for City Selection

No one city or group of cities can represent the whole United States. However, we should try to select cities that have the following characteristics:[22]

1 The markets should not be overtested.

2 The markets should have normal historical development in the product class.

3 The markets should represent a typical competitive advertising situation.

4 The markets should not be dominated by one industry.

5 Special resident profile markets should be avoided (for example, college towns and retirement areas).

6 If sales are different by region, each region should be tested.

7 The markets should have little media spillover into other markets and should receive little outside media impact.

8 The markets should have a media usage pattern similar to the national pattern.

9 The markets should not be too small to provide meaningful results or so large that testing becomes too expensive.

To this list we might add:

10 The markets should have representative distribution channels.

11 The competitive situation should be similar to the national situation.

12 Sales auditing and other research services should be available.

13 The company must be able to ship the product to the test areas at a reasonable cost.

14 The demographic profile of the cities should be "representative."

Obviously, not all these criteria are met by any one city. This list is just the standard to shoot for.

In test marketing we distinguish between the two types of test cities: (1) control markets and (2) standard markets. *Control markets* (or minimarkets, as they are called) are cities where a research supply house has paid retailers to guarantee that they will carry products that it designates. The research company (1) handles the placing of products on shelves in retail stores, (2) services these products regularly to ensure that the required in-stock condition is maintained, (3) audits product class sales, and (4) observes competitive action that would affect the test. In other words, the environment is controlled to allow for tight designs. Control markets offer the advantages of (1) speedier access to distribution and readings on results, (2) reduced cost per market, (3) no distraction of salesforce attention from other lines, and (4) greater secrecy, as most control markets are small and are not automatically audited by A. C. Nielsen or SAMI, etc. Thus, competitors must expend more time and effort to monitor your results.

The major drawback to control markets is the fact that true trade reaction to your product cannot be obtained, and this is often important to the marketer. These markets tend to be smaller, making national projections more difficult. Also, they generally do not have isolated media. This results in spillover of advertising into other

---

[22] Adapted from ibid.

areas where the product is not available. This wastes money, and in addition it can cause ill will among consumers and retailers who cannot buy the advertised product. Control markets are a fairly recent development in test marketing. The research companies who run these control markets have reported extensive use of this service. They also report success in having control market tests reasonably accurately predict national sales levels.

The alternative to control markets is the use of what are called *standard markets,* where the company must fight for trade support in the same fashion as in a national roll-out. There is no guarantee of getting retail distribution at all, let alone getting particular shelf facing and special stocking. This type of test provides a more realistic picture of the likely trade reaction to your product. It is, however, more expensive, slower, more distracting to the salesforce, and more easily monitored by the competition. This type of test is still the dominant one in practice. Exhibit 23-1 lists both standard and control markets that are frequently used for test markets in practice. The names of some of the larger research supply houses that run a particular control market are also indicated.

The Length of a Test

The average test market runs from 6 to 12 months.[23] How do you decide how long a test should run for a particular situation? The following factors are relevant:

1 The test must run long enough for repurchase activity to be observed. This gives a measure of the "staying power" of a new product or program. The shorter the average repurchase period, the shorter the test can be. Cigarettes, soft drinks, perishable foods are purchased every few days, whereas shaving cream, toothpaste, etc., are purchased only every few months. The latter type of product would require a longer test than the former. The product should be allowed to go through a number of repurchase cycles.

2 How soon will competitors react? The faster this reaction, the shorter the test.

3 The cost of the test must also be considered. At some point the value of additional information is outweighed by its costs.

The Use of Research Suppliers

Marketing research suppliers are very active in the business of test marketing. Their primary activities include (1) providing retail store and warehouse sales or shipment information through audits, (2) selling consumer panel data on purchases and attitudes, and (3) providing control market tests. They are also able to design and execute customized research for a company doing test marketing. Exhibit 23-2 presents a listing of some of the major companies providing test market services. (A more detailed description of these companies was presented in Chapter 5.) The major trend in test marketing services in the 1980s has been the use of scanner services. IRI's Behaviorscan and Nielsen's ERIM services are two examples. (See Exhibit 23-2 and Appendix to Chapter 5.)

---

[23] Scanlon, "Calling the Shots More Closely," p. 43.

EXHIBIT 23-1

FREQUENTLY USED TEST MARKETS

Standard Markets

Akron
Albany–Schenectady–Troy
Albuquerque
Ann Arbor*
Atlanta
Augusta, GA*
Austin*
Bakersfield
Baltimore–Washington, DC*
Bangor
Baton Rouge*
Beaumont–Port Arthur–Orange, TX*
Binghamton, NY
Birmingham–Anniston*
Boise
Boston
Buffalo
Cedar Rapids–Waterloo*
Charleston, SC
Charleston, WV
Charlotte
Chattanooga
Chicago
Cincinnati
Cleveland
Colorado Springs*
Columbus, GA*
Columbus, OH
Corpus Christi*
Dallas–Fort Worth
Dayton
Denver
Des Moines
Detroit*
Duluth*
El Paso*
Erie, PA
Eugene, OR*
Evansville
Fargo, ND

Flint
Fort Wayne
Fresno
Grand Rapids–Kalamazoo–Battle Creek
Green Bay, WI
Greensboro–Winston-Salem–High Point
Greenville–Spartanburg–Asheville*
Harrisburg
Houston
Huntsville*
Indianapolis
Jacksonville, FL
Kansas City
Knoxville
Lansing*
Las Vegas*
Lexington, KY
Little Rock
Los Angeles*
Louisville
Lubbock
Macon, GA*
Madison
Manchester, NH*
Memphis
Miami–Fort Lauderdale
Milwaukee
Minneapolis–St. Paul
Mobile*
Modesto*
Montgomery*
Nashville
New Orleans*
Newport News*
New York*
Oklahoma City
Omaha
Orlando–Daytona Beach

Pensacola*
Peoria
Philadelphia*
Phoenix
Pittsburgh
Portland, ME
Portland, OR
Providence
Quad Cities: Rock Island & Moline, IL; Davenport & Bettendorf, IA (Davenport–Rock Island–Moline metro market)
Raleigh–Durham*
Reading, PA*
Roanoke–Lynchburg
Rochester, NY
Rockford
Sacramento–Stockton
Salt Lake City
St. Louis
San Antonio
San Diego
San Francisco–Oakland*
Savannah
Seattle–Tacoma
Shreveport*
South Bend–Elkhart
Spokane
Springfield–Decatur–Champaign, IL
Syracuse
Tallahassee*
Tampa–St. Petersburg
Toledo*
Topeka*
Tucson
Tulsa
West Palm Beach*
Wichita–Hutchinson
Youngstown*

* New this year.

EXHIBIT 23-1 (*Continued*)

FREQUENTLY USED TEST MARKETS

Controlled Markets

Audits and Surveys**
(Based on metro and TV markets)
Akron
Albany–Schenectady
Albuquerque
Ann Arbor, MI
Atlanta
Austin
Bakersfield
Baton Rouge
Binghamton
Birmingham, AL
Buffalo
Charleston, SC
Charleston, WV
Cincinnati
Colorado Springs
Columbus, GA
Columbus, OH
Corpus Christi
Dayton
Daytona Beach
Denver–Boulder
Des Moines
Duluth
Erie
Evansville
Flint
Fort Lauderdale
Fort Wayne
Grand Rapids
Greensboro, NC
Harrisburg
Huntsville, AL
Jacksonville
Kalamazoo
Kansas City, MO
Knoxville
Las Vegas
Lexington, KY
Little Rock

Louisville
Lubbock
Macon, GA
Manchester, NH
Memphis
Miami
Milwaukee
Mobile
Modesto, CA
Montgomery
New Orleans
Newport News
Oklahoma City
Omaha
Orlando
Pensacola
Phoenix
Portland, ME
Portland, OR
Providence
Raleigh–Durham
Reading
Roanoke
Rockford
Sacramento
Salem, OR
Salt Lake City
San Antonio
San Diego
Savannah
Seattle
Shreveport
South Bend
Spokane
Springfield, IL
Syracuse
Tacoma
Tampa
Toledo
Tucson
Tulsa

West Palm Beach
Wichita

Burgoyne
(Based on metro markets)
Albuquerque
Bangor
Binghamton
Boise
Charleston, SC
Erie
Evansville
Flint
Fort Wayne
Fresno
Grand Rapids–Kalamazoo
Green Bay
Harrisburg
Lansing
Lubbock
Madison
Peoria
Portland, ME
Quad Cities: Rock Island & Moline,
   IL; Davenport & Bettendorf, IA
Rockford
San Antonio
South Bend
Springfield, IL
Tucson

Ehrhart-Babic Associates
(Based on metro and TV markets)
Albuquerque
Austin*
Bangor
Binghamton
Boise
Charleston, SC
Charlotte
Chattanooga

* New this year.
** Maintains permanent distribution, merchandising, and auditing services.

EXHIBIT 23-1 *(Continued)*

FREQUENTLY USED TEST MARKETS

Corpus Christi*
Des Moines
Erie
Fort Wayne
Fresno
Grand Rapids–Kalamazoo
Green Bay
Harrisburg
Lansing
Lexington*
Lubbock
Madison
Peoria
Portland, ME
Quad Cities: Rock Island & Moline,
    IL; Davenport & Bettendorf, IA
Rochester, NY
Rockford
San Antonio
South Bend
Spokane*
Syracuse*
Tucson

Lionetti and Meyers Research Center
(Based on metro and TV markets)
Albuquerque*
Binghamton
Corpus Christi
Des Moines
El Paso*
Erie
Fort Wayne
Fresno
Grand Rapids
Green Bay
Lexington
Omaha
Peoria
Roanoke
San Antonio*
South Bend

Spokane
Syracuse
Tucson

*Marketest, division of Market Facts***
(Based on counties)
Erie
Fort Wayne
Fresno
Little Rock
Spokane
Syracuse
Wichita

Market Audits
(Custom markets)
Albany
Albuquerque
Augusta
Baton Rouge
Beamont–Port Arthur–Orange, TX
Binghamton
Charleston, SC
Chattanooga
Corpus Christi*
Des Moines
Duluth-Superior
El Paso
Erie
Eugene
Fort Wayne
Fresno
Grand Rapids*
Green Bay–Appleton
Knoxville
Lexington
Madison
Mobile*
Omaha–Council Bluffs
Peoria
Reno–Carson City
Roanoke*

Rockford
Savannah
Shreveport
South Bend–Elkhart
Spokane
Syracuse
Tallahassee
Toledo
Topeka
Tucson
Tulsa
Wichita
Youngstown, OH*

Permanent markets
Bakersfield
Boise*
Charleston, WV
Evansville
Orlando
Portland, ME
Quad Cities: Davenport, IA, Rock
    Island, Moline, E. Moline, IL

*Nielsen Data Markets***[†]*
(Regular major markets)
Albany-Schenectady-Troy
Atlanta
Baltimore–Washington, DC
Birmingham–Anniston
Boston
Buffalo
Charlotte
Chicago
Cincinnati
Cleveland
Dallas–Fort Worth
Denver
Detroit
Grand Rapids
Houston
Indianapolis

* New this year.
** Maintains permanent distribution, merchandising, and auditing services.
† All new markets.

EXHIBIT 23-1 (*Continued*)

FREQUENTLY USED TEST MARKETS

Jacksonville
Kansas City
Los Angeles
Louisville
Memphis
Miami–Fort Lauderdale
Milwaukee
Minneapolis–St. Paul
Nashville
New York
Oklahoma City
Omaha
Philadelphia
Phoenix
Pittsburgh
Portland, ME
Rochester, NY
Sacramento–Stockton
St. Louis
San Antonio
San Francisco–Oakland
Seattle–Tacoma

(Major markets with weekly reporting, importance to all stores)
Boston
Chicago
Houston
Indianapolis
Jacksonville–Orlando

Kansas City
Los Angeles
New York (suburbs)
San Francisco–Oakland
Seattle–Tacoma

Dancer Fitzgerald Sample's recommended test markets (Based on TV markets)
Albany–Schenectady–Troy
Boise
Buffalo
Cedar Rapids–Waterloo
Charlotte
Chattanooga
Cincinnati
Cleveland
Colorado Springs–Pueblo
Columbus, OH
Des Moines
Erie
Evansville
Fargo
Fort Wayne
Grand Rapids–Kalamazoo–Battle Creek
Green Bay
Greensboro–Winston-Salem–High Point

Greenville–Spartanburg–Asheville*
Indianapolis
Kansas City
Knoxville
Lexington*
Little Rock
Louisville
Milwaukee
Minneapolis–St. Paul
Nashville
Oklahoma City
Omaha
Orlando–Daytona Beach
Phoenix
Pittsburgh
Portland, OR
Roanoke–Lynchburg
Rochester, NY
Sacramento–Stockton
St. Louis
Salt Lake City
Seattle–Tacoma
South Bend–Elkhart
Spokane
Springfield–Decatur–Champaign
Syracuse
Tulsa
Wichita–Hutchinson

* New this year.

Source: "Test Marketers On Target," *Sales and Marketing Management,* pp. 110-114, March 11, 1985.

Test marketing can be a very useful activity if executed with great care and with no illusions about the precision of estimates that it will produce. It provides the most realistic test of alternatives under consideration.

SIMULATED TEST MARKETS

The problems and high costs of test marketing noted earlier have led to the development and increasing use of simulated test markets for frequently purchased consumer goods. Simulated test markets take place in a laboratory environment and involve

EXHIBIT 23-2

GUIDE TO TEST MARKET SERVICES

If you're looking for help with test market evaluation or controlled-market testing, the following are leaders in those fields. They are not the only companies that offer such services, nor is their inclusion an S&MM recommendation.

For names of other research companies, consult such publications as the American Marketing Association's 1981 *International Directory of Marketing Research Houses and Services (GreenBook)*, AMA, New York Chapter, 420 Lexington Ave., New York, NY 10017, or *Bradford's Directory of Marketing Research Agencies and Management Consultants in the U.S. and the World*, P.O. Box 276, Dept. A, Fairfax, VA 22030.

Store/warehouse auditing services
Audits & Surveys, Inc.
Burgoyne, Inc.
Ehrhart-Babic Associates, Inc.
Lebhar-Friedman, Inc.
Lionetti & Meyers Research Center, Inc. NY
Market Facts, Inc.
A.C. Nielsen Co.
Selling Areas Marketing, Inc. (SAMI)
Store Audits, Inc./Q.E.D.
The Test Marketing Group/Market Audits (subsidiary of Burke Marketing Services, Inc.)

Consumer diary panels
Consumer Mail Panels (service of Market Facts)
Home Testing Institute
Market Research Corp. of America (MRCA)
National Family Opinion, Inc. (NFO Research, Inc.)
National Purchase Diary Panel, Inc.
The Test Marketing Group/Market Audits

Controlled market tests
Audits & Surveys
Burgoyne, Inc.
Ehrhart-Babic
Lebhar-Friedman, Inc.
Lionetti & Meyers
Market Audits
Nielsen Data Markets (A.C. Nielsen)
Store Audits, Inc.
The Test Marketing Group/Market Audits

Scanner services
A.C. Nielsen Co. (ERIM)
Burgoyne, Inc.
Information Resources, Inc. (Behavior Scan)
Lionetti & Meyers
Nabscan USA, Inc.
Selling Areas Marketing, Inc. (SAMI Scanner Service)
Tele-Research Item Movement, Inc. (TRIM),
The Test Marketing Group/Market Audits

Source: Sales and Marketing Management, p. 116, March 11, 1985.

shopping in a simulated retail store. The objective is to predict actual market sales of a product based upon the trial and repeat purchase patterns of consumers in the simulation. This is done in much the same way that trial and repurchase patterns of panel members are used to predict sales in an actual test market, as discussed earlier.

There are many research suppliers who now offer simulated test market services. Yankelovich, Skelly, and White have run such an operation for more than 15 years and have tested over 500 products. Elrick and Lavidge's COMP procedure completed over 200 studies in its first 10 years of operation. Other well-known procedures include Management Decision Systems, Inc.'s ASSESSOR and Robinson Associates' SPEEDMARK.

Although these systems differ somewhat from each other, they are basically very similar. Since ASSESSOR is a well-documented approach we will use it to describe the nature of simulated test markets.[24]

ASSESSOR costs about $25,000–$50,000 per study and takes about three months to complete. This is substantially cheaper and of shorter duration than test marketing. The steps in evaluating a product with ASSESSOR are:

1 A group of respondents, usually about 300, is recruited at shopping malls to match the target segment of the test product.

2 Respondents are taken to a nearby laboratory facility to complete a questionnaire. They are asked about whether or not they purchase any brand in the product category, unaided brand awareness, advertising awareness, brand preference, importance ratings of product attributes, and ratings of brands on these attributes.

3 Respondents are then exposed to advertisements for the new brand and the leading competitive brands in the category.

4 After the advertising presentation, respondents are taken to a simulated retail store where the test product is on a shelf display with a complete set of competing products. They are given $2 to use to buy a brand from the category if they wish. Those not wanting to buy any brand are given free samples of the new brand as a way of simulating free samples in the marketplace.

5 After the simulated shopping trip, respondents are interviewed as to what brand they purchased, if any, and their reactions to the product and its advertising.

6 The respondent then returns home with the test product with instructions to use it. A follow-up interview is conducted by telephone several weeks later. The measures taken are similar to the pre-exposure to advertising measures (preference, importance of attributes, and brand ratings), except that the new brand is now included in the brand set. Additionally, usage of the test product is determined, and the respondents who purchase the brand during the follow-up telephone interview and the having it delivered by mail. Those not wanting to repurchase in this way are asked to indicate their intention to purchase the new brand on a five-point scale if the brand were available in a store in the future.

These data are then used to predict market share for the new brand in one of two ways. First, preference judgments predict the proportion of respondents who will purchase the new brand. Market sales are estimated by adjusting this proportion to reflect the proportion of all target consumers who will have the new brand available to them for selection and who will be exposed to its advertising.

The second method predicts market share utilizing estimates of trial levels and repurchase rates that are based upon respondent's purchase levels and intention-to-purchase statements. Purchase levels are based upon the proportion of respondents who purchase the brand in the simulated retail store, plus the marketing actions that

[24] Alvin J. Silk and Glen L. Urban, "Pre-Test-Market Evaluation of New Package Goods: A Model and Measurement Methodology," *Journal of Marketing Research*, 15, pp. 171–191, May 1978. Other models include BBDO's NEWS model. See "NEWS: A Decision-Oriented Model for New Product Analysis and Forecasting," *Marketing Science*, vol. 1, no. 1, pp. 1–29, Winter 1982.

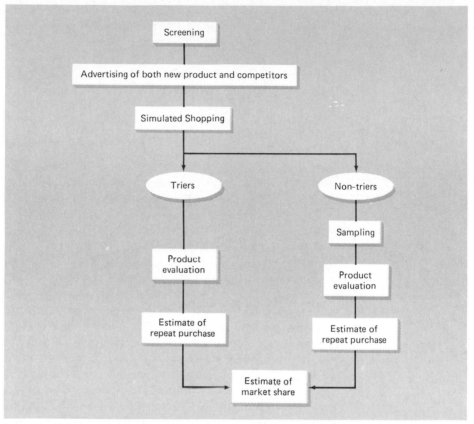

FIGURE 23-1 Most simulation models operate in the same general framework. (*Source: Advertising Age, p. M-11, February 22, 1982. Reprinted with permission of Crain Publications, Inc.*)

management intends to take with respect to distribution penetration, advertising, and free samples. The repurchase rate is estimated based upon the proportion of respondents who purchase the brand during the follow-up telephone interview and the intention levels of those who do not repurchase at that time. The purchase level and repurchase rates are then used by the ASSESSOR model to predict market share. (The mathematical details of this are beyond the scope of this book.) Figure 23-1 presents a graphic summary of the flow of a simulated test market.

The reported accuracy of ASSESSOR is very high as compared to results generated by actual test markets.[25] To work effectively, simulated test market methods must have a well-established product category in terms of substitutes and usage, and purchase rates must be the same for established brands and the new brand, and consumption and attitude formation about the brand must occur quickly enough that preference structure can stabilize in a short period of time.[26]

[25] Ibid.
[26] Ibid.

The great success of simulated test markets has led some to conclude that they will replace test marketing. To date this has not occurred, and both test marketing and simulated test markets are growing in use.

HOW PRODUCT RESEARCH CAN WORK

In developing or modifying a product, a marketer may make use of any number of the research procedures outlined in this chapter. To illustrate this, Exhibit 23-3 lists nine different studies conducted by Whirlpool and Sears in the development of their trash compactors.

SUMMARY

1 Research procedures used in new product idea generation are repertory grid and focus group interviews.

2 Research procedures used in concept development and testing are focus group interviews, monadic ratings, paired comparison ratings, conjoint analysis, and usage tests.

3 Research procedures used in business analysis are test marketing and simulated test markets.

EXHIBIT 23-3 THE NINE STUDIES UNDERTAKEN BY WHIRLPOOL AND SEARS IN DEVELOPING THE TRASH COMPACTOR

In the product development process for the trash compactor, Whirlpool and Sears either separately or jointly undertook nine marketing research studies over a three-year period. These studies were:

1 *Preliminary investigation of consumer's trash needs:* A small exploratory study tried to identify possible trash-related appliance needs.

2 *Product concept test:* Different product prototypes were tested with small groups of consumers.

3 *Market potential study:* A large survey collected data that was used to estimate the size of the potential market for a trash compactor.

4 *"Aggressive-sell" potential study:* A small survey of response to the compactor when the consumer was exposed to a persuasive message; market estimates were made.

5 *In-home use test:* Compactors were placed in a small number of homes to measure consumer reaction in actual use.

6 *Concept test:* A large national mail survey was conducted to measure intention-to-buy and to provide information to guide advertising and merchandising efforts.

7 *Name research:* Three alternative names were tested in telephone interviews.

8 *Advertising copy research:* Alternative advertising executions were tested in a laboratory setting to determine the best communication message.

9 *Test market:* A complete marketing program was tested in four cities (St. Louis, Pittsburgh, Syracuse, and Columbus).

---

4 Test marketing is frequently used but is a controversial subject in marketing research.

5 Definitions of test marketing range all the way from "controlled experiments" to "trying something out." We define test marketing as the implementation and monitoring of a marketing program in a small subset of the target market areas for the product in question.

6 Selection of alternatives to test must involve other research and judgment prior to the test market.

7 Most test markets are quasi experiments at best.

8 Test marketing may be used as a managerial control function or as a predictive research function. The latter use may involve either new-product or new-brand introductions, or the evaluation of alternative marketing programs for existing brands.

9 In projecting test market results to a national product, the researcher may use the buying income method, the sales ratio method, the share-of-market method, or panel methods.

10 Direct costs of test marketing run at about $450,000 for a two-city test. Indirect costs are also high.

11 Test marketing often yields estimates of national outcomes that are inaccurate.

12 Reasons for unsatisfactory results include abnormal behavior by salespersons and the trade, special campaigns by the company doing the test, competitive actions, and measurement accuracy problems.

13 Consider test marketing when the costs and risk of failure are high, and/or the plant investment of a national roll-out is high relative to the test, and/or the competition is not likely to respond quickly, and/or the effects of a national failure on your company's reputation would be high.

14 In designing a test market, the researcher must make decisions with respect to what information to collect, the number of cities to use, the specific cities to use, and the length of time the test should run. You must also decide what marketing research supplier services to use.

15 Simulated test markets take place in a laboratory environment where respondents shop in a simulated retail store after being exposed to advertisements for the new brand and competing brands. In-home usage of the test product follows, and purchase levels and repurchase rates are estimated and used to predict market share.

DISCUSSION QUESTIONS

1 Why are focus groups used for both idea generation and concept testing?

2 What are monadic ratings?

3 Describe the structure of a usage test for a new cake mix.

4 What is test marketing?

5 On what basis would you select alternative courses of action for use in a test market?

6 What are the two fundamental uses of test marketing?

7 How can test market results be projected to national results?

8 What information can a test market provide?

9 What are the costs of test marketing?

10 Why do test marketing results often give poor projections?

11 Under what circumstances should a company undertake test marketing?

12 What type of cities should be used in test marketing?

13 What is a control market?

14 What are the pros and cons of control markets?

15 How long should a test market run?

16 Outline the steps in a simulated test market.

17 Could consumer durable products be tested in a simulated test market? Why or why not?

CHAPTER 24

ADVERTISING RESEARCH

One of the major application areas of marketing research is in advertising. There is good reason for this, since 1984 advertising expenditures in the U.S. were $88.1 billion.[1] The 1983 American Marketing Association survey on the use of marketing research reported that 76 percent of all companies do some form of advertising research. In the consumer products area, 86 percent of companies do advertising research.[2] Marketing research is used in a number of aspects of advertising, including measuring media audiences and testing the effectiveness of advertising messages. The use of marketing research in these two areas constitutes the topic of this chapter.

MEDIA RESEARCH

One of the major decisions that marketers have to make involves the selection of media vehicles to use in an advertising plan. Thus, they must make choices between media types—television versus radio versus newspapers and so forth—and choices of specific inserts within a selected media type. For example, choices must be made concerning which specific television time or magazine to use. Both of these decisions require the availability of data about media.

The Advertising Research Foundation (ARF) suggested that six different types of data ideally would be available about media vehicles and that these data would distinguish

---

[1] *Advertising Age,* p. 48, May 6, 1985.
[2] Dik W. Twedt, 1983 *Survey of Marketing Research* (Chicago: American Marketing Association, 1978), pp. 41–44.

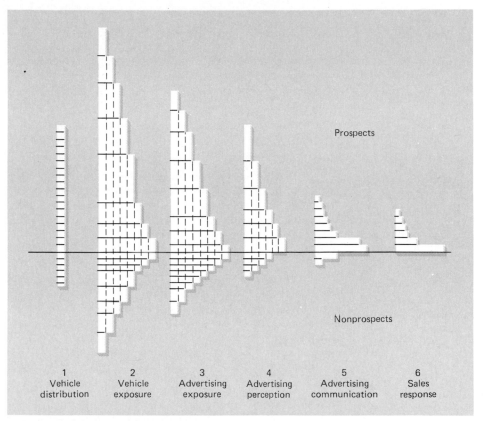

FIGURE 24-1 A model for evaluating advertising. *(Source: Toward Better Media Comparisons, © copyright 1961 by the Advertising Research Foundation.)*

between the prospects and nonprospects of the product being advertised. These data are:[3]

1 *Media vehicle distribution:* the circulation number for a magazine or newspaper or the number of television or radio sets available to carry the advertising.

2 *Media vehicle audience:* the number of people exposed to the media vehicle. Here we measure the number of readers of a given issue of a magazine or newspaper or the number of viewers of a specific television show. Media audience is typically larger than media distribution as more than one person reads the same magazine or watches on the same television set, as Figure 24-1 illustrates.

3 *Advertising exposure:* the number of people exposed to a specific advertisement in the media vehicle. People may be exposed to a media vehicle but not notice a specific

---

[3] Paul E. J. Gerhold, "Better Media Planning: What Can We Do Now?" *Proceedings 5th Annual Conference* (New York: Advertising Research Foundation, Inc., 1959), pp. 43–48, and Advertising Research Foundation, *Toward Better Media Comparisons* (New York: Advertising Research Foundation, 1961).

advertisement because of the creative aspects of the ad or the nature of the environ-ment of exposure. This number is typically much less than vehicle audience. At this point, the data we desire starts to mix both questions of media and of the creative "copy" in the advertisements. (This is also true of data types 4, 5, and 6 listed below.)

4 *Advertising perception:* the number of people who perceived the advertising in question. This could, of course, be influenced by the color and size of the ad, positioning in the vehicle, and type of product involved. The number of people actively perceiving an ad is typically less than those exposed to it, as Figure 24-1 illustrates.

5 *Advertising communication:* the number of people who comprehend specific things about the advertising, which is typically less than those perceiving the ad.

6 *Sales response:* the number of people who take buying action as a result of the placement of the specific advertising. Fewer people respond to an ad by purchasing the product than have actually received its communication, yielding the pattern of numbers for people in Figure 24-1.

In the last four categories of data (3–6), both media and message interact. It thus becomes very difficult to assign numbers related to the media alone in these cases. Because of this difficulty, media vehicle data are typically obtained for only two of the above categories: media vehicle distribution and media vehicle audience. In this section, we will follow advertising research practice by examining the first two levels in the context of media research, and leave the last four levels for our discussion of message research.

Media Vehicle Distribution

Data about media vehicle distribution are the most readily attainable and are relatively free of controversy in terms of their accuracy. In the print media the most important agency is the Audit Bureau of Circulation (ABC), a group sponsored by advertisers, advertising agencies, and publishers. ABC audits and reports on the circulation levels of its members, publications that have at least 70 percent of their circulation paid for at a price of not less than half the established price. For special audience publications distributed to the business community sometimes on a free basis, such as *Production* magazine, the circulation is audited by the Business Publications Audit of Circulation. Additionally, the Verified Audit Circulation, an independent organization, audits both the paid and nonpaid circulation of newspapers and magazines.

For the broadcast media the measurement of vehicle distribution is much less impor-tant. Over 99 percent of all U.S. households have at least one television set, while about 99 percent have radios. The average household has 4.3 radios, which increases to 5.9 when car radios are considered.[4] For television and radio, the more important research questions relate to vehicle audiences.

For outdoor media, the Traffic Audit Bureau takes measurements and reports on the number of persons passing specific locations to give a "circulation" measure for this medium.

---

[4] *Broadcasting Yearbook,* 1985.

Media Vehicle Audience

The media vehicle audience is the number of people actually exposed to the vehicle at least once. The methods of measurement at this level vary greatly by medium.

Magazine Audiences The size of these audiences are measured by so-called pass-along studies. The intent is to measure the total of the circulation of the magazine, plus all the people who read it when it is passed along to them. Two major organizations are active in this area, each using a different measure of readership. The first is the Simmons Market Research Bureau (SMRB). SMRB samples about 15,000 individuals annually using a cluster sampling procedure. The readership measurement taken uses the *through-the-book editorial interest method*. Here respondents, shown logos of magazine titles, are asked, "Pick out those you might have read or looked into during the last six months, either at home or some place else." This is verified again later in the interview, after the respondent goes through a stripped-down version of each magazine. The total size of the audience is estimated by dividing the audience size in the sample by the sampling fraction (see Chapter 8).

While SMRB is the dominant supplier, a major competitor has established itself: Mediamark Research, Inc. (MRI). MRI draws a cluster sample of about 30,000 individuals (15,000 in the spring and fall) and measures audience size with the *modified recent reading method*. Respondents are given a list of about 160 magazines and asked to note the ones they have read during the most recent publication interval. They do this in two steps. First, the respondent sorts a deck of cards containing magazine logos to indicate those read in the last six months. The cards for these magazines are sorted again to indicate those read in the last publication interval. With differences in the methods of audience measurement, and some differences in sampling procedures, it is little wonder that SMRB and MRI report different audience sizes. The result is a great controversy as to which has the correct estimate.

In one reporting period MRI's audience estimates were as high as 162 percent and as low as 34 percent of those reported by SMRB among the 104 magazines reported in common.[5] To the magazines in question, these differences can affect advertising rates. The MRI and SMRB numbers are usually greeted with great emotion. The Advertising Research Foundation investigated this and found that the differences resulted from the methodological differences in the studies and not from execution problems. Ways to make the results of MRI and SMRB more in line with each other are being investigated.

Newspaper Audiences A newspaper reader is typically defined as someone who claims to have read part of the newspaper in question on a given day. The survey method is again used. The Audit Bureau of Circulation's Newspaper Audience Research Data Bank (NARDB) provides such data. The NARDB combines data which is self-collected by cooperating newspapers in the top 100 markets. To be part of NARDB, however, the information given must meet both methodological and format specifications. In general, advertisers must rely on newspaper-collected audience data.

---

[5] "Does MRI Have The Answer?" *Marketing and Media Decisions*, p. 66, November 1979.

Another source of newspaper audience data is Three Sigma, founded in 1974, which conducts surveys on 180 newpapers to measure audience size and demographic profile. These studies are done every few years. Three Sigma is subscribed to by all major dailies and about 40 advertising agencies. In 1981, it was acquired by Simmons Marketing Research Bureau.

Television Audiences   The audience size affects television more than any other medium. Charges for commercial time and even decisions on what shows remain on the air are greatly influenced by them. The two companies dominating the television ratings business are A. C. Nielsen and Arbitron. Nielsen is dominant for national ratings, and Arbitron for local.

Television audience data are collected by four methods: (1) diary, (2) meters, (3) coincidental telephone recall, and (4) personal interview recall.

In the *diary method* viewers record the name of the shows that they watch and mail the diary back to the research firm. The major advantage of diary is that it is relatively inexpensive. It is the dominant mode in the measurement of local television audiences. Arbitron contacts over 2 million households annually to place its diaries. Local audiences are usually measured in November, February, and May, and local television rates are set from these results. These are called "sweeps" months. A major problem with sweeps ratings is that networks and stations try to hype their ratings with great movies, specials, and so on. The major disadvantages of the diary method are that respondents fail to record shows watched, or forget what they watched, or even untruthfully record what shows they watched.

These problems have led to the use of *meters* to record what channel the set is tuned to and when it is on. A. C. Nielsen uses a device called an *audimeter* for their network ratings, the Nielsen Television Index (NTI). This device is connected electronically to a computer and records what the television is tuned to, if anything. NTI gives two major measures: (1) the share of households for a show (the percentage of television homes tuned to a network program for at least six minutes) and (2) the share of audience (the number of homes watching a specific show over the total number of homes watching any program at that time). Since meters are expensive, they are used mostly for national ratings, although Arbitron uses meters in its local ratings in Chicago, New York City, and Los Angeles. Also, meters do not record whether anyone is watching the television while it is on, a problem that affects up to 25 percent of an audience measurement. Controversy as to the accuracy of NTI has raged for years, but almost all advertisers and agencies use it. In measuring local markets with its Nielsen Station Index (NSI), Nielsen uses both diaries and meters. The metered cities are the same as those used by Arbitron, except Nielsen also uses San Francisco. Recently, both Nielsen and Arbitron have begun to measure the size of cable television audiences using meters and diaries.

In the *coincident telephone recall method,* a sample of households is telephoned and asked what show is being watched at that time, if any, and asked to identify the sponsor or product being advertised. This latter question is a validity check on the response given. Ratings are calculated on the percentage of homes watching a particular program.

This method is quick and inexpensive but has some limitations. Nontelephone homes are excluded and rural homes are underrepresented owing to the cost of sampling them. Thus, the total size of the audience is hard to estimate accurately. Also, only certain hours (8:00 A.M. to 10:00 P.M.) can be measured this way, and respondents often try to indicate that they are watching socially acceptable programs.

The *personal interview recall method* involves in-home interviews with a sample of respondents shortly after the time period of interest. A list of the shows by quarter hours (8:00 A.M. to 10:00 P.M.) can be measured this way, and respondents often try to dicate which shows were watched. Respondents' poor memory and untruthfulness, plus the expense of personal interviews, are the biggest problems here.

Radio Audiences   Measurement of radio audience presents some unique problems as radios are used almost everywhere. Thus, meters have not been useful. The only major supplier of local radio audience data is Arbitron. In recent years, a number of major suppliers have failed to crack Arbitron's position. These include the Pulse, Inc.; Audits & Survey's TRAC-7; and Burke's Broadcast Research, Inc. Arbitron uses the mail diary method to gather data. During the selected seven-day period in which ratings are taken, the sample members are called twice to make sure they understand the required task and are reminded to complete and return the diary. Demographic data are also collected. The hyping of ratings by stations running contests or specials is again a problem, as it was for television.

Network radio audiences are measured by two primary services: Arbitron (using diaries) and RADAR (Radio's All Dimension Audience Research). RADAR uses the telephone coincidental method using a panel. Two telephone panels are set up, one in the spring and one in the fall. Each panel household is phoned eight times on consecutive days and is asked about radio listening for each quarter hour for the preceding 24 hours. In this way weekly cumulative audiences can be measured. Both Arbitron and RADAR also collect demographic data in order to allow audience profiles to be presented.

As the above discussion indicates, even measuring audience size is difficult and expensive. To date, little progress has been made in measuring advertising exposure at a general level in a given vehicle. No syndicated sources are available, and the advertisers usually must rely on information supplied by the media itself. Moreover, most advertisers want to know how their own ad did and not what the general exposure in the vehicle was. Thus, they are frequently more interested in copy testing for this purpose.

COPY TESTING

Copy testing addresses issues related to the effectiveness of each advertisement. A better term would probably be "message research," as copy testing suggests written parts of print ads. However, copy testing is used in practice to refer to all aspects (color, graphics, pictures, action, and so forth) of ads appearing in all media. Many marketing research suppliers provide copy testing services. The reliability and validity as well as the procedures used by these services are of great concern to advertisers. In 1982, 21 of the largest U.S. advertising agencies endorsed a set of principles aimed at improving copy testing. These principles are called PACT (Positioning Advertising Copy Testing) and they state that a "good" copy testing system:[6].

1 Provides measurements which are relevant to the objectives of the advertising

2 Requires agreement about how the results will be used in advance of each specific test

3 Provides multiple measurements, because single measurements are generally inadequate to assess the performance of an ad

4 Is based on a model of human response to communication—the reception of a stimulus, the comprehension of the stimulus, and the response to the stimulus

5 Allows for consideration of whether the advertising stimulus should be exposed more than once

6 Recognizes that the more finished a piece of copy is, the more soundly it can be evaluated and requires, as a minimum, that alternative executions be tested in the same degree of finish

7 Provides controls to avoid the biasing effects of the exposure context

8 Takes into account basic considerations of sample definition

9 Demonstrates reliability and validity

Most advertisers put a great deal of time and money into copy testing. An ad may be tested at a number of different phases of its development: as a written concept, a set of storyboards or drawings, a rough animated version, or a finished ad. Additionally, it may be tested before or after media dollars are spent on it at the level they are planned for in the campaign. The former are called *pretests* and the latter *posttests*.

Idealized Procedure

Pomerance[7] outlined one view of an *idealized* copy testing procedure by raising four questions:

1 *What measure should be taken?* The concern here is with what level or levels in the hierarchy of effects model (see Chapter 11) should be measured. Ideally, we would like to know the profit implications of our advertising. Figure 24-2 summarizes what we need to measure, and the arrow notes the direction of the ideal situation.

2 *What degree of finished form should the ad be in?* Should we test a rough sketch of the ad or a cheap film or a videotape version or the final version? Ideally we would like to test the final version since this is what people will be reacting to. However, cost and time may require the use of less finished versions. Figure 24-2 relates what measure to take with what form the ads should be in; the arrows again indicate the ideal direction.

3 *Should we measure the effect of one ad or of a whole campaign?* Clearly, we would like to know the effect of our campaign as opposed to that of an isolated ad. Figure 24-2

---

[6] "21 Ad Agencies Endorse Copy Testing Principles," *Marketing News,* pp. 1 and 9, Feb. 19, 1982.
[7] Eugene C. Pomerance, "How Agencies Evaluate Advertising," *Reflections on Progress in Marketing* (AMA), pp. 167–172, December 1964.

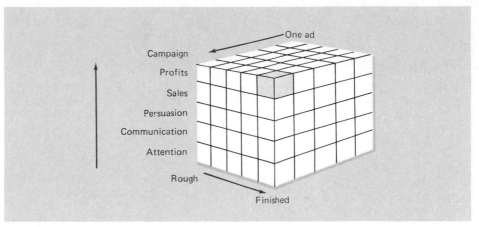

FIGURE 24-2   What to measure. *(Source: Eugene C. Pomerance, "How Agencies Evaluate Advertising," in Reflections on Progress in Marketing, AMA, pp. 167–172. December 1964.)*

shows the shaded cube as the ideal situation. We would like to measure the profits generated by a whole campaign of finished ads.

4 *How should the measurement be made?* Here the subquestions are: Should the ad be exposed in a normal advertising vehicle or in a less normal fashion? How many times should it be exposed? Should the sampling and measurement techniques be technically optimal or something less? We would, of course, prefer the ideal: repeated exposures in a normal fashion, with a truly representative sample, and so on. Figure 24-3 shows the choices available, all leading to the ideal, represented by the shaded cube.

FIGURE 24-3   What and how to measure. *(Source: Eugene C. Pomerance, "How Agencies Evaluate Advertising," in Reflections on Progress in Marketing, AMA, pp. 167–172, December.)*

TABLE 24-1   THE SEVEN BASIC ATTRIBUTES OF A MEASUREMENT TECHNIQUE

Attribute	Idealized measurement procedure (IMP)
Scope of the advertising being measured:	
a. Insertions	Many
b. Media	All relevant media for planned campaign
Response(s) measured	Natural purchase (overtime)
Conditions of exposure:	
a. Exposure environment	Natural
b. Advertising context	Natural
Condition of measurements	
a. Method of data collection	Unobserved audit
b. Measurement environment	Natural
Sampling procedure:	
a. Sample element	Individual purchase unit
b. Restrictions	None
c. Method	Probability
d. Size	Optional*
Type of comparison	Alternative advertisement or campaign
Data handling	Unweighted

*Large enough so that similar results would be obtained if test were repeated.
Source: Patrick J. Robinson, Homer M. Dalbey, Irwin Gross, and Yoram Wind, *Advertising Measurement and Decision Making* (Boston: Allyn & Bacon, Inc., 1968), p. 37a.

Robinson, Dalbey, Gross, and Wind[8] extended this type of reasoning to formulate an *idealized measurement procedure* (IMP). They designated a number of basic attributes of all measurement techniques and came up with the ideal situation; namely, many ads in all relevant media would measure natural purchase or profits; the exposure would occur in a natural environment and natural advertising context, with the measurement taken by means of an audit that is unobserved by the purchaser; the sample should be a probability sample with no geographic or media or participation biases, and large enough that similar results would occur if the test were replicated. Table 24-1 summarizes this ideal situation.

Of course, such considerations as time and money force all advertising measurement procedures, syndicated or internal, to compromise this ideal. However, the IMP is a good benchmark to work from. Deviation from it should be backed up with reasoning For example, we might decide to measure awareness instead of sales because we believe awareness is a more meaningful measure in our particular situation. Or we may not use a national probability sample because we cannot afford it. Let's now move on to commonly used testing procedures.

[8] Patrick J. Robinson, Homer M. Dalbey, Irwin Gross, and Yoram Wind, *Advertising Measurement and Decision Making* (Boston: Allyn & Bacon, Inc., 1968), p. 37a.

PRETESTING PROCEDURES

There are many different procedures used to pretest advertising. The ones we will touch on here are (1) consumer jury, (2) portfolio tests, (3) physiological methods, (4) dummy advertising vehicles, (5) inquiry tests, (6) on-the-air tests, (7) theater tests, (8) trailer tests, and (9) laboratory stores.

Consumer Jury

In the *consumer jury* procedure, 50–100 consumers from the target audience are interviewed either individually or in small groups. The jury members are asked to rank a set of ads that are typically in rough, unfinished form, often displayed on storyboards. Questions relate to such matters as: Which ad would you most likely read? Which headline is most interesting? Which interests you in buying the product the most? The respondent rank orders the ads on each of these dimensions. Alternatively, a paired comparison procedure to rank the ads may be used.

It is also common to have jury members use a numeric rating scale to rate the ads on explicitly identified dimensions. This procedure can be standardized and is thus susceptible to comparisons over time. Norms give average past ratings by product class or even the previous ads for the same brand. The McCollum/Spielman procedure to pretest television ads in a laboratory setting is an example of a service that uses rating scales with a consumer jury and gives norms. Almost all major copy testing services report some form of norms.

Rating scales allow the degree of intensity of response to ads to be measured, which is an advantage over ranking procedures. An extension of this type of rating is the Leo Burnett advertising agency's Viewer Response Profile (VRP) system for testing television ads.[9] It attempts to tap viewers' experience with the advertisement on seven dimensions: entertainment, confusion, relevancy, brand reinforcement, empathy with characters and situation in the ad, familiarity, and alienation. Thus, the ratings go beyond the ad itself to the emotions associated with it.

The reliability and validity of virtually all jury systems is a serious question given the artificiality of the exposure to the ads and the questioning procedure. Unfortunately, most services do not provide the data for a critical appraisal of these issues. For the most part, it is up to the individual advertiser to press for these measures.

Portfolio Tests

The *portfolio test* procedure involves the forced exposure of a group of target consumers to a package of both test and control ads, called a portfolio. Respondents are asked to look through the portfolio, reading whatever interests them. The effectiveness of the test ad is measured by the respondent's ability to recall the ad and then recall specifics

---

[9] Mary Jane Schlinger, "A Profile of Responses to Commercials," *Journal of Advertising Research*, pp. 37–48, April 1979.

about the ad, with the portfolio closed. Recall measures are generally unaided by any interviewer prompting, except on occasion.

Portfolio tests have been widely used in practice but have some problems. Fundamentally, there is concern that differences in recall of a set of test ads may result from differences in consumer's interest in the products involved in the test ads. To the degree that this is true, the portfolio method does not differentiate between ads on the basis of creative presentation.

Physiological Method

A number of laboratory procedures have been developed that measure various physiological responses to ads. These procedures are not the mainstream of copy testing practice but continue to attract both practitioner and academic interest.

One procedure uses an *eye camera* to track the movement of the eye as it examines an ad. The layout of the ad is then examined in the context of this movement to determine which sections receive and hold attention, which parts seem interesting, and what level of confusion can be related to sections of the ad. Unfortunately, interpreting eye movements is difficult; does lingering at a given location indicate interest or confusion? Researchers continue to work on the eye movement approach. In 1981 Applied Science Laboratories announced the development of a computer-based eye position tracking system called the EVM Series 1998EHT. In this system the eye point of gaze, pattern of movement, blink rate, and pupil diameter are recorded 60 times a second.

Galvanic skin response (GSR) is another physiological response to ads that has received some attention. GSR is measured by attaching electrodes from a recording device to respondents, who are then exposed to test and control ads. GSR measures changes in the electrical resistance of the skin. When GSR increases, it is considered to be a measure of the *arousal* that the ad causes in subjects. The major problem here is that arousal is not necessarily related to a positive reaction to the ad.

The *tachistoscope* is another physiologically related testing device. It is a slide projector with special capabilities that allow for the presentation of ads under different levels of speed and illumination. Researchers can measure the rate at which an ad conveys information or recognition. This can be especially important in magazine and outdoor presentations.

Dummy Advertising Vehicles

In this procedure, test and control ads are inserted into a magazine format with editorial features of lasting interest. Thus, the only variation in the dummy magazine in a given year is the test ads. The dummy magazine is then distributed to a random sample of households in various regions of the country. The respondents are told that the publisher is interested in their evaluation of the editorial content and are instructed to read the magazine in a normal fashion. A follow-up interview covers both editorial and advertising content. Measures taken include awareness, recall, copy readership level, and product interest induced by the ad. This procedure can be questioned on the same basis as portfolio tests except that it takes place under natural readership conditions and thus recall scores are likely to be more realistic.

Inquiry Tests

Inquiry tests measure the effectiveness of an ad on the basis of either measured sales or consumer inquiries that result directly from the ad. This may be measured by levels of coupon returns for a contest or orders received for a direct-action ad like a Book of the Month Club ad. The consumer response is a directly measurable sale.

Different creative approaches can be compared in three ways: (1) by placing the ads in successive issues of the same magazine or newspaper, (2) by placing them simultaneously in different vehicles, and (3) by placing different versions in "split runs" of the publication—half the copies of the vehicle contain one ad and the other half another ad.

Inquiry tests provide a direct measure of response with no interview being required, reducing costs and artificial reactions due to the interviewing process. On the other hand, limitations include the following: The presence of a coupon itself may attract attention and obscure creative difference among ads; some people may perceive and be attitudinally influenced by the ad but not return the coupon; and the inquiry does not necessarily translate into long-term action. This latter point is especially true in industrial marketing advertising; consumers may inquire about a new computer system featured in an ad but may not buy even after a later sales presentation. The inquiry test is most appropriate when a coupon return or direct sale is the objective of the advertisement.

On-the-Air Tests

Research services are available that measure responses to ads that are placed on actual television or radio programs in test areas. These procedures offer the same advantages and disadvantages as dummy vehicles. In television some of the best known services used are Burke Marketing Services' Day-After Recall (DAR), Gallup and Robinson's Total Prime Time (TPT), Burke's AdTel cable system, IRI's Behavior Scan, and Nielsen's ERIM.

DAR tests typically involve about 200 respondents who are contacted by telephone in any of 34 cities and who claim that they watched a particular television show the night before. Measures are taken in both unaided and aided recall fashion. To begin with respondents are asked if they remember seeing a commercial for a product in the product class of interest. If they do not, then they are asked if they remember a commercial for the specific test brand. Those who recall the ad in either fashion are asked what they remember about the specific copy points of the ad.

DAR tests dominate the television pretesting business but do have some critics. Foote Cone & Belding, Inc., the advertising agency, recently released a study comparing DAR tests and their own method for creative executions that are "thinking" based and "feeling" based.[10] They proposed a *masked recognition test* (MRT) that involves deleting all audio and video reference to the brand name in a commercial which respondents saw in its entirety the previous day. The respondent is then asked

---

[10] "FCB Says Masked-Recognition Test Yields Truer Remembering Measures Than Day-After-Recall Test," *Marketing News*, pp. 1-2, June 12, 1981.

to identify the brand in the masked commercial. The reason for this approach is that DAR tests ask consumers to verbalize the advertising message, and it is believed that this is especially difficult when the appeal is emotional. All the MRTs so far have involved on-air cable audiences who have agreed in advance to watch the program in which the ad appeared. Scores for "feeling" ads are significantly higher for MRT than for DAR.

Additionally, a study conducted by J. Walter Thompson, and supported by six major advertisers, indicated that show environment was an important influence on the effects of commercials on audiences, and the DAR scores should consider this.[11] In one instance a brand recall was 41 percent on one show and 53 percent on another.[12] This raises serious questions about reported DAR norm scores, and comparisons scores of different executions that are tested on different shows. Burke has indicated that their methods of measurement differ from J. Walter Thompson's and that their research on this issue indicates "that program has no effect on a commercial's related test score when [our] standard procedures are followed. [We are] aware, however, of some broadcast situations which can affect a commercial score, and we advise our clients not to test in these situations."[13]

Total Prime Time (TPT) is a service of Gallup and Robinson (G&R) that can test, either on a pre- or posttesting basis, commercials that appear in prime time. They survey about 700 men and 700 women in the Philadelphia area. Qualified respondents are those who have watched at least 30 minutes of network prime time the previous night. Another service that is used strictly for pretesting is G&R's In-View. Respondents are called in advance and invited to watch the show in which the test ad will appear. About 150 men and 150 women are used in In-View, again all from the Philadelphia area.

Measures taken for both TPT and In-View include:

1 Proved commercial registration (PCR)—percentage who can recall (from company or brand cues) and accurately describe the ad
2 Idea communication—the percentage of those who can recall specific sales points in the ad
3 Favorable attitude—percentage of favorable comments about the brand offered by the respondent

AdTel, a division of Burke, offers testing of alternative ads at the same time in the same show environment through cable television. By using special dual-cable systems in selected test cities, AdTel can direct an A ad and a B ad to different cable subscribers. Purchase diaries are kept by a panel of people who are in the A and B groups. Thus, the measure of effectiveness is actual purchase. Recently AdTel has expanded its services by offering results based on a scanner panel (see Chapter 5).

The late-1980s find a major technological battle being waged between IRI's Behavior-Scan and Nielsen's ERIM system for the on-the-air testing dollars. The Marketing Research

---

[11] "On-Air Ad Testing Misses Show Differences: Yuspeh," *Marketing News*, p. 4, Apr. 6, 1979.
[12] Ibid.
[13] Ibid.

MARKETING RESEARCH IN ACTION

BEHAVIORSCAN AND ERIM COMPETE
FOR ADVERTISING TESTING DOLLARS

In a nutshell, BehaviorScan tracks a new product's progress over the course of 1 year in a highly controlled electronic minimarket—one monitored by the technological marriage of UPC supermarket scanner data and meters which provide targetable TV—for a cost ranging from $145,000 to $160,000 per test. The scanners track the purchases of panels of 2500 households in each market. Panel members simply present an ID card at checkout to have all of their purchases electronically recorded, thus providing the database to track trial and repeat, buying rate, loyalty, purchase cycles, brand shifting, and demographics. Furthermore, with BehaviorScan's targetable TV technology, marketers can deliver alternative advertising campaigns to different subgroups of the panel.

A.C. Nielsen entered the fray with its ERIM, an acronym for Electronic Research fo Insights into Marketing.

While Neilsen's ERIM is a mightly close cousin to BehaviorScan, there are some differences. The biggest is that ERIM's delivery will be over-the-air broadcast, rather than cable, as is BehaviorScan. This is an advantage, according to Larry Gold, vice president of marketing of the system, who says that "ERIM is using orthodox sampling in marketing and will measure both cable and noncable households." Cable households, he notes, skew in demographics and purchasing behavior. And unlike BehaviorScan, which has installed scanner equipment in its eight markets at its own expense "for better control," ERIM will rely on the existing scanner equipment in the markets it intends to be in. ERIM will initially go up in two markets, Springfield, Missouri, and Sioux Falls, North Dakota, and eventually roll out to six to ten markets, depending upon demand.

Source: Marketing and Media Decisions pp. 76–77, November 1984.

In Action in this section outlines the dimensions of this battle. Both of these systems attempt to relate advertising to sales results, and usually do so in the context of a test market. Thus these latter tests are more expensive than communications measurements such as DAR.

Theater Tests

Television commercials are also tested in theater environments. ARS and ASI Market Research, Inc., offer such services. Samples involve 250–600 recruited respondents in selected major cities. Ads are shown in the context of a standard television show. Typical measures taken are for brand preference shift based upon before and after exposure to test and control ads and recall of the copy points in the commercial. The artificial nature of the test environment is a major concern.

Trailer Tests

An alternative to a theater test is to recruit respondents from shopping malls and take them to a trailer near the mall or even a room in the mall itself. There they are shown several ads with or without surrounding programming, and recall, recognition, and product preference measures are taken. Again, artificiality is a problem.

Laboratory Stores

Commercials may be tested for sales and attitude input in a simulated shopping environment, like the new product simulated test markets described in Chapter 23.

POSTTESTING PROCEDURES

The three major posttesting procedures described here are recognition tests, recall tests, and sales tests.

Recognition Tests

The readership of print ads is primarily measured with *recognition* procedures. The leading supplier in this area is Starch Readership Service. In the recognition method, personal interviews are conducted with a sample of 100–150 adults of each sex for each issue of a magazine. (If the magazine or newspaper has a youthful audience, a younger sample is recruited.) The respondent is asked whether or not the specific periodical has been read. For those who answer positively, the issue is opened at a page specified in advance to prevent order bias and then three measures of recognition are taken:

1 *Noted*—the percentage of readers who remember seeing the ad
2 *Seen-associated*—the percentage of readers who saw or read a part of the ad that indicates the brand or advertiser
3 *Read most*—the percentage of readers who read half or more of the written material in the ad

Additionally, these scores are ranked for all the ads in the periodical, and cost ratios are given which relate readers to the money spent on the ad. Norm scores for types of product classes and periodicals are also available.

Recognition procedures are limited by the possibility of respondents confusing ads with other similar ones, forgetting, and false claiming. Also, product interest may distort memory of ads.

Recall Tests

Gallup and Robinson offer a posttesting readership service called Magazine Impact Readership Service (MIRS). Copies of test magazines are delivered to a sample of 150–300 respondents, and telephone interviews are arranged for the next day. Respondents, who are in 10 major geographic areas, are asked to read the magazines in a normal fashion. In the follow-up interview readership is verified, and then a list of ads appearing in the magazine is read. Respondents identify those they remember. Result scores are similar to G&R's television service: proved name recognition, idea communication, and favorable attitude. Measurement goes beyond recognition to recall of specifics of the ad and its impact.

A twist on MIRS is G&R's Tip-In, which is really a pretesting service that uses a regular magazine into which test ads have been inserted to look like normal ads in the publication. Methods and measures are the same as MIRS.

Other similar recall-based readership services available are READEX, Starch Reader Impression Studies, Chilton Ad-Chart Readership Service, AD-Q, and the Advertising Index. Commonly used measures include unaided and aided recall scores.

Recall tests may understate the ad's impact as the cues given to stimulate respondent memory are not strong. This is why some prefer recognition tests, especially for nondistinctive appeals and for low-involvement products. Also, despite G&R's use of the term "impact" for their service, recall does not necessarily relate to the respondent undertaking the desired buying behavior or the advertising reaching its objectives.

Sales Tests

Sales tests measure the impact of the ad on the sales of the product. Since sales are influenced by so many factors, great care must be taken in evaluating advertisements in this manner. Thus, these tests often involve the application of the experimental and quasi-experimental procedures discussed in Chapter 12, plus the mechanics of test marketing discussed in Chapter 23. AdTel and other panel procedures can also be used.

SUMMARY

1 Media vehicle and message research constitute the major application areas of marketing research within advertising.

2 Media research focuses its attention on media vehicle distribution and media vehicle audience.

3 Measurements related to advertising exposure, advertising perception, advertising communication, and sales response—although media-related—are usually dealt with more in message or copy research.

4 Media vehicle distribution research measures the circulation of print media and the penetration level of broadcast media in households.

5 Media vehicle audience research measures the size of the audience exposed to a given vehicle. Periodical pass-along or readership studies and the radio and television ratings are the modes here.

6 Survey methods dominate print media audience measurement, while diary, meter, coincident telephone, and personal interview recall methods are important in television. Radio uses diary and telephone panels.

7 Copy testing measures the effectiveness of the ad itself. Ads may be tested in a number of developmental or finished stages as well as in natural or artificial environments. The more finished and more natural the exposure, especially repeated exposures, the more ideal the procedure.

8 Pretesting of ads occurs prior to commitments of media dollars at the level planned in the campaign. Pretesting procedures include: consumer jury, portfolio tests, physiological methods, dummy advertising vehicles, inquiry tests, on-the-air tests, theater tests, trailer tests, and laboratory stores.

9 Posttesting of ads occurs after the ad has been run at the planned level in the media. Posttesting procedures include recognition tests, recall tests, and sales tests.

10 Good copy testing procedures should follow certain principles: have relevant measures, provide multiple measures, consider models of human response to communication, allow for number of exposures, compare the same degree of finished ads, provide controls against bias in the exposure environment, and demonstrate reliability and validity.

DISCUSSION QUESTIONS

1 Why is advertising research so much used in practice? Why is this true given the great experience base among marketing managers in advertising?

2 What different types of data would advertisers like to have about media vehicles?

3 Why are some of these data so difficult to obtain? Be specific.

4 Why do the Simmon Market Research Bureau and Mediamark Research, Inc., obtain estimates of magazine audience sizes that differ? Which method of measurement is better?

5 What methods may be used to measure the size of television audiences? Evaluate each.

6 What are the characteristics of an ideal copy testing procedure? Why does practice not follow the ideal?

7 How can you measure the reliability and validity of a copy testing procedure? Why is this important?

8 How are ads pretested? Evaluate each method.

9 In posttesting recognition and recall two different measures are taken. Give an example of each and evaluate the two.

10 Why aren't sales tests the most common form of posttesting?

CASES FOR PART SEVEN

CASE 7-1: *Production* Magazine: Capital Spending Study

Production magazine is a monthly publication of the Bramson Publishing Company of Bloomfield Hills, Michigan, a suburb of Detroit. *Production* serves the production metal-working market, which includes the following manufacturing industries under U.S. government Standard Industrial Classifications (SIC) for two-digit codes:

SIC code	Business and industry	Circulation
25	Furniture and fixtures	1,388
33	Primary metal	2,515
34	Fabricated metal products	13,911
35	Machinery, except electrical	24,753
36	Electric and electronic equipment	16,990
37	Transportation equipment	12,781
38	Instruments and related products	5,730
39	Miscellaneous manufacturing industries	1,688
50	Steel service centers	669
	Total	80,425

According to U.S. Commerce Department figures, there are 130,812 plants in these markets, as of the 1977 census of manufacturers (released late in 1980). However, 108,972 of those plants employ less than 50 employees. Circulation for *Production* is based on plants with employment of 50 or greater. The Commerce Department survey also indicates that the vast majority of capital equipment investment dollars is spent by plants with 50 or more employees ($15,112.1 million of $16,785.9 million—or 90 percent).

The magazine is distributed to qualified personnel in these industries on a nonpaid basis—in other words, no subscription fee. (Qualified recipients are companies and their administrative, production, engineering, product design, and purchasing personnel.) Circulation is about 80,400 copies per month and has been stable for years. Most recipients specifically request that they receive a copy of the magazine which enjoys a very positive reputation for keeping readers current on production-related issues. The advertising rate in early 1981 was about $2800 per black-and-white page.

The job profile of recipients is as follows:

Company officials and general management	9,042
Production engineering	33,904
Production management	29,748
Product engineering	3,637
Procurement	2,496
Company names, etc.	1,598
Total	80,425

The Capital Spending Study

Every year the marketing research staff at Bramson Publishing conducts a study concerned with the capital spending plans of the industries in its circulation. The results of this study are much quoted and often used by firms as a basis for their activities for the coming year. Additionally, the study serves as a way of identifying trends in the market for the magazine's advertisers. The publishing function in an industrial market often serves as a (or the only) market research source for all but the largest advertisers.

Method and Selected Results

The description of the method used for the annual capital spending study and selected results (about 10 percent of all reported results) are presented in Exhibit 1. This exhibit is based upon a report prepared by Bramson's director of research. The questionnaire used is contained in Exhibit 2.

CASE QUESTIONS

1 What forecasting method is being used in the capital spending study? What is being forecast?
2 Evaluate the sampling plan and the sample actually selected.
3 Are there any questions that seriously prejudice responses by how the questions are asked?
4 What other method(s) could be used to make these forecasts?
5 How accurate do you think the forecast will be?

EXHIBIT 1

METHOD AND RESULTS

We mail the questionnaire to a universe of 12,000 plants in the discrete parts manufacturing industries: SIC 34, Fabricated Metal Products; SIC 35, Machinery, except Electrical; SIC 36, Electrical Machinery; SIC 37, Transportation Equipment; SIC 38, Instruments; a few selected industries in SIC 39, Miscellaneous Manufacturing and the Metal Furniture portion of SIC 25. The universe, by employment, is made up of every plant we reach employing 500 and over and every *other* plant reached employing 50–500. We mail to upper-echelon readers—presidents, executive vice presidents, general managers, vice presidents of manufacturing and/or operations, plant, works, or factory managers and superintendents, directors of production engineering, and managers of manufacturing engineering—people with lateral interests and access to the dollars and plans needed to complete our questionnaire. We mail one questionnaire per plant, using a computer program to select any one of the above titles on an alphabetical search of each plant galley.* We conducted the survey between July 22 and August 29 of this year, so the data we have is very current.

The findings we are reporting on today are based on the first 2400 returns (a 20 percent response). While we'll be adding in returns that have come in subsequent to the cutoff for this presentation, it's worth noting the results will not change more than a tenth or two of a percentage point from what we pass on today.

The first question we ask concerns spending intentions: "Next year, will your plant's spending for capital machinery-equipment—increase, decrease, or remain the same?"

Spending intentions, 1981	
1981	**1980**
43.8% to increase	57.4% to increase
18.1% to decrease	17.9% to decrease
31.4% to remain the same	24.7% to remain the same
6.6% no answer	

Now, why are your customers and prospects buying production machinery and equipment? These are the reasons (motives) ranked by the respondents:

Reasons for spending (ranked 1st or 2d out of 6)				
	Percent ranking 1st or 2d			
	1981	**Rank**	**1980**	**Rank**
New machines to reduce costs	64.6	1	69.3	2
Increase machine-equipment capacity	43.8	2	73.1	1
New models–new products	25.4	3	31.4	4
Tighter quality standards	22.7	4	36.1	3
More make–less buy	16.0	5	11.3	5
Reduce energy consumption	9.5	6	5.2	6

*Therefore, our survey of 12,000 covers 55 percent of the market of plants of 50 or more employees (21,840).

EXHIBIT 1 (CONTINUED)

Capacity utilization reported at the time of the survey, late summer 1980, was 76.1 percent. One year ago it was 84.2 percent. We believe this goes a long way in explaining the reduced pressure to purchase equipment to alleviate capacity problems.

Capacity utilization: 76.1%

One year ago: 84.2%

While low this year, respondents were generally optimistic about operating levels in 1981. So, how much will be invested in production machinery and equipment in 1981?

$11 billion on machinery-equipment in 1981

That's just about what we projected one year ago for 1980. *In 1981 dollars* it means overall spending will be down 9–10 percent.

We have two projections this year:

Two projections	
Scenario A	**Scenario B**
$11.7 billion	$10.8 billion

Scenario A, at $11.7 billion—exactly the figure we projected last year—was obtained by following procedures we've used for 12 years. Namely, we ask the respondent how much his plant is going to spend and do not question the figure further. Scenario B was developed by asking the respondent whether he had the allocation in hand and if he did not, what did he feel would be approved—100 percent, 90 percent, 80 percent, 70 percent, or whatever. We factored in these responses and cut the figure by $900 million.

Here's how the machinery-equipment dollar will be spent:

How the dollar will be spent (percent)	
Metal cutting	35.1
Metal forming	9.0
Assembly	16.3
Cleaning-finishing	7.7
Material handling	6.5
Gauging-inspecting-testing	5.0
Weld-rivet-braze	4.8
Plastic molding	2.7
Heat processing	2.6
Other	10.3

EXHIBIT 2

CAPITAL INVESTMENT PROGRAM 1981–1982

1 Next year, will your plant's spending for capital machinery-equipment: ___ Increase ___ Decrease ___ Remain the same?

2 What are the principal *overall* motives for 1981 capital investments? (Rank 1, 2, 3, etc., to show importance)
___ Increase machine-equipment capacity   ___ Make instead of buy
___ Tighter quality standards   ___ Reduce energy consumption
___ New machines to reduce costs   ___ New products-models

3 At what level of capacity is your plant currently operating? (Check one)
___ 50–59% ___ 60–69% ___ 70–79% ___ 80–89% ___ 90–99% ___ 100%
Are you planning to operate at a ___ higher ___ lower ___ same level in 1981?
Why?_____

4 Which of the following are you *actively* investigating for major cost reduction? (Check all which apply)
___ Materials costs   ___ Inprocess inventory   ___ Direct labor
___ Perishable tools-supplies   ___ Materials handling   ___ Indirect labor (maintenance, toolroom, etc.)

5 When justifying a production equipment investment, what does your company require as the minimum pre-tax, first year return-on-investment? (Check one)
___ Less than 10% ___ 20–29% ___ 40–49% ___ 60–69% ___ 80–89% ___ 100%
___ 10–19%   ___ 30–39% ___ 50–59% ___ 70–79% ___ 90–99% ___ None

6 (a) In 1981, how much will your plant invest in machinery-equipment? If you are uncertain, use your best judgment. Questions b-c-d will help us "weight" your answer. (Check one)
___ Less than $50,000   ___ $300,000–$399,999   ___ $700,000–$799,999
___ $50,000–$99,999   ___ $400,000–$499,999   ___ $800,000–$899,999
___ $100,000–$199,000 ___ $500,000–$599,999   ___ $900,000–$999,999
___ $200,000–$299,999 ___ $600,000–$699,999   ___ $1,000,000 or more
                                              Specify: $ _____
(b) Has the above amount been approved? ___ Yes ___ No
(c) If *no*, when do you expect approval? ___ Sept. ___ Oct. ___ Nov. ___ Dec. ___ Other_
(d) What percent of the indicated total do you expect to be approved? ___ 100%
___ 90% ___ 80% ___ 70% ___ Other ____%

7 What percent of the total equipment dollar will be: domestic-sourced _____% foreign-sourced _____%

8 What percentage of your 1981 capital equipment expenditure will be invested in each of the categories of machinery-equipment listed in the table on page 648?

GENERAL TRENDS—PRACTICES

1 Does your plant currently operate numerically controlled machines? ___ Yes ___ No
If *yes,* how many individual numerically controlled machines are currently in operation?
_____ (number)

	Step 1 (percent of total machinery-equipment expenditures for major category)	Step 2 (break out percentages for equipment types under each major category. These should add up to totals shown in Step 1)*	Step 3 (for each equipment type, indicate if current plans call for purchase in 1982)
Assembly Machines-Equipment	_____ %		
Automatic and semi-automatic machinery		_____ %	Yes ___ No ___
Portable power tools		_____ %	Yes ___ No ___
Other assembly equipment		_____ %	Yes ___ No ___
Finishing Equipment	_____ %		
Cleaning equipment		_____ %	Yes ___ No ___
Plating equipment		_____ %	Yes ___ No ___
Painting equipment		_____ %	Yes ___ No ___
Mechanical finishing (deburring, polishing, etc.)		_____ %	Yes ___ No ___
Heat Processing Equipment	_____ %		
Induction		_____ %	Yes ___ No ___
Vacuum		_____ %	Yes ___ No ___
Other heat processing equipment		_____ %	Yes ___ No ___
Metal-Cutting Machine Tools	_____ %		
Boring machines		_____ %	Yes ___ No ___
Broaching machines		_____ %	Yes ___ No ___
Drilling machines		_____ %	Yes ___ No ___
Electrical discharge machines (EDM)		_____ %	Yes ___ No ___
Grinding machines		_____ %	Yes ___ No ___
Machining centers (horizontal and/or vertical)		_____ %	Yes ___ No ___
Milling machines		_____ %	Yes ___ No ___
Turning machines		_____ %	Yes ___ No ___
Transfer and other special purpose		_____ %	Yes ___ No ___
Metal-Forming Machine Tools	_____ %		
Blanking and stamping presses		_____ %	Yes ___ No ___
Forging and cold heading machines		_____ %	Yes ___ No ___
Brakes and shears		_____ %	Yes ___ No ___
Sheet/strip processing/feeding equipment		_____ %	Yes ___ No ___
Material Handling Equipment	_____ %		
Conveyors		_____ %	Yes ___ No ___
Industrial trucks		_____ %	Yes ___ No ___
Cranes		_____ %	Yes ___ No ___
Gauging-Inspecting-Testing Machines-Equipment	_____ %		
Gauging-inspection equipment		_____ %	Yes ___ No ___
Testing machines-equipment		_____ %	Yes ___ No ___
Plastic Molding-Forming Equipment	_____ %		
Injection molding machines		_____ %	Yes ___ No ___
Other molding machines-equipment		_____ %	Yes ___ No ___
Welding-Riveting-Brazing Machines-Equipment	_____ %		
Welding machines-equipment		_____ %	Yes ___ No ___
Riveting machines-equipment		_____ %	Yes ___ No ___
Brazing machines-equipment		_____ %	Yes ___ No ___

*For example: An investment of 15 percent in "assembly machines-equipment" might break down as 9 percent automatic or semiautomatic equipment, 3 percent portable power tools, and 3 percent other assembly equipment.

2 Do your plans for 1981–1983 capital equipment purchases include numerically controlled equipment? ___ Yes ___ No

	1981	1982	1983		1981	1982	1983		1981	1982	1983
Mach'g center-horiz.	___	___	___	Drilling	___	___	___	Turning-horiz.	___	___	___
Mach'g center-vert.	___	___	___	Grinding	___	___	___	Turning-vert.	___	___	___
Boring	___	___	___	Milling	___	___	___	Punching	___	___	___

If *yes*, which of the following types will be purchased? (Check year and type which apply)

3 Flexible machining systems usually work efficiently on similar parts. They may be machining centers or multiple station systems with head changers, indexing devices and shuttle tables.

Do your plans for 1981–1983 include flexible machining systems? ___ Yes ___ No
If *yes*, which type will you purchase? (Check year and type which applies)

	1981	1982	1983		1981	1982	1983
Flexible machining center	___	___	___	Multiple station system	___	___	___

5 Does your plant operate production equipment controlled by computers or mini-computers? ___ Yes ___ No
If *no*, check if you anticipate installing in ___ 1981 ___ 1982.
6 Are you using computerized data systems for:

Production control	___Yes	___No	___Plan to	Materials requirement planning	___Yes	___No	___Plan to
Machine loading	___Yes	___No	___Plan to	Maintenance scheduling	___Yes	___No	___Plan to

7 Do your plans for 1981–1983 capital equipment purchases include electrical discharge machines (EDM)? ___ Yes ___No
If *yes*, which tank size and types will be purchased? (Check year and types which apply)

Tank size	1981	1982	1983	Type	1981	1982	1983
12″ x 20″	___	___	___	Numerically controlled	___	___	___
18″ x 24″	___	___	___	Wire EDM	___	___	___
Over 20″ x 30″	___	___	___	Other	___	___	___

8 Four developments will have marked effect on the requirements for industrial products in the 1980s. These are (1) energy development, (2) energy conservation, (3) information handling, and (4) a resurgent defense establishment.

Please read the following paragraphs and then answer the question which pertains to them.

Energy development: Mining and drilling for coal, gas and oil; energy-power generation; refineries; energy transmission/distribution.

Energy conservation: Design and redesign of products for efficient utilization of energy for private-public transportation, heating, agriculture and industry.

Information handling: Data collection-processing-transmission; facsimile reproduction-transmission; computer-aided functions; numerical control of machines-processes; conversion of printed-oral instructions into electronic impulses; personal-home computers; audiovisual communications; video tape systems.

Defense industries: Ordnance, aircraft, missiles and naval vessels; communications systems; equipment and systems for support and supply of armed forces and the overall defense establishment.

Question: For 1981–1983, what percentage of your capital outlay will be allocated for the manufacture of products or components for:

Energy development _____%   Information handling _____%
Energy conservation _____%   Defense _____%

Thank you very much!
Please return the questionnaire in the enclosed postage-paid envelope to Production.

CASE 7-2: "No Sweat"*

San Francisco Package Goods (SFPG) was one of the largest companies in the United States. In the previous decade, it had had many new-product successes. Their newest venture was an antiperspirant/deodorant, based on a new formulation, tentatively called "No Sweat." After a favorable employee reaction to the product, SFPG decided to conduct a concept test. Production of the new product would require considerable investment in plant and equipment, so SFPG managers planned to base much of their go–no go decision on the results of this test. A concept test, rather than an actual product test, was undertaken because production costs were so great, and also the R&D crew was still trying to make minor improvements in the product.

The SFPG marketing department was considered to be one best in the industry. Unlike many other companies, SFPG conducted its own marketing research. Bill Freeland, a recent B.B.A. graduate, was asked to prepare the concept statement and to design the testing procedure for No Sweat. His concept statement and portions of his design are presented in Exhibit 1.

The study was undertaken using the methodology proposed by Freeland. Approximately 400 phone calls were made to set up the 100 interview appointments. Two of the scheduled subjects (both male) canceled their appointments before being interviewed, making the actual sample size 98. Selected results from the experiment appear in Exhibit 2.

* Coauthored by Sheryl Petras.

EXHIBIT 1

STUDY PROPOSAL

Concept statement for a new antiperspirant/deodorant:
A major producer of soaps, shampoos, and other personal hygiene goods has developed a new antiperspirant/deodorant stick. The company has combined ingredients which have, in the past, been difficult to stabilize in stick form. The product has a unique appearance; its white antiperspirant center is surrounded by an outer ring of green gel deodorant. This antiperspirant/deodorant combination provides both males and females with the highest degree of protection available against odor and wetness. This new product will be available in a 2.5-oz size for $3.50 and a 1.5-oz size for $2.20.

Objective
Our objective is to identify the potential market for No Sweat, the new antiperspirant/deodorant created by SFPG. Given its unique appearance and its dual-action formula, we hope No Sweat will find a niche in an already flooded market. Consumer attitudes regarding specific characteristics of the product will be investigated, as well as their overall reaction to the product concept. At the request of the new-product manager, we will differentiate between spray, stick, and roll-on users in the presentation of our data.

Method
Personal interviews will be used due to the length of the survey and the quality of data that must be procured. A random sample of 50 men and 50 women will be selected from the Los Angeles phone book. Because the sample will be random, one can be assured of equal representation of roll-on, stick, and spray antiperspirant and deodorant users. Soliciting for personal interviews will be conducted over the phone between 12:00 noon and 9:00 P.M. This will ensure that all members of the population have an equal chance of being contacted.

The Interview
Interviews will be conducted without any reference to SFPG, thus eliminating a potential source of respondent bias. All subjects will be shown the concept statement. They will then be asked to give opinions regarding specific attributes of the product. Finally, intent to purchase will be measured. The respondents will also be shown the proposed package design for No Sweat. Their feedback will be recorded and used to suggest possible changes in the design.

EXHIBIT 2

STUDY RESULTS

Primary type of antiperspirant/deodorant used (n = 98):

Roll-on	47%	(46)
Stick	39	(38)
Spray	11	(11)
Other	3	(3)

Respondents were given a list of several product characteristics, then asked to use the seven-point scale appearing below to record what influence each characteristic had on purchase intent. Subjects were divided into four classes—roll-on, stick, spray, and "other" users. The table following the scale presents the average score each characteristic received within those divisions.

				Influence on purchase Intent		
Definity would not influence purchase decision					**Definitely would influence purchase decision**	
1	2	3	4	5	6	7

Characteristic	Most common type of antiperspirant or deodorant used			
	Roll-on	**Stick**	**Spray**	**Other**
Can be used by both sexes	4.2	4.0	3.9	4.4
Effective at stopping wetness	6.2	5.9	6.1	5.8
Effective at stopping odor	6.4	6.0	6.0	6.7
Product appearance	2.5	3.1	3.6	3.0
Product form (stick, roll-on, aerosol, other)	2.8	6.3	2.6	2.2
New formula	4.1	4.5	4.2	3.9
Package design	3.1	3.0	2.7	2.9
Package size	4.0	4.1	4.1	4.6
Package shape	3.9	3.8	3.9	3.6
Price	4.7	6.1	3.2	5.4

The following table summarizes the results into two categories: the data from respondents who said they would try the product and data from those who said they wouldn't. Within each group (triers and nontriers), the table presents the percentage of people who rated the characteristic: (a) 1 or 2, (b) 3, 4, or 5; and (c) 6 or 7.

Characteristic	Rating	Triers	Nontriers
Effectiveness at stopping wetness	1–2	0%	1%
	3–4–5	32	39
	6–7	68	60
Effectiveness at stopping odor	1–2	0	0
	3–4–5	30	32
	6–7	70	68
Price	1–2	20	67[‡]
	3–4–5	74	32[‡]
	6–7	6	1
Product appearance	1–2	52	74[†]
	3–4–5	36	18[*]
	6–7	12	8
New formula	1–2	2	11
	3–4–5	64	76
	6–7	34	13[†]
Total number		25	73

[*] Significant difference at 90% confidence level.
[†] Significant difference at 95% confidence level.
[‡] Significant difference at 99% confidence level.

Reasons for trial: Those who said they would try the product (*n* = 25):

Dissatisfaction with current brand	14%
Curiosity	58
Other	28

Reasons for no trial: Those who said they would not try the product (*n* = 73):

Price	25%
Satisfaction with current brand	64
Other	11

Product package results:

	Yes	No	Indifferent
Do you like the package shape?	17%	21%	31%
Do you like the package colors?	29	58	13
Do you like the lettering?	62	26	12
Do you like the package overall?	45	47	8

CASE QUESTIONS

1 Evaluate the concept statement.
2 Critique the methodology of the study.
3 What conclusions can be drawn from this study.
4 What further research needs to be done before this product is introduced? Be specific.

CASE 7-3: Executive Express*

Heather Clayton is president of Express Air, a small commuter airline company based in St. Andrew. Express Air currently provides air taxi and corporate flight services to local businesses. To boost company profits, Clayton is considering offering a regular service between St. Andrew and Bayville, a major city about 340 miles from St. Andrew. There are presently no regular flights between St. Andrew and Bayville. St. Andrew–Bayville fliers must either charter a plane or leave from Eastport City Airport, which is about 50 miles from St. Andrew. Before establishing this Executive Express service,

* Co-authored by Sheryl Petras.

however, Clayton wants to see what kind of demand there is for it. She begins by evaluating the current service and the type of travelers who currently use it. A brief description of the current service, the cities involved, and the potential customers follows.

Bayville   Bayville is a major metropolitan area of more than 6 million people. It hosts the main offices of several "Fortune 500" companies, so it is frequently visited by executives from Eastport and St. Andrew. Most of these business travelers arrive in the morning and leave at the end of the day. Bayville is also a cultural center; it has fine restaurants, museums, playhouses, and a world class symphony orchestra—making it a popular weekend vacation spot.

Bayville has two airports: Central and Lake. Central Airport is extremely busy because all major airlines land there. It is also located 25 miles from the downtown business district. Lake Airport is smaller, less busy, and closer to downtown, so business travelers generally prefer to arrive there. Both Central and Lake airports offer regular service to Eastport.

Eastport   Eastport, also highly populated, has about 4 million inhabitants. Eastport City Airport offers hourly jet service to Bayville's Lake Airport. Flights to Central are less frequent.

St. Andrew   St. Andrew is much smaller than either Bayville or Eastport, claiming slightly less than 100,000 residents. It is the home of St. Andrew College, which has an enrollment of 20,000 students. More than 800 businesses are located in the area, including several banks and consulting firms. Travelers flying from St. Andrew to Bayville must go via Eastport City Airport, and thus the trip takes about 2 hours; a 1-hour drive to Eastport (this includes parking and check-in) and a 1-hour flight to St. Andrew.

The proposed St. Andrew to Bayville service would cut travel time in half, to 1 hour (including the drive to the airport). There is a major drawback to this service, however. The St. Andrew Airport cannot accommodate jets because its runway is too short.

Since jets cannot be used, Express Air is considering two types of prop planes for the service. The first type, CASA, is unpressurized. This means it cannot attain the same altitudes that pressurized planes do. Because of this, CASA might not be able to fly above bad weather conditions to escape turbulence. CASA has 24 seats, and passengers are able to stand up inside the plane. Metroliner, the other aircraft being considered, does have a pressurized cabin. Thus, it can fly higher than the CASA and probably escape bad weather conditions. But, the 18-seat Metroliner is not large enough for passengers to stand upright inside the plane. The Metroliner and the CASA have virtually identical cruising speeds.

CASE QUESTIONS

1 Assume that Clayton has come to you for advice. What information will she need before deciding whether or not this service is feasible?
2 How would you obtain this information?
3 Assuming that part of this information would be collected by a conjoint measurement study, identify the appropriate attributes, attribute levels, and data instrument structure.

CASE 7-4: The Cupertino Group*

Express Air is a small commuter airline based in St. Andrew. It presently provides charter service to local companies. Heather Clayton, president of Express Air, is considering the feasibility of a regular service between St. Andrew and Bayville, a major business center located 340 miles northeast of St. Andrew. Currently, travelers must drive 50 miles to Eastport City Airport before catching a flight to Bayville. Clayton's proposed service would eliminate the 50-mile drive by flying directly from St. Andrew Airport to Lake Airport in Bayville. Express Air could offer three flights per day from St. Andrew, which is not many when compared to the 7:00 A.M. to 7:00 P.M. hourly service available from Eastport. Because jets are unable to land at St. Andrew Airport (the runway is too short), Express Air would employ prop planes.

Clayton had hired the Cupertino Group, a small specialty marketing research company, to research the demand for the new service. She has just received the data and is ready to interpret the findings. The survey and questionnaire results appear below Additional cost data are presented in Appendix A.

SURVEY

Findings from a preliminary telephone survey of local travel agencies and businesses:

1 At least 50 persons per business day travel to Bayville.
2 Sixty percent of the businesses get their St. Andrew–Bayville tickets through travel agencies.
3 Travel agents believe that a St. Andrew to Bayville service would be popular.
4 The majority of businesses said that they would take advantage of such a service.
5 According to the Chamber of Commerce, "the proposed service would be substantially used by St. Andrew businesses as a more efficient and economic means of transportation to and from the Bayville area."

QUESTIONNAIRE

This half-hour mail survey was given to 50 local businesspersons who had traveled to Bayville within the last 6 months. Travel agents provided the names of potential respondents. Results follow each question. (All questions were open-ended, so the response categories were created by the researchers in order to analyze the data.)

QUESTIONNAIRE

1. When was your last trip to Bayville?
   64%   within the last month
   12   more than 1, but less than 2 months ago
   8   more than 2, but less than 3 months ago
   16   more than 3, but less than 6 months ago

* Co-authored by Sheryl Petras.

2. How did you get there?

   92%   plane

    8   car

3. What was the purpose of the trip?

   74%   business

   20   pleasure

    4   business/pleasure

    2   transfer planes

4. How often do you go to Bayville per year by plane? By car or train?

   Average number of plane trips per year: 7.3

   Average number of car or train trips per year: 2.8

5. At what time of day do you usually leave for Bayville?

   96%   before 10:00 A.M.

    4   noon

6. When do you like to leave Bayville?

   68%   between 5:00 P.M. and 6:00 P.M.

   14   between 6:01 P.M. and 7:00 P.M.

   10   between 7:01 P.M. and 8:00 P.M.

    4   between 8:01 P.M. and 9:00 P.M.

    4   the following morning at 8:30 A.M.

7. How do you feel about the existing service from Eastport to Bayville?

   How is the airport?

     —Many respondents said they disliked the parking facilities

   The schedule?

     —98% were completely satisfied

   The price?

     —For most people the price was unimportant, although 11 respondents thought it was too high for such a short distance

   The service aboard?

     —Not important

8. A small aircraft leaves from St. Andrew airport and flies to Bayville Lake Airport in 1 hour. It departs from St. Andrew at 8:00 A.M. and the return flight leaves from Bayville at 5:30 P.M. that same evening. The price is $110 one way. Would you consider taking such a flight when you go to Bayville?

   70%   yes

   30   no

For the next set of questions, respondents were asked to fill in several matrices similar to the one shown in Table 1. They were told to place a 1 in the cell they liked most, and to place the highest ranking in the cell they liked least.

TABLE 1

	Time of traveling (one way)		
Price (one way)	2 hours	$1\frac{1}{2}$ hours	1 hour
$170			
120			
70			

Assume all combinations are possible. *Note:* The time of traveling includes the time it takes to get to the airport.

Data obtained from several of these matrices were analyzed using a conjoint measurement computer program (MONANOVA). For each individual matrix, the program calculated utility values between 0 and 1 (with 1 being highest utility) for every category of every variable in the matrix. For the above example the following utilities occurred:

Price (one way)	Utility value	Travel time, hours	Utility value
$170	.16	2	.17
120	.56	$1\frac{1}{2}$	.58
70	.78	1	.75

Add these utility values to get utilities of the various combinations of variables. The program assigns utility values so that the utilities for the cells in the matrix are in the same order as the rank order (1, 2, 3, etc.) given by the respondents. For example, a 2-hour trip costing $170 has a utility of .17 + .16 = .33, the lowest value in the price–travel time matrix (see Table 2). This combination was also ranked last by the respondents. The ordering of calculated utilities does not always coincide with the respondent rankings, but this program generates the values which come closest to accomplishing that task.

TABLE 2

	Time of traveling (one way)		
Price (one way)	2 hours (.17)	$1\frac{1}{2}$ hours (.58)	1 hour (.75)
$170 (.16)	9 (.33)	7 (.74)	6 (.91)
120 (.56)	8 (.73)	4 (1.14)	3 (1.31)
70 (.78)	5 (.95)	2 (1.36)	1 (1.53)

The relative importance of the variables has also been calculated for each matrix. Relative importance = (range of the utility values of variable a)/(range of values of variable a + range of values of variable b).

Relative importance of price and travel time:

Price   .52   (.52 = .62/1.20, where .62 = .78 − .16, the range of the price utility values)

Travel time .48 (.48 = .58/1.20)

TABLE A PRICE AND SORT OF PLANE

Price (one way)	Utility
$170	.23
120	.51
70	.78

Sort of plane	Utility
DC-9	.87
Metroliner	.60
CASA	.23

Relative importance	
Price	.46
Plane	.54

TABLE B PRICE AND AIRPORT OF DEPARTURE

Price (one way)	Utility
$170	.17
120	.51
70	.82

Airport	Utility
St. Andrew	.72
Eastport	.28

Relative importance	
Price	.60
Airport	.40

TABLE C PRICE AND COMFORT OF THE PLANE

Price (one way)	Utility
$170	.21
120	.55
70	.74

Comfort	Utility
Possible to stand upright, bathroom	.86
Not possible to stand upright, bathroom	.54
Possible to stand upright, no bathroom	.50
Not possible to stand upright, no bathroom	.10

Relative importance	
Price	.42
Comfort	.59

TABLE D TRAVEL TIME AND SORT OF PLANE

Travel time, hours	Utility
1	.74
$1\frac{1}{2}$	.61
2	.15

Plane	Utility
DC-9 commercial jet	.79
Metroliner pressurized prop jet (18 seats)	.51
CASA unpressurized prop jet (24 seats)	.20

Relative importance	
Time	.50
Plane	.50

This means that the importance of two variables in the decision-making process is almost the same, with price having slightly more influence. In other words, a higher price is rejected slightly more than a longer travel time. The utility values and relative importances for other pairs of variables are as shown in Tables A to E.

TABLE E TRAVEL TIME AND SCHEDULE

Travel time, hours	Utility
1	.70
$1\frac{1}{2}$	.62
2	.18

Schedule	Utility
Leave St. Andrew or Eastport: 8:00 A.M. and 5:00 P.M. Leave Bayville: 9:30 A.M. and 6:30 P.M.	.17
Leave St. Andrew or Eastport: 8:00 A.M., 1:00 P.M., 7:00 P.M. Leave Bayville: 9:30 A.M., 2:30 P.M., 8:30 P.M.	.42
Leave St. Andrew or Eastport: 8:00 A.M., 1:00 P.M., 5:00 P.M. Leave Bayville: 9:30 A.M., 2:30 P.M., 6:30 P.M.	.51
Leave St. Andrew or Eastport: hourly from 7:00 A.M. to 7:00 P.M. Leave Bayville: hourly from 8:30 A.M. to 8:30 P.M.	.90

Relative importance	
Time	.42
Schedule	.58

TABLE F SORT OF PLANE AND AIRPORT OF DEPARTURE

Sort of plane	Utility
DC-9	.84
Metroliner	.46
CASA	.21

Airport	Utility
St. Andrew	.74
Eastside	.26

Relative importance	
Plane	.57
Airport	.43

TABLE G SORT OF PLANE AND COMFORT

Sort of Plane	Utility
DC-9	.76
Metroliner	.44
CASA	.30

Comfort*	Utility
Stand, bathroom	.93
Can't stand, bathroom	.54
Stand, no bathroom	.40
Can't stand, no bathroom	.14

Relative importance	
Plane	.37
Comfort	.63

* See Table C for complete descriptions.

TABLE H AIRPORT OF DEPARTURE AND SCHEDULE

Airport of departure	Utility
St. Andrew	.66
Eastport	.34

Schedule	
Leave St. Andrew or Eastport: 8:00 A.M. and 5:00 P.M. Leave Bayville: 9:30 A.M. and 6:30 P.M.	.16
Leave St. Andrew or Eastport: 8:00 A.M., 1:00 P.M., 7:00 P.M. Leave Bayville: 9:30 A.M., 2:30 P.M., 8:30 P.M.	.40
Leave St. Andrew or Eastport: 8:00 A.M., 1:00 P.M., 5:00 P.M. Leave Bayville: 9:30 A.M., 2:30 P.M., 6:30 P.M.	.49
Leave St. Andrew of Eastside: hourly from 7:00 A.M. to 7:00 P.M. Leave Bayville: hourly from 8:30 A.M. to 8:30 P.M.	.95

Relative importance	
Airport	.29
Schedule	.71

CASE QUESTIONS

1 What do these findings mean? What characteristics do potential customers find important? Unimportant?
2 Should Clayton go ahead with the service?

APPENDIX A

Cost Data The price for Eastport-Bayville flights varies with the time of day, the flight date, and the date of reservation. Clayton plans to have a flat rate for the proposed St. Andrew–Bayville service. The fares used in the questionnaire represent the highest ($170) and lowest ($70) fare charged in the last year for the Eastport–Bayville flight, and the fare at the time the questionnaire was printed ($120). The typical fare (for weekday flights) ranges from $110 to $130.

Projected Quarterly Cash Flows for Express Air

Outflows:

Fixed costs	$ 85,000
Direct operating costs	275,000

Inflows:

Depends on fare charged and the number of passengers per flight.

Break-even:

Assume that each passenger buys one round-trip fare. At $240 round trip, break-even occurs at 1500 passengers per quarter (23 per day).

$$\frac{\$360{,}000 \text{ cash outflow per quarter}}{\$240 \text{ per flight}} = 1500 \text{ passengers per quarter}$$

CASE 7-5: Advertising Testing Services, Inc.

Advertising Testing Services, Inc. (ATSI) is a small marketing research supplier specializing in the copy testing of television commercials. ATSI is located in Princeton, New Jersey, and numbers among its clients some of the nation's largest advertisers. ATSI tests both animated and finished versions of commercials.

Procedure

ATSI's typical testing procedure is as follows:

1 Approximately 150 respondents in total are recruited from five to seven different shopping centers around the country. Typical locations would be St. Louis, Missouri; Hartford, Connecticut; Tampa, Florida; Denver, Colorado; and Charlotte, North Carolina. Potential respondents are screened to make sure they are in the target audience of the commercial being tested and are users of the product category being tested. This is done by asking potential respondents whether or not they have bought or used products in many product categories, including the one of interest.

2 Respondents are taken to a viewing area where they are shown the test commercial along with six other commercials for noncompetitive products.

3 After viewing all the commercials once, the respondent is given a personal interview.

Measures Taken

The response measures recorded in the post-exposure interview include the following:

1 The respondent is asked to name three brands from the advertising he or she has just seen. This serves as an unaided awareness measure. The order mentioned is also recorded.

2 If the test brand is not mentioned, the respondent is asked if he or she remembers the commercial for the test brand. This is a measure of aided awareness.

3 The main points from the test commercials are then asked for, to give a measure of unaided recall of the content of the ad.

4 The test commercial is then shown again to the respondent, and the main points are asked for to give a measure of aided recall. Additionally, the thoughts and feelings generated by the ad are probed, along with any confusion or lack of understanding that is generated and the believability, likes, and dislikes about the ad.

5 Finally, questions are asked about the brand itself, including an indication of liking for the brand compared to how it was viewed before seeing the test commercial and a series of rating scales on brand descriptions. Demographic data on respondents are also recorded.

Reported Results

Results are reported on all the measures taken and compared to norm scores. These norms may be for other similar product commercials that have been tested in the same way. If the user has employed the service enough, the norm may be the scores from a set of the user's own commercials. Both the norm and test scores are indexed for easier interpretation.

In comparing test results against the norm, the following guide is offered for noting significant differences at the 80 percent confidence level:

Proportion observed, percent	Differences in reported percentages necessary for significance
50	8
30–40 or 60–70	7
20 or 80	6
10 or 90	4

An example of part of a typical report of test results for a new car is presented in Exhibit 1.

EXHIBIT 1   RESULTS FOR CAR ADVERTISEMENT

	Norm*		Test advertisement	
	Percent	**Index**	**Percent**	**Index relative to norm**
Overall reaction				
Liked the commercial very much	39	100	55	141
Brand image				
Made me feel that this car is:				
of the highest quality	42	100	71	169
better driving than most other cars	52	100	59	113
for people who love to drive	60	100	81	135
my kind of car	26	100	34	130
Clarity and drawing power				
Not confusing	79	100	68	86
Convincing	26	100	28	108
Unaided awareness (% of time test ad is named in first three)	64	100	59	92

*Based upon six commercials for same car brand.

CASE QUESTIONS

1 Evaluate the procedure used by ATSI.

2 Evaluate the measures taken by ATSI.

3 In comparing test results against the norm, is the stated significant difference level in scores appropriate? From a statistical testing point of view, is type I or type II error more important here?

4 How should the reliability and validity of ATSI's results be determined?

5 What conclusions for the advertiser would you draw from the results reported in Exhibit 1?

GLOSSARY

absolute frequency   A measure of dispersion for nominal data, defined as the number of total elements appearing in a given category.

absolute precision   Precision expressed in units.

acquired source   A source which has procured data from an original or primary source.

affective component   One of three main components of attitudes, concerned with a person's feelings regarding an object or phenomenon (in a marketing model, includes liking and preference stages).

aided recall   An approach to questioning which provides the respondent with cues regarding the event of interest.

alternative forms reliability   Estimating reliability by giving the respondent two forms which are judged equivalent but not identical and comparing the two measurements for degree of discrepancy in scores, as in the test-retest approach.

alternative hypothesis   A hypothesis that states a population parameter, taking on a different value from that stated in the null hypothesis.

analysis of covariance (ANCOVA)   A dependence method of multivariate data analysis appropriate for use with an intervally scaled dependent variable, nominally scaled independent variables, and one or more intervally scaled covariates; useful in assessing the effects of extraneous sources of variation in an experiment ex post facto.

analysis of variance (ANOVA)   A method of analysis used when dealing with one intervally scaled dependent variable and one or more nominally scaled independent variables; used primarily in the analysis of experiments to determine whether treatment population means are equal.

applied research   Investigation whose aim is to assist managers in decision making.

area sampling   A form of sequential cluster sampling which samples areas in the first $n - 1$ stages and elements in the nth stage.

attitude   An individual's enduring perceptual, knowledge-based, evaluative, and action-oriented processes with respect to an object or phenomenon.

attitude scaling The various operational definitions developed for the measurement of the construct "attitude."

audimeter A mechanical device used to record the channel that a television is tuned to, if any.

automatic interaction detector (AID) A dependence method of multivariate data analysis appropriate for use with an intervally scaled dependent variable and nominally scaled independent variables; a technique which involves the repeated application of one-way ANOVA to reduce the total sample to a number of subgroups which are more homogeneous on the dependent variable than the sample as a whole.

balanced scale A rating scale providing the same number of favorable and unfavorable categories.

bar chart A graphic presentation of magnitude in the dataset depicted by the length of various bars which have been laid out with reference to a horizontal or vertical scale.

basic research Investigation whose aim is to extend the boundaries of knowledge regarding some aspect of the marketing system.

Bayes' rule

$$P(A|B) = \frac{P(A \cap B)}{P(B)} = \frac{P(A) \cdot P(B|A)}{[P(A) \cdot P(B|A)] + [P(A') \cdot P(B|A')]}$$

The conditional probability of A given B equals the joint probability of A and B divided by the unconditional probability of B.

behavioral component One of three main components of attitudes, concerned with a person's readiness to respond behaviorally to an object or phenomenon (in a marketing model, includes intention-to-buy and purchase stages).

biploar adjectives A pair of adjectives defining opposite ends of a continuum regarding some attitude or belief; used in the semantic differential scale.

bivariate analysis The analysis of two variables at a time.

blocking A method for attempting to control external effects from experiments.

breakdown method An approach to estimating current demand which begins with aggregate industry or market data and breaks down the data into units of interest to the firm.

buildup method An approach to estimating current demand that involves the aggregation of data from the customer or account level to the industry or market level.

buying income method One method of projecting the results of a test marketing program to national performance, based on income and estimated as:

$$\text{National sales estimate} = \frac{\text{total U.S. income}}{\text{test area income}} \times \text{test area sales}$$

canonical correlation A dependence method of multivariate data analysis appropriate for use with a set of intervally scaled dependent variables and a set of intervally scaled independent variables.

cartoon completion A technique in which the respondent is presented with a cartoon drawing depicting people in a situation and is asked to complete a cartoon in response to the comment of another cartoon character.

case A specific unit of analysis for a study, typically the respondent.

case history The intensive study of situations which are relevant to a particular decision problem in order to gain insight into the variables operating in the situation.

causal model forecasting methods Methods that apply statistical models to historical sales data and measure the underlying causes of sales dynamics.

causal research   A mode of conclusive research designed to gather evidence on cause-and-effect relationships.

census   A study using all available elements of a defined population.

central-limit theorem   The fundamental theorem of probability sampling. It allows us to measure sampling error, and it shows that the sampling distribution of the mean is normal when (1) the population distribution is normal for all sample sizes and (2) the sample size increases ($n \geq 30$) for nonnormal population distributions.

central tendency measures   One type of descriptive statistics, including such measures as the mean, median, and mode.

chi-square test   A test designed for comparing a hypothesized population distribution with a distribution obtained by sampling; with nominal variables in either univariate or bivariate analysis.

closed-ended question   A question on a data collection instrument with structured answers.

cluster analysis   An interdependence multivariate data analysis technique which uses as input a matrix of associations between variables or objects; the technique forms subgroupings and assigns variables or objects to these groups.

cluster sampling   Sampling in which clusters or groups of elements are randomly selected. It is composed of two steps: (1) the population is divided into mutually exclusive and collectively exhaustive groups, and (2) a probability sample of the groups is selected.

codebook   A listing of the documentation of the coding scheme and other information regarding the variables in a dataset.

coding   In the research process, establishing categories for responses or groups of responses such that numerals can be used to represent the categories.

coefficient of determination, r^2   The exact percentage of variation shared by two variables, obtained by squaring the correlation coefficient.

coefficient of multiple determination   In multiple regression, the proportion of the variation in Y explained by the regression, which can be calculated as $SS_{explained}/SS_{total}$.

coefficient of variation   An expression for the standard deviation as a percentage of the mean; formally defined as $CV = S/\bar{X}$.

cognitive component   One of three main components of attitudes, concerned with a person's beliefs about some object or phenomenon (in the marketing behavioral response model, includes the awareness and knowledge stages).

communality   In factor analysis, the proportion of a variable's total variation that is involved in the factors; defined mathematically as the sum of the squared loading of a variable on all factors (h^2).

communication method   A general method of collecting data involving the questioning of respondents, either verbally or by means of written questionnaires.

communication techniques   One type of attitude measurement procedure, including such techniques as self-reports, responses to unstructured or partially structured stimuli, and performance of objective tasks, in which the measurement process is based on some sort of communicated response by the subject.

company demand   The company's share of market demand.

company sales forecast   The expected level of company sales based on a chosen marketing plan and an assumed environment.

company sales potential   The limit approached by company demand as company marketing effort increases relative to competitors.

completely randomized design (CRD)   The simplest type of designed experiment; it involves only one independent variable, and the treatments are assigned to test units at random.

computer card   The basic device used for converting data to a computer-readable form; a heavy-stock paper card containing 80 columns for data input.

computer graphics   Computer software packages which display research data in the form of pie, bar, and line charts.

conclusive research   Research designed to help the decision maker evaluate courses of action and select the best one.

concomitant variation   The extent to which a cause, X, and an effect, Y, occur together or vary together as hypothesized.

concurrent validity   A method of assessing validity that involves correlating two different measurements of the same marketing phenomena which have been administered at the same point in time.

conditional association   The association between two variables conditional on one or more control variables.

conditional probability   The probability assigned to an event when another event has occurred or is assumed to have occurred; in symbols, $P(A|B)$, the probability of A given B.

confounding variable   An uncontrolled extraneous variable, the effect of which is to invalidate conclusions from an experiment.

conjoint measurement   A dependence method of multivariate data analysis appropriate for use with an ordinally scaled dependent variable and nominally scaled independent variables; essentially an analysis of variance of rank-order data which generates intervally scaled measures of the effects of the categories of the independent variables.

consistent estimator   A statistic that approaches the population parameter as sample size increases.

construct validity   A means of estimating validity which relies on an understanding of the theoretical rationale underlying the obtained measurements.

consumer jury   A pretesting method of copy testing using consumer ratings of ads in a forced exposure setting.

content validity   Assessing validity by the subjective judgment of an expert as to the appropriateness of the measurements.

contingency planning   Specification of alternative courses of action by an organization to meet invalid planning assumptions or unanticipated changes in the situational factors.

contrived observation   An observation technique in which an artificial environment is created and the behavior of persons put in the environment is observed.

control markets   Test market cities in which a research supply house has paid retailers for a guarantee that they will carry products designated by the supply house; also known as minimarkets.

convenience sample   A sample which is selected on the basis of the convenience of the researcher.

correlation coefficient, r   A bivariate descriptive statistic, appropriate when dealing with two intervally scaled variables, which provides a measure of the linear direction and strength of the relationship between these variables.

cross-sectional design   A research design (typically associated with descriptive research) which involves taking a sample of population elements at one point in time.

cross-tabulation table   A matrix display of the categories of two nominally scaled variables, containing frequency counts of the number of subjects in each bivariate category.

data   Observations and evidence regarding some aspect of the marketing system.

data deck   The complete set of computer cards containing all the data from a given study.

data matrix   A rectangular array of data storage with n rows and m columns, where the number of rows equals the number of cases and the number of columns equals the number of variables.

decision criteria   The rules for selecting among courses of action given various data outcomes.

decision problem A situation in which management has an objective to accomplish, two or more alternative courses of action exist which may reach the objective, and uncertainty is present regarding the best course of action.

degrees of freedom The number of independent observations on the variable of interest minus the number of statistics calculated.

dependence methods Multivariate data analysis procedures that specify a dependent variable.

dependent variable The presumed effect in a cause-and-effect relationship.

depth interview An unstructured personal interview using extensive probing in such a way that the respondent talks freely and expresses detailed beliefs and feelings on a topic.

descriptive research Marketing research aimed at characterizing marketing phenomena and identifying association among selected variables.

descriptive statistics The branch of statistics that provides researchers with summary measures for the data in samples.

deterministic causation The "common-sense" concept of causality, in which a single event (cause) always results in another even (effect).

diary method A procedure for collecting consumer purchase data or media habits that requires respondents to complete a written report of their behavior.

dichotomous question A form of multiple-choice question which provides only two response alternatives.

discriminant analysis A dependence method of multivariate data analysis appropriate for use with a nominally scaled dependent variable and intervally scaled independent variables; a technique which derives a linear combination of the independent variables such that the mean scores across categories of the dependent variable in this linear combination are maximally different.

disguised observation Observation techniques in which the respondents are not aware that they are being observed.

disproportionate stratified sampling Sampling in which the overall sample size is allocated to strata on a basis disproportionate with the population sizes of the strata.

division A geographic unit of the Census Bureau, third highest in level of aggregation; the regions are divided into nine divisions.

dummy-variable multiple regression A dependence method of multivariate data analysis appropriate for use with an intervally scaled dependent variable and nominally scaled independent variables; an extension of multiple regression to less than interval data through the creation of a series of binary variables coded as $0-1$.

dummy advertising vehicle Advertising pretesting procedure where test and control ads are inserted into a magazine format with editorial features of lasting interest; respondents are asked to read the magazine normally; response measures include awareness, recall, copy readership level, and product interest.

editing The process of reviewing the data collection instruments to ensure maximum accuracy and unambiguity; checks for legibility, consistency, and completeness.

effect In ANOVA, a difference in treatments means from the grand mean.

efficient estimator An estimator that has the minimum variance.

eigenvalue In factor analysis, the amount of variation in the data accounted for by a factor.

element The unit in a sample about which information is sought.

expected monetary gain of imperfect information (EMGII) The value of a research study net of its cost. Used in decision theory; calculated as EMGII = EMVII − cost of information.

expected monetary value criterion (EMV) Select the alternative with the highest expected monetary value.

expected monetary value of imperfect information (EMVII) In marketing research terms, the measure of the value of a study; calculated as EMVII = EMV (with study) — EMV (without study).

expected monetary value of perfect information (EMVPI) Equal to EMV(C) – EMV(UC); this represents the gain over expected outcomes under uncertainty and represents the absolute theoretical limit of the amount one would be willing to pay for perfect information. EMV(C) and EMV(UC) are EMVs under certainty and uncertainty, respectively.

expected utility value criterion (EUV) Select the alternative with the highest expected utility value; this takes into account the attitude toward risk as well as monetary payouts.

ex post facto Searching for a cause following the observation of the effect.

experiment A process in which a person consciously manipulates or controls one or more independent variables to measure their effect on the dependent variable(s).

experimental design The specification of treatments, test units, dependent variables, and extraneous variables to be considered in an experiment.

exploratory research Research designed to formulate hypotheses regarding potential problems and/or opportunities present in the decision situation.

external data Data obtained from a source other than the organization for which the research is being conducted.

external validity The generalizability of experimental results to test units other than those used.

extraneous variable Any variable other than the treatments that affects the response of the test unit to the treatments.

extreme case A response on a variable that is so far out of the ordinary that it might represent a coding or punching error.

factor analysis An interdependence multivariate analysis method that takes a large number of variables or objects and attempts to find a small number of factors in common which account for their intercorrelation.

factorial design An experimental design useful for measuring simultaneously the effects of two or more independent variables.

field operation That phase of the research project which makes contact with the respondent, administers the data collection instrument, records the data, and returns the data to a central location for processing.

fixed effects model An ANOVA procedure in which inferences about differences among treatment administered are made, but no interpolation between treatments is made.

focus group interview A loosely structured interview conducted by a trained moderator simultaneously among a small number of respondents; also known as a group depth interview.

forced scale A rating scale which does not include a "no opinion" or "no knowledge" category and thus requires respondents to indicate a position on the attitude scale.

grand mean In ANOVA, the mean of all observations across all treatment groups.

hierarchy-of-effects model A marketing behavioral response model consisting of stages which a buyer is hypothesized to pass through, including awareness, knowledge, liking, preference, intention to buy, and purchase.

history An extraneous variable referring to the occurrence of specific events that are external but concurrent to the experiment.

hypothesis A conjectural statement about the value of a variable or the relationship between two or more variables.

independent variable The presumed cause in a cause-and-effect relationship.

indirect observation Observation techniques in which some record of past behavior is used rather than observing behavior as it occurs.

indirect scale A self-reporting technique in which the respondent's judgments on several questions are combined in order to develop a measure of his or her position on the attitude in question.

inferential statistics   The branch of statistics that allows researchers to make judgments concerning the population based on the results generated by samples.

information   Data that reduce the uncertainty in a decision situation.

inquiry tests   Advertising pretesting procedure where the response measure is either measured sales or consumer inquiries that result directly from the ad.

instrumentation   An extraneous variable referring to changes in the calibration of the measuring instrument used or changes in the observers or scorers used.

interaction effect   The effect (that the total effect is greater than the sum of their main effects) which occurs when the relationship between an independent variable and the dependent variable is different for different categories of another independent variable.

interdependence methods   Multivariate data analysis methods in which no variable or variables are designated as dependent on others.

internal data   Data that originate within the organization for which research is being conducted.

internal validity   The extent to which experimental results are caused by the treatment variables as opposed to extraneous variables.

interval scale   A scale of measurement in which the distances among the numbers correspond to the distances among the objects or events on the characteristic being measured; intervals between numbers are assumed to be equal.

item nonresponse error   The refusal by the respondent to answer a question or series of questions.

joint probability   The probability that two or more events will occur; in symbols, $P(A \cap B)$, the probability of A and B.

judgment sample   A sample that is selected on the basis of what some expert thinks particular sampling units or elements will contribute to answering the research question at hand.

Laplace criterion   Select the alternative with the highest average value.

Latin square design   An experimental design useful for controlling and measuring the effects of two extraneous variables.

level of confidence   The probability of not rejecting the null hypothesis when it is true, equal to $1 - \alpha$.

levels   The categories of the independent variables in a factorial design experiment.

Likert scale   An indirect scale in which the respondent indicates the degree of agreement or disagreement with each of a series of statements; each response is subsequently numerically scored by the researcher, and a summary score for each respondent is obtained.

line chart   A graphic presentation of magnitude in the dataset depicted by the slope of a line (or lines) which has been laid out with reference to a horizontal or vertical scale.

longitudinal design   A research design in which a fixed sample of population elements is measured over time.

market demand   The total volume of a product that would be purchased by a defined customer group in a defined time period and geography given an environment and marketing program.

market forecast   The level of market demand given an expected level of industry marketing effort and an assumed environment.

market potential   The limit approached by market demand within an assumed environment, as industry marketing effort approaches infinity.

marketing information system (MIS)   The systematic and continuous gathering, analysis, and reporting of data for decision-making purposes.

marketing mix   Those independent variables over which the organization exerts some degree of control (product, price, place, and promotion).

marketing research   The systematic and objective approach to the development and provision of information for the marketing management decision-making process.

marketing research system   An information center for decision making.

maturation   An extraneous variable concerned with changes in the experimental units that occur over time.

maximax criterion   Select the alternative that maximizes the maximum payoff.

maximin criterion   Select the alternative that maximizes the minimum payoff.

mean   A measure of central tendency for interval data; the average value.

measurement   The assignment of numbers to characteristics of objects or events according to rules.

measures of dispersion   A type of descriptive statistic, including such measures as the standard deviation, coefficient of variation, interquartile range, and relative and absolute frequencies.

mechanical observation   Observation techniques involving mechanical observers in conjunction with or in place of human observers. Examples are the motion picture camera, the Audimeter, the psychogalvanometer, the eye-camera, and the pupilometer.

median   A measure of central tendency for ordinal data, defined for ungrouped data as the middle value when the data are arranged in order of magnitude.

metropolitan statistical area (MSA)   A geographic unit of the Census Bureau consisting of (a) one city with 50,000 or more inhabitants or (b) an urbanized area of at least 50,000 inhabitants and a total MSA population of at least 100,000 (75,000 in New England).

minimax regret criterion   The alternative selected with the minimum opportunity loss.

mixed effects model   An ANOVA procedure including independent variables of both the fixed and random types.

mode   A measure of central tendency for nominal data, defined as the category which occurs with the greatest frequency.

monadic rating   An evaluating procedure whereby respondents rate items on a rating scale without reference to other comparison items.

multidimensional scaling   An interdependence multivariate data analysis method which uses as input a matrix of relationships between objects with unknown underlying dimensionality, determines the minimum dimensionality of the relationships between the objects, and positions each object on each dimension.

multiple-choice question   A question which requires the respondent to select or answer from among a list provided in the question proper or following the question.

multiple correlation coefficient   In multiple regression, the correlation coefficient between the observed Y_i and the estimated $\hat{Y}_i$'s.

multiple regression   A dependence method of multivariate data analysis appropriate for use with an intervally scaled dependent variable and intervally scaled independent variables; an extension of the simple regression technique to more than one independent variable.

multivariate analysis   The analysis of more than two variables at a time.

multivariate analysis of variance   A dependence method of multivariate data analysis appropriate for use with two or more intervally scaled dependent variables and one or more intervally scaled independent variables; the multivariate extension of ANOVA to more than one dependent variable.

nominal scale   A measurement scale in which numbers serve only as labels to identify or categorize objects or events.

nonprobability sampling   A sampling procedure in which the selection of population elements is based in part on the judgment of the researcher or field interviewer.

nonresponse errors   The differences in measures between those who respond to a survey and those who do not respond.

nonsampling errors   All the errors that may occur in the marketing research process, except the sampling error.

null hypothesis   The hypothesis which states that a population parameter takes on a particular value or set of values.

O   An experimental design symbol, referring to processes of observation or measurement of the dependent variable on the test units.

observation method   A general method of collecting data from respondents in which the respondent's behavior is recorded.

observation techniques   A type of attitude measurement procedure, which includes such techniques as overt behavior and physiological reaction measurement, in which the procedure is based on observing the behavior of the subject.

omnibus panel   A fixed sample of respondents measured on different variables over a period of time.

on-the-air tests   Advertising pretesting procedures that measure responses to ads that are placed on actual television or radio programs in test areas.

one-tailed test   The situation in which the alternative hypothesis is stated such that one specific direction (one tail of the possible distribution of values) is considered.

one-way ANOVA   ANOVA applied to a CRD, in which it is applied to categories of one independent variable.

open-ended question   A question which requires respondents to provide their own answers.

opportunity   The presence of a situation where performance can be improved by undertaking new activities.

ordinal scale   A scale of measurement which defines the ordered relationships among objects or events.

original source   The source which generated the data.

overall efficiency   A relative assessment of a sampling procedure based on its statistical efficiency and cost; defined as the cost per standard error.

paired comparison scale   A self-reporting technique presenting the respondent with two objects from a set and requiring the respondent to pick one with regard to the attitude in question.

parameter   A summary description of a measure in the defined population.

performance-monitoring research   Research designed to provide information about the outcomes of marketing activities.

periodicity   In systematic sampling, a cyclical pattern within a list of elements forming the sampling frame that coincides with a multiple of the size of the sampling interval.

pie chart   A circle divided into sections such that the size of each section corresponds to a portion of the total.

population   The aggregate of the elements defined prior to the selection of the sample.

portfolio tests   A pretesting procedure using a package of control and test ads: consumers are asked to read whatever interests them; recall measures are then taken.

posterior analysis   The combination of prior information with additional information to provide revised (posterior) probability estimates, which are then used to calculate a posterior EMV.

posttesting   The evaluation of advertising after it has run in the media.

power of test   The probability of rejecting a false null hypothesis, equal to $1 - \beta$.

precision   The width of a confidence interval expressed either absolutely in units or relative to the size of the mean.

predictive validity   A means of assessing validity which involves the ability of a measure of marketing phenomena to predict other marketing phenomena.

preexperimental design   Experimental designs with inherent weaknesses such that questionable internal validity results.

preposterior analysis   A method of analysis allowing the researcher to measure the value of alternative research studies prior to undertaking the research.

pretesting   The initial testing of one or more aspects of the research design, or the evaluation of advertising prior to a fully funded run in the media.

prior analysis   The application of the decision theory approach when the probabilities of outcomes are assessed on the basis of present judgment, without benefit of additional information.

probabilistic causation   The scientific concept of causality, in which one event or a series of events results in the probable occurrence of another.

probability sampling   A sampling procedure in which each element of the population has a known chance of being selected for the sample.

problem   Those independent variables that cause the organization's performance measures to be below objectives.

profile analysis   A method of analyzing semantic differential data, in which an arithmetic mean or median is calculated for each set of polar opposites for each object evaluated.

programmed decisions   Decisions of a repetitive nature for which the manager's experience and judgment provide the key input.

proportionate stratified sampling   Stratified sampling in which the number of elements drawn from each stratum is proportionate to the relative number of elements in each stratum of the population.

q-type analysis   A case wise factor analysis.

qualitative forecasting methods   Methods that involve collecting judgments or opinions from knowledgeable individuals.

qualitative research   Questioning knowledgeable respondents individually or in small groups regarding the "why" of behavior.

quantitative research   Questioning large groups of respondents regarding the "what, when, where, and how" of behavior.

quasi experimentation   An experimental design in which the researcher has control over data collection procedures but lacks complete control over the scheduling or randomization of the treatments.

questionnaire   A formalized schedule for collecting data from respondents.

quota sample   A sample selected so as to match the population on some prespecified "control" characteristics.

r   An experimental design symbol, indicating that a randomizing process has been used in assigning test units and treatments.

r-type analysis   A factor analysis calculated by variables.

random-digit dialing   A method of identifying households in a telephone interview whereby either all seven digits are randomly generated, or numbers are randomly selected from a directory and the last one or two digits are replaced with random numbers.

random effects model   An ANOVA procedure in which interpolation of results between treatments is allowed.

random error   Bias in the measurements caused by the transient aspects of the respondent or measurement setting.

random number list   A list of numbers that have no pattern of occurrence.

randomized block design (RBD)   An experimental design in which test units are blocked on the basis of some external criterion variable, in such a way that scores within the blocks on the dependent variable are likely to be more homogeneous than in the absence of blocking.

rank-order scale   A self-reporting technique in which the respondent ranks various objects with regard to the attitude in question.

rating scale A self-reporting scale involving ordinal, interval, or ratio scales in which the respondent indicates the position on a continuum or among ordered categories corresponding to his or her attitude; includes both graphic rating scales and verbal rating scales.

ratio scale A scale of measurement which has all the properties of an interval scale plus an absolute zero point.

recall tests Advertising posttesting procedures that emphasize respondents' ability to recall, unaided and aided, ads they have previously been exposed to.

recognition method Aided recall in which the actual event is presented to the respondent.

recognition tests Advertising posttesting procedures that emphasize respondents' ability to recognize ads they were previously exposed to in an interview.

region A geographic unit of the Census Bureau, second highest in level of aggregation; the United States is divided into four regions.

relative frequency A measure of dispersion for nominal data, defined as the percentage of the total elements appearing in a given category.

relative precision Precision expressed as a percentage of the mean.

reliability The extent to which the measurement process is free from random errors.

repertory grid A method of identifying attributes which consumers can use to describe their perception of products; respondents repeatedly think of ways in which any two of three items are similar to each other and different from a third.

respondent characteristics One of three types of data which can be obtained from respondents to forecast market behavior; this type describes respondents in terms of demographic, socio-economic, and psychological characteristics.

research design The basic plan which guides the data collection and analysis phases of the research project.

research report The presentation of the research findings directed to a specific audience to accomplish a specific purpose.

response bias An inaccurate response, resulting from such factors as respondent fatigue, boredom, desire to please, etc.

role playing A technique in which the respondent is presented with a verbal or visual situation and asked how the beliefs and feelings of another person relate to the situation; also known as the third-person technique.

sales budget A conservative estimate of the expected volume of sales.

sales ratio method A method of projecting the results of a test marketing program to national performance, based on sales of another brand and estimated as:

$$\frac{\text{National sales}}{\text{estimate}} = \frac{\text{national sales of other product}}{\text{test area sales of this other product}} \times \text{test area sales of test product}$$

sampling distribution The distribution formed by a statistic that is calculated for each of all possible samples of a certain size from a given population.

sampling error The difference between the observed probability sample statistic and the population parameter.

sampling fraction The proportion of the number of sample elements to the number of population elements.

sampling frame A list of all the sampling units in the population.

sampling interval The size of the step between selected elements in systematic sampling; the reciprocal of the sampling fraction, i.e., N/n.

sampling unit The element or elements available for selection at some stage of the sampling process.

scanner data The recording of data by passing merchandise over a laser scanner which optically reads the bar-coded description printed on the merchandise.

secondary data Published data which have been compiled for a purpose other than the present study.

selection bias The assignment of test units of treatment groups such that the groups differ on the dependent variable prior to the presentation of the treatments.

semantic differential scale A self-reporting scale requiring the respondent to evaluate an object on a seven-point rating scale bounded on each end by bipolar adjectives.

sentence completion A technique in which an incomplete sentence is presented to the respondent, who is asked to complete the sentence.

share-of-market method A method of projecting the results of a test marketing program to national performance, based on sales in the test area of the product category as a whole, and estimated as:

$$\frac{\text{National sales}}{\text{estimate}} = \frac{\text{test area sales of new brand}}{\text{test area sales of this whole product category}} \times \frac{\text{national sales of this}}{\text{whole product category}}$$

significance level The specified level of α indicating the probability of making a type I error.

simple random sampling A probability sampling procedure where each element has an equal chance of being selected and each combination of elements is equally likely.

simple regression A bivariate statistical procedure, applicable to intervally scaled variables, used to demonstrate how an independent variable is related to a dependent variable and to make predictions about scores on the dependent variable, given knowledge of the scores on the independent variable.

simulated test market A laboratory-based method of forecasting product sales based upon pretest interviews, forced advertising exposure, simulated store shopping, product trial, and follow-up interviews to measure repurchase rate.

simulation An incomplete representation of the marketing system designed to explicate the dynamics of the variables operating within that system.

situational analysis The process of analyzing the past and future situation facing an organization in order to identify problems and opportunities.

situational factors Independent variables that are not under the control of the organization.

Solomon four-group design A true experimental design which controls for both extraneous variable effects and interactive testing effects.

split-half reliability Estimating reliability by dividing a multi-item measurement device into equivalent groups and correlating the item responses to estimate reliability.

spurious relationship The observed relationship between variables when one does not really exist; the relationship disappears with elaboration.

SS_B In a randomized-block-design ANOVA, the blocking effect sum of squared deviations.

SS_C In a Latin-square-design ANOVA, the column effect sum of squared deviations.

SS_E In ANOVA, the sum of squared deviations related to error.

$SS_{INT(AB)}$ In a factorial-design ANOVA, the interaction effect sum of squared deviations.

SS_R In a Latin-square-design ANOVA, the row effect sum of squared deviations.

SS_T In ANOVA, the total sum of squared deviations from the grand mean.

SS_{TR} In ANOVA, the sum of squared deviations resulting from the treatments.

SS_{TRA} In a factorial-design ANOVA, the treatment A effect sum of squared deviations.

standard deviation, s A measure of dispersion for interval data.

standard error of the coefficient, s_b A measure of the amount of sampling error present in the determination of b in a regression equation; more precisely, the standard deviation of the sampling distribution of the regression coefficient.

standard error of the estimate, s_{YX} The measure of the scatter of the actual Y_i values about a regression line $\hat{Y}_i$, more precisely, the standard deviation of Y_i about $\hat{Y}_i$.

standard error of the mean The standard deviation of the sampling distribution of the mean.

Standard Industrial Classification (SIC code) A system of classification based on the products produced or operations performed which the federal government uses in its Census of Manufacturers.

standard markets Test market cities in which no guarantees of retail distribution support are made: the traditional alternative to control markets.

Stapel scale A modification of the semantic differential scale, using a unipolar 10-point $(+5$ to $-5)$ nonverbal rating scale, designed to measure the direction and intensity of attitudes simultaneously.

statistic A summary description of a measure in the selected sample.

statistical efficiency Comparison of the standard errors generated by various sampling procedures.

statistical regression The phenomenon that outliers tend to move toward a more average position over time.

strategy Broad principles as to how the marketing program is to operate in achieving objectives.

stratified sampling A two-stage probability sampling procedure in which the population is divided into mutually exclusive and collectively exhaustive strata, and a random sample is drawn from each stratum.

study population The aggregate of elements from which the sample is drawn.

symptom A condition that signals the presence of a problem or opportunity.

syndicated source A profit-making organization which provides standardized data to an array of clients.

systematic error Error that causes a constant bias in the measurements.

systematic sampling A type of cluster sampling in which every kth element is selected from the frame, after a random start somewhere within the first k elements, where $k =$ sampling interval.

t test A test designed for comparing the sample mean with a hypothesized mean of a population, appropriate for all sample sizes when σ is unknown; also designed for comparing the difference between two means.

test marketing The implementation and monitoring of a marketing program in a small subset of the target market areas for the product in question.

test-retest reliability Estimating reliability by repeating the measurement using the same scaling device under conditions which are judged to be very similar.

test units The entities in an experiment to whom the treatments are presented and whose response to the treatments is measured.

test unit mortality Test units' withdrawal from the experiment before completion.

testing effect An extraneous variable consisting of the effect on the experiment of taking a measure on the dependent variable before presenting the treatment. The *main testing effect* refers to the effect of the first measurement on the second measurement, while the interactive *testing effect* refers to the effect of the first measurement on the test unit's response to the treatment.

theater tests Advertising pretesting procedure that exposes respondents to control and test ads in the context of a theater-shown television program.

Thematic Apperception Test (TAT) A projective technique using one or more pictures or cartoons depicting a situation and asking the respondent to describe what has happened or will happen as a result of the situation.

time-series experiment A quasi-experimental design involving a periodic measurement on the dependent variables for some test units.

time-series forecasting methods Methods which apply statistical techniques to historical sales data over time to make numerical sales forecasts.

tracks Alternative ways of processing the data from collection instruments to the computer.

tracts Small areas into which large cities and their adjacent areas have been divided for statistical purposes by the Census Bureau.

traditional panel A fixed sample measured over a period on the same variables.

trailer tests Advertising pretesting procedure that recruits respondents from shopping malls for forced exposure to ads in a trailer near the mall or in a room in the mall itself.

treatment The alternatives which are manipulated and whose effects are measured in an experiment.

true experimental design An experimental design in which all extraneous variables are eliminated or controlled.

two-tailed test The situation in which the alternative hypothesis is stated in such a way that both ends of the sampling distribution are considered (no specified directionality).

type I error (α error) The rejection of a true null hypothesis.

type II error (β error) The nonrejection of a false null hypothesis.

unaided recall A questioning approach which does not provide the respondent with cues as to the event.

unbiased estimator An estimator whose expected value is the parameter or population value.

uncertainty A lack of complete knowledge about the possible outcomes of actions, with the probabilities of the possible outcomes not known.

unconditional probability The probability assigned to an event that is independent of other events, also known as marginal probability.

univariate analysis The analysis of one variable at a time.

unprogrammed decision A decision involving a somewhat new, atypical situation in which a manager's experience and judgment are of limited usefulness.

validity The extent to which the measurement process is free from both systematic and random error.

variable A property that takes on different values at different times.

variance A measure of the dispersion of the distribution of an interval variable.

wild codes Codes that are not defined in the codebook for a particular variable.

word association A technique in which a series of words is presented to the respondent, who is to respond to each one with the first word which comes to mind.

X An experimental design symbol, representing the exposure of a test group to an experimental treatment.

z test A test designed for comparing the sample mean with a hypothesized mean of a population; it is appropriate for interval data when σ is known for any sample size, or for situations of sufficiently large sample size ($n > 30$) and σ unknown.

zero-order association Also known as total association, this is the original association between two variables, without controlling for any other variables (as contrasted with conditional association).

APPENDIX A

TABLE A-1   ABRIDGED LIST OF RANDOM NUMBERS

10 09 73 25 33	76 52 01 35 35	34 67 35 48 76	80 95 90 91 17	39 29 27 49 45
37 54 20 48 05	64 89 47 42 96	24 80 52 40 37	20 63 61 04 02	00 82 29 16 65
08 42 26 89 53	19 64 50 93 03	23 20 90 25 60	15 95 33 47 64	35 08 03 36 06
90 01 90 25 29	09 37 67 07 15	38 31 13 11 65	88 67 67 43 97	04 43 62 76 59
12 80 79 99 70	80 15 73 61 47	64 03 23 66 53	98 95 11 68 77	12 17 17 68 33
66 06 57 47 17	34 07 27 08 50	36 69 73 61 70	65 81 33 98 85	11 19 92 91 70
31 06 01 08 05	45 57 18 24 06	35 30 34 26 14	86 79 90 74 39	23 40 30 97 32
85 26 97 76 02	02 05 16 56 92	68 66 57 48 18	73 05 38 52 47	18 62 38 85 79
63 57 33 21 35	05 32 54 70 48	90 55 35 75 48	28 46 82 87 09	83 49 12 55 24
73 79 64 57 53	03 52 96 47 78	35 80 83 42 82	60 93 52 03 44	35 27 38 84 35
98 52 01 77 67	14 90 56 86 07	22 10 94 05 58	60 97 09 34 33	50 50 07 39 98
11 80 50 54 31	39 80 82 77 32	50 72 56 82 48	29 40 52 42 01	52 77 56 78 51
83 45 29 96 34	06 28 89 80 83	13 74 67 00 78	18 47 54 06 10	68 71 17 78 17
88 68 54 02 00	86 50 75 84 01	36 76 66 79 51	90 36 47 64 93	29 60 91 10 62
99 59 46 73 48	87 51 76 49 69	91 82 60 89 28	93 78 56 13 68	23 47 83 41 13
65 48 11 76 74	17 46 85 09 50	58 04 77 69 74	73 03 95 71 86	40 21 81 65 44
80 12 43 56 35	17 72 70 80 15	45 31 82 23 74	21 11 57 82 53	14 38 55 37 63
74 35 09 98 17	77 40 27 72 14	43 23 60 02 10	45 52 16 42 37	96 28 60 26 55
69 91 62 68 03	66 25 22 91 48	36 93 68 72 03	76 62 11 39 90	94 40 05 64 18
09 90 32 05 05	14 22 56 85 14	46 42 75 67 88	96 29 77 88 22	54 38 21 45 98
91 49 91 45 23	68 47 92 76 86	46 16 28 35 54	94 75 08 99 23	37 08 92 00 48
80 33 69 45 98	26 94 03 08 58	70 29 73 41 35	53 14 03 33 40	42 05 08 23 41
44 10 48 19 49	85 15 74 79 54	32 97 92 65 75	57 60 04 08 81	22 22 20 64 13
12 55 07 37 42	11 10 00 20 40	12 86 07 46 97	96 64 48 94 39	28 70 72 58 15
63 60 64 93 29	16 50 53 44 84	40 21 95 25 63	43 65 17 70 82	07 20 73 17 90
61 19 69 04 46	26 45 74 77 74	51 92 43 37 29	65 39 45 95 93	42 58 26 05 27
15 47 44 52 66	95 27 07 99 53	59 36 78 38 48	82 39 61 01 18	33 21 15 94 66
94 55 72 85 73	67 89 75 43 87	54 62 24 44 31	91 19 04 25 92	92 92 74 59 73
42 48 11 62 13	97 34 40 87 21	16 86 84 87 67	03 07 11 20 59	25 70 14 66 70
23 52 37 83 17	73 20 88 98 37	68 93 59 14 16	26 25 22 96 63	05 52 28 25 62
04 49 35 24 94	75 24 63 38 24	45 86 25 10 25	61 96 27 93 35	65 33 71 24 72
00 54 99 76 54	84 05 18 81 59	96 11 96 38 96	54 69 28 23 91	23 28 72 95 29
35 96 31 53 07	26 89 80 93 54	33 35 13 54 62	77 97 45 00 24	90 10 33 93 33
59 80 80 83 91	45 42 72 68 42	83 60 94 97 00	13 02 12 48 92	78 56 52 01 06
46 05 88 52 36	01 39 09 22 86	77 28 14 40 77	93 91 08 36 47	70 61 74 29 41
32 17 90 05 97	87 37 92 52 41	05 56 70 70 07	86 74 31 71 57	85 39 41 18 38
69 23 48 14 06	20 11 74 52 04	15 95 66 00 00	18 74 39 24 23	97 11 89 63 38
19 56 54 14 30	01 75 87 53 79	40 41 92 15 85	66 67 43 68 06	84 96 28 52 07
45 15 51 49 38	19 47 60 72 46	43 66 79 45 43	59 04 79 00 33	20 82 66 95 41
94 86 43 19 94	36 16 81 08 51	34 88 88 15 53	01 54 03 54 56	05 01 45 11 76
93 08 62 48 26	45 24 02 84 04	44 99 90 88 96	39 09 47 34 07	35 44 13 18 80
33 18 51 62 32	41 94 15 09 49	89 43 54 85 81	88 69 54 19 94	37 54 87 30 43
80 95 10 04 06	96 38 27 07 74	20 15 12 33 87	25 01 62 52 98	94 62 46 11 71
79 75 24 91 40	71 96 12 82 96	69 86 10 25 91	74 85 22 05 39	00 38 75 95 79
18 63 33 25 37	98 14 50 65 71	31 01 02 46 74	05 45 56 14 27	77 93 89 19 36
74 02 94 39 02	77 55 73 22 70	97 79 01 71 19	52 52 75 80 21	80 81 45 17 48
54 17 84 56 11	80 99 33 71 43	05 33 51 29 69	56 12 71 92 55	36 04 09 03 24
11 66 44 98 83	52 07 98 48 27	59 38 17 15 39	09 97 33 34 40	88 46 12 33 56
48 32 47 79 28	81 24 96 47 10	02 29 53 68 70	32 30 75 75 46	15 02 00 99 94
69 07 49 41 38	87 63 79 19 76	35 58 40 44 01	10 51 82 16 15	01 84 87 69 38

Source: This table is reproduced with permission from tables of the RAND Corporation from *A Million Random Digits with 100,000 Normal Deviates*, New York, The Free Press, 1955.

TABLE A-2   AREAS IN TWO TAILS OF THE NORMAL CURVE AT SELECTED VALUES
OF x/σ FROM THE ARITHMETIC MEAN

This table shows:

x/σ	.00	.01	.02	.03	.04	.05	.06	.07	.08	.09
0.0	1.0000	.9920	.9840	.9761	.9681	.9601	.9522	.9442	.9362	.9283
0.1	.9203	.9124	.9045	.8966	.8887	.8808	.8729	.8650	.8572	.8493
0.2	.8415	.8337	.8259	.8181	.8103	.8026	.7949	.7872	.7795	.7718
0.3	.7642	.7566	.7490	.7414	.7339	.7263	.7188	.7114	.7039	.6965
0.4	.6892	.6818	.6745	.6672	.6599	.6527	.6455	.6384	.6312	.6241
0.5	.6171	.6101	.6031	.5961	.5892	.5823	.5755	.5687	.5619	.5552
0.6	.5485	.5419	.5353	.5287	.5222	.5157	.5093	.5029	.4965	.4902
0.7	.4839	.4777	.4715	.4654	.4593	.4533	.4473	.4413	.4354	.4295
0.8	.4237	.4179	.4122	.4065	.4009	.3953	.3898	.3843	.3789	.3735
0.9	.3681	.3628	.3576	.3524	.3472	.3421	.3371	.3320	.3271	.3222
1.0	.3173	.3125	.3077	.3030	.2983	.2937	.2891	.2846	.2801	.2757
1.1	.2713	.2670	.2627	.2585	.2543	.2501	.2460	.2420	.2380	.2340
1.2	.2301	.2263	.2225	.2187	.2150	.2113	.2077	.2041	.2005	.1971
1.3	.1936	.1902	.1868	.1835	.1802	.1770	.1738	.1707	.1676	.1645
1.4	.1615	.1585	.1556	.1527	.1499	.1471	.1443	.1416	.1389	.1362
1.5	.1336	.1310	.1285	.1260	.1236	.1211	.1188	.1164	.1141	.1118
1.6	.1096	.1074	.1052	.1031	.1010	.0989	.0969	.0949	.0930	.0910
1.7	.0891	.0873	.0854	.0836	.0819	.0801	.0784	.0767	.0751	.0735
1.8	.0719	.0703	.0688	.0672	.0658	.0643	.0629	.0615	.0601	.0588
1.9	.0574	.0561	.0549	.0536	.0524	.0512	.0500	.0488	.0477	.0466
2.0	.0455	.0444	.0434	.0424	.0414	.0404	.0394	.0385	.0375	.0366
2.1	.0357	.0349	.0340	.0332	.0324	.0316	.0308	.0300	.0293	.0285
2.2	.0278	.0271	.0264	.0257	.0251	.0244	.0238	.0232	.0226	.0220
2.3	.0214	.0209	.0203	.0198	.0193	.0188	.0183	.0178	.0173	.0168
2.4	.0164	.0160	.0155	.0151	.0147	.0143	.0139	.0135	.0131	.0128
2.4	.0124	.0121	.0117	.0114	.0111	.0108	.0105	.0102	.00988	.00960
2.6	.00932	.00905	.00879	.00854	.00829	.00805	.00781	.00759	.00736	.00715
2.7	.00693	.00673	.00653	.00633	.00614	.00596	.00578	.00561	.00544	.00527
2.8	.00511	.00495	.00480	.00465	.00451	.00437	.00424	.00410	.00398	.00385
2.9	.00373	.00361	.00350	.00339	.00328	.00318	.00308	.00298	.00288	.00279

x/σ	.0	.1	.2	.3	.4	.5	.6	.7	.8	.9
3	.00270	.00194	.00137	$.0^3967$	$.0^3674$	$.0^3465$	$.0^3318$	$.0^3216$	$.0^3145$	$.0^4962$
4	$.0^4633$	$.0^4413$	$.0^4267$	$.0^4171$	$.0^4108$	$.0^5680$	$.0^5422$	$.0^5260$	$.0^5159$	$.0^6958$
5	$.0^6573$	$.0^6340$	$.0^6199$	$.0^6116$	$.0^7666$	$.0^7380$	$.0^7214$	$.0^7120$	$.0^8663$	$.0^8364$
6	$.0^8197$	$.0^8106$	$.0^9565$	$.0^9298$	$.0^9155$	$.0^{10}803$	$.0^{10}411$	$.0^{10}208$	$.0^{10}105$	$.0^{11}520$

SOURCE: This table is copyrighted by Prentice-Hall, Inc.   It is reproduced by permission of Frederick E. Croxton.

TABLE A-3 AREAS IN ONE TAIL OF THE NORMAL CURVE AT SELECTED VALUES
OF x/σ FROM THE ARITHMETIC MEAN

This table shows: or

x/σ	.00	.01	.02	.03	.04	.05	.06	.07	.08	.09
0.0	.5000	.4960	.4920	.4880	.4840	.4801	.4761	.4721	.4681	.4641
0.1	.4602	.4562	.4522	.4483	.4443	.4404	.4364	.4325	.4286	.4247
0.2	.4207	.4168	.4129	.4090	.4052	.4013	.3974	.3936	.3897	.3859
0.3	.3821	.3783	.3745	.3707	.3669	.3632	.3594	.3557	.3520	.3483
0.4	.3446	.3409	.3372	.3336	.3300	.3264	.3228	.3192	.3156	.3121
0.5	.3085	.3050	.3015	.2981	.2946	.2912	.2877	.2843	.2810	.2776
0.6	.2743	.2709	.2676	.2643	.2611	.2578	.2546	.2514	.2483	.2451
0.7	.2420	.2389	.2358	.2327	.2296	.2266	.2236	.2206	.2177	.2148
0.8	.2119	.2090	.2061	.2033	.2005	.1977	.1949	.1922	.1894	.1867
0.9	.1841	.1814	.1788	.1762	.1736	.1711	.1685	.1660	.1635	.1611
1.0	.1587	.1562	.1539	.1515	.1492	.1469	.1446	.1423	.1401	.1379
1.1	.1357	.1335	.1314	.1292	.1271	.1251	.1230	.1210	.1190	.1170
1.2	.1151	.1131	.1112	.1093	.1075	.1056	.1038	.1020	.1003	.0985
1.3	.0968	.0951	.0934	.0918	.0901	.0885	.0869	.0853	.0838	.0823
1.4	.0808	.0793	.0778	.0764	.0749	.0735	.0721	.0708	.0694	.0681
1.5	.0668	.0655	.0643	.0630	.0618	.0606	.0594	.0582	.0571	.0559
1.6	.0548	.0537	.0526	.0516	.0505	.0495	.0485	.0475	.0465	.0455
1.7	.0446	.0436	.0427	.0418	.0409	.0401	.0392	.0384	.0375	.0367
1.8	.0359	.0351	.0344	.0336	.0329	.0322	.0314	.0307	.0301	.0294
1.9	.0287	.0281	.0274	.0268	.0262	.0256	.0250	.0244	.0239	.0233
2.0	.0228	.0222	.0217	.0212	.0207	.0202	.0197	.0192	.0188	.0183
2.1	.0179	.0174	.0170	.0166	.0162	.0158	.0154	.0150	.0146	.0143
2.2	.0139	.0136	.0132	.0129	.0125	.0122	.0119	.0116	.0113	.0110
2.3	.0107	.0104	.0102	.00990	.00964	.00939	.00914	.00889	.00866	.00842
2.4	.00820	.00798	.00776	.00755	.00734	.00714	.00695	.00676	.00657	.00639
2.5	.00621	.00604	.00587	.00570	.00554	.00539	.00523	.00508	.00494	.00480
2.6	.00466	.00453	.00440	.00427	.00415	.00402	.00391	.00379	.00368	.00357
2.7	.00347	.00336	.00326	.00317	.00307	.00298	.00289	.00280	.00272	.00264
2.8	.00256	.00248	.00240	.00233	.00226	.00219	.00212	.00205	.00199	.00193
2.9	.00187	.00181	.00175	.00169	.00164	.00159	.00154	.00149	.00144	.00139

x/σ	.0	.1	.2	.3	.4	.5	.6	.7	.8	.9
3	.00135	$.0^3968$	$.0^3687$	$.0^3483$	$.0^3337$	$.0^3233$	$.0^3159$	$.0^3108$	$.0^4723$	$.0^4481$
4	$.0^4317$	$.0^4207$	$.0^4133$	$.0^5854$	$.0^5541$	$.0^5340$	$.0^5211$	$.0^5130$	$.0^6793$	$.0^6479$
5	$.0^6287$	$.0^6170$	$.0^7996$	$.0^7579$	$.0^7333$	$.0^7190$	$.0^7107$	$.0^8599$	$.0^8332$	$.0^8182$
6	$.0^9987$	$.0^9430$	$.0^9282$	$.0^9149$	$.0^{10}777$	$.0^{10}402$	$.0^{10}206$	$.0^{10}104$	$.0^{11}523$	$.0^{11}260$

SOURCE: This table is copyrighted by Prentice-Hall, Inc. It is reproduced by permission of Frederick E. Croxton.

TABLE A-4 TABLE OF CRITICAL VALUES OF *t*

Df	Level of significance for two-tailed test								Df
	0.5	0.4	0.3	0.2	0.1	0.05	0.02	0.01	
	Level of significance for one-tailed test								
	0.25	0.20	0.15	0.10	0.05	0.025	0.01	0.005	
1	1.000	1.376	1.963	3.078	6.314	12.706	31.821	63.657	1
2	.816	1.061	1.386	1.886	2.920	4.303	6.965	9.925	2
3	.765	.978	1.250	1.638	2.353	3.182	4.541	5.841	3
4	.741	.941	1.190	1.533	2.132	2.776	3.747	4.604	4
5	.727	.920	1.156	1.476	2.105	2.571	3.365	4.032	5
6	.718	.906	1.134	1.440	1.943	2.447	3.143	3.707	6
7	.711	.896	1.119	1.415	1.895	2.365	2.998	3.499	7
8	.706	.889	1.108	1.397	1.860	2.306	2.896	3.355	8
9	.703	.883	1.100	1.383	1.833	2.262	2.821	3.250	9
10	.700	.879	1.093	1.372	1.812	2.228	2.764	3.169	10
11	.697	.876	1.088	1.363	1.796	2.201	2.718	3.106	11
12	.695	.873	1.083	1.356	1.782	2.179	2.681	3.055	12
13	.694	.870	1.079	1.350	1.771	2.160	2.650	3.012	13
14	.692	.868	1.076	1.345	1.761	2.145	2.624	2.977	14
15	.691	.866	1.074	1.341	1.753	2.131	2.602	2.947	15
16	.690	.865	1.071	1.337	1.746	2.120	2.583	2.921	16
17	.689	.863	1.069	1.333	1.740	2.110	2.567	2.898	17
18	.688	.862	1.067	1.330	1.734	2.101	2.552	2.878	18
19	.688	.861	1.066	1.328	1.729	2.093	2.539	2.861	19
20	.687	.860	1.064	1.325	1.725	2.086	2.528	2.845	20
21	.686	.859	1.063	1.323	1.721	2.080	2.518	2.831	21
22	.686	.858	1.061	1.321	1.717	2.074	2.508	2.819	22
23	.685	.858	1.060	1.319	1.714	2.069	2.500	2.807	23
24	.685	.857	1.059	1.318	1.711	2.064	2.492	2.797	24
25	.684	.856	1.058	1.316	1.708	2.060	2.485	2.787	25
26	.684	.856	1.058	1.315	1.706	2.056	2.479	2.779	26
27	.684	.855	1.057	1.314	1.703	2.052	2.473	2.771	27
28	.683	.855	1.056	1.313	1.701	2.048	2.467	2.763	28
29	.683	.854	1.055	1.311	1.699	2.045	2.462	2.756	29
30	.683	.854	1.055	1.310	1.697	2.042	2.457	2.750	30
35						2.030		2.724	35
40						2.021		2.704	40
45						2.014		2.690	45
50						2.008		2.678	50
60						2.000		2.600	60
70						1.994		2.648	70
80						1.990		2.638	80
90						1.987		2.632	90
100						1.984		2.626	100
125						1.979		2.616	125
150						1.976		2.609	150
200						1.972		2.601	200
300						1.968		2.592	300
400						1.966		2.588	400
500						1.965		2.568	500
1000						1.962		2.581	1000
∞	.67449	.84162	1.03643	1.28155	1.64485	1.95996	2.32634	2.57582	∞

SOURCE: Table is abridged from table III of Fisher and Yates, *Statistical Tables for Biological, Agricultural and Medical Research* (Edinburgh and London: Oliver & Boyd Ltd.). Reprinted by permission of the authors and publishers.

TABLE A-5 UPPER PERCENTAGE POINTS OF THE F DISTRIBUTION*

$1-\alpha$	n	m=1	2	3	4	5	6	7	8	9	10	12	15	20	30	60	120	∞
0.90	1	39.9	49.5	53.6	55.8	57.2	58.2	58.9	59.4	59.9	60.2	60.7	61.2	61.7	62.3	62.8	63.1	63.3
0.95		161	200	216	225	230	234	237	239	241	242	244	246	248	250	252	253	254
0.975		648	800	864	900	922	937	948	957	963	969	977	985	993	1,000	1,010	1,010	1,020
0.99		4,050	5,000	5,400	5,620	5,760	5,860	5,930	5,980	6,020	6,060	6,110	6,160	6,210	6,260	6,310	6,340	6,370
0.995		16,200	20,000	21,600	22,500	23,100	23,400	23,700	23,900	24,100	24,200	24,400	24,600	24,800	25,000	25,200	25,400	25,500
0.90	2	8.53	9.00	9.16	9.24	9.29	9.33	9.35	9.37	9.38	9.39	9.41	9.42	9.44	9.46	9.47	9.48	9.49
0.95		18.5	19.0	19.2	19.2	19.3	19.3	19.4	19.4	19.4	19.4	19.4	19.4	19.4	19.5	19.5	19.5	19.5
0.975		38.5	39.0	39.2	39.2	39.3	39.3	39.4	39.4	39.4	39.4	39.4	39.4	39.4	39.5	39.5	39.5	39.5
0.99		98.5	99.0	99.2	99.2	99.3	99.3	99.4	99.4	99.4	99.4	99.4	99.4	99.4	99.5	99.5	99.5	99.5
0.995		199	199	199	199	199	199	199	199	199	199	199	199	199	199	199	199	199
0.90	3	5.54	5.46	5.39	5.34	5.31	5.28	5.27	5.25	5.24	5.23	5.22	5.20	5.18	5.17	5.15	5.14	5.13
0.95		10.1	9.55	9.28	9.12	9.01	8.94	8.89	8.85	8.81	8.79	8.74	8.70	8.66	8.62	8.57	8.55	8.53
0.975		17.4	16.0	15.4	15.1	14.9	14.7	14.6	14.5	14.5	14.4	14.3	14.3	14.2	14.1	14.0	13.9	13.9
0.99		34.1	30.8	29.5	28.7	28.2	27.9	27.7	27.5	27.3	27.2	27.1	26.9	26.7	26.5	26.3	26.2	26.1
0.995		55.6	49.8	47.5	46.2	45.4	44.8	44.4	44.1	43.9	43.7	43.4	43.1	42.8	42.5	42.1	42.0	41.8
0.90	4	4.54	4.32	4.19	4.11	4.05	4.01	3.98	3.95	3.93	3.92	3.90	3.87	3.84	3.82	3.79	3.78	3.76
0.95		7.71	6.94	6.59	6.39	6.26	6.16	6.09	6.04	6.00	5.96	5.91	5.86	5.80	5.75	5.69	5.66	5.63
0.975		12.2	10.6	9.98	9.60	9.36	9.20	9.07	8.98	8.90	8.84	8.75	8.66	8.56	8.46	8.36	8.31	8.26
0.99		21.2	18.0	16.7	16.0	15.5	15.2	15.0	14.8	14.7	14.5	14.4	14.2	14.0	13.8	13.7	13.6	13.5
0.995		31.3	26.3	24.3	23.2	22.5	22.0	21.6	21.4	21.1	21.0	20.7	20.4	20.2	19.9	19.6	19.5	19.3
0.90	5	4.06	3.78	3.62	3.52	3.45	3.40	3.37	3.34	3.32	3.30	3.27	3.24	3.21	3.17	3.14	3.12	3.11
0.95		6.61	5.79	5.41	5.19	5.05	4.95	4.88	4.82	4.77	4.74	4.68	4.62	4.56	4.50	4.43	4.40	4.37
0.975		10.0	8.43	7.76	7.39	7.15	6.98	6.85	6.76	6.68	6.62	6.52	6.43	6.33	6.23	6.12	6.07	6.02
0.99		16.3	13.3	12.1	11.4	11.0	10.7	10.5	10.3	10.2	10.1	9.89	9.72	9.55	9.38	9.20	9.11	9.02
0.995		22.8	18.3	16.5	15.6	14.9	14.5	14.2	14.0	13.8	13.6	13.4	13.1	12.9	12.7	12.4	12.3	12.1
0.90	6	3.78	3.46	3.29	3.18	3.11	3.05	3.01	2.98	2.96	2.94	2.90	2.87	2.84	2.80	2.76	2.74	2.72
0.95		5.99	5.14	4.76	4.53	4.39	4.28	4.21	4.15	4.10	4.06	4.00	3.94	3.87	3.81	3.74	3.70	3.67
0.975		8.81	7.26	6.60	6.23	5.99	5.82	5.70	5.60	5.52	5.46	5.37	5.27	5.17	5.07	4.96	4.90	4.85
0.99		13.7	10.9	9.78	9.15	8.75	8.47	8.26	8.10	7.98	7.87	7.72	7.56	7.40	7.23	7.06	6.97	6.88
0.995		18.6	14.5	12.9	12.0	11.5	11.1	10.8	10.6	10.4	10.2	10.0	9.81	9.59	9.36	9.12	9.00	8.88
0.90	7	3.59	3.26	3.07	2.96	2.88	2.83	2.78	2.75	2.72	2.70	2.67	2.63	2.59	2.56	2.51	2.49	2.47
0.95		5.59	4.74	4.35	4.12	3.97	3.87	3.79	3.73	3.68	3.64	3.57	3.51	3.44	3.38	3.30	3.27	3.23
0.975		8.07	6.54	5.89	5.52	5.29	5.12	4.99	4.90	4.82	4.76	4.67	4.57	4.47	4.36	4.25	4.20	4.14
0.99		12.2	9.55	8.45	7.85	7.46	7.19	6.99	6.84	6.72	6.62	6.47	6.31	6.16	5.99	5.82	5.74	5.65
0.995		16.2	12.4	10.9	10.1	9.52	9.16	8.89	8.68	8.51	8.38	8.18	7.97	7.75	7.53	7.31	7.19	7.08
0.90	8	3.46	3.11	2.92	2.81	2.73	2.67	2.62	2.59	2.56	2.54	2.50	2.46	2.42	2.38	2.34	2.31	2.29
0.95		5.32	4.46	4.07	3.84	3.69	3.58	3.50	3.44	3.39	3.35	3.28	3.22	3.15	3.08	3.01	2.97	2.93
0.975		7.57	6.06	5.42	5.05	4.82	4.65	4.53	4.43	4.36	4.30	4.20	4.10	4.00	3.89	3.78	3.73	3.67
0.99		11.3	8.65	7.59	7.01	6.63	6.37	6.18	6.03	5.91	5.81	5.67	5.52	5.36	5.20	5.03	4.95	4.86
0.995		14.7	11.0	9.60	8.81	8.30	7.95	7.69	7.50	7.34	7.21	7.01	6.81	6.61	6.40	6.18	6.06	5.95

Percentage points of the inverted beta (F) distribution* — values by numerator degrees of freedom (columns) and denominator degrees of freedom / probability level (rows).

df_2	P	∞	120	60	30	20	15	12	10	9	8	7	6	5	4	3	2	1
9	0.90	2.16	2.18	2.21	2.25	2.30	2.34	2.38	2.42	2.44	2.47	2.51	2.55	2.61	2.69	2.81	3.01	3.36
	0.95	2.71	2.75	2.79	2.86	2.94	3.01	3.07	3.14	3.18	3.23	3.29	3.37	3.48	3.63	3.86	4.26	5.12
	0.975	3.33	3.39	3.45	3.56	3.67	3.77	3.87	3.96	4.03	4.10	4.20	4.32	4.48	4.72	5.08	5.71	7.21
	0.99	4.31	4.40	4.48	4.65	4.81	4.96	5.11	5.26	5.35	5.47	5.61	5.80	6.06	6.42	6.99	8.02	10.6
	0.995	5.19	5.30	5.41	5.62	5.83	6.03	6.23	6.42	6.54	6.69	6.88	7.13	7.47	7.96	8.72	10.1	13.6
10	0.90	2.06	2.08	2.11	2.15	2.20	2.24	2.28	2.32	2.35	2.38	2.41	2.46	2.52	2.61	2.73	2.92	3.29
	0.95	2.54	2.58	2.62	2.70	2.77	2.84	2.91	2.98	3.02	3.07	3.14	3.22	3.33	3.48	3.71	4.10	4.96
	0.975	3.08	3.14	3.20	3.31	3.42	3.52	3.62	3.72	3.78	3.85	3.95	4.07	4.24	4.47	4.83	5.46	6.94
	0.99	3.91	4.00	4.08	4.25	4.41	4.56	4.71	4.85	4.94	5.06	5.20	5.39	5.64	5.99	6.55	7.56	10.0
	0.995	4.64	4.75	4.86	5.07	5.27	5.47	5.66	5.85	5.97	6.12	6.30	6.54	6.87	7.34	8.08	9.43	12.8
12	0.90	1.90	1.93	1.96	2.01	2.06	2.10	2.15	2.19	2.21	2.24	2.28	2.33	2.39	2.48	2.61	2.81	3.18
	0.95	2.30	2.34	2.38	2.47	2.54	2.62	2.69	2.75	2.80	2.85	2.91	3.00	3.11	3.26	3.49	3.89	4.75
	0.975	2.72	2.79	2.85	2.96	3.07	3.18	3.28	3.37	3.44	3.51	3.61	3.73	3.89	4.12	4.47	5.10	6.55
	0.99	3.36	3.45	3.54	3.70	3.86	4.01	4.16	4.30	4.39	4.50	4.64	4.82	5.06	5.41	5.95	6.93	9.33
	0.995	3.90	4.01	4.12	4.33	4.53	4.72	4.91	5.09	5.20	5.35	5.52	5.76	6.07	6.52	7.23	8.51	11.8
15	0.90	1.76	1.79	1.82	1.87	1.92	1.97	2.02	2.06	2.09	2.12	2.16	2.21	2.27	2.36	2.49	2.70	3.07
	0.95	2.07	2.11	2.16	2.25	2.33	2.40	2.48	2.54	2.59	2.64	2.71	2.79	2.90	3.06	3.29	3.68	4.54
	0.975	2.40	2.46	2.52	2.64	2.76	2.86	2.96	3.06	3.12	3.20	3.29	3.41	3.58	3.80	4.15	4.77	6.20
	0.99	2.87	2.96	3.05	3.21	3.37	3.52	3.67	3.80	3.89	4.00	4.14	4.32	4.56	4.89	5.42	6.36	8.68
	0.995	3.26	3.37	3.48	3.69	3.88	4.07	4.25	4.42	4.54	4.67	4.85	5.07	5.37	5.80	6.48	7.70	10.8
20	0.90	1.61	1.64	1.68	1.74	1.79	1.84	1.89	1.94	1.96	2.00	2.04	2.09	2.16	2.25	2.38	2.59	2.97
	0.95	1.84	1.90	1.95	2.04	2.12	2.20	2.28	2.35	2.39	2.45	2.51	2.60	2.71	2.87	3.10	3.49	4.35
	0.975	2.09	2.16	2.22	2.35	2.46	2.57	2.68	2.77	2.84	2.91	3.01	3.13	3.29	3.51	3.86	4.46	5.87
	0.99	2.42	2.52	2.61	2.78	2.94	3.09	3.23	3.37	3.46	3.56	3.70	3.87	4.10	4.43	4.94	5.85	8.10
	0.995	2.69	2.81	2.92	3.12	3.32	3.50	3.68	3.85	3.96	4.09	4.26	4.47	4.76	5.17	5.82	6.99	9.94
30	0.90	1.46	1.50	1.54	1.61	1.67	1.72	1.77	1.82	1.85	1.88	1.93	1.98	2.05	2.14	2.28	2.49	2.88
	0.95	1.62	1.68	1.74	1.84	1.93	2.01	2.09	2.16	2.21	2.27	2.33	2.42	2.53	2.69	2.92	3.32	4.17
	0.975	1.79	1.87	1.94	2.07	2.20	2.31	2.41	2.51	2.57	2.65	2.75	2.87	3.03	3.25	3.59	4.18	5.57
	0.99	2.01	2.11	2.21	2.39	2.55	2.70	2.84	2.98	3.07	3.17	3.30	3.47	3.70	4.02	4.51	5.39	7.56
	0.995	2.18	2.30	2.42	2.63	2.82	3.01	3.18	3.34	3.45	3.58	3.74	3.95	4.23	4.62	5.24	6.35	9.18
60	0.90	1.29	1.35	1.40	1.48	1.54	1.60	1.66	1.71	1.74	1.77	1.82	1.87	1.95	2.04	2.18	2.39	2.79
	0.95	1.39	1.47	1.53	1.65	1.75	1.84	1.92	1.99	2.04	2.10	2.17	2.25	2.37	2.53	2.76	3.15	4.00
	0.975	1.48	1.58	1.67	1.82	1.94	2.06	2.17	2.27	2.33	2.41	2.51	2.63	2.79	3.01	3.34	3.93	5.29
	0.99	1.60	1.73	1.84	2.03	2.20	2.35	2.50	2.63	2.72	2.82	2.95	3.12	3.34	3.65	4.13	4.98	7.08
	0.995	1.69	1.83	1.96	2.19	2.39	2.57	2.74	2.90	3.01	3.13	3.29	3.49	3.76	4.14	4.73	5.80	8.49
120	0.90	1.19	1.26	1.32	1.41	1.48	1.54	1.60	1.65	1.68	1.72	1.77	1.82	1.90	1.99	2.13	2.35	2.75
	0.95	1.25	1.35	1.43	1.55	1.66	1.75	1.83	1.91	1.96	2.02	2.09	2.18	2.29	2.45	2.68	3.07	3.92
	0.975	1.31	1.43	1.53	1.69	1.82	1.94	2.05	2.16	2.22	2.30	2.39	2.52	2.67	2.89	3.23	3.80	5.15
	0.99	1.38	1.53	1.66	1.86	2.03	2.19	2.34	2.47	2.56	2.66	2.79	2.96	3.17	3.48	3.95	4.79	6.85
	0.995	1.43	1.61	1.75	1.98	2.19	2.37	2.54	2.71	2.81	2.93	3.09	3.28	3.55	3.92	4.50	5.54	8.18
∞	0.90	1.00	1.17	1.24	1.34	1.42	1.49	1.55	1.60	1.63	1.67	1.72	1.77	1.85	1.94	2.08	2.30	2.71
	0.95	1.00	1.22	1.32	1.46	1.57	1.67	1.75	1.83	1.88	1.94	2.01	2.10	2.21	2.37	2.60	3.00	3.84
	0.975	1.00	1.27	1.39	1.57	1.71	1.83	1.94	2.05	2.11	2.19	2.29	2.41	2.57	2.79	3.12	3.69	5.02
	0.99	1.00	1.32	1.47	1.70	1.88	2.04	2.18	2.32	2.41	2.51	2.64	2.80	3.02	3.32	3.78	4.61	6.63
	0.995	1.00	1.36	1.53	1.79	2.00	2.19	2.36	2.52	2.62	2.74	2.90	3.09	3.35	3.72	4.28	5.30	7.88

* Abridged from Maxine Merrington and Catherine M. Thompson: Tables of percentage points of the inverted beta distribution, *Biometrika*, vol. 33 (1943), pp. 73–88, and published here with the kind permission of the editor of *Biometrika*.

Table A-6 PERCENTAGE POINTS OF THE CHI-SQUARE DISTRIBUTION*

n \ (1 − α)	0.005	0.010	0.025	0.050	0.100	0.250	0.500	0.750	0.900	0.950	0.975	0.990	0.995
1	0.0^4393	0.0^3157	0.0^3982	0.0^2393	0.0158	0.102	0.455	1.32	2.71	3.84	5.02	6.63	7.88
2	0.0100	0.0201	0.0506	0.103	0.211	0.575	1.39	2.77	4.61	5.99	7.38	9.21	10.6
3	0.0717	0.115	0.216	0.352	0.584	1.21	2.37	4.11	6.25	7.81	9.35	11.3	12.8
4	0.207	0.297	0.484	0.711	1.06	1.92	3.36	5.39	7.78	9.49	11.1	13.3	14.9
5	0.412	0.554	0.831	1.15	1.61	2.67	4.35	6.63	9.24	11.1	12.8	15.1	16.7
6	0.676	0.872	1.24	1.64	2.20	3.45	5.35	7.84	10.6	12.6	14.4	16.8	18.5
7	0.989	1.24	1.69	2.17	2.83	4.25	6.35	9.04	12.0	14.1	16.0	18.5	20.3
8	1.34	1.65	2.18	2.73	3.49	5.07	7.34	10.2	13.4	15.5	17.5	20.1	22.0
9	1.73	2.09	2.70	3.33	4.17	5.90	8.34	11.4	14.7	16.9	19.0	21.7	23.6
10	2.16	2.56	3.25	3.94	4.87	6.74	9.34	12.5	16.0	18.3	20.5	23.2	25.2
11	2.60	3.05	3.82	4.57	5.58	7.58	10.3	13.7	17.3	19.7	21.9	24.7	26.8
12	3.07	3.57	4.40	5.23	6.30	8.44	11.3	14.8	18.5	21.0	23.3	26.2	28.3
13	3.57	4.11	5.01	5.89	7.04	9.30	12.3	16.0	19.8	22.4	24.7	27.7	29.8
14	4.07	4.66	5.63	6.57	7.79	10.2	13.3	17.1	21.1	23.7	26.1	29.1	31.3
15	4.60	5.23	6.26	7.26	8.55	11.0	14.3	18.2	22.3	25.0	27.5	30.6	32.8
16	5.14	5.81	6.91	7.96	9.31	11.9	15.3	19.4	23.5	26.3	28.8	32.0	34.3
17	5.70	6.41	7.56	8.67	10.1	12.8	16.3	20.5	24.8	27.6	30.2	33.4	35.7
18	6.26	7.01	8.23	9.39	10.9	13.7	17.3	21.6	26.0	28.9	31.5	34.8	37.2
19	6.84	7.63	8.91	10.1	11.7	14.6	18.3	22.7	27.2	30.1	32.9	36.2	38.6
20	7.43	8.26	9.59	10.9	12.4	15.5	19.3	23.8	28.4	31.4	34.2	37.6	40.0
21	8.03	8.90	10.3	11.6	13.2	16.3	20.3	24.9	29.6	32.7	35.5	38.9	41.4
22	8.64	9.54	11.0	12.3	14.0	17.2	21.3	26.0	30.8	33.9	36.8	40.3	42.8
23	9.26	10.2	11.7	13.1	14.8	18.1	22.3	27.1	32.0	35.2	38.1	41.6	44.2
24	9.89	10.9	12.4	13.8	15.7	19.0	23.3	28.2	33.2	36.4	39.4	43.0	45.6
25	10.5	11.5	13.1	14.6	16.5	19.9	24.3	29.3	34.4	37.7	40.6	44.3	46.9
26	11.2	12.2	13.8	15.4	17.3	20.8	25.3	30.4	35.6	38.9	41.9	45.6	48.3
27	11.8	12.9	14.6	16.2	18.1	21.7	26.3	31.5	36.7	40.1	43.2	47.0	49.6
28	12.5	13.6	15.3	16.9	18.9	22.7	27.3	32.6	37.9	41.3	44.5	48.3	51.0
29	13.1	14.3	16.0	17.7	19.8	23.6	28.3	33.7	39.1	42.6	45.7	49.6	52.3
30	13.8	15.0	16.8	18.5	20.6	24.5	29.3	34.8	40.3	43.8	47.0	50.9	53.7

* Abridged from Catherine M. Thompson: Tables of percentage points of the incomplete beta function and of the chi-square distribution, *Biometrika*, vol. 32 (1941), pp. 187–191, and published here with the kind permission of the editor of *Biometrika*.

Table A-7   THE GREEK ALPHABET

Letters	Names	English equivalent	Letters	Names	English equivalent
A α	Alpha	a	N ν	Nu	n
B β	Beta	b	Ξ ξ	Xi	x
Γ γ	Gamma	g	O o	Omicron	o
Δ δ	Delta	d	Π π	Pi	p
E ϵ	Epsilon	e	P ρ	Rho	r
Z ζ	Zeta	z	Σ σ	Sigma	s
H η	Eta	—	T τ	Tau	t
Θ θ	Theta	—	Υ υ	Upsilon	u or y
I ι	Iota	i	Φ ϕ	Phi	—
K κ	Kappa	k	X χ	Chi	—
Λ λ	Lambda	l	Ψ ψ	Psi	—
M μ	Mu	m	Ω ω	Omega	—

NAME INDEX

Abrams, Jack, 317*n*.
Achenbaum, Alvin R., 623, 630*n*.
Ackoff, Russell L., 149*n*.
Albaum Gerald S., 315*n*., 322*n*., 460*n*.
Allvine, F. C., 394*n*.
Andrews, Frank M., 474*n*., 491*n*., 547*n*.
Assael, H., 391*n*., 392*n*.
Auerback, Barbara, 416*n*.
Axelrod, Myril D., 382*n*.

Babbie, Earl, 200, 253*n*., 258*n*., 455*n*., 463*n*., 469, 470*n*.
Bailey, Carl L., 616*n*.
Bailey, Earl L., 610*n*.
Banks, Seymour, 334*n*., 341*n*., 342*n*., 344*n*.
Bayer, Alan E., 415*n*.
Bellenger, Danny N., 319*n*., 380*n*., 383*n*., 621
Bent, D. H., 466*n*.
Berdy, Edwin M., 626*n*.
Bernhardt, Kenneth L., 284*n*., 380*n*.
Best, R., 322*n*.
Best, Roger J., 611*n*.
Blackwell, R. D., 308*n*., 408*n*.
Blankenship, Al, 36*n*.
Blankertz, Donald F., 128*n*.
Bloom, Derek, 143*n*., 144*n*.
Bowen, J. M., 416*n*.

Boyd, Harper W., 22*n*., 30, 166*n*.
Braden, Patricia, 81*n*.
Bradford, Ernest S., 49*n*.
Brown, Lyndon O., 29
Brown, Rex V., 122*n*.
Brunner, G. A., 392*n*.
Brunner, J. A., 392*n*.
Bursk, Edward C., 137*n*.

Cahalan, D., 393*n*.
Cambell, C., 411*n*.
Campbell, Donald T., 333*n*., 334*n*., 341*n*., 342*n*., 343*n*., 347*n*., 378*n*., 398*n*.
Caporaso, James A., 341*n*., 342*n*.
Carmone, Frank J., 536*n*., 537*n*., 538*n*.
Carter, R. F., 321*n*.
Carvey, D. W., 316*n*.
Cayley, Murray A., 13, 106*n*.
Chaffee, S. H., 321*n*.
Chapman, John F., 137*n*.
Chase, Donald A., 383*n*.
Chorafas, Dimitris N., 138*n*.
Churchill, Gilbert A., Jr., 136*n*., 167*n*., 253*n*., 507*n*., 528*n*.
Clayton, Alden G., 108*n*.
Cocanougher, A. Benton, 87*n*., 95*n*.
Cohen, Stanley, 363*n*.
Collins, B. J. K., 627*n*.
Cook, Stuart W., 311*n*., 316*n*., 329*n*.

Copulsky, William, 609*n*.
Cordell, W. N., 133*n*.
Cox, Keith K., 331, 348*n*., 349*n*., 482*n*.
Cox, M., 392*n*.
Cox, William E., Jr., 605*n*.
Crawford, C. Merle, 83*n*.
Crespi, I., 322*n*.
Crisp, Richard D., 609*n*.
Crosby, Lawrence A., 62*n*.
Crosby, Richard, 83*n*.
Crutchfield, R. S., 308*n*.
Curtin, Richard T., 393*n*.

Dalbey, Homer M., 652
Dalkey, Norman, 611*n*.
Daniels, P., 319*n*.
David, H. A., 319*n*.
Davidson, Terrence N., 474*n*.
Day, G. S., 308*n*., 395*n*.
Day, R. L., 394*n*.
Dearden, John, 149*n*.
Demby, Emanuel, 377*n*., 525–526
DeNooyer, J. Craig, 42*n*.
Deshpande, Rohit, 108*n*.
Deutsch, M., 316*n*., 329*n*.
Drake, Jerry E., 166*n*.
Driscoll, D. G., 7*n*.
Duncan, C. S., 29
Dunkelberg, W. C., 395*n*.
Dunning, B., 393*n*.

SUBJECT INDEX